Orchestrating Europe

KEITH MIDDLEMAS

Orchestrating Europe

The Informal Politics of the European Union
1973–95

with the collaboration of
Virginia Crowe, Henriette Peucker
Franco Algieri, Lorenza Badiello, Ramon Ballester

introductory historical chapters by
Richard T. Griffiths

FontanaPress
An Imprint of HarperCollins*Publishers*

Fontana Press
An imprint of HarperCollins*Publishers*
77–85 Fulham Palace Road,
Hammersmith, London W6 8JB

Published by Fontana Press 1995
1 3 5 7 9 8 6 4 2

A catalogue record for this book is
available from the British Library

ISBN 0 00 255678 2
ISBN 0 00 686263 2

Set in Linotron Ehrhardt

Printed in Great Britain by
HarperCollinsManufacturing Glasgow

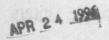

To my grandchildren:
Hugo, Georgia, Fabian, Isabella

It is the duty of the patriot to prefer and promote the exclusive interest and glory of his native country: but a philosopher may be permitted to enlarge his views and to consider Europe as one great republic, whose various inhabitants have attained almost the same level of politeness and cultivation. The balance of power will continue to fluctuate, and the prosperity of our own, or the neighbouring kingdoms, may be alternately exalted or depressed; but these partial events cannot essentially injure our general state of happiness, the system of arts, and laws, and manners, which so advantageously distinguish, above the rest of mankind, the Europeans . . .

Edward Gibbon, *The Decline and Fall of the Roman Empire*, Vol VI, chapter XXXVIII, p. 402 (1818 edition)

CONTENTS

Introduction   xi

Acknowledgements   xxvii

Glossary of Abbreviations and Acronyms   xxix

Presidencies and principal Commissioners,
relevant to the main themes, since 1981   xxxv

Presidencies of the Council of Ministers and
Meetings of the European Council   xl

The European Integration Experience
  by Richard T. Griffiths

1. 1945–58   1
2. 1958–73   37

Part I: History   71

3. The Stagnant Decade, 1973–83   73
4. Making the Market:
   The Single European Act, 1980–88   111
5. Maastricht and After, 1988–93   156
   Post Script   204

Part II: Forces   207
6. The Commission   213
7. The Member States   266

8. Institutions:
    The Parliament and the Court of Justice   340
9. The Regions   383

    Part III: Players   429
10. Firms and Federations   435
11. Players in Action   498
12. Policy-Making: Industry and Trade   556

    Part IV: State without a Country   613
13. Unity and Diversity   615
14. Conclusion   668

    Notes   699
    Index   773

INTRODUCTION

The late 1980s brought a sense of quickening tempo to the European Community after a decade of stagnation. Two landmark Treaties, the Single European Act of 1986 and the Treaty of Union at Maastricht stood out in that optimistic period. Now that the wave of euphoria has broken, and the tide receded – though not nearly to its pre-1985 level – it is worth asking what were the permanent achievements and the quality of change that each brought about. As EEC, EC or EU, the European Community has habitually moved through troughs and hollows, punctuated by much shorter bursts of energy: neither can be explained without asking what all the relevant forces – governments, Community institutions and the array of interested outside players – were doing at each point in the cycle.

How member state governments and EU bodies relate is similar enough to what goes on in national political systems to be comprehensible, and open enough to be readily accessible. Community institutions are in most cases much the less secretive of the two. But the task of weaving the influence of non-governmental players (industrial firms, financial institutions, trades unions, regions and distinct state organs such as central banks) into the recent history of a subject extending over twelve or more nation states requires a different format, almost an alternative kind of history. Robert Brenner did this for seventeenth-century England in *Merchants and Revolution*,[1] with the benefit of access to all surviving archives. But the EU, like its member governments, restricts access at every point after 1965.

Yet without a complete picture of how influence is exercised and who moves whom, we have only half the story. Present day comment lacks essential connections to the recent past, to the trends which may not be obvious today but remain latent, like nationalism in eastern Europe before 1989. Without contemporary history, studies of the contemporary world – by political scientists, lawyers, economists, or specialists in international relations – rest on a dangerously relative foundation, and students are faced with a blind spot for the 'years not taught'.

The contemporary historian (like any other), ought to contribute a distinct sort of understanding of three connected phenomena: processes as they change over time; the continuous interchange of many players; and the mutation of institutions, and the beliefs and behaviour patterns of those who work in them. These were my own concerns in a series of studies of British government during the twentieth century which developed the concept of a long and continuous game between an increasing number of players of different power, status and interests, a game in which all of them used the needs that the modern state had for their participation to draw it and its component parts into an informal framework, from which there could subsequently be no retreat to a pristine minimal state.

Their continual rivalry in the political marketplace focused on a range of goals, from naked self-interest to bargaining a consensus about what the common or national interest might be. Each one's willingness to accept a measure of interdependence ensured that the others would be more inclined to recognize some of its own claims, if only as the price of general social harmony (for which, in turn, governments and political parties were prepared to pay). As a descriptive device, I called this a 'competitive symposium' – to signify a prolonged discourse, not between equal partners but ones which recognized each other's claims and followed, voluntarily but as a precondition of membership, a code of political language and conventions of behaviour in pursuit of rational self-interest.

The competitive element was always present but was limited by the need not to risk the whole delicate balance through outright conflict. The game was therefore a continuous one, many-headed and usually peaceable, with regular prizes but no final victories, open to generally acceptable players bound by agreed rules and a shared belief that negotiated results, though never entirely binding or satisfactory, were preferable to dictation by a higher power.

Having reached a point in 1990 where a contemporary historian could not reasonably go further forward in a British context, I have tried to apply the same method on the European scale, by looking not only at the Community's history over the last twenty years but at the interchanges between a much broader range of players or constellations than is usual in the approaches of other disciplines. To borrow a phrase of Andrew Shonfield's, I hoped to study a great theme from a single standpoint, to discover an underlying coherence in the idea that the arena where these players meet could be described as informal politics, part of the overall system whose more obvious features are of course formal.

Living in a country which, more than any other member of the Community, has difficulty with the concept of being European, yet which I firmly believe has no special role and hardly any living space outside it, I am disturbed by the distorted and frequently trivial way the Community is portrayed in the press and on television by all but a handful of commentators. Apart from the brief period in 1972–4, and during the 1975 referendum, British governments have done little in their public discourse to make clear what is at stake, so that stereotypes are used habitually which provoke incomprehension if not derision across the Channel.

What is said here is meant therefore also as a contribution to perceptions: as Rudyard Kipling put it in *Something of Myself* in 1891, 'trying to tell the English something of the world outside England – not directly, but by implication . . . a vast conspectus of the whole sweep and meaning of things . . .'. (Kipling of course wrote 'Empire' not Europe.) To start with, the Community is not just Brussels, the Council of Ministers and the Commission, but fifteen member states of varying size, importance and interests, some of which are very much more effective than others (insofar as their games lie within Europe). Beyond them, but in overlapping circles, range other players at national or regional level, of different status operating from different standpoints. There is no ideal Europe, no single picture, outside the emptiness of political rhetoric; just as there is no one centre. The centre is wherever the players meet. Those from 'above' may be formally superior, but informally, when they meet as a matter of common interest, it is each one's effectiveness that counts.

The question to ask here is not 'what is Europe?', because in this dimension Europe is whatever you see, but how, informally, does the Community function, how do governments and non-governmental players act and what do they try to achieve? Does informal politics help to ameliorate the deep-rooted discords between north and south, core and periphery, small states and large, Anglo-Saxon and continental mentalities? Does it facilitate the entry of new players? Does it reduce rigidities and friction which would otherwise make the Community a less efficient mechanism for what its members want?

The Europe which questions like these throws into focus is one of interests, elites and powerful groups. It is vital to study these as they are: Europe as it is, not as people might wish it to be, as a preliminary to changing it. Players in the informal sector of a system are those who choose to enter out of self-interest, who have the willpower and resources to stay in and the capacity to make themselves heard in that highly competitive arena. Lack of resources or inability to form stable alliances condemns the rest to marginal status or, like small companies, to reliance on whatever support they can get at national or regional level. There is no democratic bias here.

But not all roads in the EU's history lead to the same outcome. The narrative from 1973 to the present given in chapters 3 to 5 is intended to make clear how the European project revived after a long stagnation, and why the Single Act led on to the Treaty of Union at Maastricht – in the context of a Europe which had been fundamentally altered by the collapse of the Soviet Union after 1989. There are other ways of telling the story because the Community's development is not teleological, not precisely delimited by the Treaties. How it evolves and what new legal texts it produces are for the players to decide.

As an historian I have tried not to confine myself to any one interpretation, whether federal, functional or intergovernmental, and to proceed empirically, taking account of all the significant players. The project assumes no hierarchy of players, no measured evolution: it examines 'punctuated equilibrium', change rather than progress, short bursts of energy interrupted by longer troughs (usually associated with recession). Of these, the economic and financial crisis of 1973–5 profoundly altered the balance between industry and labour, while that of 1981–3 had a direct effect on the behaviour of large firms and their federations towards the Community. The more recent 1990–93 recession ran parallel to a political cleavage between governments and elites on one side, publics and media on the other, in all member states, which severely impaired the Union (as the Community had by then become) and delayed completion of the internal market. Deep discontent with Community institutions seemed to be a sort of retribution for pre-Maastricht euphoria, as the last vestiges of post-War settlements disappeared, to be replaced by anguish at the threats to welfare systems and national identities, the latter at least being one long consequence of 1989.

There is a difficulty with this approach to incremental change. Existing studies of the Community and its processes take for granted a sense of progress and seek general conclusions, which the detailed evidence of what large numbers of players do does not always substantiate. Self-interest and bargaining, as Richard Griffiths shows in his historical introduction, written from the EU's own archives, bulk much larger than earlier accounts, written by committed Europeans, allowed.

At best these concentrated on peak organizations or federations. But the primary actors were not usually federations but their members, for whom central bodies served mainly to correlate the varying opinions within them. A group study of such bodies gives an illusory impression of continuity. Likewise, most large firms or banks had a presence in the Community from the 1970s onwards. But generally their interest increased substantially and in a qualitative way in the 1980s, so that they appear to be now fully engaged as players; yet the intensity and scope of their involvement differs according to what is at stake, and may diminish (as many companies' efforts did, once the internal market legislation was in place).

Either way, corporate players helped to create the Community's informal political infrastructure, as they did nation states' systems rather earlier during the twentieth century. In the European Union, however, they operated in greater freedom from the constraints of the past, because the Community is only an imperfect or quasi-state, some thirty-seven years old. Its system is different from those of nation states and the degree of informality greater, because of its institutional heterodoxy.

All this makes it necessary to examine the links and networks that have grown up, and to look at how similar informal politics operate in the European Court, the Parliament, the regions and among financial players or central banks, in their context rather than in isolation. Networks in the 1990s are growing fastest in the recently colonized commercial or financial spheres. They have always crossed borders, but here borders have ceased to count. The increase by volume is perhaps the most noticeable feature of the last decade; but the fact that major players can no longer ignore less relevant areas, for fear that their competitors will establish bridge-heads there, suggests that the quality of change is more important.

As the competitive symposium extends itself, a sort of inter-dependence becomes established. Bargaining through networks in a densely structured game reduces friction and produces results for which the formal system may be ill attuned, even on ostensibly formal matters such as easier implementation and enforcement of laws. It allows for wide, flexible participation; it reduces incon-sistencies; it gives rise to conventions, rather than formal rules, which can be adapted more easily over time. But it is not protective of weaker interests and it privileges the more efficient ones.

Like the dusty engagements in a 'soldier's battle' spread over a huge terrain, it is hard to see results. Even business participants are often unclear who is winning at any one time or what constitutes success. They might reflect with William Morris 'how men fight and lose the battle, and the thing they fought for comes about in spite of their defeat; and when it comes, it turns out not to be what they meant, and other men have to fight for what they meant under another name.'

Appreciating the game's totality is vital: without it, it is impossible fully to understand EU processes and the behaviour of players or individual practitioners; the informal constitutes the 'dark side of the moon', without which that sphere is only a disc.

It is impossible even to think of including here more than a brief selection of the sorts of cases where informal politics proliferate. But space should be made for all the players or the sense of totality is lost. Each one, whatever its size, effectiveness, status or resources, has some influence on the outcome. Until it has proved unimportant or marginal, therefore, it should be given historical space. The Community contains large numbers of games which are distinct, as well as 'nested boxes', and a group powerful in one may be outplayed in another – which is not the case in the formal system between legal entities of equivalent status.

Power of this kind is also a function of how much the EU's institutions need what players have to offer. Commission officials' willingness to consult peak organizations from particular industries and their component firms is well known; and so is their propensity to take on experts from member states or those same firms as advisers (which is ascribed reasonably enough to shortages of staff in the Directorates and the need to take account of what exists in national or local markets). Very complex forms of diplomacy govern the subsequent transactions of information and influence.

Early in the EU's history, individuals carried great clout, as befitted a relatively small Brussels elite. Today, the keys to sustained influence lie much less in personal linkages, more in tightly argued dossiers and presenting the most up-to-date information at the initial stages of policy evolution. The professionals have taken over, flanked by cohorts who constitute their own distinct groups: technical experts, lawyers or journalists.

But whoever acts, the questions remain the same: who manipulates? Who controls whom? What are effective transactions rather than ritual ones? The gains made by either side may not have obvious market connotations, especially once players have committed themselves to a long-term involvement: positional gains often outweigh monetary ones. In such circumstances it is hard to ascribe a balance of advantage, or to portray influence as a one-way process. Both sets of participants tend to shape each other, whether at the Commission/Council level, or at that of the firm and Directorate official.

It is clear from the interviews on which this book is based that the game begins surprisingly low down among relatively junior Commission officials; and that what matters is the cumulative weight of such bargaining (governed as it is by its own system of filters, access mechanisms, rules and conventions) by the time that decisions, whose basis rests on joint agreement, have become EU law or policy. This is no longer – if it ever was – a matter merely of lobbying, but of degree of commitment, indicated by when a player finds it expedient to set up an office in Brussels or to develop a department of EU affairs with a direct link to its main board.[2] The index of commitment is to be measured in terms of resources (for example, the cost of lobbying in the European Parliament), the quality of personnel involved, and the extent to which the player develops internal mechanisms for dealing with the EU in its corporate structures.

If one selects only certain categories of players, the game's totality is lost, not least because such studies tend to ignore the variety of modes of action open to all those players, ranging from direct pressures in Brussels or use of MEPs (a multinational corporation might have a minimum of fifty MEPs on its contact list at any one time, including the total membership of some key Strasbourg committees), to leverage via its own member state government's European Affairs Coordinating committees, or with its Permanent Representation in Brussels. The sheer volume of new entrants, the number of corporate offices set up in Brussels in the late 1980s, the numbers of lobbyists who, like Renaissance mercenaries, did well at Strasbourg out of the legislative boom, have done more than clutter the EU's political marketplace. They have changed it, probably irreversibly, because all the serious players (which does not include those who work sporadically or primarily through lobbyists) have engaged themselves permanently, on a large scale and with substantial resources, to the evolution of means of influence at every level. A firm cannot ignore any of these approaches, not because all means are equal, or have a commercial or even viable return, but because competitors might gain advantage there.

It is sometimes argued that players are more concerned with relative than collective advantage. My impression is that, in the more coherent industrial sectors like chemicals and pharmaceuticals, this is not so and may not even be true for the less coherent such as motorcars and consumer electronics, firstly because it is almost impossible for a large firm not to play in the EU market, secondly because the extensive range of modes available ensures that relative advantage can be defended on other levels – for example by utilizing group pressures on those perceived as playing only for their own interests, or deprecating what they do to Commission officials in order to ensure their partial exclusion or downgrading.

Given such a plethora of activities, there are substantial problems not only in deciding who influences whom but in discriminating between significant and unimportant activity. It is not much use measuring the numbers of lobbyists employed, the size of federation memberships, or the numbers of MEPs' signatures on proposed amendments; it would be better to ask what is their quality, how coherent is their representation, on which committees do they sit? Few players, from member states to SMEs, focus all their existence in the Community context; we need to know if they have changed emphasis in the spectrum running from national capitals through Europe to global markets; whether the man in Brussels reports direct to the managing director, whether players with widely different interests are adopting similar tactics.[3]

Formality and informality are not part of a syllogism, thesis and antithesis because, like ying and yang, they complement each other. All social scientists understand what informal politics is, but find its essence hard to define formally. But if they too often reduce it to formal abstractions, historians tend to avoid it altogether for lack of proper documentation. Logically, it does not constitute a system, because that would mark its clear separation from the formal: it can only be part of a system.

Two assumptions can be made about formal mechanisms: firstly, that they rely on their operators' continual good behaviour; secondly that, without informal processes, they become more rigid or unworkable the more pressures build up in the societies which originated them. No mechanism is so perfect that it cannot be disturbed by dissidents or outsiders. None can be designed to alter itself over time to meet the challenges of which the originators can have had no conception, unless it has latitude built in. Combinations of the two have a better chance of preventing systemic failure than tight legal prescription does on its own.

But what is it? Almost any habitual, voluntary practice could be described as informal. It is not restricted to individuals who know each other – though nationality or language affinity, cultural rapport and shared professional ethos are important. Whatever it is must constitute the basis for continuous relations between the players, whether governments, officials or commercial organizations. It must include everything which does not appear in legal texts, all rules and conventions which may be policed but are not justiciable.

Informal politics are defined not so much by players' status – any who wish and can establish credentials to the satisfaction of others can enter – as by the mode chosen to establish relationships. All players can choose between formal and informal modes and the shades of grey between them. There is no dividing line – only a spectrum. Rules and conventions are policed on both sides, with many nuanced penalties for infringement.

Inclusion depends on a player's willingness to accept the rules and conventions of its own club or association. To a minimum extent, all players, like member states themselves, must demonstrate an element of altruism (European-mindedness) as well as basic self-interest, not only to be proper members of higher sectoral and European-wide groupings, but to make themselves acceptable to EU institutions and officials.

Informal politics exist wherever there are 'grey areas'. As these are filled in and categorized over time, the informal may mutate, becoming, like the European Council, quasi-formal or ultimately fully formalized. But periodically new grey areas will open up as contexts or procedures change. Where interpretation is open to dispute, where there are margins of manoeuvre, where boundaries are imprecisely defined, where authorities have to exercise discretion, the informal will always flourish.

It exists most in conditions of plural bargaining where interdependence requires players to consort together to make agreements or risk losing the consensual base on which their status and the possibility of future agreements rests. It increases with the number of players, because none wishes to be isolated in the political marketplace; and it operates more easily and frequently in the Community than in nation states – whose modern forms of trilateral brokerage developed earlier in the twentieth century and have since grown older and more rigid; whose governments are also less open or willing to admit that it exists.

Its appearance is infinitely variable, but each aspect has certain common characteristics: impermanence, flexibility, subtlety. Inside groups and institutions it is disseminated as individuals are inducted, socialized and promoted, taking root most readily where there is professional training or practical experience. Political constructions damage it, for it is ultimately consensual, unlike the politics of politicians which tends to divide.

It evolves mechanisms for revision more easily than the formal system, and is closely compatible with the long Community tradition of setting markers in legal texts, to be implemented in riper circumstances at a later date. In that sense, it assumes both good faith and the continuity of ethos and convention among players, though not of course always in the same forms.

In what follows, I argue that this constitutes a distinct field with systemic characteristics, not merely a shadow or extension of the formal. But it is not a Manichean distinction: only at the ends of the spectrum are matters black and white. Unless the whole range is taken into account, analysis remains imperfect, since for want of it the strong probability is that the formal system will be less acceptable, flexible or efficient.

The formal and informal sides' interactions are present in any known political system, since the only difference between them in a tyranny and a democracy is one of proportion: they exist in both. But in open systems the informal is far more pervasive, legitimate and well-grounded, even at the point of policy initiative. Looked at in this way, not only governments but the components of the modern state – ministries, civil servants, central banks, and the state as a whole – are players. Power is exercised through shifting alliances, depending on what is at stake in the polygonal activities which surround economic activity and the social life of individuals.

But its Community aspect is not the same as that in nation states, being more open, welcome, and effective to the point at which the formal might well silt up without informal mechanisms. As one very senior Brussels official put it, 'if you were to stick to the formal procedures, it would take ten years every time . . . the more there is disagreement, the more the informal is necessary.'[4] This argues that the EU's slowly evolving statehood – which is a subtext throughout this book – will continue to differ in kind from the statehood of its members. Each player operates in a multinational range. Each of them has its own distinct global interests, its own concept of what is good for it within the European framework. It is this which it wants inserted, like a pacemaker, in the heart of Europe. No nation state has to contend with such a game, none is so much an artefact of the game.

What the EU will become is not something this book attempts to guess. Given the model of perpetual flux which the formula competitive symposium implies, that would depend on answering an impossible set of questions about the future of the nation state, which is at present still the EU's main determinant. Yet that outcome will be affected by all the players, not just member states and Community institutions, in the double game in Brussels and national territories. How power is exercised in the Community is inseparable from the sum of all their transactions, a state of affairs which national governments would not permit at home but are powerless, because of their diversity, to prevent here.

By participating, players affect each other's perceptions of one another and what each is doing. As a result, the European Union may be becoming more like a global market in political and economic terms, but not necessarily so in social or cultural respects since there is a wider assimilation at work, beyond the one that makes their behaviour patterns similar. As their perceptions change – faster with the onset of an internal market – so may their interests. Imperceptibly, the economic players may become European, whatever nation states do, whether or not a European public comes into existence to fulfil what, in national terms, remain 'unnatural communities'. Yet the Community cannot be confined to the economic sphere because there are not even Chinese walls to separate economics from the political economy. If that makes the Community into a state, albeit of a different order from nation states, then the members of it must accept the outcome of what they have helped to create.

Sources

A book like this can only be written on the basis of elite oral history. Only one major archive, that of the Confederation of British Industry, was made available to us, from 1973 more or less to the present day. In amassing our own archive of over four hundred and forty interviews, we were able to hear the views of as complete a range of practitioners as seemed possible: Commission officials, Commissioners, member state administrators, politicians and Permanent Representatives, MEPs, judges and Advocates General, regional notables, representatives of peak institutions in the industrial, financial and labour sectors, and a considerable variety of firms' and financial institutions' executives.

We should emphasize that this selection was not Brussels-oriented, but incorporated a variety of standpoints: those of twelve member states, weighted according to size, four applicants for membership, five regions in the five largest member states, and a range of firms and sectoral organizations chosen to illustrate particular cases and their diversity of ethos and orientation. The choice of retired respondents as well as those in post enabled us to cover the period 1973 to 1994, and in particular to obtain insights into less-studied areas such as the Court of Justice, and the Committee of Central Bank Governors in Basel.

There were, inevitably, some arbitrary aspects to the selection, since not all those asked were willing or available to be interviewed. We concentrated more, for example, on the European Court of Justice than the European Parliament, whose powers and informal structures are still in the process of evolution; and on certain Commission Directorates, dealing with industries and the financial sector, rather than others. The interviews themselves naturally vary in quality, but at best constitute a significant weight of evidence. Copies have been lodged at the Sussex University

European Institute, at the European University Institute in Florence, and at the Hoover Institution, Stanford, California.

These are in the form of notes, not verbatim transcripts, being the researcher's record of what took place. This creates problems of attribution. Some of the material would not have been given if the sources were to be made plain so soon after the event; in other cases, where many of the respondents agreed, footnotes would have been unmanageably long. Where a choice is made between different interpretations, attribution would have been invidious and unfair to those who spoke in good faith. Furthermore, no individual could be taken as representative of any firm or institution, let alone a whole sector of government. Hence they are referred to here, where direct quotation occurs from the notes, but only by indexed numbers; in the archives they are referred to by a general title such as 'DG3 Official' or 'Executive of such-and-such a company'.

The problems connected with oral history are well known. They include lapses of memory, vindictiveness, falsification, excessive discretion, trivia, over-simplification, lack of perspective and various sorts of distortion and hindsight.[5] The interviewer in turn has his or her limitations, ranging from choosing an unrepresentative sample to undue deference or bias in questions; not forgetting that the method is often so enticing that it may unwisely be preferred to official or other printed sources.

A distinction should of course be made between oral history, used predominantly to record memoirs of the less articulate (whose lifestyles rarely appear in documentary form), to construct alternative or 'peoples' histories', and elite oral history, whose respondents are used to presenting themselves and their views fluently. Only the latter have been used here because they offer an unrivalled insight into motivations, interpretations, factors in policy-making, and the personal or group interchanges between those who belong to one or other of a number of elites.

The advantages clearly outweigh the risks, which prudence and practice can to a large extent mitigate, though never eliminate. Elite oral history, constructed from discussion with participants in the midst of the action, provides assessments of personalities and events which may not be recorded in documents even when these eventually become available for research. More important, it gives guidance on organizational relations which may well substantially modify observations found elsewhere. No organigram can be weighted sufficiently to show the informal channels or the difference between real and ritual communications.

Some institutions have only a limited effective life before becoming bureaucratized. Some are so informal as to leave no documentary record. All networks operate differently, depending on the question at issue and the level at which they relate to others. Vast as the flood of EC documentation is, ranging from formal reports to discussion documents, these alone cannot establish what on any given question is the place each player in each game merits. Interviewing gives insights into the assumptions or ethos of a group and its collective aims which, in the case of commercial organizations, may never otherwise be fully documented.

ACKNOWLEDGEMENTS

My gratitude to the members of the research team is simply expressed: without their patient work, in five languages, the aim could not have been achieved. The insights they provided, from very different national perspectives, informed the whole enquiry, and the discussions which took place among us at intervals during the project's life had the merits of a symposium, without the competition. In that sense they were indeed collaborators, as well as researchers; but as sole author of this book, I bear the responsibility for the themes and opinions expressed.

Secondly, I must express my thanks to the more than four hundred people in all walks and at all levels of Community life who allowed us to interview them, rarely for less than an hour, and often for much more. They gave their time and responded patiently and courteously, in the knowledge that there was no other way to understand the full complexity of the processes and links involved. What follows owes them an immense debt.

A project like this, ranging across a wide field and many countries, is hard to fund. I am therefore all the more grateful to the public bodies and foundations which supported it. In alphabetical order, these were CNRS/British Council Programme Franco-Britannique, the Commission of the European Communities, the Economic and Social Research Council, the European University Institute Archive, Florence, the Hoover Institution, Stanford, California, the Leverhulme Foundation, the Nuffield Foundation, the Thyssen Foundation and the University of Sussex.

Finally I should like to thank Professor Helen Wallace of the Sussex European Institute, whose kindly but forthright critical advice has been of immense benefit and saved me from many errors.

GLOSSARY OF ABBREVIATIONS AND ACRONYMS

ACEA : European association of car producers
ACP : African, Caribbean and Pacific
AGCM : Italian competition and anti-trust authority
AGREF : Association des Grandes Enterprises Françaises
AmCham : American Chamber of Commerce
ARE : Association of European Regions
ASTER : Agency for Regional Technological Development
Emilia-Romagna

BA : British Airways
BDA : German industry federation
BDB : German bankers federation
BDI : German industry federation
BKartA : Bundeskartellamt
BMWi : German Economics Ministry
BT : British Telecom

CAP : Common Agricultural Policy
CBI : Confederation of British Industry
CCMC : Association of European car producers
CDA : Netherlands Christian Democrats
CDI : Danish industry federation
CDU : Christian Democratic Union
CEA : European insurance federation
CEEC : Committee for European Economic Cooperation
CEEMR : Council of European Municipalities
CEFIC : European association of chemicals industry federations and
firms

CEN : European centre for standards
CENELEC : European electrical standards centre
CEO : Chief Executive Officer
CEOE : Confederation of Spanish employers
CET : Common External Tariff
CFDT : French socialist trades union confederation
CFI : Court of First Instance
CFSP : Common Foreign and Security Policy
CGIL : Italian communist trades union confederation
CGT : French communist trades union confederation
CIP : Portuguese industrial federation
CLCA : Association of national car producers federations
CNAC : Portuguese Council of EC Ministers
CNB : Czech National Bank
CNPF : French employers confederation
CONFEMETAL : Spanish confedertion of metalworking industries
Coreper : Committee of Permanent Representatives
CSCE : Conference on Security and Cooperation in Europe

DATAR : French government agency responsible for the regions
DBP : Deutsche Bundespost-Telekom
DC : Italian Christian Democrats
DG : Directorate-General
DGB : German trades union federation
DGCCRF : French mergers & fraud authority
DHKI : German SMEs federation
DIHT : German Chambers of Commerce
DM : Deutschmark
DTI : Department of Trade and Industry
DVI : German industry federation

EACEM : European association of electronics industry federations
EBRD : European Bank for Recovery and Development
EC : European Community
ECA : Economic Cooperation Agency
ECB : European Central Bank
ECNA : European Aerospace Industrial Association

ECSC : European Coal and Steel Community
ECTEL : European association of telecoms equipment producers
EDU : European Democratic Union
EEA : European Economic Area
EEC : European Economic Community
EEG : European Enterprise Group
ECJ : European Court of Justice
Ecofin : Economic and Finance Committee
Ecosoc : Economic and Social Committee
EDC : European Defence Community
EFPIA : European association of pharmaceuticals industries
EFTA : European Free Trade Association
EIB : European Investment Bank
EISA : European association of independent steel producers
EMI : European Monetary Institute
EMS : European Monetary System
EMU : Economic and Monetary Union
EP : European Parliament
EPC : European Political Cooperation
EPP : European People's Party
EPU : European Payments Union; European Political Union
ERDF : European Regional Development Fund
ERM : Exchange Rate Mechanism
ERP : European Recovery Programme
ERT : European Round Table
ESF : European Social Fund
ETUC : European Trades Union Confederation
EU : European Union
EUROMNI : European association of small producers (SMEs) federations

FBE : European banking federation
FDI : foreign direct investment
FDP : German Free Democratic Party
FEIQUE : Spanish federation of chemicals industries
FEOGA : Fonds Européen d'Orientation et de Garantie Agricole

FO : Force Ouvrière
FTN : Catalan employers confederation

G5/G7 : Group of Five/Seven
GAC : General Affairs Council
GATT : General Agreement on Tariffs and Trade
GDP : gross domestic product
HA : High Authority
HDTV : high definition television
HIBD : Highlands and Islands Development Board
HNB : Hungarian National Bank

IBEC : Irish Business and Employers Confederation
IBRD : International Bank for Reconstruction and Development
IGC : inter-governmental conference
IMF : International Monetary Fund
ITO : International Trade Organization

JAMA : Japanese federation of car producers (in Europe)

KK : Netherlands Coordinating Committee

MEP : Member of the European Parliament
MFA : Multi-Fibre Agreement
MFE : Movimento Federalista Europeo
MITI : Ministry for International Trade and Industry (Japan)
MMC : Monopolies and Mergers Commission
MNC : multinational company
MS : member state

NAFTA : North American Free Trade Area
NATO : North Atlantic Treaty Organization
NEDC : National Economic and Development Council
NESC : National Economic and Social Council
NFs : national firms

OECD : Organization for Economic Cooperation and Development
OEEC : Organization for European Economic Cooperation

OPEC : Organization of Petroleum Exporting Countries
ORGALIME : European association of telecoms industry federations
ÖVP : Austrian Christian Democrats

PCE : Spanish communist party
PCF : French communist party
PCI : Italian communist party
PCPE : Patronat Catala Pro Europa
PDS : Italian democratic party of the left
PIMEC : Spanish association of SMEs
PP : Partido Popular
PS : Parti Socialiste
PSI : Italian socialist party
PSOE : Spanish socialist party

QMV : qualified majority voting
QR : quantitative restrictions

RDF : Regional Development Fund
RPR : Rassemblement pour la Republique

SDA : Scottish Development Agency
SEA : Single European Act
SEM : Single European Market
SEV : Greek industry federation
SGCI : Service de Coordination Inter-ministerial
SME : Small and Medium-sized Enterprises
SMMT : Society of Motor Manufacturers and Traders
SOPA : Agriculture Confederation
SPD : German socialist party

TNCs : trans-national corporations
TUC : Trades Union Congress

UDF : Union Democratique Français
UGT : Spanish socialist trades union federation

UNICE : European confederation of industries
UNIFE : European railway producers federation
UNRRA : United Nations Relief and Rehabilitation Administration

VCI : German chemicals industry federation
VDA : German association of car producers
VER : voluntary export restraints
VNO : Netherlands industrial federation

WEU : Western European Union
WTO : World Trade Organization

ZDH : German association for craft business (SMEs)
ZVEI : German consumer electronics industries federation

Presidents and principal Commissioners relevant to the main themes since 1981

President (81-84)	External relations	Econ. and finance
Gaston Thorn	Wilhelm Haferkamp (Lorenzo Natali)	Francois-Xavier Ortoli

Industry	Competition	Transport
Etienne Davignon	Frans Andriessen	Georgis Contogeorgis

Science/ Research	Telecoms	Internal market /Financial institutions
Etienne Davignon		Karl-Heinz Narjes (int. market) Christopher Tugendhat (financial institutions)

Regional policy	DG XXIII (enterprise policy, tourism,...)
Antonio Giolitti	Antonio Giolitti

Presidents and principal Commissioners
contd.

President (85-88)	External relations	Econ. and finance
Jacques Delors	Willy De Clercq (Claude Cheysson)	Alois Pfeiffer

Industry	Competition	Transport
Karl-Heinz Narjes	Peter Sutherland	Stanley Clinton Davis

Science/ Research	Telecoms	Internal market /Financial institutions
Karl-Heinz Narjes		Arthur Cockfield

Regional policy	DG XXIII (enterprise policy, tourism,...)
Alois Pfeiffer	Carlo Ripa di Meana (Abel Matutes)

Presidents and principal Commissioners
contd.

President (89-92)	External relations	Econ. and finance
Jacques Delors	Frans Andriessen (Abel Matutes)	Henning Christophersen

Industry	Competition	Transport
Martin Bangemann	Leon Brittan	Karel van Miert

Science/ Research	Telecoms	Internal market /Financial institutions
Filippo Maria Pandolfi	Filippo Maria Pandolfi	Martin Bangemann (Leon Brittan)

Regional policy	DG XXIII (enterprise policy, tourism,...)
Bruce Millan	Antonio Cardoso e Cunha

Presidents and principal Commissioners
contd.

President (93-94)	External relations	Econ. and finance
Jacques Delors	Leon Brittan Hans van den Broek (Manuel Marin)	Henning Christophersen

Industry	Competition	Transport
Martin Bangemann	Karel van Miert	Abel Matutes

Science/ Research	Telecoms	Internal market /Financial institutions
Antonio Ruberti	Martin Bangemann	Raniero Vanni d'Archirafi

Regional policy	DG XXIII (enterprise policy, tourism,...)
Bruce Millan	Raniero Vanni d'Archirafi

Presidents and principal Commissioners
contd.

President (95-99)	External relations	Econ. and finance
Jacques Santer	Hans van den Broek Leon Brittan (Manuel Marin) (Joao de Deus Pinheiro)	Yves-Thibault de Silguy

Industry	Competition	Transport
Martin Bangemann	Karel van Miert	Neil Kinnock

Science/ Research	Telecoms	Internal market /Financial institutions
Edith Cresson	Martin Bangemann	Mario Monti

Regional policy	DG XXIII (enterprise policy, tourism,...)
Monika Wulf-Mathies	Christos Papoutsis

Presidencies of the Council of Ministers and Meetings of the European Council since 1970

Year	Country	European council meetings	
1970	Belgium Germany		
1971	France Italy		
1972	Luxembourg Netherlands		
1973	Belgium Denmark		
1974	Germany France	Paris, 9–10 December: Decision to create the 'European Council'	
1975	Ireland Italy	10–11 March, 11–17 July, 1–2 December,	Dublin Brussels Rome
1976	Luxembourg Netherlands	1–2 April, 12–13 July, 29–30 November,	Luxembourg Brussels The Hague
1977	United Kingdom Belgium	25–26 March, 29–3 0 June, 5–6 December,	Rome London Brussels
1978	Denmark Germany	7–8 April, 6–7 July, 4–5 December,	Copenhagen Bremen Brussels
1979	France Ireland	12–13 March, 21–22 June, 29–30 November,	Paris Strasbourg Dublin
1980	Italy Luxembourg	27–28 April, 12–13 June, 1–2 December,	Luxembourg Venice Luxembourg
1981	Netherlands United Kingdom	23–24 March, 29–30 June, 26–27 November,	Maastricht Luxembourg London
1982	Belgium Denmark	29–30 March, 28–29 June, 3–4 December,	Brussels Brussels Copenhagen
1983	Germany Greece	21–22 March, 17–19 June, 4–6 December,	Brussels Stuttgart Athens
1984	France Ireland	19–20 March, 25–26 June, 3–4 December,	Brussels Fontainebleau Dublin
1985	Italy Luxembourg	29–30 March, 28–29 June, 2–3 December,	Brussels Milan Luxembourg

1986	Netherlands	26-27 June,	The Hague
	United Kingdom	5-6 December,	London
1987	Belgium	29-30 June,	Brussels
	Denmark	4-5 December,	Copenhagen
1988	Germany	11-13 February,	Brussels
		27-28 June,	Hanover
	Greece	2-3 December,	Rhodes
1989	Spain	26-27 July,	Madrid
	France	8-9 December,	Strasbourg
1990	Ireland	28 April,	Dublin
		25-26 June,	Dublin
	Italy	27-28 October,	Rome
		14-15 December,	Rome
1991	Luxembourg	8 April,	Luxembourg
		28-29 June,	Luxembourg
	Netherlands	9-10 December,	Maastricht
1992	Portugal	26-27 June,	Lisbon
	United Kingdom	16 October,	Brussels
		11-12 December,	Brussels
1993	Denmark	2 1-22 June,	Copenhagen
	Belgium	29 October,	Brussels
		10-11 December,	Brussels
1994	Greece	24-25 June,	Corfu
	Germany	15 July,	Brussels
		9-10 December,	Essen
1995	France	June	Cannes
	Spain		

The European
Integration Experience

RICHARD T. GRIFFITHS

1

─────────

1945–58[1]

In 1945 western Europe counted the cost of yet another continental conflict, the third in the space of seventy years involving France and Germany. Yet by 1958, these two countries had formed the core of a new supranational 'community', transforming intra-state relations in the space of thirteen years. It represented a development to which many in 1945 would have aspired but which few would have dared to hope would be realised so quickly. This evolution marked the beginning of what is commonly referred to as 'the process of European integration'.

It is worth pausing to consider the double connotation of the word 'integration', since the expression is used to imply both a sequence of institutional changes (all involving the surrender of national sovereignty) and the enmeshing of economies and societies that it is intended should flow from these measures. To be more precise, 'integration' was one of the goals of the European Coal and Steel Community (ECSC), founded by France, Germany, Italy and the Benelux countries in 1952, and of the European Economic Community (EEC) and EURATOM, both founded by the same six states in 1958. Nonetheless, we should realize that this term intentionally excepts many other types of institutional change on the grounds that they are 'inter-governmental', and do not involve the surrender of sovereignty. It also marginalizes other sources, institutional or otherwise, of Europe's growing 'interdependence'.

The 'process of integration' is given pride of place in the memoirs of those most closely identified with it. This is because they were convinced of the historical importance of their achievements, but also because they were eager to win the propaganda war against the existing inter-governmental alternatives, which they perceived as weak and incapable of sustaining further development.[2] The institutions and workings of the new supranational communities were pushed further into the limelight by the writings of a generation of political scientists, attracted by the novelty of provisions in the Community and the dynamic inherent in their operations. Their attitudes have subsequently been projected backwards onto the past in a series of histories which concentrate on the struggle for supranational, even federal, institutions, but which mostly exclude developments elsewhere. Yet the EEC came onto the scene relatively late in the day and although the ECSC had been created six years earlier, it was limited in its economic impact. Insofar as the economic boom of the 1950s and the trade expansion that accompanied it had been caused by institutional changes, its origins lay elsewhere. The EEC's creation witnessed the end of western Europe's financial and commercial rehabilitation and not the beginning.

Since the late 1970s, a new generation of historians, trudging in the wake of the so-called 'thirty year rule' – the period before which some national governments grant access to their archives – have been rewriting the history of this period. Much of this work has still to be assimilated into mainstream accounts but, once it has been, its main achievement will have been to widen the perspective and context of analysis and to rediscover the complexity of the past. This, in itself, has often constituted an antidote to the simplistic 'high politics' analysis (and sometimes straight federalist propaganda) of existing accounts. However, thus far historians have been less than successful in agreeing on a coherent 'alternative' explanation to federalist accounts.

One casualty of the new history has been 'American hegemony theory', at least in its early chronology. The 'hegemonic leadership' theory argues that the existence of an American political hegemony allowed for the reconciliation of lesser, more localized national differences. Thus, at the height of its relative economic, political, military and moral power, the United States is supposed to have used its good offices to establish a liberal world order and, more particularly, to have supported 'integrative' solutions to world problems that mirrored its own history and that seemed to underpin its own success and prosperity. The new, revisionist literature has demonstrated the limits of hegemonic power and has raised awareness of the degree to which Europe has been able to resist American influence. Equally, it has underscored the 'European' as opposed to the American motives in seeking to 'change the rules' of European inter-state relations through institutional innovation and reform.

Secondly, historians have stumbled into the 'actor-agency' dilemma already familiar to political scientists. Initially, much of the literature focused on the actors: the ideas that drove them, the positions of political power they occupied and their role in the nexus of key players, together with the political processes which they adapted or invented to accomplish their ends. The need to find peace in western Europe and to build a bulwark against totalitarianism formed the 'real world' components in this analysis. Subsequently, historians working usually in governmental archives have found a more prosaic subtext to these events. Far from an heroic, visionary quest for a better future, they recount the story of an entrenched defence of perceived national interest. This version of history is often juxtaposed against the earlier approaches but the two are not necessarily irreconcilable. The international agreements that underpin the integration 'process' were usually submitted to parliamentary scrutiny and the threat of rejection placed constraints on too cavalier a surrender of sovereignty on issues of real public concern. Moreover, the whole idea of 'supranationality' is to adapt the rules of future political behaviour, to determine a new 'how' for the political process. It may remain a primary goal even if it requires a surrender of consistency or elegance in the short-term.

This version of 'perceived national interest' is itself the outcome of domestic political processes and is susceptible to changes in the balance both within governments and between governments. It is some way removed from the concept of national interest as formulated by 'realist' or 'neo-realist' scholars, who argue that the state is a unitary actor, intent on maximizing its interests, whose foreign policy behaviour can be understood from an objective reading of its relative geo-political position. Within the literature of integration this type of analysis made its appearance in the early 1960s[3] and has recently been revived. In its current version, the viability or survival of post-War, democratic states lay in their ability to satisfy a 'consensus' built around comprehensive welfare provision, economic growth and agricultural protection. According to this critique, only when these goals can not be met in any other way do governments agree to surrender sovereignty, usually emerging stronger as a result.[4] Aside from postulating an implausible degree of coherence in collective decision-making, this version of events both exaggerates the dangers confronting European states in what was, after all, the middle of the greatest economic boom in modern history, and the importance of supranational mechanisms in resolving residual commercial challenges.

Despite the awesome destructive power of the weaponry deployed during the Second World War, Europe's post-War productive capacity was not as damaged as has often been claimed. Although the image of utter devastation still persists, the material damage was concentrated on areas of infrastructural investment (mainly transport and housing) and much less on productive capital. Most historians now accept that Europe's industrial capacity was larger in the late 1940s than it had been in 1938 and, in some respects, better adapted to the needs of the post-War era. Without taking this into account, it is impossible to understand Europe's rapid industrial recovery. Already by 1947, most western European countries had surpassed their pre-War levels of industrial output. Germany, the main exception, was not to do so until 1950, by which time western Europe as a whole was producing almost 25 per cent more than in the pre-War years. Although the expansion of manufacturing was remarkable, serious problems still remained. Basic industries, such as coal and steel, struggled to recapture pre-War levels and the neglect and destruction of transportation systems also caused major bottle-necks. Agricultural production was not as severely weakened within western Europe, but recovery was much slower than it had been for industry. Although a poor harvest in 1947 reinforced the negative image of the condition of European agriculture after the War, this was a serious but isolated incident and output rebounded quickly. Even so, it was not until 1950 that production recovered to its pre-War levels.[5]

The impact of all these changes was to widen the productivity gap between Europe and the USA. In industry alone, the USA had emerged from the War with double the output of 1938 and, despite the dislocation of adjusting to peacetime conditions (and a short-lived recession), had added further to this position by 1950. Without closing the gap, it was felt that Europe would be unable to repair the trade imbalance with the US and would be unable to sustain acceptable standards of welfare for its peoples. This problem was aggravated by the impact of the War on Europe's trading relationships, both with each other and with the rest of the world.

American wartime planning had aspired to a world multilateral trade and payments system. The Bretton Woods conference, held in July 1944, decided in favour of the restoration of the gold-exchange standard (based on gold and convertible reserve currencies) but with two important safeguards. Firstly, it created the International Monetary Fund (IMF) to aid countries against speculative attack. Secondly, it agreed a set of 'rules' to govern international monetary behaviour. In December 1945, the US proposed complementing the arrangements for world monetary order by the creation of the International Trade Organisation (ITO) to ease trade conditions and to co-ordinate national countercyclical policies. Its constitution, in a much watered-down form, was agreed in Havana in 1948. However, the ITO never came into existence because the US Congress, unwilling to surrender so much control over its protectionist arsenal, refused its ratification. This left the temporary and far less comprehensive General Agreement on Tariffs and Trade (GATT), agreed in 1947, as the main regulatory body for commodity trade. It is important to note that in both areas, the agenda for action was a global one. There was little place for new regional discrimination and every intention to eradicate existing trade preference areas, usually between colonial and metropolitan powers.[6]

Instead of a multilateral trading system, Europe's trade and payments had returned to the pattern of bilateralism and autarky that had characterized the 1930s. Indeed the pervasiveness of frontier controls between countries and across products surpassed anything that had been seen in peacetime since the start of the free trade movement a century earlier. Europe's commercial problems stemmed from several different sources. The effect of the dislocation of the War on many economies made it difficult to divert production to exports at the expense of investment or already low levels of consumption. Moreover, the liquidation or destruction of foreign investments which, even by 1950, were still earning 75% less in real terms than they had been in 1938, removed an important source for covering import requirements. These two developments aggravated trade imbalances but the problem was further complicated by shifts in the direction of trade. Germany had provided many countries with imports of fuel and raw materials, semimanufactured and investment goods upon which their own industries had depended. Because German recovery was inhibited by the occupying Allies, this source of supply was much diminished. Moreover, agricultural goods, and particularly grain, were no longer available in the same quantities from eastern Europe. Indeed the only area capable of compensating for this shortfall in supply was North America. Thus the trade deficit with the dollar area increased enormously compared with before the War, at a time when the disruption of colonial economies also meant that Europe was no longer able to earn dollars from triangular trade. The scarcity of hard currencies forced countries to restrict imports and control trade through bilateral agreements, augmented with quantitative restrictions and exchange controls. The effects of these problems, and the measures chosen to cope with them, reduced the relative levels of internal trade in peacetime in western Europe to possibly their lowest point in the twentieth century. The share of internal trade as a proportion of Europe's total imports and exports fell from almost 48% in 1938 to under 35% ten years later.[7]

It was against this background that, early in 1947, there occurred a sharp deterioration in western Europe's balance of payments. It was probably occasioned primarily by the ambitious inflationary investment plans initiated in pursuit of domestic reconstruction but was aggravated by the impact of poor harvests on Europe's terms of trade. Yet it was this second factor, with its associated images of hunger, high prices and social discontent, that formed the prime means publicly to legitimize the massive dollar investment programme announced by the American secretary of state, General George Marshall, at a speech at Harvard University in June 1947. The announcement of the Marshall Plan has often been associated with the 'Truman Doctrine' of March 1947, which pledged American help to the Greek government in their struggle against the Communists in the civil war. Together, they have come to symbolize the start of the Cold War. Yet Marshall Aid marked another fundamental shift in American policy. It represented a recognition that Europe's reconstruction could not be managed within a global, multilateral framework, but rather that the continent's rehabilitation was a prerequisite for the functioning of wider arrangements.[8]

The failure of a global strategy was underlined within months of the announcement of Marshall Aid. When, in 1945, the Anglo-American loan agreement had been signed, one of its clauses had stipulated that the United Kingdom would reintroduce sterling convertibility by mid-1947. This would allow countries to use their sterling reserves for multilateral settlements and thus reduce the pressures on the dollar. On the appointed day, supported by new loans, the British government duly announced the return to convertibility and found itself immediately confronted with a run on reserves. Within seven weeks, the experiment was abruptly curtailed. Nothing else could have demonstrated so eloquently that it was not currency or liquidity that the system needed, but one currency in particular (the US dollar) and in one area (western Europe).

Of course there was a realization that special transient arrangements would be needed to assist recovery from wartime destruction. In November 1943, for example, forty-four governments created the United Nations Relief and Rehabilitation Administration (UNRRA) for the provision of immediate relief in the form of food, clothing and shelter, as well as the raw materials and machinery necessary to restart agricultural and industrial production. In mid-1946, the UNRRA decided to wind up its operations by the spring of 1947. Before then, in June 1946, another Bretton Woods institution, the International Bank for Reconstruction and Development (IBRD or World Bank) had commenced operations, although it was another full year before it made its first loan. Marshall Aid, however, was an implicit acknowledgment that IBRD funds would be no match for the task at hand.

The United States began its active intervention in Europe's structural problems with the European Recovery Program (ERP). In comparison with the $4 billion that the United States had contributed to European reconstruction in the first two years since the War through the UNRRA and other programmes, over the four years of its operation Marshall aid allocated to Europe nearly $12.5 billion: $10 billion in grants, $1 billion in loans and $1.5 billion in 'conditional aid', which was used to lubricate the limited intra-European Payments Agreement of 1948. Not only were the sums contributed far larger than had previously been considered necessary, but ERP was important in enabling countries to adopt longer-term and more secure planning frameworks for their investment strategies, by giving recipient countries a commitment to provide financial aid and other assistance on a four-year, rather than an ad hoc, basis. On the American side, the Economic Cooperation Agency (ECA) administered the scheme. In Europe, sixteen states formed the Committee for European Economic Cooperation (CEEC) to decide on accepting the aid and, in 1948, continued their existence as the Organisation for European Economic Co-operation (OEEC).

The dollars were made available for vital import requirements. Only 17% was spent directly on imports of 'machinery and vehicles', the rest went on raw materials and agricultural products. The importers, however, paid the equivalent in domestic currency to their governments who were free to use the money on capital projects. This mechanism freed domestic funds for capital formation and, since ECA approval was required before the funds could be spent, it allowed US planners to influence directly the direction of economic change. In addition, for example by refusing funds to Italian firms that dealt with non-'free' (i.e., communist) trade unions, it also permitted their intrusion into the politics and societies of European states.

The macroeconomic impact of the ERP on European economies has recently been questioned. Certainly it did not save the continent from ruin and starvation since, by the time its funds came on stream in mid-1948, that moment had long passed. Instead, it contributed to the maintenance of already high investment levels, with the greatest relative impact in the first two years. However, funding was not on a scale sufficient to explain the super-growth of the 1950s. It is true that in 1948 and 1949, the contribution of ERP funds to gross domestic capital formation touched 30% in Germany and Italy, but in both countries the global figures were particularly low. The more usual level was around 10%, as it was also for Italy and Germany in 1950 and 1951; a useful but not decisive contribution. New calculations suggest that aid directly contributed only 0.5% per annum to annual growth in this period. Indirectly, the flow of funds for raw materials itself released resources for investment and the secure planning horizons might also have contributed to raising investment and output targets. The ERP also reduced the tension of the said structural adjustment. At a time when demand exceeded supply by 7.5%, an addition of 2.5% to GNP reduced the potential conflict about how wealth should be distributed between labour and capital.[9]

Not unnaturally, the Americans were reluctant to see their funds siphoned off into competing national schemes, each presumably demanding further measures of national protection. They insisted from the start that the funds be allocated according to pan-European criteria and in the service of a pan-European plan. The European criterion for aid assessment was adopted. It was taken as the size of the dollar gap rather than any estimate of size of income or degree of damage. A European plan also emerged, aimed at the previously prescribed goal of balance of payments equilibrium by 1952. However, a closer reading of the European plan demonstrates that it was little more than the aggregation of separate national plans. The Americans had more success in encouraging measures for the freeing of trade and payments from national constraints and protectionism. Although the causes of the economic growth of the 1950s, and the even more spectacular expansion of trade that accompanied it, are many and complex, at an institutional level it was the ERP, through the OEEC, that laid the foundations.

In October 1949, the ECA administrator, Paul Hoffman, made a major speech to the OEEC in which he called repeatedly for 'integration' as the price for a continued, generous level of dollar aid. 'The substance of such integration', he went on, 'would be the formation of a single large market in which quantitative restriction on the movement of goods, monetary barriers to the flow of payments and, eventually, all tariffs are permanently swept away.' Although the OEEC had experimented in 1948 and 1949 with some limited multilateral payments schemes and was at that moment considering a (modest) start to a programme of quota removal, Hoffman's speech had the effect of concentrating minds wonderfully.

In case the OEEC was in doubt about the direction of American thinking, another ECA official, Richard Bissel, produced an outline for a European Payments Union (EPU), a discriminatory soft-currency zone, which in its detail went far beyond the usual policy advice. The Americans also pledged themselves to providing a sum of $350 million for the EPU's working capital. It is interesting to note that the EPU was a recognition that another American creation, the IMF, was incapable of supervising Europe's transition to convertibility. However, its rules and objectives were oriented towards the attainment of full, non-discriminatory currency convertibility. The sterling crisis of 1947 had demonstrated that any such move would rapidly have drained the IMF of its loanable funds. All the IMF could do was to recognize the serious structural problems facing the continent and sanction the discriminatory currency practices that were already commonplace.

The European Payments Union (EPU) embraced all OEEC members and came into operation in September 1950, its structure being an interesting innovation in the OEEC, which is commonly known as an 'inter-governmental' institution. In order to resolve conflicts, the EPU included a Special Restricted Committee of five persons chosen by lot from a list of nominees proposed by the member states, with the proviso that none of the committee members could be citizens of the countries involved in the dispute. The committee reported to the OEEC Council which then pronounced judgement. The Managing Board of the EPU, comprising seven representatives and one American observer, adjudicated using majority voting. This, too, was at odds with standard OEEC procedure, but since the Board was responsible to the OEEC Council, serious disputes were likely to end up before them anyway.

Of the initial $350 million granted to the EPU, some $80 million was immediately allocated to countries with 'structural' payments problems, while the remainder provided the working capital of the Union. This money was necessary to bridge the gap in the arrangements for debtors and those for creditors. The system worked thus: for each country, a margin of deficit was calculated (equivalent to 15% of the value of trade) that would receive some automatic credit on its intra-European transactions. This figure was demarcated according to five steps. In the first step, the debtor received 100% credit; in the second, he received 80% credit but had to pay the rest in gold or dollars. The amount of hard currency payable was increased until the fifth step, when only 20% was covered by credit and the rest in hard currency. Beyond that, all transactions took effect in hard currency. Overall, within the EPU allocation, a debtor could rely on a credit covering 60% of any deficit. A similar situation prevailed for creditors within the Union but although the overall position was the same (60:40), the steps were not synchronized, with the effect that creditors received hard currency from the Union earlier than the debtors were paying it in. It was to cover this gap that the dollar funding was intended.[10]

No sooner had the EPU been installed than it was put to the test. The German economy already had a huge deficit in autumn 1950 and the situation was rapidly deteriorating. With the exhaustion of its quota in sight, the EPU extended an extra credit line and, in February 1951 acknowledged the need for a reintroduction of quotas and the creation of state monopoly import agencies. By the summer of 1952, the crisis had been weathered and an upturn in exports allowed Germany to reopen its markets. Similar, though less violent, crises hit the United Kingdom and France in these early years and it was the EPU that provided the means whereby countries were not forced to adopt violent deflationary measures. Moreover, although in every case there was some backsliding in the commitment to hold back levels of import quotas, the fact that EPU and the OEEC's 'trade liberalization' scheme (of which more below) were in existence, acted as a control over a more drastic and dislocating return to temporary protection.

From a low point in June 1952, when the combined reserves of the OEEC states stood at $7.8 billion, the position steadily improved until mid-1955 when they reached $13.4 billion. Against this background, the conditions within the EPU gradually 'hardened'. In place of a ratio 60:40 between credit and gold, in mid–1954 the coverage was changed to 50:50 and in 1955 only 25:75. By this stage much of the EPU's work had been done and many countries had introduced de facto convertibility on current account transactions (though this step was not formally taken until December 1958). Meanwhile, the EPU's main customer was France and, although the job could equally have been done by the IMF, the operation held France within the European institutional orbit at a time of political upheaval fuelled by colonial unrest, and when more 'integrationist' experiments were being discussed.

The mirror of American concern on payments was its determination to remove quotas on intra-European trade. The obvious multilateral forum for dealing with the issue was the General Agreement on Tariffs and Trade (GATT) agreed in Havana in 1947. Yet GATT was fatally flawed. It was dependent for its existence on regular renewal by its members. Moreover, the rejection of the ITO had signalled that the US Congress was wary about agreeing to anything that might affect levels of protection for US industry. At a time when the major dysfunctional element in the world economy was seen to be the inability to pay for dollar imports through the sale of goods on the American market, it was inconceivable to envisage a reciprocal tariff negotiation that did not require for its success concessions by the United States. Although at Geneva, in 1947, GATT partners negotiated cuts of 19% in their registered tariffs on manufactured goods, at Annecy, only two years later, the meagre harvest was estimated at 2% while at Torquay, in 1950–51, it climbed marginally to reach 3%. In both these latter cases, a major factor was the reluctance of the USA to negotiate reciprocal tariff reductions. With success on tariffs beyond them, the members of GATT refrained, perhaps wisely, from tackling the enforcement of prohibitions on quotas, which were seen as even more harmful to trade than tariffs. It was for this reason that the USA accepted a regional solution to the removal of quantitative restrictions (QRs) or quotas on intra-European trade.[11]

At the end of 1949, the OEEC adopted the target for removing import quotas directed against each other, on 50% of their 'private' trade, by the end of the year. This target also applied separately to each of the three groups: food and food stuffs, raw materials and manufactured goods. Under prompting from ECA officials, who argued that something a little more spectacular was necessary to convince Congress to continue aid at the present high level, the target was raised first to 60% and subsequently to 75%. The 'trade liberalization scheme', as it became known, had several drawbacks that made the commitments, and the achievements, less than at first sight. Firstly, the operation referred to 'private trade' and exempted, therefore, imports on government account. This had been done so as not to interfere in 'domestic' political decisions but the effect was to remove from the operation of the scheme entire swathes of trade, mostly in agriculture but sometimes also in fuel, controlled by monopoly government purchasing agencies. Secondly this bias in the operation was compounded by the fact that the initial obligation to remove QRs evenly over broad product categories was dropped once the targets were further raised. An over-performance in raw materials, for example, could and usually did compensate for an under-achievement in agriculture. Furthermore, the Liberalization Code allowed a country with balance-of-payments difficulties unilaterally to reimpose restrictions if necessary, causing a rebound effect on its trading partners and undermining the EPU's 'discipline' in the process. Finally, the whole operation excluded tariffs, which were considered the preserve of GATT, so that QR removal was often accompanied by the re-imposition of (partially) suspended tariffs. The initial agreement bore all the hall-marks of the compromises necessary to secure its passage through the OEEC Council.

In October 1950, the OEEC Council agreed that by February 1951, members should remove QRs on 75% of imports from other members, but it was there that further progress stalled. The crisis atmosphere engendered by the payments problems in Germany, the UK and France meant that for them even the 75% target had to be temporarily shelved. Such circumstances obviously inhibited the pressure for further advances. Discussions were also constrained by increasing disenchantment by the 'low tariff' countries of the Benelux, Scandinavia and Switzerland towards the failure to tackle tariffs, and therefore to deal with all frontier barriers to trade. Finally, as QR removal advanced, it threatened to touch the hard core of protectionism in sectors deemed by governments to be politically, socially or strategically vital to the national interest.

By the mid-1950s, reflecting their less strained balance of payments positions, most OEEC countries had satisfied their 75% targets. Many had also relaxed their quota regimes towards the dollar area, although not to the same extent. Yet when the decision was taken, in January 1955, to progress towards 90 per cent liberalization, the 'low tariff' countries made their agreement conditional upon action being taken by the Organisation to deal with high tariffs. Although they did not get their way, the target was nonetheless renewed and when, in December 1958, France finally attained it, private trading within western Europe had, to all intents and purposes, been purged of quantitative restrictions. There remained residual quota discrimination against the USA and, of course, state trading in agriculture was widespread. Nonetheless, for an experiment with such tentative beginnings, the achievement in reducing tariffs was remarkable.

Hoffman's call for 'integration' back in October 1949 acted as a catalyst for a pan-European programme of action on trade and payments. Yet, even at the time, there was an awareness that there existed another path to 'integration' and that it might even be preferable. Whereas Hoffman sought to increase Europe's degree of multilateral cooperation in carefully defined but meaningful areas, secretary of state Dean Acheson preferred a strengthening of political mechanisms that would weaken the ability of national veto-rights to prevent desirable initiatives. In fairness, one should add that he preferred this path because he considered that it would be easier for European countries to comply than it would be for them to accept a more concrete programme. For both men, the ultimate goal was a 'Europe' that mirrored more closely the political model of the United States of America. The 'new' continent could still show the old how to throw off the last shackles of its *ancien régime*.

The concept of 'integration' in political or institutional terms had also entered the mainstream of debate in western Europe. During the Second World War, Resistance movements had been forced, partly by the pan-European model espoused by the fascists and the Third Reich, to produce a cogent alternative that also transcended national frontiers. Their thinking was shaped by several factors that pointed the way towards international institutional reform. The failure of the Versailles Treaty and the League of Nations to prevent the reassertion of aggressive nationalism suggested that the foreign policies of nation states required stronger constraints. Similarly, the 'beggar-thy-neighbour' policies that characterized separate national responses towards the Great Depression suggested that there, too, some higher disciplinary force was necessary. These ideas had inspired the original surge of post-War institution-building, but for many observers the strengthening of inter-governmental organizations was not enough. They argued that national units were too small to guarantee security and prosperity in the modern world and too recalcitrant to guarantee freedom from assault. Solutions lay in the pooling of national sovereignties, thereby effectively proscribing the use of national means for economic or military aggression.

After the War almost every country witnessed the creation of national 'European' movements, even though they often disagreed on both aims and tactics. Some dedicated themselves to the task of leading opinion, while others had more populist aspirations. Some saw progress as incremental, like a ripple effect from a core of commitment; others wanted a swift adoption of new political structures; some took a view that it was good for others but not necessarily for themselves. Various national federalist groups, more geared towards mobilizing mass opinion and characterized in their approach by a certain 'constitutionalism', formed the European Union of Federalists in 1946. Another organization formed at this time, intent on mobilizing support for a new form of European political organisation, was the Socialist Movement for a United States of Europe. However, the lead in galvanizing public opinion was the United Europe Movement, inspired by Winston Churchill's Zürich speech in September 1946, calling for a United States of Europe, and founded by his son-in-law, Duncan Sandys. It was this body that, in May 1948, sponsored the Congress of the European Movement, held in the Hague.[12]

The Hague Congress, which created the Council of Europe, was supposed to create a new momentum towards higher federalist goals. Instead, its creation was its own greatest achievement. Whether the British government, or Churchill in opposition, had ever held more than a fleeting interest in actively associating themselves with the construction of a European federation is highly questionable. Embroiled in an organization with a federation as its goal, the government rapidly proceeded to distance itself from other countries' impulses towards 'integration', and in the process became the focus of opposition. The Council of Europe became torn between the 'federalists', who wanted to move quickly towards new constitutional arrangements, and the 'functionalists', who believed that new arrangements would be workable only if the surrender of sovereignty were a functional necessity. The latter envisaged that progress would take place cautiously, on a step-by-step basis, but since the UK was the leading exponent of the functionalist school, the position boiled down to one of no progress at all.

These developments quickly paralysed developments in the Council of Europe and certainly robbed the European movement, in its various guises, of direct political influence. Only in Italy, under the leadership of Altiero Spinelli, was there an attempt to convert the federalist cause into a mass movement, the Movimento

Federalista Europeo. Spinelli soon became disenchanted with the MFE, but his enthusiasm for supranationalism remained undiminished. When the head of the Italian government, Alcide de Gasperi, asked him to draft a federalist plan for controlling European institutions, Spinelli seized the chance. His efforts resulted in the introduction of the 'federalist' clause 38 into the European Defence Community treaty (see below). This, however, represented the pinnacle of the MFE's achievements. As the EDC faded, so the movement's influence began to ebb.[13]

Whilst popular movements cannot claim credit for initiating 'the process of integration', they nonetheless provided a pool of new ideas and a vocabulary that decision makers could draw upon when confronted by immediate political problems. This occurred most dramatically when, in May 1950, the French foreign minister, Robert Schuman, announced his plan to form a coal and steel pool which embraced Germany. When this call was answered by the Benelux countries and Italy as well, the way was cleared for the 'Six' to embark upon a series of institutional experiments built around the concepts of supranationality and surrender of sovereignty.

It was by no means preordained that six countries would become irrevocably associated with each other in a series of supranational communities, nor that those six would be France, Germany, Italy, the Netherlands, Belgium and Luxembourg. To appreciate how 'the Six' reached that stage, we have to go back to the creation of Benelux, and the reaction of France, especially, to that development.

Benelux was the oldest of the post-War experiments in regional integration in western Europe. It linked Belgium and Luxembourg (whose own economic union, the BLEU, dated back to 1921) to the Netherlands, first through a monetary agreement concluded in 1943, and then by a customs union treaty signed a year later by the three governments-in-exile in London. Before the War the BLEU and the Netherlands had conducted approximately 10% of their trade with each other, although there had increasingly been an imbalance in favour of the former. The greater wartime damage in the Netherlands served to accentuate the Dutch deficit, which doubled between 1947 and 1951. Despite the manifold difficulties, the customs union came into force in January 1948, when all tariffs were abolished to be replaced by a common external tariff. However, trade was still impeded by the widespread imposition of quotas, especially on the side of the Dutch. To remove these, even if only towards the BLEU, threatened to aggravate the deficit. Progress was only made possible by two further measures. Firstly, Belgium granted ever greater credit extensions (which it was willing to do if it meant securing the Dutch market from Germany, while the latter's industry was still operating at artificially low levels) and eventually the problem was subsumed into the European Payments Union. Secondly, the Dutch were able to secure preferential access to the Belgian agricultural market. They had wanted completely free access, since this would have helped remedy their trade deficit, but they had to make do with a provision which left Belgium's domestic protectionism intact.[14]

From its inception, the Benelux experiment attracted considerable attention from policy-makers in France. This should be no surprise since before the War Belgium had been France's largest European trading partner. Just as Belgium hoped to supplant Germany in Dutch markets, so France to needed to expand into the German vacuum to fund its own modernization plans. However, whereas the Benelux tariffs lay close to each other at the lower end of the range when they agreed to a common external tariff, it was realized that any union with France would be behind highly protectionist walls. Moreover, the Netherlands required the German market for its agrarian exports and its traditional shipping services. This required a reciprocal ability to purchase German imports; something that would be impossible if the Netherlands agreed to the arrangements proposed by the French.

From 1944 onwards there was continuous French pressure to break open the Benelux. It was headed off by the creation of a joint consultative body, known as the Conseil Tripartite, which arranged swaps of raw materials in the early post-War months, attempted to co-ordinate policy towards Germany (difficult given the different national provisions) and provided a forum for French attempts for a customs union. These efforts to break open the Benelux were countered by a demand that the move could only be considered if West Germany were to be included; a demand that ran counter to the reason for the French wanting the union in the first place. In 1947 the French used the CEEC conference in Paris to bluff the Benelux partners into daring to turn down the option of a customs union. They had hoped to use American leverage, who themselves wanted to use dollar aid as a way of securing their goal of closer regional integration.

Instead the study group for a pan-European customs union was created to deflect some of the pressure. They deliberated until the end of 1948 but ultimately failed because no decision had yet been taken on the German economy and its position in any future schemes. More immediately, the French found their challenge to move to the immediate formation of a customs union accepted only by the Italians. The fact that France's primary goal remained the Benelux was reflected in two further approaches in 1948 to persuade them to join. Both were refused.[15]

By December 1947 the first feasibility study for the Franco-Italian Customs Union was ready. It was surprisingly optimistic and a second commission was established to investigate how it could be implemented. In March 1949, Sforza and Schuman signed a treaty that would effectuate a customs union in a number of stages. A tariff union was already envisaged for 1950 and full economic union about six years later, but through fear of Italian competition, in particular in agriculture, the French Conseil Economique (a tripartite advisory body representing labour, industry and agriculture) thrice rejected the treaty. The government drew the inevitable conclusion and demurred from presenting it to parliament for ratification.[16]

It was whilst the issue of the Franco-Italian customs union was still alive that the French economy was confronted by a highly localized but serious problem; a balance-of-payments deficit with Belgium. From such unpromising beginnings was born FRITALUX, the name given to the grouping of France, Italy and the Benelux. The French solution to this trade imbalance had been a devaluation against the Belgian franc, with all the help from the Belgians in managing these 'broken exchange rates' that this move implied. From there the idea developed to a 'mini payments union' with a flexible exchange rate mechanism. Thinking in this direction was reinforced by the prospect that US dollars would be available to sponsor regional integration initiatives, which served to lubricate the discussions long after the exchange rate realignments of September 1949 had resolved France's original problems. Given the advanced stage that the talks between France, Italy and Belgium had reached and the implications all of this would have had for Benelux, it is amazing that it was only in September 1949 that the Dutch were actually informed of what had been happening. They immediately declared that they disliked the idea and would only consider it if it were supplemented by a customs union, which would also embrace the newly sovereign West German state. The French, whilst not rejecting the idea out of hand, argued that the union would better be created first and that Germany could join later. The Dutch feared this would never materialize and that entry, if it were ever agreed, would be surrounded by so many exemptions and escape clauses that Germany might not be willing, or even able, to join. There the negotiations stuck until the spring of 1950, when it became clear that the Americans had decided to do something else with their cash – provide the initial capital for the EPU.[17]

With the exception of the Benelux itself, the episodes discussed in this section all ended in failure. Yet they reveal several imperatives guiding policy in the immediate post-War period. The first was the motivation in all the modernization programs to utilize the breathing space created by Allied control over the post-War German recovery, to supplant the German position in both domestic and in foreign markets. The second was the fear of unrestricted German competition. Towards the end of 1949, Allied controls were already being relaxed; yet the powers of the new supervisory authorities were ill-defined and as yet untested. With or without the complication of the Dutch insistence on surrendering frontier controls against Germany, which a customs union would imply, the re-emergence of German industry was already a certainty. It was upon meeting that challenge, either politically or economically, that the entire commercial future of Europe depended.

The coal and steel sectors of western Europe took time to recover from the War. These key industries figured prominently in govern-mental recovery programs, such as the Monnet Plan in France. It was not accidental that the first major broad-based plan to integrate a specific industrial sector was the European Coal and Steel Community (ECSC). Coal and steel were important traded goods and essential industrial resources. Since they were largely similar products, they were easy to control and had a long history of being subjects of international cooperation. However, neither the timing nor the authorship of the first proposals for integration was accidental. The French initiative stemmed from an acceptance that this plan would, realistically, be their only method of establishing any control over German re-industrialization. French plans for the reconstruction of their steel industry had been based on an attempt to secure markets which had previously been German and also upon guaranteed access to German coal supplies. In 1950, the US policy of relaxing controls threatened to release excess German steel capacity upon a market that was already showing signs of becoming glutted. If, at the same time, German coal was redirected towards German mills, and coal supplies to France were priced relatively unfavourably, the adverse effects on France would be compounded. The Benelux countries, and to a lesser extent Italy, were pulled into the arrangements because they could not afford to remain aloof from a powerful producer bloc being created on their borders.

The Schuman Plan, as it was known, had been prepared in the French Planning Commission by Jean Monnet's staff. It was launched on 9 May 1950, on the eve of talks with the Americans and the British on future controls of the Ruhr's industry, and was clearly aimed at seizing the policy agenda. The British had been neither consulted nor informed of the proposals beforehand, but quickly ascertained that the organizational form implied too great a surrender of sovereignty, and that they required an entanglement in continental Europe of a nature that was inconsistent with their other foreign obligations. French attempts to persuade them to partici-pate, the sincerity of which has been questioned, were quickly abandoned and, in the summer of 1950, negotiations began. The treaty of Paris, establishing the European Coal and Steel Community, was signed in March 1951 and came into effect in July 1952.[18]

The stated goal of the treaty was to rationalize the production and sale of coal and steel. To this end, all import and export duties, subsidies and other discriminatory measures on the trade of coal and steel were immediately abolished. Although rules for pricing were established, in 'normal' circumstances the market was supposed to be competitive. The Community also managed funds for subsidizing firms hurt by the creation of the ECSC and for retraining workers. These were aimed particularly at the Belgian coal industry, some sectors of which were penalized by a combination of thin seams and high labour costs. Over a transitional period, efficient producers paid a levy to enable Belgian mines to adjust to the lower prices. Moreover, because of the heavy weight of fixed costs, the industry was extremely vulnerable to fluctuations in demand and therefore many of the remaining provisions were intended to come into effect in 'abnormal' circumstances; namely, to mitigate the impact of price falls in times of recession. It is curious that although cartel practices were prohibited within the community, the ECSC's marketing policy in the rest of the world was identical to those that would have been followed by a private cartel.

The innovation in the treaty, and the reason why it inspired such interest among proponents of deeper 'integration', lay not in the settlement of a potential political and commercial problem but in the manner of its resolution. The ECSC was administered by an organizational structure which bore many outward similarities to that of the future EEC. It was controlled by the High Authority (HA), a supranational organization comprised of nine independent members assigned by each of the participating nations, which was free to initiate reaction where it had competence and rights to do so at extremes of the business cycle.

The HA co-operated with a Consultative Committee recruited from producer, labour, consumer and distributive interests. It also worked closely with a Special Council of Ministers, in which each country would have one vote, whose role was designed to increase as decisions on coal and steel impinged on wider economic and security issues. The HA was ultimately responsible to the Common Assembly comprising 78 members drawn from national parliaments. Although the HA was the most powerful governing body, the Council could block certain decisions and the Assembly could force the resignation of HA members.[19]

It is hard to judge the immediate economic impact of the ECSC. The overnight removal of trade controls, without the transitional periods common to most European agreements, was certainly a success. However, for coal and steel, traditional barriers were less important as regulators of trade than they had been in the past or than they were for other sectors of the economy. The coal trade was covered by international agreements in which tariffs did not really play a role; Italy, with a rate of 15%, was something of an exception. For steel, both France and Germany had already suspended tariffs before the treaty was signed and the Benelux tariff had long been fairly low. Again, only in Italy, where an *ad valorem* tariff of 11–23% had been levied (and which was allowed to remain intact over a transition period) did tariffs have a protectionist intent.

More important was the impact of the ECSC on pricing. The ECSC eliminated the practice of dual pricing and created a base-point pricing system. Although price controls and subsidies were not fully abolished, even small progress on this front eased trade. Moreover, the discriminatory transport-pricing policies of ECSC members were eliminated. By volume, coal and steel were among the most important traded goods, so reduction of cross-border rates of about 30% made a major impact in deregulating transportation. The opening of the coal and steel trade also expanded imports of steel products into France and the Saar, which jumped from 27,700 tons in 1952 to 117,600 in 1953 – a period of low demand with trade barriers in effect for the first few months. In fact, throughout the 1950s, total intra-community trade grew much faster than production or trade with non-members; intra-ECSC trade in treaty products increased 171% from 1952–7, while production increased only 43% and extra-ECSC trade only 51%. In addition to these concrete effects, the ECSC defined the pace and structure of the debate over future initiatives undertaken by the Six. The next initiative took place in the area of defence and security policy.

Although they were soon to be overshadowed by the Cold War with the Soviet Union and its satellites, it is important to remember that security and defence policies had initially focused on the need to inhibit future German aggression. The Treaty of Dunkirk, signed in March 1947, was a long-term Franco-British alliance directed against Germany. When the Brussels Pact was signed a year later and the Benelux countries joined the alliance, they modified its exclusive orientation against Germany by a commitment to ward off aggression from whatever source.[20] In the intervening twelve months, the announcement of the Truman Doctrine had highlighted a more immediate and dangerous threat to peace and security from the Soviet Union in the east. Yet the fact remained that had the Soviets invaded, the new alliances were ill-placed to stand in their way. Some have even argued that their very frailty was intended to demonstrate the necessity for American troops and equipment, backed by nuclear weapons if necessary, to be committed to Europe's defence. Indeed, the secret so-called 'Pentagon Talks', which embraced the USA and Canada, started soon afterwards. These discussions came into the open in the summer of 1948 and were widened in their scope, culminating in April 1949 with the signature of the Atlantic Pact, forming the North Atlantic Treaty Organisation (NATO).[21]

American strategic planning in this period recognized that it would be impossible, even with US troops already on the ground, to defend Europe from Soviet aggression. In the event of an attack, the best scenario was a withdrawal behind the Pyrenees to Spain and across the Channel to the United Kingdom, from which points the reconquest of Europe could begin. A defence line at the Rhine or the Alps was not considered to be plausible before 1957 at the earliest. The only way to bring that date forward was to increase the European defence effort, and to employ the latent military strength of West Germany. Two events accelerated thinking in this direction: the victory of the Communists in China and, more importantly, the loss of the nuclear monopoly signified by the detection of the first Soviet atomic test in autumn 1949. These plans were made public in the crisis atmosphere surrounding the Communist invasion of South Korea which triggered the start of the Korean War. In September 1950, Acheson demanded the rearming of West Germany within NATO whilst pledging both an increase in the number of US troops stationed in Europe, and assistance for an arms build-up elsewhere.

The European reaction to events in eastern Asia was rather more sanguine than that in the USA, and few really saw any link between the Korean war and an increased threat to security in Europe. Given the fact that the rise in raw material prices which had accompanied the outbreak of war had undermined ECSC members' balance-of-payments positions and weakened their recoveries, they were reluctant to undermine progress further by increasing defence budgets. Still less did they see any immediate necessity for German rearmament. In France especially, this reaction was acute. If the idea of facing a resurgent German industry had filled French policy-makers with dismay, their alarm at the prospect of a reconstituted German army was even greater. Since much of the French army was involved in Indo-China, Germany would soon have the largest army in western Europe.

Within the French planning ministry, an alternative strategy was hurriedly put together. If supranationality had provided a vehicle for controlling German industry, could it not serve to control its rearmament as well? In October 1950, the prime minister René Pleven announced that France would accept German rearmament only in the context of a European army, under the control of a single minister of defence. Initially, the Americans were horrified at the delay to the formation of German divisions that acceptance of the French proposals would imply. Although talks on the Pleven Plan started in February 1951, parallel efforts continued to find a formula for the integration of the German army into NATO. When these failed, in summer 1951, the US not only tolerated the French scheme but became an enthusiastic advocate. A European Defence Community (EDC) would become the agent for carrying forward the process of integration in Europe.[22]

At this point, only five of the six ECSC countries were involved as full participants in the negotiations. After the switch in the American position, the Netherlands finally joined too, its change of heart prompted by a fear of losing American cash and goodwill and the hope of securing a defensive line (the Rhine-Ijssel line) that would not abandon most of the country to advancing Soviet forces. In May 1952, the treaty establishing the EDC was signed in Paris. It was not particularly elegant in design, nor particularly egalitarian in intent. To neutralize the danger of independent German military adventure, the army was to be made up of national units of battalion size only. Having thus fragmented German military capacity, the French then went on to remove their own colonial armed forces from Community control. By defining Germany as a potential war zone, the treaty also proscribed the manufacture of certain war equipment on German soil. Despite the modifications made during the negotiations, the EDC did not make much military sense. Nor did it much appeal to the other members of the Six. But the treaty's greatest failure lay in its primary task of making German remilitarization acceptable to French public opinion. Successive French governments shrank from presenting the treaty to parliament for ratification and when they eventually did so, in August 1954, it was rejected.

The EDC is an interesting example of the limits of American hegemonic leadership. American pressure was instrumental in securing a higher priority for European defence spending and for obtaining recognition that German troops were necessary. Yet, ultimately, the American administration had to defer to the French political agenda. Moreover, having done so, they failed to secure French acceptance of its own government's creation, despite the fact that Europe's defence was impossible without the USA. Certainly, this point was repeatedly made and never more clearly than when secretary of state John Foster Dulles threatened an 'agonizing reappraisal' of the American defence commitments to Europe if the issue were not resolved quickly. Moreover, French security objectives in their colonies were utterly dependent on US assistance. From 1950 to the fall of Dien Bien Phu, the United States covered 70% of the costs of France's colonial war in Indo-China.

Despite all the possibilities for leverage that this dependence implied, the Americans still failed to secure the acceptance of a policy with which it had become increasingly identified.[23]

Part of the problem with the EDC was the question of control: to whom would a European minister of defence be responsible, who would decide how and when the European army would be used and who would decide the foreign policy that the existence of the army was supposed to support? The treaty had indeed envisaged an assembly and its first task would be to design a new, democratic model for political control. The existence of these clauses had been introduced on the insistence of Alcide de Gasperi and were a triumph for Altiero Spinelli's federalist movement. In September 1952, the foreign ministers decided not to wait for the ratification of the EDC treaty but to move ahead immediately with the preparations for a 'European Political Community' (EPC). Six months later, right on schedule, the *ad hoc* assembly produced a draft treaty for the EPC. Meanwhile the increase in Gaullist representation in the French parliament had led to the coalition government dispensing with the services of Schuman as its foreign minister. This, more than anything, symbolized the abandonment of supranationality as the leitmotif of French foreign policy. Within the new environment, however, the EPC merely complicated an already difficult situation. For French socialists, the EDC was acceptable only if the elements of democratic control were strengthened. But any concessions in this direction would antagonize the Gaullists and others for whom the treaty was acceptable (if still unpalatable) only if the elements of national control were reinforced. Thus the French made desperate efforts to add protocols to the EDC treaty in the vain hope of finding the magic combination that would allow their parliament to ratify it.[24]

Within the Netherlands, the EDC had created problems of a different nature. The European army had been accepted only reluctantly and the government was not interested in increasing its entanglement with premature experiments in political federation. Thus, when the EPC was launched, the Dutch made their acceptance conditional on its being given specific economic tasks. Their foreign minister, Jan Willem Beyen, attempted to get the EPC treaty to include provisions for the automatic creation of a customs union. In the subsequent inter-governmental talks on the EPC, which lasted from the autumn of 1953 until the summer of 1954, the Beyen Plan received only qualified endorsement. In theory, it was acceptable to Belgium and Germany only if it were widened to embrace a complete common market and only if provisions were added for economic policy coordination. The Italians, however, were willing to accept the idea that the creation of a common market was one of the tasks of the EPC (which left open the option that the EPC might do nothing) but were not willing to countenance it as a separate protocol. But the French were unwilling to accept it at all. With an economy lurching into deficit because of colonial wars, while government abandoned many of the 'liberalization' measures that had previously been adopted, the time was evidently not ripe for discussing the automatic removal of protectionism.[25]

The EDC was never a very stable construction. It was also utterly inadequate to carry either the ambitions of the European federalists or Dutch designs for a permanent and fair removal of trade barriers. When the EDC collapsed in August 1954 on the French refusal to move to ratification, it seemed at the same time to dash all hopes that the Six might move towards further integration.

In the wake of the EDC's collapse, there was an intense surge of diplomatic activity to resolve outstanding sources of Franco-German conflict. One success of this was the decision, based on a British initiative, to create a German army under the umbrella of NATO and under the auspices of the Western European Union (WEU) which was now to embrace all six ECSC countries, as well as the UK itself (ironically, this was a solution that could have been reached almost four years earlier). Another potentially thorny issue in relations between the two countries had been the disputed status of the Saar, pre-War German territory under French administration, later incorporated into a customs union with France. The French government had wanted to give this area 'European' status but, under a new agreement, France accepted that it would be bound by a plebiscite to be held in October 1955. In the event, the populace rejected the European option and the territory was transferred back to Germany in January 1957.

Another source of inconvenience, if not tension, had been the French desire to secure markets for its agricultural produce in Germany. This question had become trapped into the so-called 'green pool' negotiations for the creation of some form of European agricultural organization but, after their failure and the transfer of the agricultural brief to the OEEC in January 1955, the first bilateral agreement to emerge was the Franco-German wheat agreement. Among the other agreements dating from this period, possibly the next in importance was that to canalize the Moselle river, thereby improving trade between the two countries. France's partners reacted to this flurry of activity with some ambivalence. Whilst they could see the potential gains in easing relations between the two countries, they could also see the danger that if France no longer needed 'integration' to control Germany, their own interests could easily be ignored in the ensuing rounds of bilateral dealing. Under these circumstances, the Benelux governments began to consider ways of relaunching the 'European agenda'.

At the headquarters of the ECSC in Luxembourg, Jean Monnet was also concerned at the drift in events. Unaware that the French government was indifferent to his fate, he decided to make his continuance as chairman of the High Authority contingent upon progress on the European front. Rather than start afresh, or pick over the wreckage of the EDC disaster to see what could be salvaged, he considered that the best approach would be to build outwards from the existing community. This could be extended into inland transport in general, into other classical energy forms (particularly electricity generation) or, and this was to be the key to its success, into atomic power. Nuclear energy was seen as an exciting new prospect where there had been little time for entrenched interests to emerge; yet the costs of developing it were too heavy for a single country to bear. This last consideration, however, had not prevented most industrial nations from embarking on experimental programmes of their own. The French government, especially, was extremely keen on developing nuclear cooperation and particularly wanted jointly to construct an isotope separation plant, a necessary but expensive component in developing enriched uranium for future reactors and nuclear bombs. Unknown at the time, it was in December 1954 that the French nuclear energy agency began to implement a five-year programme to manufacture a French nuclear bomb.[26]

The question of a nuclear community, EURATOM, was one of the items on the agenda when the foreign ministers of the Six met in Messina in June 1955 and it was adopted for further study alongside a patchwork of other initiatives (the main one of which was a common market, which we will return to below). The first results of this study envisaged that EURATOM would acquire a monopoly of all nuclear material and its transformation into products for fission. EURATOM would also build and control its own nuclear installations, including an isotope separation plant, financed from a common budget. Finally, it would administer a common market in all these materials and equipment. The one point it did not touch on was the relation of this structure to national military programmes, such as the one already underway in France. At this juncture the French suggested a moratorium on the manufacture and testing of nuclear weapons for five years, which did not affect the French programme because it would not be ready for such tests until after this period. The military problem was part of a wider one that, mid-way through the negotiations, was beginning to sap EURATOM's rationale. It was never envisaged that EURATOM would be the sole European nuclear programme, merely that it would assist and facilitate (and to some extent control) parallel national programmes.[27]

EURATOM's future was further enfeebled by the intervention of the United States. Back in 1946, the McMahon Act had tried to limit the spread of nuclear technology by classifying the fruits of US atomic research as secret. Paradoxically, by prohibiting collaboration of any kind, it had effectively prevented the Americans from exercising any control over developments that were already taking place. In his famous 'atoms for peace' speech to the United Nations in December 1953, Eisenhower had signalled a change in US policy which held out the prospect of the United States providing 'fissionable material' for projects designed to promote the peaceful use of nuclear energy. In February 1956, it offered 20 tons of enriched uranium to EURATOM at half the cost at which any European venture could hope to supply it. Aside from the noble aim of promoting peace (and deflecting attention from the fact that the 'new look' strategy could turn much of central and western Europe into a nuclear battlefield), the offer would displace UK competition and provide an outlet for the surplus of three US separator plants. It would also demonstrate American backing for a new supranational initiative. Finally, it would ensure that EURATOM would not build its own separation plant.

If EURATOM was not to build a separation plant (and right to the bitter end France tried to ensure that it should), then the French were determined to retain a separate national programme, keeping both peaceful and military options open. Moreover, France was only willing to surrender the sovereignty necessary to run a parallel operation, which in reality was not very much. The only limitation on its freedom of action was a four-year moratorium on testing. Parallel to these developments was a move in the OEEC for nuclear cooperation. Thus when EURATOM was formed, robbed already of most its substance and denuded of much supranational responsibility, one of its first acts was to pay the subscription of the six for joining the OEEC's 'Dragon' scheme to build an experimental reactor, an act which also absorbed much of its operational budget.

EURATOM had carried all the hopes of – and been the target of favourable propaganda by – the Action Committee for a United States of Europe, founded by Monnet in October 1955. It was only a 'success' in the sense that a treaty was signed at all. The other treaty signed in Rome in March 1957 was that establishing the European Economic Community (EEC). It was lucky to get onto the Messina agenda in the first place and, ironically, it was EURATOM that helped keep it there.

During the EDC negotiations, the Beyen Plan for the creation of a customs union had received varying degrees of support from five of the six governments. The Beyen Plan had at its core the creation of a customs union according to a rigid timetable over a period of 10–12 years. In order to accommodate countries in economic difficulties, the plan contained provisions for temporary escape clauses whose implementation and execution rested with the institutions of the EPC. There would also be an adjustment fund to assist countries with structural problems. Although the Beyen Plan failed because the French Assembly rejected the EDC treaty, the discussions about its merits had served to test the range of political opinion and to anticipate many of the technical problems. Firstly, the step-by-step approach to tariff cuts was condemned as too inflexible, making it more likely that countries would have difficulties in following the schedules. A less rigid programme, albeit with intermediate and final targets, was preferable. Secondly, the safeguard clauses were thoroughly disliked, by Germany and Belgium in particular. They argued that repeated backsliding followed by justification and appeals procedures would eventually destroy the community. Instead they urged far-reaching measures of policy coordination to prevent economies moving too far out of step, thereby removing the occasions for invoking these clauses. Thirdly, although the Dutch were heavily preoccupied with commodity trade, it became apparent to all that progress would be impossible unless capital and labour mobility were also dealt with. These were valuable insights, and all would eventually find their way into the Treaty of Rome. But there was one more factor in the summer of 1954: French politicians were implacably opposed to the idea of the EEC in whatever shape or form.[28]

The Dutch government was inclined, rightly or wrongly, to ascribe trenchant French opposition to the complexion of the government then in power. Once the Mendès-France cabinet had fallen, the Dutch considered that the main obstacle to persisting with the initiative (or indeed to expanding it by incorporating agriculture) had been removed. Thus, when the idea of a 're-launch' of European integration gathered momentum, the Dutch government made its support for the Benelux memorandum conditional upon the inclusion of a customs union in the list of demands presented at Messina. However Monnet, especially, was reluctant to risk a prompt rejection of a new European initiative because it introduced an immediate challenge to French protectionism. Curiously, the German government had had similar reservations and its delegation to Messina came armed with negative instructions on the customs union in order not to isolate the French. In the event, after a particularly indecisive meeting, an agreement was reached to establish study groups, under the overall direction of Henri Spaak, to investigate all the components of the Benelux memorandum.[29]

Once the talks commenced, it became obvious that the French were primarily interested in atomic energy. However, the Germans, having been willing to back the French at a critical moment, entered the common market negotiations with conviction, as did the Belgians. Various pointers to the moment at which France decided to take the common market issue seriously have been offered by historians, but the most credible seems to be January 1956, when a new Socialist coalition led by Guy Mollet came to power. To dispel any tendency towards backsliding, from that moment the German delegation insisted that, whenever it was appropriate, there should be a 'Junktim' between the common market treaty and that for atomic energy.

The second revelation during this early phase of negotiations concerned the position of the United Kingdom. Surprised at having been invited at all, the UK had joined the initial talks without a prepared position, other than to express a loose preference for a free trade area over a customs union. Opinion within the cabinet soon afterwards veered towards a rejection of a closer European entanglement and when, in November 1955, Spaak announced that the talks had proceeded sufficiently to start preparing a final report, the UK delegation elected not to take any further part, but to judge the report when it appeared. In reality, the decision had already been taken to reject the common market option and, at the prompting of the Americans (and to avoid being saddled with any blame when the negotiations failed), the announcement was made the following month. But the common market negotiations did not collapse.[30]

The 'Spaak Report' was approved by the ministers of the Six in May 1956 and negotiations proper were then able to start. But the French government's conversion to the common market did not mean that it did not have to placate significant parliamentary opposition when the treaty came up for ratification. Thus a great deal of time and emotion was expended on what were ultimately peripheral items in the treaty. For example, France demanded that elements of its own expensive social legislation (equal pay for men and women, overtime pay for work beyond forty hours a week) be incorporated into the treaty to equalize competitive conditions. Once these demands had been conceded, the French delegation returned with a proposal for sharing some of its current colonial development costs in return for access to these countries' markets. Even with such concessions in place, the government negotiated special provisions to allow France to commence lowering its tariff barriers later than the rest whilst still enjoying the benefits of market access elsewhere. None of these provisions added to the elegance of the treaty, but they all helped to condition acceptance by the French Assembly.

A second circumstance also helped to shape the negotiations, although not as decisively as some authors have suggested. In October 1956, together with the British and in collusion with the Israelis, the French launched an attack on Egypt in order to wrest control of the Suez canal from Arab nationalists. The invasion outraged public opinion and attracted the condemnation of both the USSR and the USA. On the brink of achieving their military objectives, the British cancelled operations, leaving both powers tasting the bitter ashes of political defeat. In a gesture loaded with symbolism, Adenauer travelled to Paris for talks with Mollet in the course of which both leaders announced the outlines of the compromise (largely agreed before the Suez crisis) that would set the common market treaty back on its tracks. Suez did not rescue the common market, nor did it finally convince the French government to accept it, but it did convince Spaak that the days of the current French government were numbered. If any treaty were to be certain of ratification, it had to be concluded and presented quickly. As a result, many questions that had not been resolved or that looked unlikely to be resolved quickly were left for the community itself to work out later. This accounts for the odd mixture in the treaty between detailed provisions on some issues and more procedural outlines on others.

At the core of the common market treaty lay the creation of a customs union in three steps, each of four years, with the possibility of a three-year overrun. Spelled out in precise detail, each phase would be marked by the completion of part of the removal of tariffs on intra-area trade and the erection of a common external tariff. With the exception of some troublesome items (list G), the new tariff schedule had also been calculated. By contrast, the details of the agricultural clauses concerned the way in which the steps towards a common policy were to be achieved but said little about the shape of the policy itself. This reflected a realization by the Dutch that if they pressed for more concrete clauses, they would be unlikely to be happy with the outcome. Yet the move was also viewed favourably by federalists, who saw the entrusting of future tasks to community institutions as a positive step towards supranationality. Few at the time paid much attention to the clause at the beginning of the treaty linking progress towards a common agricultural policy at each stage to further progress towards the common market. Yet this link was to form a 'Junktim' of its own and to underpin the implementation of both elements in the treaty.

In order to manage the community and steer its future development, the Treaty of Rome modified the supranational structure agreed for the ECSC. A European Commission, headed by independent commissioners chosen by the member states, would have sole rights of initiative across a wide range of policy issues. Only when these had been approved by the European parliament could the Council of Ministers take decisions. Moreover, after the second stage, the Treaty foresaw that the ministers would reach decisions by majority vote rather than by unanimity.

The Treaty of Rome, signed in March 1957, was the product of a society that had already reduced many of the cruder barriers to international trade, that wished to get rid of them altogether and that wanted to ensure they would not re-emerge in the event of a subsequent recession. In addition it reflected an ambition to deal with other competitive distortions (state aid to industry, restrictive practices and other invisible trade barriers) by eliminating them at source. This required a more sophisticated institutional structure than previous inter-governmental organizations. This implication was willingly accepted because the Treaty was seen as more than a simple economic agreement; for some, at least, it carried the hopes for a future federal European state.

1958–73[1]

The explicitly federal implications of the EEC made it superficially unattractive for the rest of Europe.[2] A variety of political, economic or security reasons confined the supranational course initially to a limited group of countries, albeit a group that comprised more than half of western Europe's output and foreign trade. Nonetheless the outsiders still constituted a sizeable market of considerable sophistication, one that had shared with the Six the same pan-European movement towards commercial liberalization and growing interdependence. Among these smaller trading economies, in particular Denmark, Sweden and Switzerland, there existed the same drive towards a further relaxation of protectionism that had motivated the Benelux countries, and this drive was reinforced by the fear of what might happen once the mutual preferences, implied by the formation of the customs union by the Six, began to take effect. The government of the United Kingdom was particularly concerned about the possibility of an economic division of Europe and, at the end of 1956, tried to neutralize the effect of EEC preferences with a proposal for a wider industrial free trade area to be constructed inside the OEEC.

The initiative was launched at a particularly testing moment for the Six, since the common market negotiations had still to be concluded and then ratified by national parliaments. The Commission of the EC itself did not begin work until January 1958. If the free trade area offered non-member states a solution to their dilemmas, for the Six it posed a distinct threat. Distrust of British motives suffused the following negotiations but there were more prosaic reasons why the Six were reluctant to embrace the UK initiative. For example, the French, in the final stages of the common market negotiations, obtained a set of favourable conditions and safeguards that they could not replicate in the free trade area. Moreover, the French, Italians and the Dutch had obtained some 'compensation' for the opening of their industrial markets through the prospect of a common agricultural policy, but agriculture was exempted from the British plan. Finally, those who hoped that the Community institutions would rapidly develop in a federalist direction were worried that their energies might be dissipated by the Free Trade Area.

The Free Trade Area negotiations dragged on for nearly two years, before finally being terminated by the French in November 1958. Under de Gaulle, France had decided to embrace the Treaty of Rome without recourse to its opt-out provisions. This commitment was worth infinitely more to Adenauer than the dubious prospect of a free trade area and thus the move received German acquiesence, if not support. The Commission, especially under its first president Walter Hallstein, had never liked the British plan and was generally pleased to see the back of it. Indeed by the end of the year, among the Six, only the Dutch government and the German economics minister, Ludwig Erhardt, could be numbered amongst its supporters. In the face of the opposing coalition there was little they could do.[3]

The failure of the free trade area negotiations left the UK without any coherent strategy towards the Common Market. In the absence of an alternative, the idea of forming a smaller free trade area amongst the 'outer Seven' (Britain, Denmark, Norway, Sweden, Switzerland, Austria and Portugal) rapidly took over. With the exception of Austria and Portugal, these were already relatively low tariff countries which shared a desire to maintain tariff autonomy towards third countries. They therefore preferred the concept of a free trade area to solve Europe's trading problems, rather than the more restrictive principle of a customs union. Formal negotiations started in June 1959 and culminated, in January 1960, in the Stockholm Convention establishing the European Free Trade Association (EFTA).[4]

EFTA's ambitions and its structures were simpler from the start than those adopted by the EEC. It was essentially designed to 'build a bridge' to the EEC, thereby obtaining through bilateral negotiations *en bloc* what the previous multilateral negotiations had failed to deliver. The differences can be summarized as follows:

* The EEC wanted a customs union, EFTA did not.
* The EEC had to build a common external tariff, EFTA did not, but did require instead a 'certificates of origin' regime. The common external tariff meant that the EEC needed a common commercial policy, whereas EFTA did not.
* The EEC wanted to eliminate the cause of trade distortions at source and required the machinery to do so; EFTA instituted a procedure to deal with complaints if and when different national practices were felt to have distorted trade.
* The EEC wanted a common agricultural policy; EFTA excluded agriculture but relied instead on bilateral agreements to expand agrarian trade.

In a way, EFTA was almost designed to disappear in the form in which it had been cast. It was only the subsequent failure of the 'bridge-building' strategy that forced it to assume the identity of an individual trading organization in its own right.[5]

Even before the establishment of EFTA, the Macmillan government had begun to consider applying for full membership of the European Community. By late 1959, it had become increasingly apparent that the UK would be unable to negotiate a settlement which aimed at a parallel removal of barriers within the EEC and EFTA *and between* the two blocs. The 'Hallstein Report' of 1959 which outlined the EEC's foreign policy perspectives left little room for a purely commercial settlement in Europe. Moreover, the United States, faced with a mounting balance of payments problem, made clear that it would not accept the discrimination implied by an interim settlement unless it conformed with GATT rules. That meant that any solution ended in a forseeable time and according to a fixed schedule, with the complete abolition of trade barriers. At the time the most that was on offer was a Benelux plan for the mutual exchange of the next scheduled tariff cut.[6]

Throughout 1960, the number of voices from the press, business circles, and certain politicians calling for a reappraisal of the UK's relations with the Six, grew considerably. However, the strongest statement seeking a drastic change in course came in May 1960, from an interdepartmental committee headed by Sir Frank Lee. It advanced the view that Britain should abandon attempts to negotiate loose economic agreements with the Six and instead seek full membership of the EEC. The Committee's arguments, based more on political than economic considerations, can be summarized as follows:

* The offer of a purely commercial 'bridge' between the EEC and EFTA would never be acceptable to the Six.

* The UK would face a relative decline in its political significance if it remained outside the EEC.

* The danger of a European federation would be mitigated if the UK joined while de Gaulle, who was notoriously anti-federalist, was still in power in France.

* Special arrangements for UK problems, such as Commonwealth trade and domestic agriculture, could be negotiated.

Macmillan was anyway predisposed to accept these arguments. Although he had been its victim, he had been impressed by the power and influence of France and Germany within the EEC. He saw in it the reinforcement of traditional great power diplomacy within which Britain could easily function, somewhat missing the point that the attraction of these arrangements to both Adenauer and de Gaulle was their exclusivity. Yet it was more than a year later before a formal application was made. This was primarily because of the daunting array of individuals and organizations which had to be persuaded of the desirability of EEC membership (from the party to the parliament, the press and public, not to mention the Commonwealth and EFTA). Macmillan also faced the 'presentational difficulty of explaining why a policy which had been repudiated inflexibly since 1948 had now become both desirable and necessary'.[7]

In July 1960, Macmillan appointed Edward Heath as lord privy seal, with special responsibilities for Europe. His major task in the ensuing year was to appraise the attitude of the Six, and France in particular, to the prospect of British entry. There would be little point in even considering a membership application if the French remained determined to keep Britain out. However, by summer 1961, it was evident that the French would not discuss possible concessions to UK interests prior to a formal commitment to negotiate. Indeed many, including President Kennedy, felt that de Gaulle had no desire whatsoever to share French leadership of the Six with Britain.

This placed the Macmillan government in an extremely difficult position. Speculation in the press and business circles had already anticipated an announcement on Britain and Europe. Thus, rather than make an open commitment to EEC membership, it was decided to open negotiations with the Six to see whether suitable arrangements could be made. It was hoped that this fine distinction would put an end to public uncertainty, and keep Britain's options open in Europe. The formal announcement was made in the House of Commons on 31 July 1961.[8]

The three major problem areas of negotiation with Brussels were the Commonwealth, EFTA, and British agriculture. In each case, Britain held outstanding commitments which, in the absence of special arrangements, were incompatible with EEC membership. The negotiations that opened in October 1961 proceeded extremely slowly due to a mutual unwillingness to offer concessions. It was not until May 1962 that the first specific agreement was reached on Commonwealth industrial goods. By the end of July, arrangements for most Commonwealth countries had virtually been finalized, although these often fell short of Commonwealth demands. However, it was the issue of agriculture which finally brought the negotiations into deadlock. The British system of guaranteed prices and deficiency payments to farmers was manifestly incompatible with the artificially inflated prices of the Common Agricultural Policy (CAP). Disagreement on the best means to reconcile the two dragged on into December 1962, when the EEC Commission appointed a committee under the direction of Commission vice-president, Sicco Mansholt, to explore possible solutions.

In the meantime, de Gaulle had become increasingly concerned about the political consequences of British membership. Although Macmillan was aware of these views, neither he nor any of the delegations in Brussels anticipated de Gaulle's unilateral statement, at a press conference on 14 January 1963, that Britain was not yet ready for the full commitment of EEC membership and that therefore there was no point in prolonging the negotiations. De Gaulle referred to the deal with the United States on Polaris nuclear weapons as evidence of Britain's 'special links' outside the Community structure. However, it is now clear that such objections were used to mask underlying fears of a British challenge to French leadership of the Six. The veto came as a monumental blow to British aspirations in continental Europe and the wider world. It also generated considerable illwill and mistrust between the Six, which in turn impaired the prospects of further political initiatives. Finally, it also served to repudiate the approaches of other states for membership or association with the EEC.

The applications of Denmark, Norway and Ireland[9] for EEC membership had been essentially a reaction to Macmillan's decision to negotiate with the Six. Denmark was the strongest supporter of this decision, as it provided the opportunity to bring its two largest customers, the United Kingdom and West Germany, together in a single market. The breakdown of the British negotiations was crucial to the Danish position. Although de Gaulle had offered prime-minister Otto Jens Krag membership for Denmark separately, this was turned down after consultations with the British.

Norway was somewhat less enthusiastic in applying for EEC membership. Einar Gerhardsen's goverment was uneasy about opening Norwegian fisheries and agriculture to foreign competition but the simultaneous application of important trading partners like Denmark and Britain led many to the view that Norway could not afford to remain outside. Before any application could be made, the constitution had to be amended to provide for the transfer of sovereign powers to an international organization. This amendment was passed without difficulty by the Storting in March 1962, followed soon after by the EEC announcement opening negotiations. Only one meeting at ministerial level had taken place, however, when the collapse of the UK application brought the Norwegian case to an equally abrupt end.

Ireland's membership application was perhaps even more closely linked with that of the United Kingdom. Ireland had not taken part in the EEC/EFTA split of the late 1950s, but had special trading arrangements with Britain dating back to the time when it formed part of the United Kingdom. Edward Heath specifically mentioned Ireland in his opening speech to the EEC governments in October 1961, expressing the hope that their trading relationship would be 'subsumed in the wider arrangements of the enlarged Community'. The EEC Council of Ministers signalled the start of negotiations with Ireland in October 1962 but, as in the case of Norway, substantial negotiations never actually opened.

The return of de Gaulle to power in France on 1 June 1958 was decisive for the EEC's development. Given his long antipathy towards the integration efforts of the Six, nobody expected him to look favourably upon the new supranational organization emerging in Brussels. After all, he viewed France's participation in the ECSC, the EEC and EURATOM as the humiliating policies of a previous regime 'more concerned with pleasing others'. Thus it was with considerable relief that 'Europeanists' saw his early recognition of the Rome Treaties. In part, this reflected the support in French industrial and especially agrarian circles for the EEC. It also marked an appreciation of the usefulness of the Treaty, and its safeguards, for the liberalization of the French economy upon which the regime embarked at the end of 1958. However, it soon became evident that the General had his own concept of 'Europe' which differed markedly from the federalist ideal.

At a press conference in May 1960, de Gaulle launched his proposals to develop political cooperation among the Six. He announced his intention 'to build western Europe into a political, economic, cultural and human grouping organised for action and self-defence ... through organised cooperation between states, with the expectation of perhaps growing one day into an imposing confederation'. The use of the phrase 'une cooperation organisée des Etats' was particularly significant and reflected a desire to ensure that any future political integration of the Six would not be at the expense of French national sovereignty. De Gaulle obtained the support of Adenauer for this position on 29 July at a meeting at Rambouillet. Central to the plan was the establishment of a permanent political secretariat of the Six in Paris, responsible to a Council of the Heads of Government. It would comprise four permanent directorates; dealing with foreign policy, defence, economics and cultural affairs. There would also be an assembly of delegates from the national parliaments.[10]

The scheme ran into strong opposition from federalists such as Walter Hallstein and Paul-Henri Spaak who feared that the inclusion of defence and economics within the competence of the new organization would tend to undermine both NATO and the existing Economic Community in Brussels. These problems were discussed by the heads of government of the Six in Bonn in July 1961. The outcome of the meeting was the 'Bonn Declaration', which tried to allay doubts about the plan by including references to political union as a means for 'strengthening the Atlantic Alliance' as well as an affirmation of the intention to 'continue at the same time the work already undertaken in the European Communities'. However, the Declaration had been cleverly drafted to conceal the many points of disagreement, and the illusion of consensus proved to be short lived.

The preparatory work was entrusted to a new commission, chaired by the French ambassador to Denmark, Christian Fouchet. Its brief was to submit 'concrete proposals concerning meetings of the heads of state and the ministers of foreign affairs, as well as all other meetings that might appear desirable'. In November, the French government presented a draft *Traité d'union d'Etats* which became known as the Fouchet Plan. The Fouchet Plan adhered firmly to de Gaulle's earlier position and, as such, represented some backsliding from the text of the Bonn Declaration. Most notably, the draft treaty included the key issues of defence and economics within the scope of the Political Union, despite the earlier protests by France's partners. Negotiations among the Six on the Fouchet Plan commenced in early 1962, with numerous redrafts of the treaty submitted by the Five. However, as the negotiations progressed, a further point of disagreement emerged among the Six, over the issue of British participation in the Fouchet negotiations.

At this time, simultaneous negotiations were being held in Brussels on Britain's application to the EEC. The Dutch, in particular, were adamant that the UK should also be included in the discussions on political union. Their foreign minster, Joseph Luns, saw British participation as essential to ensure the primacy of NATO and to keep a check on French ambitions. This was in stark contrast to the French position, that Britain would have to make a separate membership application to the Political Community, if and when it came into existence. Throughout the spring of 1962, this divergence of opinion became an ever greater source of antagonism among the Six. Meantime, the British themselves had begun to take a more active interest in the Fouchet negotiations, which, after all, coincided with Macmillan's preferences for Europe's organization. In April, at the Council of the Western European Union, Edward Heath made a long statement indicating Britain's desire to participate directly in the discussions. Coming at a crucial stage in the Fouchet negotiations, his announcement had the effect of rallying Belgian support for the Dutch position. Spaak now declared that he would not sign any proposed treaty until after Britain had been admitted to the EEC. The negotiations were then formally 'suspended', and the Fouchet Plan was abandoned.

The failure of the Fouchet Plan represented the first of many political complications to emerge among the Six in the 1960s. Moreover, by stiffening French resistance to British intervention in continental affairs, it had a marked effect on the atmosphere of the Brussels negotiations on British accession. Four weeks after the suspension of the Fouchet discussions, de Gaulle held a press conference in which he defended the Fouchet Plan and delivered one of his most scathing attacks on European federalism. His response to Belgian and Dutch intransigence was to proceed with negotiations on a political treaty with Germany alone. The summer and autumn of 1962 were marked by a number of high profile meetings and state visits. This process culminated, a mere fortnight after the collapse of the first British membership application, in the signature of the Franco-German Treaty of Friendship and Co-operation – a treaty which has also been described as a 'bilateral version of the Fouchet Plan'.

Despite these external threats, and perhaps partly even because of them, the early years of the EEC were startlingly successful. In 1958, it had yet to start its day-to-day operations and still had to recruit its staff. Although its president, Walter Hallstein, was welcomed in Washington almost as if he were a head of state, his position as the head of the secretariat of Europe's smallest and newest international organization meant he was virtually shown the tradesmen's entrance in the United Kingdom. Nonetheless, the Commission quickly became a formidable force in European politics. This was partly because it was remarkably well-staffed. For example, Walter Hallstein himself had been involved in European affairs since he had led the German delegation in the Schuman Plan negotiations. Sicco Mansholt, an ardent federalist, had served as an agricultural minister (not usually a post renowned for its length of political tenure) for over a decade. Hans von der Groeben had already served as his country's representative to the High Authority of the ECSC. Each of these men recruited highly skilled and experienced personal staffs.

Its success, however, was more than a question of personnel. At an organizational level, the Commission was quickly able to establish its own priorities and, still more importantly, to implement them. This, in turn, was facilitated by the compactness of the Commission itself, as evidenced by its small number of portfolios. Only later, when the EEC was merged with the ECSC and EURATOM, did its focus become blurred; it was then further diluted by the addition of new commissioners to satisfy new members in 1973. It is also undeniable that political factors played an important part. Early support from the Americans had certainly helped to increase the legitimacy of the new organization. Additionally, foreign policy challenges, an area in which the Rome treaties had given the commission an important role, presented themselves in the form of GATT trade rounds and in preparing the response to UK initiatives. Finally, the favourable economic climate provided new opportunities in the shape of an accelerated creation of the common market and thus created new areas for the Commission to exercise its influence at an early stage.

I once asked a senior official with a lifetime of service in the Commission, what the difference was between an inter-governmental organization, with a large and efficient secretariat, and a supranational community, controlled by a Council of Ministers (often voting with unanimity) and a large and efficient Commission. He replied that often there was no discernible difference, especially if there were sources of disunity within the group. However, if the political or economic constellation were favourable, a supranational community could respond more quickly and effectively to issues to which an inter-governmental agency might not be able to respond at all. He argued that the first Hallstein Commission was fortunate to find itself in such a situation.[11] Small, uncertain, and untried, the new Community soon found itself basking in a golden age, and inspiring a whole branch of theorizing among political scientists into the bargain.

The Six's first step in economic integration was the building of a customs union for industrial goods. All tariffs and quotas on trade between members were to be reduced gradually to zero and a Common External Tariff (CET) installed. The first 10 per cent tariff cut on intra-EEC trade took place in January 1959 and, according to schedule, bilateral quotas were multilateralized, while those quotas that were extremely restrictive (less than 3% of output) were expanded. At the same time, the benefits of the tariff cuts (other than those on tariffs already below the planned CET) were extended unilaterally to other GATT members. This was partly to anticipate criticism in the GATT that the EEC would develop into a closed organization and partly to cool the row that had erupted after the failure of the free trade area negotiations, which would have been aggravated had the Six immediately begun tariff discrimination against the rest of Europe.

The next two tariff cuts of 10% each were to take place in July 1960 and December 1961. Hallstein suggested accelerating the schedule, ostensibly to take advantage of the favourable economic climate but also to accentuate the EEC's own identity at a time when there was still an active interest in subsuming its commercial arrangements into a wider European grouping. As a result, in May 1960 the Council of Ministers decided to proceed, on schedule, with the July reduction but to make the next cut a year early, in December 1960. Similarly, in May 1962, the Council decided that the state of the economy allowed the 10% cut scheduled for July 1963 to be brought forward a year. Due to these accelerations, tariffs between the EC members were dismantled completely by July 1968, two years ahead of schedule.[12]

The creation of a customs union by the Six also implied a common level of tariff protection towards the outside world. This too was completed ahead of time. The first problem was to define the tariff itself. The CET should have been calculated as the unweighted average of tariffs in four areas, but for a number of products (mostly in the semi-manufactured and petro-chemical sectors) this formula was opposed. Due to lack of time in the Treaty of Rome negotiations, these goods had been consigned to List G and left to be decided by January 1962. Because of the need for a complete tariff schedule before entering GATT negotiations, this operation was completed by March 1960 and the outcome, moreover, was far less protectionist than had originally been anticipated.[13] Because the timetable of internal tariff cuts had been accelerated, so too was the realignment of national tariffs. In January 1961 and July 1963, the margin between national and projected rates was reduced by 30% each time, and the gap was finally closed in July 1968.

Although the Commission boasted that the level of the CET was moderate and its incidence considerably narrower than the British tariffs, Paxton stresses that 'in practice, the common external tariff as originally fixed was higher and more restrictive than the average incidence of the 1957 tariffs.' Germany had already in the mid-50s been concerned that their first post-War tariff had been fixed at too high a level and had already engaged in some unilateral reductions of their own. The Dutch too had been alarmed at the upward revision of tariffs on semi-manufactured goods especially. Neither country had been happy with the upward drift in protection that the CET implied. They therefore welcomed the call in 1958 by US under-secretary of state, Douglas Dillon, for a new multilateral tariff round in GATT. So too did the Commission. The Treaty of Rome had constituted a single bloc from four, already large, trading entities. Under GATT rules which applied to negotiations between major suppliers, this enhanced its importance and its international recognition, especially in relations with the United States. Moreover, since the Treaty also allocated the Commission a specific role in preparing and negotiating foreign commercial policy, the Dillon Round immediately promised it a prominent role in the national policies of the Six.[14]

The Dillon Round was delayed by the need firstly to construct the CET and then to get it approved by the GATT. Once underway, the Commission suggested a 20% 'linear' reduction in the CET, subject to reciprocal concessions by other countries. This idea foundered on the inability of the US to react to an offer framed in this way, but it is far from certain whether it would have been endorsed by the Six anyway. Thus the negotiations proceeded bilaterally on a product-by-product basis. No less than 4400 bilateral deals were made covering trade worth $4.9 billion and resulting in tariff cuts of about 7%. This outcome, however measured, was twice a good as that of the previous 'round' in Geneva in 1956 but was still considered disappointing. However the Dillon Round did have one important side-effect in that it convinced the Kennedy administration, in framing the 1962 Trade Expansion Act, not only to reopen tariff negotiations but to empower the US to negotiate across-the-board tariff cuts.

The Kennedy Round lasted from May 1963 to June 1967 and resulted in the largest tariff cuts in modern history, although the across-the-board method was not employed, since the EEC argued that the disparity in US tariffs, compared with those in Europe, would lead to inequitable results should that method be used. Nonetheless, over 8000 deals were made with a trade coverage of $40 billion and an average reduction of 35%. In over two thirds of cases, with the steel and chemical sectors especially heavily represented, tariffs were reduced by more than half. Textiles, on the other hand, recorded only minor gains. Equally, little progress was made in grains, meats and dairy produce which were rapidly being embraced by the Common Agricultural Policy (CAP) and where the French, especially, were reluctant to make concessions. The need to conclude the CAP, and the 'crisis' that had accompanied it, served to delay progress. More importantly, it prevented the trade-offs that might have made deeper cuts possible elsewhere. None-

theless, despite the tensions that inevitably accompanied the
process of establishing a single position, the Commission emerged
from the exercise with its international status considerably enhanced.

The Commission also suceeded in making the EEC the focus of
international relations with the wide range of African territories that
had made up the previous French and, to a lesser extent, Belgian
and Dutch empires. These countries were overwhelmingly dependent on Community markets for both exports and imports, and on
the metropolitan countries for much of their capital. Their future
had been introduced at a late stage into the Treaty of Rome
negotiations as a way of reducing the burden of their upkeep on the
French budget in return for France's renunciation of its bilateral
preferences (or, more to the point, the multilateralization of those
preferences). Thus the Six would remove tariffs and quotas on
imports from these areas in the same way as those on intra-trade.
By March 1963, tariffs had been reduced by 50% for manufactured
products, by 30% for most of the liberalized agricultural products
and 35% for the remaining agricultural products. It was not
foreseen that these reductions would be strictly reciprocal, but
protection retained by the overseas territories had to be applied
equally to the Six.[15]

After a five-year period, the association agreements were put on a
new basis with Yaoundé I, negotiations for which lasted from mid-
1961 to July 1963. These negotiations were difficult insofar as many
territories had ambivalent feelings towards their colonial and ex-
colonial masters and towards the prospect of neo-colonialism on a
European scale. Moreover, the European member states were far
from identical in their views of these countries. Whilst France
shared with the Commission a desire to renew and extend the
association, the Dutch were rather critical. Large Dutch economic
interests in Commonwealth Africa led them to demand an agreement that could accommodate these territories and they linked the
outcome of Yaounde I to the question of British accession. Only
when the French veto blocked this possibility could real progress be
resumed. The principles of the agreement were:

* Free trade area, dismantling of tariffs and quotas
* Technical and financial aid payments and capital liberalization
* Freedom in rights of business establishment and services

In 1969, after only six months' negotiations, Yaoundé II was concluded to govern the relationship for another five years. These talks were much easier since many of the earlier problems had passed, though not without traumas: in essence, France and Belgium had accepted their post-colonial status. The issue of widening the association had been resolved by the Arusha Convention of July 1968 which put relations with Kenya, Tanzania and Uganda on a new footing. Finally, and most tellingly, the agreements had had positive effects on the development of the African territories concerned.

The preferences established by the association clauses and by Yaoundé I and II have prompted much criticism. Non-associated countries in Africa, Asia and Latin America were opposed to the arrangements. So too were the United States and the United Kingdom. From the very beginning, the arrangements were condemned as incompatible with GATT and this discussion remained alive throughout the period. George Ball, then US secretary of state, suggested that it 'tends to result in a poor use of world resources'. What he said was true, but efficiency in the global allocation of resources had not been the Commission's main objective. Its first General Report defended its association policy in unambiguous terms:

> It was the duty to promote the economic and social development of the Overseas countries and territories associated with them by letting these countries and territories share in the prosperity, the rise in the standard of living and the increase in production to be expected in the Community.

The trade-off between access to industrial and agricultural markets had been a central cornerstone in negotiating the EEC. Yet there was so little chance of agreeing on the form of the policy or the level of protection during the negotiations that, unlike the sections on the customs union, the clauses on the Common Agricultural Policy remained largely procedural. Ehrard, who was anyway opposed to much of the Treaty of Rome, argued that the vagueness of the clauses proved that they were designed to be forgotten. The key to ensuring that this did not happen lay not in the paragraphs concerning agriculture but in article 8 which made progress through the three stages towards the customs union contingent upon equivalent progress in agriculture.

As commissioner in charge of agriculture, Sicco Mansholt started his work by rallying national agricultural pressure groups behind a European policy. In June 1960 he submitted his first proposal to the Council of Ministers. This foresaw free trade in agricultural products within the Community but with uniform target prices and variable levies on imports. In addition there would be structural policies designed to raise productivity. In 1962, after intense negotiations, market unity, Community preference and financial solidarity emerged as the principles of a future CAP. However, this still left important issues such as the level of support prices and the financing of the system to be settled before the CAP could become operative. Meanwhile a regulation was passed establishing the FEOGA (Fonds Européen d'orientation et de garantie agricole) whose provisions extended until mid-1965.[16]

The level of common prices as well as the financing of the CAP proved to be very controversial and the fierce negotiations almost brought the EEC to the brink of collapse. It took until the end of 1964 before German reluctance to accept a target price for grain below their prevailing national level could be overcome and before a common price level for cereals could be introduced. Proposals for common financing of the CAP were submitted in March 1965. Since these envisaged augmenting the EEC's institutional powers, through increasing the budgetary competences of the European Parliament and the introduction of majority voting, France flatly opposed the move. In summer 1965, it withdrew its representation from all EEC meetings and, with this 'Empty Chair' policy, precipitated a major crisis within the Community which was only resolved in January 1966 with the Luxembourg Compromise – usually described as an 'agreement to disagree'.

The Luxembourg Compromise stipulated that the Commission would consult with governments before adopting any important proposal, notwithstanding its rights of initiative enshrined in the Treaty of Rome. More significantly, it stipulated that if a country felt its vital interests to be at stake, even on issues normally decided by majority, the Commission was bound to continue discussion until unanimous agreement was reached – or drop the proposal altogether. Although at the same time the financing of the CAP was resolved, with a fixed scale of contributions agreed to run until January 1970, these events emphasized that the balance of power lay not with the Commission, but with member states.

Relatively high price levels within the CAP soon led to serious problems. Besides raising the cost of living, high guaranteed prices contributed to a rapid growth of agricultural surpluses. By the beginning of the 1970s, the EEC had turned a deficit in wheat and barley into a surplus of 10% above requirements. An equilibrium in butter had been transformed into a surplus of 16%, and a 4% surplus in sugar beet had been bloated to closer to 20%. Mansholt responded in 1967 by calling for more emphasis on structural policies that would allow a reduction in prices, but this appeal foundered on violent opposition from agricultural organizations. The Council of Ministers capitulated to pressure by rejecting any consideration of price cuts and by diluting considerably the proposals for structural policies.[17]

One of the principles of the CAP was that the same price and marketing conditions prevailed throughout the Community. Thus, when the CAP began, unified support prices were expressed in units of account (u/a), a measure of value equivalent to the US dollar. However, changes in exchange rates between currencies would also require an alteration in producer prices expressed in the national currencies concerned. Thus, when the French franc was devalued in 1969, domestic producer prices should have been raised by an equivalent percentage. Similarly, domestic returns for German producers should have been reduced to make allowance for the revaluation of the deutschmark. However, governments were reluctant to adjust farm prices in the direction of, and to the degree indicated by, fluctuations in exchange rates. As a temporary

solution they therefore established a system of Monetary Compensation Amounts – i.e., subsidies and levies for imports and exports –
to bridge the gaps that had emerged between domestic and
'common' European prices. Later this *ad hoc* provision was virtually
institutionalized by the introduction of special exchange rates, the
so-called 'green' rates, that applied exclusively to agriculture and
allowed the agricultural support prices expressed in national currencies to diverge.[18] This procedure increased the costs of the
CAP, perpetuated and aggravated distortions in competitive conditions in national markets, returned effective control of agricultural
prices to national governments and undermined the entire logic of
having a 'common' policy. Indeed, divergences in national prices
sometimes exceeded those experienced before efforts at price
harmonization began in 1967.

On balance, the major achievement of the first fifteen years of the
CAP was the removal of arbitrary quantitative controls that had
characterized intra-European trade since the late 1920s and early
1930s. It also erected an external regime that created an EEC
preference zone (although this could also have occurred without
common policies). Finally, it attempted to implement a single
system and level of protection throughout the Community. All these
factors generated a sizeable increase in intra-European trade, but at
considerable cost. Nobody in the post-War period questioned
whether agriculture should be protected and all economic protection has to be paid for in some way. The 'consumer pays' principle
chosen for the CAP was, in its nature, a regressive tax on food that
augmented the cost of living. The effect of this was compounded by
the increasingly high price levels that repressed domestic consumption whilst stimulating output. As production swung towards structural surpluses, so the costs of intervention, buying and storage
increased and ate into the funds intended for structural renewal.
The solution of disposing (or dumping) the surpluses on the world
market also served to undermine relations with external trading
partners who had already been disconcerted by being squeezed out
of EEC markets and who now had to sustain the impact that the
sporadic sale of large commodity stocks had on the fragile levels of
world prices.

The removal of tariffs and quotas ahead of their original schedules was, as we have seen above, a milestone in the histories of both the EEC and EFTA. Since EFTA, too, had in 1961 and again in 1963 decided to accelerate its own timetable, within the blocs of the Six and the Seven tariffs had vanished completely by 1969.[19] Yet, as it was understood at the time, the dismantling of tariffs and quotas was a necessary but not sufficient condition for ensuring free competition:

* Both organizations allowed the retention of some quotas for cultural and similar reasons.
* Both faced customs formalities for the restitution and reimposition of indirect taxes (and EFTA also had to contend with certificates of origin).
* Both saw individual administrative and technical obligations assume a more restrictive character.
* Both had to confront the effects of methods of levying taxes on business, incentives for investment and the granting of subsidies – which all acted to distort competition.
* Both still had to tackle the problem of cartels and restrictive practices.

EFTA ducked many of these issues by only investigating complaints made by governments (and there were not many), whereas the Commission dedicated itself to eliminating these sources of trade distortion in principle. Yet the EEC only really started to address these problems at the end of the 1960s and even then made very slow progress. Even discounting the new protectionist measures introduced after the 1973 oil crisis, the Commission's own judgment in 1981 is revealing: 'The customs union, the implementation of which is intended to ensure the internal market, is proving to be increasingly inadequate for the achievement of this aim.'

As tariffs and quotas were dismantled, so the impact of non-tariff barriers became more apparent. Some argue that their incidence became more prevalent as business turned to new protective devices to compensate for the loss of traditional forms of protection. However there have been no historical studies to substantiate or deny this. The Treaty of Rome stressed the need for a general system to protect competition from distortions (art.3(f)) and developed the areas of policy, the competences of the Commission and Council, and the rules and procedures in articles 85ff. Articles 85 and 86 declared that agreements between enterprises, together with dominant market positions capable of distorting trade, were incompatible with the Common Market. Furthermore, they prohibited dumping and state subsidies (though the latter came with a long list of exceptions). Lastly, state monopolies (art.37) should be reshaped, and fiscal as well as legal dispositions should be adjusted.

All these provisions remained sketchy, however, and it was the task of the EEC institutions and Commissioner, Hans von der Groeben, to flesh them out. Given the different interests and perceptions in this field, the problem was formidable, but it was by no means the only one. Competition policy was ambiguous as a concept, and the possible negative sides of a stringent competition policy were much resented. On the other hand, it could be articulated in more positive terms by suggesting that what Europe needed was more, rather than less, concentration in the interests of maximizing efficiency.[20]

On the question of state monopolies, the Commission could, after the first stage, recommend measures for reshaping them, which it did in several cases, usually by proposing gradual modifications which increased imports, eliminated the disparity of margins and adjusted to market conditions. There is insufficient evidence available to judge the impact of these rulings but in some cases, such as tobacco, it was shown that imports from other member states increased considerably. Yet given the facts that the Commission tried to work with, rather than against, member states, and that these had often and publicly voiced firm opposition, analysts generally agree that the policy of the Commission in this field was rather cautious. Moreover, celebrated successes such as tobacco need to be counterbalanced by equally significant setbacks: the reintroduction of a French petroleum monopoly represented a de facto break of the standstill agreement of art.37, to the effect that no further state monopolies should be introduced.

State subsidies also presented a thorny and difficult problem, the more so since subsidies were poorly and ambiguously defined in the Treaty. Generally, subsidies were deemed incompatible with the Common Market since they could distort trade between member countries. Yet industrial or regional policies were seen as necessary adjuncts to a mixed economy – and this implied financial aids. Thus it was necessary to distinguish between 'adjustment' and 'unfair government aid' and the Commission had the power to scrutinize existing state subsidies. Should they distort trade, it could ask that they be abolished or amended. It could also rule that the subsidy was compatible or necessary. Similarily, new 'other' subsidies could be introduced with a qualified majority vote of the Council.

The Commission became active in this field early in 1959 and demanded information on the financial aids in use among the member states. Following this, it had some success in persuading governments to amend and/or end subsidies – as in the case of German synthetic rubber, or on the more rapid depreciation allowances for French producers buying French equipment – together with similar practices in Italy. Moreover, considerable progress was made in the early 1960s in completing the inventory of existing aids and agreeing on information procedures. Yet as late as 1974, so Cairncross and Giersch argue, the praxis of state aid was still not transparent and, on the whole, EC policy failed adequately to tackle the problems of state aid. Matters grew worse after the Luxembourg compromise, when the Commission's attitude can best be described as pragmatic awareness of the difficulty of successfully challenging determined member governments. Difficulties with financing subsidies from the EEC's own funds contributed, though this problem diminished over time. Not surprisingly, the level of government subsidies showed little inclination to decline. What is more, the Community had still failed to define uniform criteria and conditions for judging the admissibility of aid.

The Treaty of Rome empowered the Commission to submit proposals on restrictive business practices and dominant positions which were able to distort competition – i.e., cartels and imperfect competition. It did so in 1960, and in 1962 the Council adopted Regulation 17, which was called by Swann/McLachlan 'an obscure legal document'. It reaffirmed the prohibition on restrictive business practices (art. 85 (1)) and ruled that they could be dissolved. It also subjected the firms concerned to a fine. First of all, though, it provided a notification of such agreements and a procedure to determine the action taken. This succeeded in attracting the notification of more than 35,000 restrictive agreements, most in the hope of securing acceptance and many involving fairly innocuous trading practices. By the end of 1962, however, Commission officials had isolated almost five hundred as constituting serious impediments to international trade.[21] Even so, many of the 'traditional' cartels had not registered at all.

After some struggles with the Council, which initially refused to give the Commission regulating powers, a policy emerged via a combination of exemptions, rulings of the EJC and Decisions by the Commission; which tried to ban price fixing, market sharing, production quotas, vertical distribution agreements, certain aspects of the exploitation of commercial property rights, and collective exclusive dealing. Implementation of this policy, however, remained fraught with difficulties. Obviously, restrictive agreements which the participants felt unlikely to be accepted were rarely notified. The villains of the piece were secret, large, international, horizontal producer agreements where the Commission had problems in securing evidence and prosecuting cases. Progress on this front was halting and sporadic but, since there is still no assessment of the prevalence of cartels in the 1960s, it is difficult to assert the effectiveness of the Community's efforts. The contemporary merger boom and the spread of multinationals in these same years complicated matters; and to some extent these new commercial arrangements built on tacit measures of cooperation existing earlier.

The Spaak Report (1956) had argued that the advantage of a Common Market 'lies in the fact that it reconciles mass production with the absence of monopoly'. It was assumed – and hoped – that European enterprises would adapt to the new situation by becoming bigger entities, enjoying economies of scale and enhanced productivity. Herein lay the route to improved competitiveness, above all, through the example of US firms. Throughout the discussion on the 'technological gap' and the 'American challenge', the size of US enterprises was seen as the main reason for their superiority over their European counterparts. On the other hand, the Treaty of Rome hoped to avoid dominant positions – or at least their abuse (cf. art. 86) – and to ensure competition. The European Communities had to find some way through this dilemma to define their policy.

The Commission initially adopted a largely passive stance: in 1963, the question of 'concentration' was handed to a group of experts who produced a first memorandum in 1966. Although this reiterated the need to preserve competition, it laid more stress on the positive aspects of concentration. The Commission's first aim was to reduce impediments to certain forms of merger. The reason may have been the poor results of cross-frontier mergers within the EEC (only 257 in the period 1961–9) compared with domestic mergers (1861) and those involving third countries (1035) At the same time, the Commission demanded powers to control mergers that threatened to acquire a dominant market position. It did not acquire these powers then, and when it did, in 1973, it was only in the form of rights to prior notification. The intervening years had been marked by complex legal arguments on the way in which the relevant articles were to be applied, arguments that could have been avoided, 'if there had been any real political will amongst the member states for a merger policy'.

It was obvious that the dismantling of tariffs by both the EEC and EFTA, as well as the EEC's introduction of a CET, was going to have some impact on the international pattern of trade. Modern customs union theory predicted two effects from the dismantling of tariffs and the introduction of a CET: *trade creation*, that is a shift from higher-cost producers to other EEC sources whose goods had become cheaper with the dismantling of tariffs; and secondly, *trade diversion*, that is a shift from lower-cost foreign sources to higher-cost EEC sources that benefited from tariff preferences whilst the external tariff was maintained. Intra-area trade would expand; in the first case because of a more optimal use of resources and in the second at the cost of less optimal sources. Much empirical research has been done to determine the balance of advantage.[22]

Trade within the blocs rose considerably. That of the EEC increased from $7530m to $49,830m between 1958 and 1971 and within EFTA in the same period from $2800m to $11,190m. In both cases, trade between bloc members grew faster than their trade with the rest of the world. EEC exports to EEC countries rose from 32.1% to 49.4% in these years while the percentage share for EFTA exports to EFTA countries rose less dramatically from 17.5% to 24.3%. Before trying to apportion the balance of advantage, one has to consider that increased intra-bloc dependence is not exclusively a function of the manipulation of commercial conditions. In a period when the growth centre of world trade lay in the exchange of increasingly sophisticated manufactured goods, it would not be surprising to see developed economies in close geographical proximity doing particularly well. Equally, performance within groups may be determined by differential growth rates. EFTA, which included the relatively sluggish UK economy, may appear less 'successful' than the EEC, with the rapidly-expanding German economy at its core. For example, EC exports to EFTA fell from 21.1% to 16.6% whilst the share of EFTA exports to EEC countries rose from 22.8% to 25.4%, despite the maintainance of tariffs or the deflection of agricultural trade.

Singling out an EEC-effect is not easy and the various attempts that have been made to do so have been much discussed. The so-called ex-post models cover a period when the EEC was in operation, and try to find out what the world would have been like if the EEC had not existed. To estimate trade in such cases, one has to rely on some ceteribus-paribus assumptions, so that the findings are always problematic. Hence Sellekaerts's warning 'that all estimates of trade creation and trade diversion by the EEC are so much affected by ceteribus-paribus assumptions, by the choice of benchmark year (or years), by the method to compute income elasticities, by changes in relative shares and by structural changes not attributable to the EEC but which occurred during the pre- and post-integration periods (such as the trade liberalization among industrial countries and autonomous changes in relative prices), that the magnitude of no single estimate should be taken too seriously'. Notwithstanding this destructive comment, it has to be admitted at, despite the different methodologies employed, most studies suggest that trade creation outweighed trade diversion, so that a net gain was achieved. Furthermore, Davenport has stressed the fact that 'the divergence in estimates is relatively limited, with the majority clustered in a range going from $7.5bn to $11.5bn for trade creation and from $0.5bn to $1bn for trade diversion.'

Very few estimates break this 'gain' down into individual national components. Two studies that do this come to broadly similar conclusions. The Benelux countries benefited least, since they already had the lowest tariffs and because the mutual Benelux preferences had to be diluted in the common market (a case of trade erosion). There is a noticeable gap between these countries and the other three. Despite having the next lowest tariffs, Germany benefited the most, reflecting both its export structure and its ability to make inroads into the markets of partner states. France and Italy followed close behind.[23]

Some authors contend that these calculations underestimate the impact of trading blocs. They stress that increases in market size and the impact of certainties in irreversibly reduced frontier barriers to trade induced a favourable investment climate and economies of scale, at least in sectors engaged in trade. Indeed, in the Italian case, the difference between a hyper-efficient export sector and a more backward domestic sector had led to the economy being analysed in terms of 'economic dualism', even before the full impact of the EEC was felt.

Growing commercial interdependence especially among the EEC states prompted concern among their governments over whether or not to tie their currencies closer together. The implications of moving to convertibility in 1958 quickly became apparent because the US balance of payments deficit remained acute. In the 1950s, this had been the main source for replenishing reserves. By the early 1960s, however, central banks in the EEC member states held about all the dollars they wanted. Yet the inflow of dollars continued unabated, attracted by the investment opportunities offered by the rapidly expanding EEC economies, or seeking a quick return by exploiting the relatively high interest rates on offer in Europe. Some of these funds were exchanged for US gold, some remained in the vaults of European central banks, and some were held by the private banking system. The latter formed the basis for the so-called Eurodollar market and provided a growing wash of international liquidity highly responsive to changes in, or rumours of changes in, market conditions. International speculation in foreign currencies became a daily fact of life. In such circumstances the desire for some preemptive, collective defence mechanism assumed a higher place in the aspirations of the Six.[24]

Unfortunately, as Tsoukalis has pointed out, the Treaty of Rome provided 'very little, if any, guidance with respect to monetary policy'. This was hardly surprising since conventional wisdom at the time assumed that the multilateral arrangements enshrined in the Bretton Woods agreements could be fulfilled – and did not envisage their imminent demise. Expectations were high, but the Treaty's provisions for monetary integration or cooperation (arts 104ff.) were rather pale and dim, stipulating the liberalization of payments on both current and capital accounts. Within a framework of overall equilibrium in the balance of payments, member states were enjoined to pursue policies directed at high employment and stable prices. To accomplish this, it was seen as necessary – and apparently sufficient – that there should be a loose coordination of economic policy accompanied by the creation of an advisory monetary committee to observe, report and comment on current problems. Although exchange rate policy fell within the purview of this body, it remained a national prerogative. Should countries face difficulties, the Community could offer financial assistance in addition to making recommendations, but no fund for this was created.

The first decade of the EEC's existence brought various proposals but few achievements. It was characterized by almost uninterrupted balance of payments surpluses for the EEC-members and a parallel decline in the position of both reserve currencies, the dollar and sterling. After the devaluations of the French franc in 1958, the payments situation within the Community attained some equilibrium. The small, five-per-cent revaluations by the deutschmark and the guilder in 1961 stemmed largely from the size of their respective surpluses with non-members. The only internal EEC crisis was the Italian deficit in 1963–4 which was resolved by non-Community credits and without recourse to changes in exchange rates. Several initiatives for institutional change and closer monetary integration came from the European Parliament and the Commission.[25] Suggestions for closer consultations and the creation of a separate committee of central bankers were accepted in 1961 and 1964 respectively. However, more radical proposals, if not rejected outright, found little positive support among the member states, partly because monetary reform was seen as an issue that required the involvement of the USA and the UK, and partly because the ever-open question of British membership of the Community made several members reluctant to press ahead with more drastic schemes.

Nonetheless, the increasing outflow of dollars and the need for a common line by the 'surplus' countries (which included all the EEC states) kept the issue of regional monetary reform on the agenda. In 1964 the French finance minister Giscard d'Estaing proposed the creation of a new reserve unit to eliminate use of the dollar and to serve the needs of intra-European trade. This idea was killed by a combination of the point-blank refusal of the US to contemplate such arrangements, the reluctance of some EEC partners, and a policy conflict within the French government. Jacques Rueff, architect of the French reform programme of 1958, favoured instead an attack on the pre-eminence of the dollar, through using the 'rules' of the international system rather than through changing them. Since the dollar was convertible into gold, France decided in 1965 simply to do just that; a decision that provoked d'Estaing's resignation. Although member states shared France's underlying concern, they were uneasy about these tactics; and varied in their degree of susceptibility to American diplomatic pressure. On this last point, West Germany was particularly sensitive to US pressures, since the country depended upon the large American troop presence for its security.

A further impetus towards creating a Community attitude on monetary problems came from the decision in 1964 to adopt a common 'unit of account' for determining national prices. This implied that domestic prices would need to adjust proportionately to any future change in exchange rates. Although such adjustments were considered unlikely, the Commission wanted mechanisms to reduce the chances further still. At this point it faced opposition on the grounds that tying down one part of the monetary equation made no sense without tightening other components – a line of argument which had already been voiced by German delegations at various international gatherings for over a decade. They demanded economic policy coordination as a prerequisite for monetary union.

The essential underlying assumption that international parities were somehow immutable was punctured by the crises of 1967–8. When sterling devalued in November 1967, a two-tier gold market was introduced in March 1968. As speculation built up against the franc, France introduced exchange controls in spring 1968. Germany provided a safe haven for funds but the government denied that an overvalued DM had caused the problem. Instead, in autumn 1968, it imposed extra taxes on exports and took fiscal measures to encourage imports. The Bundesbank's stubborn refusal to revalue, despite massive pressure, worried all concerned and pressure for a realignment of exchange rates could not be avoided. But it was a symptom of the depth of the conflict that when the decision was made, the action was not coordinated. France, unilaterally, devalued by 11.1% in September 1969. With German honour thus satisfied, the DM was allowed to float that same month and was formally revalued by 9.3% the following month.

These events produced a surge of interest in regional solutions. The Commission tabled two memoranda in the course of 1968, and in February 1969 the so-called 'Barre Report' was submitted. Although the reports differed in emphasis and tactics, they agreed on creating a new reserve unit, improving policy coordination and a establishing a mutual aid system. The Council of Ministers responded, since it also 'recognized the need for fuller alignment of economic policies in the community and for an examination of the scope for intensifying monetary cooperation'. Even so, there was no immediate follow-up. Meanwhile, the need for some initiative was underlined by the situation created by the 1969 currency realignment. Since neither France nor Germany had wanted national farm prices to change in line with the new exchange rates, (rather than allow the CAP to collapse) the Commission had to produce a system of 'green' exchange rates to preserve the fiction of common price levels.

It was some relief when, prompted by the German chancellor, Willi Brandt, the Hague summit of December 1969 endorsed the aim of 'Economic and Monetary Union' (EMU) and set up the Werner Group. Although Brandt's proposal seemed a major departure from the usual German line of insisting on the primacy of prior policy coordination, the Werner Group very soon found itself embroiled in old conflicts. Two schools of thought prevailed: the 'monetarist', which saw fixed exchange rates as a means of forcing policy coordination, and the 'economist' school, represented by Germany and the Netherlands, which saw the maintenance of fixed parities as impossible without convergent economic policies. The Werner Report, submitted in October 1970, adopted a compromise position. It called for the realization within ten years of complete and irreversible convertibility, closely aligned exchange rates, the full liberalization of capital movements and the creation of a common central banking system.

To achieve these ends it recommended a narrowing of the margins of fluctuation (from 1.5% either side of par) and a better organization of policy cooperation, especially in the area of foreign monetary policy. It took until March 1971 before the measures were approved. Although the French endorsed the monetarist approach, they wanted to avoid at all costs any discussion on the political and institutional aspects of EMU. But it was exactly a commitment on these aspects that Germany and the Netherlands saw as the price for their concessions. As a result, the resolution approving the goal of EMU left the questions of the transfer of power and institutional reform undecided.

Thus nothing was in place when the Bretton Woods system experienced its next, and ultimately terminal, crisis. In 1970 the USA, still experiencing mounting balance of payments deficits, had eased its monetary policy; consequently, speculative funds flowed back to Europe and, in particular, to Germany. The thinking of the

German Bundesbank now moved quickly in the direction of a DM revaluation as a means of reducing the attraction for foreign funds, but there was still the question of how to reconcile this with maintaining parities within the EEC. In spring 1971, the German finance minister, K. Schiller, apparently against the feelings of the majority within the Bundesbank, proposed a joint flotation of all EEC currencies against the dollar. This was resisted by those countries that did not want their currencies dragged upwards in the slipstream of the DM. Instead something reminiscent of the 1966 Luxembourg 'agreement to disagree' was decided. The DM and the guilder floated, while other countries introduced capital controls. The decision by Nixon to suspend dollar convertibility in August 1971 only reinforced the divide. Italy now joined Germany and the Netherlands in advocating flexibility of exchange rates, while France, Belgium and Luxembourg preferred a system of exchange controls. Action was further delayed by a general agreement that the key to a global currency realignment lay in a dollar devaluation and not in a revaluation of other currencies. Thus another four months elapsed before the Smithsonian Agreement validated a change of most EEC rates against the dollar of between 7.5 and 16.9%.

The Smithsonian Agreement also allowed currencies to float by 2.25% on either side of the new central rates, which implied that EEC currencies could diverge by as much as 9% before triggering intervention to stabilize the exchange rate. This prospect produced a compromise whereby European currencies would maintain a tighter rein on their rates with each other, whilst moving jointly against the dollar: the so-called 'snake in the tunnel'. The system was also briefly joined by the aspirant members. However, there was still no mechanism to produce convergent policies, nor were convergent policies adopted. Soon the new rates appeared as unrealistic as the old ones they had replaced. In June 1972, sterling left the snake and floated downwards. Ireland and Denmark, heavily reliant on the UK market, immediately followed suit, although Denmark rejoined after four months.

These mutations notwithstanding, the 'success' of the system prompted new moves, agreed in October 1972, to reinforce EMU but, significantly, no agreement was reached on the second step towards attaining the ultimate goal. Meanwhile divergent policies continued to exact their toll. Attempts to get the UK to rejoin the float in January 1973, when it joined the EEC, were rebuffed by a government that did not want to sacrifice recovery for exchange rate equilibrium. The following month, the Italian lira was forced out of the system. The fact that Sweden joined was little consolation. However, the final blow to the system (and to the chimera of economic and monetary union by 1980) was the fate of the French franc which in January 1974 was also left to float. As Tsoukalis comments, by this stage a group comprising Germany, Benelux and Scandinavia had to be understood as 'little more than a DM Zone'.

The 1966 Luxembourg Compromise had allowed the Council, and thus the EEC, to resume its work by postponing the introduction of majority decision-making and allowing the right of national veto. For many observers who had looked for further progress towards supranationality and contributed to a body of neo-functionalist literature to rationalize their aspirations, the Community appeared interesting but no longer exciting. Moreover, the issue of UK membership again strained relations among the member states. The second British application in May 1967 – followed by applications from Norway, Ireland, Denmark and Sweden – was again aborted by a negative French vote in December 1967. It was clear that on this particular question France was immune to the feelings of its European partners. The Five tried to maintain pressure on France by using the WEU for initiatives to extend cooperation to the political as well as monetary field. This 'rebellion' could only be prevented by de Gaulle's intervention, using the so-called 'Soames Affair' (in which the British had leaked details of confidential conversations with the General that suggested a revival of a free trade area to include agriculture) which produced another 'Empty Chair'. The mood deteriorated further: if the Community were ever to be enlarged to embrace the UK, something in France itself would have to change.

In fact French attitudes shifted surprisingly fast. It is possible that there were objective factors behind the change. For example, new concern about German economic power emerged, especially as

France's balance of payments weakened. Germany's refusal to revalue during the monetary crisis of 1968 reinforced the fear about the balance of power within the Community which may have produced a feeling that the UK could serve as a countervailing force. Secondly, the Warsaw Pact's invasion of Czechoslovakia had led de Gaulle to repair relations with the USA. It has been argued that this made it senseless to persist in seeing the UK as an Anglo-Saxon 'Trojan horse' in the Community. Although both of these arguments are plausible, until evidence is provided to the contrary it seems most likely that the contemporary view, which attached the greatest importance to the shift in power from de Gaulle to Pompidou, was closest to the truth. Although the government was still 'Gaullist', under Pompidou it contained four ministers who were members of Monnet's Action Committee for a United States of Europe. Whatever the ultimate reason, in July 1969 Maurice Schuman announced that France was willing to countenance some European *rélance*. Proposals linking the completion, strengthening and enlargement of the EEC would be forthcoming at the Hague summit in December.[26]

The Commission quickly wrote the Hague summit into its hagiology calling it a 'turning point in its history' (EEC Bulletin, 1/ 1970). It would be churlish to deny that much was accomplished, although different countries laid different emphasis on different parts of the package. France was most interested in completion of the Community and, specifically, the financing of the CAP. The others were primarily committed to enlargement. Nevertheless the decisions at the Hague, taken together, represented an ambitious programme for future development. It was agreed to find a definitive financial arrangement for the CAP by the end of 1969. By July 1970, ministers had requested a report to deal with possible developments in the field of political unification. By December 1970, they wanted a further report on Economic and Monetary Union (EMU). Last, but undoubtedly not least, it was agreed to open negotiations with candidate-countries.

Implementation of the agenda began immediately after the conference. Between 19 and 22 December, agreement was reached on financing the CAP and on the EEC's financial resources. The latter involved allocating to the Community all receipts from levies and customs duties, as well as national contributions to cover any deficits, and their gradual replacement by receipts to be calculated on the basis of an assessment of harmonized VAT. Committees were installed to draft the requested reports. Two major reports were published in 1970: July saw the publication of the Davignon Report on political unification, while October saw the Werner Report on Economic and Monetary Union. The fate of EMU has been dealt with in the previous section, but the cornerstone of Davignon's recommendations was foreign policy coordination, described as 'European Political Cooperation' (EPC), which rested upon regular meetings of foreign ministers and high officials. Its first achievement was to produce a concerted position during the Conference on Security and Cooperation in Europe that produced the famous Helsinki Accord in 1975

However, the Hague summit's main achievement was to re-open enlargement negotiations. Within the UK, a range of studies had attempted to balance a calculable economic 'loss' (attributable entirely to the structure and funding of the CAP and the structure and direction of UK foreign trade) against potential economic gains (as the economy benefited from both the static and dynamic effects of customs union). Most managed to arrive at a favourable result. Nonetheless, the negotiations did result in the adoption of new policy areas, noticeably in the creation of a regional fund, from which the UK was likely to emerge as a net beneficiary, in an effort to redress at least part of the transfer problem. These measures, however, stopped short of any automatic redistributive mechanism. No such problems arose with Denmark or Ireland, which were expected to emerge as net beneficiaries from the system.

The membership negotiations were sucessfully concluded in June 1971, following a top level meeting between Edward Heath and Georges Pompidou the previous month. Negotiations for a series of industrial free trade agreements with the remaining EFTA states ran in parallel and were concluded in subsequent months. January 1973 thus represented not only the moment of the first Community enlargement but the closing of a passage of history that had begun in 1958 with the failure of efforts to secure industrial free trade in western Europe. The moment was marked by an optimism scarcely dented by nagging differences on monetary policy. However, 1973 was also the year in which the inflationary boom of 1971–3 was savagely punctured, one of the immediate casualties being the prospects for Economic and Monetary Union. But although it was not immediately apparent, other treasured assumptions that had marked the 1950s and 1960s were destined to be discarded: economic growth, full employment, efficacious Keynesian economic management, technological leadership, to name but a few. It was in these new conditions that the Community had to absorb its three new members.

PART ONE

HISTORY

The Stagnant Decade, 1973–83

There is a received picture in Britain of a Community slumping from the high point of optimism reached at the Hague in 1972 into a dismal decade of inertia, relieved only by fractious competition among its member states. Like all received pictures it contains truths. The aspirations of 1972, such as the Davignon Report's attempt to address the issue of political cooperation for the first time since the mid-1960s,[1] and the Community's first enlargement in 1973, did little to break the pattern of self-interested national bargaining vying with rare bursts of collective altruism. Worse, the recession set off in 1973–4, and renewed in 1980–82 after an uneasy remission, brought internal problems and a pan-European sense of relative decline. Yet EC institutions sustained the idea of integration with an often surprising momentum in the interstices, so that the astonishing regeneration of the mid–1980s has to be explained not only in terms of a sudden shift around 1984 but in an accumulation of long-planned strategies at different levels within the Community and among different categories of players in the game.

The accession of Britain, Denmark and Ireland on 1 January 1973 occurred while the optimistic mood survived, so that the immediate consequential processes of adapting EC institutions and negotiating the informal areas took place against a background of goodwill, buoyed up by affinity between Edward Heath's government and that of Georges Pompidou. But ministers and officials in Brussels had also to adapt to – or frustrate – the expectation of two new small states (Denmark and Ireland), both with a high agricultural content to their economies, and one large one (Britain) whose predominantly industrial economy, currency and financial institutions were, by the end of 1973, manifestly in disarray, and its industrial relations close to civil disorder.

Yet in the years of Britain's final negotiations, the climate of opinion both in the EC and in the Heath government had been optimistic, even euphoric. To French observers, Heath seemed not only willing to pay the full price of entry but to bring for the first – indeed in retrospect the only – time a genuine willingness to follow European models of industrial policy and industrial government. In turn, Heath saw his DTI and regional innovations as material for the EC to emulate.[2] The fact that an anti-EC wing already existed in his Conservative party seemed unimportant, for Enoch Powell, then the chief critic, was not to turn to outright hostility until 1974. The fact that all Britain's initial advantage was subsequently lost should not obscure the possibility that, had the oil crisis not struck then, and had Heath not lost the February 1974 election, Britain might have fitted into a novel triangular relationship with Germany and France in a way quite different from its actual halting, semi-detached progress thereafter.

Denmark, in spite of some internal opposition, could take advantage of the experience of other small states in northern Europe, and its economic linkages with West Germany; Ireland (whose emergence from a long period of introspective isolation which stretched back to the late 1920s had now begun) increasingly found a political ally in France. But British entry posed questions for the future of the Franco-German entente, and since the accession terms represented an act of will by the Heath government, with the close support of business, banking and industry, rather than the nation as a whole, Britain's long-term stance under the next Labour government remained problematic – something which not only French and German governments but those of Benelux and even Italy watched with trepidation.

The new entrants' responses differed from the beginning. As the Commission recruited new staff, experts and linguists, the Irish took up the offers speedily and successfully, the Danes less so, and

the British with marked reluctance. Whitehall's resistance to transfers, and fears among expatriates for their promotion, lost a great
potential advantage during the next decade.[3] Due to the lack of full
cooperation between ministries, for example, Britain found its
former colonies losing out on the share of Yaoundé/Lomé aid even
as late as 1981, when they gained only 11% of the total despite the
existence of an informal system of apportioning on a geographical
basis, because the form had been shaped originally with
Francophone Africa in mind, on which UK representations subsequently made small impression. The Labour party also refused to
take the seats allotted to it in the Parliament, as trades unions did in
the Economic and Social Committee (Ecosoc) – again in contrast to
the other entrants, ensuring an illusory Tory parliamentary contingent at the first direct elections in 1979.

Meanwhile, the new Commission President, from France,
Francois-Xavier Ortoli, encouraged the Paris Summit momentum
on three broad fronts. As free trade agreements came into force
with EFTA countries (Austria, Sweden and Switzerland, followed
by Norway, Iceland, and Finland in January 1973, together with
Portugal in 1974, newly liberated from dictatorship) it seemed for
the first time since Messina that the 'real Europe' could be
achieved. Discussion began with North African countries about
long-term trading relationships, although nothing tangible was
likely to emerge until the Council had agreed its own policy for the
European side of the Mediterranean. By July 1973, EC and ACP
countries started to negotiate both renewal and extension of the
Yaoundé Convention, clearly necessary in terms of former British
colonies, and despite this potent source of Anglo-French tension,
what emerged as the Lomé Convention between the EC and forty-
six Third World states was signed in February 1975.

Secondly, the Commission began serious planning for the Social
Fund and the new European Regional Fund (which was to have an
important impact on the British budgetary question in the early
1980s, and on the attitude of poorer member states who began to
argue for what in the end became 'cohesion').[4] July 1973 brought
the 'Social Action Programme', with involvement by management
and unions in all member states. Thirdly, using the EPC

machinery, the Nine successfully aligned their national policies at the CSCE meetings in Helsinki, an essential precursor of the final accord with the USA and the Soviet Union in 1975.[5]

The era of détente in Europe seemed assured, not least because these three developments seemed to be an external sign of the 'fundamental bargain' made with the United States, that American firms which had already set up within the EC boundary should be treated as Community ones, offsetting the disadvantages of discrimination and trade diversion outside. But a currency crisis in January 1973 had forced the lira to float outside the 'Snake' (as sterling and the Irish punt had done since June 1972). The lira's exit forced the remainder to stop supporting the dollar, then close to its floor against EC currencies. Despite French efforts to push Britain into the Snake,[6] the Snake had, in effect, left the 'tunnel', and the last attempt to shore up the vestiges of Bretton Woods ceased, ushering in a dangerous era of violent fluctuations and huge capital movements, later styled 'casino capitalism' by Susan Strange. The crisis forced the EC to forgo plans for the first stage of monetary union. Nevertheless plans for a European Monetary Fund surfaced briefly and the Economic Policy Committee emerged at the end of 1973.

That summer, the Commission won Council support for its first industrial and technology policy. But Ortoli reported to Council in indignant terms on the lack of progress with the internal market, intra-EC trade being still obstructed by a mass of quantitative restrictions and technical barriers. Member states, he implied, were responsible for the bureaucratic delays which obfuscated the customs union and which, intentionally or not, had increased since enlargement. While the EC prepared for the next GATT talks in Tokyo, it was clear that its own commitment to total harmonization, lacking member states' consensus on the means, had created a vast backlog of work. The Council however showed no disposition to take up Ortoli's more flexible alternative, which threatened the physical and psychological barriers to free trade in which each state still had such vested interests.

On 6 October 1973 the Israeli-Arab War began, closely followed by the oil crisis and rampant monetary instability, leading to the first full-blown European recession since 1947. OPEC countries' use of oil supply and price as weapons to deter Western support for Israel had not been entirely unforeseen (at least by the Heath government) but there was little short-term action that any EC state could take, certainly not to look for strategic energy alternatives unless, like the Netherlands, they possessed gas reserves. Italy suffered most (and received help with its oil supply from Holland and Britain) but none escaped the initial shock, and even when OPEC restored production levels, the price rise (initially from $5 to $11.65 a barrel, but finally $14) induced serious cost inflation and balance of payments problems, with lasting consequences for industry.

The *sauve qui peut* among member states in late autumn and winter was such that for many observers (unaware of the oil companies' swap agreements) the EC seemed to have lost its rationale as an economic, let alone a political, organism. Commissioners argued for a common energy policy, but Council ministers demonstrated themselves quite unable to broker a solution. The IMF Committee of Twenty did no better: only Italy and Britain tried out its recommendation that members should accept their oil deficits and not shift payments problems onto each other at the world economy's expense. The USA, West Germany and Japan all deflated, the latter most drastically. Meanwhile, EC-USA relations almost ruptured over ECOFIN's agreement to borrow $6 billion from IMF facilities with Saudi Arabian-OPEC underpinning.[7] Although ECOFIN eventually got its money, thanks largely to the UK delegation, the US Congress vetoed further funding and it became clear that, without American backing, the EC could stand alone only on a limited scale and then only if it were united, well-briefed and determined.

Such conditions proved rare during the next ten years as the Nine's economies diverged sharply. Large reductions in output and working time occurred, and in Britain a three-day working week was introduced. Once the immediate crisis had passed, the underlying problems of meeting external deficits emerged, with almost insupportable consequences in Britain and Italy, together with contingent problems of recycling Arab petro-dollars into OECD investments. The effect was like that after an earthquake: a primary shock followed by disorientation, secondary shocks, immediate crisis responses, and then, at very different times, adaptation and reorganization.

Taking the decade as a whole, the far-reaching consequences of this 'mid–70s crisis' can be seen to have been decisive in re-shaping European nations' ideas and policies for the remainder of the century. It shifted concern from full employment to inflation (with notable impact on the relative strength of unions as against management, and on the EC's concept of a 'social area'), and led to new power relations in each society's major centres of economic activity: finance departments became dominant over those of trade and industry, central banks and the financial ethos superseded industrial priorities, and accountants gained ascendancy over both engineers and personnel managers. Finally, this crisis created a prolonged, pervasive questioning of the cost, priorities and effectiveness of state social service provision which, in the second oil-induced recession after 1980, brought about a revaluation of the state's role itself. In this sense, (with the notable exception of France) it caused the end of that series of post-War settlements established in the late 1940s, and completed what the collapse of Bretton Woods in 1971–2 had begun: the Community's severance from the long post-War boom.

Britain's essay after 1979 in new-right economics and social politics – usually called 'Thatcherism' – thus turned out to be only the most urgent and extreme case of a wider trend that was to be replicated, in different national contexts, right across the Community and EFTA. The post-War corpus of ideas which had infused economic growth and political institutions since the 1950s ceased first to have absolute validity, and ended by being virtually obsolete – as the EC's experience of prolonged high unemployment in the 1990s recession demonstrated.

Within the Community, it was soon clear that as currency cooperation in the OECD had been lost so had unlimited access to cheap energy and the belief in the automatic efficacy of neo-Keynesian macro-economic management. As the IMF's Committee of Twenty noted, currency cooperation could not be restored until the USA resolved its trade imbalance, or until the surplus countries, Germany and Japan (which had restored themselves to surplus by mid–1975) reduced theirs. As the DM and yen rose, the dollar and sterling declined and, with the IMF's relaxation of its rules in 1976 (to help out those with the severest problems), international coordination appeared lost in the impasse. France now floated the franc, leaving only four member states clustered around the DM in the 'Snake' from which the EFTA countries rapidly distanced themselves.

Certain industrial sectors suffered most: shipbuilding, textiles, above all steel. Car producers and consumer electronics did not escape and, in the general retrenchment of capital investment, a rapid loss of competitiveness ensued *vis-à-vis* Japan and the Pacific rim 'tigers' of South Korea, Taiwan, Singapore and Hong Kong. Low growth, low investment, inflation and unemployment were common to all, but in Europe, as elsewhere, responses varied widely, inhibiting any EC-wide industrial policy.

The West German economy readjusted faster than any other in Europe. After twenty-five years of holding the DM's value down, to the benefit of trade and industry rather than of the consumer, the Bundesbank allowed the DM to rise, as did interest rates. The subsequent restrictive monetary policy, in conditions of restored price stability and independence from the dollar, made West Germany the natural basis for the 'Snake', but this was at the expense of domestic growth. Banks took the lead in the rationalizing process that followed, generally to the detriment of large over-stretched firms such as AEG and Volkswagen. However, the harsh social consequences of this monetary policy were offset at government level by the SPD/FDP coalition, based on corporatist understandings with unions to cushion austerity measures.

Meanwhile, on the diplomatic front, and despite the fall of Willi Brandt in 1974, the *ostpolitik* survived under Helmut Schmidt, insuring stable relations with East Germany as well the Soviet Union, the USA and France. The Franco-German entente remained in place, since all three German parties accepted *westpolitik* as the only way to balance that in the East.

In France, after Pompidou's death, despite the Gaullists' preference for Chirac (RPR) rather than the UDF leader Giscard d'Estaing, it was the latter who succeeded as presidential candidate against the socialist challenge of François Mitterrand, in spring 1974. Giscard's government held to the 6th plan, hoping to sustain both planned growth and industrial restructuring during the emergency. But being a liberal by inclination, Giscard also wished to diminish the Gaullist emphasis on state direction, while deflating the economy and reducing France's dependence on external sources of energy. This was a policy which required heavy investment in civil nuclear development, yet which, for fear of a recurrence of the 1968 disorders, proceeded via monetary means rather than by direct wage cutting. It led first to negative growth, then, in 1975, to reflation, and ultimately to a 38 billion franc budget deficit, together with high unemployment accompanied by a weak currency.

In 1976, Giscard replaced Chirac with Raymond Barre (a former Commissioner) as prime minister, who had the more robust aim of cutting feather-bedded state industries down in size, reducing wages, and liberalizing prices. After strikes and much industrial conflict, the Plan Barre achieved surprisingly good results, notably with the rationalizing of steel production into two massive new holdings, Usinor and Sacilor.

In contrast with France, Italy, which had tried to avoid deflation, experienced 26% inflation in 1974 and suffered a steady fall in the lira. A period of political instability saw the regional electoral success of a much-reformed Communist party in 1976 (though it remained excluded from participating in the governing Christian Democrat–Socialist coalition). A strategy of terror mounted by the extreme left culminated in the murder of Aldo Moro, prime minister, in May 1978, and led to reinforcement of the right and extension of political warfare and corruption into almost every level of administration, finance and industry – with long-term repercussions through to the 1990s. Beset by crisis, with constant recourse to the IMF and West German support, Italy failed either to restore confidence in its institutions or to meet the external criteria for fiscal reform.

In Britain inflation continued to rise until it reached 23% in 1976,[8] thanks to a period of drift under a Labour government with only a small majority, preoccupied with instituting its Social Contract with the trades unions and sorting out the aftermath of a massive secondary banking crisis. Only in 1976–8, after Britain's referendum on EC membership, and under the direction of James Callaghan and Denis Healey, did Britain achieve some control of inflation and a sounder monetary policy, together with an industrial strategy which, by the late 1970s, had had some effect on microeconomic industrial adjustment. For economic and political reasons therefore neither Britain nor Italy took much part in determining EC-wide patterns before 1980.

Recovery across the Community was correspondingly varied and patchy, depending on the sector and the level of demand, and was nowhere so strong as in Japan or the United States.[9] Currency fluctuations also fragmented agricultural markets and disrupted the CAP, so that the system of monetary compensation amounts (MCAs) grew ever more complex and had to be bolstered by export levies. Attempts by the Commission to reduce guaranteed prices were rejected by the main beneficiary states, so that MCAs, having been merely a temporary expedient, became an integral part of the CAP in six zones of varying price levels. This in turn caused a rift in the Franco-German entente, since the French government believed MCAs worked to the advantage of countries with stronger currencies.

Increased complexity reflected an institutional crisis. The oil shock and member states' nationalistic responses produced in Brussels a mood of deep gloom: Ortoli declared that the Community had lost its vision and that its institutions were near collapse. Indeed at the OECD Energy Conference in Washington, in autumn 1975, the EC exposed all its differences, and the UK insisted on a separate seat. At home, members applied individual trade safeguards, many of which the Commission was forced unwillingly to accept. Collectively the EC turned protectionist, imposing a 15% anti-dumping duty on Japanese ball bearings. Of greater significance, it agreed to the Multi-Fibre Agreement's cartel arrangements on September 1977 in order to keep the EC textile industries alive. There was infighting over fisheries, and a wine war between France and Italy which the Commission had to take to the European Court.

Whatever the language still used by EC institutions, the reality lay in national defensiveness, absence of a common energy policy, and inability to address new issues collectively. The EC's outward appearances by 1976–7 had come to depend on the Franco-German understanding represented by Schmidt and Giscard, and on the DM core of the 'Snake'. It was hardly surprising that, within the wider periphery, EFTA countries went their own ways, Austria for one set of reasons,[10] and Sweden for another. (Norway's electorate had of course already voted against its government's entry application in 1972.) Only the two Iberian states and Greece showed signs of wishing to join: all three, unlike the EFTA countries, seemed on balance to be assets of doubtful value.

Nevertheless, the Community's level of activity maintained a certain momentum with the Commission's establishment of its science and technology policy, its social action programme (which included provisions for disabled workers and equal pay for women) in December 1975, and further limited advances in the free movement of goods in the few sectors, such as pharmaceuticals and medical services, that were still profitable. The Regional Fund took off in March 1975, albeit with smaller resources than were originally envisaged, thanks to disagreements between the main payer, West Germany, and Italy, Ireland and (for different reasons relating to budgetary adjustment) Britain. The ECJ handed down several important rulings on transport and demonstrated a clear commitment to integration which put it, in national governments' eyes, on the same side as the Commission.[11] Political cooperation also broadened out after Helsinki into bilateral agreements with Comecon countries and Yugoslavia, and in a continuing commercial dialogue with the Mahgreb countries of North Africa.

Even these limited gains came about primarily not because the Commission initiated policy but because the Council of Ministers willed it.[12] When the heads of government, jockeyed by the French Presidency, agreed at the Paris Summit in December 1974 to establish the European Council, they went beyond the founding treaties to formalize the existing informal, occasional inter-governmental mode of regulating business, over and above the EC's existing, and Treaty-based institutions. This Council's subsequent request to the Commission, Parliament and Coreper to prepare one report on European Union, and to Leo Tindemans, Belgian prime minister, to produce another, together with the agreement by seven states to introduce direct European Parliament elections and to increase the Parliament's powers, showed how priorities stood. Although the decision for direct elections had been very controversial in France, being referred on grounds of national sovereignty to the Constitutional Council, France had taken the political lead with German acquiescence and Italian support – the latter predicated on the assumption of political influence with France and economic support from Germany.

Meanwhile, without becoming any more *communautaire*, or any less hostile to harmonizing laws and taxation, the British won an acceptable (though actually useless) formula on their budget contribution at Dublin in March 1975, an apparent redress which probably helped Harold Wilson's last government to gain its referendum on retaining EC membership in June, after which Labour MEPs at last took their seats.

This emphasis on inter-governmental supremacy, as the recession began to lift, indicated that European integration would proceed without fundamental alterations in the balance of power or the patterns of activity set in the mid-1960s. France returned the franc to the 'Snake' in July 1975, and at a minor but not unimportant level acquired some support from Ireland, during the Irish Presidency. The restructuring of basket case industries was to follow the EC pattern of crisis cartels, first set out by the Commission in the case of steel in April 1975, followed by textiles, then the aircraft industry (1977), and shipbuilding (1978). Only in the novel areas covered by the Regional Development Fund was the Commission able to extend its informal autonomy by remedying grosser inequalities between north and south, core and peripheral regions, so that what had earlier been only an attempt to recuperate the Italian Mezzogiorno, became a more general policy of aiding poorer and peripheral regions.

The interplay between the Council and the Commission led to a flurry of activity, ranging from harmonizing company law to reports on a passport union and special rights for EC citizens. Most

Commission draft directives at this time derived from the twin themes of harmonization or the internal market, free of border restraints, but those on worker participation and company law were clearly intended to restore an earlier tripartite balance between the social partners which the recession had severely damaged.[13] In a series of tripartite conferences, the Commission sought to inspire some sort of interdependence rather than sectoral competition, firstly between financial interests and secondly between management and labour – all to no effect. The Council rejected the directive on co-determination and the Vredeling Directive on worker consultation within large firms, and the ETUC discovered that the EC saw the 'social question' only in terms of markets and industrial survival.[14]

This failure of an earlier dream can be attributed both to the real loss of union influence, especially in labour-intensive industries such as engineering, metalworking and textiles, and to the implicit defensive alliance between management and union leaders to safeguard what employment still remained. But it also emphasized how the earlier consensus had been eroded, and how the Commission was now powerless to restore it.

As Etienne Davignon observed in his report on European Union, it was becoming increasingly difficult to resolve even apparently specific issues without reconstructing the general political conception of what Europe should become. What had appeared to exist in 1971–2 had largely disappeared. The McDougall Report, for example, recommended in 1977 that member states should concert macro-economic policy and structural adjustment, together with the Commission's regional strategy. But what might in the 1960s have been the beginnings of a genuine attempt at redistribution between core and deprived periphery was rejected by a Council whose members could not agree on what macro-economic policy might be, and therefore refused either the powers or the money. The ERDF itself had become 'a pawn in the debate over far wider issues'.[15] At this stage, the total of 1.3 million units of account was split 40% for Italy, 28% UK, 15% France, 6% Ireland and 6% Germany. In 1981, Greece entered the arena with 13%.

Yet something more integrated could still be discerned, in direct suffrage for the European Parliament and the consequent distribution of seats (December 1975), in the strengthened budgetary system, backed now by the Court of Auditors with power to investigate members states' spending practices, and in the institutional reports on EU, accompanied by the Tindemans document. Under the Dutch Presidency in November 1976, the European Council accepted a cautious statement about an incremental road to European Union. Six months earlier, under the Luxembourg Presidency, the Council had accepted no fewer than eighteen directives on the removal of technical barriers to trade, and resolved some of the fisheries disputes by extending EC limits to 200 miles in the North Sea and Atlantic.

But very many directives remained for approval, and the emergence of a common fisheries policy led to often violent disputes between members and with Nordic countries, which were not finally settled until 1983. At the same time, with the second Portuguese revolution[16] and Franco's death, the issue of extension surfaced again, in circumstances prejudiced rather than eased by the case of Greece.

Greece, freed of its military junta, had been encouraged to apply in mid–1975 by member governments who had backed the government-in-exile and who saw membership as a safeguard of the new democracy's future. The implication at that point had been that similar support would extend to Spain and Portugal;[17] and Spain's centre-right government under Adolfo Suarez did indeed formally resume negotiations in mid–1977, after the first democratic elections, with the consent of the centre-left. The Socialist government in Portugal, led by Mario Soares, followed suit in 1978.

At this stage, Greece, liberated from military dictatorship in 1974, under prime minister Karamanlis, (who was widely liked in western Europe) stood furthest down the road to EC membership, untainted by the suspicions of member states, that the military might intervene as in Spain, or the Communist party return to power as in Portugal. The Commission on the other hand regarded all three rather more dispassionately, and recommended against early Greek entry, but the Council, mindful of the dangers of hostilities with Turkey's military government in the Aegean, over-rode it and opened negotiations in July 1976, ignoring Greece's very different level of social, political and economic development.

Member states differed, depending on whether they looked at the political arguments or the economic ones: on the latter they were harder and more sceptical in the case of Spain, and by association Portugal. Spain also suffered from the outright opposition of French farmers in the south, some unease in Belgium and Holland, and uncertainty in Italy, torn between agricultural interests and Mediterranean solidarity.[18] At a time when the largest entrants from 1973 had not still fully been assimilated, Spain represented too sizeable a risk, whereas the dangers of incorporating Greece seemed relatively small and apparently containable when it came to the CAP and regional funding.

Debate among member states had centred upon Spain's potentially large new markets and the investments that could be made there, which seemed likely to offset the budgetary drain and to be especially profitable for Germany. But they also took account of the world strategic situation – in the tail end of Nixon's presidency, the threat from the Greek Left to leave NATO and abrogate American air bases, and the economic conflict between France and Spain.[19] In the end they compromised, agreeing to deal with Greece quickly and to delay the Iberians at a pace acceptable to France and Italy. Delay stretched into the 1980s, exacerbated by Greece's own bout of factious campaigning to get more financial advantage before Spain and Portugal actually came in.

In the event, negotiations opened with Portugal in 1978, Spain a year later, and proceeded desultorily. In a speech in June 1980, Giscard linked Iberian entry to solution of the EC's own problems – i.e., the Greek Kalends – an attitude which derived retrospective justification from an attempted coup by sections of the Spanish army in February 1981. Although the king's firm stance and the rally by the great majority of senior commanders revealed that Franco's 'bunker' had become obsolete, the excuse of unripe time continued, prolonged by Colonel Ynestrillas's failed coup in October 1982, until Mitterrand's political turnabout in 1983.

Sporadic moves towards a more comprehensive currency

alignment revealed similar discords and inertia. Ideas about a European Monetary System had been aired even in de Gaulle's day, when Giscard d'Estaing had been finance minister, with the support of the Banque de France. Additionally, EC central banks had always cooperated together, albeit secretively, both in the Governors Committee (established at Basel in 1964) and on the EC's Monetary Committee where, with finance ministers, they provided advice to the Council. Monetary Union had been latent as an ultimate aim since 1957 and had been recommended by the Werner Committee in 1970 as an aim realisable by 1980.

Such dreams had faded fast after the end of Bretton Woods. But French re-entry to the 'Snake' and the evolution of a system of managed rates around the DM anchor encouraged hopes of a zone in which, crucially, the franc and lira might be stabilized. The liberal Giscard's long intent was to abandon the policy of habitual devaluations as acts of French policy. France was, in fact, forced out of the 'Snake' again early in 1976 and the DM had to be revalued later that year. But in the face of continued, variable rates of inflation, the new Commissioners of 1977, and above all the President, Roy Jenkins, were avid to restart the immobile machine and again set their sights on EMU.

Jenkins's proposal for a European Monetary System (EMS) reached Council at a moment in late 1977 when Japan's trade surplus and its aggressive competitive edge seemed only too clear to a Community locked into a pattern of weak growth and high unemployment. Among member states, Britain was now far more amenable to the imposition of an external discipline, its chancellor, Denis Healey, having imposed a measure of budgetary restraint and money supply control after the IMF's intervention in November 1976. There is evidence of consultation between the UK Treasury, Bonn and Paris, at ECOFIN meetings. But at this stage both Banque de France and Bundesbank opposed it. Among bank governors, only Gordon Richardson and Paolo Boffi of the Banca d'Italia supported it (the latter seeing progress to EMU as a restraint on his own reckless political class). These two however drew indirect support from German industrialists who wanted a lower DM – as in fact occurred in the early 1980s.[20]

They would have got nowhere without Franco-German concertation. Initially sympathetic to the Bundesbank's view, put by Otmar Emminger, that EMS would weaken the Bundesbank's independence and its capacity to control inflation through domestic price levels, as well as impose stresses on the DM as core currency that would ultimately force West Germany to become a leading political force,[21] Helmut Schmidt tried at first to share the burden with France, Italy and if possible Britain. Callaghan declined, but Giscard accepted, taking this as a first step towards EMU. The Italian government hesitated. But for three months the scheme stalled on France's unwillingness to accept what looked like a West German initiative.

Schmidt finally accepted the DM's anchor role in February 1978 during the French elections, but since it was a political-economic initiative rather than a fiscal discipline, it was agreed that EMS should be handled by the Council, not the Commission.[22] Germany's conversion owed much to Schmidt's perception that, as the dollar fell steadily during 1978, President Carter had abdicated the role of Western leadership and that something had to be found to fill the gap. Thus at the Bonn Summit in July 1978 (before the Bremen Meeting where EMS was given its final shape by heads of government, with bank governors filling in the details), West Germany reluctantly agreed to reflate, under US pressure.[23] A stimulus of 1% of GDP was thus given, with some success. But Germany met massive retribution later, when the second oil crisis seriously weakened the DM and aroused a new surge of inflation.

On the macro-economic level, German unease at a rising DM coincided with the Plan Barre's anti-inflationary aims. But EMS was intended by the Commission and the main participants to lead on to a full exchange rate mechanism (ERM) from which would emerge a European Monetary Fund or pan-European Central Bank with pooled reserves – with the ecu acting as a reserve currency.[24] Delayed because of objections, by Ireland among others, it finally came into force on 1 March 1979. Britain, though a member of the EMS, refused to join the ERM. By 1981, despite severe balance of payments problems, worst in Belgium, Denmark and Ireland, all had regrouped except sterling and the drachma, hoping to enforce discipline on their unruly domestic economies. (In the event, since sterling rapidly became a petrocurrency when North Sea oil came on stream, only massive EC intervention could have sustained Britain as a member, even if its new Conservative government had been willing at first to measure sterling against the DM rather than the dollar.)

Yet despite the appearance of stability guaranteed by EMS, German reflation, and Carter's new energy policy, the second oil shock initiated another recession and four realignments more occurred before 1982. Since West Germany would not revalue, the weaker currencies had to fall, causing growing resentment among their governments. Central bankers, led by the ever-reluctant Bundesbank and with Council assent, postponed the Monetary Fund indefinitely.

In the brief period of renewed optimism however, and before the French Presidency of the Community opened in January 1979, Giscard determined that French political leadership should be re-established lest West Germany fulfil the role that Emminger feared, or the Commission take advantage of its enhanced status.[25] In French terms, reform of EC institutions, crucial to preparations for the next stage of enlargement, therefore implied reducing the Commission's initiating role, subordinating the European Parliament's ambitions, and putting the Council firmly and formally in control. This involved a revival of de Gaulle's early concept of a Directoire, with greater sway for the larger member states.[26] Hence the appointment of the Comité des Sages set up under the French Presidency, with a brief to examine the reform of institutions, while retaining the Council's role, together with the Luxembourg Compromise, except in cases where qualified majority voting (QMV) had been unanimously accepted.

The three 'wise men', Berend Biesheuvel (NL), Robert Marjolin (France) and Edmund Dell (UK) could not but be influenced by the inter-governmentalism of the time: the way the EMS had been instituted, the impact of Franco-German leadership on smaller members, and the Atlanticist dimension set by the Group of Five.[27] Moreover, their report in October 1979 reached a Europe in which members were either self-absorbed, like Italy and Britain, or on the defensive like Belgium. It was not a time for visionary thinking outside the limits set by France and West Germany.

Nevertheless, despite the French Presidency's leverage, the Committee did not simply follow Giscard's agenda, but tried to measure the validity of small states' complaints (Luxembourg, Denmark and Ireland) against the larger ones. In particular, they examined the methods used to operate the European Council, and the suggestion of a two-tier Presidency in which large states would serve for longer periods. In the end, the three accepted the logic that the Council should give 'overall direction', setting out the EC's priorities, but that the Presidency should not be extended beyond the existing six months for each member state in rotation.

This report was a symptom of the prevalent malaise rather than a factor in what followed. The Commission had not, despite Jenkins's attempts, recovered its old influence as it had existed under Hallstein. It now suffered criticism from West German leaders as much as French ones – often directed at individual Commissioners for their national partiality – criticism whose validity both Jenkins and Emile Noël, Secretary General since 1958, had to admit, yet could not easily remedy, and from the European Parliament President, Emilio Colombo, who saw it becoming 'renationalized'. The Spierenberg Committee claimed that it had become too large and recommended that the number of members of the Commission should not increase pro rata with future accessions from Mediterranean countries.[28] Worse, from Brussels' point of view, despite manifest delays, some of the big states were not prepared to ease their veto powers under the Luxembourg Compromise, even though some of the smaller ones, led by Belgium, might have been.

The conflict between the Council and the Commission, latent ever since 1965, produced a condition of immobility, on which the diversity of reforming ideas made little impact – hence the *lourdeur* of which Giscard frequently complained. In practice, most initiatives were decided by the leading member states, even if the initiative came from the Commission or outside: EMS, Greece's accession, and responses to the Tokyo/GATT round. Such CAP reforms as occurred were possible only because of Franco-German agreement: the Three Wise Men could not have operated without this backing. And whenever the European Parliament asked for more competence, it aroused deep antipathies among both Gaullists and British Conservatives.

But the European Parliament could and did play successfully on West German *Länder* aspirations, and those of Italian regions whose politics had sprung vigorously into life in the 1976 local elections. Even before the Parliament used its single, ultimate weapon and rejected the EC's budget in December 1979,[29] it had induced the Council of Ministers to address three important issues: economic disparities, convergence, especially of the regions, and the EC's transport infrastructure – with a future common transport policy in mind. The European Parliament's sense of its own dignity and tactical responsiveness increased with direct elections, while some sense of common identity on EC matters also developed between parties in certain countries. This had long been true in West Germany and Benelux and it became so under Italy's *pentapartito* governments, before and after Aldo Moro's death. Karamanlis's creation of New Democracy can be seen as a bid to create a similar centrist governing philosophy in Greece. What may be called 'insider parties' tended during the 1980s to find similar affinities inside the Parliament, while the 'outsiders' (all communist parties save in Italy,[30] both main parties in Britain, many French socialists and the majority of Gaullists) emphasized inter-governmentalism at the European Parliament's expense.

Meanwhile the ECJ began to accumulate a body of judgments which increasingly underpinned the Commission's initiating role. In *Kramer* (July 1976) it ruled that EC institutions' competences within the EC extended under the treaties to the international engagements required to fulfil them. In March 1976 came the *Simmenthal* judgment that defined direct applicability to mean that EC legislation had to be implemented uniformly in all member states, not only through transposition but implementation and enforcement – which implied a direct obligation by governments towards individuals to implement directives. This had a stringent effect not only on backsliding states (Italy being already notorious) but also gave recourse to individuals or firms prejudiced by their own government's failure. The Court's 1978 judgment against

Distillers' policy of pricing one brand of whisky differently in different countries forced the company to withdraw from the UK market altogether. And in the area of state aids, where member states had frequently disobeyed rulings with impunity, especially in declining industries such as steel and shipbuilding, the legal revolution begun in the 1960s continued, leading to a sharp increase in the number of instances where the Commission dared to intervene.[31]

By giving *effet utile*, that is interpreting the treaties to give the law its fullest and most efficient effect, with consequences often not obvious in the original texts, the ECJ thus widened the scope of EC law and extended Commission or other competences. Its continuous activity thoughout the 1970s was probably the most important single factor in keeping the sense of 'Community' alive in an era of inter-governmentalism.

Simmenthal was perhaps inherent in the Treaties, but *Kramer* seems in retrospect a more creative interpretation, as does the ECJ's October 1978 opinion in the 'foreign policy arena', that the Commission had competence to use international trade sanctions or embargoes to achieve the EC's agreed aim. In the *Roquette* judgment (October 1980) the ECJ laid an obligation on the Council of Ministers to ask Parliament's opinion – and to wait for it. But all these were overshadowed by the consequences of *Cassis de Dijon* 1979,[32] which established the principle of mutual recognition of members' own national standards and health or other regulations. The court ruled that a product which was lawfully produced, subject to minimum standards, and distributed in one member state could not be banned from sale in another unless it constituted a clear risk to public health.

The political extent of this battle was not won immediately. In the always contentious area of foods, exclusions and evasions continued, even though the criteria were outside the food standards arena: France ignored both the rules and the ECJ's judgments by banning lamb imports in 1980, Germany restricted beer under its ancient production regime, and non-fizzy mineral water,[33] Denmark for ecological reasons prohibited beer and soft drinks unless sold in recyclable containers, Italy rejected German pasta, not being made with *grano duro*, Belgian margarine was to be sold only in cubes not rectangles, and so on. Whatever its logical consequences for the generic harmonization policy, the *Cassis de Dijon* judgment and its sequel, the pressure vessels case which Arthur Cockfield used in the mid-1980s, could not solve all cases. Indeed similar obstacles survive today, in complicated, obscure forms (such as the effects of the German waste and recycling law) requiring in most cases to be abolished one by one.

Yet it is hard to overestimate the significance of the new approach in which the establishment of basic standards and mutual recognition replaced harmonization. From that point on, the Commission sought to collaborate more effectively with member states' own technical departments and standards agencies, and to relegate Article 100 (harmonization) only to areas essential for the EC as a whole. By insisting on the overriding aims of the Treaty, the ECJ had given the Commission a powerful instrument to break up the huge log-jam of draft legislation stacked up by a decade of unsuccessful detailed harmonization. It may even have saved the EC's original ethos from the delays for which the Council and its members were to blame; it certainly helped to recover momentum and renewed the internal market's attractiveness. It also established a golden rule: that future directives and rules should be simpler, less specific, and aimed at setting basic standards in a general context within which national agencies could operate: if they wished, more but not less strictly.[34] A long search for general EC competences thus led to an early definition of what subsidiarity (a phrase harking back to 1957 if not the 1890s) might eventually mean.

The second OPEC oil shock forced the crude oil price to over $20 a barrel at the end of 1979, helping to precipitate a severe and prolonged recession. Domestically, the EC's endemic budgetary crisis was reinforced by the new British Conservative government's determination to revise downwards its net contribution. Margaret Thatcher's single-minded advocacy of 'our money' galvanized the next Dublin Council in November, so that the fractious disputes about the EC's budget overran into farm prices and the common fisheries policy. Thatcher took the subsequent compromise solution with ill grace, letting it be seen as merely a temporary expedient.

In that same, particularly gloomy, year, the EC's international context was disrupted, firstly by events in Iran (the Shah's fall, the seizure of American hostages, and the end of Carter's presidency), then by the Soviet invasion of Afghanistan (roundly condemned by all EC members in January 1980) and thirdly by the new Reagan presidency's apparent intention (with Thatcher's support) to revert to an arms race in order to counter and if possible permanently impair Soviet superpower capacity. Tensions rose at the same time in the Middle East and in Poland, where Solidarity's early successes – though partially reversed by General Jaruzelski's military dictatorship – exposed both the limits of Soviet power in eastern Europe and the unstable nature of Comecon, the state trading system linking Soviet and satellite states.

The EC coordinated its responses to these crises rather more successfully than it had done in 1974, though the EC's London Report pointed out the shortcomings in its political cooperation processes.[35] But the possibilities of cooperation were limited both by the recession and the 'sovereign debtors' crisis (Mexico, Brazil, Argentina, Poland) which lasted well into 1982 with consequences lasting to the present day (Brazil's debt, for example, had increased from $63.5 billion in 1980 to $116.5 billion in 1991). The recession laid serious, long-lasting burdens on European industries which found themselves at the same time exposed as inefficient, over-manned and technologically backward in competition with Japan and the new Asian 'tigers', while the debtors' crisis tested the banking systems almost as severely as the 1974 liquidity crisis. Steel suffered worst of the industries: this time, however, the British steel strike, and its outcome – defeat for the unions and harsh rationalization – provided a contrast with the EC's crisis cartel solution, following the 1975–6 model, which was instituted in October 1980.

Such a conjunction of severe economic and strategic problems encouraged EC governments to respond in a piecemeal fashion and inhibited their feelings of commonalty, except in the most defensive, protectionist sense.[36] Germany's earlier attempt to reflate and act as the EC's motor led to pressure on the DM, a deficit and high interest rates. French policy in 1981–3 moved rapidly in the other direction. A period of frequent realignments followed in which, given the existence of capital controls in most member states, domestic players rather than world markets set interest rates, allowing France until March 1983, together with Italy and Ireland, to devalue apparently without penalty, whereas Germany, Belgium and Denmark emphasized currency stability. But when France reversed its policy in March 1983, it become clear that Italy and Ireland would have to follow. Even the Netherlands, which had stuck with the DM, would have to switch from neo-Keynesianism to the disinflation, industrial adjustment and supply-side policies already being put into effect in Germany by the Kohl administration.

It was hard for the Commission, whatever its responsibility for macro-economic guidance, to check such defensive, protectionist activity during the recession despite the consequences for employment and the existing industrial base. They found it easier to maintain the EC's coherence and integrity by brokering the lowest common denominator of member states' most urgent needs, by sponsoring crisis cartels and national schemes for industrial support. The criteria for permitting state aids to industry were made less stringent, especially for shipbuilding, ship repairing and textiles: this despite the fact that state aids should have ceased altogether in the former case. On the industrial side, delays built up in establishing even the most urgent standards for TV systems, video-recorders, telephone systems and mobile telephones. In the computer field, despite demands from the ten or more world-ranking firms for the Commission to set an EC norm for interfaces, progress was painfully slow. It was not surprising that the Spinelli and Dahrendorf plans for scientific and technological policy also ossified.

The Community appeared to be reverting to national and inter-governmental activity. Yet at the same time, its weaknesses were emphasized, weaknesses which could only be remedied by collective action. The EC might have been able to limit the danger from Japan by 'voluntary export restraints' (VERs) for a time, but for all its protests, it had little leverage against the Reagan administration, high US interest rates, and the embargo imposed by the White House on EC equipment, first for the Siberian gas pipeline, and then on all high technology supplies for Comecon. Neither did it have a easy defence against US criticisms of the CAP or EC steel subsidies, which were avidly fostered by American producer lobbies, culminating in the imposition of countervailing duties on EC steel exports in June 1982.

In conditions of growing protectionism, not only between the EC and US, but between the US and Japan (which was, of the three, the most successfully impervious to liberal trade), the Community slipped away from its initial consensus on industrial policy[37] argued by Davignon and Willi Claes in 1977–8. This had defined goals for the emergency reconstruction of the most stagnant industrial sectors: steel, textiles, aeronautics and defence-related high technology (to which were added infrastructure development and large industrial projects under the 'Ortoli Initiative'). In that period, a genuine attempt had taken place to break away from sustaining 'national champions' (mainly in Germany and France, but also in the Netherlands and Italy). Some of that legacy nevertheless survived as the recession threw the emphasis back onto those markets – electronics, telecoms and cars – most at risk. Davignon's lead – at a time when his was the most vigorous in the Commission college – went into research and development arrangements such as ESPRIT (information technology), or RACE (communications), which had the effect of sharing the work among the twelve major telematics corporations, but also marked an important new stage in Commission-industry relations.

As for those mergers which came under competition policy because they implied abuse of market dominance, the ECJ gave an interpretation of Article 86, beginning with the *Continental Can* case in 1972, and extending it with *Philip Morris* in 1981, which was controversial but confirmed the Commission's powers.[38] But for several years, member states blocked the Merger Regulation proposed by the Commission, being unwilling to see its competence confirmed in detail. The Commission's struggle to define the nature of the European market and to curb state aids and illegitimate mergers led, however, towards liberalization and the internal market initiative, a contrast to the macro-industrial policy for structural adjustment embodied in the Commission's other defensive measures or crisis cartels. The latter proved easier than the former, in contemporary conditions: at the request of France, backed by Britain and Benelux, and despite German reservations, the Council agreed unanimously in October 1980 that a 'manifest crisis' existed in the steel industry. It was easier to protect than to adjust and, as in the case of managed trade, temporary relief became semi-permanent accommodation (see below p.573).

Among member states there existed no single view of what industrial policy should be, and certainly very little common ground between traditional French and German standpoints. Neither was this surprising in the economic climate of the time. Lack of clarity here contrasted with the developments in competition policy, where most member states wished to retain competence for their national regulatory agencies. Thus the Commission had some ground on which to act in the general interest, declaring that there should be a European industrial outlook, even if it fell short of being a synoptic policy.

A cluster of hopes, in training and professional skilling, assistance for small and medium-sized enterprises (SMEs), transport, regional policy and social action continued to reappear in all Commission documents. Meanwhile 'anti-trust cartels' provided time and space for firms penalized beyond the average by the costs of modernizing to produce plans for reconstruction. At a deeper level, belief in the internal market and liberalization spread outwards from the crisis sectors and high technology industries, influencing firms' behaviour and through them, national governments.

The Commission also proposed, in November 1981, that anti-trust cartels should be read as part of an EC-wide strategy and not confined to the cases in individual countries.[39] But this was not enough when set against the reality of member states' defensiveness[40] or companies' breaches of competition policy, even if the Commission was not opposed to stronger linkage between managed industrial decline and managed external trade – especially given the renewed US response to Japanese competition in a range of hi-tech areas. The EC had to respond to the structural challenge, had to modernize and adjust more quickly, even if the costs were high. The problem was to recapture member states' conviction that this was best done on a Community rather than a national basis.[41]

For all these reasons, hopes seemed to lie in the concept of the single internal EC market, flanked by components in research and development, regional policy and sectoral adjustment – a concept which member states, racked by rising unemployment and a sombre awareness in 1983–4 that they could no longer keep all their national champions alive, seemed more prepared to accept than after the first 1973 oil shock. This could of course also be read as a fulfilment of the Commission's original plan for industry in March 1970, put tentatively in the Colonna Report on harmonization and industrial change, coming to fruition a mere fourteen years after the event.

Nine elections also took place in the EC during the period 1980–83,[42] causing substantial political changes, especially in France at a time when domestic conditions were overshadowed by deflation, rising unemployment, and industrial discontent. Meanwhile, in a number of countries, notably the Netherlands, West Germany and Italy, public protests grew about the installation of Cruise missiles and the effects on NATO of the American arms build-up. In a much longer timescale, and in various ways, most member states also followed Britain's lead in profoundly questioning their welfare systems' efficacy, relations between state and industry, and the state's role itself.

How different the responses were can be seen by comparing Britain and France. Whereas the Thatcher government in 1980–83, beset by strikes in most basic industries, an over-valued currency, and historically high interest rates, abandoned thirty years of neo-Keynesian macro-economic management and instituted deflation and tight control of money supply, reducing state expenditure at the height of the recession, France embarked on what has been described as 'socialism in one country' after Mitterrand's PS/PCF victory in the May 1981 presidential election. While the rest of the EC watched the Thatcher experiment with a mixture of horror and fascination, as market liberalism gave birth to the privatizing of state industries on an unprecedented scale, Mitterrand's government abandoned the Plan Barre (whose austerity had been partly responsible for Giscard's unpopularity) and introduced a new policy of widespread nationalization.

Pierre Mauroy's government, a coalition of Socialists with four Communist ministers, sought to reflate the economy by redistributing wealth in order to generate higher spending among poorer groups, and hoped to increase employment by classic job-creation programmes, including reductions in working hours. The price was high in terms of currency instability, while the budget deficit multiplied seven-fold in two years. Inflation stayed stubbornly high and the trade deficit nearly doubled.

The crux in France came with the major currency crisis in March 1983, following two earlier deliberate devaluations. Whereas the Ceres left of the PS (like the British Labour party's left in the mid-70s) had been advocating protection, regardless of what EC partners thought or would permit, Mitterrand and the new finance minister, Jacques Delors, after an initial reconsideration in June 1982, changed radically the government's whole economic policy to one of increasing austerity. The second package included not only a substantial enforced devaluation, but a budget freeze, a stabilization of the franc, and an end to public sector recruitment.[43] Mauroy was replaced as Prime Minister by Laurent Fabius, and the remaining Communist ministers resigned.

France's experience seemed to prove that no member state, even one with France's record of political leadership, could act continuously contrary to the global trend – in contrast to the United States which, having first instituted 'Reaganomics' as the antithesis of New Deal interventionism, had actually arrested its industrial decline by an expansionist fiscal policy close to classic Keynesianism. But Mitterrand's *grand tournant* also affected the EC's political balance. In 1981, French socialism had consorted uneasily with Schmidt's brand of social democracy in West Germany (even if some German commentators remained sceptical about its validity, assuming that Mitterrand was at the time finessing his own Socialist left and his Communist allies in the 'common programme'). But once Mitterrand accepted failure in 1983, and adopted a policy closer to market liberalization and EC integration, revulsion from protection and isolation removed many of the French objections to EC enlargement, to solving the British budget problem, to reform of the CAP and EC institutions, and above all to completion of the internal market.

Mitterrand's transition from a 'worker's Europe' to 'no Europe without a social Europe'[44] occurred as Helmut Kohl became chancellor, leading a CDU/FDP coalition. With Hans-Dietrich Genscher as more or less perpetual foreign minister, and continued domestic principles of low inflation and monetary stability, Germany's EC position barely changed. Balancing the *Ostpolitik* in the framework of EC integration again took the form of a low profile foreign policy, acceptable to both centre-left and centre-right in Germany, which avoided any semblance of desire to lead the EC, and set increasing emphasis on integration – to be achieved by the same Franco-German entente as before (see chapter 7).

The fact that by 1983–4, political and economic conditions had been created which made France a willing collaborator, not only in economic but in all dimensions, provides one major explanation for the EC's subsequent regeneration. In achieving that, Kohl's personal support strengthened Mitterrand, especially during the crucial French Presidency in 1984, as Schmidt's had Giscard in the late 1970s, while governmental and institutional linkages supplemented the rapprochements between individuals. But that this could happen was only clear by mid–1983. At that point, the British had to accept that there was no advantage in pursuing bilateral Anglo-German or Anglo-French alternatives, a point already demonstrated when the foreign secretary Geoffrey Howe played a Gaullist card in May 1982 and tried to use the veto to prevent a settlement on agricultural prices, only to fail for lack of a minimum number of allies in the Council of Ministers.

Taken together, the years 1980–83 were a period of fluctuation in the EMS,[45] nine elections, national defensiveness, distortion of competition, and the introduction of often blatant means to evade free movement of goods. All went far to undermine collective faith in the efficacy of EC legislation and rules. Trade rivalries and different responses to the Soviet Union seemed at the same time to align the continental EC states against Britain and the United States. Spanish entry to NATO in May 1982, and Greece's factious game-play once Andreas Papandreou's left-wing Pasok came to power in October 1981, suggested the existence of a new north–south cleavage in Europe, to add to the existing ones of large versus small states, socialist versus non-socialist governments, and the wealthy core versus peripheral regions.

At the centre, the Commission, under the genial but lightweight Luxembourger president Gaston Thorn, could find no obvious consensus about the EC's future nature and functions. Some talked of a two-tier system and variable geometry or core-periphery models,[46] while others turned back to de Gaulle's model of a Directoire.

On the other hand, some operations at Brussels were steadily becoming more collegial, if not among foreign ministers, at least among their finance colleagues on ECOFIN. The evolution of Coreper, the informal association of member states' Permanent Representatives, into a flexible instrument preparing policy for the Council, together with increasing specialization in the Council and its Secretariat, ensured that majority voting was coming into more frequent use: 90 times in 1979–84, as against 35 in 1974–9 and a mere 10 in 1966–74.[47] Informal processes and pressures induced compromise and diminished the use of the veto: even France helped to vote the British down when they essayed the Luxembourg Compromise in May 1982. This represented a trend towards a philosophy of incremental momentum, of 'getting things done', about which Mitterrand and Thatcher, its foremost opponents, were evidently aware. The process long predated the 1980s revival, and owed much to the other, more integrationist states of Benelux, Italy, Ireland and Germany, albeit each for different reasons.

The pursuit of the internal market centred on three consequential proposals: firstly, the Commission's own report on regenerating industry, reforming CAP, and solving the budget issue (June 1981), secondly, the committee set up by the Council to draft amendments to the Treaties, to which were added, thirdly, the topics of strengthening the internal market, energy policy, industrial innovation and research, together with proposals on Mediterranean agriculture and job creation, especially among the young. These can be seen as preparatory to the November Council Meeting in London under the British Presidency. But the French also put alternative proposals in October, and in a parallel action, Genscher and Emilio Colombo submitted independently to Parliament in November a draft European Act and statement on integration.

The London Summit might therefore have been the occasion for renewal. That it was not can be attributed partly to Britain's budget problem and partly to the principle of unripe time.[48] Nevertheless, Mrs Thatcher became the first Prime Minister to address the Parliament, and a number of concessions were made to its demands for greater powers over the budget process. (These did not stop the Parliament threatening Council with ECJ proceedings in September 1982 for its failure to institute a common transport policy. The European Parliament now saw itself, conjoined with the Court, as one means eventually to subvert inter-governmental dominion.)

Meanwhile, exposed to the recession and confronted by the greater spectre of American and Japanese inroads into their markets, industries and businesses, especially the larger and multinational firms, began to campaign more publicly than in the past for a more effective industrial policy, and for the long-promised internal market. Until around 1981, these efforts had, with the exception of a small number of individual multinationals, largely been on a national scale, in the context of member states' own industrial policies – or lack of them,[49] but such was the divergence between German policy and the French socialist experiment, or between Britain's deflationary neo-liberalism and Italian support for the state sector, that in 1981–3 they began to involve themselves more directly. As a result, influence tended to slip away from ministers, downwards towards the interest groups.

Lobbying of the Commission by industrial players became a notable feature during the Thorn Presidency, encouraged by some of the Directorates' entry into more specialized policy-mongering, and by the appearance of contentious issues such as the Vredeling Directive on worker participation which required of companies large expenditure and sophisticated rebuttal techniques. Sectoral institutions across Europe in the chemicals and car industries, and the varying national peak bodies – CBI, DVI, Confindustria and Patronat – had for some years secured a point of leverage in DG3 (responsible for industry), particularly in Davignon's day, though rather less so with his somewhat hide-bound successor, Karl-Heinz Narjes. But this had never generally obtained with the Commission, and to judge from British sources (the only ones currently available),[50] they and their members had habitually resorted to their home governments, especially in Germany. They had enjoyed varying success. In France they were generally subordinated to an administrative definition of French interests. In Italy they had largely had to make their own way to Brussels. Furthermore, from a position of influence in the 1970s, in Britain after mid-1980 the CBI found itself isolated from government in a way unprecedented in post-War history – yet still having to defend UK membership on the UK political stage, as if it were an open issue.[51] (Operations of these networks are considered in chapter 10.)

In spite of the problems which national peak organizations encountered at home, their European counterpart UNICE was not their preferred choice for activity when it came to trying to influence the Council of Ministers or the Commission.[52] On the one hand, their members could use the sectoral bodies which already represented each industry; on the other, they could form new organizations of leading industrialists, such as the European Round Table or the group around Guido Carli, governor of the Bank of Italy, which included important heads of banks such as Alfred Herrhausen (Deutsche Bank). The heads of large companies, many of them French, members of AGREF, the association of larger, private sector companies, notably less protectionist and conservative in their own outlook after Mitterrand's 1983 turnabout, now looked to links with MEPs in the Parliament, such as the Kangaroo group, or developed their own specific companies' commercial strategies: of which the Albert Report and Wisse Dekker's report on behalf of Philips (Netherlands) are prime examples.

But whatever the mode of activity (which in the case of national organizations frequently overlapped), the central issues remained the same: abolition of non-tariff barriers and establishment of the internal market. The CBI's European Steering Committee had indeed held this in its sights continuously from as early as August 1974, and from March 1977 was working closely with the French Patronat. Again, if it is fair to generalize from CBI records, governments used these peak organizations to achieve similar national ends, which in itself encouraged them to address Brussels more directly.[53] But on the whole, these semi-public efforts took care to keep industry's initiatives free of the political vortex during the confused infighting among member states in the period 1979–83.

Much of the industrialists' work overlapped. Wisse Dekker remained a leading member of ERT while drafting his report, *Europe 1990*, with Philips' backing. According to the CBI, 90% of their proposals coincided with his. *Europe 1990* also foreshadowed the internal market White Paper in 1985, but since it was begun in the recession under the guidance of firms in the front line of exposure from American and Japanese competition, it was set in a defensive mode, tinged with protection. Fears of the social consequences of 10–12 million unemployed at a time when trades unions' bargaining strengths in Brussels appeared to be reviving, conditioned its aims of reducing costs without hitting either wages or salaries. So many Ministries of Labour, Commission officials and MEPs felt soured by the way that the Vredeling Directive had been emasculated by a combination of industrial federations, UNICE, and the American Chamber of Commerce's European Committee,[54] that they were prepared to listen to ETUC arguments about the 'transaction costs' of ignoring the social partners – that is, predisposed to avoid electoral unpopularity and industrial relations conflict.

The CBI (which had fought Vredeling all the way with support from its government and Conservative MEPs) could see that its 10% divergence from the Dekker Report lay not only in its labour market policy but in important questions about how to address all non-tariff barriers together, how to incorporate financial markets, and how far to liberalize and deregulate, rather than erect new barriers where the Euro-borders met the outside world. How effective all this was in the general array of influence bearing on the

Single European Act in 1985 is a question for the next chapter: here it should be noted that it aroused the interest of all the allies against Vredeling, among American firms, in the long-established European Committee of AmCham, and also among Swiss firms such as Nestlé and Ciba-Geigy, which were already habituated to working in the EC.

Older pressure groups joined in, under new banners: Jean Monnet's Action Committee, which he had dissolved in 1975, was refounded in 1979 by Leo Tindemans and Max Kohnstamm, primarily to campaign for European union, but it included industrialists whose main interest was the internal market. When in the second half of 1982 the European Parliament produced a resolution for European Union, the Commission responded with its own proposals for reinforcing the internal market. At the Copenhagen Summit in December, heads of government were finally persuaded to call on the Council of Ministers 'to decide on the priority measures to reinforce the internal market'.[55]

Of this, Arthur Cockfield would remind them, in his foreword to his White Paper on establishing the internal market, three years later. At the time, it led to a modestly constituted Internal Market Council and the beginnings of a concerted plan by DG3, together with officials of the largest member states, whose outward face could be read in a host of Commission papers arguing this as the only way to recover competitiveness;[56] and (since EMU was always a contingent matter) currency and monetary stability. Under the German Presidency the plan gathered momentum,[57] and at Council level culminated in the 'solemn declaration' on EC Unity at Stuttgart 19 June 1983.

Soon afterwards, in September, once the drama over French restraints on the entry of Japanese VCRs had been resolved, the French government produced a memorandum *Vers une espace industrielle Européenne*. A Commission mandate of sorts now existed to prepare something more specific for the Athens Summit in December. But too much Council time was being consumed by the acerbic British budget question (from which the French government took advantage to delay Spanish accession, reform of the CAP and structural funds). The hostilities which had attended the messy

EMS general revaluation in March had also not entirely disappeared. The European Parliament was dissipating its energies on dreams of European Union inspired by Stuttgart (which Thatcher regarded as itself an illusion[58] and which Mauroy also condemned as eroding the national right of veto). Systemic reform depended that summer on three assumptions: that West Germany would not drop its opposition to increasing the Community's revenue by 1% on VAT until the reform process had actually started (even at the risk of the EC's temporary bankruptcy), that the British would not shout too loudly, and that Greece would handle its first Presidency competently.

On these assumptions and inspired by Stuttgart, senior officials in the Commission such as Fernand Braun (DG3) and Paolo Cecchini, Maurice Carpentier, Peter Klein, and Riccardo Perissich, prepared something more dynamic and far-reaching than Commissioner Narjes' long catalogue of directives-in-waiting since the mid-1970s (which was not actually published until mid-1984). They were able to capitalize on work done in some Departments of Industry, notably in Bonn, London and Paris and on the technical harmonization and the implications of *Cassis de Dijon*, so that by October, Narjes could outline 'a more general common approach' on mutual recognition, rather than total harmonization, to the Internal Market Council. Since Britain, France and Germany now had the clearest policies in this area, Cecchini invited top officials from the Economics Ministry in Bonn, the DTI, and the French Industry Ministry to meet him at the Chateau de Namur, 15–16 October, and here, under very informal Commission auspices, a text was agreed and immediately translated into the three languages. This was fed indirectly to the Steering Committee texts for Athens, as a prototype 'declaration for the internal market'.[59] It was lost of course, in the Athens debacle, illustrating both the powers and limits of sub rosa Commission work. But its substance emerged eventually in the EC resolution, 7 May 1985, which indicates the strength of such little-seen trends.

There had been no reason before Athens to think these preparations inadequate. Greek demands had already apparently been appeased with a careful devaluation of the drachma and a scheme of transitional financial support. Greece now took 16% of the regional development fund budget. No fewer than seven special Council meetings took place to sort out in advance the reforms of CAP and the structural funds, together with forms of EC-wide cooperation on the technological challenge to competitiveness, a balanced package involving increased revenue, better budgetary discipline, and prevention of future imbalances to meet the British criticisms. Such a comprehensive package might conceivably have been steered between the British Scylla and the French Charybdis.

Instead a combination of Greek inexperience in the Presidency, and Pasok's factious demands for yet more cash support, together with Papandreou's erratic chairmanship, shattered Summit conventions and these tenuous agreements. But it should be added that other heads of government also played disingenuous roles:[60] with the French Presidency coming up, Greece was not to have the glory. Nevertheless the fiasco was so total that it proved impossible even to draft an agreed communiqué.

Confusion among member states did not necessarily imply total failure. Within six months, under the French Presidency, all these questions had been brought into line, largely by Mitterrand, now at his peak, yet ever conscious of the need for West German backing. France and Germany were finally able to meet even Britain's demands. But the passage was hard despite the fact that Commission, Parliament and most member states were within reach of each other. After Mitterrand's speech on federalism at Strasbourg in May 1984, and Lord Carrington's swift riposte on the budget, it needed the spectre of EC bankruptcy in March and Mrs Thatcher's refusal of the 'best offer',[61] before ministers finally conceded guaranteed thresholds on CAP farm prices, in order to phase out slowly the onerous MCAs.

At the Fontainebleau Summit of 25–26 June (just after the European Parliament's second direct election) the deadlock broke on the CAP and the budget reforms, together with Britain's contributions.[62] Germany, which was to pay most of the debit, won a special subvention for German farmers. 'Own resources' were increased to the necessary 1.4% on VAT revenues, leaving loose ends to be tied up in Dublin in December with a final cash

subvention for Mediterranean agriculture and the acceptance of an.
– as yet unformulated – integrated Mediterranean programme.

That in turn removed the southern French farmers' objection to
Spanish accession.[63] Spain's and Portugal's negotiations, so long
delayed by pretexts, were rapidly concluded in March 1985 and
the Treaty of Accession was signed in June, providing for entry on
1 January 1986. Meanwhile meetings with EFTA ministers saw
the beginning of negotiations on the European Economic Area
which, however difficult at times, began what was to be a steady
enhancement of mutual economic relations over the next five
years. The EC itself came closer to a standards policy, and simpler
border formalities with the adoption of a single Community
Customs document. France and Germany declared that they
would abolish border checks,[64] and set off on the road to what
became the Schengen agreement.

But the impetus went further. The Council at Fontainebleau
appointed two committees to examine the EC's future: one
chaired by James Dooge (an Irish senator) on institutional affairs,
the other by Adonnino (an Italian parliamentarian) on the
prospects for a 'People's Europe'. The latter – a sop to the
Parliament and its draft Treaty of Union – implied, however
vaguely and rhetorically, the existence of a European citizenship
and European representation. Fontainebleau thus meant more than
Mitterrand's re-establishment of his own and French leadership in
Europe: it cemented the Franco-German core, so that Spanish
and Portuguese entry could at last be agreed, it ensured that
Jacques Delors (though not Mitterrand's first choice) would
become Commission President from 1 January 1985, and it
removed the barriers against Iberian extension by promoting a
package of reforms acceptable to all (even to the Dutch who
disapproved of Germany's payoff). But above all it restored
momentum to a more widespread European process.

What had begun in 1982 at several levels of individuals, firms,
associations, member states, and Commission officials, had been
brought into a conjunction. The aims of once-divergent bodies
and their leaders coincided sufficiently, as a result of these accumulated trade-off and incremental agreements, to make possible

the convening of an inter-governmental conference on the internal market in 1985.

It may not be possible until the documents are available to say certainly which of the actors was the prime mover or indeed whether the explanation should focus on circumstances rather than participants. Quite possibly it will depend on which segment of the wider process is examined. As can be seen from the next chapter, claims can be made for each of the main players. What matters more is that the combination of external challenges to the EC, the 1973 oil shock and strategic fears, the harsh recession and a pervasive disillusion with the system as it had stagnated, led to the entry of more and more players to the arena, while those already in it found a deeper commitment necessary. Their networks expanded and became denser, more continuously effective, notably in industries most threatened by foreign competition: cars, textiles, chemicals, electronics and steel producers. Similar developments, bringing in the same players, were taking place concurrently in many, if not most, national political systems.

Large and multinational firms had sought influence at the EC's centre but had not been present on this scale before the 1970s, nor switched so much of their corporate resources from national to Community level. Financial institutions, which already watched the process, would follow once the internal market was seen to involve services and monetary union (EMU).[65] They did not of course outweigh member states or Community institutions because they were not competing on the same level, nor usually for the same ends, but as the temporary failure at Athens demonstrated, the conjunction of all these was needed before regeneration could take place in the *annus mirabilis* of 1985.

New linkages were growing among the states; between France and Italy, France and Ireland, Germany and Italy, and in the core of those countries whose currencies followed the DM. Some even believed it possible that Britain might become a normal partner. A new world economic boom had started, which seemed matched in political terms by the arrival in power of Mikhail Gorbachev in March 1985: Gorbachev, whose aims had been hinted at earlier, both by his own speeches in England in December 1984, and in Russia by the fact that he had been manifestly the candidate of Yuri Andropov and those reformers who envisaged regeneration arising from a reborn Soviet state.

When President-Designate of the Commission Delors visited each of the other nine members' capitals in the late autumn of 1984, he put four proposals (rather in the Monnet manner, 'Europe is in a mess – where do we start?') Only on the internal market were there signs of general consensus. Whatever conjunction existed at the EC centre (i.e., whenever ministers and heads of government met) was not yet matched in their domestic contexts. The process was neither secret nor predetermined: it operated on many levels with disjunctions, and moved like evolution itself, in fits and starts – more fits at IG level, more starts at official. Some hopes turned into dead-ends, like the Adonnino report; others, like the Dooge Report or the new language of 'cohesion'[66] proved unexpectedly fruitful. There was no prime mover, and there were no obvious state boundaries within which the game could take place. But the players, wittingly or not, had begun to create them.

4

Making the Market:
The Single European Act,
1980–88

Like cooling steel, recent history sets easily into patterns which then resist remoulding. The combination of media reports, expert and specialized commentaries, interviews, articles and memoirs, leads to a received wisdom which successive generations of political scientists, contemporary historians and biographers advance piecemeal. Some seek for a synthesis from which to theorize, others highlight what they take to be particularly significant episodes or individuals. At present, the consensus suggests that the Community experienced a great regeneration around 1985 with the Single Market White Paper serving as its dynamo; then, in a mood of euphoria, member states and the Commission took a leap at Maastricht, which they knew to be contingent on the internal market, only to find themselves isolated from their national publics and from each other. Recession and political disarray followed hand in hand.

Chapter 3 suggested that a variety of players at different levels of activity were engaged, as early as 1980–81, in a struggle to break out of the inertia which had blanketed EC activity since the first oil shock. But what were the aims of each of these, and who contributed most, in that exuberant period after Fontainebleau?

The fact that EC archives are not yet available is not an insuperable difficulty, but it makes it harder to separate underlying trends from less significant details. It is not clear, for example, whether the oligopolistic tendencies among firms in this stagnant decade were caused by the failure of small and medium companies to adapt quickly enough, or by large ones exercising their advantage through concentration and monopoly power, often in collusion with their national governments. Yet the internal market was advocated by players who took the latter assumption for granted, together with its logical extension to the concept of a single currency. Nor is it obvious that the Single European Act was the only way to remedy the collusive, anti-competitive state of mind which appeared to envelop European business and industry in the face of the American and Japanese challenges.

The account given here takes a historical perspective on a very complex and still-continuing process; and is intended to show not only the relative importance of the players (the Commission, member states, the European Parliament, industrial or financial bodies) but their motivation at the time. Seen in this way, the significant points in the narrative are those where the greatest measure of agreement was reached between them, prior to more public action.

In the second half of 1984, following the breakthrough at Fontainebleau, the British budgetary question had apparently been resolved, the EC's financial system had been unblocked, aspects of the CAP, such as the wine market, had been reformed, and the Regional Development Fund expanded. The Esprit Programme introduced a more coherent policy on technology, while the single customs document launched a substantial assault on frontier barriers. Jacques Delors, an ardent integrationist with a considerable reputation as former French finance minister, had been chosen as the new President of the Commission. He could in turn be expected to demand a higher standard of Commissioners and overall competence than had been the case in the previous ten years.

The recession had also ended, providing a two-fold spur to activity: firstly because of the upturn in global demand and secondly because so little had been done since the mid–70s crisis to improve European industry's competitive performance *vis-à-vis* the United States and Japan. General economic convergence led member states towards a common awareness of the likelihood of takeovers looming from outside the EC, and the continuing loss of EC companies' share of world and European markets. Meanwhile, as international trade recovered, the EC's defensive strategies and member states' endemic lapses into protectionism came under fiercer scrutiny, particularly from the USA, where American trade negotiators in the Reagan administration began to use much rougher language towards both the EC and Japan than they had under President Carter; but also from Britain, where inflation control, privatization of state industries, and widespread assaults on the labour market were becoming the keynotes of a novel sort of industrial regime – one which Mitterrand's 1983 turnabout suggested other EC states might conceivably follow. On a more general level, the development of competition law and its enforcement, mainly in Germany (for France and Italy barely had a competition policy other than the one the Commission tried to police),[1] led to a climate in which linkages became possible between what the German government was trying to achieve and the Commission's long-term industrial policy. American and Swiss companies in the EC soon became aware of this new climate, generally earlier than their EC national counterparts.

At the same time, the ERM moved into its 'classic' phase, being transformed after March 1983 into a de facto DM zone with a core of currencies (those of Denmark, the Netherlands, Belgium and Luxembourg) linked to the DM, matched by an increasingly hard French franc . Realignments were still possible, but within progressively narrower limits, less frequently, and on principles established by the anchor country – in effect by the Bundesbank. This system served better those states which embarked on new, more market-oriented economic policies than those who tried (as France had done briefly in 1981–3) to proceed on their own. (Germany had, after all, abolished exchange controls two decades earlier.) For roughly four years, the ERM acted as an external, neutral arbiter, which suited not only governments but industrial and financial interests, because it disciplined inflation and wages and also helped to wean governments away from what these players saw as endemic overspending in pursuit of electoral support.[2]

Because the British government believed it had already solved its problems, however, Margaret Thatcher saw no need to relinquish sterling's greater margin of manoeuvre, and the more that ERM currencies converged, the less desirable entry seemed.[3] Britain already had a free capital market, having abolished exchange controls in 1979, and the wild fluctuations of sterling in this period of increasingly deregulated financial markets suggested that the EMS would have little bearing on the four freedoms envisaged in the future single market; rather the reverse, for British Conservatives and many City economists expected that financial markets would force realignments, whatever governments did to prevent them. The ERM also seemed to inhibit policy flexibility towards interest rates (now the main, indeed the only monetary weapon used in London) and the supply side measures which the government believed were required to reduce labour restrictive practices and rigidities in wages. It seemed therefore that an historic cleavage inside the EC was being perpetuated, though not necessarily, as it was conceived in Britain, to the internal market's disadvantage.

But member states aligned themselves on different axes in response to the other major feature (apart from global recovery) which encouraged ideas of regenerating the EC. Mikhail Gorbachev came to power in March 1985, after the brief Chernenko inter-regnum, evidently bearing a mandate from Yuri Andropov and the Soviet state institutions to reform the system from above. For France, Britain and Germany, this offered chances of playing novel roles, especially insofar as there would be trading prizes in the Comecon states. Yet at the same time the new gravitational pull eastwards imposed stresses on the Franco-German understanding. From France's point of view, political leadership in the EC needed to be re-established to offset West Germany's likely economic predomin-ance in eastern Europe. Smaller member states, which had only reluctantly acceded to the French Presidency's conduct at Fontainebleau, could be expected to take advantage of this shift in balance, and to assert themselves more in future.

In asking what each member state wanted of the internal market, and through what general framework they approached the problem of EC regeneration, it is simplest to take the largest first, according to their relative political weighting in the European Council which, growing up outside the treaties, had by now partly superseded the inter-governmental functions of the Council of Ministers.

FRANCE

Until 1981, France's general interest had been to maintain the link with whatever government existed in West Germany, and the coherence of its worldwide policy (for example, in Africa with the Lomé II Agreement 1979), while preventing EC institutions – the directly elected Parliament and the ECJ, but above all the Commission – from acquiring power to deflect or subordinate French interests. Two years of Mitterrand's socialist and counter-cyclical, counter-GATT programme, the first such essay since Leon Blum's Popular Front in 1936, put in question not only the Socialist government's economic standpoint but the nature of France's polity and its existing relationships within the EC. After the *grand tournant* in 1983, however, the whole French state machine was realigned in a strongly deterministic European project, and Mitterrand assumed at Fontainebleau, as Giscard had done earlier, the role of 'chef d'état de l'Europe'.[4]

The new 'grand project' of integration and European Union was not immediately accepted by the Socialist party, despite the Communist ministers' withdrawal: Jean-Pierre Chevenement and the Ceres radicals represented a powerful strand whose influence was not easily downgraded – although in the end, once the Socialist programme proved to be unrealizable, they adopted the European project with almost equal fervour. But the transformation was implemented directly from the Elysée through an increasingly well-coordinated state administration; and it received substantial backing from French industrialists, appalled at the economic consequences of the previous two years.

Its corollary, as in the 1960s, lay in modernizing French industry, banking and the economy, through the internal market and a stable exchange rate within the ERM. Mitterrand had two years in hand before the next parliamentary elections, four years before the presidential one, and he could rely on West German understanding that any attempt to break out of the 'lourdeur des affaires communautaires' could be successful only if France and Germany were conjoined.

In French eyes the project had four facets. Firstly, having accepted the ERM and the need for convergence, France should, if the ERM was to function properly, look beyond mere stabilization accompanied by periodic, often traumatic realignments, to a tight alignment of parities as the way to eventual Monetary Union and a single currency.[5] Secondly, the social element should be enhanced but given an appropriate market-led ethos, more acceptable to West Germany and Britain than the original 'workers' Europe'.

Thirdly, the Parliament's reopened debate on European Union should be assimilated – but by member states at Council level – in order to restore the EC's institutional coherence. This ran counter to long-standing opposition to any increases in the Parliament's competence by the Conseil d'Etat, Paris bureaucrats, and the Trésor. It even involved some support for the Spinelli initiative. Yet the problem of the indivisibility of French sovereignty, which had for years made prior acceptance of EC laws problematic, may well have been obviated by Delors's 1985 *coup de génie* in putting forward simultaneously the means to satisfy both economic and political projects. Political union, which was West Germany's major ambition, would thus become a complement to economic integration[6] – in contra-distinction to the British dislike of both.

French defence policy provided a contingent element, since West Germany appeared willing at the same time to be associated with a revival of the 1963 Elysée Treaty and a renewed WEU. Geoffrey Howe's alternative paper, put forward at Stresa, served as a further stimulus for launching the Franco-German proposed treaty on European Union in 1985, the fruit of what Simon Bulmer calls their 'complex interdependence', before the British initiative could acquire allies.[7] Finally, having relinquished his earlier dreams of a Europe wider than the EC, Mitterrand now seemed content to see the EC as the core, to which EFTA, Mediterranean and even Comecon states could adjust. France's role was to serve as mediator and adjudicator, a motor for scientific and technological advance, and a liberalizing influence.

There was even talk of extending QMV and Commission (but not Parliamentary) competences.

Yet Mitterrand gave no direct indication which of these four should predominate.[8] A substantial part of the entire project design depended on how far he could recreate a centre-left governing party at home and undermine the right, utilizing the deep divisions between Giscard's UDC and the Gaullists. Ambiguity served also to disguise the extent to which the project required West Germany and the EC itself to be shaped according to French terms.

WEST GERMANY

From its inception, the EC had formed an essential framework for West Germany's process of political and economic rehabilitation, until in due course it became the precondition for whatever followed. Since Adenauer's time, federal governments, usually in coalition, had used it as part of their increasingly elaborate balancing act between *Ost-* and *Westpolitik*, between the USA and Russia, West and East Germany and between West Germany and France. On the basis that this would prevent German isolation in the future, they had developed the EC's most technologically resilient and efficient industrial economy. That secure basis helped determine the German vision of an ideal EC: a community to ensure peace and security in Europe, an economic entity based on free trade, and a community of values and common action (*Werte- und Handlungsgemeinschaft*).

Each of these principles reinforced the more general balance of West Germany's other external relations: whatever German unity emerged in the future was to be understood in its European dimension, not as a purely national phenomenon. Public opinion seemed benign; no anti-EC party existed, nor was there any serious questioning in public of these aims – rather, there was a consensus in West Germany that their country represented the very model of an EC state. The price, that West Germany would always be the largest contributor to EC funds, was – not always unanimously – accepted but it was extended with each new state's accession, in 1973, 1981, and later with Spain in 1986; each time, the justification to domestic objectors being put in terms of German manufacturers' access to these lucrative new markets.

But the Federal Republic as a whole was not notably integrationist, and suspicions existed in Bonn, and even more in some *Länder* such as the CSU-dominated Bavaria, about the use that Free Democrats and their leader, Genscher, made of their long hold on the Foreign Ministry. The Christian Democratic majority of ministers in Bonn did not directly take up the Genscher-Colombo initiative (see above, p. 102), as if remembering Schmidt's phrase (in a speech in 1977) that 'Germany did not want to be in the front row'.[9] German governments went only so far as this complex web of interests dictated. Indeed, the Federal administration often acted as a brake so that, following the 1970s experience, if France were to induce Germany to follow, the deals had to be made via the Chancellery.

Germany's tenure of the Presidency in the first half of 1983 indicated that the reactive, formal and legalistic approach to eventual European Union, based on experience of Federal government, decentralization, and citizenship rights, would continue under Helmut Kohl's Christian Democrats. No one, least of all the Bundesbank, had forgotten Germany's ill-fated reflation initiative, taken under American pressure in 1978–9, with its inflationary consequences. Thus the West German interpretation of Stuttgart's 'solemn declaration' did not represent full endorsement of what the French government currently desired.

Any estimate of West Germany's overall aims depends on which source is chosen: Chancellery, government, Bundesbank, *Länder* governments, or the conjunction of chancellor with the core of foreign, economic and agricultural ministries. As far as industrial policy was concerned, the view of the Economics Ministry (BMWi) and Bundeskartellamt (BKartA) favoured free trade, open competition, and completion of the internal market, starting preferably with deregulation in transport, energy and telecoms, in preference to a single overall initiative. Informally however, the outcome depended on an intricate process of cohabitation and bargaining between the Bonn bureaucracy, leading industrial firms, and the banking system, which was to be brokered at all levels in the Federal Republic. (So content were German companies with this system of 'patronage government' that few bothered to open offices in Brussels until the late 1980s.)

The Bundesbank wished monetary policy to come within the Treaties but strongly opposed EMU (as Otmar Emminger's letter of protest had shown in 1979) even at the level of a future Treaty preamble, it being a matter for member states to safeguard their monetary sovereignty, whilst at the same time taking account of the EC's common interest. Issues relating to foreign policy or defence which required positive responses were treated cautiously; like Schmidt before him, Kohl showed himself willing to accept a steer, either from the European Council, or from France acting in lieu.

The principal weakness of this complicated, decentralized policy-making was that it inhibited German initiatives and thus disguised Germany's latent strength (which was, paradoxically, German politicians' intention). It also put the onus informally on the Chancellor either to concert policy in advance with France, or simply to acquiesce in what French governments did (the case of Schmidt's decisiveness over EMS is unusual). Finally, it tended to irritate British ministers, making any closer relationship with them unlikely, even if that had not already been excluded in the 1980s by personal antipathy between their two leaders.

BRITAIN

The case is apparently simple, especially as expounded in Margaret Thatcher's memoir, *The Downing Street Years*. In fact it was ambiguous, full of nuances, and hidden passages reflected in contrasting accounts.[10] In an assessment of the economic significance of membership, made in 1979, the Treasury had noted that Britain had become a European country visited by 7 million EC tourists, with 42% of its export trade to, and 44% of its exports from, Europe and 2.5 million jobs directly dependent on the EC.[11] Free trade within the Community, after deducting the costs of the CAP (£250 million) and the common fisheries policy (£150 million) added a net total of £120 million to the British economy; furthermore, 59% of United States foreign direct investment went to Britain and the EC – a matter of the greatest significance also for Scotland and Northern Ireland.

By 1984, on the other hand, Britain's post-War settlement, expressed over three decades of neo-Keynesian macroeconomic management and tripartite industrial and labour policies, had been largely replaced by a deflationary fiscal and monetary policy, and what may be called the obverse of an industrial one, concerned with privatizing the state sector and forcing flexibility into the labour market. Contested with little success by a demoralized Labour party and a trade union movement suffering rapid membership decline, the new values in politics, finance and industry contrasted sharply with EC social initiatives such as Vredeling, or the defensive industrial cartels associated with Davignon. Britain had long been hostile to the CAP and was to remain so. Whenever 'own resources' or institutional reforms surfaced, Thatcherite politicians tended to read the worst into Commission initiatives.[12]

Assuming that the imbalance in the British budget contribution and the CAP's iniquities represented the EC's true face, Margaret Thatcher tended always to present herself as the purveyor of financial discipline and sound book-keeping. She publicly construed Stuttgart's 'solemn declaration' as meaningless and attacked the Spinelli Report for absurd idealism. But she was determined to increase Britain's share of world trade and financial services after decades of decline, and therefore endorsed the internal market as a free trade landmark.[13] So, for more complex reasons of inward investment and new technology, did the DTI: thus the core of civil servants in Whitehall were encouraged to assist the Commission in its 1983 harmonization plan (see p. 106) and later in preparing the government paper *Europe and the Future*.

Nigel Lawson, chancellor of the exchequer 1983–8, realized that Britain's ERM entry would add the exchange rate weapon to his very limited armoury, once the strict monetary policy based on £M3 had been abandoned in 1983.[14] But the Bank of England's support for entry, which had been strong up to July 1983 under the Governor, Gordon Richardson, evaporated under his successor, Robin Leigh Pemberton. Lawson's failure on his own to convince the prime minister that sterling should join the ERM led, after the 1984–5 sterling crisis, to sterling's 'shadowing' of the DM, an irregular and informal policy about which Thatcher later claimed not to have known.[15]

The Conservative party had failed to evolve a coherent EC strategy when in opposition in the late 1970s and its leadership remained obsessed with Britain's contentious budget contribution until mid–1984. Nothing of note therefore appeared in the 1983 election manifesto. Geoffrey Howe's growing interest, which led to what in Conservative party terms was a surprisingly open paper, *Europe and the Future* (July 1984, defended by Howe at the party's autumn conference) dated only from Stuttgart. Meanwhile, beyond Whitehall and Westminister, layers of antipathy remained in both political parties. The popular press reflected the adversarial mood and helped to shape perceptions in a very different way from 1972–5, so that the level of public ignorance actually increased.

Industry, which had strong interests in the internal market, could make no impact on this political combination. The CBI monitored EC developments closely but had lost much of its earlier influence with the prime minister in the early 1980s; City markets showed little interest at that stage (though the Bank of England soon picked up its significance for financial services and insurance). Even in Parliament it was the House of Lords Select Committee that investigated rather more than committees in the Commons. Meanwhile, whatever civil servants and diplomats thought, ministers' policies were effectively defended during the British Presidency in 1981, so that Labour's poor handling of the office in 1977 was forgotten. But Britain's partisan nationalism nevertheless antagonized other member states.

Up to 1985, the Conservative political animus lay not primarily against the Commission (indeed Thatcher supported Delors for the Presidency) so much as the EC's integrationist ethos, so that the second Thatcher government saw no merit in moving beyond free trade and the internal market. Stronger supporters of the latter, such as Geoffrey Howe, Leon Brittan, and Michael Heseltine, thought in terms of detailed legislation and constitutional conventions, rather than the prevalent EC way of operational texts to be interpreted later. Yet there was evidence of change at the top of the Conservative party in 1983, and again at the Dublin Summit in December 1984, even on the subject of QMV. Probably as a result of the Athens debacle, Thatcher herself prepared to concede some extension, though preferably only after prior inter-governmental agreement.[16]

As French and West German politicians saw the future in terms of their own recent history, so did British leaders, who envisaged a market-led project in which they, like the Americans, could hold on to their early deregulatory lead. They opposed not only the idea of a two tier EC but what was later styled 'variable geometry'; and they construed the single market itself as the only important aim, unconnected to EMU or political union. But they were realistic and prepared to concede trade-offs such as QMV to attain that primary aim.

ITALY

Since 1957, Italy's relationship with the EC had reflected an underlying formalism, a largely juridical approach, so that by the 1980s several distinct government institutions existed, each with a separate function, joined neither by political coordination nor synoptic thinking, apart from what was provided by a governing majority led usually by successive factions in the Christian Democratic party (DC). Despite political society's apparently widespread enthusiasm for the EC idea, there had been little continuous involvement over the years – hence the importance of a few individuals and interest groups, together with giant firms which, for lack of government support, maintained direct links in Brussels. Except in the industrial north, and on the left (mainly in the unusually open Communist party), political and civil society rarely engaged with each other. In default of a coherent, incorrupt and efficient policy-mongering bureaucracy (as existed more obviously in northern Europe), sustained policy depended on the vagaries of political brokerage which sustained the *pentapartito*, the long-running coalition.

Thus what appeared to be Italy's prompt responsiveness to EC thinking compared badly with the Rome government's actual implementation of legislation (highlighted by the high number of ECJ judgments against Italy). This indicated that Italian institutions had not been permeated by EC values, even when the Commission or Council tried specifically to do so, as they did in reclaiming the endlessly backward Mezzogiorno administration. Because the Italian parliament had in effect been excluded from the EU coordination process as a result of party bargains, a substantial democratic deficit existed. An uninterested public and an inward-looking bureaucracy confronted a tiny elite of insiders in the Foreign Ministry and the Italian Permanent Representation in Brussels. But the most effective of these were usually not party men. Those with a career in Rome in mind tended to stay apart from Commission colleagues who in turn found them deficient in European ideals.

Italy's initiatives therefore tended to come from a few leading politicians in the Foreign Ministry such as Emilio Colombo. If the activists were outside government, like the Independent MEP Altiero Spinelli, their work had little resonance in political life. Even if the evolution of increasingly powerful regional administrations (often run by the PCI in a relatively incorrupt and efficient way after the 1976 elections) produced regional linkages to Brussels (see below, chapter 9), this led to significant conflicts over competence with the Italian Constitutional Court and, in the 1980s, a renewed bout of government centralization. Any hopes that EC membership might be a means to reform Rome itself could not yet be fulfilled.

Italian reformers however welcomed the Parliament's attempt to relaunch political union. The undoubted effect of the EMS in curbing Italian inflation, together with the firm support of the Banca d'Italia and the heads of the largest industrial firms, ensured enthusiasm for the internal market project. Socialists as well as Christian Democrats concurred. Italian industrialists, members of the ERT, or Confindustria (which used the newspaper it owned, *24 Ore*, selling 300,000 copies a day, as its advocate) took an active part. The only real opposition came from the banks and the insurance sector, both of which were deeply uneasy about the price of adjustment; and, in an ill-focused way, from Parliament whose MPs resented their exclusion from the process.

Foreign and Economic Ministries, Banca d'Italia (one of the few wholly untainted institutions), giant firms such as Fiat, Ferruzzi and Olivetti, and even small firms in the North eager to escape the state's tainted bureaucracy, could agree that the internal market would bring opportunities, long overdue restructuring, and administrative reform. But there was no detailed plan, no prior decision as to whether to follow the Davignon or the 'Anglo-Saxon' interpretation, so that in no other member state were the practical details of the 1985 White Paper so far reaching in their effect on how the discussion would evolve. Meanwhile, on the way to the Single European Act, the byzantine games played out on the EC stage and under the Italian Presidency (including the crucial Milan Summit 1985), reflected both the sum of domestic political strategies and Italy's bilateral bargaining with France and Germany. In short, Italy presented a genially positive face to the EC, excusing its shortcomings in implementing legislation or coordinating policy on the grounds of overload, while the political parties milked EC resources – not always for local advantage. This state of affairs was almost the exact antithesis of that in Britain.

THE NETHERLANDS

Since the 1950s, the EC had been a fundamental article of faith in Dutch political and public life. Seen originally as a means to contain Germany, it became, once post-War hostility had diminished, a larger replica of the Netherlands itself, a legally based form of collective rule. Given that Dutch involvement in Benelux's economic integration pre-dated the Treaty of Rome, this worked well in the 1960s while the EC still behaved as a collective, and when two Dutch former prime ministers filled senior posts in Brussels. But it was threatened, firstly by de Gaulle's intransigence, and secondly by the advent of the Franco-German entente, which Dutch leaders saw as inevitably prejudicial to the aspirations of small and medium-sized states.

The Netherlands was wholly opposed to the developing practice of settling issues between heads of government (inter-governmentalism) and its governments deliberately set themselves up to act as the guarantor of small states' rights under the Treaties. In Dutch hands, the Presidency served as a means to help the collective machine run smoothly, with none of the directive tones supplied by Giscard or Schmidt. Many of late 1970s' and early 1980s' changes seemed, to the Dutch, undesirable: the Franco-

German understanding, the advent of the European Council, the EMS, and the backlog of delay in dealing with Commission proposals. The Dutch therefore sought QMV on a wider scale. But unlike the Belgians, they stuck to a conception of the EC which had been implanted much earlier in the Beyen Plan (see p. 31): they tended to accept whatever ideas the Commission proposed, believing that course of action to be a correct reading of the 1957 Treaty.

A few giant companies dominated industry and treated such initiatives as Wisse Dekker's report (see p. 138, above) as part of their corporate strategy. The VMO's outlook paralleled the country's 'instinctive political attitude, never really discussed'; which envisaged the internal market in terms of controlled adjustment rather than full liberalization – though the VMO did lobby extensively for telecoms deregulation.

Further, progressive integration was taken for granted by Dutch public opinion, together with an increasing role for the European Parliament, while progress to EMU and political union ranked as high as abolishing trade barriers. Progress was to come according to agreed procedures and deadlines, beyond the capacity of larger governments to adjust. Given its open economy, the Netherlands strongly opposed protectionist tendencies and looked outwards to international as well as European trade. Successive governments supported NATO, were generally favourable to the USA, to liberal tax regimes, and FDI rules, and were adamantly against state intervention – thus coming closer to the British interpretation than that of Germany, despite having linked the guilder to the DM since 1973.

Long habituated to ideas about social harmony, decentralization of state power and tripartism, Dutch governments supported any Commission proposals to give organized labour greater advantage *vis-à-vis* capital and management, and still vested some hope in Ecosoc as the forum to discuss employment policy and the social dimension. In spite of a decentralized system of administration which required endless harmonization, the Dutch impetus was often effective on the European Council.

BELGIUM

As with the Netherlands, the EC was never a matter of dispute. Belgium received great economic benefits and a status which no small country could have achieved on its own. The price – if it was a price – had to be paid in terms of the impact of EC federalism in a country whose increasingly polarized ethnic divisions reflected its nineteenth-century social evolution and the creation of the state out of two distinct elements. Whether EC membership actually accentuated the process of transforming the unitary state of 1970 into a federal one in 1990, ('a federal state composed of communities and regions') is unclear, but all relations with the EC and its institutions became politicized, though not necessarily in a contentious way. Each Belgian Presidency had to replicate the domestic role of government in a sort of permanent arbitrage between decentralized units.

For the majority of Belgians, their polity pre-figured what the EC would eventually become: a cooperative framework of states and institutions with a strong regional dimension and a common citizenship. These assumptions underlay the Belgian Presidency's conduct of EC crisis management in the case of Poland, Libya and the Falklands war in 1982. On the other hand, because of complex national competences and Flemish/Walloon rivalries, long delays in incorporating EC laws were inevitable – and much criticized by the ECJ.

All-party consensus prevailed on matters concerning the economy and integration, partly because 70% of Belgium's trade lay within the EC and partly because the EC was taken for granted as the prime source of Belgian status in the world. Any moves towards reinvigorating it, including the internal market, were welcome. But on balance, Belgian governments followed the lines set by Davignon and recommended by Dekker, because of the relatively huge part still played by their declining steel, coal and textiles sectors.

LUXEMBOURG

Living in a tiny country with no pretensions to any of the usual connotations of power, Luxembourgeois had long held a deep fear of being swamped by their neighbours. They had always been eager to propagate the idea of integration, emphasizing that progress should be achieved by legal instruments and collective action. A long history of close cooperation with Belgium and the Netherlands, predating the EC itself, showed itself in the currency link with the former dating from 1922. Despite its small population, Luxembourg had no problem with all the roles required by its status as a member.

Precisely because it was so *communautaire* and disinterested in larger states' rivalries, Luxembourg had been able shrewdly to manage its Presidencies. In 1976, it helped to institute the Troika, and in 1980 to stage manage the EC-Arab talks, the North-South dialogue, and the evolution of CSCE during the Solidarity crisis in Poland.

As a fully open and integrationist state, wedded to free trade (on which its industries had developed and its banking sector had become a leader in the EC in the 1970s), Luxembourg welcomed the internal market, especially the free movement of capital which greatly benefited its own financial services. It also sought EMU, after the 1982 currency crisis in which Belgium had devalued without joint consultation. (From then on it was clear that the Belgian franc would be tied to the DM inside the EMS.) Luxembourg had wisely reduced its dependency on the steel industry and expected unequivocal benefits from EC regeneration. Yet potential problems existed, chiefly in the field of harmonization, for its banks had no wish to fit in with German requirements on taxation – especially withholding tax – nor to change the laws on banking secrecy: the Luxembourg economy benefited too much to envisage a truly level playing field.

IRELAND

Entry to the EC had offered Ireland the chance to break out from its narrowly constructed, protectionist, rather bigoted provincial identity, to become a distinct European nation. By 1980, largely through its EC links, it had also escaped the long shadow of the United Kingdom and its poor and backward economy had experienced a greater recovery, and greater politico-cultural benefits than either of the other 1973 entrants. In the early 1980s, Ireland also enjoyed regular trade surpluses[17] and financial transfer payments.[18] In its economic aspect at least, the public was united: 83% had voted in favour of entry in the 1972 referendum and 68·7% were to vote for Maastricht in 1992, despite the fact that previously undreamt-of legal and constitutional implications had emerged.

New affinities with France began to replace the ancient ambiguity of cohabitation with Britain. In its first presidency in 1975, Ireland was able to stand up on the international stage as Garret FitzGerald addressed Commission-Council relations directly, having negotiated ably with the United States in Henry Kissinger's day. It also subsequently played a mediating role during the second oil shock, despite problems with the European Parliament.

Agriculture benefited unequivocally from increasing specialization while industry drew in foreign investment, particularly from Germany, to replace its formerly sheltered sectors – though this came at the expense of local capacity. Despite the disruptions so caused, Irish governments retained their interests in liberalizing their domestic markets. But EMS membership, the only alternative to linking the punt to sterling, produced a hardening currency, welcome for its disinflationary effect but unwelcome in its impact on domestic production in the early 1980s. Some of this disadvantage was offset by transfers from the EC's Regional Fund because all of Ireland still qualified for assistance.

Manufacturing and food processing would have suffered in any case from global changes. The prospect of a link between the internal market and structured funding helped to mediate this, and to curb any hankering for a repetition of the failed experiment in protection during the 1960s. Wisely, Irish governments used EC money and technology transfers to address structural failures. This was the overt reason for going forward to the single market, as the Dooge Committee recommended. But, as the Fine Gael party saw, structured change would be the real means to modernize the economy in the European dimension, to which a purely national market was an obstacle.[19] This insight passed in due course to

Charles Haughey's Fianna Fail government which, despite its historic tendency towards isolation, was content to accept that the country's future lay wholly in the EC.

That there would be costs in unemployment, rising national debt, and disruption of rural society was not denied. The EC could moderate the pain, increase economic and social cohesion, and restore a measure of real independence to offset the surrender of formal sovereignty. This was a synoptic viewpoint, in sharp contrast with Britain's, shared by farmers, trade unionists and most of industry, despite the predicted impact of EC imports on domestic market share: in the late 1980s and with the support of the Irish Labour party, it was to lead on to support for EMU and European Union.

DENMARK

Denmark, like Ireland, found itself faced by economic readjustments after entry in 1973, but without a basis of political consent. The EC had until then been presented as a superior sort of EFTA, a customs union with a few 'political dreams' attached. Membership was already a contentious subject and this was not alleviated by the first, unfortunate, Danish Presidency, which took office after only six months' membership experience, at the time in 1973 when the oil shock hit the EC. The Social Democratic party remained as divided as the British Labour party, while fears persisted among the Six that the Danes would use the EC as a milch cow. These were dispelled during subsequent Presidencies: in 1978 by an unsuccessful Danish attempt to launch a growth programme, and in 1982 when, in Copenhagen in June, the odium for lack of progress fell on Britain.

Denmark's complex and devolved decision-making processes ensured that in the absence of public consensus the passage to the internal market would be difficult. The White Paper's mixture of economics and politics, and disputes between the government and the Folketing over whether EC affairs counted as foreign or domestic, made it hard for the government to take decisions and helped to produce an appearance of obstructionism.[20] At home, government usually won its case but at the price of later electoral retribution. To get the Single Act through, it had finally to by-pass the Folketing majority (80 to 75) with a national referendum (56.2% in favour, 43.8% against).

The internal market offered clear advantages to industry and consumers, yet morbid fears persisted about the EC's bureaucratic centralization, and the portents of harmonization, as a threat to ecological purity from an overweening EC state. Without a clear mandate, the government confronted a range of domestic pressure groups which feared liberalization. But the Confederation of Danish Industries favoured the single market, in order to achieve a stable market for its few but globally oriented medium-sized companies. For them the EC was the home market, and although they disliked talk of industrial policy, they remained fiercely antiprotectionist. But the Confederation represented a small sector of the population with only 300,000 employees, fewer than Siemens employed in the EC.

Swayed by these pressures, and different oppositions, the government alternated between alliances with Britain (for example on aspects of the Dooge Report), and a claim similar to the Netherlands that institutional reform was essential to restore the EC's dynamism. Denmark (whose currency link to the DM owed more to economic *force majeure* than political affinity) was seen therefore as *contre*: against inter-governmental action, political union, and EMU. It voted against an IGC in Milan in July 1985 but then later conceded, anxious not to be the only member state left out.

GREECE

Seven years after the end of the military dictatorship, the Karamanlis government from 1974 to 1981 attempted to modernize the Greek economy and transform Greek attitudes through the medium of the EC application. But this project (with intrinsically similar aims to those of Turkey) was undermined by the rapid rise of Andreas Papandreou's ostensibly socialist but in practice populist-left party, Pasok, from 1977 to its election success in 1981.[21] At once the Accession Treaty, hard won at home by Karamanlis with Franco-German backing in the Council of Ministers, came into question. It was the Pasok government and its leader, according to other members states' opinions, who were responsible for the Athens debacle in December 1983 and, more persistently, for blocking the Commission's new plans for standard-setting and mutual recognition.

Much of this could be ascribed to the inexperience of a small, relatively backward state emerging from a harsh military dictatorship; a measure of local demagoguery and political-administrative corruption was predictable. But Pasok's 'third world orientation' and Greek reactions to the Turkish invasion of northern Cyprus in November 1983 estranged Greece from the EC's mainstream, as could be seen from factious behaviour of large states during the Greek Presidency.[22] Greece's blatant exercises in renegotiation to gain maximum advantage early in 1982, and again before Spain was finally allowed entry, left Greek membership with few admirers and appeared to prove that Greece was prepared not only to milk the EC but to hold up its essential business in order to do so. Paradoxically, this helped to convince the waverers, notably Margaret Thatcher, that some measure of QMV was essential (see above, p. 122).

Yet the Greek government had serious problems to overcome at home, having to confront very inward-looking factions and an avowedly sensationalist press. There was good evidence of a will to do its EC duty, as the Pasok government eventually settled the quarrel over air bases with the USA and moved away from its third world policy, while the Turkish invasion helped eventually to introduce a period of learning on both sides. The appointment as secretary general of CEN (Centre Européen des Normes) of an able Greek engineer went some way to persuade the government of the internal market's virtues. EC policy was managed by a small bureaucratic elite, running a weak, highly politicized state apparatus, often in confrontation with a volatile public opinion on which all opposition politicians capitalized. Greece's final decision in favour of the Single European Act therefore represented acceptance not only of the internal market but of a change in Greece's destiny, a western style of modernization rather than a traditional one, for which Pasok would have to educate their public.

*   *   *

Something should be added about Spain and Portugal, even though the internal market was to be part of the EC *acquis* that any new member would have to accept.

SPAIN

The small political elite who managed the long-delayed application process, firstly from Suarez's centre-right basis, then after the 1982 election under the Socialist government of Felipe Gonzalez,[23] knew that entry would be a harsh challenge but that there was no alternative if the Spanish economy were to develop to EC levels and standards. (That there would be a second, more difficult, challenge with EMU/Maastricht in 1991 was not foreseen, although the peseta's entry to EMS/ERM was always taken for granted, given the importance of creating an integrated financial sector). From the EC's side, it was recognized that Spain needed a long period of transition before convergence could be completed, or there would be a balance of payments crisis, accompanied by devaluation and inflation.

Restructuring and upgrading the industrial base, together with banking and insurance, were the preconditions of adjustment, in which using not only EC support but attracting foreign direct investment from member states, the USA and Japan would be essential. Paradoxically, the Franco legacy lay less heavily on the economy than the effect of compromises made during the transition to democracy in the late 1970s, notably the Moncloa pacts made in October 1977 between the government and opposition parties acting variously on behalf of trades unions and management, which had accepted mild inflation, wage rigidity and employment security as the price of social peace. Trades unions' growing powers, a highly restrictive labour code and index-linked wages soon produced much higher inflation which, despite the Banco de' España's austere monetary policy, stuck at 20–22% in the early 1980s, inhibiting inward investment, dividing the administration and setting the Bank against the Economics Ministry.

The Gonzalez government's turnabout in 1984 (which can be compared to that of Mitterrand in 1983) made it possible to reduce money supply and public spending and to bring inflation down to

15%. Thereafter unemployment rose steeply, signifying that the Moncloa pacts' legacy was dead. As the shocked unions wavered, a recovery began, leading to a boom which accompanied Spanish entry on 1 January 1986. Four years of rapid growth to 1990 brought high demand, high consumption, and a revolution in production – in which the long-sought foreign investment, led by West Germany, was a prime cause. That this policy mixture would lead to overheating became clear towards the end of the 1980s, but apart from joining the ERM no precautions were taken, despite pressure from the CEOE (Confederation of Spanish Employers) for matching supply side reforms,[24] which alone could make realistic Spain's targets for 1992, open banking and free capital movements.

Since the accession negotiations were handled by the government, on the same basis of consent that occurred among the players on economic policy, Spain's consequent acceptance of the internal market was taken for granted. The political parties, economic sectors (apart from agriculture which was seriously hit in the later and hasty stage of accession bargaining), and the Spanish public, increasingly well informed of the advantages by a liberated and lively press and television, accepted the package as a beneficial whole, so that there was no perceptible domestic opposition to the terms of the Accession Treaty. EC member states, however, could be in no doubt that Spain, with 8 votes on the Council of Ministers, would henceforward rank as a substantial European player, likely to be demanding on matters of regional funding, Mediterranean agriculture and social cohesion.

PORTUGAL

As the revolutionary years 1974–5 receded and memories of the forty-year dictatorship and the long preoccupation with African colonies rather than Europe faded,[25] Portugal looked to the EC to help it discover late twentieth-century normality. Shorn of imperial ambitions, the country had no future except in Europe: this much was a matter of agreement between centre-right (PSD) and centre-left (PS). Yet a still-strong Communist party and a nationalist Catholic right conditioned the balance of attitudes. Apart from the main banks (now state-owned) and a few large but declining industries such as shipbuilding and repairing, the Portuguese economy was still based in the south on Mediterranean agriculture and in the north on small firms, mainly concerned with textiles. A backward infrastructure, low levels of education, and a GDP per head of only $3500, below that of Greece (which most observers at the time expected to perform better), ensured that its transition would be prolonged and difficult.

But the small political elite had no difficulty in convincing a public tired of isolation and the heavy burden of having lost a colonial empire, that EC membership was the only way to avoid being relegated to the impoverished periphery and swamped by Spain. The problem lay in deciding between the primarily economic hopes of the minimalists (who included both the communists and the socialist left, as well as the nationalist right) and the centre, which accepted a broader measure of integration. Overall, apart from the ardent federalists, who included President Soares, a concern with sovereignty and national identity inhibited support for monetary union, as it did in Britain, though more so perhaps because of frequent escudo devaluations to aid exports. Living in the shadow of Spain, the Portuguese were jealous of small member states' rights, yet conscious that, if they were to benefit and complete the process of modernization, they had to show themselves to be good Europeans.

Yet by 1985, Portugal possessed not only an open economy – partly as a result of the tough IMF-imposed programme in the mid-1980s – but an international awareness and important links with southern Africa and Brazil. Though few, its Brussels representatives were to prove themselves able and cooperative. Community decisions were all made at the centre, almost uninfluenced by civil servants and not at all by parliament. The public, conditioned by the ten-year-long liberal PDS government of Cavaco Silva, accepted integration and seem barely to have distinguished the EC from the world at large.[26] The influence of industry and farming interests, along with the small role assigned to consumers, can be compared with the situation in Ireland, but the survival of a strong Communist party ensured a stronger role for organized labour.

Like Spain, soon to be Portugal's largest trading partner, the country was to experience boom years up to 1990, buoyed up by German and Spanish investment. But at the time when the date was set for completion of the internal market, there appears to have been more widespread awareness than in Spain of how far the abolition of tariffs, free movement of capital and transition to the CAP would affect all aspects of Portuguese economic and social life. Hence, while in favour of the internal market, the Portuguese government argued that it was not yet ready, and remained defensive, arguing for a higher levels of support for social cohesion, regional funds and Mediterranean agriculture, while at official and presidency level living up to the 'good European' expectation.

On the central issue of the internal market, all ten member states had thus come roughly into line – albeit for different reasons – by the end of 1984. So had the other major players across Europe, industry, finance, even labour – insofar as that had recaptured its European presence. But it needs to be asked to what extent these rather than governments actually determined the outcome.

Financial sectors certainly took little part in the internal market process. The Fédération Bancaire Européen (FBE) had had to react so far to only one major Commission proposal, the first banking Directive of 1977. So long as the quiet years continued neither side wished to stir things up. In the absence of Commission activity, there seemed no urgent need to react to competition from American and Japanese banks, while insurance companies and stock exchanges barely stirred. Even when banks did get their fingers burned in the 'sovereign debtors' crisis, they tended to seek global remedies via spreading and insuring risks.

Even central banks involved themselves only when the Single Market White Paper had been assimilated and monetary union come into focus as a consequence. But deregulation, particularly in Britain after 1983, led to an exuberant period of often ill-judged growth and acquisitions, followed in due course by competition in all markets for capital and financial services; excess capacity ensued, followed by retrenchment – and the same choice that had already faced key industries, between managed and market-led restructuring. Thus the market cycle, as much as changes in the formal financial environment, ensured that they would enter the EC game in the end.

Political scientists and contemporary historians dispute how far 'industry' can be seen as a coherent player in this game.[27] Up to the late 1970s there was certainly no consistent evidence that large or multinational firms, though they were regular players at official level, had been recognized in formal Community bargaining. Insofar as they operated informally, they did so at national government level or through personal links with officials in DG3, so that with the exception of American and Swiss MNCs, which tended to go direct to both the Commission and the Parliament, influence seeped almost imperceptibly into both member states and Commission plans. The results of what they did therefore varied, being at national level more effective in France, Germany and the Netherlands than in Italy and Denmark; and at Commission level, more with DG3 than DG4. Indeed a presumption existed in most of the sectoral federations that DG4's competition brief inhibited informal links with corporate interests, and that any formal ones should run via UNICE. Since those directives which got through the early 1980s log-jam were still framed in terms of technical harmonization, usually in the food processing industry, and since DG3 perpetuated the industrial sponsorship ethos to their satisfaction, firms and federations themselves saw no need to do more.

But when Etienne Davignon rebuilt DG3 on the Spinelli model, adding to it technological development and foreign trade elements, together with rationalization of the steel industry, this complacent attitude changed rapidly. The twelve major information technology firms willingly took part in Davignon's research initiative which led to the promulgation of ESPRIT in 1984. On a wider scale, European corporations who benefited substantially from it generally saw the grand structural adjustment plan as a benign way to offset otherwise unacceptable political and financial imperatives from the recession of the early 1980s: redundancies, real wage cuts, benefits reductions, and some of the heavy cost of high-technology capital investment.

Considerations such as these led inevitably to firms' preoccupation with the internal market's potential advantages, and complemented what was always in France, and also now in Spain, a thesis about general modernization. If CBI records are typical,[28] this recognition can be dated to 1980–81; that is, contemporary with Davignon's initiative.[29] However, at first its impact was confused by the vigorous polemic over Vredeling. UNICE however was not to be the vehicle, but instead a 'high level' informal group, aiming directly at Brussels and heads of government.[30] Neither were sectors or peak organizations chosen for permeation: few of them were as yet so well based in Brussels as the Americans, and AmCham's European Committee. But the informal groups, of which the European Round Table (ERT) became the most influential, had greater effect in the earlier period, 1982–4, when they operated informally, than afterwards. Having, as it were, gone public, they became animators, adjuncts to, rather than initiators of change. The influence of the firm has therefore to be measured in the interstices, in rivalry with louder views coming from the Parliament such as de Ferranti's Kangaroo Group, and the 1981 Nicholson Report which claimed that the EC was ignoring industrial uncompetitiveness.

Yet this is to measure matters only on the EC stage. Some member states had gone down the Davignon road much earlier – Britain with the Labour governments' late 1970s Industrial Strategy, France with the Plan Barre, Germany with the Modell Deutschland. Though sectors of British government took a different view in the early 1980s, the DTI was still eager to engage the CBI's services in its 1981 campaign for the internal market: clearly (despite the rupture between the Thatcher Cabinet and the CBI) a basis for general consensus still existed, at least in the high technology race. Something similar occurred in West Germany as the heads of much of industry came to a central standpoint on the internal market. Their French counterparts followed suit around 1983. AGREF (the Association des Grandes Enterprises Françaises), noted the conjuncture. The idea grew rapidly, according to one French company executive: 'Europe is a kind of domestic market ... the foreign markets are in America and south east Asia.'[31] The CBI and DVI, together with support from the CNPF or Patronat and Confindustria, therefore took part in Delors's later 'vast consultation' with heads of enterprises across Europe.

Governments in effect used their giant firms and federations to influence the Commission, complementing what national representatives were already doing in the Council of Ministers. Who used whom, and who if any one actually set the agenda, is almost impossible to decide without access to EC archives.

What matters here is that in this game, private associations like ERT were encouraged by governments and the Commission to behave as privileged actors; individual industrialists, usually with their firms' long-term strategic advantage in mind, willingly took up the roles. UNICE, which began to call for QMV as a solution to the log-jam problem in February 1984 came later, counted for less, and was used by the Commission rather as a source to disseminate information and Commission messages. (Even less can be ascribed to the 'Jean Monnet Committee', reborn at the end of that year.)

The European Round Table (ERT) stands out, firstly as a collection of industrialists who led firms that were highly important, being multinationals oriented towards investments (which the Community could hope to stimulate by incentives) in telecoms, road and rail transport, and research and development. Secondly, they acted as an influence personally on Jacques Delors before, and for a short time after, he took up the Commission Presidency in January 1985.[32] It was first established with Pehr Gyllenhammer (Volvo) as chief executive – a useful non-EC catalyst – and its members included Umberto Agnelli (Fiat), Wisse Dekker (Philips), Pierre Defraigne (France), John Harvey-Jones (ICI), K. Durham (Unilever), H. Maucher (Nestlé), C. Nicolin (ASEA), A. Riboud (BSN France), D. Spethmann (Thyssen), Sir Peter Baxendale (UK Shell), R. Fauroux (St Gobain), B. Hanon (Renault), O. le Cerf (Lefarge Coppée), H. Merkle (Bosch), L. von Planta (Ciba-Geigy), W. Seelig (Siemens). It had valuable links with Davignon and his successor Narjes, Fernand Braun, and Ortoli, and in that sense furthered the Commission's idea of a pan-European, synoptic approach which was neither socialist nor corporatist. Its main general proposal was for a 'Marshall plan for Europe' (January 1983), the result of much debate about how to achieve reindustrialization; its main special report was written by Wissi Dekker, on behalf of Philips, in 1984 and published in January 1985.

Private and informal influence had had most effect before these publications, during 1983, in particular on the Franco-German element in the Stuttgart Declaration.[33] Specifically, ERT focused directly on decision-makers (unlike the coordinating body, European Enterprise Group), proclaiming the importance of non-tariff barriers and the lack of standards, which the internal market was intended to remedy. Its suggested solutions – contained in slim, well-produced pamphlets, somewhat tinged with protectionism – were aimed at political leaders, in contrast to the more detailed literature from UNICE. What mattered most was its animator status, given the point already reached by the Commission and the German, British and French industry ministries. As Maria Green suggests, its influence was used in the direction of a unified rather than a common market, and to bring a much needed pragmatism to the debate;[34] however, its later, more formal work also fed back into those member states which had stimulated it in the first place, so that it tended to replicate national lines of thought, whether for defensive adjustment or free market openness. This probably explains the CBI's 10% area of disagreement with the Dekker Report and the DTI's rather greater degree of divergence, enhanced of course in Margaret Thatcher's speeches. In its crudest form of differentiation, the British version embodied an unrest-cure with contingent unemployment and bankruptcies while the German and French ones propounded a state- and industry-managed restructuring at minimal social and economic cost.

Given the momentum among governments from mid–1984 onwards, ERT's later contributions have to be seen as supererogatory, part of the heightened climate of awareness about venture capital, completion of 'missing links' in the infrastructure (such as the Channel Tunnel or the EC-Scandinavian road/rail bridge) and the individual projects such as the European Technology Institute, for high-grade postgraduate training.[35]

As for the firms themselves, who in a mere three or four years were to flood into Brussels to establish influence in what now appeared to be the epicentre of commercial advantage, it is impossible to isolate their individual weighting.[36] Most had a vested interest in the process, as they demonstrated in the wave of mergers, joint ventures and takeovers – in consumer durables, office equipment, metals, agribusiness, airlines (though these mergers all failed), press and television and venture and finance capital – which occurred even in advance of the Single Act, 1985–6, usually with Commission support.[37] Firms in the lead here included Thomson, Zanussi, Olivetti, Pechiney, Ferruzzi, Cerus (Olivetti), and entrepreneurs such as de Benedetti, Maxwell, Berlusconi (several of which, as a result, became grievously over-stretched by the early 1990s).

American firms, feeling themselves losing market share world-wide to the Japanese, especially in semi-conductors, banking and financial services, were meanwhile extracting special concessions in the United States and many varieties of protection from the compliant Republican administrations of Reagan and Bush. As a result, there emerged a barely veiled policy of trade through bilateral agreements which seemed to have become, by 1985–6, as great an impediment to the current GATT round as anything emerging from France or the EC. The situation generally worsened with the US Trade Bill of 1987. In the critical areas of cars, semi-conductors, telecoms, and consumer electronics, the EC reacted less stringently (since American companies, organized in AmCham's European Committee, had long since operated within its borders)[38] than it did against Japan. Nevertheless, the Commission disliked the mid-80s regimes of VERs, quotas and tariffs, imposed by member governments acting together in Council, which officials believed only emphasized the bankruptcy of inter-govern-mentalism and the virtues of the Commission-led internal market process.

The Commission had developed its own scheme in 1983 in the limited field of mutual recognition and standards introduction: 'limited' (in DG3's view) meaning the most that member states would permit. Thereafter, it seemed as if Stuttgart had produced only rhetoric, of little value in daily transactions. Narjes's long summary of uncompleted items emphasized the backlog, without shaming the Council into advancing the project. Fontainebleau gave no particular encouragement to the internal market. As late as November 1984, when Delors put his four questions to the member governments, he himself was inclined towards institutional reform: it was the negative responses to that which convinced him that only the internal market could proceed.[39] His first speech to the Parliament, on 14 January 1985, with its call for 'completion of a fully unified internal market by 1992 (with) a realistic timetable' may have represented a Commission-led breakthrough.

But that ignores the fact that the 1983 efforts by officials had only been postponed. One close participant points to 'the Commission's internal dynamic which . . . used the multinationals; and also the pressures coming from the Parliament to get away from "non Europe"', which pre-dated Delors' activity. Allowance should also be made for the ECJ's influence: what had begun with the *Continental Can* case 1972 (see above, p. 96) was renewed in the *Philip Morris* case of 1981, when the ECJ used Article 85 rather than 86 to lay down the considerations pertaining to cases of mergers and concentrations. The issues of merger regulation and limiting state aids did not disappear from the Commission's agenda with the Council's rejection of the Draft Merger Regulation; that this area of the internal market required the work of two far-sighted Commissioners, Peter Sutherland and Leon Brittan in 1986–92, may in fact be a tribute to the delaying capacity of certain governments and industries. Then, as later, the many-faceted interaction of President, college of Commissioners and Director-Generals, has to be seen as itself a competitive symposium operating on a much longer time cycle than those of national governments or firms.

Delors' questions offered the twelve governments four choices of how to recapture the EC's momentum: monetary union, foreign policy and defence cooperation, institutional reform, and the internal market. Apart from France, no member government chose anything but the latter; yet few supporters felt strongly about it. On the evidence of his own writings, Delors reckoned that it would take two full four-year terms of office: the first up to 1988 to get the Single European Act, the second to 1992 to complete it;[40] so his *rélance* to the European Parliament was to be read both as a proposal for a Europe without internal borders, and a long, politically radical project for what that Europe was to become.

The concept of a single market had by then been agreed between Delors and the key Commissioner, Arthur Cockfield, who had been appointed by Margaret Thatcher to succeed Christopher Tugendhat who was now out of favour. That combination, and the greatly enlarged competence which Cockfield requested at DG3 (financial institutions, company law, VAT and indirect taxation) set him in a position of greater directive power than Davignon had ever possessed. Cockfield could therefore provide sole authorship as well as conceptual force for DG3's work in preparing the White Paper, and a unique preponderance in the Commission college. Davignon's pragmatism and Narjes's preparatory work infused what was done, but the logic and intricate cooperation between Directorates owed most to their successor.

Thatcher had given Cockfield a brief 'to make the internal market work'. His early investigations led him to agree with Delors that any target date before 1992 would be unrealistic. He had no illusions about the lukewarm involvement of most governments, even though the Luxembourg Council (following the Dooge Committee Report) endorsed the target. Consequently the White Paper had to contain a precise schedule of all the components, amounting to nearly 300 items for legislation, a deadline (1 January 1993), fully elaborated concepts of mutual recognition harking back to *Cassis de Dijon*, tax harmonization (a favourite of Cockfield's) and some measure of supervision to keep member states in line during the process of implementation. The programme had to be coherent, interlocking, yet distinguished from the social, environmental, competition, investment and monetary issues which were contingent on it, but which, for political reasons to do with member states, could only be incorporated later.

Member state governments may have been unanimous in their welcome for some sort of internal market; but how much they foresaw of the White Paper's actual details or its contingent elements is unclear. Cockfield took his tutorial mandate to the limit, composed the document as if the political will already existed (as the founding fathers had done in 1957) and wisely circulated it only ten days in advance, giving time for governments, civil servants and permanent representatives to evaluate it but not to draw up counter-proposals. He prefaced it by citing every endorsement that ministers had given, from Copenhagen and Stuttgart onwards: they had willed the ends, here were the means. Despite this care, and despite the low-key, almost bureaucratic tone, objections were at once raised, from other Directorates and from some of the industrialists, who sensed how far it reached beyond the Dekker Report. But Cockfield refused to tone it down. Indeed, being well aware of its impact on financial services, he used other industrialists and City of London figures to propagate what he claimed was the only way to end 'this prolonged period of uncertainty'. He was rewarded when, at the Milan Summit, the Council instructed the Commission to prepare a plan of action, within the timescale which Cockfield had envisaged from the beginning in his critical path analysis. From this point on, ministers began also to come to terms with QMV, which had been evaded at Dublin the year before and which Cockfield and Delors knew would be essential.

During the French Presidency in 1984, President Mitterrand had also made a tour of European capitals with a 'relaunch of the EC' in mind. From this came two significant understandings, the first between Germany and France on institutional reform, (even though France still hesitated at the further powers for the European Parliament apparently required by both Germany and Italy), and secondly between Germany and Italy on market liberalization.[41] The British government, secured temporarily in the Fontaine-bleau budget concessions, grew uneasy about suggestions in Paris about an EC of different speeds, if not necessarily a two-tier approach, especially when, addressing the European Parliament on 23 May, Mitterrand presented, with some panache, a view of Europe's federal destiny and a mordant commentary on how to face *le défi Américain* – the US challenge.

Much detailed diplomacy was necessary before the Twelve could broker even the beginnings of a compromise, ready for the Milan meeting in October 1984. Mitterrand was now reforging the entente with Germany, hoping that Maurice Faure's presence as rapporteur of the Dooge Committee (consisting of heads of governments' personal representatives) would maintain France's version of how institutions should be reformed during the Irish Presidency. Because of British preoccupations, QMV remained a central issue for the Dooge Committee, whose deliberations were mainly concerned with institutional and constitutional issues.[42] But the Committee's high-level membership, and its reluctance to discuss issues of detailed policy, made it an unsuitable vehicle for inter-governmental competition to set the social and political matrix of the internal market, which may well have influenced Margaret Thatcher to look to Cockfield for a more cautious and and empirical approach. In the end, after sifting the potential impact of various important consequences of the internal market, including the Luxembourg Compromise, the numbers divided seven to three on the key question of QMV.

The Dublin Summit which considered Dooge's interim report had therefore to fudge the main issue for lack of a consensus; and gave a very nuanced, even contradictory line for Milan. But there was enough acceptance by the majority – which did not in fact exclude Britain – to indicate that the seven to three tally, reaffirmed in relation to the need for Treaty amendments and an IGC (during the March 1985 Council meeting in Luxembourg), could be adjusted. Britain was in the process of modifying its position and making overtures to France about a common front. Geoffrey Howe put an able defence of a British plan for QMV *without* an IGC, at Stresa, in May.[43] But his proposal was pre-empted when Mitterrand and Kohl drew up their 'Treaty of European Unity', to coincide with the fortieth anniversary of the end of the Second World War. What appeared in London to be fresh evidence of the Franco-German entente angered Thatcher and may have contributed to her being manoeuvred into opposition at Milan; she seems not to have been aware until too late that Kohl had also concerted his tactics before the Summit with fellow Christian Democrats in Rome and probably also indirectly with Craxi and the Italian Socialists.[44]

The Milan Summit took place after assiduous lobbying by all the minor players. But Italy held the Presidency, and the leaders of the *pentapartito*, Giulio Andreotti (DC) the foreign minister, and

Bettino Craxi (PSI) the prime minister, sought above all to have an IGC in order to ensure that political cooperation and wide-ranging institutional reforms were incorporated. This would have been impossible without amending the Treaties. The Italian proposals were intended to ensure better decision-making, more Commission power of initiative, a Court of First Instance to ease the ECJ's overload, and larger powers for the Parliament – a substantial part of which went beyond what Kohl and Mitterrand had agreed. After a confused debate, Craxi called for a vote under the simple majority procedure covered by QMV, and obtained the required and predicted seven to three result: Britain, Denmark and Greece being in the minority.

The British were scarcely surprised at this outcome. Later on, Thatcher argued that her willingness to cooperate had been misconstrued. But for the other heads of government, having an IGC was crucial. At the time, Thatcher accepted that her prior element of acquiescence in QMV (even on the basis that there was no need for an IGC), and the importance for Britain of limiting further progress to no more than the White Paper's proposals, justified all-out participation once the IGC had been set up by the the majority. (As Howe put it: 'member states had to be checked from hanging more baubles on a mobile Christmas tree.')[45] But before the IGC opened at Luxembourg on 9 September, the White Paper was already being subsumed in the wider Commission design.

Cockfield had envisaged that his White Paper's approach to the demolition of three sorts of barriers – frontier, technical and fiscal – should continue to guide the internal market's evolution, whatever came out at the IGC. Only later would tax harmonization, for example, be incorporated. He had confined it deliberately to the industrial sectors to be liberalized and had not touched on competition, regional policy or the agricultural implications, since he did not intend it to serve as the basis for a more general (and potentially over-ambitious) policy. Nor did he imagine that the internal market would lead directly to EMU (though the Dooge Committee had considered reform of the EC's monetary system). These dimensions became clear later, for example in his introduction to the

Report of the Cecchini Committee, which had been set up to convince member states that the single market would produce not only great but *quantifiable* benefits.[46]

How much was in fact afterwards made to seem contingent on the White Paper can be gauged from Cockfield's later phraseology[47] and the fact that he responded to a question by Cecchini, whether or not to state flatly that the single market required monetary union, by asking him 'not to overload the boat' at that stage.[48] At the same time, other Directorate officials, looking ahead, were preparing their own complementary proposals in the fields of competition policy, mergers, state aids, and overseas trade.

But while pressing the White Paper on governments prior to the Milan meeting, the Commission Presidency and some member states were also engaged in widening the whole concept to include what they regarded as a more balanced programme, including socio-economic policy, environmental action, institutional reform and political integration (which Delors had already outlined to the European Parliament in January), together with social cohesion in the light of Spain's and Portugal's accessions. All this stood in clear contrast to the British interpretation, but in line with the opinions of Laurent Fabius and Elizabeth Guigou, who were in charge in Paris. In October, Delors criticized the British 'supermarket approach', and set out his own conception of a 'real Common Market' including political solidarity, EMU and cohesion. Here in essence lay the idea of a European developmental state and of an economic space not restricted to the Ten, because these had imagined from the start that it would, in due course, be extended to EFTA countries.[49]

It was these proposals which Luxembourg's Presidency, the next in line, set itself to implement, as an essential adjunct to fulfil the single market according to the contingency formula. Over time, through intricate negotiations in the IGC, Luxembourg's subtle and neutral approach served to reduce the suspicions of both the Danes and the British. However, the Danish government promised its people a referendum (and Craxi in turn pledged that the Italian parliament would vote only after the European Parliament had given its approval, thereby conveying to the European Parliament a sort of informal competence).

The outcome owed something to cooperation within the 'Troika', as Luxembourg eased the agenda from drafts to final texts with few votes but always 'noting where the majority lay'. But the primary momentum came from the fact that all twelve governments wished to see the internal market come to fruition. Some participants concluded that the British alternative scheme's intention had come about and that in this area the national veto had already died.[50] Ireland's assent (postponed for two years for legal reasons, to meet the Irish courts' insistence and followed by a referendum) was actually taken for granted by the Belgian Presidency in 1986, as if QMV already existed.

Five IGC meetings sufficed to bring the documents to two Council meetings in December 1985. Divisions and alliances between states varied according to the issue being debated. Real disagreement however centred on four main questions: which single market decisions were to be taken by QMV? How far should cohesion extend, and in what form? How should cooperation and codecision with the Parliament operate in foreign affairs? What place should be given to EMU?

None of these was susceptible to a simple solution and the wider implications of each ran on to Maastricht and beyond. The text on EMU divided France, Belgium, Italy and Ireland, all of which thought it too weak, from Germany and the Netherlands which wanted the relevant articles attached to but not incorporated as an integral part of the Treaty. Britain did not want either, or indeed any reference to EMU, certainly not before the internal market's complete freedom of capital movements had been achieved.

The arguments had no empirical basis, except in current practice in running the EMS and ERM, Britain not being a member of the latter. But the eventual compromise rested on promises from France and Italy to liberalize their exchange control provisions – promises which were turned into a guarantee of abolition before the single market deadline came, at an ECOFIN meeting in June 1988, just prior to the Hannover Summit. Meanwhile, the preamble of the SEA was given three indents referring to the 'objective of EMU', together with a chapter stating that the member states should cooperate to ensure the convergence of economic and monetary policies.

On this somewhat ambiguous basis, EMU was to be included in the pre-Maastricht process. The Single European Act retained majority voting for all EMS decisions, so that Britain could still exercise a veto, even though it was not in the ERM. Nevertheless, two years later at Hannover, the UK government did concede that the Central Bank Governors Committee, chaired by Delors, might examine ways of setting up the future European central bank, and the 'concrete steps' towards EMU long sought by France.

An increase in structural funds (coherence policy) to appease Ireland's and Greece's fears about the impact on their economies, eased the Act's passage, up to its ratification by nine governments in February 1986, and by Ireland more than a year later. Some member states seem not to have realized how large these sums would be, when measured afterwards in relation to Iberian needs. It also brought a trade-off between the German federal government and the *Länder* (led by the Bavarian and North Rhine Westphalia prime ministers, Franz-Josef Strauss and Johannes Rau, which gave the *Länder* increased rights of participation in decision-making in Bonn). These were to be a foretaste of the regional compromises made at Maastricht in 1991. Success in the IGC negotiations, reform of the CAP, and extension of QMV to financial services' liberalization, satisfied British ambitions. The Italians got their extra powers for the Parliament,[51] the Netherlands and Belgium achieved an extension of political cooperation, Germany a clearer definition of regional policy, and France its hopes of EMU. From all this stemmed the mood of euphoria leading on to Maastricht.

But that was only the legal framework: much space remained for Commission interpretation. Officials' creativity during the next six years improved on what had actually been agreed, while members transposed what eventually became the 285 legislative enactments, in order to meet Cockfield's deadline of 1st January 1993. Among the twelve governments, opinions inevitably varied. (Margaret Thatcher particularly resented the way the Commission used Articles 100 and 235 to obtain ECJ confirmation of its interpretation.[52]) It was not clear until the Hannover Summit in June 1988 that all the heads of government had 'irreversibly accepted' the SEA: indeed the Act deliberately had not made the 1 January 1993 deadline a legal obligation, so that the internal market would not be final until all its provisions had been transposed and implemented. Whereas transposition had nearly been completed by the 1st January 1993, implementation still fell far short.

At the time of Hannover, 194 out of 285 legislative items remained to be completed. But the breakthrough on exchange control abolition had come. The legislative programme no longer depended on each six months' Presidency (which was as well, since the Greek government attempted to turn the proceedings after Hannover in the direction of social policy, training and worker consultation, which would inevitably have aroused industrialists to make a renewed 'Vredeling offensive'.[53]) Member states' mid-term failures to transpose legislation were already being remedied by an informal system of mediation, *réunions paquets* (see below, p. 628). Great as the delays were to be, even beyond 1992, the main technical problem after Hannover lay not with visible barriers but the implicit ones, created out of 'exceptions' through which member states continued to defend their *chasses gardées* long after they had conceded the former. Although Hannover represented a political landmark, 'beneath its calm surface, the battle between liberals and interventionists for control of the 1992 project was at last launched.'[54]

In the two and a half years after the IGC, the game between states, Commission and industrial players continued,[55] complicated by the entry of new players from Spain (which played a part in the second Banking Directive). Most of the advantage, however, accrued to the Commission, which did not seek to hide its wider design but only to nuance it for different audiences as the next stage – harmonization of VAT, excise and corporation tax – approached.[56] The Commission concentrated, for example, on reducing national restraints on air transport and the carriage of goods, and on the agreement over car imports with Japan. Officials accepted that some implementations would be delayed beyond 1 January 1993, particularly by Mediterranean countries (especially those concerning Spain's financial services and Italy's state industries), but relied on the states' commitments, sealed at Hannover, to limit delays to an acceptable level.

Having been very largely excluded during the bargaining process from Milan to Luxembourg, the Parliament also increased its part during later stages of the single market negotiations, as Cockfield steered his enactments through. Some 260 legislative items remained after the Act's second reading, together with a host of amendments, and in the process MEPs acquired a power through practice which they were later to consolidate at Maastricht. This extended informally to areas where MEPs had no direct competence at all.[57]

The financial sector also emerged as a player, now that EMU's shadow lay over the internal market. Banks and insurance companies, at least in the northern states, joined the various action groups and some even took part in public campaigns for 1992 through their domestic press and television. Huge financial gains were being made in these sectors by 1988, much greater than Cecchini had forecast; more in France and Germany than in Britain, but most of all in Italy and Spain, where the least open markets operated.[58] Harmonization affected all securities markets and stock exchanges, and Spain went through its own 'big bang' in 1989–90, as London had done eight years earlier. Nothing was invulnerable to foreign access, not even long-closed insurance and mortgage finance sectors.

Previously, these had been heavily protected areas: in Germany, insurance protection law meant that all policies were similar, with strict tariffs, so that innovation was impossible. This was in complete contrast to the competitive market in Britain, which regulated intermediaries, not policies. In France it remained a criminal offence for non-French companies to sell any sort of insurance. Some liberalizing had been achieved by the EC on life and non-life policies, but full market freedom was not actually achieved until 1990, after nearly twenty separate Commission drafts. Until then, the governments of Germany, France, Belgium, Italy, Denmark and Luxembourg resisted any change, to the unconcealed fury of German companies and all multinationals. It was no wonder that Cockfield avoided legislating for this sector, relying, as 1992 approached, on the single market's momentum to do the job.[59]

Talk about 'Europe à la carte' and 'variable geometry' during the Presidencies of the Netherlands, Britain, Belgium and Denmark in the years 1986–8 revealed how fortunate the EC had been in the previous year under Italy and Luxembourg. Britain was evidently keen to prevent the emergence of a contingent social policy dimension. As the Thatcher decade neared its end, and as she herself attempted to limit any broadening of the single market concept, Britain seemed once more to be at loggerheads with the rest. Among member states, it seemed as if the impetus had been lost.

The breakthrough under Germany's Presidency at Hannover can be explained partly because of France's occlusion, during the tense period of 'cohabitation' between Mitterrand (who during a long duel between Elysée and Matignon managed to retain power over foreign and EC affairs) and Jacques Chirac's RPR government, and partly by a convergence of opinion between Bonn and German industry on the substantial opportunities for Germany offered by the internal market. The Hannover Summit also indicated that West Germany had committed itself to political, if not yet monetary, union.

Even then, some elements remained uncertain, such as harmonizing VAT, which was fought out between Cockfield (who sought a 17% rate) and the responsible Commissioner, Christiane Scrivener (who proposed a 12% one), at ECOFIN meetings under the Greek Presidency in late 1988. The British government again objected to the principle of harmonization, but in the long run, when Norman Lamont was at the Treasury in July 1992, accepted it as an irreversible matter – one essential for raising government revenue during the 1990s' recession.

The years 1988–90 were good ones in the EC, which saw a rise in corporate profits, individuals' living standards, and their expectations (at least for those in work, and above all in skilled or professional work), as the boom swept towards its crescendo. European directors of Ford, IBM or Exxon had long seen what Cockfield's timetable presaged, as did some Japanese multinationals, and were now eager to set up inside the EC before the 1992 deadline. More and more giant firms such as Rhône-Poulenc (chemicals) and Philips (electronics), and Daimler-Benz (cars), opened offices in Brussels, where lobbyists multiplied, *pari passu* with the Commission's output of SEM directives, giving greater complexity to the game. Many of the deals or joint ventures made in this period (British Leyland-Honda, Fiat-Sikorsky and Westland Helicopters, together with Siemens-GTE (USA), CGE-AT&T, and Telefonica-Fujitsu (in telecoms)) suggest that multinationals were actually demonstrating what a single market implied and perhaps defining what EC industrial policy and trade policy in the future should be.

But the most obvious result of Hannover was a renewed mood of optimism, and a determination to consolidate the entire project of monetary and political union. Cecchini had dealt largely with once-for-all benefits deriving from the original White Paper. But by 1989–90 it seemed that, if the single market *did* help to solve the underlying problems of the EC's overall adjustment, the gains to be expected after 1993 would be vastly greater – at least for the northern European states – than he had predicted, not least because adjustment could provide means to counter US, Japanese and south-east Asian firms' market penetration.

In that sense the achievement of an internal market, though the direct consequence of the Single European Act, cannot be isolated from the wider process which culminated at Maastricht in December 1991. For a relatively short period, member states accepted what had already become common sense in the business and financial communities, that the internal market's likely gains offered greater advantage than earlier economic defensiveness. There could be no value in being the last to come in or the least conciliatory, since the game had ceased to be a zero sum matter; such defensive stances risked being overruled or gaining nothing, whereas the propensity to bargain represented an attractive alternative.

Yet member states' ratification of the Single European Act hid a number of individual government reservations and, in the British case, perhaps also misconceptions about what had been accepted by the others and the Commission as logical corollaries. Hannover marked a point of *political* assent to the concept of a rule-based system in which sectional opting-out or evasion would become unprofitable, just as the pledge on EMU provided the necessary technical accompaniment (apart from Britain and Denmark) to avoid unmanageable distortions in the new market and the CAP. That in turn brought huge pressure on Britain and Spain to enter the ERM if they wished financial liberalization to reach its apogee.

The way the internal market was made cannot be isolated from the international context and the Gorbachev era of apparently ultimate détente, followed by the collapse of the Soviet empire in 1989–90, which opened up the countries of eastern Europe to new forms of exchange with the EC. West Germany's leadership at Hannover prefigured its likely stance two years later as the Wall, and its accompanying psychological walls, came down.

Peter Sutherland, the Commissioner responsible for competition policy, had been appointed to lead the high-level Group on Operation of the internal market, in order to assess how best to achieve the full benefits Cecchini had promised. In his report, analysing post–1992 problems in managing the internal market, he pointed out that the Community's main functions would now be to administer the rules, monitor member states' compliance, improve their means of doing so, spread an understanding of the law to ensure consistency and transparency, and generally help to create a climate of shared responsibility in which the Commission would henceforward rely on member states' competence and expertise, and on their courts for enforcement. The Single European Market was to become the core of a new EC geography which would in turn redefine the relative positions of Commission, member states and ultimately regions. But even in his chosen areas of goods and services, a great deal remained to do.

If this represented a new stage of partnership between them, it was clear from what Sutherland said that the Commission would have to accept some informal degree of diversity in practice among the Twelve, whatever its formal legal standpoint. The advance on the previous decade was nevertheless enormous, whether the Single

European Act is depicted as the result of a tacit contract between all twelve member states or of a number of parallel decisions by each government about relative advantage. Either way, each player would respond to the rules, not because of the sanctions (which were negligible and had often enough been evaded in the past) but because of the severe and increasing costs of not doing so. Nevertheless, a number of substantive contingent questions remained to be settled, including the emphasis to be given to competition policy, and the Commission's place in developing industrial and external trade policies, research and technology programmes. The Act nowhere stated that Article 115, which gave powers to take protective measures against non-European imports, would be removed; neither did it lay down details about progress towards monetary union – if it had, its passage would have been immeasurably harder.

Political problems also remained. When the British government argued for its own draft proposals for single market management before the Edinburgh Council in December 1992, several EC ministers contested the UK's underlying philosophy, on the grounds that it reverted to the inter-governmental style and failed to acknowledge the Commission's leading role.[60] Representing France, Elizabeth Guigou also objected to the UK's unwillingness to face up to the free movement of people, without imposing passport formalities. Yet on this obstacle to the Act they had already signed, the UK, Denmark and Ireland stood fast against the rest. Single market issues thus ran on, into and beyond Maastricht, to be affected by the recession of the early 1990s and member states' increasing unease at the consequences of events in eastern and south-eastern Europe.

Taking the process from the early 1980s as a whole, it is clear that the closer the internal market came to fruition, the more it suited both member states and the Commission to cooperate and enjoy the heady mood of harmony after so many debilitating, stagnant years. In this sense, the mid–1980s represented a turning point. Afterwards the Community showed itself better able to face up to extended competition, to direct American and, later, Japanese investment (US investment had decreased during the recession of the early 1980s, as had European companies' own investments in the EC). The majority of governments, in sharp contrast to their behaviour in the 1970s, also began to turn away from the defensive, non-tariff barriers which they had erected earlier on to delay harmonization.

Four deep modifications occurred in this period. The quality of EC governance improved, thanks very largely to better implementation and enforcement of the law; the financial sector became freely involved; competition policy was made congruent to the assault on intangible barriers to the internal market; and officials began to conceive of policies for industry, trade, social affairs and competition as a whole. In this sense, the internal market cut off both commercial players and their governments from the frustrating recent past.

5

Maastricht and After,
1988–93

The West German Presidency in the first half of 1988, and especially the Hannover Summit in June, appears in retrospect even more significant than it did at the time. Not only did that Presidency oversee the conclusion of many of the EC's long-running battles, such as that over the abolition of exchange controls by France, Italy and Spain, but it witnessed what Arthur Cockfield called 'the irreversible acceptance' by member states of the single market. It also settled the budget saga for the succeeding four years, after one of the most prolonged and divisive crisis in the EC's history, which had ramified into the CAP, now that France had become a net payer; and this, despite protests by the *Länder* governments and German farmers that Germany was already paying too much, and would pay more once 'cohesion' had been incorporated by the coming Inter-Governmental Conference (IGC).[1]

The Hannover Summit confirmed Delors's second term of office from 1989–93, with British approval (Helmut Kohl having failed to put forward Martin Bangemann's name, despite its being 'Germany's turn', because of a political trade-off with the Free Democrats in Bonn). Delors would also chair the Central Bankers Committee which was to recommend rules for operating the future European Bank. Coming after a number of minor but irritating disputes over the CAP and the purity of beer, these achievements suggested that the Franco-German understanding had been enhanced. Insofar as there remained arguments, these were internal: the first being between Chancellor Kohl and Foreign Secretary

Genscher about how to react to the Gorbachev reforms in Russia, and the second between the Bundesbank and the Bonn government over EMU.

But Hannover also demonstrated how consistently Germany (shortly to be reunited) would react when external events forced it to engage in the international domain. Whatever the different approaches to *Ost-* and *Westpolitik* advocated by Kohl and Genscher, Germany's political elite was still agreed that 'the coming Germany' had to be embodied and understood in its European dimension, that is, within a European political union. From the 1985 IGC to the next, at Maastricht in 1991, this basic line did not change.

What did change was firstly that Germany's advocacy of political union acquired a novel assertiveness, which tended to undermine French certainty of how the dual understanding would operate in future. Secondly the grounds on which the French, led strongly after an initial period of reluctance by Mitterrand, would seek to redefine the partnership also changed. It is perhaps necessary to emphasize the French government's increasingly urgent search for monetary union, even more than the German desire for political union. The Mitterrand-Kohl agreement to balance the two, in order to retain their informal parity, despite Germany's increase in size and status as a result of reunification, and to bind this new Germany firmly into a deeper, as well as larger Community, was to be the single most important phenomenon between the two IGCs. Neither that nor Maastricht would have happened without French fears of what a united Germany would otherwise become.

The price, on France's side, was political union; on Germany's it was monetary union. After Kohl's about-turn on EMU to meet French demands in 1988, the German government (though not the Bundesbank) showed itself positive about the common currency even though it would involve losing the deutschmark – that is, so long as the new one was based solely on principles of economic stability and was managed only by the new Central Bank. Fluctuations in their relations continued, of course, at diplomatic levels: however these were repaired by the Kohl-Mitterrand proposal to have a second IGC on political union, made in April 1990 before the Dublin Summit, and strengthened during that IGC where foreign and security policy, and later European defence, were concerned. Much less consensus was obtained about EC institutions' power, for elite German opinion valued an increase in the European Parliament's democratic functioning so highly that the government tied it to its consent to EMU, as the only way to defuse domestic hostility to the impact of Monetary Union on the deutschmark.

From the French point of view, these attempts to tie EMU to Bundesbank management criteria, and to strengthen the Parliament, could be made acceptable if Germany were induced to accept a fixed schedule of progress leading from the ERM to complete monetary union on France's terms. The French government also hoped that the Common Foreign and Security Policy (CFSP) could be extended to cover defence but on French, rather than NATO, terms: Mitterrand wisely gave instructions not to raise this question too early on. A substantial reordering of France's domestic priorities would be involved in approaching the question of political union, but not of a size to require major or public changes in the machinery of French government.

All this contrasted sharply with the British case. Margaret Thatcher's last two years were increasingly overshadowed by her belief that a grand conspiracy had come into existence, manoeuvred by Christian Democrats, renegade Socialists and the Commission led by Delors, with the aim of imposing Brussels' sovereignty on a permanently embattled offshore island. But whatever her forays may have gained tactically in 1988 and 1989–90, they were mostly pyrrhic victories ending in acquiescence, for lack of allies. Meanwhile, on the domestic front, she was gradually manoeuvred towards acceptance that Britain should join the ERM by an entente between her chancellor, Nigel Lawson, and the foreign secretary, Geoffrey Howe, which, for lack of a true cabinet majority, she was unable to rupture.

On top of this came German reunification which she vigorously, and probably unwisely, attempted to delay by enlisting Mitterrand's support during his period of uncertainty of how to react – as if a French president with his personal background had not been aware of its implications. Such tensions had already showed themselves in her speech at Bruges on 20 September 1988 – which became celebrated in retrospect for the tone of its delivery and its reception by the Conservative Eurosceptics rather than its actual content – accepting 'Britain's destiny is in Europe as part of the EC' (but an EC that was imagined as a commonwealth of free independent nations working in harmony together, with a free trade policy covering the whole of Europe.) The text represented a modification of what she had herself accepted in 1985–6 but was consistent with a more general 'Anglo-Saxon' view that the EC was essentially an economic vehicle.

Like so many of Margaret Thatcher's deep-rooted beliefs, these fears rested on a basis of evidence which was inevitably heightened and distorted by her personal perceptions, now ingrained in a long-running administration.[2] She encountered other EC heads of government only at summits, and had become isolated, largely because she no longer listened to the complex skeins of Whitehall advice. She was aware of this isolation, aware also of the strength of the EC majority, how her tactics often united them against her, and perhaps of how much less Britain counted with the United States under President Bush than it had done with Ronald Reagan. Yet she seemed unwilling or incapable of acting otherwise than Napoleon in his last campaign of 1814, winning many of the tactical battles but sliding to long, remorseless retreat. She was unwilling above all to examine her lifelong preconception about what 'Germany' really was.[3]

No such inhibitions restrained the Commission after Delors's second term began, though he was to be dogged, in the press of several nations, by his assertion that by the year 1998, thanks to the Single Act, 80% of economic, and possibly fiscal and social, legislation would emanate from Brussels. This claim seemed to be heightened by Delors's address to the Trade Union Conference in September 1988, which Thatcher used to justify her neo-Gaullist defence of national sovereignty – so long at least until the rest should have considered more carefully where all this would lead.[4] The Commission, of course, had considered carefully, as the whole edifice built on the 1985 White Paper demonstrated. But it could not control how its proposals to the Council would be interpreted outside, in the press and on television in the twelve member states. British politicians could argue that in implementing the single market programme, the Commission often acted by stealth or resorted to rarely used powers such as Article 90, to force member states to open their telecoms markets to other EC competitors.

Views like this derived from evidence of various kinds: Commission documents such as the internal guide on how to infiltrate the mass of single market legislation through Coreper and the Council of Ministers; or the steadily increasing agenda of items contingent on the internal market. Delors's campaign to represent the EC, not only at G7 meetings but at all functions dealing with external trade and GATT, appeared to aggrandize the Commission *vis-à-vis* member states. Indeed the Greek Presidency's rather presumptuous initiation of direct talks with the Soviet Union in 1988, as if 'representing the EC', can be seen as a small state's rejoinder; one that was reiterated by the Spanish Presidency early in 1989 over trade with Japan. That the Commission did retract, as it had done often in the past, on some of its more contentious positions in order to take a more emollient line, was less often remarked.

For example, concessions made by Delors and Christiane Scrivener, the Commissioner responsible for taxation, on VAT harmonization, which the British in particular had resisted, appeared in any case to accrue to the member state holding the Presidency, or to the European Parliament. In strategic terms, a grand design clearly did exist by 1989, on which the Hannover Summit's accord allowed the Commission two priceless years to expand. But this might have happened in any case, without the Commission's driving force, since preoccupation with Euro-sclerosis did not automatically vanish in 1988. It was certainly accelerated by the entry of financial institutions as significant players, and employers' determination Europe-wide to use the internal market's four freedoms firmly to re-establish managerial rights and enforce further deregulation of wages, security of employment and conditions of work, to the inevitable detriment and dismay of trades unions.

The Commission, led very strongly by Delors during the period 1988–91, provided a focus for what might otherwise have been diverse activities. Delors's speeches and the agenda he outlined each

January to the Parliament increasingly embodied a particular view of the inexorable unity of economic and social spheres; put simply, that EMU and the Social Charter should run in tandem. The argument that the EC needed a new deal (with undertones of Roosevelt's New Deal) to safeguard concertation (as long as that had genuine economic content) and to give some hope of a return to full employment, required the Community to examine training and education, technology and structural cohesion, together with redress for unemployment and support for the areas of late 1980s industrial devastation.[5]

The embryo of an EC-wide supply side policy contained a built-in presumption that, while post-War neo-Keynesianism may have been misguided, the answers that Keynes had provided were not.[6] Whether interpreted as a compromise between the requirements of financial and industrial capital or as an innovative response to the EC's uncompetitiveness, the Commission set out a strategy in which industry, trade and social policies complemented each other in the search for adjustment in a guided, not a wholly open, market. Some of its manifestations are discussed later: industrial policy and trade, competition, and state aids, monetary union (which depended on member states reforming their public finances according to selected convergence criteria) and the Social Chapter.

The existence of such a massive agenda, unprecedented in the EC's history, represented a drawing together of many disparate strands of policy-making within different Commission Directorates, by an unusually powerful and comprehensive direction. Given a second term of office as President, for the first time since Hallstein, Delors made clear what he intended in his speech in January 1989 to the European Parliament: 'History', he declared, was 'knocking at the door . . . it will not be enough to create a large frontier-free market nor . . . a vast economic area. It is for us, in advance of 1993, to put some flesh on the Community's bones and to give it a little more soul.'

Naturally enough, each Directorate strove for a greater role in this grand design,[7] which in turn contributed to demands for greater competence by the Commission, and also by the Parliament. The appearance, as much as the reality, affected member states' perceptions, so that 'Delors II' became for some a synonym for aggrandizement.

Answers to the question whether Delors did in reality overstate the grand design in the second Presidency, depend on when the estimate is made. At the time of Hannover, the build-up was incomplete. But in 1990–91, the run-up to Maastricht paralleled the final run-in of the single market programme, together with the waves of legislation from the Single Act itself, then going through every member state's parliament. The popular press and public opinion in member states only woke up to this concatenation in 1991–2, and there was a very widespread reaction which fed through during the process of ratifying Maastricht and EMU (which was itself a follow-up to the SEA).

But for the political elites in each member state, and the Brussels milieu, the Delors peak came a year earlier; the factor which merited blame was that the IGC was ill-conceived, badly prepared and badly conducted, not on EMU, but on the political side. There was, for example, no central EU body like the Spaak Committee and no think-tank to prepare what actually went on at Maastricht; ministers went into the negotiating chambers often without full texts, in a changing set of circumstances. But the fault lay not only with the Commission's excess of zeal to get everything included: ministers were equally over-ambitious, for instance in their desire to merge CFSP and defence.

Spain's entry in 1986 also introduced a novel element, for Spain rapidly became not only a major beneficiary but an increasingly adept player. The Gonzalez government focused on a narrow set of aims, clearly intending to take its place alongside the existing big four[8] – an outcome which seemed to have taken place after Spain joined the ERM in 1989, but above all in the triumphal year 1992 of Expo-Seville, Madrid's tenure as Europe's cultural capital, and the Barcelona Olympic Games.

The Spanish phenomenon also highlighted what was initially a less obvious part of the grand design: the extension of regional funding from a policy of subsidizing poor areas, such as Italy's Mezzogiorno and most of Greece (often without tangible returns), to one by DG16 intended to raise the standards of infrastructure, production, investment and commerce to those of the rich core. This gave the well-organized, politically articulate regional govern- ments in Catalonia and northern Italy their cue to ask for political as well as financial recognition when the IGCs began work.

Member states' consent for the agenda and the Delors II agenda budget which was to pay for it depended on resolving a string of apparently unrelated issues in the two years before Maastricht. This was the harder to deliver since the Twelve no longer grouped in broad agreement, as they had on the Single Act, but divided into aggregations, northern or Mediterranean, large and small, rich and poor, those with great bargaining skills and those with less. Generally in this period it suited the 'northern' members to appease Mediterranean demands – in short for Germany to pay. Delors's appointment of three liberal-minded Commissioners to the principal jobs in January 1989 (Leon Brittan to DG4, Martin Bangemann to DG3, Frans Andriessen to DG1, while keeping the protectionists Manuel Marin (Spain) at Fisheries, and Vasso Papandreou (Greece) at Social Affairs) may have encouraged them to do so.

The two principal issues need to be treated separately: monetary union first, then 'political cooperation' (foreign policy and defence), together with the whole area of the 'interior ministry matters' – policing of borders, cooperation on crime, terrorism, drugs and illegal immigration – which came together as a result of much wider developments in Europe and 'near-Europe'. All were, of course, contingent on achievement of the single market. But the Commission could integrate the agenda and take a leading role only on the first of these; the other two touched on member states' sovereignty far more directly and had to be argued out by ministers and heads of government in the context of a Europe that was changing, after the collapse of Soviet power, more rapidly than at any time since establishment of the 'Peoples' Democracies' had cut old Europe in two in the late 1940s. Even France and Germany could not agree on the details of so wide a range.

On both aspects, the Commission lacked the force to recreate the coherent agenda that had been given it earlier by industrial and financial organizations in Brussels and member state's capitals during the single market negotiations. These players did not lack interest, but they tended to dispute the agenda among themselves, with those expecting advantages in the internal market facing up to the still-protected national champions, secure for the present in their state aids and government procurement contracts. On the question of Japanese car imports for example, the old peak organization actually broke up, to reform itself under a new title and without one of France's leading producers (see chapter 10). Apart from these relatively novel rivalries, firms and financial institutions were already deeply engaged in preparing for 1992's consequences – to which monetary union seemed a remote adjunct; main boards were more concerned with the wave of mergers and acquisitions which reached its apogee in 1988–90.[9]

Organizations such as ERT and the European Committee of AmCham still argued the industrial point of view, especially on monetary union, but managements across Europe did not seek direct inputs to the IGC and appear not to have followed their course in detail. They reacted to the post-Maastricht crisis as if the world had changed little since the Single Act. The ERT, which did succeed in getting some of its ideas into the Maastricht texts, continued to publish pamphlets such as 'Rebuilding confidence, an action plan for Europe' (December 1992), which prescribed neo-Keynesian remedies for revival and employment, with talk of 'concerted action' and 'strong leadership' by governments in partnership with industry, as if the 1988–90 harmony between member states still existed.[10]

The agenda for the IGC was very much more complex than in 1985 because of the range of issues it had to consider, and the diversity – often incompatibility – of outlooks among member state governments. Heads of government and the Commission, often as rivals, therefore developed the agenda at one remove from the corporate players (who restricted themselves to monetary union and its consequences), and at several removes from national parliaments, media and the public. As a result, the long-running process was shaped by bargains, trade-offs and concessions which were different in kind from those of the internal market IGC in 1985. This may not have been intended to be an evasion of public debate, for many of the issues genuinely appeared too complex to explain in straightforward language, or were too confidential. But what, in retrospect, seems a clear failure of all those in the negotiations to educate their publics, meant that the new treaties, launched in 1992 in very altered circumstances, would shock public opinion – notably in Denmark, France and Britain.

There is no need to re-tell in any detail the Soviet Union's collapse, the failure of former People's Democracies (which began when Hungary opened its border with Austria to East Germans fleeing to the West and ended with the collapse of Communist authority in Prague and breach of the Berlin Wall on 9 November 1989), nor the reunification of the two Germanies. But all three events conditioned everything that happened in Europe thereafter. They affected EFTA, as Sweden and Finland reacted both to the removal of a forty-year-long threat and to the new-found independence of the Baltic States and Austria, with the return of growing normality, to what had once been Habsburg dominions. Above all they affected former West Germany and France, the EC's central nexus, because the implications of a united Germany encompassed all the other eleven. The break-up of Yugoslavia, the collapse of Christian Democracy in Italy, and the undermining of the political right in Britain can be traced to the same origin, as can the growth of largely refugee immigration through east and south east Europe's porous borders, with its direct consequences of racism and xenophobic nationalism.

In the years 1989–93, many of the vestiges of post-War settlements, in welfare programmes, industrial relations and state benefits, also died. Each country described its own parabola of declension: the new – or perhaps nineteenth-century Liberal – thought, first enunciated by the new right in Britain and the United States, passed through a sort of contagion, causing questioning, then fiscal and moral panics, and finally a scaling down of promises and expectations. The true fiscal crisis of European states, heralded in academic literature in the early 1980s, burst a decade later. Coinciding with disillusion after Maastricht, it had a corrosive effect on what remained of late–1980s' aspirations.

Four Summit meetings stand out as markers on the road from Hannover to Maastricht. The first, in Madrid in June 1989, brought together the Delors Committee's report on Monetary Union and the first draft of the Social Charter. The meeting was noted for Nigel Lawson's attempt (speaking for a divided leadership) to be explicit about the terms for Britain to enter the ERM, though his government opposed both EMU at any point beyond stage I and the Social Charter. Defeated on the question of whether to have an IGC, and reduced to near-isolation by the accommodations between the Spanish Presidency, Germany and France (which had been made explicit in the Kohl-Mitterrand letter in favour of political union) Britain had to accept not only the IGC but EMU stage I in July 1990.

At the next Summit in Strasbourg in September 1989, with overwhelming support from the Parliament and smaller states such as Belgium, the French version of monetary union was accepted, with a date for that IGC (but not for the one on political union) after the West German elections and under the Italian Presidency at the end of 1990. Mitterrand had won his second seven-year term in 1988, and although his narrow Socialist majority forced him to govern with centrist approval, he had the firm support of his finance minister, Pierre Bérégovoy, in a period of stability, growth and falling unemployment – which he used to get the European Bank for Recovery and Development (EBRD) off the ground, with his protégé Jacques Attali as head. By then, the Commissioner for Social Affairs, Vasso Papandreou, had seventeen draft directives ready on all the aspects of industrial relations and conditions of work which had been stultified since the early 1970s.

The third meeting, in Dublin in June 1990, took place very much in the shadow of the Franco-German commitments to common foreign and security policy and to a second IGC on political union set out jointly by Kohl and Mitterand in April. The Irish prime minister Charles Haughey capitalized shrewdly on Ireland's affinity with France, which was seeking to strengthen the European Council, extend QMV and inhibit the pretensions of the Commission and the Parliament. This also suited Helmut Kohl, whose government was prepared to pay the price so long as political union could be kept in tandem with its monetary counterpart.

Once again, the British Cabinet hesitated on the margins, its prime minister profoundly uneasy at the implications of the Kohl-Mitterrand agreement which had been made without consultation with either NATO or their EC partners. That lack of consultation had offended other governments as well: however the weight of the Franco-German entente lay heavy on them all, and was on the basis of this declaration that EC foreign ministers prepared for Dublin and its sequel, the summit in Rome, which to a large extent set the IGC's agendas. All Thatcher could do, given Britain's eleven to one minority, was – sensibly enough – to veto a Franco-German proposal for a large dollar loan intended to prop up the collapsing Soviet Union.

Italy took over the Presidency in July, before the Conference on Security and Cooperation in Europe (CSCE) meetings with the Soviet Union. Soon after, Giulio Andreotti became prime minister (Craxi having destroyed de Mita's liberalizing government of 1989, together with the DC's reformist programme which, in retrospect, was Christian Democracy's last chance to save itself from shameful eclipse). Under his direction, the principle of two concurrent IGC's for monetary and political union was established. After careful consultation with the German and French governments, Andreotti proposed a special 'informal' Council, to meet in Rome in October: his intention being to agree a target date for EMU stage II in 1994, with a further wide-ranging IGC the following year.

So hot was this pace that the Italian leader's motives need analysis. It has been argued that, with the help of his own MEPs and other Christian Democratic parties, Andreotti set a truly Florentine trap for Margaret Thatcher, while her attention was diverted by the July G7 meeting in Houston and by GATT negotiations, so that she went largely unprepared into the October special Council.[11] Certainly her political nemesis was welcomed widely across the EC – in what one French diplomat described as a mood of *soulagement*. Yet there is no evidence among member states, whose policies were much more finely balanced than their leaders' statements usually allowed to appear, of a desire to marginalize Britain. Concessions on stage II, and even some consideration of the chancellor of the exchequer John Major's 'hard ecu scheme' had not been ruled out. But the Italian coalition was committed to transferring power to the Parliament. Andreotti may also genuinely have been concerned that the agenda for December was too vast for one meeting, since he attempted to agree much of it in advance at bilateral meetings and in the encounters of Christian Democratic parties in the late autumn. The German government had agreed not to bring forward the subject of the next set of GATT negotiations, hoping thereby to avoid antagonizing France (whose farming lobby passionately opposed the Blair House Agreement), while helping Andreotti's fragile *pentapartito* administration. The German government's concession of a firm date for EMU stage II, made during the October special Council, certainly strengthened France's tentative acceptance that the two IGCs on monetary and political union should coincide.

Some of this can be ascribed to German and French governments' calling in of past favours to Italy. But Italy also provided a skilful chairmanship which falsefooted British and Danish opposition. There was no discussion of GATT. Instead, proposals on political union and EMU stage II for January 1994 were confirmed, in advance of the IGCs. Thatcher had failed to seek alliances for her point of view and found no support except from Ruud Lubbers of the Netherlands.

France and Italy emerged with their governments' main aims agreed. The real winner was Helmut Kohl who had been hoping for an uncontroversial reunification after the successful East German elections in March, and before public opinion during the West German elections began to question the terms. At the year's end, Germany in effect paid for USSR approval of reunification and the new Germany's continuing NATO membership with a massive hard currency sum to cover the withdrawal of Soviet troops from the former East Germany. In the same month, the five new *Länder* were absorbed in the enlarged Federal Republic, under Article 23 of the 1949 Basic Law; and once Kohl belatedly acknowledged the existing Polish border (cutting off the original pre–1914 East Germany for ever), the Soviet Union was excluded from central Europe for the first time since 1944.[12]

The fact that the two IGCs which began after the Rome meeting were to be concurrent, starting under the Luxembourg Presidency and ending under the Dutch one at Maastricht a year later, did not imply that they would resemble each other. The one on political union and Interior Ministry questions remained very largely a matter for inter-governmental negotiations. The question of monetary union involved the Commission to a far greater extent, and its influence permeated many of the texts. But the two were intimately linked, as Andreotti had argued; at the same time, the agenda was complicated by the issue of the reform of EC institutions, and by cohesion and the budget cycle after 1992 (which was essential for future cohesion funds), together with the Social Chapter, to which both were closely related.

I. EMU

The EMU IGC's history is inextricably linked to that of the ERM.[13] Even though the Single European Act stated the goal of eventual monetary union, nothing precise had been set down or accepted on the detailed matter of how transition to a single currency would take place, or when, or the shape and rules of the eventual European Central Bank which would administer it. The devil lay in precisely this detail, for which the ERM provided the only non-theoretical guide. Yet the ERM was the product of a very different conception, and had been disputed during its ten-year course between France and West Germany. The conclusions on which EMU's architects would build were to become further confused by the entry of Spain and Britain.

The EMS had been created by decisions of the Council. But the ERM was formally an agreement between central banks (and therefore not part of the Community). Yet it had always had a high political content, whatever its economic effect on the economies of participants; and in that sense was to be compared not with the Gold Standard, as it had operated in Europe in the four decades up to 1914, but with the Gold Standard as governments rather than central banks had manipulated it in the 1920s.

Having been affected principally by movements of the French franc during the frequent realignments of the early 1980s, the ERM had been mistrusted by the Bundesbank for reasons expressed during Otmar Emminger's tenure of office. But in the years after the French economic *grand tournant* of 1983, the ERM became a DM zone. Mitterrand and Delors, as his finance minister, took a decision which was politically strategic, as well as economic – a decision followed in due course by the Belgian and Danish governments and rather later by Italy and Ireland. For four years, in what can be seen as its 'classic period', the ERM rested on the Bundesbank's credibility, together with West Germany's willingness to behave as if the DM were indeed the anchor currency; and it achieved a generally accepted and widely welcomed reduction of inflation and state borrowing among members. It thus served as the monetary agency for what were becoming accepted concepts of prudence and discipline, necessary components of economic restructuring. Whether or not causation actually worked in this sequence is another matter: the gains appeared, at a time of rapid growth, to justify the sacrifices in output and employment that accompanied it.

France's January 1987 devaluation however, which was forced on an unwilling government by the international markets as the American dollar fell steadily, altered this benign pattern.[14] As Bernard Connolly observes, 'the ERM had become an inescapable symbol of attachment to sound policies. But lack of complete credibility made it economically costly.' French acceptance of the price for hard currency status was overtaken by a desire not to peg the franc to the DM, like the guilder or krone, which would have been politically unacceptable to French public opinion, but to fence the DM inside an increasingly rigid ERM structure which would lead logically and remorselessly to monetary union and a single currency – and thus to the disappearance of deutschmark primacy. French ministers evidently believed that this could be done, despite the global development of money markets where billions could flow across the exchanges in a matter of hours. They assumed continuation of the climate of opinion that had seen the G7 arrange the Louvre Accord in February 1987, in order to stabilize the dollar and yen against European currencies, whilst promoting world economic growth.

But the Bundesbank objected because of the implications for West Germany, and its criticisms carried great weight so long as the Reagan administration did nothing to remedy the dollar's fall and the American budget imbalance. Having been pressed by Bonn to loosen its monetary stance, the Bundesbank reacted instead by raising interest rates in early October 1987, an action which helped to precipitate the New York Stock Exchange crash on 'Black Monday'. The clash between Bonn and Frankfurt did not diminish until Hannover in July 1988, when the heads of government agreed on progressive reduction of interest rates. But this added new pressures to currencies in the ERM, since it had been agreed that capital would become fully mobile in France and Italy by 1990; so that it would cost their governments and central banks more and more, in each year before EMU took effect, to resist currency flows and speculation, particularly by the vast American 'hedge funds'. Strengthening the ERM's operations failed to limit these accumulating risks.[15]

Edouard Balladur had already proposed, in conjunction with Giscard, during the period of cohabitation, that a prototype of the European Central Bank (ECB) should start work before the final move to monetary union; and to plan it, the Committee of Central Bankers, under Delors's chairmanship, was to be appointed at Hannover. But in the shorter term, two years of overshoot in West German money supply, together with signs of a speculative bubble in Japan, rapid overheating in Britain, and the Netherlands' government's unease about shadowing the deutschmark, presaged trouble which the G7's pardonable overreaction on 'Black Monday' did nothing to allay.

With the Bundesbank apparently sulking on the fringe of a political vortex, stubbornly pushing up German and therefore ERM interest rates, the ERM's deflationary classic phase ended in recrimination between Bonn and Frankfurt, and growing signs of inflation in Britain and Spain. (Denmark, isolated in its own peculiar cycle, experienced both inflation and stagnation, with repercussions on public opinion which were to be of great significance in 1992).

Meanwhile, the Committee of Central Bank governors, chaired by

Delors, met between autumn 1988 and April 1989. They took part already having much common ground, both as professionals of a high order with a common discipline and as believers in the ERM's proven effects on inflation, as well as the likely benefits of lower transaction costs and risks to be gained from monetary union. It is inherently unlikely that they ignored the political effects of a future ECB on members' national sovereignty; but the possibility of national divergencies was offset by a measure of theoretical agreement: the conceptual ground had been well prepared in economic terms by the Padoa-Schioppa Report.[16] This highlighted a basic inconsistency: following the completion of the internal market after 1992, which would be accompanied by full capital mobility and a more or less fixed exchange rates in the ERM, member states would still retain monetary autonomy in their national spheres.

Put simply, Padoa-Schioppa argued that it would not be in the interests of weaker economies to conform and bear the pain; instead they would act as backsliders or deviants, forcing the stronger partners to react, and thus prejudicing the whole. Prudent central bankers, inherently suspicious of what politicians would do to appease their electorates after the experience of the fifteen years since 1974, rated the collective good higher than national sovereignty. The fact that Karl-Otto Pöhl chaired the technical group and both he and Robin Leigh-Pemberton, governor of the Bank of England, signed the Delors Report seemed to indicate that unanimity had been achieved.[17]

To a large extent it had: all the governors accepted that a prototype ECB should start work, in order to begin the process of inducing equality of discipline and practice in reducing inflation as soon as possible. All could reasonably expect their governments to have accepted by then that no one country could bear the costs of doing this alone especially when taken together with contingent problems, such as wages and other labour market rigidities, and that if collective action were not initiated, at the next recession the EC might lapse into another *sauve qui peut* like 1974. The differences between them related mainly to highly technical problems. But the political issues of whether this new single currency, provisionally styled the ecu, would be too soft (as the Bundesbank feared) or too hard, as the British government suspected, and whether it would eventually be intended to stand up against the dollar and yen as an equivalent world currency, were not and probably could not be argued out.

The one fundamental disagreement in the Delors Committee concerned the mode of transition to EMU. It was finally concerted between Pohl and de Larosière (Banque de France) with some mediation from Carlo Ciampi, governor of the Banca d'Italia, and help from the Netherlands and Spanish central banks, in time for Delors to present his report on 19 April 1989, in advance of the Madrid Summit. At that stage, it was sufficiently uncontentious to convince 'respectable financial opinion' in the EC, which in Britain included both *The Economist* and the CBI. But when Delors introduced it later that month to Ecofin, he added a timetable: there should be three stages, the first to begin as soon as possible. All twelve currencies should move within the ERM's narrow bands by 1 January 1993, the date for completing the internal market. In stage two, exchange rates in the ERM should become almost rigid, and all central banks should be given the same degree of independence as the Bundesbank. Finally, in stage three, exchange rates would be permanently fixed, under an ECB entirely responsible for the monetary policy of the single currency. There would then be binding conventions on member states' budgetary deficits, modulated – for example in the Spanish, Portuguese or Greek cases – by new EC cohesion funds.

Little debate took place in Ecofin, which had rarely been a forum for technical monetary matters, and the Spanish Presidency pushed ahead to start stage one on 1 July 1990. The governments of France, Germany, Spain, Italy and Belgium concurred in this timetable (though the Bundesbank held strong reservations); those of Italy, Greece and Portugal were appeased with cohesion promises. Finance ministers from Denmark, Netherlands and Luxembourg argued only over the detailed schedule. British delegates again were isolated. At Madrid, the whole package went through in the wake of Spain's ERM entry within the 6% bands, (at a surprisingly low rate because Carlos Solchaga, the finance minister, had previously 'talked the peseta down'). Meanwhile, as Lawson told in his autobiography, he and Howe jointly forced Margaret Thatcher to set out the conditions for British entry, despite her protests up to the last moment of arriving in Madrid.[18] The Bundesbank gloomily went its way, raising West German interest rates further to contain domestic inflation.

Then the Berlin Wall came down. Very large numbers of East Germans had already escaped, mainly through Hungary's un-officially opened border, raising the spectre of mass migration from East to West Germany. The situation could be compared with the strong, demand-led inflation experience before the Wall had been built in 1960–61. Bonn poured huge funds into East Germany to forestall such a threat to the DM, and later promised to exchange one deutschmark for each individual's now almost worthless ostmark at a rate of one to one, a burden on West Germany which ensured high domestic interest rates for the foreseeable future.

Neither of the logical consequences, an ERM realignment or revaluation against the DM, or very high interest rates for all other member currencies, actually occurred. The first broke on French objections, since the *franc fort* policy had not yet acquired complete credibility, the second on German political reality. Karl-Otto Pöhl's outspoken protests against the currency swap were ignored, being politically inconvenient before the crucial autumn elections. He was, in fact, threatened with constitutional revision of the Bank's statutes if he did not give in. As a direct result, the DM's credibility was impaired.

ERM partners in 1990, however, concerned themselves more with the effect of rising German interest rates on their own borrowing and their domestic economies, for while the German government expected to bear 80% of unification costs, it was not willing to internalize the consequences for other Community members. The result, if the Bundesbank held to its primary duty of monetary stability, could only be a steady rise in German rates to which the rest would have to adjust. Yet the British government – or rather its chancellor, John Major, fearful of losing the chance should Thatcher change her mind – chose this moment finally to enter the ERM in the narrow bands, on 5 October 1990. It was a bad time, with the dollar still falling and the ERM now nearly rigid, and a worse choice of parity. Yet the British chose not to take the advice of other member states which the ERM's informal conventions prescribed – and which might perhaps have counselled caution.[19]

Meanwhile, despite these huge potential sources of tension, member governments concerned above all with passage to EMU went ahead, like Captain McWhirr in Conrad's *Typhoon*, hoping to win through the storm to the hypothetical calm beyond. The German government's price for accepting the principle of EMU in such conditions was to be France's overt support for reunification and rapid progress to political union, so that the new, larger Germany could cement itself firmly into the Community. This can be read as the second stage of the Franco-German bargain made in 1987.

France's government could accept this, whatever Mitterrand's initial doubts about reunification, and whatever the impact on French public opinion, because few wished to unleash visceral images of Germany's past being propounded at this time by Thatcher herself and Nicholas Ridley (except, that is, in languages such as Dutch and Danish which the international press agencies did not read). On that basis, Kohl and Mitterrand agreed their highly important joint declaration of April 1990. It followed, apparently naturally, that EMU would come about via the ERM-convergence path, and according to Delors's timetable. Franco-German clarity of aim contrasted with Britain's disarray at the top as Margaret Thatcher fell from power in November 1990, the result of a palace coup within her own Conservative party.

All this time the Bundesbank was constrained not only by its duty to the currency but by its charter obligation to support the Bonn government's policy in the last resort. Whatever its Directorate felt about Kohl's pre-election promise that reunification would cost the West German electorate nothing, the bank could not oppose the chancellor's direction outright. In due course, with the CDU/CSU triumphant in the elections, Pöhl resigned. His lonely gesture and his subsequent explanation, though cogent, had less general effect on events than the new British prime minister's tone; for John

Major's talk of bringing Britain to a more pro-EC orientation, and signs that his Conservative party might even align with Kohl's CDU and the European People's party parliamentary grouping, seemed remarkable after eleven years of marching in another direction.

It was widely assumed during the IGCs that year that the ERM had become the 'glide path to Monetary Union'.[20] But that this represented a political as well as an economic judgment was not clear until after Maastricht, in spite of the most unwelcome paradox that developed shortly afterwards, when the peseta went to the top of its ERM range and the French franc to the bottom – the exact reverse of what their relative stabilities indicated should happen. France encountered the greatest economic pain, for despite inflation being almost as low as in Germany, interest rates stayed higher and contributed both to slow growth and persistent high unemployment, and to the government's repeated attempts to reduce rates rather than let the franc rise.[21]

At the heart of the problem lay the fact that with reunification of Germany costs and prices would eventually rise; unless the Bundesbank permitted higher domestic inflation, France and the other members would pay the price via the ERM. Acceptable though the arrangement might be in 1990–91 while Bérégovoy pursued the *franc fort*, and while Mitterrand sought to reincorporate Germany *coute qui coute*, its long term survival could not be taken for granted during the next three years. It also depended entirely on monetary union remaining the agreed end. Yet twelve years of ERM practice offered no precedent for resolving such tension. *Any* realignment at this stage – even by Britain, now locked into its initial misjudgment – would imperil the 'glide path' thesis. As for the Spanish paradox, the others could neither ignore the thesis nor rethink the ERM's logic. Only the Bundesbank's council dreamed, as they had since 1987, of a different path to EMU through gradual evolution of a cluster of low-inflation currencies such as the guilder, Belgian franc, Danish krone, and now the French franc, linked to the DM.

Governments across the EC chose to ignore protests from industry and trade unions about high interest rates, and focused primarily on the IGCs. But the French and German finance ministers did induce the Spanish government, against the advice of the Bank of Spain, to depreciate the peseta (contrary to the ERM's presumed doctrine that the government should not manipulate the exchange rate but content itself with cutting state spending, wages and public consumption). The Spanish government conformed, fearing to antagonize Germany, its main investor, suspecting that if it did not Spain might lose access to the cohesion funds which alone could help its economy fulfil the EMU convergence criteria . The Spanish government's version of perceived national interests triumphed over its central bank's fiscal prudence.

In order to bring EMU to the speediest conclusion, the French government and the Banque de France argued during 1990–91 for even more than Delors had: instead of achieving convergence first, according to generally-agreed criteria, a strict timescale should be imposed, *pari passu* with the IGC at Luxembourg. Margaret Thatcher's replacement by the relatively inexperienced John Major facilitated this move, which was incorporated in the Commission's draft treaty on EMU and the ECB's draft statutes in December 1990. Thereafter, the two IGCs ran in parallel into a maelstrom where *raison d'état*, economic logic and deductions from very recent history surged inextricably around two conflicting propositions: on the one hand, that EMU would produce automatic convergence and was therefore a precondition for economic union (advocated especially by Italy and Belgium which most needed the external discipline); and on the other, the contention of the Bundesbank and Chicago monetarists, that convergence and completion of the internal market were themselves the preconditions.[22]

Within this grand argument lay others, such as the shape of stage two and Britain's proposal for a 'hard ecu' rather than an irreversible single currency. (This proposal originated with Sir Michael Butler, and was taken up by Major when he was chancellor. Like Howe's scheme in 1984 for a Single European Act without an IGC (see p. 144), it had certain advantages, one of which was that it made a rigid schedule unnecessary. But, like Howe's earlier scheme, it came too late. In any case, it would have implied a long delay in stage three. Though acceptable to Spain and possibly others, it ran into outspoken German opposition on the grounds that the 'hard ecu' would constitute a 'thirteenth currency'.

Inevitably a compromise emerged, even in such a Manichean struggle: the timetable should be absolute, but so should be stage two's move to narrow bands and the convergence criteria themselves, the assumption being that each member state would thus be forced to adjust its own inflation, budget deficits and public debt ratios. To meet British objections, the Maastricht Treaty's EMU sections added that the Commission should monitor member states' performance, as it was already doing in their progress towards the internal market.

Governments' various alignments in the EMU IGC were composed by a sort of logic outside time and public opinion, far from the actual recession which was beginning to affect industrial players in the second half of 1991.[23] Stage two was set to begin on 1 January 1994, stage three in January 1997 or up to two years later, a date from which John Major obtained his celebrated opt-out clause with Kohl's direct assistance.

Only one event disturbed the tenor of compromise, when the Netherlands Presidency introduced a proposal that the four convergence principles should be achieved before making any move to set up an ECB. This was attacked both by the French and the Commission, with support from Italy and Greece, whose governments saw the external agency which was to help them reform their public finances evaporating. Yet this was what German ministers, primed by the Bundesbank, actually wanted. It also pleased the British whom at this stage the German government wished to carry with them. The ECB was not therefore to take its final form during stage two, but only a European Monetary Institute (EMI), whose precise relationship to the existing array of central banks was far from clear. Convergence seemed assured, and in fact developed most markedly at first among the more widely divergent members like Spain, Italy, Belgium and Britain. Commentators in the United States assumed parities already to have been fixed so that 'hedge funds', managed by men like George Soros, had a straight gamble on whether EC governments would hold to this resolve.

The denouement came quickly, as the Bundesbank pushed rates higher to cope with German domestic inflation in the second half of 1991. For the next year Pöhl's successor, Helmut Schlesinger, pursued the lonely path of rectitude to maintain the bank's reputation against manifestly political pressures from Bonn and other EC capitals, all of which watched the struggle between Frankfurt and Bonn with increasing dismay.[24] Speculators inevitably targeted those currencies, the peseta and the lira, whose governments had most to lose from the deflationary regime and were most likely to have to devalue long before 1997.

Substantial issues affecting members' sovereignty had been traded, as British, Dutch and Danish ministers constantly pointed out. Yet the pass had been sold with the Central Bankers' Report. All the more scrutiny was therefore imposed on the political union IGC, at a particularly fractious time of quarrels over agriculture and GATT, and the siting of the EC's new institutions such as the EMI. Meanwhile the Commission's interventions brought accusations of overbearing behaviour: a proposal in May 1991 to make detailed regulations within existing laws earned the criticism that Delors sought to make it the 'thirteenth state'. Delors himself, nearing the end of his second term, needed to keep in line not only the IGCs – the second of which was largely outside the Commission's scope – but the future budget on which the promised cohesion funds (and thus the acquiescence above all of Spain) depended. Yet in the second IGC, the Commission had to be a broker between member states whose tolerance had already worn thin.

The first IGC did nevertheless settle the fundamental issue of where power would lie: in Michael Artis's phrase, 'it was the culmination of an unparalleled effort to think through the implications of monetary union and to strike realistic bargains in the interests of realizing this good.'[25] Whether the Commission's powers of enforcement, or the logic of convergence and the timescale, would be adequate to reach that point was another matter, when the ERM reached its foreseeable long crisis in 1992–3.[26]

II. Contingencies

REGIONS

Although the aim of creating 'a more favourable business environment through the definition of a common industrial policy as
a whole', which was set out by the Commission in its paper on
industrial policy in 1990, belongs to a distinct history, it affected the
IGCs in a very broad sense, since it touched on key matters like
trans-European networks for research and development, initiatives
for training, liberalizing civil aviation or telecoms, the differing
competences of the Directorates concerned with industry and
member states, and the attempts to iron out economic and social
imbalances in the Community. Since the imbalances, especially in
the infrastructure, had a strong regional formation, a leading
managerial and supervisory role had to be envisaged for the
Commission. DG16 already had a claim to be the residuary legatee of
such a role, by virtue of its responsibility for the Regional Fund.

But the more politically salient regions, above all certain West
German *Länder*, led by Bavaria and North Rhine Westphalia, wanted
a more tangible sign, outside the Commission's competence. So
great was their influence on Bonn, in the sensitive period before the
East German *Länder* were assimilated, that an argument developed
for instituting an entirely new political structure, one avidly
welcomed by Spanish, Belgian and Italian regions. The Maastricht
Treaty therefore embodied a new Committee of Regions, similar to
the old Economic and Social Committee. At the time of signature,
what this committee would become remained speculative (see
chapter 9). But that it could be a useful sounding-board for the
ambitions of different sorts of regions, ranging from German *Länder*
to the partly autonomous Spanish regions was not in doubt. Hence
the interest of trade union confederations, now once again linked
under a regenerated central body, the ETUC, across the north–
south divide in order to further the Treaty's Social Charter.

SOCIAL CHARTER

The Charter's roots can be traced back to the previous period of trade union influence nearly two decades earlier; more directly to the report from the Commission working group in 1979. It was also influenced by the high levels of tripartite consultation in the EFTA countries which were already requesting membership, such as Austria, displayed in the 1989 Kreisky Report. If, as the Commission forecast, these states were soon to enter the EC, then the Community's labour market arrangements should be compatible with the conditions they already enjoyed. So argued the Netherlands, who were the leaders in this particular field. Delors and leading members of the ETUC such as Ernst Breit (DGB), Bruno Trentin (CGIL), and Nicolas Redondo of Spain's UGT drew up the Social Charter, which was then adopted as part of the IGC agenda by eleven member states to one in December 1989. Its intention was to renew the earlier 'social dialogue' and compensate for the deleterious impact of the internal market and industrial restructuring, of which rising unemployment – forecast to reach 13% across the EC by 1992–3 – was the first consequence.

The Charter itself set out twelve categories of workers' rights, based usually on the West German model of *mitbestimmung*, which were presumed to facilitate the emergence of a single European labour market, more flexible and endowed with higher skills.[27] The Charter embodied the Vredeling directive under another, non-compulsory form, and was likely to arouse opposition from UNICE and the European Committee members of AmCham because of employers' predictable fears about higher costs, restrictions on the rights of management to hire and fire, and the imposition of standard contracts of employment. Indeed Delors told one British chief executive that the Charter was meant to be 'the instrument for levelling the (labour) field'.

In spite of a proposed directive linking progress on rights to the cross-border mergers on which large companies were now keen, the only coordinated opposition came from Britain and Denmark. With their higher labour costs and legally protected markets, the governments, and in many cases the trade and employers federations of France, Germany and the Benelux countries, saw the Charter as a way of balancing the 'Anglo-Saxon advantage' which was initially predicted to derive from the internal market. Italy and

Spain also wished to avoid disruption from trades unions at a sensitive period while their governments pruned public finances. The Charter thus stimulated systemic conflict between very different approaches to industrial relations, labour law, social security, welfare and pensions.

Yet there existed a strong case for arguing that the Charter would actually facilitate the internal market transition of which, according to the Commission, it was now a component (just as Structural Funds – doubled in size to 50 million ecus in 1989–92 – would ease the problems of declining industry and long-term unemployment (including the British coal industry)). The case for harmonizing laws on health and safety had been agreed already and if there were to be derogations they would be for the poorer countries, not Britain or Denmark. Thus the issue rested on the legal weight to be given to rights such as adequate information for employees about company strategies.

On the European Companies Statute (the heir to Vredeling) the Commission set out three basic models: that of Germany, the Franco-Belgian factory council model, and the British tradition of voluntary arrangements or bargains. From the list, all large and medium-sized firms would have to select one. It was perhaps unfortunate that the Commissioner in charge was neither much liked nor diplomatically skilled, because the Commission college let Vasso Papandreou, with her forty-seven directives, take the brunt of UNICE's attack,[28] while keeping in reserve a still-tripartite but more voluntarist alternative.

Much depended on the powers that trade union confederations still maintained at national level, in what was inevitably a subordinate part of the Maastricht arena, even for the more committed member states. Mitterrand's phase 'no Europe without a social Europe' carried little weight even with social-democratic governments in 1991. During the IGC, the Dutch Presidency did its best for the Social Charter. But Britain, its government relatively united on Thatcherite principles, refused, on this matter, to accept QMV at all.

There being no choice, if the Charter were to be salvaged from a British veto, the other eleven governments proceeded with it as if it had been part of the Treaty, in a masterpiece of informal politics which the Netherlands Presidency then turned into a Protocol. John Major, taken aback by the long-term prospects if the Commission were to choose (under Article 100A of the Single European Act) to launch fresh legislation under a QMV heading, presented this opt-in by the majority of eleven to the House of Commons as if it had been a successful opt-out by the one.

REFORM OF INSTITUTIONS

Bargaining about the Commission's competences surged up on these issues, often for financial reasons, because many of the trade-offs included compensation, through the proposed cohesion funds, for member states which expected to do badly out of EMU as well as the internal market. But behind disputes about the EC's swelling budget rested issues of sovereignty and institutional reform. Insofar as the cost of regional equilibrium would rise, for example, the 'northern' member states who paid the most required supervision of the allocation and spending of both structural and cohesion funds.[29] At the same time, the collapse of Communist regimes in eastern Europe required a response. If there were not to be a rush by Western countries to take easy advantage of newly democratic, politically inexperienced states with weak economies overloaded with Comecon debts, the Community had to act together. So it did; but it was the Commission which coordinated the West's rehabilitation and loan programme, first for Poland and Hungary, then for all of eastern Europe. Fears that the Commission would thus slip into defining a sort of Community foreign policy led Mitterrand at Strasbourg to sponsor the grand concept of a European economic entente, a case which – like the Kohl-Mitterrand declaration on EMU and EPU – revealed the Council's increasing habit of reaching major decisions in principle, usually on a Franco-German basis, preempting in practice both the Commission and Parliament.

Even before the IGCs began, change and reform of institutions touched other spheres, such as the European Court of Justice.[30] Any extension of QMV proposed at Maastricht would also greatly complicate member states' tactics, obliging them to calculate more carefully than they already had to, under the Single European Act, when constructing alliances or trading advantages if they wished to mobilize a blocking minority. But some power also adhered to the Parliament, as its President, Enrique Baron Crespo, with Kohl's support, demanded that the political IGC should confer on it the right to initiate legislation, and amend more of, or reject, what was put before it. Italian, Dutch, and Luxembourg ministers, as well as those from Germany, supported this challenge to the prerogatives of the Commission and the Council.

The Parliament had already conducted its own attempt to set the IGC's agenda, when its first 'assizes', held in Rome in November 1989, debated the proposals which Baron Crespo was later to advance in his semi-official meetings with ministers before and during Maastricht. These included not only greater rights to initiate, amend or reject legislation, but definitions of citizenship – basic rights on which might eventually be constructed the idea of a European public. In addition, it asked for enlarged competence for the Commission in social and environmental cases, and that European political cooperation (EPC) should be brought within the Treaties.

III. *Political Union*

The second IGC's origins derived from two sources: member states' long concerns with foreign policy from which, unlike EMU or the Social Chapter, Britain could not and did not wish to dissociate itself; and from the threats to their national security represented by cross-border crime, drug smuggling, terrorism and illegal immigration. Consciousness about the latter grew as the internal market and abolition of economic frontiers approached, and on the former with every stage in eastern Europe's metamorphosis. Although the IGC had not been envisaged initially as having a defence element, events in 1989–91, including the incipient break-up of Yugoslavia, led that way, as did economic aspects of both the Community's foreign and security policy (CFSP) and the internal market, via defence procurement, state aids to industry, and mergers such as the Siemens/GEC takeover of Plessey.[31] Meanwhile, thirty-five years after the French Assembly had killed off the EDC, the French government wished to come back into the centre of European defence, even if that meant it had to reconsider aspects of NATO, so long as it did not have to rejoin NATO's Military Committee. But defence as a separate theme could not be brought within the Treaties since it had been specifically excluded in 1957.

Mitterrand therefore sought an enlarged status for Western European Union (WEU) as the main plank of France's CFSP proposals.[32] But since the dilution of NATO was a highly sensitive subject, his proposals remained vague – as did their embodiment in the Treaty (see p. 193). Not only did they have a direct impact on other member states in NATO, they invited an unpredictable Russian response. France's defence industry, long the most successful of any EC exporters, also stood to gain substantially, to the dismay of British and German competitors and those parts of the Commission concerned with the single market and competition policy. If defence was to be touched on during the IGC, not only Britain's fears about NATO but Germany's concerns with its own new status and the problems of eastern Europe and Yugoslavia had to be addressed.

Interior Ministry issues were also brought into sharp focus by events in eastern Europe, above all the profound uncertainty about what would emerge from the former Soviet system after the onset of civil war in Yugoslavia. For the first time since 1961, the possibility of a flood of refugees and asylum seekers confused the patterns in which legal and illegal immigration had largely been contained. Unlike 1961, heavy structural unemployment in western Europe was beginning to change the outlook of governments which had previously been willing to accommodate large numbers of refugees. For the first time since the 1960s, the prospect of economic migrants, rather than refugees, from eastern Europe reappeared. In mid–1991, while the IGC was in progress, the International Labour Organization estimated that roughly eight million legitimate immigrants were living within the EC's borders; on top of that had to be added the illegal ones, and asylum seekers whose numbers had risen from a mere 70,000 in 1983 to 350,000 in 1989 and nearly half a million by 1991 – even before the Yugoslav conflicts.

Refugees and asylum seekers were one thing, illegal migrants another. But the conditions of the time fostered confusion, so that the two easily became conflated, in certain political movements, and by the popular press. Nations' rights to defend themselves against crime or drugs, recognized in Article 36 of the Rome Treaty, had been reaffirmed in the Single European Act. But the Schengen Agreement, made between France, West Germany and the three Benelux states in 1985, prefigured a Europe of open borders, where the southern and eastern members – Greece, Italy and Spain – would stand in effect as frontier guarantors for the rest against most sources of illegal immigration.

The political IGC therefore had to encompass a vast area, with no clear long-term aims, where member states argued not only over the practicalities of ID cards, data protection, and the so-called 'right of hot pursuit', but their likely impact on national public opinions. This was especially so in Britain and France, but became more so in parts of Germany and Spain; Italy felt the force of it once refugees began to pour in from Yugoslavia and Albania. Even among the Schengen countries, discords developed, for example over Dutch permissive policies on soft drugs, which French interior ministers referred to in outspokenly critical terms. Sentiments which had rarely been voiced in public now became commonplace, throwing doubt on the competence of other member states to keep out, variously, Moroccans and Algerians, Albanians, Yugoslavs or Somalis, and economic refugees from behind the fallen Iron Curtain.

Three main influences shaped this IGC: the efforts of the Parliament (by far the weakest); the Commission's attempts to set the agenda, which dated back to 1986, if not 1985; and the aims and ambitions of member states. The well-attested tendency for EC states to grow more to resemble each other might have led the Maastricht negotiators to expect the same sort of consensus levels that had been obtained in 1985. Earlier frictions between Commission, Council and Parliament had indeed lessened during the late 1980s. But north–south differentiation seemed to have increased, as Spain's successfully aggressive tone during the bargaining indicated, and the distinction between countries with sound fiscal regimes and others who were lax demonstrated. The ancient gulf between Britain and the majority, with all its philosophical undertones, remained, albeit softened by Major's 'Britain at the heart of Europe' pretensions. Even subsidiarity, which for most states already meant devolution not to national but to regional capitals or even municipalities, meant something different to British Conservatives – though not to many Scots and Welsh.

How divergent the larger member states' aims were can be gauged from the table of their desiderata compiled by the *Economist* in December.[33] But whereas smaller and Mediterranean states had more cause than they had had over the Single European Act to defend particular national interests, the activities of Germany, France and Britain were complicated by their adjustments to changing perceptions of the outside world.

As in the past, the German government supported a Common Foreign and Security Policy (CFSP) having, at that stage, no conceivable alternative. French foreign minister Dumas and his German colleague Genscher explained in their October 1990 proposals for a CFSP that they were prepared to include majority voting in the Council. In December 1990, they widened their approach to include a common European defence, building on what had been done in Western European Union (WEU) since 1984. The German-French paper of February 1991 spelled out the WEU's function as a bridge between the European Union and NATO. For both Bonn and London it was also important to guarantee that any European defence pillar in the framework of the WEU would not undermine NATO. However, the Germans had the additional aim of tempting France back into full membership of NATO.

Conduct of this part of the negotiations, though in the hands of foreign ministers at their monthly meetings, and deputies or permanent representatives on more frequent special occasions, reverted in the last six weeks to heads of government level. In Paris, it was the responsibility of Dumas and Guigou, but never far from Mitterrand himself: in Bonn, rather less harmoniously, it lay between Kohl and Genscher.

For the French government, it was vital to reinforce the EC in

French colours rather than allow the Dutch Presidency, aided by Belgium and Italy, to make EC transactions more accountable to the Parliament and more detrimental to national sovereignty. The French were playing for very high stakes: not only for EMU but for a French rather than a NATO-based version of CFSP – at variance, for example, with what the Netherlands required. If defence were also to be included, an alternative had to be found to the organic image of a tree from whose trunk all the branches would spring.

One of the French negotiators, Pierre de Boissieu, brought forward the idea of a temple, whose pediment would rest on three *distinct* pillars: EMU (which mattered above all other elements to France), foreign policy, and home and justice or Interior Ministry matters. This had the inestimable advantage that neither of the latter need add to Commission competences – negotiations between governments would suffice. Even so, it would need advance concertation with Germany if a move in foreign and defence policy apparently so at variance with France's twenty-five year stance were to be accepted by French public opinion.

Germany's representatives regarded strengthening Community institutions and a stronger position for the European Parliament as so important that they were prepared to link them to their consent to economic and monetary union. They were also well aware that EMU was subject to growing criticism inside Germany, and that public support for bringing new fields into the Treaties, such as asylum policy for refugees, combating terrorism and international crime, derived from *Länder* administrations, not Bonn. *Länder* governments, of course, sought a significantly stronger role for themselves, and the principle of subsidiarity. Remembering how their views had been ignored when the Single European Act was ratified five years earlier, and relying in part on the example of what Belgium's ethnic regions had already achieved in the EU context, these sought confidently to replicate in the Community the division of powers between 'Bund' and 'Land' in the federal system itself.

Less obviously, fear motivated German leaders that if the new treaties were not signed quickly, conditions in the mid–1990s would deteriorate and encourage the rise of instability, fierce nationalism, and ethnic discord in central and eastern Europe. To avoid that, and the repercussions on those of German origin living in the former Soviet Union (and therefore entitled to citizenship of the reunited Germany), Kohl would be prepared to make substantial concessions.

It was not however clear that the British would even sign. One vital preliminary had been the ousting of Margaret Thatcher, for, in spite of an initially obdurate stance, John Major and Douglas Hurd skilfully let it be seen in private among the foreign ministers that they were not opposed *à l'outrance* to political union, but rather that they were men of goodwill as well as firm principles, shackled by the Thatcherite faction in their Conservative party. Such hints were reinforced at the personal level by links with the CDU between Chris Patten and Volker Rühe[34] and informally by Whitehall officials. By November, confronted with preparations by the other eleven governments for an 'opt-in' strategy on EMU, British ministers allowed it to be thought that they were prepared for concessions so long as they were permitted to opt out when stage three finally arrived. There was also some common ground with Germany, given British resistance to the Delors II budget package and demands for greater parliamentary audit over spending, as well as for the ECJ actually to be able to fine member states who ignored single market judgments.

In the end, Major was able to extract large, even remarkable concessions, partly because he was not Margaret Thatcher but more because it suited the other large state governments – principally Germany's – to make deals which safeguarded essential interests before too much time elapsed. But this was done at what seemed a high price to the southern states then facing up not only to completing the single market but to the Community's next extension in favour of EFTA countries which were already completing their political and economic reorientation.[35] Brokerage between governments conscious of the need to safeguard their national interests, rather than Commission control of the agenda, characterized the second IGC, together with a determination to get everything into texts, agreed and signed, before it was too late.

As the IGC ground remorselessly on, under enormous pressures from world events and domestic public reactions, a series of interlocking, contrapuntal elite bargains were made, by men and women who were often by now over-tired, working late at night in cabals and closets using an arcane jargon, assisted by increasingly exhausted officials. Although within each government's apparatus, the issues appeared clear (and some of those engaged now admit that there was insufficient discussion by some national EC affairs coordination systems, leading to a lack of direction on essential questions),[36] their outcomes proved simply too complicated or obscure to explain in public language.

Yet since the web of alliances seemed to preclude national vetoes, while most participants believed the Luxembourg Compromise dead, national publics – or perhaps better, national media – came to feel that 'their' governments could do little to reverse the momentum. A pervasive sort of disillusionment spread, most strongly in Denmark, which may have been the first genuine expression of European-wide public opinion. It ramified in Britain and France, to say nothing of Italy, where the failure to educate or explain led (with good reason) to deep fears about higher taxes, sacrifices and assaults on work-place security as a result of fiscal reform.

Shifts of perception occurred, the results of a changing external environment, among the main players during the IGC. German diplomacy now had to operate in an entirely different way, given its borders with eastern and central Europe, a factor which explains President Bush's transfer of interest as early as 1990 (and which disturbed Mrs Thatcher on her last visit to see Bush at Camp David). Her fall removed the principal – indeed the only – exponent of a bilateral diplomacy involving Britain and France, intended to contain a newly united Germany, but it did not alter Britain's reliance on NATO and the CFSP framework; nor the fact that on matters such as Community support for Slovenes and Croats against Serbian claims to a greater Serbia, or EC extension to eastern Europe as well as EFTA, Germany would now insist on being heard.

The orientation of France towards the Community also changed, signified in 1991 when the Quai d'Orsay abandoned its line on 'variable geometry', even if the phenomenon was interpreted in a variety of ways by French analysts at the time. Under Mitterrand

and Edith Cresson, France committed itself firmly to the internal market, not in the form of Anglo-Saxon liberalization – which Cresson, as a member of a Socialist government, frequently lampooned – but as a defence against Japanese competition and a means to adjust (an echo perhaps of how de Gaulle had assessed the EEC's mid–60s harmonization policy). An element of protectionism grew, while unemployment rose in 1991–2. Yet as its one method of containing Germany, France set itself to become less particularist and more truly European, a step well beyond the already-significant turning point of 1983–4.

Documents flooded into the IGC, starting with the Commission's agenda and member states' own proposals. Others, with less formal status, included the Martin Reports and recommendations from the Parliamentary Assizes. Having been hyperactive in the preparatory period, the Commission appeared to miss several chances of imprinting its own agenda, possibly because Delors and the college were preoccupied with the many separate issues ranging from the early trade negotiations in eastern Europe to disputes over the budget. Whatever the reasons for the loss of focus, the proliferation of member states' general plans, which varied from relatively 'soft' Spanish proposals to the more forthright German draft Treaty of March 1991, caused serious problems for the Luxembourg Presidency.

To contain the flood, and induce greater precision, the Presidency wrote what it styled a 'non-paper' in April, summarizing the state of play as if it had actually encompassed majority opinion. Later, on 20 June, in time for the Council Meeting, this was rendered into the negotiating text for a draft Treaty. As was normal in these circumstances, Council did little more than endorse what was going on, because actual progress was held up by three points of principle.

The first, the use of the word 'federal', conveyed a host of different meanings to different audiences. But it was employed to signify the desire (*inter alia* of the Commission, the Belgians and the Dutch) to incorporate the Common Foreign and Security Policy (CFSP) into the Treaties, rather than leave it subject purely to the governments of member states, given the existing overlap of foreign policy with the EC's own trade and external relations. About that France still remained uneasy, and Britain adamant. The second issue, of national as against Community jurisdiction, came up on nearly all the Interior Ministry matters. No easy precedents existed to guide twelve-nation cooperation, for the Trevi arrangements had been both obscure and hard to evaluate, and only five members had joined the Schengen Group. Since only the Netherlands wanted such questions made justiciable at the ECJ, Luxembourg's 'non-paper' proposed to keep them, like CFSP, as a distinct inter-governmental sector *outside* the Treaty.

The third argument followed the long debate – essentially about national sovereignty – over whether the three elements (including EMU) should be conceived of as a tree – its trunk the new Treaty, its branches the elements – or a temple, supported on three pillars, not all of which need have their legal being within the EC's framework. Germany, Belgium, Italy, Spain, Greece, Ireland and the Netherlands wanted the tree, but the Luxembourg Presidency realized that this majority could never actually win against a minority which included Britain and France. The draft Treaty therefore adopted the temple model, to the dismay of the Commission, the European Parliament and some national parliaments.

When, somewhat late in the day in September, the Netherlands Presidency tried to reopen this fundamental issue with an entirely new draft Treaty, it failed, for the document proposed by the Dutch was itself a compromise between the prime minister and his foreign minister, which was seen as disastrous by all but the Italians. Ruud Lubbers withdrew the Dutch text and restored the Luxembourg one on 8 December, on which the foreign ministers worked for a further five weeks, until the climactic Council session of 10–22 December.

Apart from the word 'federal', for which it was tacitly agreed an alternative could probably be substituted at the end, (since the British appeared to fight less hard on the substantive issues of citizenship and judicial and home affairs), the major areas for later bargaining centred on the Presidency's role in the CFSP, whether QMV would apply, whether it should include defence, and if so whether it should be approached via NATO, or WEU, or both. European political cooperation during the Gulf War had been minimal, but it had improved slightly during the Kurdish crisis and the early stages of Yugoslavia's disintegration.[37] But NATO's own first revision of its role, in the light of the Cold War's end, was taking place at the same time, in November, and foreign ministers had to wait until that was complete. Ireland's government also had severe problems with the country's traditional neutral status.

Despite a variety of reservations, faced with this sort of choice, most members (with the possible exception of Ireland and Denmark) were prepared to accept WEU as a part of the new Union, which could conceivably be advanced during the prospective 1996 IGC. But Britain and Germany were not. In finding a compromise, British ministers had a coadjutor in the Italian foreign minister, de Michelis, while France lent its weight to two contiguous proposals, one with Germany and Spain, the other only with Germany. During the last month, Britain, the Netherlands, Portugal and Denmark let it be seen that they would accept WEU as a bridge between NATO and the EC, and on that basis, Luxembourg and the Italian ministers were able to draw the threads together into a formula which, characteristically, was full of ambiguity ('the EU requests WEU to elaborate and implement decisions', as 'an integral part of the EU's development', but only in so far as 'shall be compatible with NATO'). Defence remained in the hands of member states, responsible, in the words of Article J4(1) of the Maastricht Treaty, for 'the eventual framing of a common defence policy, which might in time lead to a common defence'. For the moment, this sufficed.

Joint action would be taken, not in defence as such, but only on CFSP if and when member states had 'important interests' in common; and the Council, not the Presidency, would determine whether or not the decisions in any case should be by QMV. Given the extent of French accommodation to a European concept of defence, and Britain's not inconsiderable movement, even this much may be reckoned surprising, given that it formed an evidently incremental part of an evolutionary process, albeit under inter-governmental control. What those increments might be was demonstrated by the WEU's move to Brussels.

On Judicial and Home Affairs matters, diversity reflected member states' geography of mind. Because of their philosophical commitment to Community ideals, the Netherlands, Belgium, Italy and Spain wanted this pillar incorporated; France, Germany and Portugal preferred it to be under the Council's competence, and Britain, Ireland and Greece wanted there to be no doubt but that it would remain subject to national veto. Denmark disliked the whole project, but was prepared to settle for the latter. Slowly Luxembourg jockeyed the texts into line around the Franco-German average, with the addition of visa policy but not cooperation on police, drugs or terrorism. So it stayed until the final stages. But acquiescence hid many national reservations, as the sequel showed.

Meanwhile member states tried to include a range of new subjects in the EC's competence, ranging from public health and cross-border transport networks to education, culture, tourism and youth issues. Some were incorporated, if not in binding form then in shadowy headings on which more might be built in future. Industrial policy was included, and also citizenship (the product of a Spanish initiative), as well as reiterated demands from the Parliament to incorporate the European Convention on Human Rights together with a common but very limited form of citizenship which would at least allow voting rights to all in EC and municipal elections. Britain's representatives, having contested the subsidiarity principle like most other matters, allowed it to appear in Article 3b in a neutered form, knowing that, as Richard Corbett puts it, proof of its efficacy depended entirely 'on how far the ECJ is willing to get involved in what is essentially a political judgement, to be made on a case by case basis'.[38]

The Commission and Parliament sought QMV on all Maastricht business, save constitutional questions such as new members' accession and Treaty changes. Some member states gave them support but the debate foundered on the earlier objections to increased competences for the institutions. Britain opposed it outright, successfully, and in the end QMV was only extended to some environmental areas and a handful of new titles (including education and training, health and development), as well as parts of what became the Social Protocol. On powers of parliamentary 'co-decision', Britain and Denmark began in opposition, supported by France, Portugal and Ireland. France then shifted ground, partly in reaction to the Netherlands' abortive draft treaty which would have conferred a right to reject or veto legislation if the cooperation procedure had been completed, partly because the concession was not a painful one to make, A number of items were added to the existing scale, together with a 'assent procedure' for future Treaty revision.

On other demands from the Assizes, the Parliament largely won its case, though whether from force of persuasion is doubtful. The Commission's tenure was allowed to run in parallel to the Parliament's five year-cycle and the President's appointment by the Council was to be subjected to 'consultation'. Since this began on 1 January 1995, Delors was later to win a short third term of office. But Spain, supported by France, would not accept a freely elected Commission President, nor a limit of one Commissioner per state, nor the Parliament's right to sack any member of the college. In turn, the Commission successfully fended off any erosion of its own powers where the right to initiate legislation was concerned.

Under its two Presidencies, the IGC was characterized by endless brokerage, elite bargains and the private councils of ministerial alliances. At the final Council meeting, John Major duly won his *coup de génie*, the result of painstaking work by a gifted team of ministers and officials, making what appeared at that time to be the first real gains for the British position since 1986. But on matters of substance, they failed to shift the other eleven: the convoluted form of words which replaced the word 'federal' did not disguise the key phrase 'ever closer union'. Neither did Major's presentation in London remove the fact that the turning point came with Helmut Kohl's personal intervention, agreed beforehand with Mitterrand, supported by the Italians, and brokered by Ruud Lubbers of the Netherlands (for the Dutch regarded it as more important to prevent a British veto than to protest at such special terms). The amendment of 'federal' and the rewording of 'subsidiarity', like the opt-out on EMU's third stage, were as much the gift of others as a famous victory.

The British government, in any case, now committed itself to the next IGC date in 1996, preceded by a reallocation of European Parliament seats to allow for the proper representation of the newly-enlarged Germany. Major had not only accepted the Committee of Regions but also – a point of some significance for a unitary monarchy – what was existing practice in Belgium and Germany: that a state could substitute a regional minister for a national government one, so long as he or she held the title of minister and had full authority to act.

Since the Commission was soon to be made the scapegoat for the Maastricht Treaty of European Union, it has to be asked whether it was responsible for this outcome. The answer must be that praise or blame should be shared with member states. Delors and the Commission college had done all that was possible to set the agenda and had opened the bidding high, in summer 1990, to establish the essentials: EMU and the Social Charter. But it was an exaggeration, chiefly of nationalist newspapers, to claim that they aspired to dominate the IGC or to give the Community full federal powers. The President's power lies in presentation, strategic vision and charisma, hand in hand with tactical skills (which are often not seen and therefore underrated). Delors had the extra advantage that he set out and defended strict principles but with an immense variety of flexible tactics, each used to justify the other. Because his immediate predecessors had been less successful, each fresh success added to his own legitimacy. (Indeed, even in the sour aftermath in 1992–3, the college held together and supported him, because the Commission cannot work unless it represents the 'general interest of Europe', which he exemplified.)

But the outcome, though remarkable given the international and economic context of 1991, remained confederal. The Community crept a little nearer to statehood insofar as the Union Treaty provided for a single currency; but for most close observers Maastricht amounted to little more than the Single European Market *bis*. For all the skilful drafting and ingenious compromises, the temple was not a unity, and its three pillars varied in strength. Member states, having frustrated the Dutch draft, still ruled.

That there now existed a juridical route to EMU, very precise in its terms, and apparently irreversible, did not of course imply that economic realities had been abolished, as the 1992–3 crises in the ERM revealed (see chapter 11). On defence, France's transformation had been crucial. The old sixties' taboos had been exposed to the light and largely overcome: defence could be expected in future to run parallel to CSFP. Deep problems of coherence remained, and whether integration and cooperation could be held in balance. The European Union, to give it the new Maastricht Treaty nomenclature, was still a variable one, likely to remain so as new applicants began to queue up outside the temple doors. Those who did so, on the other hand, were to have no option: Maastricht declared that they must accept all the *acquis communautaire*, the accumulated legislative inheritance, as it stood at the time when they were admitted.

What had been done at the centre required assent and ratification. The high contracting parties had long since styled themselves as member states, yet the Maastricht Treaty had been negotiated by individual ministers acting for their governments, who had now to ensure that their national parliaments and publics followed where their bargains led. Yet during the Maastricht negotiations, no one raised the question about the difficulty of ratification, which simply had been taken for granted. No one asked if it was wise that the Danish government should have its referendum first; no one argued, at least in public, that the case had to be proved; no one hinted that the onset of another deep recession might prejudice the answer they all expected; no one asked what would be the consequences of making the Commission the scapegoat if anything should go wrong, given that the world outside these small elites was not accustomed to discriminating between what it did and the transactions of member state governments. Only four months after the Treaty's formal signature, the Danish electorate rejected the Treaty – by the very narrow margin of 50.3% to 49.7% – and set off a train of responses, among parliamentary parties, media, and sections of national public opinion in other nations, which almost wrecked the entire process.

Because of Denmark's unique political culture and the vigour of its local forms of political association, its government had prepared its case for the referendum: nearly half a million copies of the Treaty were circulated to a population of 5 million – but with little explanation of the contents. Until then, EC affairs had been dealt with by government in consultation with the Folketing, excluding the players and interest groups, because the public did not conform to the generally favourable opinion about the Community prevalent among, say, the Benelux countries. Danes had, after all, suffered nearly a decade of economic stagnation, and were now confronted with what seemed to be a poor choice: that economic recovery (thanks to the internal market in 1992) would become part of a trade-off where national independence was surrendered for mere influence. This gloomy outlook was worsened by widespread reports of Delors's remarks that future institutional reform would reduce small states' parity of tenure in the Presidency. Poul Schluter's bizarre, over-sophisticated tactics meant that a very diverse Danish public made judgments as much about domestic issues of unemployment or minority interests as Maastricht itself.

As the foreign minister, Ellerman-Jensen, later admitted, the result forced the Danish political class to face up to its public and try, unsuccessfully, to reconvert them. In the end, the Community's need to extract itself from the Danish dilemma, rather than Britain's parliamentary problems ratifying the Treaty, discovered a way out at the Edinburgh Summit in October 1992. Given special provisions and even more opt-outs than Britain (on common defence, WEU, EMU, citizenship and Interior Ministry matters, together with an assurance that there would be no more institutional reform before the EFTA extension had taken place), Denmark finally voted 'Yes' on its second round in 1993.

Generally, European politicians had had serious doubts about the British and Danish exemptions, particularly the older generation such as Davignon, Barre and Schmidt. What insiders felt, however, differed profoundly from how these events were interpreted in the media, according to public concerns or antipathies. The year-long appearance of haggling had already caused incomprehension, especially where national governing parties, such as the French Socialists, British Conservatives, or Italian Christian Democrats, had seen their electoral hold seriously eroded. The European Parliament itself equivocated for some months before giving the approval on which

Belgium and Italy had staked ratification – thereby absolving either from the difficult process of national education (which was in any case barely needed in Belgium). The Parliament's debates, however, were positively learned compared with those conducted 'lower down' and 'further out'.

In a period of very rapid adjustment to the medium-term consequences of 1989–90, the process of winning consent became quite unexpectedly problematic as the matter of Europe fed domestic debates, exposing recondite texts to often crude interpretation. In some countries, national interest as defined by the party in power triumphed: Spanish and Portuguese governments simply refused opposition parties' demands for a referendum. Long public habituation to the EC made referenda unnecessary in the Netherlands and Luxembourg. There was at that stage no talk of a referendum in France, and only later in Germany was it claimed that Maastricht conflicted with the Basic Law.

But even the Netherlands had problems. Although the Single European Act had been welcomed as a vindication of small states against large, there had been problems with public opinion over the Schengen Agreement. The government had been humiliated over its Maastricht Draft Treaty, and was disturbed at its failure to increase EC institutions' accountability. Nevertheless, there was none of the revulsion which developed in France; there was, rather, a growing interest, stemming from the republican tradition, in the regional and local democratic elements of the Treaty.

Spain was already afflicted by the recession, the peseta's imbalance and deep worry that EFTA enlargement would shift the EC centre of gravity northwards. Its parliament ratified Maastricht however, as did the Portuguese one, both centre-right and centre-left parties in the latter being aware of the need for CFSP, given Portugal's continuing links with Latin America and Southern Africa.

In Ireland, a judgment by the High Court involving the Constitution and Community law[39] forced a referendum in June 1992. The government fought its campaign on the huge cash benefits provided by the EC, leaving the public to sort out the social implications of enshrining a religious prohibition in the Constitution. While the Catholic bishops wisely stood aside, the clerical ultras opposed the

Treaty. Since industry and unions left no doubt where national interest lay, the 68% vote in favour was never in doubt. Yet the Irish public found themselves in a disconcerting vacuum, surrounded by systemic change, with few pointers save an awareness that, whatever the country's earlier emancipation after 1973, it had recently become a more insular economy, a disadvantaged part of the EC's periphery. Greece on the other hand ratified the Treaty first, and by the largest majority of all.

France went through an increasingly hot public debate on the EC's future for the first time in twenty years. As the Socialist party declined abruptly in popularity, Mitterrand replaced Cresson with Bérégovoy, hoping to hold business and the financial sector in line and to maintain a steady franc. Bérégovoy succeeded but at the price of public antipathy. The mood then turned inwards, to preoccupations with unemployment and France's endangered identity, while the left and the divided right-wing parties pointed up the Treaty's defects and identified the Commission as a scapegoat.

Immediately after the Danish vote, Mitterrand decided on a referendum; but at a time of disillusionment and apathy towards the EC, the fact that a French government had acknowledged its reduced international status, while Britain and Germany had made more obvious gains than France, outweighed the Treaty's beneficial elements. The campaign lagged and was barely revived by the spectacle of ministers canvassing on holiday beaches in August. Only Mitterrand's final broadcast, and the support of both Giscard and Barre, ensured a Yes vote on 20 September by a margin almost as fine as that in Denmark: 51.05% to 48.95%.

As Alan Lamassoure (EC Affairs Minister) put it later,[40] the success of 'Europe as space' had not been balanced by the construction of 'Europe as a power'. Instead, all the benefits had flowed to other member states, on the trade and industrial side, apparently to France's disadvantage. This malaise was slowly generalized into a sense of deep alienation from an overweening EC, and conflated with the growing, indeed overwhelming, opposition to the Socialist government and a feeling that French politics had become the private preserve of ageing, corrupt prima donnas who left no space for younger alternatives.

The government's rather lame answer lay not in proclaiming the remarkable adjustment to the new Germany, but in proposals for a renewal of the EC around its existing *acquis*, greater subsidiarity, and a focus on institutional reform *before* the next round of EFTA countries' accession, so that the Commission would be reduced to its primary role of animator not director. Thus the EC's elected leaders were to constrain the rest to accept the European ideal, even at the price of 'variable geometry', rather than bow to recalcitrant members' lowest common denominators. The alternative seemed to be acceptance of a merely economic area under Anglo-German hegemony.

Public opinion in Britain might have been won over by a campaign of public conversion, as it had been during the Labour government's referendum campaign with majority Conservative help in 1975. Instead, it had to focus at second-hand and in stereotyped terms on the Conservative party's parliamentary dilemma. During a prolonged, often dismal passage, the Maastricht Treaty was assailed by two categories of objection: that it would undermine the idea of Britain and impair its sovereignty on one hand, and – from the Labour side – that Conservatives had rejected its most important element, the Social Protocol, which would not, as for the Eleven, be the EC's main defence against the consequences of a decade of new-right economics.

Between them, the Thatcherite faction and the Labour opposition delayed the Bill and discredited the government, so that to get it through, John Major had to promise his back-benchers not to ratify until a second, successful Danish referendum had taken place. The adjustments that this required during the British Presidency in 1992 shifted Major's government into an oppositional stance very much at odds with the tacit understandings given at Maastricht when Britain was granted its EMU and Social Protocol concessions.[41]

In Germany, the Bundestag voted for the Treaty by 543 to 17 with 8 abstentions, and the Bundesrat by a similar percentage in December 1992. But the government was obliged to concede further rights of participation to parliament and *Länder* governments, in the shape of a two-thirds parliamentary majority where future EC decisions by the federal government were concerned.

Manfred Brunner, a former chef du cabinet for Bangemann (then a
Free Democrat politician, and subsequently leader of a small anti-
Maastricht party), and four Green MEPs then brought a case
before the Constitutional Court, arguing that the 'democratic
deficit' in the Treaty threatened Germany with a loss of *Staatlichkeit*
(statehood), and of parliamentary competence. Given the ineffective
defence put up by Bonn ministers, there was no choice but to let the
case proceed, and Germany found itself therefore the last to ratify
in October 1993. When the judgment came, it favoured the
Treaty, but with certain important conditions which amounted to
making Treaty amendments – valid only for Germany – after the
event.[42]

During the intervening year, while the Soviet Union unravelled
and some of its component parts such as the Ukraine lapsed into
economic anarchy, the contrast between Germany's current, inward-looking position, especially where immigration, rights of
asylum and investment in eastern Europe were concerned, and its
potential one as the ERM's anchor currency and the strongest –
albeit recession-threatened – economy, affected the momentum of
both EMU and CFSP. The German media and public swung in a
powerful reaction in defence of a supposedly threatened DM.
Questions were asked about what economic advantage Germany
still derived, being by far the largest contributor to EC revenues,
and with a group of very poor *Länder* from former East Germany to
nourish, at a time of substantial pain from the recession. Subsidiarity doctrine as expounded by *Länder* governments as yet
offered little to assuage what amounted to a cleavage between
political elite, media and public.

Whether late, as in Germany, early as in Denmark, or constant as
in Britain, the Maastricht debate served as a catalyst for each
member state's own evolution at a time of most intense and rapid
change in their economic and geopolitical contexts. It touched each
one's perceptions of what the nation state was and its role in the
world. The Maastricht debate in Germany had one thing in
common with that in France and Britain: it concerned national
identity at a time when the nation was changing profoundly and a
redefinition was in any case necessary, if not desirable.

At the same time, but for quite different reasons, the Italian political vortex led to near-disintegration of the existing order. Belgium and the Netherlands suffered in different ways; in France, the Socialist party suffered catastrophic defeat in the 1993 elections. Meanwhile, member states set out on the four-year path to economic convergence, with forebodings that were loudest in Spain and Italy, whose currencies were most at risk.

The Lisbon Summit in June 1992, though well-enough managed by the Portuguese Presidency, allowed most of the difficult decisions like CAP reform to be deferred. However, it did reach the stage of offering negotiations to EFTA countries and may have helped sway the second Danish referendum. Nothing else was settled, except economic sops to the newly associated Visegrad group – Poland, Czechoslovakia and Hungary – because of north–south deadlock on the budget and disputes over the location of EC agencies such as the EMI.

The Edinburgh Summit in December 1992 came after the first and most serious crisis in the ERM (see chapter 11), widespread doubts about EMU's future, and much mutual recrimination in the CFSP arena. The lira, peseta and punt had been devalued and sterling withdrawn altogether from the ERM. Despite being joint anchor currency, the franc was also troubled. The British seemed obsessed with making the concessions to Denmark which would sway the second referendum and thus allow the Treaty through the House of Commons. The Spanish government meanwhile played its hand aggressively, and successfully, for more cohesion funds, and this in turn affected the next round of negotiations with the EFTA applicants.

To a marked extent, the British Presidency allowed itself to appear partial as a result of domestic politics and loss of direction at the top;[43] a bad omen, because the Danish one which followed (the normal order in each year having been reversed) found itself too busy repairing its own damage, so that only under the Belgian Presidency, in the second half of 1993, was there space for regrouping.

Meanwhile, although Delors won his reappointment for the two years to the end of 1994, the Commission, stung and humiliated by the assault which lasted throughout 1992–3, played its cards with caution. This stalled period saw a loss of momentum, particularly in competition policy and industrial restucturing, together with renewed demands for protection by member states against eastern European and south-east Asian imports of steel and semi-conductors. Conclusion of the GATT round by the end of 1993 appeared highly problematic.

It may not in reality have been a policy vacuum but this was certainly how it appeared in public.[44] Not until the White Paper on economic, industrial and employment policy, which had been conceived under the British Presidency but took twelve months to mature, was presented to the Council in December 1993 (see chapter 12) can the Community be said to have begun to emerge from this tangled period – of which the currency market surges, the ERM crisis of June 1992 to summer 1993, and the Yugoslav three-handed civil war were only the most obvious signs.

Postscript

Much of the internal market remained incomplete on the eve of its introduction. Two-and-a-half-years later, some items of legislation still remained to be implemented in every member state [1] Benign effects of the internal market which could have been expected in 1993–4, as Europe emerged from recession, were also discounted, possibly excessively, so that the arrival of '1993' appeared disappointing. Nevertheless, the real gains from the internal market made by industrial and financial players, together with fears that political and social discord would upset what they had striven for since the early 1980s, led many major companies and their federations to dissociate themselves from the general anti-Commission, anti-Maastricht, anti-EMU tirades in 1993–5. From the business perspective, a period of consolidation was required, time to react to the opportunities in research and deregulation of industries; not a new vision and certainly not another contentious IGC in 1996. Differences about long-term strategy therefore grew between the business players, most of whom saw the Commission as on their side, in the context of the 1993 White Paper and its sequel, and their governments, who were increasingly caught up in the very different social and political questions opened up in the early 1990s.

The Commission Presidency's *cellule de prospective* had already undertaken a series of enquiries in each member state about the conditions which would affect business once the internal market opened on 1 January 1993. Its findings included major social trends such as ageing, the problem of providing public services and the consequences of prolonged high unemployment, as well as cultural difficulties, such as the need to maintain diversity in an increasingly homogeneous Europe. Slow economic growth, increased external competition and the danger of trade wars between the three major trading blocks dominated the economic agenda; the failure of consensus in the Council of Ministers and serious problems on the EU's eastern, south-eastern and southern borders, the political one.

But the report identified two further problems in the EU itself: firstly, a lack of momentum, caused by the break-up of consensus among governments, the Commission's post-Maastricht subordination and the need of business players for a long period of consolidation; and secondly, a pervasive malaise in political life, something beyond the so-called 'democratic deficit'. The fault lay not with the failure to install subsidiarity, since no one could properly define what was implied, but rather with governments' weakness to implement even what had already been decided, let alone fulfil the promises made by all twelve to their increasingly disillusioned electorates.

After the often-acerbic and prolonged negotiations with EFTA countries for the European Economic Area, the accession round in 1993–4 turned out to be easier than had been predicted. But hopes that all the EFTA members would come in had already ended when the Swiss voted not to proceed with the EAA. Internal opposition, mostly from rural areas and more from women voters than men, ensured that the subsequent referenda would be closely fought in Austria, Finland and Sweden and that Norway would vote against as it had done in 1972. British ministers almost prejudiced the outcome by insisting, unsuccessfully, that despite the numbers of new entrants, the exisiting blocking minority on the council should remain. Yet Britain was also a leading exponent of admitting applicants from central Europe: Poland, Czech Republic, Hungary and perhaps Slovakia. Wide differences between them, however, in their performance according to Western economic criteria, indicated that they were unlikely to be admitted as a collective; and the assurances that the German government above all sought to give them only began to evolve in the years between the Summits at Edinburgh (1992) and Essen (1994).

Within the EU, rivalry between member states and the Commission continued into the Presidency of Jacques Santer; but several of the most serious post-Maastricht engagements resolved themselves or were resolved during Delors's last two years; above all the long and contentious GATT round which was finally, under the Balladur government, accepted by its most dedicated opponent France, thanks at least in part to pressure from the German side of the entente. Trends in the Commission's approval of state aids, particularly to the embattled national airlines of France, Spain, Portugal, Belgium and Greece unfortunately suggested that competition policy had been tempered to member state advocacy more than would have been admitted in the prime of Commissioners Sutherland and Brittan (1984–92), at least in the fields of civil aviation, telecoms and energy supply.

Less obvious problems also surfaced in the informal agreements made between national governments and corporate players on how to handle aspects of the internal market or environmental problems. That these, and the large numbers of new ones being planned in 1994–5, constituted new trade barriers had already been exposed by German and Danish arrangements under the packaging area; yet since they did not require notice to the Commission under the Information Directive, the Commission seemed likely to have to resort to novel means of restraint.[2]

Finally, member states' own alignments shifted in the light of domestic changes; Germany's elections, which sharply reduced Kohl's majority and weakened the 1994 German Presidency; Mitterrand's terminal illness, announced months before the French Presidential election in April–May 1995 and the revival of Gaullism under his successor, Chirac; the collapse of the Berlusconi government in Italy; and the travails of the Gonzalez government in Spain, assailed by the exposure of widespread corruption. In spite of schemes for Franco-German cooperation during their two Presidencies in 1994–5 the efforts came entirely from the German side, in particular the CDU. After the Corfu Summit, July 1994, when their joint candidate for the Commission Presidency, Jean-Luc Dehaene was vetoed, tension seemed to grow inside that entente.

All this added to the number of sensitive subjects piling up for the next 1996 IGC under the Presidencies of the Netherlands and Luxembourg. Since it is impossible to conceive of an IGC actually failing, or stalling in disorder, the likelihood is that after much struggle, ultimately between Germany and Britain, a more modest agenda will be set, and very large issues delayed. The existence of multiple speeds will become more evident, informally if not formally, and the concept of *unicité*, the unity of the temple, will decay. Until the member states resolve the crisis of identity which currently afflict all the five big states and the majority of smaller ones, it seems inconceivable that the European Union can experience another *rélance* like the decade-long revival which began in the early 1980s.

PART TWO

FORCES

It is the dealing between political, industrial and financial players in the extended, informal area of the European Community's political economy which provides the main focus of this book. The formal, Treaty-based side, prescribes the rights and duties of what are canonical institutions: the Commission, the Parliament, the Court of Justice, together with specially-created forums such as the Economic and Social Committee (Ecosoc) and the Committee of Regions, which appear in the next four chapters. But each of these, like the member states from which they derive their powers, functions and public legitimacy, has an informal aspect which suffuses their relationships with each other and with the non-governmental players in the game.

Constitutions prescribe how things will be done according to formulae which are justiciable. But few imagine that they do more than define the boundaries of legitimate action. The infilling is frequently a matter of informal politics. Builders who interpret the plans drawn by constitutional architects find their own ways to modify them as circumstances dictate. They discover for themselves that outside the ideal cosmos, prime movers vanish in the day-to-day search for competitive advantage. So it is with the EC's range of players, of different orders, status and capacity, as they express their inherent competition in ever-shifting patterns of rivalries and alliances.

Insofar as the word 'player' can ever sum up this aggregation of individuals, institutions and corporations, or indeed member states, it embraces a range of motives from the most obvious self-interest to awareness of the sort of Europe other players desire – if it did not, there would be no point in each seeking a European Union presence. EU institutions, on the other hand, have a prime duty to define Europeanness. But among them, primacy is contested between the Council, the Commission and the Parliament, while authority to adjudicate a question of law is reserved ultimately for the European Court.

Of these rivalries, the primordial tension lies between the Commission, which guards jealously its right to initiate policy and legislation, and the twelve – now fifteen – member states. Although that right was laid down in the Treaty of Rome, ever since the 'empty chair' crisis in 1966 it has been the subject of competition between them, on the Council's side to curtail the Commission's aspirations, and on the Commission's to gain more precise and far-reaching application. Advantage sways to and fro over decades. Dormant at times when the Commission was most beleaguered, largely absent during the mid–1980s euphoria, Council-Commission antagonism re-emerged in the context of Delors II, the Maastricht IGCs, and the subsequent years of pessimism and disillusion when rancour spread among the twelve to create serious doubts whether some member states willed any further progress.

No picture of the EU could therefore be attempted without assessing how these two sets of basic players engage across the whole front of legislative, managerial and political activity. But since both are and always were conditioned, domestically and at the European level, by other players outside government – firms, banks or financial institutions, trades unions, and all their sectoral and peak organizations – these too must be included, together with relatively new players, such as the more self-assertive regions.

Each one has its range of motivations, since it represents its own or its members' self-interest, but within a European context which requires it to play according to certain rules or conventions. Searching for advantage, threatened or constrained by others, and by their own dependency on national, European and global markets, reaching out to new dimensions in the media and the capture of public opinions, faced with choices of strategy and of where to apply leverage, they find themselves in a highly political market regulated at one and the same time by EU law, informal rules and conventions, and the balance of power at any given time.

There is no ideal measure from which to deduce the relative weight each ought to be given: regions, for example, are in practice widely different and cannot simply be willed to coequality because the Maastricht Treaty provided for a Committee of Regions; neither can small firms easily be given facilities by the responsible Commission Directorate (DG23) to compete for political space with the giants. The Treaties seek to give proportionate weight to member states in the Council of Ministers, as well as appropriate numbers of MEPs; but small states and large states, whatever their formal position, have widely different aims and their effective powers change over time, according to their domestic political situation. Tensions and competition between them are normal, but particularly sensitive in the Community context because the polity is still too new for dissent about the share of power under its constitution fully to have been accepted and internalized by each.

Yet it does not appear that the EU has been a zero sum game; rather the reverse, since all sorts of players have been prepared to compromise and accept a higher interest (while at the same time striving to inject their own version of the EU interest into the endless series of discussions). Member states have usually, in the long run, been prepared to accept that nothing moves without an organizing principle provided by Community institutions which on their own they could hardly or only sporadically supply. In the last resort, progress depends on trading advantage. But in the troughs and hollows between waves of enthusiasm, when self- interest flourishes, the players stall, obfuscate or obstruct. Momentum falls off again until threats (such as foreign competition) force them once more to comply.

The Commission

The Commission's aim, in the simplest terms, is to confound Engel's view of history that the product of many separate wills is something that no one willed; and to ensure instead that some part of what each player desires is met. It must search for the elements of a general will and define it where it does not already exist, and lead mutually antagonistic players to accept commonalty in Community aims and ideals, on the assumption that its members continue to accept the Treaties as the best available means of achieving what they want. It is, at heart, an Enlightenment artefact, based on the triumph of rationality over the molten magma of human chaos.

But what makes it move (because, despite all the blockages, like Galileo's earth, *eppur si muove*)? The original Treaties, (unlike Rousseau's, a legal social contract) are now very distanced, having been created in a different era, part of a conjuncture which can never be repeated. Fear and greed provide traditional answers, the Hobbesian nightmare of unrestricted rivalry in which European states discovered that after World War I, despite the influence of the United States, they could only make general agreements that would stand for a matter of four or five years after the Paris Peace Conference. Even in the 1950s, Europe was not a United States, ripe in its eighteenth-century experience for a constitution drafted by a like-minded body of Enlightenment gentlemen. Neither have its nations been able to rely collectively on the muscular flexibility of American political institutions in the nineteenth and early twentieth centuries. The European experience has instead resembled Alice in Wonderland trying to play croquet with flamingoes.

The interplay between member states in the Council of Ministers and the Commission illustrates the two aspects of an endless rivalry of discourses. But whereas the states meet as formal equals, and have evolved comparable systems for coordinating and representing their interests in the Community, the Commission is a single entity built on three levels: the college of Commissioners and the President of the Commission, the seventeen (now twenty) individual Commissioners, and a varying number of Directorates General (at present twenty-four, since the addition of a consumer affairs Directorate in 1995).

Looking from a different perspective, of the 17,000-odd officials which compose it, perhaps 1500 constitute a mandarin elite of policy-makers or policy-mongers, headed by the twenty-four Directors General who are responsible to 'their' Commissioners; their activities in turn are coordinated and to some degree managed by the Commission President. Whether or not this elite can be seen as the source for an emerging European political class, or merely as the expression in institutional terms of separate national political traditions, needs to be asked, as does the question of whether the Commission can act as the executive of Community projects in default of what the fifteen members fail to do, or whether the pattern of their rivalry is so confusing that one cannot establish a general rule.

I. *The Centre of the Centre*

Nothing in the EEC/EC/EU's history leads one to imagine that there is a single centre of power or master of the game. There may not even be a 'centre of the centre' (to use Gramsci's phrase) within the Commission, for Presidents have differed and power is not necessarily transferable. In any case, depending on the players' standpoints, the location of the hypothetical 'centre' varies. But in recent times, under Jacques Delors, as at the beginning when Walter Hallstein was President, there was a particular concentration of informal power at the Commission's geographical centre. Whether it will continue under his successor, Jacques Santer, remains to be seen.

In the long argument about the influence of individuals in history, it is important to distinguish between the power conferred by appointment to an office and the powers added or subtracted by the individual during tenure. Roy Jenkins's establishment of the President's right to speak for the EC, as Giscard d'Estaing saw, could be put to greater (though undesirable in Giscard's eyes) use in the future, as it was during Delors's decade. This in turn offered chances to a vigorous far-sighted President which were not available to Delors's weaker predecessor Gaston Thorn. Yet beyond the bare facts that the President is chairman of the college of Commissioners, aided by the Secretariat General and the Legal and other services, and acts as the Commission's representative to the Council of Ministers and its Presidency, the formal aspect reveals only that there exists a substantial area of informality which he can exploit. What matters, from his appointment until the transfer of powers to his successor, lies in the interstices.

The appointment itself is in the hands of heads of government, with all the blindness of chance conveyed by twelve sets (in 1994) of domestic preoccupations and reactions to EC-wide alliances. Delors was not an obvious choice in 1984, nor is it obvious why Margaret Thatcher voted for him. Jean-Luc Dehaene in 1994 had Franco-German backing and the assent of most others, yet his candidature fell to a British veto because of fears that as skilled an operator as the Belgian prime minister might be able to assume Delors's full mantle. The final appointment, Jacques Santer, was no member state's first choice.

The fact that governments of whatever ideology in small or large, northern or Mediterranean states should, by convention, agree or at least accept the final outcome, tends to ensure that the successful nomination will be someone few would have put as their first choice – though this has rarely been so clearly demonstrated as in the latter case. Until the dispute at the Corfu Summit, July 1994, the decision tended to reflect what the Franco-German entente – or Schmidt and Giscard – had decided between them. It is possible that inflation of quality has occurred: in 1976 and 1980 there were only three likely candidates,[1] whereas in 1994, several serving prime ministers had their hats in the ring. But conditions generally militate against the candidature of anyone with notable talents or identified with a leading programme, or of the 'wrong' nationality. Even afterwards, these constrain the new President who would be wise, for the first six months (like Delors in 1984–5) to consult the member states, sell the result to the Parliament, balance the Commission appointments, and work very hard in comparative obscurity.

The President's job is to represent the Commission and to keep the college together, and is expressed in what he chooses to expound in public speeches. Probably his most urgent role is to keep the show on the road[2] in the direction given by successive generations' interpretation of the Treaties. He need not have a master plan, his leadership can be passive (as were those of Rey, Malfatti, Ortoli and Thorn – Mansholt was only briefly in office). He certainly does not command a great machine. In a normal four-year tenure, given the lack of time and formal powers, media exposure and member states' countervailing tactics, it has been hard to construct a controlling group inside the Commission – indeed perhaps only Hallstein and Delors have ever tried. One measure of success must therefore be how effectively the President fits with the college, which is the collective Commission organ, and the key Directors General, to provide a working majority for the Commission as a whole, sufficient to deny member states the chance to split what is by nature an ill-assorted congeries of Directorates whose functions, even in the late 1980s, were imprecisely distinguished. Wherever qualified majority voting does not obtain, the opposition of a single nation can defeat a united Commission. However skilful Roy Jenkins's leadership was, he could not have established the EMS in 1978–9 without a political lead from both Schmidt and Giscard.

This is a roundabout way of saying that Delors's three terms 1985–95 have re-established the Presidency in a way not known since the historically remote case of Walter Hallstein, an equally determined but rather more dogmatic figure. Delors was able to set both short- and medium-term agendas without loss of coherence or momentum, and to imbue both with a long-term philosophy capable of surviving the severe post-Maastricht depression (as Hallstein failed to do in 1967). The recipe lay in an ethic of dedicated work (for there was no remission, no study leave, and very little holiday); a blend of knowledge, energy and conviction constantly refreshed by an expanding torrent of new ideas, and an ability to give conceptual substance to the Community even in times of disarray (witness his reiterated statement that it had 'the wrong mix between economics and society').[3] But while those qualities explain the good years to 1990, when the Commission's de facto capacity to intervene, even to lead member states, was generally accepted, for a complete picture one needs to add the skills of retreat and defence in depth, to account for the survival of so much of his grand design through the dark period 1992–4.

All would-be leaders depend on mobilizing disparate groups, and have to use a full keyboard of roles from Yogi to Commissar. While the Commission as a whole performs the tasks of information search, reflection, and bargaining with other players as preliminaries to evolving policy, only the President together with the Secretary General and the head of the Legal Service has a picture of the whole activity. Delors gave a public lead, partly through influence with the rotating member-state Presidencies, partly by declaratory speeches to the Parliament and partly through television interviews. But his leadership within the Commission was couched more often in Delphic hints, to be interpreted by his cabinet and given flesh in prolonged bouts of argumentation between them and the Commissioners' chefs du cabinets, whose job it is to test the general line within the organization.

Delors may have seemed an *éminence grise* to British observers, unused to how a top-flight, French-trained administrator works, because he chose to be so, as Père Joseph was to Cardinal Richelieu. The historical analogy is fair, for though Delors was far from unique among bureaucrats brought up in the Christian Democratic or Christian Socialist traditions, he guarded a particularly strong moral and ethical element, based on his own experience as a lay Catholic intellectual, sensitive to the Jansenist tradition as well as that of the 1891 Papal encyclical *De Rerum Novarum*, without losing a socialism more associated with Mendés-France's organic outlook on society than French socialist dogmatism. Yet he remained abstracted, more interested in ideas than most members of his chosen protective cabinet shell, drawn from trusted, normally French, officials like Pascal Lamy and François Lamoureux. This vision sought to extend legal boundaries on a grand scale, very different from most politicians' pragmatic immediacy. He disliked open conflict and reacted with some difficulty to the reverses after Maastricht, having been too long protected from obvious failure. He preferred to marginalize aggressive Commissioners, and to fix matters indirectly through their cabinet chefs. On the other hand, as Jean Rey did with Mansholt and his agriculture plan, and as all successful leaders must, Delors relied on individual Commissioners like Natali for support; he let Arthur Cockfield have his head with the single market White Paper, and eventually, after disputing nearly every case, did the same with Leon Brittan over competition policy.

All Presidents have to accept the Hallstein lesson that, like Popes, they have no legions to confront member states head-on and must therefore persuade or catch them with silken nooses. But in addition, Delors's Presidency was characterized by the creation of an epidermis, sensitive and protective as skin itself to outside forces, and a complementary set of personal modes of action: Chairman of the college, interlocutor between the Directors, coordinator of information, and administrator of a bureaucracy which was and is by comparison with most member state administrations, under-staffed and inordinately overstretched. Informally, his role ranged from overall shaping of the legislative process to inducting newly appointed officials, and covered fields which under Santer's tenure may be reassigned, such as senior promotions in the Directorates (formerly the purview of the Secretary General) or the coordination of Commissioners' own cabinets.

Although Delors's two and a half terms have been criticized, it was the second which became the subject of greatest hostility by member states. Within the Commission, views have been more nuanced, varying from dislike to veneration, depending on the standpoint and political culture of the observer: few, if any, have denied his mastery of administrative techniques or his capacity to compose a harmonic ideal from apparently discordant strands.

Insiders assert that Delors suffered the misrepresentation common when outsiders assess very complicated institutions. What seemed biased or temperamental to one set of observers may represent long-term subtlety to another. But there is enough evidence to suggest that, although manipulative (witness his interference with Ray McSharry's conduct of GATT negotiations), his Presidency was rarely irresponsible or short-sighted. Many of his alleged Florentine manoeuvres were designed to ensure that, though in any bargain there will always be losers, there need be no wholesale slaughter. (For example, when German investment in Portuguese industry during the EC's late-1980s support programme seemed likely to push Portugal above the limit of regional funding under Objective One, he advised the college not to pursue the letter of the law and rescind so useful a programme prematurely.)[4] 'No partner, players, region or sector should suffer excessively; subsidiarity is a concept for the EC as a whole, not for member states themselves.'[5]

Insofar as it is the Commission's duty to stand guardian for, as well as to interpret, the Treaties, Delors's responsibility seems to have been to define what states, being members, ought properly to desire. From that derived phrases such as 'I have twelve countries to manage',[6] with its conscious reference to civil services with long national administrative traditions who see their art as managing democracy. Delors's method was to put others through the same logical process as himself, rather as Neville Chamberlain did with his cabinets.

The practice of lucid and didactic discourse – its insistence on collectivity and the balance of rights and obligations between more and less powerful entities – invested with ethical overtones and almost monastic style, could be deduced from Delors's background. His technocratic, self-tutored formation, his early experience in the office of the Plan and the Banque de France did not conform to the classic *grandes écoles* route, neither did his membership of the European Parliament, or his tenure as minister of finance in the crucial year 1983. His Catholic background made him sympathetic to moderate Christian Democrats in Germany, Belgium and Italy, especially those critical of free market ideology, hence his close link and strong working connections with Kohl rather than Mitterrand.

In practical orientation Delors was always better versed in financial matters than industrial ones, and he lacked the broad international background of a Hallstein. A combination of intellectual rigour and powerful feelings about balance in society prevented him from understanding Thatcher, who appeared to be an aberration, acceptable in an American but not a European context. He lacked natural allies, despite his links with the Paris administration, but he made a virtue of this by running in parallel a series of transnational networks and personal links – which enabled him, for example, in the two years before Maastricht, and again in 1993–4, to set large sections of what became the Council's agenda. (A fluent German speaker, he took care to throw the Commission's weight behind the West German government during reunification with East Germany to the point of helping to provide EC finance, which in turn – as chapter 5 suggested – assisted Mitterrand and France's political class to accept the outcome as inevitable.) He also used his power to appoint national nominees to particular offices in the college to marginalize or cut down Commissioners whom he could not exclude – putting Vasso Papandreou and Manuel Marin to the periphery and depriving Bruce Millan (DG16) of responsibility for cohesion funds.

Like Commissioners, the President has a small margin of manoeuvre in favour of 'the country he knows best'. It is doubtful if Delors overstepped this on behalf of France as often as was alleged, save in the cases where governments leaned directly on him, as they did often in cases of state aid (see chapter 11), or in the financial sphere (Britain's exit from the ERM (see p. 537) and the loan to Greece. All Commissioners are likely to be telephoned in contentious cases, but over Renault's state aids repayment[7] and Spain and Italy's steel subsidies, some bias did intrude. As Frans Andriessen put it, 'There is only a college if there is collegiality'; however, during Delors II, it frequently appeared as if the President was acting 'on behalf of the shareholders', in the Philips/KLM and Air France/Scania deals for example, in order to reduce Dutch or French unemployment. Yet bias is a relative concept and such cases need to be compared with equally corrupt bargains among members states particularly from the Mediterranean.

A Commission President who aspires to give even indirect leadership will arouse hostility, especially if he has personal quirks such as a fondness for 'traditional hunting methods' or an innate mistrust of the Anglo-Saxon approach, allied to a marked distaste for the majority of British Conservative ministers after 1981.[8] Yet alien and self-indulgent as Delors conceived Britain to be, he seems never to have imagined it other than as part of the Community.

No President of the Commission stands alone, but surrounded by a cabinet of his own choice and Commissioners in posts of his choice. Gaston Thorn had to be a broker, given Davignon's more commanding status, while Jenkins opted for an inner group; neither was able to create the elaborate 1980s apparatus. Delors was fortunate in having Cockfield and Natali in key posts early on. The team may have been weaker in his second term, despite the presence of Andriessen, Bangemann and Brittan, partly because of divisions between the latter pair in an otherwise harmonious college; it was restored by the more united quadrumvirate van den Broek, Brittan, van Miert and Bangemann in Delors III. But he could ensure that his cabinet contained a remarkable array of talent throughout the decade even if the majority of them were drawn from France. (He chose, for example, Jerome Vignon to run the *cellule de prospective* or think-tank, and put Jean-Charles Leygues, Lamoureux's successor in 1991, in charge of the industrial dossier.) The formal Secretariat and Legal Services, whose main purpose for the President is to provide neutral support and ensure legality, were also supplemented by informal contacts with protagonists in each Directorate, notably in DGs 1, 2 and 3.

As well as being an organization in its own right, the Secretariat is a vital adjunct to keep the college in hand, and to prevent individual Commissioners or Directors General going their own ways. Some subjects are peculiarly sensitive, and hard to assign to any one Commissioner: hence the practice of 'donating' specially contentious matters like the cohesion funds, or the final stages of EFTA admission in 1993 to the Secretary General, at that time an English official, David Williamson. The Secretariat is also vital in helping to spread the load and legitimate it; it had acquired a significant profile during the thirty years when Emil Noël held the post. Noël's voice was in fact often decisive in meetings of the college, and always important where internal promotions were concerned. But Delors allowed Williamson much less say on promotions, so that the role concentrated more on harmonizing the transaction of business as if he were a British cabinet secretary. Commissioners and Directors General cannot be ordered about like ministers under a Napoleonic or presidential system.

As a result, what was lost (temporarily) on one side, has been made up on another. In 1995, the Secretariat is probably stronger than it was ten years earlier, for instance in activity as chair to the External Affairs triumvirate. The fact that even a President as apparently powerful as Delors had to place himself in the hands of the services, whose ethos of loyalty is to concepts fundamental to the house including 'the duty of proper service and furtherance of good government'[9] (without which the college itself might disintegrate), indicates the tenuous nature of his power, and how little of it may be transferable to his successor.

Outside the Commission buildings – distributed across a swathe of central Brussels – range non-concentric circles of advice and acquaintance. For a time in 1984–5, Delors used the European Round Table as a whole, but later relied on a few, selected from its members. Such contacts no doubt added insights but could be misinterpreted: Delors's interpretation of Giovanni Agnelli's advice about the Social Charter 1989–90 may have hinted at more approval than a wider circle of industrialists would offer later.

There are few precedents in this unpoliced terrain. Members of the college act as seems best, each with his or her own concept of the EU's interest. Rules are no more than current practice which varies according to the times and the membership. Some Commissioners and some Presidents become benchmarks during their term of office and this was the case with Cockfield – massively knowledgeable and self-evidently fair – whereas Vasso Papandreou lost credibility through being partial and argumentative, and became a byword for what was unacceptable.

In the creation of an effective network of influence, a President's cabinet and his organizing methods will always be central. His cabinet should (as Delors's did) provide intelligence from all points of the Commission and the means to regulate business and weekly college meetings, beginning with the preparatory conclaves of chefs du cabinet (a point at which proposals either go forward or fail, lacking substantial prior agreement). During most of Delors' tenure, Pascal Lamy played the role of animator and interlocutor between Commissioners' cabinets and Directors General (often taking a more extreme position to give Delors greater flexibility later on); not necessarily at the start of a policy but as soon as it became salient. Lamy could also, as sherpa to the G7 group of nations for example, carry medium-term strategy, like the 1993 White Book plans for industrial and employment recovery, to a wider arena. By monitoring, husbanding and coordinating the Commission's general work through its weekly agenda, Delors's large and intensely hard-working cabinet[10] in effect gave him control of the college agenda and, indirectly, much of the work undertaken by Commissioners' own cabinets.

The intricate details of this system, where individual loyalty was less to the patron than to the EC cause,[11] do not belong here. Its aim was firstly to mobilize agreement among as many Commissioners as possible and to prevent them chasing hares beyond the set overall policy; secondly, it was designed to get as much business prepackaged as possible, leaving only the hard questions for the college; and thirdly, to give a discreetly-veiled political steer downwards to officials in the Directorates. Its net effect has been substantially to reduce diversity of action among Directorates and to increase momentum across the whole Commission, as had been envisaged by the Treaty's signatories in 1957. But to achieve the coordination necessary to produce successively the Single European Market, the Delors II proposals for Maastricht and the *rélance* in 1993 required a fiendishly complicated set of informal practices, with new links continually added to remedy weaknesses as they emerged.[12]

The physical and human geography of the Commission, however, resists change. It took a decade even to start rationalizing 'external affairs' under DGs 1 and 1A in 1992–4 (which was then reorganized under Santer), just as it required fifteen years to mould DG3 (industry) to cope with the internal market. Although DG4 (competition) had teeth from the beginning, through the land mark decisions by the ECJ in 1962–3, another twenty-five years was required to turn it into an effective instrument capable of taking on member states in the area of state aids. Nevertheless Delors's informal networks facilitated a degree of controlled planning previously inconceivable in a loose, fissile and often discordant Commission. Collectivity rather than fiefdoms, cooperation not trade-offs weighed more heavily in 1994 than in 1984. But personal rivalries flourish still, as was demonstrated by the challenges for Delors's post made in 1994 by a number of contenders who resembled angry samurai. Even after Santer emerged as the survivor-victor, Leon Brittan and van den Broek continued the struggle over who should have central and eastern Europe in his portfolio.

Formally, though the concept of a President's overview means no more than the conduct of the college chair, drawing threads together, informally it involves influence over the agenda, the conduct and order of debate, the powers of presentation and summing up (although a Commissioner can *insist* on a point being included). Few major issues between 1985 and 1995 were not presented by Delors in person to the Council of Ministers or deliberated according to his formulations.

The patent need to keep collegial a college composed of seventeen national nominees with politicians' egos and rival policies tends in any case to require from the President expertise in mitigating quarrels or healing scars. But without Delors's tightly controlled overview, momentum might well have fallen off after the Single European Act, so that the wider agenda might have been lost before Hannover, let alone Maastricht, as poorer states clamoured for cohesion money to make the deal worthwhile, and as member states' trades unions took up the Commission's Social Chapter as if it had been a guarantee against the dominance of industry and the financial triangle of Frankfurt-London-Paris. Without Delors's leadership, it is hard to imagine that the Community could have reacted as quickly as it did to events in eastern Europe in 1989, before and during the Paris Summit, or engaged itself in lending and providing know-how through Community support schemes Phare, Tacis and the rest.

Setting the agenda for the Maastricht IGC during Delors's second term seemed to abolish the diversity – or rather vacillation – that had existed in Thorn's day. That Delors judged it necessary to set such a pace must be read as the necessary counterweight to member states' own diversity or lack of interest. But it was resented, not only by national politicians. Industrialists were to be found in 1991–2 complaining that Commission plans 'were being defended and fought for' in contrast to the early period of open dialogue. Delors found it expedient to reveal a penitential face after Maastricht, when sub-groups opened up discussion on subjects such as Japanese competition or 'the EC and Russia in Europe'. But at the centre, in tribute to the legitimacy created by past success, the college held together throughout, being aware 'that the Commission could not work unless it represents the general interest, which Delors exemplifies. The alternative is suicide.'[3]

None of this occurred in secret. The Commission is a far more transparent body than the Council or most national governments and it would have been impossible to conceal informal manoeuvres, given that Delors's cabinet members sat behind the Commissioners in the Council meetings. Nevertheless, despite the clear advantages it brought, his style of management created resentments and concern about 'control'. From outside the Commission, the President's apparatus seems to resemble the Treasury in all national capitals, a vast fortress, looming over the whole bureaucracy; but from inside it is seen to be merely a small blockhouse manned by a few against the unfriendly hordes outside.

Unlike any previous President, Delors had time to create an informal organization (not a machine) which enabled him to know, survey and influence a far wider range of business than any of his predecessors. Its limits ought therefore to be pointed out: above all the difficulties of allowing for reflection about long-term trends (characteristic of all cabinet governments), and of ensuring continuity once the originator retired. In an attempt to meet the first, Delors set up the *cellule de prospective*, whose reports on the internal market's effects and the linkage between industrial, trade and technology policy were intended to shape the agenda after

1993. Whether the system lives on with sufficient vigour to be as effective under his successor is impossible to gauge. It is hard as yet to imagine all Delors's intellectual capital, and the charisma which ensured his treatment as an equal, albeit of a different order, in the European Council, being transferred to Jacques Santer.

The centre of the centre is a variable quantity, dependent ultimately on an individual, over whose appointment member states hold sway. Delors's appointment in 1984 may have owed something to coincidence. But that he presided over the Single European Act, the hydraheaded internal market, the Maastricht Union Treaty and the *rélance* after, should be attributed to his willpower in the difficult first two terms, the system he created, and the degree to which he extended the Commission's external role. Insofar as he sought power too much (as he himself admitted in elegiac mood) and forgot about 'leading without leading and being seen', his organizational legacy may have been impaired. The proof, like much else in the EU, will be seen in how the next generation of Commissioners under a President who is a natural arbiter, rather than a leader, interpret and implement the unwritten rules he left behind.

II. *The College*

As the outside world tends to see it, the Commission consists of the seventeen – now twenty – individual Commissioners and the college they constitute, usually represented in public by their President. Formally, the latter must fulfil three principal duties: to guard the Treaties, to initiate legislation (whether proposed by member states, Directorates or the Parliament), and to manage the spheres directly assigned to it by the Treaties, such as the Common Agricultural Policy, the Regional and Social Funds, and the internal market. None of these is simply demarcated: the legislative initiative, though legally clear enough, is continually under siege from the Council and individual states such as France and Britain for one set of reasons, Germany for another.[14] Member states administer the Funds' expenditure and oversee the Community's regional projects, and all players contest the guardianship role. Tensions also exist with the Parliament, though the majority of disagreements come over legitimate differences of policy, as in July 1994, when the Parliament voted down proposals for liberalizing the European telecoms markets, despite the tenor of Article 90. Each corner of this disputatious triangle tends therefore to overplay its hand to obtain the minimum it really wants.

Because the practicalities of jurisdiction have never been finally settled, the Commission can hardly be called a *Rechtsstaat*. Being a multilateral, non-sovereign body, relatively open and transparent, its functions could in theory be sub-divided into the *technical* aspects of preparing legislation or policy measures (research, synthesis, editing of legal texts, consultation among interests and technical experts); and their *political* implications (brokerage between interests and officials, prepackaging policies for the college, transactions with the Council). But in practice the two are inextricably entwined, so that there can be no final resolution of opinion about the Commission among member states between those, like the Netherlands, Belgium or Italy who would prefer it to be the Community's prime mover, and Britain, France, Germany or Spain who wish its political dimension reduced.

Such tensions affect the behaviour of individual Commissioners in the balance they hold between their national identity and their oath of impartiality between states. They extend through their cabinets, and permeate the Directorates below.[15] After whatever secret soundings governments – or rather the prime ministers and foreign ministers who usually take charge – choose to take, member states nominate Commissioners, two for each large state, one for small, as they do the President. Any assumption that the college will somehow reflect a European average is therefore conjectural, depending on twelve–fifteen sets of national party balances and the interplay of merit, availability and Buggins's turn. A sort of Darwinism may be in operation, as it is with the President's post: whereas in the 1970s the field was small, even in large states, competition has increased steadily into the 1990s thanks to the job's higher status and the clearly unfavourable results for a state of making a second-rate nomination. But the field is still mainly confined to politicians of the governing parties, or ex-ministers for whom there is no longer a space in domestic political life. Nominations depend on heads of governments' personal choice and sometimes whim.[16] But the European Parliament has now taken up its rights under Maastricht to question them individually before they take up their post, and its vigorous conduct of this examination in January 1995 seems to have ensured that future nominations will at least come better briefed.

Having nominated their Commissioner, member states' power is in theory expended, cut short by his or her quite formidable oath not 'to take instructions'. The Commission President guards the right to allocate portfolios, for the best of which there has always been sharp competition. In 1994–5 Santer's dilemma of finding suitable posts for all twenty became almost intolerable and prejudiced logical demarcation. Heads of government have frequently intervened: Margaret Thatcher ensured that the single market job went to Cockfield and recommended Brittan for competition (but failed to get the post that Tugendhat wanted), while Genscher intervened to give Brunner the energy portfolio in 1977. When Cheysson left, Mitterrand insured that Pisani went to DG8. When Gundelach died, Denmark insisted that he was succeeded by Dalseger. In fact these are exceptions, but important ones, and in some areas a sort of prescriptive right exists, so that although the informal convention requires that no large member state may ever occupy the post of Agriculture Commissioner because the dossier is so sensitive, there has normally been a French Director General. Such *chasses gardées*, of which development (DG8) is a case in point, long Cheysson's fiat, run with a bias towards Francophone Africa, do not necessarily attract the best candidates. Insofar as they exist, conventions may easily be broken. It is normal that no Commissioner serves two terms in the same post, yet a French Commissioner remained at DG2 from 1964 to 1984 and a German in DG3 for nearly as long. It is up to each President to assess which are the key roles during his term, and to trade them among a field over whose composition he has had no say, in order to get the best, least disruptive, service for the college.

What briefing a Commissioner gets has remained in the President's hands. Before 1984, this was rarely regular or consistent, but in November/December of that year, before launching the internal market initiative, Delors held a series of preparatory seminars for his new appointees at Royaumont Abbey near Paris. Even so, it was never in his power to insist on how a Commissioner would conceive his or her role, only to manage their collective view within the college. Commissioners bring to the job what sense of mission they already have, to blend with or impose on the ethos of what become 'their' Directorates General. People in middle age with considerable political experience do not easily change their natures, simply because they swear 'not to take instruction'. Nevertheless it is curious that there are no signposts to the customs of the House. Commissioners find out by trial and error, discussing and doing. As Emile Noël pointed out 'there is no arch priest to instruct how things work. It is necessary to ask in the middle range . . . among heads of division about principles: these have knowledge, as it were, from the interior.'[17] But many more recent generations of Commissioners understand the system better, having already represented their member states in other capacities.

In a four- (now five-) year tenure, Commissioners have to come to terms with both the portfolio and the permanent officials, relegating national affinity to second place and party ideology to third. One of them from a large state declared that he saw himself partly as national by inclination – that is, aware of what action would mean for his nation – partly as European, but that in his decisions he would seek 'to advance Europe and his nation state within it, even if the former were uncomfortable for the latter'.[18] Some from the Benelux countries operate above the national political dimension almost entirely. Yet again, others respond passively to structural weakness or failures by their home governments to put up the best profile (a common explanation for the surprising failure of many German Commissioners to play a hand commensurate with their country's economic weight), or simply replicate domestic politics on the European stage. Vanni d'Archirafi's relaunch of the single market early in 1993 represented both a Commission tactic during the weak Danish Presidency and a personal attempt to recover Italy's prestige as a member state once the tide of corruption prosecutions rose against the old political regime.[19]

But the majority of Commissioners show themselves partisan from time to time, especially in the matter of state aids (where it was almost 'normal' in the late 1980s). Habitual defensiveness in the national interest by Commissioners risks alienating the college majority and making others more not less prepared to find a Commission-led compromise. Wiser Commissioners prefer not to set markers in their own country's interests, but to win over others likely to be affected further down the line – as it might be Italy or Spain where Fiat or Séat was concerned, some time after the Renault state aids case. Blatant assertion of national interest – Vasso Papandreou being nominated as a case in point – is self-defeating, leading to loss of credibility and marginal status. On the other hand, subtler tactics, followed ultimately by a willingness to compromise, can produce surprising gains: Spain has done very well since 1986 out of a sometimes scarcely veiled self-interest.

No Commissioner can expect to remain free of all pressures. It was a British Conservative cabinet minister who declared to one, 'we put you there and we expect you to deliver the goods' – but the statement could have come from half a dozen capital cities. Both Christopher Tugendhat and Arthur Cockfield were judged by Thatcher to have become too assimilated to particular Brussels viewpoints and were withdrawn.[20] But some are more beholden or vulnerable. The surprising thing is that more do not bend more often, for all Permanent Representatives send their governments' reviews of Commission projects to 'their' Commissioners. The practice is technically a breach of convention as well as the formal rules, but it serves as another useful informal link between a Commissioner and the outside world, since the national government will probably have done its homework well. The review's quality will count more when he makes his case to an ever-critical college than his degree of (probably well-known) obligation.

It is not obvious cheating which matters, although each member state has its own blacklist of Commissioners whom it believes cheat regularly, over matters ranging from energy subsidies and state aids for the steel industry to support for farmers. Cheating exists of course, but is partly obviated by the conventions of behaviour, for outrage creates its own reactions. The college, after all, decides by a simple majority, which tends to iron out unconventional practices: adversarial tactics become too predictable, unwelcome and thereby easier to defeat. A greater danger is that the college slips into bargaining the terms on which a member state, in breach of European law, might settle – yet this too has been turned to advantage, by Davignon during the late 1970s steel crisis and by Brittan and Delors, in unwilling association over competition policy in 1990–91. Structural funds' allocation and cases concerning state aids cause the only *regular* strong advocacy today.

National positions permeate in less direct ways, some of which may even be beneficial. It serves the Commission well, sometimes, to be steered away from unnecessary confrontations, by Commissioners versed in their own political cultures. A Commissioner, speaking of 'the country I know best', may warn, 'you proceed with this at your peril', to which others usually listen. Cockfield, who set a high standard by being harsh to his own nation state, warned against treating the design of London taxis as a barrier to trade: it no doubt was, but the outcome was not worth the battle. What seems the locus for national intrusion, such as Permanent Representatives' briefing of Commissioners and officials, may in fact be an informal two-way valve, through which the Commission's views and plans (backed by the complaints of subordinate players who have been tutored by the Commission as much as by national opinions), feed back to the governments which imagine it is they who wield the influence.

Aside from what they bring with them, Commissioners have a margin, like any minister, between active and passive acceptance of what their Directorates have in their pigeonholes. Unlike ministers, they are largely isolated from their national media and publics. Some activists go far beyond what is expected: in the case of competition policy, Andriessen, Sutherland and Brittan in succession uncovered the full force of what had been only latent in Articles 85 and 86. So, above all, did Cockfield with his internal market White Paper.

Patterns develop, suggesting that Mediterranean Commissioners tend to be hierarchical and less flexible than northerners, to use think-tanks less, and to launch initiatives without sustained bureaucratic preparation.[21] Small state Commissioners can play a high game and raise their country's profile in the process. Belgium was fortunate in having Davignon, the Netherlands in Mansholt and Andriessen, Ireland with Sutherland and McSharry. Small state Commissioners tend to have more affinity with Directorate officials (and they with them) than those from large states whose interests usually clash. The former will gain proportionately, given that all Commissioners are short of underpinning and time, and were often discouraged by Delors from acquiring powerful cabinets which they might turn into private fiefdoms.

Governments have their ministerial pecking orders, the unwritten table of precedence that runs from key to major to minor posts. In this sense, DGs 1, 2, 3 and 4 count for more than 9, 10, 11 and 12 during the preparatory stages of policy in all chefs du cabinet meetings. But in the college, each of the (now twenty) Commissioners has one vote only, and unless a proposal has eleven or more supporters it is barely worth putting to the Council. Key members of the college have therefore to balance weight (measured by portfolio repercussions) against numbers. The requirement to act together becomes in itself a guarantee against national excess or personal and departmental rivalry. To take the perennial division between DG3 (industry) and DG4 (competition): after recurrent disputes in 1989–90, Martin Bangemann and Leon Brittan evolved a *modus vivendi*, not primarily because of Delors's diplomacy but because, to convince the college majority, each had to learn enough of the other's case. Having gone through the intellectual exercise, and the bruising encounters with member states which followed, both came to accept a measure of common interest which has in turn infused the broader industry/competition/trade area (see chapter 12). Lines of such affinity or broader consensus, always reached after hard bargaining, prove more effective than inner groups or dominant Commissioners have done in the past.

Commissioners are put in charge of what until now have been fragmented fiefs, constructed to fit the existing array of individuals appointed rather than bureaucratic logic. They have then to confront problems of boundary definition, overlap and poaching. Boundaries can only be rectified with difficulty at the start of each new Commission every four–five years, so that the incentive to settle informally is strong. The alternative to alliance-building is to pile up proposals without firm majorities, as was done in the 1970s with harmonization directives unlikely to get through the Council. This is in no one's interest, particularly since the Commission's power and status wanes with failure, just as its momentum grows with successes. (As distinct from the Community as a whole, Commission success tends to be measured by proposals agreed in the Council and Parliament rather than their final implementation by member states' courts and administrations).

But the mobilizing of a college majority is rarely a simple matter, for Commissioners do not stand alone as individuals. They depend on their cabinets, without which they are isolated and likely to walk naked into the college. Each cabinet serves both as infrastructure for all college business and as a private office. But it also keeps a Commissioner in touch with member state politics, its parliament, and media comment, and may well act as a vehicle for personal advancement there.

Over time, the cabinets' significance has varied. In the 1970s, Directors General attended the chefs meeting, as if it were a sort of parliament, rather than a committee, and often found themselves subdued or even excluded from 'their' Commissioner. Delors abolished this practice to protect the functions of the Directors General and to bring Commission cabinets more under central surveillance. Mobilizing a majority now starts when proposals are near the top of Directorates, and depends not only on Commissioners' own diplomacy, but on the way the President's own team works through cabinets, chefs du cabinets and chefs specialisées. The sort of coordination which Delors constantly arranged (his cabinet and the Secretariat acting as advance guards for the college) certainly prevented the diversity which he feared would thrust the college back to the fruitless coalition-building of 1980–84. But the 1984–94 decade was one that encouraged common action: there might have been other, equally successful ways to harmonize the Commission's energies.

The balance between chefs and Directors General is itself conventional not formal. The former stand or fall with their

Commissioners, but their power to shape Commissioners' activity is as great in their own sphere as is that of the President's own chef, and is consequently often resented by long-serving Directors General. Chefs du cabinet also represent one means by which member state influence can permeate the college itself, as it does through promotions to Directors General, in which all national governments take a close interest. Here merit vies with ideological affinity, compliance and contacts: it is said that seven Directors General were dismissed during Delors's tenure and at the peak of Delors II in 1989 nineteen of the twenty-seven posts (or their service's equivalents) were held by nationals of the five largest states.[22]

National interest thus intrudes via procedures, as it does with personalities, especially in disputed cases where the Commission, having full competence, is the last court of appeal; it also appears in areas such as competition, or the regional geography of eligibility for structural assistance. One notable case occurred in 1993, when Padraig Flynn, the Irish Commissioner, spoke out in favour of his government's refusal to settle for a lesser allocation than had allegedly been promised from the structural fund's budget, against Bruce Millan, the Commissioner responsible for regions, DG16.

But these are, in the overall context, no more than significant exceptions, and are offset by an array of conventions (e.g., that no Commissioner can have a Director General of the same nationality) so complex and incremental that they have to be policed by the Secretariat. In any case, it is usually worth a member state's while to reserve its main fire for the next stage in the Council, and the lobbying of MEPs.

Reading out in the college a Permanent Representative's brief is a solecism that 'would be noted'. The constraints of peer review operate in what is an enforced *noyau*, whose members have no real social interchange, who work very long hours in enforced proximity and feed off endless corridor gossip. Since individual success is equated with proposals passed into law, personal ambition and European idealism lead equally to a politics of alliances, trade-offs and Florentine diplomatic manoeuvres. A Commissioner needs support not only from his cabinet and the relevant Director General but from the interest groups concerned who, if not consulted or squared along the way, will use every other available route to oppose, from their national capital and media to their MEPs.

The college is not yet a government, though it may in due course become a government without sovereignty. Neither is it a cabinet serving under a prime minister. Commissioners are too diverse by origin, language and function, too open to outside influences, too dependent on arbitration among officials and by the Commission President above, ever to acquire the natural loyalty that is supposed to exist in national cabinets. They are bound, however, by a common interest in the Commission's success and may become loyal to a conception of European interest if it is enunciated by a gifted President. Lacking that, they may settle for Thorn's 'somewhat folkloric arbitration', when 'Senatorial courtesy' proved a recipe for delay. Cockfield was only following normal practice in his decision to keep his 1985 White Paper close, giving time only for one full discussion in the college, hoping thus to avoid making major concessions before confronting the Council. The late 1980s and the 1990s have seen more votes and less courtesy. Yet the college is actually more coherent, even on matters of political cooperation (and despite the EU's experiences during the Gulf War and the Yugoslav civil war), than it was in the early 1980s thanks to a generally accepted opinion that without central coordination the Commission itself is stultified. In that sense, Delors's legacy has been institutionalized.

The Commission is also likely to be outflanked by the Council and the Parliament if it fragments. In the absence of precise legal delineation, Commission powers have continually to be safeguarded, and at the same time made palatable to the forces which would erode them – whether at the level of governments or national media and public opinion. Its influence rests on a capacity for intelligent listening, reflection, expertise, careful preparation of texts, without which power seeps away like mercury through clay jars. Leadership has become an endless game of innovation, where the options available to other players, such as secrecy, are rarely available (save in the matters of appointment and college votes), and where the Commission is popularly required to behave in a more upright way than member states, if only to counteract the obvious accusations that it is neither accountable nor democratic.

There is an understandable tendency for the college to remain discreetly anonymous, which member states have taken advantage of recently. They can then more easily take the hard decisions in the Council and, if criticized at home, blame the Commission. Since the Maastricht IGC, national media have, in their search for scapegoats, investigated more closely and, for lack of alternative, the Commission has had to accept this role. Delors's skilful use of television interviews, provided by networks eager to display controversy, may have given a sense of benign purpose to the Commission which has been emulated successfully by individual Commissioners on their national and other networks. But the success of their interventions in changing entrenched prejudices, say in France about state aids, in Italy on non-compliance with the internal market legislation, or in Britain about the threat to sovereignty, have been limited since they had no European public or media of their own to appeal to for support.

After the period of deep unpopularity after Maastricht, something of the earlier benign image was briefly restored with the 1993–4 programme for recovery, employment and labour market reforms. Given the Commission's open access to media players, which journalists enjoy, the programme's emphasis on social, environmental and cultural factors, and its comparatively simple programme for jobs and competitiveness, near enough to popular recollections of the Keynesian post-War era to be acceptable, it recovered some of the lost ground – though less in Britain and Denmark say than in Ireland or Spain, and much less among national politicians than business and financial communities. But, as Santer's Presidency opens, the scapegoat syndrome may in any case be returning. The Commission seems to have settled for fewer proposals now that the surge of internal market legislation is past and for cautious recognition of national realities where implementation and enforcement are concerned. Its legal and bureaucratic authority is not enough to produce political consent, nor to overcome rooted national objections to the long-term implications of what was done in the decade 1984–94.

Some degree of criticism was perhaps deserved, because in public the Commission has often resembled the stereotypes its enemies use; except to officials and the players who regularly meet Commissioners, it can appear as if it were indeed a close corporation, unconcerned about wider constituencies once the major interest groups have been appeased.

Being so often on the defensive, aware that the other players have multiple means of reopening settlements at later stages of the game, the Commission has had to construct, or assent to the imposition of, conventions governing its relations with them, from preliminary contacts at the level of junior officials extending up to the rules of comitology which govern the setting up of those committees which are not specifically within the Commission's jurisdiction.[23] Mistakes cannot be afforded. Texts must be made legally watertight according to advice from its own Legal Service. This produces a measure of caution, if not dependency (for the Service's function is to interpret the Treaties). Few cases are important enough to risk ignoring the Service's advice and possibly a confrontation with the European Court where judges' knowledge that such warnings had been ignored might be enough to determine the judgment.

The Commission also reserves rights of access by, and consultation with, the non-governmental players, which permits some of them an essentially private admission to a privileged discourse about policy. Officials in charge of dossiers make explicit judgments about which individual sector's peak organizations, enterprises or financial institutions are to be preferred, on grounds of their expertise or dominance of a certain market or sector (thus implicitly downgrading other contenders). Quite junior officials thus judge some players to be better Europeans than others – more expert, more representative or more powerful – and able to contain rivalry among their members.[24] Commissioners themselves benefit from the existence of such filters since they rarely need to see even the largest companies unless a major point of law or principle is involved. The useful fiction of independence and impartiality is maintained, without losing the advantage of tapping corporate experience or dissent, before firms' lawyers scrutinize the texts which the Commission formulates.

There remain risks either that these informal relations will become so elaborate that they defeat both sides' intentions, or that they arouse such suspicion about 'corporatism' that their effects are discounted politically. It is quite possible that what the Commission achieved in the years 1983–91 was an aberration, the result of a conjuncture between all member states, anxious about modernization and competitiveness, and the direction set by a remarkable Commission Presidency. In retrospect, those eight years may have been an Antonine age, already being overwhelmed by renewed struggles at all levels in the Community.

The original role envisaged in the Rome Treaty ended in the mid–1960s (if it had ever really been instituted, at a time when fewer member states were more easily able to sort out the agenda in advance). In past recessions, after all, the Commission has invariably lost the influence it gained in periods of economic growth. It is no longer even true to say, as one former German Commissioner put it, that 'Commissioners discovered the European interest together, negotiating the bumps in the road together signalled by their special knowledge of conditions and circumstances in their home state,'[25] since a far more complex political market place has superseded it; to use Tönnies' distinction, the Community has become more of a *Gesellschaft* than a *Gemeinschaft*.

The college has to uphold the law as it is, not as it would have it be, or risk being arraigned by the Court (as, for example, over its failure to implement Community transport policy). It has also to accept the Maastricht-inspired new powers of the Parliament, as well as the Council's power of decision. Even a measure as long prepared and backed by the Treaties as telecoms liberalization, was delayed in 1992–4 because certain member states did not wish it to be instituted. In the mid–1980s, Delors had habitually used the Parliament as a sounding board for the Commission's yearly programme (which was in turn a sop to try to restrain its ambitions for a wider role). But German, Belgian and Italian backing for the Parliament's new powers at Maastricht ensured that that aspect of the Commission's triangular gameplay foundered.

It has to take a long, cautious line, to mobilize maximum support at each level of business and remember never to ignore or directly to confront a member state. The European Companies Statute provides a case in point. Based on German legal principles, it was intended to provide a model for corporate and workplace relations within larger companies, and thus serve as a symbol of the era of harmonization. But it ran head-on into opposition from other systems, notably the British adversarial one. It became obsolete with time and was modified in the hope that it would help to promote cross-border mergers, but this, too, met opposition, because of member states' incompatible laws. Even in 1994, when the basic thesis about compatible corporate behaviour had at last become acceptable to many business players, huge pyschological barriers still existed at political level.

Where member states themselves err, judged by Community law, it is unwise for the Commission to try to impose Machiavelli's exemplary punishment (even where it has the competence to do so,[26] say in commercial negotiations, trade agreements, national monopolies or mergers). It cannot make any national player act without its own prior agreement, or, where QMV applies, without a Council majority. As the reception of the 1993 White Book indicated, if it tests out policy by making a full public disclosure the result may confuse rather than persuade member states, for the various publics to whom the Commission is appealing cannot distinguish between Commission and Council, between the tentative and the real. There are too many distinct audiences to aim at, in contrast to the tactics available to a national government.

But above all, the Commission fears a free-for-all by member states, such as the Bérégovoy government threatened, in order to ward off what it saw as a drive by DG4 for 'the simple abolition of monopolies in the name of liberal ideology'. That would rapidly erode the fundamental mutual benefits which explain why member states need the Commission in the first place. Thus a decade is barely enough for it to edge ahead with the improvement of European drinking and bathing water. Commissioners have to accept, as part of the natural order of things, member states' derogations, delays and failures to implement.

Since 1958, their principal strategy has been to draft the text of a directive, get it signed at an appropriate moment, and hope for full compliance to evolve over the years. Whatever the tactics in the Commission's hand (which range from straightforward public statements about long-term intention to subterfuges – such as making revelations to a member state's press about how badly its national government behaves in Community terms), the Commission's strategic advantages are all long-term, and usually indirect. In contrast, those of member states are always immediate. It did appear in 1988–90 that the Commission was trying to call France to order on competition cases, and using the reaction of the French press. Until then, France had run almost level with Italy in the penalty stakes under Article 92, with ten to twelve cases a year in front of the Court, as against Italy's fifteen. After 1990, this fell to three or four. But the response came from changes in outlook and national government policy about France's place in the Community (see chapter 11), not as an answer to DG4's sustained campaign; in subsequent bargaining the French government was able to ensure that its compliance did not unduly damage the French firms concerned.

This is not to deny the direct effect on states of prolonged exposure to Commission arguments, and the indirect weight of corroborative advice from firms or financial institutions with an interest in European markets. But there is hardly any question of Commission leadership, except in formulating policy and setting the agenda. The Council decides, even if there are states such as Italy, Belgium, or the Netherlands (and occasionally France) which for different reasons may be willing to accept from the Commission what they would like but cannot initiate, out of concern for domestic public opinion. The fundamental problem remains of how to act when member states are, according to the Commission's interpretation, backward or in default.

The abuse may of course disappear of its own accord before the ripe time to remedy it arrives.[27] Alternatively, the Commission itself may temper the effect for social or employment reasons on poor and backward regions, depressed urban areas, or member states caught up in difficult elections.[28] A willingness to bargain at any stage of any game has become endemic. But this has its informal advantages: it is also in the interests of firms or states to bargain, as the French authorities did after the UTA-Air France merger almost reached the ECJ. An awareness that Air France would do better from an out-of-court deal also made the subsequent Sabena-Air France settlement easier.

Qualified majority voting (QMV) has ensured that less watering-down of directives occurs in the Council to meet member states' objections. But that may be because the texts reach Council in better shape as a result of prior consultation by the Commission. Where a member state can make its point in the Council by abstention, there is also less need to overstate its case in public – as happened in the past – in preparation for partial withdrawal or tactical compromise. Since abstention does not derogate from unanimity, but does make a gesture sufficient for domestic public opinion, both the Commission and the Council may appear to have become more successful.

Yet there seems to have been no diminution of national suspicion about the Commission, whether it is accused of bureaucratic aggrandizement or interference with national sovereignty. Some of the most unpopular proposals come from member states (for example, Denmark's requirement on the curve of a cucumber, or Britain's attempt to curb the shooting of song birds in Italy and France). But there is little to be gained even if the Commission Secretariat publishes in the *Official Journal* (destined for only a specialized audience), a reasoned analysis showing that only 25% of directives arise solely from within the Commission. (Some officials reckon that the correct figure is as low as 15%, albeit including most of the major proposals.)[29]

A former British Treasury minister defined the Commission thus: 'it should be indispensable and show member states that inter-governmentalism is not always valid, because it cannot achieve what is needed; only the Community as a whole, conjoining the two, can.'[30] Other respondents in the interviews here assert that if it had been no more than that, the single market might still be bogged down in harmonization disputes, American and German investment would have had free rein in eastern Europe, and the current form of competition policy, a touchstone of 1990s' industrial policy, would still be in abeyance. The capacity to draw up policy and to set the agenda on which the Council will deliberate goes a long way to determine the outcome. The problem for member state governments which dislike the connotation, is that like a classic civil service, the Commission acquires the power to fulfil its innovatory role without any matching accretion of formal, legal sovereignty, save what they themselves concede. Hence the inter-governmental nature of member states' preparatory documents for the 1991 IGCs and their retention, in contradistinction to those from the Commission, of two out of the three Maastricht pillars.

III. *Directorates and Officials*

A Commissioner may be appointed knowing little of the Breydel building's interstices. One of them admitted, 'When I came to office, I did not believe I could have achieved so much. This may have been due to ignorance of the competence I was able to achieve, using informal means. The dichotomy between the real and the formal is much greater than the strict formulation of the law suggests.'[31] By virtue of long service, Directors General know better, just as they understand what a member of the Delors cabinet meant when he spoke of collegiality as the essential virtue: 'If this were ever lost, the Commission itself would fail and become a sort of Council of Ministers with warring state representatives.' Functionally, and in terms of the ethos generated over decades, the Directorates differ among themselves to a degree which requires a centre to exist.

Officials cannot simply dream up policy and offer it to the Council to determine. They lack the technical understanding of complex industrial, labour or environmental problems, they are not attuned to what industries, unions or political parties are doing, and they are out of the political loop which would illuminate what member states are likely to accept. Commissioners, especially long-serving ones, are scarcely better off.

They must therefore take advice from a great variety of formal and unofficial bodies representing players' interests in the economic, political and social life of fifteen nations. 'You cannot present a utopia', one of them pointed out; according to another, 'you are selling an idea, you must consult people beforehand.'[32] But in the relations between Commission and organized interests, formal and informal ways of interaction should be distinguished. Formal consultations are organized through the involvement of interest groups in a range of committees and expert working groups. The conditions under which the Commission allows interest groups to enter into an informal dialogue are much more difficult to regulate.[33] For all the Commission's attempts to regulate what it would like to see as an 'open and structured dialogue' (see p. 463, fn 27), it has so far succeeded only in setting the general rules for lobby organizations' access to officials and Directorates, which is not at all the same thing as ensuring equal treatment of all interests. The Commission has fixed a catalogue of minimal requirements and expects the interest groups to establish a 'code of conduct' on this basis. Needless to say, they have not yet reached agreement, not least because national industrial federations fear the Commission's preference for European-wide ones.

All Directorate activities are relevant to studying the Commission, but only a limited number of the twenty-four appear here – those concerned with industry and business, financial services, research and technology, monetary policy, trade and the regions. Their functions, size and profile change over time; for example, after a long period of overload, DG1's concerns with eastern Europe, EFTA enlargement, trade and a common foreign policy, on top of its 'external affairs' brief, were divided, in 1993, apparently logically between three Commissioners: Brittan (external economic affairs and trade [DG1]), van den Broek (external political relations, membership extension and security [DG1A]), and Manuel Marin (the southern Mediterranean, Middle East, Latin American and Asia, all as part of DG8 [Development]). This failed to lessen overload and introduced much duplication, so that it had to be unwound in 1995 under Santer. In reality, the division of portfolios has more to do with Commissioners' personalities and their increasing numbers than rationality, and the whole area is long overdue for reform.

Something of what these Directorates do is shown in later chapters on competition, industrial policy, financial sectors, trade, regions and policy implementation (see chapters 9, and 11 and 13). Here it is enough to say something about each one's ethos, its links with outside players and the collectivity of senior policy-makers. Two initial points should be made: firstly, despite the presence in Brussels of 17,000 officials (15% of whom are concerned only with translation), crucial areas are thinly staffed and overburdened. Yet because of budget constraints and member states' unwillingness to pay more, it has become very hard to increase establishments or even redeploy existing staff. Similar financial constraints govern salary levels, since these were fixed in ecus in the budget set before the ERM's 1992–3 turmoil (the ecu, being based on a basket of currencies, has depreciated 15% against the DM since). There are also endemic problems of misplaced establishment and waste: when DG13 (telecoms) moved from one building to another in 1989, 200 more officials were found than the Personnel Directorate knew existed.

Secondly, access to the highest rungs of the promotion ladder, and of course Commissioners' own cabinets, is determined not only by merit but by who a candidate knows and the convergence of what he believes in with what member states actually desire. This appears to have worsened since Delors began, around 1985, to take a closer interest in promotions, to the detriment of the Secretary General's former role. Parachuting officials from national capitals into senior (A1 to A3) levels occurs frequently, as does removal or lateral movement of officials whose faces no longer fit. Of the twenty-three Directors General in service at any one time from 1985 to 1995, seven are said to have been dismissed, four retired early, one was sidetracked, and two more were badly bruised.[34] This is only surprising to northern European observers. In addition, having lost control of the flow of central Commission papers downwards to officials and of information upwards to chefs du cabinet, Directors General are now more remote than in Jenkins's time from 'their Commissioners', a state of affairs far from the 1979 Spierenberg Committee's recommendations that all these appointments should be made with career officials carrying substantive authority.

What has been lost by separate fiefdoms has of course been absorbed by the centralized system, to the advantage of the

Commission as it faces the Council. Unity in the Directorates also diminishes as the efforts of players from outside penetrate, in their attempts to mould each Directorate's ethos and policy (which was no doubt part of the intention). Over the decade, central adminis-tration has been given a Napoleonic cast of mind (even if in practice it is not especially sympathetic to France), and this in turn has encouraged other member states who have done relatively badly in the most senior levels – led by Britain – to counter the trend by trying to inject highly qualified, politically acute nationals, in pursuit of a more equitable geographical balance among the influential positions.

Informal quotas exist but mainly at entry, so that member states like Ireland, which took its chances immediately after accession in 1973 (unlike Britain), did well, as did Spain after 1986. (For Whitehall, for many years Brussels lay outside the promotion process as a sort of colonial backwater. Even in 1994, seven years after the effort inspired by Margaret Thatcher and the Cabinet Office, British nationals held only 3% of top posts as against 5% by Germany and France. Though the percentage improves lower down, at 12% it is still short of the declared 15% target).

There is, despite all the good intentions, no completely neutral or ideal system of entry. The long-standing *concours* brings in young and politically inexperienced technocrats, who frequently find alien the role of interlocutor with outside players and are apt to see themselves as a planning elite. The entry requirements also favour countries which have compatible educational systems. But over twenty years of an official's induction, training and maturity, national idiosyncrasies inevitably diminish.

It is at the top, above the A4 level, that imbalances have been most blatant and where, until recently, French predominance seemed assured. Some change has occurred; German governments' earlier acquiescence (because coalition politics in Bonn dictated a share-out on party lines similar to those operating in Belgium or Italy) may now be giving way to a new assertiveness, particularly where posts dealing with eastern Europe are concerned. Spain, despite being a late entrant, has made a series of excellent appointments and has done proportionately better since 1986 than

Britain after 1973. Nearly all small states have tended to do disproportionately well.

But these numbers mean little without asking to what degree French or Dutch officials, say, find themselves cut off from their home base once they are in Brussels, or how quickly Italian, Portuguese and Greek ones, those who do not regard Brussels as a staging-post for domestic ambitions, progress up the ladder. British and German senior officials can in their member states' eyes remedy national imbalances because they are comparatively better integrated with their home civil service, and the business and banking elites.

The underlying importance of nationality (as well as the reasons for member states' concern with senior appointments) lies in the overall tenor of how things are done, and the evolution of a general policy line in each Directorate, as individual officials seek to define the Community's ultimate interests through their work and their contacts among the players. Despite this, canons of public service have improved markedly during and after the 1980s. Administrative Darwinism, and cross-fertilization as officials or *stagaires* returned home, have had an impact on the less well-grounded traditions (notably in the systems of what northern states sometimes disparagingly term the 'Club Med'). Political patronage has diminished among contingents from Spain, Portugal, and Greece, though less obviously from Italy.

National identity survives most obviously in social life, in the clubs which officials join and in the restaurants or pubs they frequent. But it matters much more at a quite different level, among the expert representatives of member states or those seconded from firms to serve on the vast array of working groups (some two hundred and fifty in total), which range from central bank officials at DG15 to technocrats from the chemical or pharmaceuticals industry. Seconded by firms, universities or national administrations to work with Commission officials in charge of dossiers, and paid by the Commission as individuals not as employees, they do not subscribe to a written professional code. Naturally, they have their own expert opinions about whatever subject their group is engaged with, which tends to exclude partisan advocacy. But since nothing in the Community is politically neutral, they are vulnerable to a double suspicion: that they will represent too directly the interests of the firm, federation, or national government that sent them, and that by putting a certain sort of expertise at the Commission's service they will add flesh to a bare skeleton, in their own image. It was, after all, a Commission official who declared, 'the main thing is to have an important idea, and then find a specialist in the area.'[35]

In looking at different Directorates, one should distinguish between the current mood or climate of opinion, which naturally rises or falls with relative success or failure in determining the Commission's agenda and ethos, and the long-term policy identification. Not all twenty-three *have* an ethos (DG24 is too recent a creation), certainly not in the sense of principles for which officials would go to the stake. However, those relevant to this book – that is DGs 2, 3, 4, 6, 11, 13, 14, 15, 16 and 23 – display both the continuity and capacity of self-defence against other Directorates which characterizes a strong ethos.[36] There being no easy basis for comparison, the selected ones are taken *seriatim* and, since their scope changes with each new set of Commissioners, from a 1994 standpoint.

DG2, which assesses the Community's economic and financial developments for the Monetary Committee as well as the Commission, has one deep aim; the construction of an integrated EU economy – hence its close interest in the ERM as a precursor to EMU. In a world riddled by the conflicts of rival economists and monetary theories, it offers probably the widest scope for ideological argument. Yet because there is so little common ground among the economists it employs, it lacks the weight that derives from conviction. Despite the high quality of its staff, its discourse with the Commission has been interrupted constantly by interdisciplinary quarrels, so that its effective role has been limited to commentaries to which neither the Monetary Committee, central bank governors nor the Commission has any obligation to respond.

DG3 has a clear sponsorship role towards all the Community's industries, dating back over twenty years, which includes giving advice on restructuring, rationalization, mergers and competitiveness. Its natural frontier with DG4 became barbed with the latter's development of an assertive competition policy; but it now tends less than it did towards protectionism during recessions. It sees itself as an advocate to the Commission on behalf of manufacturing and services, a role originally developed in counterpoint to agriculture in the late 1960s. But its modern era dates from about 1970 and the onset of the US challenge. Under Altiero Spinelli, it extended to the introduction of high technology as well as the single market; it then lost both functions and concentrated on the emergency steel cartel and straightforward sponsorship during the mid-1970s recession. Under Etienne Davignon, it recovered research, technology and foreign trade and reached its apogee under Arthur Cockfield, as 'majority shareholder', in the 1985 White Paper; but during the years of drafting legal texts for the internal market, it lost its long-cultivated links with actual industries.

Its main work in the early 1990s recession on general industrial policy, assumed – as in German theory – that all sectors would be treated equally. But this idealistic assumption was soon diverted by member governments' pressure to a (French-style) preoccupation with European champion firms in the most threatened sectors: cars, textiles, computers, defence-related companies and, once again, steel. The 1990 plan survived only in the five-year programme which had already been applied to Portugal. Finally, in 1992, it lost the internal market to DG15 but in return acquired a deeper commitment to research and high technology.

Under Martin Bangemann, a Commissioner whose apparent economic liberalism soon melted to reveal a bent towards protection for key sectors, it has become hard to sustain an ethos about the virtues of 'advanced markets' in fostering competitiveness. Its officials, trying to act circumspectly as industry's allies are, especially in a recession, subjected to the same political constraints as any national department of industry. Though the markers set down by Commissioner Spinelli, Davignon and the long-serving Director General Riccardo Perissich survive, and distinguish enlightened adjustment from mere defensiveness, DG3's ethos offends both the advocates of competition policy and the free marketeers. At the same time, its protective instincts and propensity towards reciprocity (if not actually VERs and tariffs), incline it towards alliances with DG5 (employment, social affairs and industrial relations) DG1A (trade) and DGs 12 and 13 (research, technology and telecoms).

DG3 officials no longer argue on behalf of European champions fighting against American and Japanese competition, as they did habitually in the 1970s, and occasionally, on trade questions, in 1990–92. National markets have become historic legacies, with the relevant one today always being European; but in arguing how the latter should develop, DG3 tends to speak of guided or assisted adjustment, at least cost to the economy in bankruptcy or unemployment.[37] To a large extent its relations with federations and individual firms have become the model for how these should operate in other Directorates. Constrained in the mid–1990s by the problems of ailing state corporations, whether national airlines or energy producers, telecoms or steel industries (all of which fall under other Directorates), DG3 finds itself enmeshed in the wider politics of state and industry, condemned to propose only what the college majority can defend. In short, it could be called the advocate of managed capitalism.

DG4 stands in contrast. As a result of the ECJ's landmark decisions in 1962–3, it was one of the earliest Directorates to acquire a sense of mission and the means to start enforcing it. But for another twenty years, competition law was confined to agreements between firms, restrictive practices, and abuses of dominant market share – a fundamental but relatively unspectacular field. Its much more salient modern form, preoccupied with mergers, take- overs and state aids, only developed after 1980 in the hands of three like-minded Commissioners, Andriessen (Netherlands), Sutherland (Ireland), and Brittan (UK). Building on the seismic shift towards market economics which first touched Britain, then Germany, the Netherlands, and Denmark, its senior officials were able with such leadership to develop a more aggressive ethos and a more adventurous interpretation of Articles 85 and 86 of the Treaty of Rome.

DG4 had always possessed strong powers of enforcement, and was therefore potentially puissant, rather than merely influential *vis-à-vis* member states' business organizations and firms. But it inclined towards legalism under its long-serving Director, Claus Ehlermann, until the increasingly Anglo-Saxon input produced a mood of embattled dedication which was bolstered by the addition of a Merger Task Force, and buoyed up by an expanding record of success in the years up to 1993. Initially isolated, DG4 was increasingly supported during Delors II by other Commissioners such as Pandolfi and eventually, where mergers were concerned, by Delors himself.

DG4's current ethos can hardly be separated from its trio of Commissioners and their presumption that markets were to be interpreted as real markets, whether worldwide, EC or part-EC, according to the nature of the product and its size, and not according to prior definitions made by nation states or the European Union. While not, as was sometimes claimed, hostile to *all* monopolies, it favoured in principle competitiveness as well as competition: it would, for example, accept research and development collaboration between firms but not their collusion. It recognized nevertheless that there should be a balance between giant companies and member states on one hand, SMEs and poorer states or regions on the other, so that although market-oriented it did not instinctively exclude transitional support operations.

This tendency – evangelical, puritanical and assertive – did not obscure the earlier legal, German anti-trust tradition, which had been responsible for a remarkable approximation of national law to Community law. But it did produce a much higher level of political conflict, so that since 1993, its recent role has been hard to sustain. Whether it has already experienced reversal is as yet too soon to judge. Even at its peak, it made little impression on the state monopolies in energy supply, although it had greater success with telecoms. Given the high policy content of its chosen cases, it could in the end aim only 'where there was space to obtain a judgement'. Critics allege that this stance was too controversial to last, too dependent, particularly in the financial sector, on individual cases (such as the Eurocheque case 1984, which first applied competition rules to banks and financial services), so that DG4 was led willy-nilly into some spheres rather than others (such as the economically more significant banks' interest rates cartel).

On the other hand, after 1985 DG4 did begin to address vast issues in the *state* monopoly sector which had previously been avoided. It also opened up the argument in service industries between (German) national regulation and (British) self-regulation, which ranged from stock exchanges to travel agents. It also encouraged member states to concern themselves not with the European context but the global one, in which all non-state players now operate.

DG11 (environment) has an ethos sometimes seen as fanatical by others, concerned for example, with data protection or lenders' civil liability for the environmental damage caused by industries which borrow from them. Yet what to one group of professionals appears dangerously amateur can be vociferously welcomed elsewhere. Its ethos is still evolving, as part of broad, still-fluid politics, subject to the flux caused by a series of eccentric or little-known Commissioners. From the standpoint of industrial and financial players, it has not been able yet to establish clear principles of action, other than that member states should be defended in cases of their market restraints, say on packaging or recycling, if these can be shown to serve a good environmental cause.

DGs 12 and *13* (science, research and development, telecoms, information technology and innovation) hang together, as facets of industrial policy. Their ethos derives from principles established in the Davignon period, the rationalizing of electronics around chosen Eurochampions in the mid-1980s, and the 1981 twelve-company agreement which established ESPRIT, RACE and the intergovernmental programme EUREKA for cross-border research and development. Like DG3, it habitually seeks to privilege giant EC firms, while taking some notice of SMEs through the schemes SPRINT, STAR, and VALOREN, all of which aim to transfer high technology to small firms or regions. Since 1993, it has extended SMEs' participation in R and D investment programmes such as VALUE (human capital and mobility through relations with universities). Both DGs are active if minor players by comparison with DG3, and tend indirectly towards a protectionist point of view.

DG15 (financial services) now stands closer than any other to DG4, having been made responsible for implementing the internal market in banking, pension funds and stock markets. Its functions include direct taxation, corporate law and financial institutions generally, from the angle of the internal market. Like DG4, it aims to draw up the basic principles in texts which set out member states' obligations, with a schedule for implementation, but leaves highly technical financial matters to them to implement, in the context of world-wide deregulation, making only spot checks using outside consultants. Lacking DG4's powers of enforcement, it must use the best levers available in a very arcane area, previously barred by member states' political objections and by practical factors, such as the difficulty of altering banking law. Its ethos is best defined as the application of good practice, achieved by working alongside member states on the assumption of a common interest in modernizing these sectors. So far, it has had surprising success (see chapter 11) but implementation has been delayed by parliamentary difficulties, especially in Italy.

In matters such as banking liquidity ratios, the BCCI scandal, or the rights of creditors in bankruptcy, DG15 has followed the ECJ's 1986 principle of minimum harmonization: 'the Commission is not interfering, only seeking to remove obstacles to trade.' But in parallel, as the internal market developed, it has also tried to ensure the adoption of new financial techniques, defining protection, backwardness and two-tier operations as enemies of the internal market. What is relatively easy in banking, where all member states subscribe to a general common interest, becomes harder with insurance or the securities market, the former being heavily guarded, and the latter being highly vulnerable to investors' loss of confidence. Few member states are yet prepared for the loss of most of their stock exchanges, and for a future where only one may survive in each. DG15 therefore has no fixed idea about what is good, save to accommodate global change without unacceptably high costs. Its ethos stands closer to that of Japan's financial sector than those in the Anglo-Saxon/American world.

DG16 began life as the Directorate charged with managing and overseeing the Regional Development Fund, also handling related research funds, according to strict criteria about which regions qualified as deprived. Up to the late 1970s, most choices of projects, implementation, and all supervision remained with member states. Its first twenty years could, without undue unfairness, have been characterized as watching money pour unrequited into Italy's Mezzogiorno. One great change came with the shift from projects to programmes, which was taken under Commission auspices, while another was in the mid–1980s, when member states started to tighten up supervision, aware of what, from Italian and Greek experience, the prospect of Spanish and Portuguese entry implied. Its modern existence began when the regional funds were doubled in the EC's 1989–93 budget.

At the same time, the Single European Act stimulated more creative reflection on what regional policy might be, not as something laid down by member states, but developed in-house by the Commission in order to infuse the programmes with a common dynamic. (Possibly because of these ambitions, responsibility for coherence funds was retained by the Secretariat.) The year 1989 brought the formal regional development plan, covering training, help for SMEs and infrastructure, which offered a chance to use the new money in ways likely to establish virtuous precedents for what was expected to be a further budget increase in 1994–9.

At that point there was neither time nor political leeway to formulate a philosophy of regions or regionality. But the Commissioner, Bruce Millan, familiar with the Scottish Development Authority's work in the 1970s, saw possibilities of repeating the joint work on industrial policy by governments, local authorities and local industry, banking and trade unions, which had characterized the SDA's best work outside the habitual public–private sector demarcation line. DG16 might become a sponsor for deprived regions, as DG3 already was for industry, given the EC's double interest in eliminating regional imbalances and fostering overall harmonization. Millan and his officials envisaged nothing less than partnerships with regions and municipalities to raise not only the physical but also the administrative standards of local governments in areas such as Galicia, Epirus, Calabria, or Tras os Montes, long dominated by almost eighteenth-century landed elites. DG16 might be the cipher for an EC developmental state, bringing such remote areas more completely into the Community and thereby enlarging the internal market, in return for which the major states, led by Germany, would continue to pay the price.

Regions, as chapter 9 shows, are a risky venture, where value for money is near-impossible to monitor. Even modest ambitions to modernize or to redress imbalances touch on member states' sovereignty; grander ones to improve the quality of local administration or democratic politics may imply a highly unwelcome dimension of subsidiarity. Such thinking was never publicly formulated, for it clearly implied that some member states and very many local authorities were not to be trusted not to pillage EC largesse. Instead, the public emphasis fell on 'advanced regions', including the *soi-disant* 'Four Motors', as agencies to propagate DG16's more radical aims by example and best practice; together with the need to supplement Ecosoc by a democratically constituted Committee of Regions, which was incorporated in the Maastricht Treaty.

Finally, *DG23*; this was set up with the aim of improving both the economic environment for small- and medium-sized firms (SMEs) and their competitive performance. It was intended to be a sponsor, like DG3, if SMEs had a collective voice. But they rarely attained this, even in the most highly industrialized states, except through the European peak organization UAPME. The manner in which DG23 has acted in the recent past, under a Portuguese Commissioner with other concerns in DGs 9 and 17, and a German Director General who has made no secret of his preference for the German *bund/land* model, has not appealed widely to a sector which has no collective identity and is not keen on deregulation, especially when accompanied by injunctions to adopt the German pattern of small suppliers linked to large buyers.

The limited voices SMEs do possess have tended to ask – from what is easily denigrated as a 'Club Med' standpoint – for aid, grants and special treatment. Despite the prescriptions of Community industrial policy, it has been hard, at least until the early 1990s, to stimulate what, politically, remains an incoherent mass. The Commission's one tentative reform, the introduction of *fiches d'impactes* in order to monitor programmes and their effects, contains potentially hostile implications (like the EC's fraud squad at the Court of Assessors). Deregulation of labour markets might be the best assistance the Commission could provide, but that battle is not yet fought. At present, DG23's main thrust is on the training side and in transnational partnership programmes, reflecting member states' own current received wisdom. To quote an Anglo-German Foundation report, there is 'a major mismatch between the actual emphasis of (EC) policy . . . and what SME owners think that emphasis should be'.

Cursory as this *tour de table* is, and restricted only to the Directorates most closely concerned with the cases raised in later chapters, it may serve as introduction to demonstrate both the substantial divergences between Directorates and how their activities since 1985 have coalesced, partly as a consequence of the internal market's evolution, and partly following the centralizing process of the Delors decade.

The Directorates no more resemble ministries than the Commission does a government. Commissioners differ far more than the members of any national cabinet, who share a political culture, language, and normally a party background, while their departments inhabit a long-standing political-administrative milieu. Officials and Directors General need to eliminate possibilities for internal discord by meeting players' objections at the lowest possible level, in a way which rarely occurs in a national ministry. Their obligation to produce dossiers or analysis and present them in a competitive environment to ensure greater weight *vis-à-vis* the Council as well as the college, is quite different.[38] Commission policy and its outcomes (the legal texts offered to the Council and the Parliament) invariably represent the mean of many discussions, whereas government plans derive from party programmes, electoral mandates and prime minister's or ministers' instructions.

But they share a distinction – common, for example, in the British system – between 'managerial' and policy-mongering departments – although in some Directorates policy-making would be a better term. Diplomatic conduits and screens against publicity also exist for dealing with the non-governmental players, including a natural presumption that it is easier to deal with peak organizations – sectoral federations and associations of industries or services – whose job it is to filter their members' views, even if the resulting consensus represents no more than the lowest common denominator of an industry's opinion. Commission officials at all levels prefer first to hear majority opinions, say of the chemical or banking industries across Europe, in order to be able later to check at will among leading firms, and double-check with member governments' departments. This is infinitely preferable to fending off a host of individual rival views, corporate lawyers and lobbyists.[39]

On the other hand, a well-researched, objective initiative by a skilful lobbyist, presented to the official in charge of a dossier, may save him or her from having to do the full *tour de table*. Access is not a privilege entirely in the Commission's hands, but something which has to be won, and continuously defended. That way comes continuity, and the discipline of representativity. Where, on the other hand, a peak organization articulates itself poorly, the Commission's gift of privileged access may even improve its performance over time, as players conform to what officials require in their own long-term interest. This occurred in the car industry, which reconstituted itself in 1991, leaving the most obstructive and critical producer outside (see p. 472).

Despite the rivalries and ideological disputes, as in most cabinets, Commissioners tend rarely to push an argument to the limit, knowing that to do so will arouse resistance from all the others and perhaps endanger the college's coherence. The vertical process of policy evolution in Directorates, the strict practical and social limits set on horizontal concertation among officials at any level below that of the centre and Commissioners' cabinets, the isolation and rivalries of Directorates, also compare with national governments. So does the President's capacity to reallocate functions or to set up new agencies such as the Merger Task Force (in DG4) or the Eco-taxation working group. While some functions of policy evolution and interchange with outside players are devolved to levels much lower than would occur in a national ministry, the overall process is closer to the sort of democratic centralism practised in the civil services of centralized states such as France or Britain.

Just as the Commission Secretariat has a duty to ensure good government, openness, and promotion within the organization on merit (the latter being a role which may conflict at times with what President or Commissioners seek), so the Legal Service acts as adviser to all elements in the Commission, the President, the college, individual Commissioners, Directors, and deputy Directors General, whilst remaining responsible for the Commission's own legality. In formal terms, it must scrutinize all the texts produced by the Commission and give opinions based on its interpretation of the Treaties as well as understanding of cases, precedents and opinions coming from the Court of Justice or the Court of First Instance. Given this guardian role, it is invariably drawn into the consultation process, informally by the Directorates, and semi-formally in the meetings with chefs du cabinet and chefs specialisées which precede the Wednesday meetings of the whole Commission college.

The Legal Service has a formal requirement to attend the college and to help its membership find ways round difficulties, through alternative or more precise formulations. But, informally, elaborate games take place; while the Service seeks a better text, the chefs du cabinet or Commissioners try to elicit a formula to make possible and legal what they have already decided to do; and have ways to put the lawyers under pressure or create difficulties for a small department. Yet if doubts remain, the Service must insist, since the EU is a Community based on law and legal texts: very many, perhaps a majority of officials and Commissioners have legal training and understand too well the implications of standing without full legal certainty in front of the Court to ignore such advice.[40]

Under an activist, vigorous Commission President, the Legal Service, like the Secretariat, tends to speak more softly, because a function once almost insulated from outside notice has been exposed to political scrutiny, even to the exercise of influence by member states.[41] After 1991, but before the Maastricht Treaty ratification, some member states developed the technique of putting the Commission on the defensive, having to justify each of its proposals whenever the Council questioned it (whether or not it fell under the Commission's competence), hoping thereby that even a minority in Council could force it to withdraw.[42]

This touches on a much wider issue: that Maastricht's third, Interior Ministry pillar is ill-constructed from the point of view of parliamentary scrutiny or legal redress. Concerned about the rights of individuals, which the ECJ had vindicated in a series of cases (see chapter 8), Delors and the Commission proposed that the ECJ should be given power to supervise agreements made under this pillar, even though it was reserved for member states. So far, the effort has not been rewarded. It should be added that the subsidiarity principle, with all its potential legal ramifications, was embodied in the Maastricht Treaty without prior agreement by the Legal Service or even examination of what it might signify in a legal context.

Responsible as they are to the whole Commission, the Director General of the Service and his deputy have a special relation to the Commission President. But while the President may test out proposals, he does not use the Service as a channel to the ECJ, for the ECJ is not normally a means to further Commission policy.

But it can be used as an informal player, as it appears to have been in the case of the far-ranging Community initiative to set up a European Economic Area for EFTA countries. Whether inadvertently or by design, the Legal Service advice permitted the Commission to proceed with a text which was later declared incompatible with the Treaties by the ECJ.[43]

The Commission can find itself isolated, for example when member states or Parliament are taking it to Court, and it has to rely entirely on the Legal Service's advice. The Commission can also find itself being used to transmit certain messages, in which case the Legal Service acts as would a barrister on behalf of a Directorate (usually DG4) in proceedings against a member state for infringement. Here it has to defend the house view whether or not that takes account of its advice. It also acts as *amicus curiae*, the co-guardian of the EC's legal rectitude, giving the ECJ an opinion which is in fact a Commission-derived view.

Even in this sheltered, arcane area the outside world intrudes, occasionally, in the form of players seeking advantage, but more often via academic commentaries and scholarly critiques of the EC Law Reports. These necessarily engage the Legal Service, since they raise issues of textual interpretation, not only according to the contexts of individual cases, but also 'the broader interests and concepts of the legal order and the Community of law . . . which are fundamental to the house; hence they are guardians of and for the Commission, loyal to it in institutional terms, as a house and an institution'.[44] It is hardly surprising that, where the Commission's competence is concerned, the Service sometimes disagrees with the lawyers serving the Council, or the Parliament. Much more recently, it has argued in the same sense as it did over the Maastricht third pillar, in favour of the rights of individuals disadvantaged by their own governments' actions or failure to implement the law (as in the case of *Factortame* 3).

Self-evidently, the Commission is not only a legal entity with a range of competences, but also a range of people who compose it. Diversity has just been increased with the arrival of three extra Commissioners, attended by cohorts of officials, from Austria, Finland and Sweden, whose 'Europeanness' may differ from those already in post. Are these, by virtue of belonging to a peculiar *noyau*, engaged in a common set of functions, defending and furthering a European interest, to be seen as a distinct European order – a sort of twentieth-century Knights Templars – or are they better portrayed as disparate bureaucrats brought together by nothing more tangible than thirty years' service? To put it more narrowly, is there within the 17,000 a smaller mandarin elite with a strong ethos, akin to national civil service elites, which might be the embryo of a European political class?

Any answer can only be impressionistic. The Commission has ways of isolating or disgorging people at all levels who 'go too far' or display 'excessive affinity'. But the fact that member states' influence permeates senior levels of the Commission through interference with appointments or challenges to its legal competences suggests that such an elite would more likely to develop among the juniors, whose entry is by merit and whose national affinities are likely to disappear during their working lifetimes. Training, induction and the early responsibilities conferred by heavy dossiers, together with the hybrid social environment, create a sort of convergence. But is this a deeply European one, as Europeanness was understood by the hierarchy before 1973? There are suggestions in the interview evidence on which this book is based that the pristine 1960s vision has been replaced by a more mundane attitude to doing a particular job in a European context. This is to be expected as the Commission enters what may be its early middle age.

The workload, interchanges with the outside world, the waves of hostility from which officials who read even the *Financial Times*, *Le Monde*, *La Repubblica* or *El País* are not immune, encourage pragmatism and a preoccupation with the art of the possible. Brussels has never functioned as a social milieu to integrate different nationalities and languages, only a cultural and gastronomic one. The sixty-hour week, the absence of embassy parties and a notable lack of leisure preclude even the trappings of a social class. In that sense Brussels is a workplace not a capital city, a sort of permanent salesmen's conference. This does not preclude group behaviour – the Danes, the Irish, and the Spanish in particular tend to group together. The military religious orders of course had their distinct chapters and recognized customary distinctions; Alain Touraine's proposal that the global economy now coexists with growing cultural differentiation may be extended to suggest that the concept of European tasks is compatible with maintaining national identity.

That there *are* European tasks is accepted as much by non-governmental players as it is in Brussels or in national bureaucracies, not only in Europe but in America and Japan. In the nature of their work, civil servants are used to taking part in their own competitive symposia and acting, as do Commission officials, on behalf of a hypothetical national interest which they, as well as politicians, help to define, albeit usually under the labels of 'public' or 'state' rather than 'government' interest.

The majority of officials interviewed appear to see themselves not simply as bureaucrats, but as an elite charged with implementing an historically unique project whilst managing the political economy of an entity having the characteristics of a new sort of state. Yet they lack the time, consideration and resources which civil servants enjoy within the majority of the member states; from which they find themselves, in general, cut off – sometimes terminally. Their careers often end prematurely and in frustration. There are inevitably some, usually from the larger states, who accept the Commission as if it were a civil service owing some responsibility to its progenitors, the member states. Others, particularly from small states, envisage it as the means both to integrate their country and to bring it into the European mass.

Without endorsing any speculation about national characteristics, because in the end there are only good officials and bad ones, it does appear that each member state government regards its nationals inside the Commission in a different way. For example, Ireland has, since 1973, filled all its own quota of places and overflowed; Irish officials, sharing a similar professional formation, have in common an opinion that the EU represents the best hope of modernizing a still peripheral economy. But like Belgians, Portuguese, or Danes, they retain their roots, their casts of mind, their party affinities. Officials from these three countries could well agree the substance of a view that 'EC membership has brought Ireland not only money but also innovation and a broader perspective and this is easier to take than from Britain [or France, or Spain, or Germany], since EC ideas are not tainted in the same way'.[45] Very much the same could be said in the case of Greece.

Belgian officials may be more overtly European, more aware of the EU as a guarantor of their own federal state, which presides uneasily over two antipathetic cultures. As one Belgian former Commissioner said, 'all the EC's history has been marked by individuals, and the risks to institutions when there are no good men to run them.'[46] At the risk of creating stereotypes, the Dutch appear to see the EU for good or ill as a reflection of the Netherlands: they would like it to be truly international but find it depressingly short of a common interest. One of them lamented the erosion of commonalty – 'that after all this time of European integration, national consciousness, instead of weakening, is becoming more rigid and vivid in all member states.'[47] Appointments and secondments are not the answer, for despite nearly thirty years of interpenetration, the Commission is still widely unpopular in the Netherlands – though this is less true among those aged under forty (and one may add that, in Denmark, Portugal and Greece, those below middle age also display far greater fluency in European languages than their seniors).

If there is a measure of homogeneity among small members, with Luxembourgois in the lead for obvious reasons, the reverse obtains among officials from the big five who are unlikely ever to think alike, so long as the French are brought up in one tradition of service to ministers, the British in another, rather less partisan one, and the Germans are taught to distrust the separation of powers. The extent of European affairs coordination in Paris, Bonn, London, Madrid and to a lesser extent Rome, indicates that a conscious effort to inculcate views about priorities for an ideal Europe is propounded by ministers and Permanent Representatives, and carried directly or indirectly in their national language press.

How successful this background noise is, compared with what is produced by EU institutions, and how long an exposure to the latter is required to block it out, can be answered only by an as yet unwritten social history of the Commission. It could be argued, for Italy and perhaps also for Britain, that 'the only true Europeans are to be found in subsidiaries of large national corporations'[48] whose recruitment literature, training, induction programmes, and promotion to the top are all coloured by the need to be familiar with European affairs.[49] But main board executives, or their European legal departments, do not constitute a political class; if they did, cross-border promotion, once hailed as the onset of 'European management' would have become more fashionable. Perhaps the only true Europeans are those who are appointed by American, Japanese or Korean companies as their executives. Even when senior executives speak of the EC as their 'national territory', they do so in strategic not personal terms. Like Commission officials, when they retire, it is not to homes in 'Europe'. Companies' enormous recent interest, like their new offices in Brussels, owe everything to the internal market's opportunities. Even peak institutions regard 'Europe' as the ground on which to pursue member firms' economic advantage, not their managers' political or social destiny.

It remains to be seen how officials or business executives' work experience in the EC will, over the next, post-Maastricht generation, alter the way large numbers of individuals see the world.[50] For the chemicals MNC, Rhône-Poulenc, like many others, the 1992 internal market set deadlines and gave an EC colour to how problems were discussed; however, the subsequent recession turned managers' eyes away to GATT and the international dimension. Renault was very European in the late 1980s under one chairman, much less so after 1990 under another, at a time when sales in the US declined. Awareness of Europe does not specifically foster a European political class, and within member states it may only be a manifestation of 'a series of different two-class societies, the elite informed and the rest ignorant. Only since the SEA has there grown up the beginnings of an intermediate group.'[51] The elite is informed precisely because its training and responsibilities oblige members to be, whatever they personally think of integration.

Until member states come closely to resemble each other (a process which awareness of the EC's laws and Commission practice does not necessarily stimulate) all the coordinating systems, regular flights to Brussels or training courses are unlikely to do more than confirm this distinction between codes applicable at work and in economic life, and individual's private political and cultural beliefs. At present the most likely candidates for a European class are not even the practitioners (least of all ministers, however much acquaintance with EU procedures may facilitate decision-making) but those observing or trying to obtain influence – the MEPs, lawyers, journalists and lobbyists who resemble Renaissance mercenaries, willing to enlist under any banner, and whose chief asset is their ability to transpose themselves, chameleon-like, into the nationality of their patron. To them should be added academic commentators in the fields of business studies and public administration.[52]

The Commission and other EU institutions offer a series of career commitments which do not preclude national identity and affinities. The Commission's very structure, with its habitual brokerage at every level, inhibits the evolution of a genuinely European interest, except insofar as the results of bargains are then presented by the college majority to the Council as if they really were. Since the consensus on which majorities are based is likely to include strong elements of what member states, regions or commercial players would wish to see (if not, the texts are unlikely to pass through the Council or be approved by the Parliament), the European interest appears to be the end product of the game, rather than the organizing principle. The plurality of interests, now more numerous than the founding fathers could have imagined, is the main determinant, and may have become so as early as the mid–1970s. Behind the rationally designed classical façade wind narrow passages leading to closet rooms where Florentine bargains are made. But that is how modern states evolved in the sixteenth and seventeenth centuries.

The Commission's faults are not difficult to list, the litany having been repeated frequently enough since the mid–1960s. After a decade when stronger efforts at reform had been made than under the previous three Presidencies, the evidence of low-quality administration and poor management supervision is still not hard to find and Commission sources are open enough about the defects. But the stereotyped abuse common in the British popular press tends to ignore the fact that significant improvements in both aspects *have* been made: that the Court of Auditors' 1993 and 1994 reports exposed fraud on a grand scale in the CAP administration says as much about the Court's new astringent approach and processes of investigation as it does about the deep roots of agricultural corruption.

Waste and inefficiency are harder to detect or treat. The perception that EC legislation is not enforced properly in several member states undermines business support for the single market and saps the will to admit Community competence into areas where it could help economic performance. The Commission's unique bureaucracy requires a dynamic force at the centre if it is not to lose clear articulation. It is not, in that sense, a policy community, being, in Henry James's phrase 'too loosely hung about', and it has little, if any, historic memory, so that it quickly loses touch even with the recent past. Delors's greatest contribution was to activate the organization. Santer's greatest challenge is to reconstruct that dynamism in ways suitable for the later 1990s. The Commission's history, its earlier failures to reform, and the way the Spierenberg Report was ignored, augur badly.

Agreement on the good points is harder to find, unless one asks, what would happen if the Commission did not exist? As the next chapter suggests, member states would find it impossible to act in its stead, which is the main reason they continue, in some cases very reluctantly, to work with it. The Commission is both conscience and guardian; guardian of the temple whose pillars were so rudely bodged by member states at Maastricht, and conscience in reminding them of what they once agreed they ought to do. It is both a think-tank and a seminar, a fount of ideas and a forum for discussing them with the interests they affect. It is also a manager of certain economic mechanisms, such as the CAP and the RDF, and a policeman, watching for economic malpractice. After nearly forty years of activity, it is very hard to imagine that any other construction would be able with this degree of effectiveness to formulate ideas, give them practical form, and mobilize a consensus or a majority in their favour.

If there has been convergence, a degree of integration, and some implantation of European ideas among the twelve member states (as they were until 1995) some of the credit goes to the Commission. Of the Internal Market White Paper, Arthur Cockfield advised 'go for the best, in order to get what is *practicable*'. Like a minor state rich in economic resources and professional skills but surrounded by powerful neighbours, the Commission has little real power but great, albeit indirect, influence. Its strongest card is the need the member states have for what it offers. But the two cannot be separated: what the Commission can do to irradiate the Community depends on member states themselves accepting that it should. The ways open to it are pointed up only by what they will permit.

The Member States

The Council of Ministers, on which each member state is represented, is the Community's principal decision-making body. Formally, it agrees, amends or rejects the Commission's proposals for legislation (many of which actually derive from its own members or the Parliament's requests), and it has the final say where the Parliament's amendments are concerned (for that process, see chapter 8). Informally it is the most obviously 'powerful' of the EU's three main institutions yet, at the same time, it is the one where the power of member states has most clearly, and from the beginning, been channelled and demarcated.

The term 'the Council' applies to meetings of the fifteen member states' ministers, whose varying formation depends on the policy area under review: foreign ministers for foreign affairs and also a general co-ordination function, finance ones for financial matters, agriculture or industry ones for their departmental specialities. But it also applies to different levels of meetings, the Council working groups attended by officials of the relevant member states, and to Coreper, the Committee of Permanent Representatives in Brussels, which prepares its agenda. At a very different level, heads of government meet in the European Council (less frequently—usually twice a year). These meetings, which as late as the 1970s were still informal, are clearly distinguished from those of the Council of Ministers not only because its meetings are of a different order of importance, attended as they are by prime ministers, presidents, and chancellors often together with foreign ministers and the President of the Commission but because the European Council is reported to by, and instructs, the Council of Ministers.[1] Only since the SEA has the European Council been given a formal status; it was not incorporated into a Treaty structure until Maastricht and the Treaty of Rome does not mention it. The Treaty of Maastricht gave it a central role in the EU and for the first time gave operational responsibilities either to the European Council itself, in the case of the CFSP, or to the Council 'meeting in the composition of the heads of state or government' in pursuance of EMU. Being the final forum for decision in the most difficult cases, it is sometimes seen as the epitome of intergovernmentalism.

The General Foreign Affairs Council normally meets monthly, as do some other formations such as Finance and Agriculture. Others meet less often. Coreper meets weekly, sometimes for several days, and its many working groups sit constantly. The Council chair is taken by member states, equally, on a six-monthly rotation, despite their great variations in size.[2] By right, the Commission is represented as a participant at Council meetings, by its President and/or the relevant Commissioners. The European Parliament is not as yet represented, even unofficially. Proceedings, as befit the transactions of sovereign states, are confidential, although summaries of their discussions and decisions are subsequently given to the press and public.

The legislative process, which is the most formal kind of transaction, can be set out schematically (see figure 7.1, below).

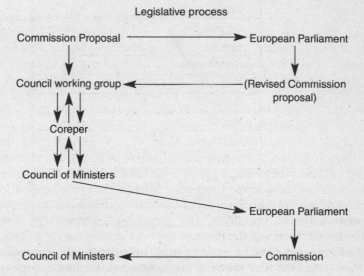

Legislative process

FIGURE 7.1

There are three modes of decision, according to the Treaty's requirements for different classes of legislation.

1. *Unanimity*. An abstention does not prevent unanimity, but does allow a member state to register dissent.
2. *Simple majority*. This requires, since 1 January 1995, at least 8 member states in favour.
3. *Qualified majority* (QMV). This depends on the proportionate weight allocated to each member state which, to a limited extent, relates to the size of its population.

Member states' weighted votes, as of July 1994, are:

Member States	No. of votes
United Kingdom	10
Germany	10
France	10
Italy	10
Spain	8
Belgium	5
Greece	5
Netherlands	5
Portugal	5
Sweden	4
Austria	4
Denmark	3
Ireland	3
Finland	3
Luxembourg	2
Total	**87**

FIGURE 7.2

For a measure to be adopted by qualified majority, fifty-four votes (out of the total of seventy-six) are required. A blocking minority of twenty-three votes, up to the end of 1994 implied a minimum of three member states. However, enlargement of the European Union in January 1995 meant that the number of votes would increase to accommodate whichever of the applicants finally voted for entry, once the negotiations had been completed (see chapter 13). The votes proposed were as follows: Austria and Sweden (four votes); Norway and Finland (three votes): Norway's population subsequently voted against joining the EU by a narrow majority; the figures for QMV votes and for the blocking minority votes are shown in figure 7.2 (see p. 268).

There are four types of legislation which the Council and the Commission may make:

1. *Regulations* have general functions and are directly applicable in all member states. They do not have to be confirmed by national parliaments in order to be legally binding. If there is a conflict between a regulation and an existing or future national law, then the regulation prevails.
2. *Directives* are binding on member states insofar as their result is concerned, which must be achieved within a stated period, while the method of implementation is left to national governments. (In the UK this may take the form of primary legislation, Statutory Instruments made under relevant specific powers, or an Order under the European Communities Act 1972.) In itself, a directive is not justiciable in the member states, but particular provisions may take direct effect if the directive is judged not to have been implemented.
3. *Decisions* are specific to particular parties whether member states, public bodies, companies or individuals, and are binding (in their entirety) on those to whom they are addressed. Decisions imposing financial obligations are enforceable in national courts.
4. *Recommendations* and *Opinions* do not have binding force but state (with considerable informal weight) the view of the institution that issues them.

The principal Council meetings, with their dependent committees are served by the independent Secretariat, and Coreper, the working groups and specialist committees. Related to these are committees constituted and served in different ways, such as the Central Bank Governors and their alternate representatives.

The agendas of all Council meetings are prepared in various ways by Coreper, acting in two forms: the Permanent Representatives (ambassadors) in Coreper 2 deal with foreign affairs, Ecofin, the development of industry, and ministerial meetings under Maastricht pillars two and three (CFSP and Interior Ministry matters) while their deputies (Coreper 1) prepare all the others, save agriculture, which is done by the Special Committee on Agriculture. The Council Secretariat, which in 1994 numbered 2200 total staff – one seventh the size of the entire Commission – is a quite distinct and separately housed bureaucracy from that of the Commission and unlike the Permanent Representatives meeting in Coreper, independent of any member state.

I. *The Council of Ministers*

The Council's primordial purpose is to reconcile the interests of member states, which naturally differ among themselves according to the issue under discussion:[3] those governments, like the French and British, with activist foreign policies may not agree with others, more passive in outlook, on, say, the Yugoslav civil war, while in the agricultural area or in trade and industrial affairs those inclined to protectionism and state aid will tend to confront the market-oriented free traders.

Undisputed consensus among the fifteen nations in the EU is so rare as to be almost non-existent. Yet nothing, apart from subjects entirely within the Commission's own competence, can happen without their assent, which in the absence of an overriding external force, has to be mobilized or brokered by the EU's institutions. There are times when, for some members, the EU may be only a secondary virtue; but the Community is never less than a vital area, a framework for policy-making and problem-solving, without which

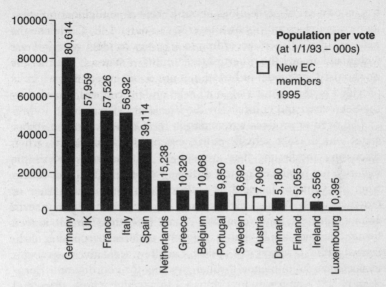

FIGURE 7.3

nothing in common would be done – save in the aftermath of major wars (as at Paris in 1919) or (as Europe's mid twentieth-century history suggests), in the face of a grave external threat (NATO's formation in 1949).

From the Commission's point of view, mobilizing the member states, as Stanley Baldwin once said of cabinet government, is like driving pigs to market. To make an initiative stick (as opposed to simply piling up fruitless directives, as happened in the 1970s) it must be supported by administrative skills (control over the agenda, expertise of presentation) and guided by a well-defined, broadly supported aim (assessed through access to media, populations, players and institutions), and the weight conveyed by the Commission college majority.

But it is then for the Council to dispose, initially through member state representatives in Coreper and then in the Ministerial Meetings. States' points of view are necessarily different from that of the Commission; as nations they inhabit a wider world. Each one has its own set of perceptions about European and global realities, its own practices and its own interests to defend. Each chooses to make its own alliances according to affinities or identity of interest within and among the other fourteen member states. Thus there is no standard, no model of how things are done, except that which is provided by the Council's formal rules and procedures, guarded by the Secretariat and enforced by the Presidency-Chair.

The need to produce agreement in the Council among member states who are not actually equal, except as a legal fiction, when discussing the issues that are subject to unanimity or simple majority, has produced quite a different set of rules and procedures from the Commission and its college. Negotiations take place in Coreper, where Ministerial meetings are prepared, and then again among ministers; however, that they take place according to agreed forms does not imply that states' own national procedures concerned with EU affairs are similar. Each one seeks, in its own way, to maximize its influence through systems for coordinating European policy, which may be compared to a wedge whose sharp end points to Brussels. It is scarcely surprising that the forums where governments engage are rife with informal mechanisms without which the formal, rule-based system could hardly function.

Since the Council of Ministers is not only the important formal body where member states discuss proposals from the Commission and other business but is the forum from which emerges a commonly agreed public presentation of the EC, its transactions have always shaped public perceptions of member states about what the EC is. This public role, however, is now shared with the apparently more adversarial (because highly publicized) summit proceedings of the European Council which are, in fact, less antagonistic than they are made to appear by media reporting (which tends to emphasize how personalities conflict and how states jockey for power).

Such images are not wrong, only partial. They ignore the continuous nature of the negotiating process, from the original Commission proposals, up through the working groups to Coreper and on to the Council and the European Council. States' positions differ, of course, when an item first comes on to the agenda – but these tend to change thereafter. In any bargaining process, players abandon initially extreme stances as they circle inwards, as they make or break temporary alliances, respond to persuasion or trade advantage. Hard line, confrontational attitudes are rare in Coreper and Council meetings and were unusual, even in the 1980s, given the immense amount of business which member states have to deal with if the Community's momentum is not to be checked. (That they may *wish* to stultify it and the Commission has not been a significant danger in general since the late 1970s.)

Formally and informally, the preparatory process in Coreper is intended to settle as many of the problems as possible in advance, so that these (which are called 'A points') can be taken as read by Ministers, leaving the substantial areas of disagreement to be dealt with by discussion in the appropriate council. The confrontational image ignores not only how the agenda is prepared, but the bargaining that takes place after meetings, designed to get agreement between what states have shown they want and what the Commission still hopes to obtain. Because meetings are confidential and revelations in the press come afterwards, usually with an eye to domestic audiences, there is considerable space for manoeuvre. Whether formal or informal, the sequences are systemic and allow individual states, via their ambassadors or ministers, the fullest opportunities to defend their interests and play for what they want by advocacy or objections, by making concessions, or by mobilizing blocking minorities.

The Council, as it stands today is, and always has been, a negotiating and decision-making body and is thus not an ideal forum for giving collective leadership and creating collective loyalty.[4] It depends on the Commission to put forward proposals, although if there is a sufficiently widely-held view in the Council, it can try to induce the Commission to bring another proposal, or to adapt someone else's as its own. The Presidency, helped by the Council Secretariat, has a responsibility to manage business to this end, although ideas can also come from any member state.

The Council is not necessarily more than the sum of its member governments' previous positions, acting as they do in the service of party-defined perceptions of their national interests. Anything which sets small states against large, or touches on competence and subsidiarity is likely to produce dissent, if not actual retreat. Foreign policy questions on the other hand may bring habitual dissenters such as Britain back into the centre; the threats of conflict on European borders from North Africa to the Arctic Circle via the Aegean, Balkans and Ukraine increase collective awareness.

As positions change during the negotiating process, collectivity tends to grow. The Council is, after all, not the only forum where member states meet each other – they often meet bilaterally, many of them in NATO; the largest have their encounters in the G5 or G7 meetings, while the political parties which form their governments have their regular European-wide colloquia, all of which contribute to continuity and inter-state political trading. The Presidency has an essential guiding and coordinating role, while the Secretariat, which works for the Council as a whole (but for the Presidency), has a measure of indirect influence as well, largely through its influence on the Presidency, which relies frequently on its experience and expertise – especially if held by a small country. The Secretariat is also responsible, with the Presidency, for the terms in which outstanding points of difficulty are put for further negotiation and decision to all levels of the Council, ranging from working groups through Coreper to the Council of Ministers itself. The Legal Service, through its duty to interpret the law, can help the Presidency by formulating texts in ways which deal with tricky institutional and judicial points. These in turn can conceal important policy issues, such as the British government's refusal to allow appeals to the ECJ in immigration cases.

It is important to distinguish the Council, which is both inter-governmental and supranational, from the European Council, which is purely inter-governmental. Neither, in the electoral sense, is a democratic body; rather they are assemblies of sovereign entities, like a conclave of medieval kings, each secure in his divine right (in modern terms, divine right is signified as being election by whatever system prevails in each country). Council Ministers whose mandate is based on domestic coalitions, inevitably cast a different shadow from those representing single-party governments, and the size and stability of domestic majorities profoundly affects behaviour. There is no need to look further than Italy in 1993 or Britain during the prolonged Maastricht debate in the House of Commons for examples of such domestic constraints in action.

Member states' systems of coordination (see p. 292) are shaped to produce the best effect in the Council, against which there is no sufficient appeal, save to the same heads of government meetings in the European Council. Here, in a variety of forms, 'the machinery is repaired to ensure future locomotion; here new lines are given to the Commission to follow, or current lines amended.'[5] Not all member states downgrade the Commission role so explicitly, but none pretends that the Council is other than the place where national interests finally operate and are preserved, or not, in what then becomes, temporarily, the common European interest. Its confidentiality (which Denmark's Presidency tried to limit slightly in 1993, but without lasting success) is explained less by the secretiveness endemic in certain member states than by the plain fact that it is an international negotiating forum as well as a legislature. So the Council hides its discords and in its publicity often misleads the outside world about what has been said,[6] despite the promises made at the Edinburgh Summit in December 1992. Its procedures often baffle legally minded observers, even sometimes the ECJ, and one foreign minister has called it 'the least open legislature in the world.'[7] But openness is not its primary purpose: bargains between sovereign entities are usually made behind veils.

Being an aggregation of government representatives not parliaments, its constituent Councils operate like cabinet committees; some, such as Ecofin, with a greater sense of collective identity than others (for example, foreign ministers in the General Affairs Council). Ministers find themselves arrayed in small enforced societies, as temporary members of interlocking clubs which require intricate, insider knowledge of how things are done; these are groups where status accrues to the best informed. Some display a sort of camaraderie, some a high level of professional etiquette. Metaphorically speaking, the rooms they meet in have few doors (to the Commission and the home base) and fewer windows, though the Parliament is in the process of enlarging one. Tunnel vision, as well as the sheer volume of business involved in attaining agreement between the twelve member states at Maastricht, may explain why the question of selling the results to national publics, parliaments or press was not raised during the IGCs in 1991.

As in cabinet committees, ministers depend on their own advisers and civil servants. Their need to succeed is therefore most obvious when prime ministers meet in the European Council, for unlike ministers in the Council, these can hardly break off to take fresh instructions, without loss of face. Again the fiction of collectivity matters, although leaks are common: usually with the aim of pointing up scapegoats when member states have to explain their conduct to national parliaments or media – witness the Dutch and French governments during their difficult Maastricht referenda campaigns, or Margaret Thatcher's behaviour as recorded in the last, injudicious chapters of her memoirs *The Downing Street Years*.

No minister has a higher loyalty to a 'European government' or to any hypothetical European public: all allegiances are to their own state. In that sense, the Council is directly descended from the European Conferences of the early 1920s, not from the 1930s federal dreams. Because of the nature of most of the business they deal with, ministers in turn have a greater natural affinity with outside players – regions, firms or even lobbyists, thanks to national systems of corporate interchange – than they do with their own public opinions. These players, in their approaches, seek to make the outside world both more comprehensible and easier for ministers to control.

How ministers behave in the Council depends partly on whether the political cultures from which they come are consensual or adversarial and partly on whether their own governmental systems allow for consultation with non-governmental interests. Both conditions influence the form of coordinating European policies employed by each government, so that what German, Dutch, Belgian or Danish ministers say will already have been affected by broad consultations, in contrast to the ministers from highly centralized states like Britain or France. This has worked to the long-term advantage of regional players and to the disadvantage of trades unions, whose relative decline since 1974 has not been compensated for by the existence of Ecosoc (see chapter 8).

It remains essential for players representing industry or any other sector to inject their versions of what policy (and the European interest it embodies) ought to be at this level, whether or not they have already done so at Commission level; and if they have, to supplement it here in order to prevent opponents gaining a late advantage. This would normally take place by making their weight felt with their own governments, rather than by approaching ambassadors whose job it is to represent the nation's unified view; but in extreme cases such as Greece and Italy, where players consider themselves excluded by the national machinery, they try to develop their own supplementary methods. Either way, whatever the Council eventually decides to do will have been influenced to some degree by what these players seek – but to a very much lesser extent than in the case of the Commission.

Within the overall structure, ministerial meetings have their own pecking order, as the Cabinet Committees do in any national administration. Agriculture is of more importance here than in most member states because of the subject's political significance in France, Germany and Spain. General Affairs (foreign policy) and Ecofin vie for primacy, the latter because the state of its economy is crucial to all member states, the former because it deals not only with external relations, foreign and security policy, but also because it has a horizontal coordinating role and covers issues not dealt with elsewhere. The Foreign General Affairs Council is serviced by the Political Committee for CFSP issues, as well as Coreper (the small 'Political Cooperation' Secretariat having been amalgamated into the General Secretariat). Both foreign and finance ministers meet once in each Presidency, informally and without officials; though this is hardly in secret since journalists are often aware of what goes on. Ecofin, as well as Coreper, is served by the Monetary Committee and the Economic Policy Committee[8] and indirectly by the Committee of Central Bank Governors which meets in Basel. But while these contain great reserves of expertise, they have been overloaded with work on ERM/EMU since the turmoils of 1992–3, and their freedom of action is limited by what member states will delegate.[9]

The agencies of all these bodies are open to influence, in the first stage by the Commission, then by member states and the Presidency. The Council has its own informal lunchtime procedures in each of its formations, where many of the bargaining processes take place. Once an item has moved into this network however, the Commission's relative influence diminishes. On some indirectly related committees such as the one comprising Central Bank Governors, its representatives attend by convention rather than right. Where it has a policy – and there are few instances in which it does not – it must rely even more than in the Council on expertise and the power of argument to get a hearing in what are highly professional worlds.

Again, the level of inter-state bargaining depends on the issue. Ecofin members are freer from it than most, 'having a common interest in merging their economies', through the ERM and eventual EMU. Financial ministers are familiar with the issues and share a common expertise 'because in any country a finance minister has few friends and all share the same dilemma *vis-à-vis* spending departments':[10] events such as Britain's rebarbative entry to the ERM are exceptions. Its informal lunchtime procedure, where officials are not present, actually includes a separate dimension for states which are members of G5 and G7, at a very much more confidential level, because they are outside the Community's procedures. This excludes a majority of member states. The freedom of capital movements, propagated at Hannover in 1988, was arranged in Ecofin; something which might have been harder to do had other ministers or heads of government actually been present.

With the increase in qualified majority voting, once the Maastricht Treaty added thirty articles providing for QMV to the fifty already in the SEA, the tactical assumptions on which voting in the Council was based, altered. In 1986, the British government studied the impact of qualified majority voting and, having seen which issues created problems and where it would be in a blocking group, proceeded to ratify the SEA. Its decision was vindicated, at least down to the anguished debate on extension in 1994, because vital national interests had not often intruded. Few instances of voting had occurred[11] thanks to the emergence of the 'informal majority' in which member states made their points and then either abstained (which allowed 'unanimity' questions to be adopted), or made an entry in the minutes to record their objections.

Such gestures lessened the number of confrontations, if not their intensity, because simple arithmetic revealed where a member state could not win. But since then the scope for alliances has grown with the accession of three new members, and the calculation that two large states and one small one sufficed to create a blocking minority has had to be modified. Whereas an alliance with twenty-three weighted votes was enough up to the end of 1994, the new figures, which include Austria, Finland and Sweden, require 64 not 54 for a qualified majority and 27 out of 90 for a blocking minority. This allows the eight smallest states, with a combined population of 44 million, in theory to frustrate the wishes of the eight largest, who have between them a population of 328 million (see figure 7.3, p. 271).

Changes in the voting formula, which appeared obvious and necessary to observers as well as participants long before the event, ought to have been automatic. But the relative weighting accorded to West Germany had not been modified when reunification came because of the political implications for France, Britain and Italy, (with Mitterrand particularly being opposed to any change). So the German government carefully took this into account and asked only for an increase in the number of its MEPs proportionate to the new, formerly East German *Länder*, paying what seemed then to be a permanent price. That the rules could be varied to meet political objections may subsequently have encouraged the British government (which welcomed EFTA countries' accession but disliked this consequence) to try to hold the clock still. The explosion in February and March 1994, however, won Britain only an illusory concession. Logically, revision of the whole voting system may be long overdue, given the outcome of its population rationale for Luxembourg at one end of the spectrum and Germany at the other; but the Council is still governed by a certain inertia, for change is never in the immediate interests of a sufficiently large majority. Not even a démarche by the largest states could force through reform, given the pivotal position of medium-sized ones like the Netherlands.

How member states manoeuvre and what bargains they make with each other in the Council's many meetings is not expounded in public and analysed as it would be in a nation state, for lack of a truly European press or television. Instead, it is largely conditioned for member states' own publics by what their representatives and journalists say afterwards, and by the gloss their governments put on Council decisions. Competition between them therefore colours the aftermath of all meetings, even when the official announcements have been agreed. But the fact that political capital can be made out of leaks or portraying another government as greedy (say that of Spain in asking for more cohesion funds to offset fears that new EFTA entrants would benefit unduly from the internal market at no cost to themselves) or self-interested (Germany's approach to competition rules, in giving state aid to steel factories in former East Germany) does not mean that the Council's discussions are barbed to the same degree.

For all its limitations, the Council has been successful over the last twenty-seven years in regulating the divergent wills of six, then nine, then ten, then twelve, now fifteen sovereign states. It does so now far more comprehensively than before 1984. For example, in advance of their admission it was possible once the European Economic Area had been negotiated to provide means for EFTA countries to have associate status, to help them acclimatize their economic and legal systems, rather than leaving them severely outside the pale, as occurred during the six years that Spain and Portugal had to wait. But as the EEA case itself demonstrated, collective affinity, like consensus, comes only after hard bargaining, and always in the shadow of the Hobbesian nightmare of 'a war of all against all'.

COREPER

Coreper, the Committee of Permanent Representatives, is the forum where member states' ambassadors or deputies meet. It has existed from the beginning of the Community as an informal body where specific proposals or papers on general policy emanating from the Commission could be prepared in a way suited to the most effective transactions by the Council. It is not a Secretariat but a convocation; and is serviced by the Council Secretariat and the committee system of the Council.

Its status grew as a result of the Luxembourg Compromise in 1966, and again with the additional powers acquired at the Paris Summit of 1974. It has since been the body preparing all Council business (apart from the separate organizations for the Agricultural Council, and Ecofin's Monetary Committee). Because it negotiates a settlement on some issues, leaving the Councils freer to spend time discussing the more important or contentious matters, it has been seen by the federally-minded as a bastion of member states' inter-governmentalism, and by the Commission as a distorting filter between the college and the Council. Relations however improved substantially during the Delors period because member states had an interest in formulating the Single European Act and the consequential internal market legislation. Member states' Permanent Representatives therefore had strong reasons for working closely with the Commission Secretariat General.

Coreper's purpose at its weekly meetings is to prepare the agenda for each Council and to allocate items appropriately. It also sets up and monitors the working groups which meet continually to process the items as they arrive from the Commission. It is not a neutral mechanism but a negotiating body; during its bargaining process, points that are agreed become 'A points', which the relevant Council will usually (though it does not have to) adopt automatically. The residual 'B points' remain for discussion and decision. What serves as a valuable means of saving Council ministers time also shapes the prior conduct of business in the college of Commissioners, which has its own view on what should rank as 'A' or 'B' points, and whose informal diplomacy (conducted either through the President and individual Commission cabinets, or via the Secretariat General) is aimed at ensuring that result.

Such a process is not democratic, as MEPs often complain. But since it cannot be, the more important question is, in whose interest does Coreper operate? If it increases the efficiency of the Council and improves the chances of achieving a consensus among member states, then it works in the interests of better supranational administration; if, however, Coreper serves the interests of the more powerful, effective or aggressive member states, then it is indeed a stage in inter-governmental brokerage.

Now that the comitology procedure exists to resolve the intricate procedural issue – loaded with political significance – of who will chair the informal committees (none of which is referred to in the Treaties), the opportunities for member states to act on the basis of unregulated self-interest have been curtailed, just as much as have the Commission's ambitions. But it can still be argued that since Coreper is made up of fifteen highly professional officials, chosen by their own governments to carry out a critically important function, they are bound to act in their national self-interest. Against that, it can be said that it is not for ambassadors to decide what is in the European interest, only for ministers; and the freer ministers are to argue out the important or contentious cases, the better the European interest is served.

The second criticism, made from the parliamentary standpoint, that Coreper is a cleverly designed filter for accommodating or deflecting Parliament's demands (thus permitting the Councils more easily to ignore them), has to a large extent been met by the Maastricht provisions (see chapter 8). Both criticisms derive from an unreal expectation about Coreper's responsibilities. Coreper exists to meet the needs of a body – the Council – which is in itself far from ideal but for which no satisfactory replacement has yet been found. The fact that the numerical majority of business items, being 'A points', do not reach the Council's highest levels because they are passed automatically, is to Coreper's credit, rather than an index of democratic deficit.

Because national ministers have to fly to and from Brussels, it is the members of Coreper, the national ambassadors, who form the permanent apex of a member state's wedge of influence and states take great care to choose adequate representatives. In addition to being negotiators on behalf of their own ministers in the Council, the ambassadors have three major functions: firstly, to serve as envoys to the Community and its institutions as a whole and in part. They are the peak of the negotiating pyramid, of which the working groups form the base, constantly available to serve their country's interests in the negotiations which are the *raison d'être* of the Council's machinery. They are supported by large staffs, posted to Brussels from the relevant national ministries and they act as the final filter of all issues before these go to the various Councils for approval or argument. Ambassadors can also stand in for a minister who for some reason cannot be present at a Council Meeting. Secondly, they act as national representatives who meet – usually informally – in Brussels and who regard it as part of their job to influence the Commission and each other, outside the formal range of meetings. Thirdly, they report systematically to their prime ministers and governments at home, with whom they maintain continuous contact, just as ministers do with them. Fourthly, and comparatively recently in some cases (such as France), they provide a means of access to the Council for their own non-governmental players in Brussels, complementing whatever national arrangements apply, to further their aims if possible, and to keep them more in line with government policy.

From the standpoint of member states, whose EU coordinating systems are compared later on, the ambassadors' function is to be a supportive alter ego for their respective ministers and, if need be, for prime ministers and presidents should an issue reach the European Council. Their permanent representations are the Community branch of each of their ministries in Brussels, defending and explaining their interests and standpoints, and feeding the national base with information on the feasibility of positions and proposals in the Community process.

As interfaces of information and brokers of positions, ambassadors have progressively become more interesting (and open) to non-governmental political entities. However, states with a strong tradition of centralized administration can admit this only with difficulty: thus a Dutch member of the permanent representation will admit to the practice much more easily than his French counterpart.

In terms of career origin, ambassadors (Coreper II) are mostly diplomats, their deputies in Coreper I being officials or experts from technical ministries (such as industry), as befits the nature of their work. The former deal with weightier political issues, the latter with more departmental ones.

Ambassadors compose probably the only genuine social network in Brussels, for in addition to the normal impulses of diplomatic life, they bear the mark of Cain: they fight unpopular battles on behalf of their ministers, which only their colleagues know is not their personal fault. They also share a central assumption that Council debates, save perhaps those on the budget, should not inherently be zero sum games.[12] Whether they help home-based ministers to draft papers or merely follow national government instructions, or whether they operate their own information and intelligence networks among their nationals on the Commission staff, depends on each nation's house style.

There is no easy means to compare their relative effectiveness, apart from gossip about what each thinks of the others. Non-governmental players' opinions are vitiated since very few address Permanent Representatives other than their own.[13] But on the evidence of what is said by executives of large multinational companies, the British are ranked highly in terms of the information service they provide directly to firms' headquarters (especially the quality of their insights into how the Community operates). This applies *mutatis mutandis* to Ireland and Denmark. France has recently made efforts to be more helpful to firms while taking care not to prejudice the state's central direction; this may be what Spain's representation aims to emulate but at present it gives virtually no information to non-governmental players.

In contrast, Belgian and Luxembourg companies, being close geographically to the Community's core, ask for less and have fewer contacts. German ones, because of the system of consultation in Bonn and the services given by *Länder* governments' offices in Brussels, used to fall in the same category but have become more demanding since the Cold War barriers fell to reveal vast investment opportunities in eastern Europe. Countries which are less well served, according to business sources, include Greece, Italy (where the function is performed by the Institute of External Commerce), Portugal, and in the past for very different reasons, the Netherlands (where the function has improved markedly since 1985).

Much depends on the individual ambassador; those from Britain, Ireland, Portugal and Belgium being highly regarded at the time of writing this (1995). In earlier days, the French ambassador Boegnor ran his office almost without rein from Paris (and with Spierenberg could claim to have created Coreper itself), but conditions have changed greatly since then. Italy's Permanent Representative is evidently hampered by the diversity of briefings from Rome. But none of them exists outside the format of national coordination: they are the mirror both of the member state and the Council whom they serve. This excuses to officials and ambassador colleagues the tenor of the instructions they are often required to pursue.

THE EUROPEAN COUNCIL

In the 1960s, the General Affairs Council (GAC) – comprised of foreign ministers – still dealt with many EC domestic matters as well as external affairs. But as the volume of business grew inexorably, and as proceedings in the highly contentious Agriculture Council led to demarcation disputes, more technical councils had to be constituted, covering everything from trade to transport. Once direct elections to the Parliament had been instituted and the Regional Fund developed, the GAC's role as a council of last resort ended, despite a series of stop-gap reforms in 1974.

A process in which decisions endlessly escaped upwards, so that serious clashes of interest between member states could be more easily resolved, led to heads of government meetings in an ultimate power centre, above the Council and outside the Commission's range of influence. After the 1960s, the tone of these informal summits became increasingly inter-governmental. France in particular required that ministers of member states should control what was done in foreign policy matters. Regular meetings were still rare in the late 1960s and the first actual summit only took place in 1969, at the Hague, after de Gaulle's fall. But thereafter discussions ranged widely over the whole EC spectrum.

At Paris in 1972, questions were raised about the meeting's status – 'not being in the Treaty' – but since the proceedings went well, nothing more was done. Two years later, at Copenhagen, the combination of the oil shock, Danish inexperience and the sudden unprepared arrival of OPEC foreign ministers late at night led to confusion in which heads of government spent their time drafting a communique designed to disguise a non-event.[14] After the post-mortem, member states agreed to give their encounters semi-formal status under the title European Council, which was then formalized in the period of Schmidt and Giscard.

By that time, heads of government attended the European Council, with foreign ministers, the Commission President and one other, usually the External Affairs Commissioner. This arrangement was given legal standing of a sort by the Single European Act in 1986. During the informal part of its existence, the distinction between the Council and Summit Meetings ran between the GAC (foreign ministers) which dealt formally with foreign affairs under the title of 'political cooperation' and the Summit 'conference' on foreign affairs. In fact, apart from the venue, they ran concurrently but with separate Secretariats and agendas in order to appease Quai d'Orsay sensibilities. In the later 1970s, Roy Jenkins found it 'a surprisingly satisfactory body, mainly because it is intimate'.[15] But even before the British budgetary offensive began to obsess its meetings after 1979, it had become necessary to give the European Council greater formality and proper links to the Commission. In a body which was intrinsically outside the treaties, despite being legally recognized in 1986, until incorporated fully at Maastricht, informality plays a much larger part than in the Council of Ministers. But the internal market project brought formal and informal systems closer together at the Summits of Luxembourg December 1985 and Hannover June 1988.[16]

Being the apex of the organization, the European Council has since been served by the Council Secretariat. It has no published agenda nor minutes, and its texts are drafted by the political cooperation secretariat. French and English are habitually spoken, and occasionally German. Its grand plenary sessions fit oddly with evening conclaves and working lunches. It meets in often over-crowded rooms with over-long agendas, with too many chiefs – most of whom are not habituated to Brussels' procedures – so that its work can be vexatious or embarrassed by speakers' ignorance. It is above all hard to engage in real discussion, given the very tight weekend schedules; and it is devastating for those who attend if it is seen to fail. But while it will always be clear that, unless things are settled beforehand in Coreper, two-day meetings are usually far too short, there is time enough for bilateral deals between individual heads of government, such as the 1991 opt-outs, provided that the other member states accept them afterwards. On the other hand, a carefully constructed deal can break down when faced with determined objections from even one member state, as happened during the Corfu Summit in June 1994, which dealt with the choice of Delors's successor.

Depending on one's ideological standpoint, the European Council can be seen as a logical extension of national sovereignty or as the apogee of inter-governmentalism. Taking into account its deep reliance on preliminary, often bilateral, talks between France and Germany, or among Christian Democrat prime ministers, it appears to downgrade the importance of the Council of Ministers and the Commission. But any matter that comes before it must first have been through the whole procedure, from Commission to Coreper to the Council. At that point it is classed as sensitive or highly political, which is sufficient for consideration by the European Council. Some fundamental issues have never reached its agenda, because they have been dealt with on the basis of consensus by the Council of Ministers. It is only in cases where questions are seen by governments to be prima facie too sensitive to be fed into any of the usual Community channels that problems arise, especially if ministers use the European Council as a way to give the Commission a political push while at the same time indicating the sort of solutions they wish it to produce.

Given that the Community has long passed the stage of being a purely economic entity, it would be remarkable if there were no forums where heads of government could meet, even if the circumstances are constrained by time and publicity. Until now, the European Council's formalized informality has ensured that it can act – on the great majority of occasions – as a Community forum. But its meetings are also the principal vehicle for whichever country holds the Presidency to display its version of what the European interest is at that time. From the point of view of centralized states it is hardly surprising that ministers tend to claim for it 'the role of impulsion and stimulus in the EC', and justify it as 'the supreme instance of seeking consensus which concludes each Presidency and sets goals for the future. The subjects are not necessarily the biggest, but the most difficult ones'.[17]

Since the late 1960s, the more federally inclined states, led by the Netherlands, have feared that inter-governmentalism would lead to an increase in national antagonisms which could be relieved only by bilateral deals. This may well be true. But the European Council (which can act as an IGC in its own right, since the Presidency takes the chair) has increased the EU's political dimensions. What has been lost in legal coherence has been remedied because governments who have not resolved their differences in the Council have often done so here. The Council has been powerless and, since 1979, unwilling, to prevent this.

After its meetings, the European Council issues a guidance document which frequently disguises differences and 'offers a decent air of ambiguity that keeps the whole thing moving'.[18] The European Council now controls many significant areas of Community business, such as the appointment of the Commission President.

II. Member States

Whatever the original treaties intended at the time, policy initiatives are the product of a reciprocal relationship between the Commission and member states which is too complex, too dependent on signals and nuances, simply to call dualism. The Commission for example is not in a position to refuse to take up ideas *tout court*, merely because they originate elsewhere with member states, and throughout the process of legislation or policy-formation the larger ones have privileged if informal access to the game.

As one French observer put it, there are two types of state; those that keep a low profile and concentrate on a few areas of interest – such as Italy, Spain, Ireland, Greece, Portugal, or Denmark. These are countries that often gain by exerting leverage on those who want always to be involved in the middle and at the start of all deals: France and Germany. Britain can be seen as in a third category of states which are in at the start and at the finish but do not attend the troublesome middle. The Netherlands comes closer to the first category, while Belgium and Luxembourg slot in between the first and the second.

What each member state, at any given time, thinks its nation has both gained from and contributed to the Community is intrinsically easier to measure than absolute gains and contributions.[19] There is no intention here to attempt the latter or to do more than suggest, by comparing their systems of coordinating Community policy, how high they rank the European Union in the context of defining national aims, and, by a brief look at their conduct when they hold the Presidency, how effective they are at implementing European policy and defining the European interest. But it is worth pointing out that in the game of comparative advantage, public appearances are not good currency.

German governments, which have not in general either gained spectacular victories or obviously influenced the Community's tenor (other than in the field of competition law), have nevertheless benefited greatly over decades from the stable environment the EC/EU has provided, while contributing an underlying politics of low inflation and economic adjustment. Having made solid economic gains throughout the Community's history, with the exception of 1980–82 (see p. 89), German governments after 1987 have ensured that progress to EMU, though made on French terms, should be matched by advances in political union. Since then the basis on which EMU is currently pursued has shifted from French to German (or rather Bundesbank) requirements.

This contrasts with France, which apparently gained most in the thirty years after 1957 yet has had, in the end, to accommodate a fixed currency, a competition policy directed against state aids, slow reform of the CAP and fisheries, and an erosion of protection. While it is *unlikely* that what one former French minister formulated as France's deep intention – that the EU should always be strong enough 'to face the U.S. without giving in'[20] – has been modified, it is with a degree of self-mockery that another recalled the proposition 'that France's positions are necessarily correct and other member states should reasonably be rallied to them'.[21] He added that, in practice, whatever the degree of state coordination, due to the ideological and social divisions inside France, its European policies have frequently fragmented, leaving the President, who, like late eighteenth-century monarchs, has always taken supreme responsibility, looking vulnerable. Some French observers, looking at Britain, recognize greater institutional efficiency when it comes to negotiating the national policy in Brussels.

Yet British governments are not seen as sharing the common assumption that the EU is an organism whose evolution depends on coexistence within the confines of a structured long-term game. Instead they appear to prefer the idea of an antagonistic partnership, governed by self-regulation, which is fundamentally opposed to a hybrid EU *Gemeinschaft* underpinned by law, and in which physical qualities count above metaphysical images.[22] Put in a different way, it is easier for a member like Britain, with largely negative aims, not to participate and to cede little, though this is always at the risk of being left to assimilate itself later, from a disadvantageous position.

By appearing tough and relentless, the Spanish government, on the other hand, has won great advantages since 1986 (although that is not the picture generally held in Spain). Yet, so long as face could be saved, it has always compromised in the end, usually by others creating the illusion of raising the ground to a suitable level rather than forcing Spain to reduce its bid.

However many points of comparison there are between the general outlook of the fifteen member states, they have few general features in common. National diversity still explains the underlying ethos with which each one approaches the Presidency, while symbolic arguments (for example over the siting of European agencies during 1993) bring out national characteristics in exaggerated forms.

However much the inter-state market is regulated by formal rules or conventions, however much the Council's agendas are shaped and influenced by the Commission, the member states see the Council as the culminating stage of a negotiated game. The SEA did initiate a change of approach to safeguarding national interests, partly because member states discovered how much each had in common, and partly because industry, commerce and, rather later, financial institutions, discovered their own routes to the EC without abandoning the alternative route via national capitals. The European champion succeeded the national champion and, though the former may now also be secular decline, the relationships between corporate interests and vested national interests have not disappeared, nor are they likely to.

But the element of fundamental national interest remains. In defining this, all governments would emphasize national security, identity (usually in terms of language, culture, immigration, and faith), conduct of fiscal and domestic economic policy, and law and justice; some would add the currency, and specific areas such as agriculture or fisheries. All three of the latter are of course already subject in part to EU law or controls.

Until the substantial extension of QMV in 1986, it had been widely assumed that a member state still had a last resort in the Luxembourg Compromise – so the British government claimed in its 1975 referendum campaign and reiterated in 1986, in unison with the governments of France, Denmark and Greece. Since Maastricht, however, it has become clear that there are two sorts of national veto: the first where the Treaties leave specified areas subject to unanimity, and hence to a legal veto. But there are fewer such areas than before and the long term tendency is for them to be diminished.

The second lies with the Luxembourg Compromise, which was evolved in 1965–6 to safeguard 'very important national interests', without which, in de Gaulle's time, there could have been no forward movement whenever interests diverged. The Compromise was still alive in the early 1980s, but curtailed, since it depended on mobilizing a minimum of support: witness Britain's unsuccessful attempt in April 1982 (see p. 100). It was last used effectively by Germany, with French connivance, in the case of cereal prices in 1985. But it is certainly not dead and may have experienced a renaissance in 1993–4 during the Balladur government's strategy towards GATT. In the centre of proposals for the 1996 IGC, ways to reduce the use of the veto ('super QMV') while safeguarding essential national interests are already being discussed in Brussels.

Failing the essential-interest argument, there is the qualified majority case, which depends on the weighted votes in Council, calculated by a formula which Britain unsuccessfully attempted to hold rigid during the EFTA enlargement debate in March 1994. No state can stand alone in this area.

In practice, the known resistance of a state *à l'outrance* might well encourage others to give it – and the EC's internal stability – the cover of a blocking minority or abstentions in sufficient numbers to achieve the same effect. No case defining the Luxembourg Compromise has so far come before the ECJ, and the view of one former President of the Court, Klaus Guttman, that only the four largest states could be certain of stopping a measure, received no support outside Denmark. In an informal sense, the Compromise may be similar to the House of Lords' budget veto used in 1909 after a lapse of over 200 years – an ultimate weapon of greater danger to the firer than the target. After all, there is, as Britain demonstrated at Maastricht, and as Denmark showed afterwards, a variety of other ways in which a state can impede a measure if it really objects to it, and achieve satisfaction from heads of large state governments that the EC's own procedures deny (to the fury of some more federally minded states, notably the Netherlands).

The systems which have evolved to coordinate policy towards the Community reflect and complement the underlying perceptions of each nation's interest in the EU itself. In this context, a nation's weight lies not in physical size or economic assets, nor the status given it by the non-EC world. Weight is made up of the effectiveness of national leaders in the Council and Permanent Representation in COREPER, taken together with the efficiency of national coordination systems.

NATIONAL COORDINATION

The simplest means to compare systems is to set them out in order, starting with that of France which has had the longest sustained influence as a model, followed by Britain's (which is often taught as a model in France), and see how the others differ from it. This is best done by an organigram with an informal evaluation attached (see figure 7.4, below).[23]

France's system works on the assumption that EC affairs are an integral part of national policy and should therefore be a mirror-image of what goes on in Paris, while reserving priority for the three ministries most continually involved: Foreign Affairs (Quai d'Orsay), Economy and Finance, and Agriculture. While a certain amount depends on ministers' own personality and seniority, much is regulated by the ministers' cabinets, by the permanent officials and by the SGCI (see p. 295). It is no longer true to say, as Couve de Murville did in the 1960s, that a minister's only aim 'est faire triompher les intérêts nationaux dont on à la charge'. That led to too much rivalry between ministries at home, requiring frequent presidential intervention, as well as increasing the risk of other member states, knowing their rival's position, ganging up against France in the Council of Ministers.

Each minister's cabinet is responsible for the coordination of what goes on in his domain and for linking it with the national coordinating body (the SGCI), and for the exchanges with the prime minister's office in the Matignon. It also links up, to whatever degree is required, with national business or financial players, especially the state-owned ones, and supplements service level contacts with opposite numbers in the Commission, or, in certain cases, other member states (chiefly Belgium and Italy, where similar cabinet systems exist). The permanent civil service handles the application of EC policy, save in cases where there is likely to be ECJ litigation (for example concerning state aids: the Matignon involved itself closely in the Renault case – see p. 522 – in order to try to mobilize DG3 against DG4).

French governments have habitually taken the view that there is a primary need to present national policy to greatest effect and to prevent any rivalries affecting negotiations in Brussels. This is of course true for any member state, but especially France where foreign affairs have frequently been disputed between Quai d'Orsay, Matignon and the president in the Elysée. Although France's administration was the first to structure EC affairs, it was

France: Coordination System

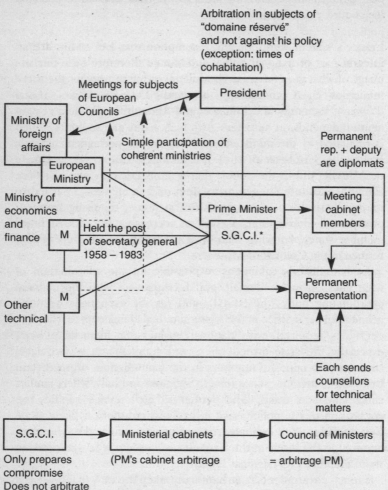

FIGURE 7.4

not thought necessary until 1987 to have an over-arching organization which could pull together not only policy formation but the implementation of what had been agreed in Brussels. The system changed, partly because ministers were sometimes tempted to try to negotiate in advance (or renegotiate afterwards directly with the Commission on their own behalf, especially in periods of cohabitation between a Socialist President and a centre-right government). Training new officials in EC affairs took on a more systematic form in the mid–1980s, when specialized courses in European politics and law began at the Institut d'Etudes Politiques de Paris. The engineering *grandes Écoles* were understandably less preoccupied with such issues, but the École Nationale d'Administration carried a full range from 1990.

While the rivalry of foreign and finance ministers had been mitigated in Giscard's time, that of foreign and European affairs ministers ramified throughout the early Mitterrand years and was only partly resolved during Edith Cresson's tenure of the latter office in 1988–90.[24] Since then, advantage has varied according to personality: from the Elysée in Elisabeth Guigou's day, to the present centre of influence at the Quai d'Orsay, to which European affairs is at present subordinated.

Overall coordination rests with SGCI (Service de Coordination Inter-ministériel, originally created for OEEC in 1948, and modified many times before being assigned to Guigou at the Elysée forty years later).[25] Even here, it is hard to resolve the different approaches of the Quai d'Orsay and the Trésor – the powerful elite within Economy and Finance – often supported by the Banque de France. Over and above the SGCI, it can be difficult, even for a like-minded inner group, to define the ultimate French interest – subject as that has been to frequent disputes between a president from one party and a prime minister from another.

In contrast to Germany, where only the chancellor's office serves as a last resort, the system provides several levels for policy disagreements to be resolved. The system is logical and routinely efficient, ensuring maximum coherence and effort in any Council of Ministers meeting. Where it has broken down in the past, it has done so for political rather than administrative reasons. The system is generally resistant to attempts by other ministers to gain particular influence and tries to be impervious to pressure from non-governmental players. That in political terms it is vulnerable to groups of large firms such as AGREF, or demanding interest groups like the agricultural lobby, emphasizes the advantages of size to the detriment of small or medium-sized enterprises, and of direct action in a state whose high level of centralization has never entirely eliminated civil society's insurrectionary element. Some of the corporate players are now beginning to take advantage of the greater openness shown by the French Permanent Representive in Brussels instead.[26]

European Council matters like special relations with individual member states, headed by Germany (less regularly with Spain, Italy and Britain), have always been part of the President's reserved domain. Officials' power is limited: the Elysée secretary general and his cabinet have a brief to ensure that no minister has made arrangements in the Councils which would inhibit his master at summit meetings, 'so that potentially dangerous subjects (like steel and ship-building) do not develop into time bombs on which there would be automatic conflict with Spain or Germany.'[27] Even so, the system came under severe stress in 1989–90 during German reunification, an issue with vast implications for France which caused Mitterrand to hesitate while the alternatives were disputed between Guigou and Attali. The uncertainty was ended only when Mitterrand and Kohl agreed their celebrated letter and the schedule for the 1991 IGCs.

At the sharp of the end of the wedge in Brussels, the Permanent Representation takes its instructions from the SGCI, the Quai d'Orsay and the president, in that order. The ambassador reports routinely to SGCI, from which Brussels information is filtered outwards to other ministers, and he oversees the two *cellules* where regional or non-governmental business players can meet officials on the ground.

It is worth noting how, despite so much effort, rivalries still exist, drawing their strength from frequent discord at the very top of government on the always-contentious subject of France's position in Europe. However good the SGCI is, its success depends on how well ministers' personalities fit, as well as on the party and presidential-

PM balances. It is not intended to broker political compromises and cannot prevent the hard cases rising upwards. Moreover the mechanisms are so intricate that they depend on some goodwill, and concomitant expertise in other cabinets. It is hardly flexible, compared to the systems in Britain or Denmark, and often waits too long for the Commission to make the first move, rather than reacting early (probably as the vestigial legacy of an earlier contempt for Brussels' Directorates' low-grade initiatives).[28]

Neither does SGCI control the entire process: ERM management is reserved for the Trésor and Banque de France, while the mergers and fraud section (DGCCRF) covers the area of competition as if it were 'counsel for companies presenting their dossiers to the Commission'.

Finally, the Conseil d'Etat has only recently, in a succession of celebrated cases (*Alitalia, Nicolo,* and *Philip Morris/Rothman*) accepted the French state's responsibility for incorrect application of any EC directive. Not until the early 1990s has it been possible in the ultimate legal analysis for the French system to accommodate itself to EC legal primacy – and some would argue that this has still not finally occurred. The concept of norms remains in doubt and the centralized Fench state retains a very different conception from federal ones of what subsidiarity means (an attitude of course shared by Britain). It is worth adding that the French parliament has only recently been given a measure of involvement, having for years been provided with only routine information about the decision-making process.

On the other hand, with such an apparatus, it has been easier when the time came, as it did in 1990–91, to reverse long-held policies or attitudes in the Paris administration, and to educate it in a more EC-orientated way. SGCI can mobilize French MEPs even across political party divisions, and has generally been successful in coordinating the national positions which will be put in Brussels as a preliminary to finding solutions acceptable to France.[29]

A. Other Centralized States (Britain, Spain, Portugal, Greece)

BRITAIN

If France's system has been subject to ministerial rivalry and

Britain: Coordination System

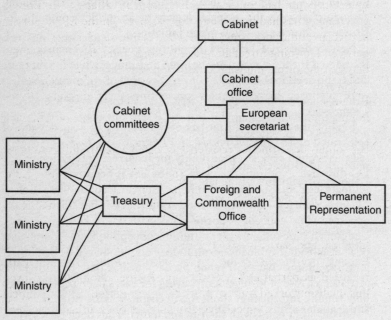

FIGURE 7.5

feuding, Britain's has suffered from the deep-rooted, fundamental conflicts in British political life, reflected in its media, about British national identity in Europe. This took the form of party divisions in the 1970s and reiterated disputes in the 1980s, between the prime minister, Margaret Thatcher, and the Foreign Office or Treasury ministers who had to deal with European affairs. No French government has had to undergo this passage. On the ERM entry in particular and, since 1993 on EMU, a line of cleavage has run between Downing Street and the Treasury, and a more general one between the prime minister and the foreign secretary.

Formally, the Foreign Office has been at the centre since Britain's accession in 1973, when Edward Heath gave it this role, hoping thereby to change the outlook across the whole of Whitehall and to create an elite accustomed to making headway in Brussels.[30] But other departments resisted his extension of the promotion network to Brussels and this failure was compounded under the Labour governments of the late 1970s, when the EC was conceived in terms only of economic policies, under the Treasury's brief.

Early on, however, the Cabinet Office took up a central coordinating position, partly as a reflection of its habitual domestic function, and partly to offset the Foreign Office's influence which Labour governments of the 1970s, followed in the Thatcher years, regarded as partial and overweening. At the administrative level, this dualism worked well over a twenty-year period. But in political and Cabinet terms, especially party political ones, it had to accommodate to almost insuperable ideological cleavages.

Conservative leaders in opposition years, and in office after 1979, concentrated on the CAP and budgetary reform until about 1983–4 (see p. 107). By then, after the Falklands War, the Foreign Office's political influence had been curtailed, the foreign secretary himself being only one of the three main ministerial figures on the ODE Cabinet Committee. The impetus for political coordination depended at that stage on the prime minister, for administration on the Cabinet Office, the European Secretariat, and Charles Powell, seconded by the Foreign Office to number 10 Downing Street – who in his capacity as special adviser also played Horace Wilson to Thatcher's Neville Chamberlain.

These tensions diminished in the mid–1980s, thanks to the work of officials connected with the Single European Act and to Thatcher's own enthusiasm for the project. But they recurred in the late 1980s as the prime minister reacted after the Single European Act to her sense of having been encompassed by Brussels. Her revival of interest in getting a larger share of British nationals into the Commission dates from this period. The political initiative returned to Cabinet members generally and to the Ministerial Committee when John Major took over in 1991.[31] In contrast, at the administrative level, it can be said that the Cabinet Office European Secretariat has played a more intensive, continuous and coherent role than the equivalent in any other member state; Whitehall culture is now largely supportive and coherent, and officials had no problems during the 1991 IGCs in negotiating directly with their equivalents in other member states.[32]

One explanation for the effectiveness of British officials in the European context rests on the Whitehall ethos itself, according to which ministers trust their civil servants to get it right once the initial policy framework is set. Another suggests that success lies not so much in coordination, in the French or Spanish manner, but in the brokerage process of sorting out problems, distinguishing the important matters and sustaining the idea that all departments have to keep Brussels in their sights. 'The spirit of solidarity exists, people trust each other to be reasonable, don't have to keep going to Ministers to decide issues, don't push disagreements, don't much hide things from each other.'[33]

This may of course have been part of a general civil service reaction to the novel pattern of ministerial-Whitehall relations during the 1980s. The Cabinet Office always tried to provide the sort of atmosphere in which habitual Treasury-Foreign Office rivalries would not escalate. But this function was easier to sustain when any divisions were likely to be exploited from above, and when Brussels was conceived of as the adversary rather than the exemplar. Consequently, the volume of informal business handled by what remains a small unit compares with that of the SGCI: two hundred meetings a year, and a circulation of around three hundred papers.[34]

The industrial and financial players stick to their post-War departmental sponsors; industry, employment or defence. Because of 1980s' political conflicts, ministers' support is regarded as evanescent; on the official side, only a few large companies make direct contact with the Cabinet Office and usually without achieving much impact. Large companies or financial institutions' own direct links to Brussels are consequently enhanced, while SMEs have to be content with the research, development and framework strategies offered by the DTI. Both Houses of Parliament are kept informed by the Cabinet Office and their Scrutiny Committees' comments are taken very seriously. Meanwhile the Permanent Representation makes no attempt to disguise the value it puts on contacts with British nationals working in the Commission, rating this and the Commission's employment of five to six hundred British experts as one effective means to remedy the disadvantage inherent in the lesser numbers of British officials employed there.[35]

In contrast to the SGCI, the European Secretariat's brief is to react, as a company would, to early stages of the evolution of Commission policy, and to incorporate what is known into the tactical planning of Council meetings, 'to ensure that, whenever the UK needs a policy on an EC issue it has one; that that is consistent with the government's broader policy, is realistic, and is properly followed up in practice.'[36] Essentially reactive, this works well for a country whose government knows better what it does not want than what it desires from the EC. It is flexible but centralized, complementary to the domestic interplay between Whitehall and Downing Street, efficient if illogical, and more effective in the short than the long term. It suits a Britain which has not in twenty years sought lasting alliances, except on the occasions when the politicians have lacked essential information or ignored it, as at Milan 1985 and Rome 1989.

Spain

Spain is included as a centralized state, not in terms of the state's formal structure, which is *decentralized*, especially at regional level, but in relation to the process of coordinating European policy.

After six years of waiting, Spain's government was not in a position in 1986 to affect the internal market's evolution other than as part of its own transitional negotiations. In any case, Spanish interests were straightforwardly defined by the Gonzalez government as being to redress the imbalances *vis-à-vis* France and Italy, and to take every advantage of membership to accelerate modernization, adjustment and investment in the national administrative machine as well as in industry and the financial sectors. ERM entry in 1989 was predicated, firstly, on the assumption that only an external discipline could remedy the political system's failure to run a stable fiscal policy and lower the rate of inflation and, secondly, that it was necessary at the same time to open up and liberalize the state sector and the labour market. As Quevedo put it, 'no sirve de nada cambiar de lugar si no se esta dispuesto cambiar de vida.'[37]

Since its long relative isolation ended with Franco's death, Spanish governments have presumed that their projects of reform coincided with the EC's own development. With earlier modernizing episodes, under Carlos III, the nineteenth-century Afrancesados, or Franco's own technocrats (who were mainly members of Opus Dei), having been short-lived, Spain could not afford that the EC should falter, nor that it should shift its centre of gravity markedly north or eastwards by too rapid membership extension. (Since 80% of its external trade now lies with the EC, the same is true of Portugal, at least in economic terms.)

The belief that a state's bargaining strength depends on the coherence and effectiveness of its coordinating apparatus is widely shared.[38] Contrary to the appearance of decentralization, Spain's coordination therefore followed that of France, with the aim of inhibiting contrary voices, whether from the banks, the unions or the more vociferous autonomous regions. Formally this has been done by the State Secretary for the EC (Carlos Westendorp) acting for the Foreign Ministry, covering the three levels of central and regional administration and political parties (although the parliament has no role as such in EC decision-making). Economic issues fall under another State Secretary and the two are jointly coordinated by a junior on the Council of Ministers or Cabinet.

There has not yet been much time for specialized training of civil servants who, in any case, work wholly to ministers' direction. While emphasizing their sovereignty, especially where regions attempt to influence policy, informally ministers make a virtue of their openness to industrial and financial players, or academics, and are accessible to a lively national press and television to a greater degree than their French or British counterparts. But in fact ministers try to press corporate players into line, and use the interplay with them to propagate their own vision of Spain as a European power. That they also hold up Catalonia as the model of what a region should be – but in Madrid's terms – owes more to the electoral necessity of a government with a bare majority than a belief in the virtues of European regionality. Nevertheless, this was well received, at least in regions other than Catalonia, until recession hit the whole of Spain in 1991.

Outside state institutions, and for the Spanish public generally, there is not much evidence that this prescription is widely believed to have been effective. A long-standing pessimism appears pervasive after the glories of Expo Seville and the Barcelona Olympic Games in 1992, a sense 'that Spain cannot win against the EC, yet cannot succeed without it', which encourages the conclusion that Spanish enterprise, lacking transnationals or MNCs able to fund high technology research or the development of new products, could compete only if linked to dominant foreign/EC investors in technology (Volkswagen/Séat, Alsthom/Maquinaria Terrestre y Marítima). This in turn reinforced the argument about cohesion funds after 1990, that without large transfers of money and technology, Spain could not possibly accept the Maastricht Treaty.

As a result, the belief held in the mid-1980s by Miguel Boyer, Minister of the Economy and Finance (who together with Carlos Solchaga represented the liberal end of the nominally social-democratic government), that concerted adjustment depended on there being no heavy losers through bankruptcy or unemployment, survived into the government's coordinated programmes for the 1990s. But in the deep recession which followed, this fitted badly with what by 1994 was the highest EC unemployment rate, and the most parlous conditions in steel and textiles. It has so far proved impossible for a long-surviving, still nominally social-democratic government to sustain at one and the same time policies of liberalization, freer trade, anti-inflation and reform of the taxation system. Policy coordination continues to be beset by regions' alternative claims (see chapter 9), by unions and employers' discontent, wholesale corruption in the ruling party, and a failure to privatize Spain's basic and long-outmoded state industries.

Madrid's undoubted centralizing power is thus expended, adequately insofar as the wedge of influence touches points towards Brussels (probably more than adequately where regional and coherence funding is concerned), but inadequately at its home base, where political dialogue alternates fitfully with confrontation. The formalities of consulting the regions or the social players conceal great disparities of treatment by different ministers (e.g., in agriculture between Romero and Solbes). Regional leaders often claim that Madrid speaks for them in Brussels in order to curtail Catalan and Basque ambitions at home.[39] The prime minister, rather than any single minister, presides over what amounts to a form of democratic centralism. The system, which certainly won impressive victories on cohesion at the Edinburgh Summit 1992, and over fishing rights at Essen in 1994, is itself a product of a particular time and government and may well be modified under a centre-right government. Yet in historical terms, it seems to be part of a much more ancient lineage.

PORTUGAL

In Portugal, EC affairs are also the monopoly of central government, apart from its legal obligation to consult the regions of Azores and Madeira. As in Spain, policy is only for ministers and not civil servants: parliament remains marginal and there is little space for consultation with industry or labour in any structured form either in Lisbon or at the Permanent Representative's office in Brussels where it is, if anything, discouraged.[40] In any case, during the early 1990s recession, the government's austerity programme was hard for either to stomach. Coordination is vested in the Council of EC Ministers (CNAC) with the prime minister in the chair giving direction to the inter-ministerial committee (comprising himself, the foreign minister, and economic affairs ministers in that order).

Within the Ministry of Foreign Affairs, the Director General for

European Affairs takes charge of the coordinating process, which also encompasses the Department of External Trade. Unlike Britain or France, the Portuguese government aims only to have a view on the questions which affect it: filtered through a highly nationalistic context, Portuguese influence is focused on its Commissioner, whatever his post in the college, rather than officials in the Directorates.[41] At home, the Industry Ministry consults the different individual sectors sufficiently to keep his Cabinet colleagues aware of how the players are making their own dispositions.

Portuguese public opinion sees the EC as a source of political stability, and the basis for innovation and change – heralded by vast projects such as the VW/Ford plant to build a four-wheel drive vehicle. Its political elite, conscious of social and cultural problems and a loss of national identity after the three African colonial wars ended in defeat in the 1970s, sees an equal need for Portugal to develop an EC-related mission elsewhere, probably in Brazil, and possibly again in black Africa. In Portugal, as in Britain, Europe still means different things to different groups, and a sense remains that sovereignty is threatened until Portugal's new late twentieth-century identity has had time fully to develop.

GREECE

In Greece, the cleavage between EU-federalist rhetoric and the reality of centralized state control seems to be absolute, for the state itself is run by party leaders in power almost as if Greece lay outside the EU. The politics of *clientilismo* prevails, even down to the state schools, characterized by an understandably defensive Hellenocentrism which is reflected in the Greek government's attempts to use their Commissioners or officials as if Brussels were another Athens. Since there are no perceptible institutional links to industry, the federation of industry (SEV) and the banks have created their own direct contacts in Brussels in a simulacrum of the black economy which now constitutes perhaps 50% of Greece's GDP.

A line of tension separates this entrepreneurial dimension from a party-controlled state which attempts, through its command of central power, to control much of the nation's economic life. As far as departments are concerned, the Foreign Ministry is responsible for EU affairs, since few outside it know or understand Brussels. Yet intense departmental rivalries impair its credibility and the Greek Permanent Representation needs to be unusually large, both because of its distance from Athens and to carry out its role as mediator between the departments. Being politically partisan, the civil service can and often does influence ministers; but since the Foreign Ministry is itself in the end subordinate to the prime minister's office, it seems unlikely that even a clear-sighted or vigorous minister can make much impression on the inward-looking pattern of party-dominated centralization.

Yet Greece, having seen its weak democracy strengthened, and its ties to the West put beyond domestic revanchism, continues to seek elusive modernization as its entrepreneurs strive to escape from a deeply conservative, nationalistic, xenophobic and state-heavy environment. Meanwhile its two political classes, one looking westward, seeking to erode state control and bring reform by liberalizing the banks and introducing a single currency, the other focused on the potentially hostile states to the north-east and south-east and highly resistant to EU intrusion, impose their rivalries on the Community.

B. Federal or De-Centralized States (Germany, Netherlands, Belgium, Denmark, Luxembourg)

GERMANY

Germany is fortunate in that EC membership has never seriously been contested. The image of German membership presented to its own people is as a paragon of altruism in EC affairs, an exemplar to the less committed, and a paymaster for the most backward economies (in return for which German industries can rely on access to these markets). Only since 1991 has there been serious criticism of the consequences in two areas: the Bundesbank's interest rate policy, as a result of German reunification, together with the ultimate impact of EMU on the deutschmark, and secondly, the cost of cohesion policy, to say nothing of the EC's endemic losses through fraud and waste.

The system of coordination might have been designed to foster

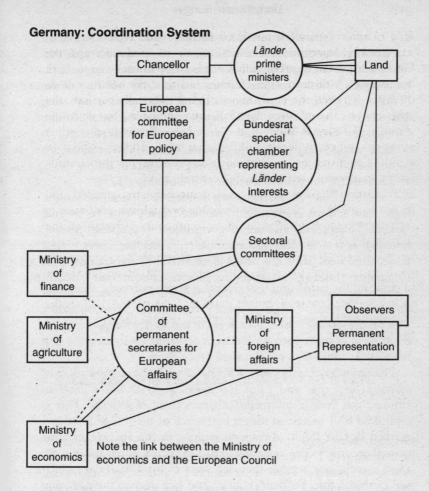

Germany: Coordination System

Chancellor

Länder prime ministers

Land

European committee for European policy

Bundesrat special chamber representing *Länder* interests

Sectoral committees

Ministry of finance

Committee of permanent secretaries for European affairs

Ministry of agriculture

Ministry of foreign affairs

Observers

Permanent Representation

Ministry of economics

Note the link between the Ministry of economics and the European Council

FIGURE 7.6

this climate of opinion, for in conformity with West Germany's 1949 federal constitution, it takes all sectors of opinion formally and informally into account. Broadly speaking, as in most other systems, the Foreign Ministry handles political matters, the Ministry of the Economy (BMWi) addresses those dealing with the economy. Both link directly to Coreper and thence to the General Affairs Council and Ecofin; both report twice yearly to the Bundestag.

As far as economic players are concerned, the BMWi maintains a continuous dialogue and, while reserving its rights of action, rarely acts against the interests of a sector or even a major firm.[42]

Consultation on all government enactments is prescribed in the Basic Law and has consequently increased vastly with the internal market. This process also serves government as a testing ground, covering as it does peak organizations representing industry and trade, employers (BDI and BDA), SMEs (ZDH) and Chambers of Commerce (DIHT), but in return governments inevitably accept the need to mobilize consent for their policies. One consequence of this quite stylized two-way process is that interests tend to attract wider representation: beer producers in the south, for example, see themselves as spokesmen for Bavarian demands for a direct voice in Brussels in addition to the Bavarian office there.

The informal has become formalized and the combination of technical expertise and rules (*Ordnungspolitik*) makes it hard to emulate the flexible informality characteristic of Britain. This is replicated in Brussels, so that at both ends of the wedge there is a marked lack of ability to respond rapidly, in the absence of clear central control.[43] The same combination recurs in parliament, for 1600 associations register their interests in the Bundestag, which acts both as a filter for their requests and as a stage in the gathering debate from *Länder* up to Federal Government. Indeed, such has been the weight of *Länder* claims for statehood (*Staatsqualität*) and self-determination (*Selbstbestimmungsrecht*) since the 1992 changes in the Basic Law triggered by Maastricht, that any government coordination has to take account of it as if subsidiarity were already an EU reality. Since in Bonn itself, under the Federal Constitution, each Ministry retains full responsibility (*Ressortprinzip*), the system lacks a prime mover save, in the ultimate resort, the chancellor.

Until the mid–1980s, chancellors from Adenauer to Schmidt had left the main decisions on Community policy to their foreign ministers or the Council of Ministers, retaining only a watching brief vested in the European Affairs Section of the chancellor's office. Policy-making occurred within lines of sectoral demarcation and each sector – BMWi, Finance, or Agriculture – could challenge any attempt to dictate by the Foreign Ministry. The result was not however the lateral resolution of problems hoped for in a federal system, but an increase in protective or defensive rivalries, enhanced by the sharing of ministerial appointments inevitable in coalition governments. Only partly mediated by the Inter-ministerial Committee of State Secretaries, these procedures were and are time-consuming and extremely complicated. One result was, at least until 1988, that German Presidencies found it hard to define what they sought during their six months' tenure, other than to avoid paying more into EC funds. Notable bargaining successes, such as winning the European Monetary Institute for Frankfurt in 1993 came only in the wake of unification.[44]

In emergencies, Chancellors began to develop ways to intervene, after 1973; these strategies have been strengthened since 1984, during Kohl's tenure of office. But these sporadic intrusions are restricted to fundamental issues (as defined by the Chancellor) such as the introduction of the EMS, or the 1990–91 commitment to EMU – both decisions having been taken despite the opposition of BMWi, the Finance Ministry and the Bundesbank. On a regular basis, it has failed to prevent the Permanent Representative being put in the position of advocating as German policy the often ill-coordinated views of at least four main departments, overlaid by the personal rivalries of Bonn and certain of the more vociferous *Länder*.

Naturally, once Kohl took charge of the internal market programme at Hannover in 1988, the major firms and financial institutions showed their preference for the highest possible level of concertation with the chancellor and his advisers (*Kanzlerrunde*), to a BMWi which was in any case in slow relative political decline. By the late 1980s, most had opened their own offices in Brussels, showing a greater degree of independence from central government and the Permanent Representation than their French counter-parts.[45]

Kohl's activity during later stages of the internal market pro-gramme had the adverse effect of alienating German trade unions, especially since he was also instrumental in allowing the British at Maastricht to opt out of what had been the unions' main compensa-tion for the internal market's rigours, the Social Protocol. The coordinating system thus produced disadvantages for Germany from which centralized states do not usually suffer, without neces-sarily enhancing domestic conciliation. This has only partly been offset by more post–1992 civil service and ministerial attempts to improve their contacts with non-German Commissioners, as well as German officials and experts below Commissioner level in the Directorates, since the effort has been spread thinly, and given equal consideration to the Parliament and MEPs. It has not been productive, for example, to define which are useful Directorates by moral-political criteria, nor to over-play relations with some to the detriment of others.

In the end, whatever their general outlook on federal Europe, German governments have had to work through inter-govern-mental mechanisms in recent years with a frequency which might have surprised and saddened Kohl's predecessors. The govern-ment's ability to act decisively, which has become ever-more evident in the last four years, is still constrained by its machinery, more than those of the centralized or intermediate states; this deficiency is remedied by formidable preparation and a remarkable degree of technical expertise in the formulation of its desiderata. A system as integrated as Germany's is hard to change, even in informal ways: it serves both as a reflection of, and a permanent influence on, the nature of German industry and industrial society.[46] To a far greater degree than in Britain for example, which is generally regarded in Germany as ethically incorrect if not anarchic, German governments have effectively resisted what Fred Hirsch saw as the 'moral depletions' of modern capitalism. This legacy is unlikely easily to be given up in the wake of unification.

THE NETHERLANDS

The Dutch system derives from an older history than the post-World War II Federal Republic; and its independence, resentment of the pretensions of central authority, and bias towards consensual agreement long predate the EEC.[47] It is highly decentralized, coordination taking place not at civil service level but under the Council of Ministers in the Hague according to collegial forms set out in the Constitution. The prime minister has a role but only as a middle-man, not arbiter. Given departmental ministers' records of stubborn defence of their interests, particularly in the Foreign Office, a resolution of inter-departmental problems may take so long as to be incomplete by the time policies reach the Permanent Representation. A 1993 law gives the prime minister slightly more responsibility as a broker, but the departure from Brussels of the foreign minister van den Broek at the same time allowed him more actual scope for manoeuvre. Even after reaching agreements, ministers are prone to reopen issues, so that the industrial or financial players may be left uncertain whether to lobby widely and risk delay, or merely to accept the infrequent rewards of their regular links with the Economic Ministry.

This slow, solid and federalized style has been adopted by some of the largest Dutch companies themselves, such as Shell and Philips, in their internal administration. At ministerial level, service on the Coordinating Committee (KK) is arduous and time-consuming and is normally left to juniors, who maintain frequent contact with the Dutch Permanent Representation in order to test Commission programmes. So finely balanced is the system between ministers that it can only be changed at election times; and despite a compromise achieved in the late 1960s, the KK itself is regularly divided by the rivalries of Foreign and Economic Ministries. As a result the Permanent Representation sometimes has to arbitrate in Brussels according to its assessment of what is going on at home.

Defenders of the Dutch system see it as being predictable and stable, and far closer to EU ideals than centralized systems. Yet they acknowledge that it is open to spoiling tactics by other member states – notably with the Netherlands' draft Treaty at Maastricht.

The federation of industries (VNO) admits that consensus building on this scale is ill-adapted to the policy-making cycle in Brussels, and suspects that it may lead ministers to misunderstand the bargaining techniques of other member states.[48] Complicated and tardy though the process is, however, the Netherlands wins more of the Brussels games than might be expected. The principal defect appears to lie at the level of ministers' rivalries and personal competence which cannot be remedied, however good the civil service, rather than in the factionalism of local authorities which frequently puts KK-agreed solutions at risk.

DENMARK

Denmark, too, despite the appearance of having only a few participants in its small policy community, has historic reasons for mobilizing consensus in a decentralized society with over 2000 separate interest organizations.[49] Since its entry in 1973, parliamentary control has been crucial, and the coordinating body, the Market Committee is, uniquely, responsible to the Folketing rather than to the Cabinet or prime minister.

Luxembourg and Denmark share a fear of being swamped by giant neighbours; but whereas Luxembourg claims near-total identity of interest with the EC (save on the tender subjects of banking and withholding tax harmonization) and has a very simple form of coordination, Denmark has so far tended to resist EC intrusion, viewing it as a threat to national identity and language because of the widespread feeling that 'economic actors these days have powers that neutral states cannot counter'.[50] As the referenda showed in 1992, Danish opinion appears to define the Community interest as a zero sum game at the expense of small states. Like Britain, but for rather different reasons, Denmark tends to be *contre*. Because of the prevalence of minority governments, and in the light of the first Maastricht referendum, ministers and civil servants habitually look for what is acceptable; as the result of the second referendum suggested, they do not have powerful administrative means to mobilize consent. Danish responses therefore are often slow to reach the Permanent Representation and governments appear to lack flexibility in the fast-moving EC currents. Policy-making is led by the foreign minister or industry minister, according to the matter in hand. Compared with livestock or fishing, manufacturing industry was a late comer in the nineteenth century and links with this sector have never flourished on a corporate basis, so that the industry federation (CDI) rarely seeks to influence government, preferring instead to concentrate on media and public opinion. But it has twice-yearly routine meetings with the Foreign Ministry which has, informally, been more receptive since the mid-1980s. Firms or banks have no direct links to the Market Committee itself, and like the CDI rely largely on written communication to Brussels.

Based as it is on parliament, in a small but very diverse society, the system is largely free of party political argument. On the other hand, it is demonstrably slow, and is often out of phase with the EU (and on some financial directives, with the European banking community as well). Although the political culture has changed since the long period of social democratic rule came to an end in 1980, it is still the case that if the prime minister or Cabinet have to take charge, the system rapidly reverts to being over-politicized.

BELGIUM

Belgium is taken last because, like Luxembourg, its system is relatively straightforward. After Germany it is the most clearly articulated of this group, judging by its governments' regular success in overcoming the fissile tendencies of a nation made up of three communities, three regions, and two asymmetric ethnic groups, where national law does not necessarily override community laws.[51] Up to about 1980, it was relatively centralized, in that the Foreign Ministry took all unresolved issues to the Ministerial Council for arbitration. The foreign minister's leading role since the days of Paul Henri Spaak rested on wide public acceptance that European integration was in Belgium's objective interest. But in the late 1970s a succession of weaker foreign ministers, and the growth of the Flemish Socialist party, led respectively to criticisms of the system and a need to form coalition governments.

By the late 1980s, largely at the behest of Jean-Luc Dehaene, the prime minister, the focus shifted, so that coordination occurred at both ends of the wedge – among ministers and with an effective

Permanent Representation, both of whom are, of course, located in Brussels. Public opinion, which still regards it as vital for Belgium that the EC should function well and not be dominated by larger states, acts as a unifying factor on both. Illogical as it may be, the system works well, albeit with side effects which would be insupportable if Belgium were not at the EC centre: for it requires continual efforts by politicians and administrators to keep these balances. Belgium is in fact a vestigial state, a federation which, unlike the EC, is in the process of losing statehood, 'where', as one official put it, 'the rules of the game have to be respected by everyone in good faith' if centrifugal forces are not to erupt and confront each other.

C. Intermediate States – Ireland and Italy

IRELAND

In Ireland, EU matters are coordinated by the Foreign Ministry, but power is also shared with Agriculture and, to some extent, Industry. The Coordinating Committee has only a general brief under the Secretary of State in the taioseach's (prime minister's) office and departments act very much on their own, within the general policy steer which derives from the head of government. In a state where nearly a third of the 3.5 million population lives in Dublin, the government is leader in EC affairs, arbiter of Irish interests and the largest single employer. Although a sort of tripartite corporatism, similar to the post-War Austrian example, brings together the social partners, and although industry and finance have well-serviced links to government departments, the system (like the overreaching national debt) is state-centred and gives the civil service a major role in resolving internal tensions.

In that sense, and in defining EC matters as mainstream Irish ones, the system resembles that of France. But unlike France, Ireland still confronts problems of hard economic adjustment, similar to Portugal and Greece.[52] However much cohesion funds may provide a palliative, EC money needs to be backed by domestic reform policies which have to be negotiated with weighty vested interests, chiefly in agriculture and food-related industries. Since the political parties still align themselves according to archaic affinities, the problem for any government is to hold the balance between the EC's requirements and Ireland's perceived needs on one hand, and between imposing and bargaining domestic solutions on the other.

Ireland will, for the foreseeable future, seek relief in the EU as neutral arbiter in dealing with its internal problems of unemployment, inequality, declining prosperity, high national debt, continued emigration, and threats to the rural economy. In terms of techniques, Irish governments seek always to be helpful, to build on what affinities they have with congenial member states, even with Nordic ones. As a result, over the last twenty years Ireland has been able to break out of its narrow dependency on Britain and also, to some extent, the United States.

ITALY

Italy comes last because it is a singular case, having undergone, since 1993, an unpremeditated and unprecedented political *épuration*. Community reports have often noted the mismatch between the Italian government's swift and optimistic responses to EU legislation, and the reality of its implementation – whose delays are not necessarily due to incompetence, but rather to administrators' and above all politicians' convenience.[53] Because the governing elites' focus has been on Rome first, the regions second, and the outside world third, and because government itself was sustained from the Second World War until the 1990s by an inward-looking Christian Democrat-led anti-Communist coalition, the EU and even Italy's presence in Brussels has had to wait. From this hierarchy of power flowed the evidence of fragmented policy-making and lack of preparation even for large-scale Foreign Ministry initiatives. On what has happened since 1992, it is hard as yet to comment, because the outcome – reform of the whole governing process and the administration – is still uncertain.

In theory the foreign minister has primacy, but in practice ministers make their own links with the Community. The former guards what he can, in the absence of the densely textured coordination which ministers in other states enjoy. The civil service, lacking the long administrative traditions of the other four large states, has no independent role. Outside certain state institutions and the majority of intellectuals who have long hoped the EC would provide a stimulus for the reform of institutions and of Italian political life, the political class has not interested itself sufficiently to play for an Italian national interest, except on certain foreign policy questions, and has been content to let the major companies and financial groups handle their own affairs in Brussels.

Across the whole machinery of government, there is little sense of the need to promote Italian interests in Brussels, except where what already exists (such as structural funds for the south) is threatened. The fact that certain regions took a lead similar to that in Catalonia (with German *Länder* in mind) in the late 1980s had repercussions in the rapid growth of the Northern League, and its ascent to power in 1994 as part of the short-lived Berlusconi coalition.

Most Italian initiatives in recent years, like de Michelis's 'pentagonale' solution for south-eastern Europe, have come from the Foreign Ministry or the Banca d'Italia (the Padoa-Schioppa Report being an important element in making the intellectual case for EMU). But Italian officials in Brussels are acutely aware of how little the Commission or member states now trust Italy, and how the Directorates find it hard to form continuous links with Rome. Because there is a fundamental lack of coordination, banks or industry go their own way. Lacking its own clear channels to government, Confindustria remains weak in comparison with CBI or DVI, while the large firms, as in Denmark or Greece, make their own way to Brussels (Fiat was one of the first in the EEC to open an office there).[54] Since these have so far functioned well, and since the Italian public has appeared quite uninterested – for lack of successive governments' lead – there has been until recently no stimulus for changing a system of complex and endless bargaining in government and parliament.

Italy has therefore slipped into what might be called disorganized coordination and an isolation which is unlikely to change until its political system is rebuilt. To paraphrase Marco Giuliani, the present chaos is itself a form of equilibrium which the EU has no choice but to accept, since it is beyond the Commission's power to reform a member state. The EJC does not accept excuses, ever since the *Leonesco* (milk subsidies) case in the 1960s, but cannot discipline a member state either, except by a Maastricht Article which has not yet been used, permitting an unspecified fine. The price that Italians pay for giving the impression of being unprepared on essential points in negotiations, and administratively disorganized, is lost influence, posts not filled, project money in jeopardy, and the delays and confusions imposed on their unfortunate Permanent Representation.[55] Recently, irritated by delays and failures, officials in the Commission have hinted that regional money could be transferred elsewhere if it is not better spent in future.

Yet, as its response to the Hannover Agreement on freedom of capital movements showed, Italian governments can react quickly and effectively when they choose to do so. Hence the faith invested by institutions which have a keen interest in using the EU as a *deus ex machina*, the Banca d'Italia and the Anti Trust Authority. Both look to the ERM and eventual EMU or to competition policy as neutral external disciplines. The competitive system works only if players demonstrate a sense of commonalty and reciprocity: continued displays of self-interest, masked by verbal assurances, risk loss of Brussels' interest and eventual member states' disregard.[56]

THE PRESIDENCY (see p. xxxv for Presidencies since 1971.)

Systems alone, however efficient, do not automatically bring success, neither does their weak implantation always imply failure, as the Italian and Greek cases suggest. They provide a necessary precondition for continuous advantage, not only in the member states' game of influencing legislation or policy outcomes but also, using to their fullest effect the six-monthly tenures of the Presidency.

From 1986–1994, the Presidency came round to each state once in six years. From 1995 onwards this period became seven and a half. For six months, it confers a unique status on the holder but at the same time it imposes a cluster of problems: the time is rarely enough to achieve substantial reform or change, while a member's ability to take the chair with flair and efficiency will determine whether it is remembered with respect or rancour.[57] Over the last twenty years, the Presidency's role has been much enhanced, both in the Council of Ministers' policy-making and in dealing with external affairs, and in the European Council's informal activity outside the Treaty's framework (whose heads of government summits now attract more public attention than meetings of the Council itself).

Today's Presidency needs to produce compromises for both levels even if it does not originate them. (Thus the arrangements for the Danish opt-outs of Maastricht in December 1992 were proposed by Britain as President, but with the advice of the head of the Council's Legal Service, Jean-Claude Piris, and the political weight offered by Helmut Kohl's ability to persuade France and Spain to concur.)[58] Its activities attract more media attention than in the past; it needs to rely on its own Secretariat and the Legal Service and to employ a discreetly persuasive manner, rather than a *tutelle* towards the rest, for it has no legal authority over them, only the weight of recent custom. Each of the others, after all, has its own programme for every summit, which it urges on the current Presidency.

From preliminary meetings, and a sense of what is possible, the President-state will decide what its government considers should be the main themes making up its version of the European interest. It is up to it to decide on ways of presenting them, guided by past practice and, since 1981, by an increasingly close association with the previous and the next President-state, referred to as the Troika (instituted to provide a means of rapid response, after the Soviet invasion of Afghanistan, through which the Presidency could speak more authoritatively on behalf of the EC).

The Presidency's formal powers are restricted to the chairman's role, setting the agenda and priorities, and the ways of handling business. It has authority to call a vote (or not, as seems best when other member states ask for one); it can conduct negotiations on behalf of the others and put forward its own answers – which may be acceptable, like the Luxembourg non-paper in 1991, or not, like the Dutch paper which followed later in the year.[59] Finally, it can sum up, usually after a *tour de table*, giving a collective view which is rarely contested even when member states disagree. (But when they do, they often win, such is the pressure to move on to the next business). Particularly when there has been disagreement, this summing-up determines whether the proposal lives or dies. The Presidency can also, if agreement is not reached, still invite the Commission to re-examine (that is, make alterations) to meet outstanding objections. With fifteen members, the Council is now moving into a new dimension, because the old round-table atmosphere barely applied even to twelve. Inevitably, with such numbers, the Presidency depends more than in the 1960s on its Secretariat; but it is in the position, when handling subsequent discussions with the Commission, of giving its own interpretation to the Council debates.

For every Council, the Presidency needs to prepare a range of compromises, since the first proposal is rarely the one finally accepted and is usually put in order to draw out dissent or to save face, allowing member states to declare to the home press that they did their best. So-called 'confessionals' may take place apart from the main sessions, if the Presidency (occasionally at the Commission President's suggestion) wishes to bring together small groups, hoping to put an obdurate minister on the spot to justify his objections. In recent years these have become effective, even intimidating, means of speeding up progress with the agenda. The whole point however is to corral member governments without attempting to coerce them, for none must be seen to give way without a reason acceptable in their domestic contests. From this requirement stems the argument for secrecy and the resistance to publishing Presidential compromises, which would, in Bagehot's phrase, 'let the daylight in on mystery'.

The Presidencies face a choice between trumpeting the grandiose themes that attract popular attention and the practicalities of what can be done in six short months. The previous incumbent will argue for continuing with its unfinished business, while the next partner in the Troika is already looking ahead to its own. The choice naturally reflects the current state of domestic politics in the President-state. If the government is in full control at home, the programme will flow more easily: Germany was able to do better at Hannover in 1988 than during the second half of 1994; a British government under pressure performed rather worse in 1992 than one with greater authority in 1986.

The Belgian Presidency, for example, though rather late in latching on to the Commission's economic White Paper in 1993, subsequently piloted it effectively, while restoring its own European image to a public disturbed in the period of post-Maastricht tension by severe cuts in state expenditure at home. A small state, more than a large one, can use the Presidency as a lever to let the collective carry responsibility for what has to be done anyway. Conversely, domestic discord can easily unpin an otherwise authoritative Presidency. An external crisis may have the same effect: having been expected to have learned from its earlier accident-prone essays, Greece was thrown badly by the Macedonian issue in the first half of 1994. Portugal on the other hand made a name for itself by taking one important long-blocked directive (on life insurance) and getting it accepted against the odds.

Despite changes in presentation, which make the Presidency's programmes more explicit than in the past to the Parliament, as well as to national publics, Presidencies tend to be discrete experiences easily diverted by international crises such as the Gulf War or Yugoslavia. The Troika and the Commission provide guidance, but the main preconditions for a strong Presidency are that it should be lucky enough to avoid the EC-wide waves of recession – in 1974–5, 1980–82 and 1991–3 – and that its own machinery of government should be effective: the business transacted has increased so vastly and the timetable has been so much accelerated that a President-state has to commit administrative and political resources undreamed-of before the 1980s.

In the case of France, so long the procedural exemplar, it has been said 'EC affairs are not foreign affairs, except for the most important questions and negotiation of treaties. All other details . . . are really matters of internal policy . . . The general goal [of the Presidency] is to give Europe a political dimension, in order to counterbalance economic liberalism.'[60] French governments have never been wary about setting out their national interests as they did at Fontainebleau in 1984; but if this is done too blatantly, as occurred during the 1992 tenure, or in the Belgian government's 1993 approach to airline deregulation,[61] bias tends to rouse the others. Without firm support from allies, the British were both shamed and constrained to show themselves more impartial and altruistic at the Edinburgh Summit in the second part of the 1992 Presidency than in their earlier meetings, for example in Bath.

The best Presidencies, defined in the sense of those which settle the most outstanding business, are characterized by well-matured consultation with all member states beforehand, not only the Troika; by clearly expressed aims; and by painstaking and diplomatic brokerage throughout. Inevitably some states count for more than others; they stand in an international order, represented by the G5 (which includes only France, Germany and Britain) and the G7 which includes Italy, as well as in NATO or CSCE negotiations. Smaller states act so as to seem to lead Europe, but the largest scarcely need to do so, although mutual jealousies ensure that stereotyped criticisms will recur: the Franco-German entente was accused of pre-empting the Presidency and the Council at the Corfu Summit in July 1994, as it was earlier after the Stuttgart declaration 1983, and following the Kohl-Mitterrand letter on political and monetary union.

Yet member states' very diversity inhibits any one Presidency from launching grand strategies of change or reform without the sort of preparations that went into the IGCs in 1985 and 1991. In spite of the Troika's undoubted value in providing some continuity, the Presidency's procedures are now so complex that it is hard to see how modifications which ought to have come many years earlier can be delayed. At the 1996 IGC, the case for altering the length of tenure, allowing more time for the largest member states, may be unanswerable. But the legal fiction of parity conveys a different reality, that with one state having one vote on issues subject to a veto, the small states will not as yet allow the great overhanging wave of reform to break to their own disadvantage.

As things stand, the ideal Presidency requires a sustained focus which may in fact be easier for small states to provide, who have less expected of them and less to lose. Belgium, Ireland or Luxembourg may lack formidable diplomatic machines but they are accustomed to being catalysts among the larger states. They are also not subject to the ultra-decentralized coordination regimes in place in the Netherlands or Denmark.

But a quality which ought to be called EC altruism is required as well. The three Benelux countries, Ireland and Italy, as well as France and Germany when they act together, find it possible to merge self-interest with the collective in the EC's interest; which is harder for Spain or Portugal to emulate and apparently almost impossible for Greece and Britain. The Irish government, for example, managed to put together a deal on export credits for the aircraft industry in 1984, *vis-à-vis* the threat from Boeing in the United States, despite French opposition and the lack of a clear Council majority – and duly got the credit because it had shown it could transpose itself to the European level. Any would-be acceptable President-state has to be aware of what moves the others, whether in the majority's eyes something should go ahead, whether it could be implemented, and whether it is likely to be accepted. The fact that the Council accepted the coherence funds bargain in 1991, and its extension at the time of negotiating entry of EFTA countries in 1993–4, demonstrated how versed Luxembourg and the Netherlands were in the first case, and Belgium and Germany in the second.

Effectiveness, not measurable until after a Presidency has finished, is thus the sum not only of what a national government does during its tenure but of how well its administration and senior civil servants, its diplomatic channels, party balance, and even its media and public opinion interact to support a sustained programme. Authority is a pyramid with a domestic base; but its apex is in the clouds of Brussels where no Presidency can do all the work but must rely on Commission experts and officials and working groups, Directorates, and its Secretariat and Legal Service. National entities inevitably behave differently in such circumstances, just as they have different bargaining techniques, but unless they accept that they can succeed only with wide support – for which trade-offs have to be made – they achieve little.

COOPERATION AND ALLIANCES

Spanning the EU's entire history, prevalent throughout and some-times decisive in its impact, the Franco-German understanding (link, or entente, or axis) stands out above all others. It has been described both as a marriage of convenience and the 'motor of Europe', neither of which adequately explains its protean nature, its variation over time, and the interplay of personality, of institutions and separate national identities.

What exists in the 1990s is quite different from the late 1950s phenomenon, which was the creation almost entirely of Adenauer and de Gaulle, enshrined with great flair and imagination by the latter in the Elysée Treaty in 1963. Their coming together owed everything to pre-War memories, wartime experience, concepts of a post-War settlement and France's difficulties in adjusting to the growing Economic Community. The first stage had already ended by the time the general left political life. The second was well under way by the time that the USA lurched into the Vietnam war, and the dollar began its long fall, which ended in the break-up of the Bretton Woods system in 1970–72. That first international crisis to disrupt Europe's post-War settlement altered the nature of Germany's external relations with the United States, the Soviet Union and indeed the EEC, more than it affected France. But by then, the Franco-German understanding had become a matter of routine involvement of administrators as well as heads of govern-ment, and an important stage in the pre-formulation of the matters being discussed by the embryo European Council.

Earlier sentiments relevant to the era of the Second World War could still be revived. But partly because both publics expected it to continue (the press having given it a sort of mythical status), partly because it had acquired institutional momentum, in the 1970s the entente became densely resilient under the stewardship of Schmidt and Giscard – though it could still be ruptured if the chief protagonists changed, as happened in 1981 to 1983 during the Mitterrand administration's first, radical phase. From mid–1983 until the Berlin Wall came down, Kohl and Mitterand embodied the routine interplay of normal bilateral relations, predisposed towards integration, and, in the longer term, enforced mutual evolution between the two leading EC states.[62]

Nevertheless, the entente remained an act of political will. French and German governments agreed to agree but not because their domestic interests coincided; deep down, they disagreed on most major issues. Their leaders' choice, reiterated over decades, reflected a mutual understanding between Giscard and Schmidt, and then between Kohl and Mitterrand that, without political agreement, both their states had much to lose if things were not resolved according to their preferences. On the personal level, each of these pairs evidently learned from the other; Kohl provided patience and stubbornness, Mitterrand skills of argument, diplomacy and a finesse that Kohl's early years lacked. Agreement, however, never excluded strong feelings about particulars, such as the appointment of Commissioners, especially in 1994–5 when Kohl's insistence that Bangemann should return to DG3 indicated that the German government had adopted a more assertive tone.

But an entente is not a motor nor is it the start of an effective cartel unless it remains unchallenged by other states. Insofar as the focus of integration changed from harmonization to regulation in the SEA period after 1984, it did so in response to more complex conjunctures of players and forces. Apart from highlights such as the introduction of EMS, which also owed much to the Commission President Roy Jenkins, Franco-German accords are better described as the core around which other member states could, if they chose to cluster, produce effective majorities if not always unanimity. The entente's history comprises cycles of starts, peaks and divergence: the latter usually at the initiative of French presidents, more obviously single-minded than German chancellors, who had always to bear in mind the other necessary dimensions of West Germany's post-War diplomacy – the USA, the USSR, and East Germany.

From French governments' point of view, since EC affairs frequently created tensions in France and threatened a particular view of indivisible sovereignty, some things were done more easily as the apparent result of accords reached between two leading heads of government than if they had appeared as impositions by the Commission or the EC collective of member states. In this sense, the Franco-German link served very slowly to wean France from that side of de Gaulle's Presidency represented by the Fouchet Plan. Once Mitterrand had turned – or been turned – away from the Socialist reforms to accept, in 1983, the EU's ultimate sovereignty and France's vital role as a second-ranking power inside it (a double severance from the past), the conditions came into existence for a remarkable transformation of attitudes that ran, almost without a break, until 1992. Even so, the high points of both their Presidencies at Fontainebleau 1984 and Hannover 1988 represented an alignment of separate national interests in two matters – reincorporating Britain after the budgetary crisis, and furthering the internal market – rather than triumphs of Franco-German diplomacy. Much more importantly, their mutual adaptation to the consequences of German unification in 1990–92, for which the political evidence can be found in the Kohl-Mitterrand approach to EPU and EMU, and in France's dedication to the strong franc *coute qui coute*, indicated that by 1992, France was ready to adapt yet further, to the plain fact that Germany had become the single most powerful state in the EU.

Without Mitterrand's eventual acceptance that the EU should bless German unification as if it had been the natural outcome of European integration, Margaret Thatcher's essay in delaying both might conceivably have had some effect.[63] Mitterrand, after all, hesitated crucially in the first few months, having failed to foresee what the outcome of the Wall's demolition would be. Thereafter, both partners could accept the Maastricht process (at the top, if not at the level of public opinions); France because the trade-off between EMU and EPU seemed to follow its prescriptions; Germany because the long incremental process towards the two had a certain resemblance to the growth of the First Empire's legal framework in the two decades after 1871 – the last period of her modern history to be relatively free of controversy.

Besides these fundamental adjustments, the accommodation to Britain's apparent reintegration during the single market period, once the budget sore had been healed in 1984, ranks as secondary. For France's government in the early 1990s, the problem has been to achieve domestic change in line with the direction given from the top while the French schedule of EMU was enshrined; for Germany's government, how to contain itself *vis-à-vis* other member states' difficulties and delays, while achieving political union, all the while without discussing (in public at least) the underlying issue of 'what was good for Germany'. German politics suffered an internal tension as a result, between what the foreign minister, Hans-Dietrich Genscher, was prepared to concede to ensure that the incorporation of former East Germany under the 1949 Basic Law's provisions was accepted, and the markers set down by Kohl to prevent either the EU from extracting too high a price for acceptance or Genscher from offering future German neutrality as a card in the game.

High as the stakes were in the autumn of 1991, the Franco-German link held. Generous though Kohl was to Major's Maastricht opt-out requirements, there was never a serious probability of an Anglo-German rapprochement, only a German need to keep Britain in, even at the price of some slackening in the common EC momentum. Thus Kohl conceded again at Edinburgh in 1992 on structural funds (to appease Spain and Ireland) and to the Danes because of their nuisance value.[64] These developments led most commentators at the time to assume that German governments would continue to keep their main activities within *Europapolitik* centred on the West. Of far greater significance was the United States' recognition of Germany's new status, foreshadowed by George Bush (to Margaret Thatcher's dismay at their last Camp David meeting, 24 November 1989)[65] and later confirmed by President Clinton's 1993 recognition that the EU, though junior, had become a *distinct*, and not merely a joint, NATO partner; it was now an organization in which Germany, not Britain, had become the lynchpin.

This third mutation of the Franco-German link has at the same time witnessed very large disagreements about ultimate aims. These have so far been put to one side in favour of beginning to implement the schedules for EMU and EPU, the start of CFSP, and even defence cooperation. But they remain, as revealed by French politicians' signal lack of response to pre-planning of the 1996 IGC suggested by Christian Democrat leaders in 1994. The fact that in his declining last year, Mitterrand was unwilling or unable to match this German initiative, which appears to have had Kohl's tacit support, suggests that the only important legacy of the Elysée Treaty, which was still alive on the twentieth anniversary in 1993, was recognition that the original had been a *compromis*: a preliminary contract to proceed *au tant que possible*, with a political rather than a legally binding endeavour. In this marriage of convenience the partners need not love each other, but they have to learn ways of living, not only with each other but, in the French case, finally inside the EU house. French acceptance of GATT under Edouard Balladur, a prime minister of the right, and the appointment of a Franco-German Economic Council to help coordinate economic and monetary policies in the internal market during EMU stage two, represented unprecedented steps. Yet under a Chirac Presidency, a fourth, Gaullist, mutation may well occur.

On the German side, however, expectation that German governments would explore possibilities outside the EU only very tentatively were confounded by the demands for recognition of Croatia once the first round of the Yugoslav civil war began. Since then it has become clearer that the reunited Germany has begun to surmount the costs of reunification faster and more easily than was predicted in 1992–3. Furthermore, there has been activity in regard to the admission of the Visegrad Group, above all Poland, which goes well beyond economic advantage, and appears to be driven by a clear understanding of Germany's long-term needs not to have an EU border with the vestigial Europe further east. This is no sense revanchist, but indicates that the overriding problem is to redefine where 'Europe' really is, and what should be Germany's place within these new metaphysical borders.[66]

As a motor, the link has worked but in a more limited sense than media commentators outside Germany and France usually assume. It helps to set many of the details of agendas before the European Council and before some Councils of Ministers. It has been responsible for pivotal innovations such as the EMS, the Stuttgart declaration, the Kohl-Mitterrand letter, the common platform on the Maastricht pillars, and the defence of the French franc in

1992–3 in which the German government helped, although it had not offered the same terms to sterling, the lira and the peseta.[67] But it by no means excludes other corresponding ententes, since some northern member states bend towards the German orbit, as some Mediterranean ones do towards that of France.

Detailed economic cooperation, in contrast, has been remarkably slight.[68] There are, for example, no privileged relations between the Bundesbank and the Banque de France. Discord can erupt on almost all topics from location of the EMI to monetary policy,[69] from the north-south debate to GATT, from immigration problems to the importance of regions. Current threats to the Community as a whole, ranging from the Balkans to the Mahgreb, are seen through different lenses, and French opinion, preoccupied by Muslim fundamentalism in Algeria, has little sympathy with Germany's perceived need to include Poland, its agriculture, and its 40 million population within the Community's borders.

The link exists primarily between heads of state; but had it not existed, had these agreements not been reached, it is hard to imagine how the other member states would have reached the place where they now stand. Had Germany or France, separately, led a broad alliance, excluding the other, the EU would surely have split from top to bottom. It remains therefore a basic building block, just as the deutschmark with its penumbra of currencies (now including the French franc) constitutes the future EMU. The Franco-German link can also be used by other players, as for example Delors did very skilfully via his personal affinity with Chancellor Kohl to increase the Commission's influence before the Council's regular meetings.[70] But it does not determine how the member states will react, if for no other reason than that it is intended, like a marriage, primarily for mutual understandings. It is certainly not in the inherent interests of any other member state except insofar (as one Spanish observer put it) 'that it ensures a European Germany and not a German Europe'. When challenged on an issue requiring unanimity, as it was by John Major at Corfu over Jean-Luc Dehaene's nomination, it had no greater power than any other alliance between member states and it depends absolutely on being renewed by personal compatibility between two leaders. Nevertheless, like a coiled spring, it has the capacity to recover: soon after Corfu, it contributed to a similar result to the original intention, but by other means.

The Franco-German link has had one other long-term consequence. Apart from a few months in 1973, when it seemed possible that Edward Heath might extend his personal and public cordiality with President Pompidou to make a triangular match with Willi Brandt, it has tended to exclude Britain. As E. M. Forster put it in *Howard's End*, marriage creates an imperceptible glass wall between the two people concerned and the rest. In 1989-92, feelings certainly existed in the newly united nation that Germany no longer needed the French *tutelle*; but they were counterbalanced by even more widespread fears that if Germany made this clear, it would encourage Germans to go their own way, a *Sonderweg* (as Edmund Stoiber, the Bavarian prime minister once put it). The elaborate framework Kohl and Mitterrand began to construct for Maastricht signified, at this level, a Franco-German compromise to contain each other. Whether it can survive their separate countries' crises of national identity, sparked by the end of Europe's ideological divisions and divergent domestic responses, depends on both sides continuing to elect heads of government who accept the entente's preconditions. So long as they do, Britain, Italy or Spain, undergoing their own post-1989 crises of identity, have no immediate recourse.

No other link, affinity or alliance between member states, not even the original Benelux arrangement, has had this continuity or significance. There are of course groupings, of Mediterranean states, poorer states, peripheral ones, just as a very broad north-south differentiation exists; but these are primarily matters of how member states behave, not necessarily determinants of what they do (see chapter 13). Britain can be considered as a self-excluded state, while Greece is sometimes described as 'the brotherless country' – a sort of Israel within the EC. There are unifying factors which tend to bring together majorities of seven to ten member states: such as GATT, justice and home affairs, and the Social Chapter. Others fragment: defence, the environment, transport, competition, prevention of fraud and waste.[71]

Equally, all member states have preferred friends who may at times be allies, as Denmark has been sporadically for Britain. Germany has a particular penchant for Spain, Italy has long tried to play for German and French support at the same time, with recently diminishing success. Spain has tried a similar game, so far with greater luck. Small states regularly seek liaisons to bolster their positions, as Portugal does, fearing Spain as a mightier neighbour.[72] Ireland or Greece do the same, often with France, for much the same reason. For some, the EC itself may be an ally, as it is for Portugal and perhaps the Netherlands against Franco-German dominance. The Netherlands also looked to Nordic countries prior to their accession. Yet all this is no more than the chiaroscuro of states' normal external relations, heightened by the EU context. It is barely open, even to small states, to play the field at will; liaisons require both partners to have at least a minimum genuine national interest in common.

The facts of membership and geography condition what affinities can develop. But they do not relieve states of other normal foreign policy concerns, with countries on Europe's periphery or in the international sphere; neither do they automatically diminish a nation's distinct self-interest. Some groupings, such as the (predominantly Mediterranean) beneficiaries from structural funds, appear to have formed a concatenation of self-interests rather than an alliance. Since nationalism, often in gross forms, appears to be increasing *pari passu* with events since the end of the Cold War, together with the potential for mass migration on Europe's southern and eastern borders, there is no particular reason to expect more general patterns of affinity to develop. Member states are conjoined as much by the far wider process of economic homogenization and by the regulatory functions of EU institutions as they are by links of national interest: the grandest alliance so far in the EU's history has been their unanimous support for the Single European Act in 1986.

III. *The Struggle Continues*

According to the prophet Isaiah, Joseph and the angel wrestled all night and still vied with each other when the dawn broke. In the sense that competition continues within the Community, despite the new title European Union, the image applies. But as far as member states are concerned, the struggle has several faces. They compete generally among themselves according to the dictates of national self-interest, but also in groups of varying size, on lines set by affinity or choice. In a distinct dimension they compete with the Commission and to a lesser extent the Parliament, some more outspokenly than others, wherever the ultimate European interest has to be defined. Yet none of these rivalries is – or can be – pursued *à l'outrance* because, even at the nadir in 1966, each of them was aware of a greater national interest in the whole. If it were not so, the Community would surely have sunk to the level of earlier unsuccessful attempts such as the Danubian Federation, or broken up altogether.

Two disciplines also condition the process: EU law, interpreted finally by the Court, which member states can evade, ignore and on rare occasions defy, but never escape save by complete secession; and the peer-group pressure of majorities whose most effective sanction is to proceed with something on their own, as a result of which the dissenting state would eventually suffer. This would obviously operate in the fields of research and technology, less obviously in monetary union. The experience of the internal market also suggests that states which try to protect previously sheltered sectors find subsequent adaptation to world markets harder than if they had accommodated to EU intentions earlier on. Both forms of discipline operate through informal channels: indeed it is hard to see how the Community's political fabric would be strong enough formally to discipline a member state even where the legal power exists.[73]

In this general framework, the main source of tension and creativity in the Community lies between the member states and the Commission. Tides ebbed and flowed even in the Delors decade; the Commission's influence surged in 1984–90, fell back in 1991–3, then began to recover as the 1996 IGC came into focus. Within these broad movements, shorter term fluctuations occur. It is not necessary to go back to the empty chair crisis or even to the British budget protest to suggest that an aggressive defence of a special interest can delay or disrupt long-planned Commission initiatives. At the Edinburgh Summit 1992, the French government threatened not to ratify the agreement on increasing the numbers of MEPs to allow for the former East German *Länder* unless the Parliament accepted the construction of its new chamber in Strasbourg; in 1994 the Italian government threatened, successfully, to renege on the Summit decision to increase EU revenues in the 1995–9 budget unless the fines it faced for ignoring limits on milk production were reduced.

It was predictable, for example, that member states would seek a successor to Delors who had his administrative gifts and capacity for negotiation but without his urge to declaim an overriding Community vision; someone who would try to ensure that DG4 under Karel van Miert would be less aggressive in defining competition policy and the state aids field, particularly where national airlines were concerned.

Their governments succeeded on both grounds, even if the majority's first choice for President failed. Equally, the number of cases of environmental infringement referred by DG11 to the ECJ declined, accompanied by an increase in bargained settlements, some of which could be described as Commission retreats. Of greater political significance, three of the largest member states at the end of 1994 engaged in pre-emptive moves to limit the Commission's initiating competence at the forthcoming 1996 IGC.[74]

In the closing months of his Presidency, Delors's attempt to finesse these offensives by setting an agenda based on industrial reconstruction and fuller employment, starting with the 1993 White Paper, seemed deeply defensive, especially once member states had defeated its proposal that the Commission should raise money in the form of bonds and lend it for infrastructure works, bypassing the European Investment Bank, as if it really were a developmental state. The college had already been outflanked by Spain and Ireland over the re-allocation of structural funds in July 1993, despite the efforts of Bruce Millan at DG16.

Something like a member states' revanche was to be expected at the end of a deep recession, and a period of unprecedented growth in the Commission's authority. It would have been hard even for the college at its peak under Delors's second term to defend itself, let alone the interim one of 1992–4. One French respondent put it straightforwardly: 'bilateral relations between member states touch more and more EC subjects, for ever longer times in the preparatory meetings . . . it is sometimes helpful for them to interpret largely the Commission's competences, on other occasions they may wish to restrain them'.[75] Either way, they are in an advantageous position. Of course the Commission can retaliate or can try to impair member states' credibility: no government likes to be exposed by its own media as leading the list of backsliders, or as being environmentally unsound. But few member states are EC-pure: most have something to disguise and such ammunition has a limited range. Using it can also lead to counter-strikes by national governments, such as the battle to influence the Commission's first report on member states' performance in implementing the internal market, and the imposition of hidden controls, in the form of new time-consuming tasks – being extra bureaucratic procedures, *fiches* and unread notices in the *Official Journal*.[76] Hesitancy pervades the margins of Commission manoeuvres, for example in the case of aid to defence-related industries, where it has never acted without consulting member states about their overriding national interest because it lacks the expertise to make what would need to be an overwhelming case.

During the 1991 IGC, the college pressed in vain for member states to create a hierarchy of legal norms, 'to order the EC's legislative activity in a comprehensive and coherent way, to avoid the existing legal vacuum at EC level in which national regulatory initiatives relating to implementing EC laws are left'. Had they agreed, member states would have eliminated the often ambiguous Directive, with its bargains and derogations, leaving only Treaties, general laws and administrative measures. But they saw this as a stratagem to deprive them not only of an important aspect of legal sovereignty but of their room for manoeuvre, both during the legislative process and afterwards, when it came to implementation and enforcement. Both sides take a different view of what is, at heart, the best way to define the European interest. What the college defined as a means to simplify the law and provide for subsidiarity (because the administrative measures would have been passed under the Council's criteria, to be adopted by member states) appeared to the states to be a major source of aggrandizement.

Much the same applies to liberalization and competition policy and their logical extension to state telecoms and energy companies: there are to be no clean cuts or Gordian knots (see chapter 11). The Commission sees itself as a Gulliver tied down by hundreds of Lilliputian ropes,[77] far from being free to rampage in member states' sovereign back yards. National bureaucracies mistrust it. Until recently, going to the Commission was considered in Paris 'as a sort of treason' and even today few *énarques* like the idea of a high-level *tour exterieur*. In Bonn, administrative weight is considered the due property of Commissioners, not officials.

At all levels and on all occasions, the struggles go on: when the college meets the countries' cabinet ministers at the start of each Presidency, and again at mid-term meetings; in respect of individual Commissioner's powers (Henning Christophersen forestalled a strike against DG11 in October 1992 by requesting that no one member of the college should be singled out); or when a state mobilizes its Commissioners against another Directive which threatens it (as DG4 was blocked in 1992 in its attempt to prevent Spanish state aid to build a new steel mill in the Basque country).[78] More generally, it seems that as part of a post-Maastricht counter-blast, some member states in the second half of 1992 mobilized their forces, including MEPs, to trim back the internal market to what had been envisaged five years earlier: the Commission was not to become regulator of the whole internal market with power to use Article 90 to improve liberalization in telecoms and energy.

That was a particularly contentious area, associated with a single far-sighted Commissioner in DG4; but on a range of issues (including waste and fraud, where the Committee of Auditors in its November 1993 report put the Commission in the dock) there were signs of a critique, aimed not only at the Commission's existing policies, but its bureaucracy (target of a particular German attack in mid-1994). In the British government's case, criticism was levelled at its methods of initiating policy by White Books and working them up into detailed instruments for further progress with the aid of experts and working groups, and the support of Permanent Representatives in those member states already known to be in favour. (Margaret Thatcher had already taken particular exception to what she saw as moves to bring in Social Protocol measures under health and safety or social security provisions, and to use advisory committees, set up according to comitology procedure, to build up 'a library of declaratory language to justify subsequent proposals'.[79])

What matters here is not the truth of such accusations, but how they and all informal strategies are perceived by what amount to partner-rivals. Thatcher complained that procedures agreed at Hannover were being evaded; the Commission – had it been as frank – could equally have claimed that some member states were distorting the spirit of what had been laid down when the Single European Act had been signed in 1986. Where member states are in default, it is ultimately for the Commission to give a lead or see the Treaties frustrated; if there is no other way, it is perhaps not to be blamed if, say, it tries out the long-delayed Company Statute under QMV rules, or bans a certain sort of pollutant under internal market harmonization, in preference to (unanimous) environmental procedure.

Member states have many recourses, if they wish to do nothing or create delays, as the Nestlé-Perrier case (see chapter 11) shows. They can ignore or obstruct (as some Mediterranean members did in 1992 on the imposition of VAT on yachts registered before 1985), paralyse for long periods the introduction of free movement across borders, originate contrary proposals such as Sunday non-working, or the 48-hour week, in order to have imposed on others a level playing field based on their own customs. Or they can simply block an existing informal procedure. (During the steel crisis in 1992–3, member states most at risk of processes against state aids opposed the use of 'comfort letters' to make informal decisions, fearing these would acquire a more formal character over time.[80]) It is, after all, easy to insert small impediments. 'The Commission is like a very big company which has a clear global strategy with some generally well-defined goals, but which, after that, has within it an extraordinary multitude of quarrels and rivalries.'[81]

Wrangles touch even the Central Bank governors and their alternates, who normally invite Commissioners to their meetings – but do not have to. In no area is this more evident than in the matter of setting up committees for detailed implementation of proposals where the Commission and member states' spheres meet. This is not a sterile constitutional debate, for the Council has to define precisely what functions are to be ascribed to the Commission, and the manner of committees may well help to determine their outcome. It had been an area of such exhaustive disputes that in the run-up to Hannover both sides agreed on a new set of rules to be styled 'comitology'. Complicated as the procedure is, it does now serve to minimize friction; but the Council usually has its way, because while the federally inclined states such as Germany and the Netherlands prefer advisory committees (which enhance the Commission's role), the majority prefer ones which do not.[82]

Comitology can be interpreted as a stage in a process which, since 1988, is leading to practical issues being extracted from the Commission's scope, leaving it to consider 'policy', according to criteria set by member states: a case in point being the implementing of supervision of financial conglomerates. The fact that these are often arguments over political territory, not the substance of policy, is not the point here.

The Commission has its own recourses: it can try to exploit national media, either to confront a government with unpalatable Brussels statistics (such as the league tables for failure to transpose laws, which so upset Italy in 1992, or the fact that of 535 proposals made in 1991, the Commission itself had originated only thirty (6%), the rest coming from member states themselves, either in the Council or through the application of international agreements). DG4 skilfully mobilized the press as part of its celebrated campaigns to regulate mergers (de Havilland) and state aids areas (see chapter 11). But explanations often come too late to mitigate bad publicity (the cases of British prawn-flavoured crisps, defence of the *tilde* in Spain, the proposal on curved cucumbers – a Danish idea – or the 'pure food' member states' prohibition on 'raw milk' (i.e., French) cheese being obvious instances.) The Commission has never had the personnel or the time to try to educate the hypothetical European public, regarding that as a matter for the European Parliament, if it is to be done at all. The Commission's representatives and bureaux in member states exist only to give information and directions to customers, not to act as political propaganda centres.

The Commission's own quirks and tendencies make it an easy target for caricature, or for nationalistic criticism veiled in self-righteousness. When the ECJ overrode the 1617 German law on purity of beer, since it constituted a barrier to trade in foreign beers, the Bonn minister responsible ended his statement of acceptance by saying, 'but all good Germans will still drink German beer'. Much as they wanted France to accept the GATT Uruguay round, some member states continued to attack the Maastricht Treaty at the end of 1993 for giving the Commission additional powers, even though those powers were useful to the chief negotiator, Leon Brittan, in his negotiations with the Balladur government.

In exercising what the college and the Commission President have seen as their true role – to defend the Treaties – the Commission has always had to persuade, wait, work on public or academic media opinion, and try again, while fending off often-justified accusations of waste, peculation and corruption (even if these are usually carried out at the level of member state administrations). Article 90 of the Rome Treaty gives it powers to bypass member states and the Council where the Commission has sole competence: but though two Commissioners threatened it in the late 1980s it has only recently been used, and confirmed by the ECJ.[83]

Most of the armoury, from their influence over senior appointments to their occasional tactics of swamping the Commission's agenda via Council requests, belongs to the member states. Few of the Commission's campaigns are as successful on their own account as those which are taken up and subtly manipulated by member states in order to bring pressure to bear on their own backward (or sheltered) sectors, making the Commission the scapegoat, without offending their own electorates or public opinions (Spanish banking, Italian insurance, Greek environmental issues). On few occasions do things go well for the Commission if member states are not at heart willing and, in the case of the internal market, pressured by their own industrial organizations. It could be argued therefore that the Commission has two roles: by collating what is desirable and possible, to act as taster of the food before it is placed in front of the sovereigns; and to serve as scapegoat when things go wrong.

De Gaulle, Giscard and Thatcher all, in their own times, wanted the Commission to be a subordinate executive to implement what member states desired. That it has remained very much more can be explained partly by the consistent support of a minority of states, partly by the conjuncture of 1984–5, which set aside many of the earlier objections in favour of a common good, at a time when all member states felt threatened by industrial and financial competition from outside Europe. A third explanation lies in what the Commission has become since the administrative turning point in the early 1980s, when its focus shifted from harmonization to regulation. It is not in the ordinary sense a civil service, not even a Whitehall or Tokyo civil service, but something closer in style to a central bank, with a specific guardian role, legal competences, technical expertise, singular authority and perhaps even prestige. Like a central bank it is demonstrably weaker in spheres further away from its legal competence and more open to political challenge. Member states can subject it, as they do their own central banks (even in Germany), to a variety of restraints. Yet they remain sensitive to the sense of continuity and ethos which the Commission, like central banks, displays, in defence of very long-term objectives which member states, ruled by changing governments, cannot always admit but accept the need to be reminded of.

Unending contests take place over boundaries and competences.[84] If it had not been so, the 1960s federalist dreams might have been more successful. The great issue is who actually takes the lead when the Community falters because member states have not acted in the European interest as defined by the Commission. The game between the Council and the Commission is like a 'soldiers' battle' which, like the Battle of Borodino in Tolstoy's *War and Peace*, takes place over a confused field where men fight hand to hand, cut off by noise and smoke from any overall direction, until at nightfall one side claims the victory. Personalities and alignments, national perceptions of interests, define what is to be in the group interest and when member states and Commission will find themselves on the same side. In the last resort, member states who created the Community and its institutions could, if they wished, destroy it. But so long as they live and cooperate within the Community, obey its laws and acknowledge that its institutions act in their higher interest, as they or their governments could not easily do alone, it is more than a zero sum game.

It is nevertheless a *political* marketplace. Disillusioning as the experience since Maastricht has been, and the failure yet to complete the entire internal market, member states do expect collective answers to continue to emerge, even in the problem areas which recall their own total failure to act together in the 1930s: technological competition and structural unemployment. Something like Pascal's wager operates in the Community: collectivity may yet be possible in the fiscal and welfare crises afflicting all of them. National governments take the Commission to task, try to curb or mould its work, attempt to take back competences and impose new duties, hoping that what the Commission defines as the EC's path will in the end represent their own version of the European interest. In this tension lies the essential dynamism which ensures change, as the Community's legal form moves from one Treaty to another.

Institutions:
The Parliament and
the Court of Justice

I. The Parliament

If the founding fathers' intentions had been fulfilled, the inherent tension between member states and the Commission would have been moderated by the existence of a strong, democratically elected Parliament, not so much to initiate legislation as to act as a second chamber to review the combined legislative functions of the Commission and the Council.[1] But the 1957 cuttings took over twenty years to root, even after the introduction of direct elections. The fact that the European Parliament did not acquire broad powers of review until the Maastricht IGC, and that widely different forms of election to the EP still exist throughout the Community today, say as much about its own inadequacies as about the jealous attitudes of some member states and the Commission's fears for its originating role, which have continuously denied it the full status of a second chamber.

The struggle to acquire what its leading members thought to be the rights and duties appropriate to a Parliament began in the 1960s, with repeated requests under Article 138(3) for composition by direct election, which were always fobbed off by the Council. In the 1970s, the Parliament changed tactics, accepting that, in the set pattern of inter-governmental brokerage, it could not hope for more than the consultation procedure for amending legislation which had finally been agreed with the Council in September 1976. Even this limited power worried France and Britain, which were wholly opposed to the idea of a tripartite system, especially since it was advocated by the traditionally federal or federalist states, the Netherlands, Belgium, Italy, Luxembourg and West Germany.

These contrary currents prevented the adoption of a uniform system for candidates' election, eligibility, constituencies or voting – even when direct elections did begin in 1979 – so that even today Britain operates a first-past-the-post system of voting, with MEPs tied to very large constituencies, while France votes according to party lists, which allow dual membership of the Parliament and the National Assembly as well as in local government. All that can be said in favour of this diversity is that, bizarre though some of the results can be, the numbers of European parliamentarians for each member state are rather more representative of their total populations than are their weighted votes in the Council.[2]

The Parliament thus grew up as a sort of shuttle-cock, bounced between the Council and the Commission and the centralized or federalist states. Yet this alone does not explain its apparent lack of legitimacy as the 'Parliament of Europe' which the debate about a widespread democratic deficit in the Community has emphasized. Although this deficit is apparently reflected by steadily falling percentages of those who bother to vote for it every five years, it is by no means clear that the fault lies with the Parliament itself, rather than the Community's overall structure.[3] As the 1994 elections demonstrated, voting for the Parliament is universally conflated with national political contexts because voters have no other way to express their preferences. Until – if ever – they elect a European government, elections will habitually be seen either as mini-referenda on the national ruling party or, if they take place at the same time as national elections, as a dependent clause to them. The Maastricht Treaty's optimistic prescription (Article 183a) that political parties, because they are intrinsically suited to transnational activity, should work for integration on the European scale, 'by focusing a European awareness and expressing the political will of the union's citizens', has not occurred. The explanation may, however, lie in the existence of national political systems and particular political cultures rather than parties and the Parliament as such.

Powers have, of course, been conferred on it. Those to scrutinize the EC's budget, acquired in 1970 and 1975 over and above the Treaty's original power to reject the budget as a whole (and by a two-thirds majority to dismiss the Commission college), were used successfully in the late 1970s, in contrast to the earlier blunderbuss instrument, rejection of the budget, which did occur in 1979 and 1984 but without lasting effect, since interim financing of the Commission's work continued. The 1975 powers to vet the spending for economic and social purposes were extended under the Delors I package in 1988; and since Delors II (Edinburgh 1992) the Parliament has had influence over the allocation of financial priorities.

Together with the Court of Auditors, it can monitor how the budget is actually managed, so that the power of discharge (last used to censure the Thorn Commission in 1984) has been transmuted into a doctrine of financial overview.[4] The budget is economically of small account but frequently a matter of intense political argument; more importantly, further powers were acquired as a result of ECJ interpretation, notably in the *Isoglucose* case 1979. (The Council had gone ahead impatiently, without waiting for the Parliament to give its opinion; but the Court ruled that it had a duty to wait for it to do so and was at fault; the test of 'within a reasonable time' conferred some implied power of delay in areas covered by the procedure.) Delay or threats to delay subsequently became a useful strategy for negotiating amendments with the Council, after a first reading debate but before voting on the measure as a whole.

Yet the Parliament was slow to take advantage until, in the mid–1980s, the SEA deluged the process with its three hundred items of legislation (finally reduced to 286). It was the SEA's practicalities which drew it out of its ineffectual advisory sphere and put it on the threshold of supervision by providing a cooperation procedure which allowed it put forward amendments at second reading. The Council then had to take account of these opinions and return with answers, but it did not have to select all of them, and the answers were not always in the form Parliament originally prescribed. Nevertheless, if the Commission also accepted these amendments, the Council was put more on the defensive, having to reach unanimity to overturn them; if the European Parliament rejected a measure, the Council either had to vote for it unanimously or drop it altogether. This gave substance at last to the Parliament's desires but still left it dependent either on winning Commission support for amendments or seeing a measure lost altogether.

At that stage, some member states still resisted any increase in what could be seen as the second chamber role. Britain was trying to divert the European Parliament into monitoring the Commission and member states' own implementation of the internal market.

But the Maastricht Treaty, coming while Parliament was learning to use its new powers, added a further range of powers at the insistence of member states such as Italy and Belgium: it extended *cooperation* and gave a right of *co-decision* in certain areas (see pp. 344–6).

The European Parliament had begun campaigning before Maastricht (see p. 191), starting with its Martin Reports after the 1990 Parliamentary Assizes held in Rome, which gave ammunition to the favourable member states. But it had no formal place during the IGC; informally, in Maastricht's inter-governmental bargaining, it was marginalized as an actor, and MEPs' attempts to enlist their national parliaments' support came to little – beyond the Benelux states, Italy and Germany – so that, despite the substantial gains achieved by the latter's advocacy, MEPs afterwards felt disillusioned.[5]

MEPs generally tended to blame the Commission for not striving more effectively on their behalf, as well as the usual suspects, Britain and Denmark, who had by now been joined by Portugal. The tide had seemed strong, given the pervasive sense of guilt in at least two large states, together with widespread media support for their campaigns. Less clear, though evident long before, were countervailing factors such as the European Parliament's track record of disorganization, MEP's poor attendance,[6] their tendency to suffer from isolation and tunnel vision, and the inordinate costs of an institution whose meetings and staff rotate between three cities, Brussels, Luxembourg and its main seat in Strasbourg. (In

EEC Legislation from Start to Finish
(Directives and Regulations)

I The Consultation procedure

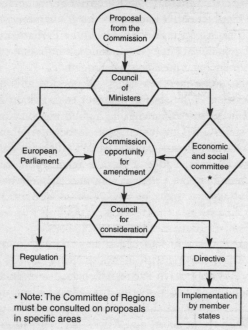

FIGURE 8.1

that long-running opéra bouffe, the Edinburgh Summit 1992 put a cap to the European Parliament's aspirations to move *en masse* to a new building in Brussels by confirming the ancient three-city compromise, to the immense relief of the mayors and citizens of Strasbourg, where another new building began, and Luxembourg).

But in fact the European Parliament emerged with at least half a loaf; that is, some of the functions associated with a normal national parliament. MEPs can now put oral or written questions directly to individual Commissioners when they attend, or to the Council, and expect reasoned answers. (Their criticisms of the Committee of Governors' EMS Report, for example, brought a visit by Wim Duisenberg, in the summer of 1992, who gave careful replies, and opened up a wide discussion of the ERM afterwards at a private

II The Cooperation procedure

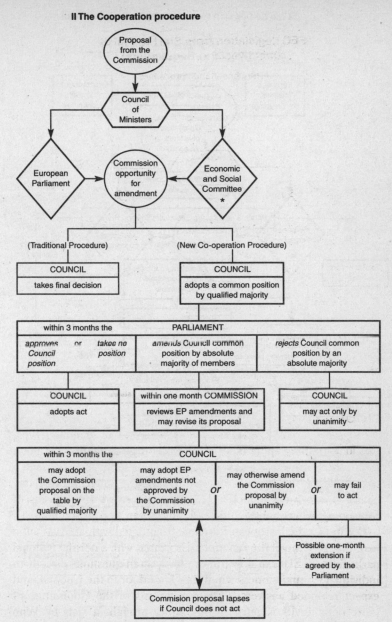

* Note: The Committee of Regions must be consulted on proposals in specific areas

FIGURE 8.2

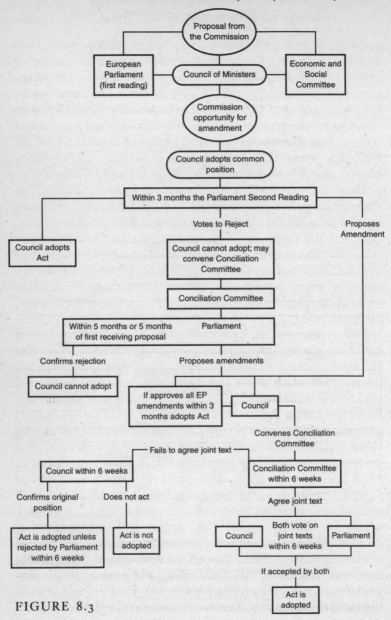

III The Co-Decision Procedure (EP has power of veto)

Proposal from the Commission

European Parliament (first reading)

Council of Ministers

Economic and Social Committee

Commission opportunity for amendment

Council adopts common position

Within 3 months the Parliament Second Reading

Votes to Reject

Proposes Amendment

Council adopts Act

Council cannot adopt; may convene Conciliation Committee

Conciliation Committee

Within 5 months or 5 months of first receiving proposal

Parliament

Confirms rejection

Proposes amendments

Council cannot adopt

If approves all EP amendments within 3 months adopts Act

Council

Convenes Conciliation Committee

Fails to agree joint text

Council within 6 weeks

Conciliation Committee within 6 weeks

Confirms original position

Does not act

Agree joint text

Act is adopted unless rejected by Parliament within 6 weeks

Act is not adopted

Council

Both vote on joint texts within 6 weeks

Parliament

If accepted by both

Act is adopted

FIGURE 8.3

meeting.) It was consulted in 1994 before Jacques Santer was proposed to succeed Delors, and subsequently put him through a testing examination, validating his appointment by a surprisingly narrow majority of 260 to 268.[7] In 1995 it extended its formal powers by vetting individual Commissioners in the same way, rather than treating the college as a whole. But although there was some talk of vetoing them altogether, because of a range of dissatisfactions, the Parliament eventually approved them by 416 to 103, thanks to Santer's placatory programme and support for 'social Europe'.

Some of the Maastricht Articles remain partly unfulfilled. The Parliament's success in requesting new legislation from the Commission has so far been limited, when compared to what the Council does and the extent of co-decision or negative assent remains ambiguous. Non-mandatory consultation (the 1976 process) has, however, been tightened up, so that it is harder for the Council to ignore or reject amendments without giving reasons. Of rather greater significance, fourteen areas have been added to the cooperation procedure.

An informal process had already developed with the internal market legislation, in which the Council was forced to manoeuvre and make concessions if it wanted to avoid large amendments or even the rejection which would bring unanimity into play. Now, what might occur at the later stages tends to be telescoped informally into the period before Parliament's amendments go to the Council, to prevent rejection or the interplay of another stage. What may be called strategies and mediation come into effect, where the non-governmental players can have some weight through sympathetic MEPs.

At the same time, the European Parliament has found itself working as a conciliator between the Council and the Commission, which was tending regularly to support its amendments. Co-decision, which at present covers external agreements, the internal market, education, culture, research and development, public health, consumer protection, EC citizenship, and environmental programmes, may have imprecise borders, but could widen if skilfully used in the future; that is, if used often enough to keep the mechanics of its conciliation committees working, but not so often as to be condemned as factious.

These novel features have accentuated what was already a growing phenomenon: the surge of lobbyists appearing in Strasbourg, scenting advantage for those clients who had done badly out of earlier stages in the process of brokering Commission legislative proposals. They also emphasized the need for parliamentary groups to mobilize absolute majorities, which in turn enhanced political groups' identities and the likelihood that these would form structured coalitions. Yet it is too soon to take an optimistic view or claim that this system now works well. Genuine collaboration between the three institutions is far off, and the medium term seems likely to witness a continuation of the old competitive struggles. Late in 1993, the Council Secretariat sent Permanent Representatives a report, warning that the Parliament's proposed new rules of procedure went far beyond what Ministers had envisaged at Maastricht or would now tolerate, and should therefore be rejected.

They had two things particularly in mind: firstly, the European Parliament's claim of the right to vote on the forthcoming GATT agreement, and secondly, its predicted request for the Commission to turn procedural ideas into legislation before the 1994 parliamentary elections. Uneasiness among member states about how the Parliament is using its powers has increased since then, not only in Britain but in France and Spain, on the grounds that MEPs have been concerned with extending its influence, rather than its effectiveness. But member states' preemptive strike may also have been directed at MEPs' attempts to penetrate the two closed pillars of Maastricht, outside their ambit, and to prevent a circuitous move to make immigration or CFSP becoming justiciable by the European Court. The Parliament, after all, has exercised its right of supervision by taking the case for the abolition of border checks between member states to the European Court, to the annoyance of the British government which wishes to retain them, and to the pleasure of Commission officials keen to implement this element of the Maastricht Treaty.

As was the case before the introduction of comitology procedures to prevent the Council and Commission vying over the form of committees, the European Parliament sets its legal claims on cooperation, the Council on consultation procedures. Maastricht has eliminated many of the ambiguities, and much of what used to be each one's tactical recourse to different Treaty Articles, seeking a legal base for one or other point of view. But grey areas remain. In the current mood of frustration, the Parliament seems to be aiming to use cooperation as the precursor to wider co-decision at (if not before), the 1996 IGC – which would in the end mean that it became a full second chamber. At present the Council will not concede this. If the Parliament is to succeed, it will have to rely on its political weight, its affinity with the Commission, and the goodwill of those member states who are favourable to its claims.

Up to now, the Commission has seen the Parliament as the natural antithesis of member states, few of which are actively integrationist. Commission and Parliament are rivals in another sense for the legislative initiative, but this dimension has always been much less barbed than the continuing disputes between Parliament and the Council, which in the end always come down to the problem that, if member states have reached an answer on the basis of QMV, there is every reason not to consult fully 'because it opens up the decision to all the activists once again'.[8]

The Parliament has perhaps more informal weight inside the Commission than commonly appears. Delors himself, a former MEP, chaired its Economic and Monetary Committee in the late 1970s with great success and used the European Parliament skilfully in his diplomacy in 1984–94. More formally, the Neunreither Committee, composed of European Parliament Bureau members, Directors General, and Council Secretariat officials, meets each month to discuss the cooperation procedure and the legislative programme. Although the Commission and the Council dominated Neunreither up to 1989, subsequently the Commission has begun to use the Parliament as an outrider, resting some of its case in the Council on the opinions already given by large European Parliament committees or plenary majorities. Equally, MEP members use Neunreither to back the Commission as well as to further their own ends. One outcome of their growing mutual interdependence is the increase in European Parliament amendments which, with Commission support, are now accepted: 30–40% of the total, including a radical tightening-up of the Directive on car exhaust emissions. But there is no way of evaluating the significance of these as a whole, only their numbers.

The Council now appears to treat the European Parliament less frequently with indifference or contempt, a change which probably dates from the Hannover Summit 1988, because the growth in negotiated package deals began with that German Presidency. If the European Parliament were to deal promptly and decisively with a matter, the Council could use that to persuade the member states who required it settled quickly also to accept other unpalatable contingencies; then, in due course, the Council might do the European Parliament a favour.[9] Such informal deals were already complex and wide-ranging by the time of Maastricht, thanks to the efforts of Spain's Presidency in processing outstanding items of what had by then been reduced to a total of 286 pieces of internal market legislation.[10] Moreover, the Parliament readily responded to the Council's post-Maastricht offensive against waste, bureaucracy and fraud, this being a matter on which MEPs had always wished to be active (seeing it as a means of pursuing the second chamber role).

The balance in this rivalry has shifted more in the European Parliament's favour than could have been predicted before 1986, with highlights such as the draft treaty on Political Union, the Cecchini Plan, the Erasmus scheme for cross-border student exchanges, the campaign for 'Social Europe', and the demand for subsidiarity. However, in 1993 the Prag Report observed that, while the shift amounted to a significant extension of democratic control, the Council remained aloof, as if negotiating under duress with a subordinate body.

Reports like Prag, done for and by the European Parliament, can have influence on the media and public opinion, as do its public auditions, and committees of inquiry on subjects such as racism or xenophobia, which do not readily attract the other institutions. Only the European Parliament could have inspired a discussion on the future of Europe's media in the era of IT and the information superhighway in January 1994, and related it to the dominance of certain network owners – in particular Berlusconi in Italy and Murdoch in Britain – with anti-trust proposals. By September, the

Commission had made ready a proposal to determine the permissible boundaries of interest in monopoly conditions. Whether something so radical could ever be made acceptable to the governments concerned, however, still depends on whether they would choose this way of doing what they themselves have so far feared or been unable to touch.

What the European Parliament wishes to become is something that its President can pronounce on during his visits to member states, just as its MEPs do in their own fifteen capital cities. It is their job to link it to member states' parliaments and propagate its values without arousing nationalist resentment among MPs unfamiliar with its work, as well as to monitor what in the latter's opinion is relevant to Strasbourg's future. But it has to be said that the European Parliament finds sympathy on the question of the democratic deficit more readily among member states' Permanent Representatives than their parliaments. A sense of what the negotiating positions are for Council meetings may be gleaned by MEPs after Coreper – though not in such a way as to permit Parliament extra leverage at another stage.

Until now, the Parliament's Presidency has alternated between the largest groups, the European People's Party (EPP) and the Socialists, thanks to the large parties' voting power. Enrique Baron Crespo, the 1989–92 President, rarely went beyond the demands of protocol in his regular meetings with heads of government and is said to have missed chances both of substantial discussions during Maastricht and of educating member state publics in what the Parliament stood for at a time when they were captive audiences of the Maastricht drama.[11] But he established a diplomatic routine, as Roy Jenkins did for the Commission, in a way which his successor Egon Klepsch (Germany CDU) could exploit. A seasoned, if little-known operator in the EC's corridors, Klepsch used his spokesman's position and the reports of leading committees to draw the Parliament closer to Delors in the harsh post-Maastricht period, and to cultivate the Franco-German entente without ignoring Britain or the Mediterranean states. The post is now held by a clever and ambitious German Social Democrat, Klaus Hansch, in the crucial period which includes the next IGC. Abel Matutes (Spain, Partido Popular) is at present a possible successor.

Fourteen Vice Presidents constitute the Bureau, with the addition of the heads of political groups and five Quaestors making up the enlarged Bureau. Though elected, these officers succeed according to an informal rotation. Chairs of the main committees carry greater weight, especially if they can inspire their members to take on an important subject and produce incisive reports. Success here engenders more success, for MEPs are keen to join popular committees like foreign affairs and security (now chaired by Baron Crespo), external economic relations (chaired by W. de Clerq of Belgium), or culture, education, youth and media (la Pergola, Italy). But it is to the technical ones, such as industrial policy (P. Brummer, Netherlands) and the groups on trade or the internal market, that lobbyists mostly address themselves, hoping for substantial advantage. Their influence is enhanced by the attitude of Commission Directors General who tend to see them as workshops, useful for advice or opinions, and as an extra means to mobilize corporate players' acquiescence.

Outside the formal bodies, loose, often temporary intergroups come together on particular issues across party lines. Though often lively and far-sighted, these have proved hard to hold together without a fuller infrastructure and against the activities of party group whips, who dislike such collaboration. All without exception display a professionalism quite at variance with the period before direct elections began, when it was not in the interests of national delegations to depart too far from member states' line of argument.

The European Parliament's influence on other Community institutions lies in its capacity to mobilize an absolute majority of 260 MEPs. Hence, in the end, party groups and their whips do matter as long as the European Parliament's organization remains ill-coordinated and sometimes wayward. Individual MEPs are (with the exception of those from Spain, France and to a lesser extent Portugal) largely beyond national government restraints, so that, for example, responsibility for the surprising result in the debate in June 1994 on EFTA countries' admission (when 486 MEPs turned up and voted by majorities of between 374 and 377 in favour of admission and 121 to 124 against, and between 58 and 61 abstentions, despite the summer holidays and the end of the session) has to be assigned to the parliamentary whips, as well as interjections by member states and the Franco-German entente.[12]

In these spheres, the European Parliament can as yet have no greater weight *vis-à-vis* the other institutions than the moon does, moving only tides on earth. For ten years, Delors used to give it a full presentation of his programmes each January, but for the rest of the year he paid it less attention, at least until the hard passage after Maastricht. However, the growth of a sort of interdependence since then may have become irreversible, now that sub-structures like the Conciliation Committees have grown to fill the interstices. Commission officials attend these in order to be able to frame compromise proposals to the Council as and when needed, so that over the years the mode leading to co-decision has acquired a momentum of its own. But in formal terms, the Commission has no mediating role.

The SEA allowed the Parliament greater involvement in political cooperation. Regular quarterly meetings take place between Baron Crespo, chair of the Foreign Affairs Committee, the Council Presidency, and member states' Foreign Ministry representatives, at which the Presidency's plans for CFSP are also discussed. By association (if no more), the European Parliament has thus been drawn into the Troika, giving it a vague status which rises to co-equal whenever enlargement – for which an absolute majority is essential – is discussed. Parliamentarians even assert tangential powers, having applied political cooperation to the sphere of human rights by holding up association agreements with Israel and Turkey in the late 1980s, until they removed discriminatory trade and other barriers (in the first case against Palestinian fruit traders, in the second Turkey's Kurdish population). For good measure they intervened on similar grounds against Syria and Morocco in January 1992.

But all this has been a slow, painstaking process, where the use of ultimate weaponry, such as taking the Commission to the Court (for default on transport policy or lessening the use of irradiation in foodstuffs) has, by contrast, been unproductive. (Nevertheless, the Parliament's action in the ECJ to ensure open frontiers, which particularly affects Britain, is a real source of leverage.) The European Parliament still lacks even that limited leverage against the

Council. Nevertheless the very recent proposals for the 1996 IGC emanating from German CDU sources suggest that one side at least of the Franco-German entente may be ready to envisage early status for the Parliament as a second chamber, and Klaus Hansch has put forward his own demands for 1996 which include a power of legislative veto.

It has been suggested that the European Parliament will only become a real parliament when it develops pan-European parties, derived from a voting base which itself is European. The latter is still remote, but pan-European parties have grown up in the last seven years (in particular since the partial shift of British Conservatives towards the EPP,[13] and the mutation of the Italian Communists into the PDS to become members of the Socialist group). Among the eight principal groups, only three so far have reached this stage, the EPP (centre right), the Socialist/Social Democrats and the Liberal and Reformist group which at present includes the French UDF (which gives some sign of being ready to enter the EPP) and Ireland's Fianna Fáil.

State of the European Parliament

Number of MEPs, 1994, and 1989 in brackets

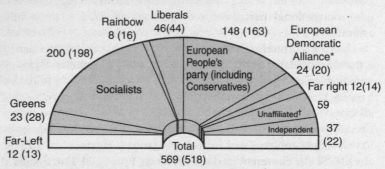

* Irish Fianna Fáil and French Gaullists; many spilt into other groups
† Mainly new right wing Italian parties still negotiating which group to join

FIGURE 8.4

The Socialist group is the most coherent because its underlying social democratic persuasion is reinforced every three years by pan-

European congresses, and it enjoys a strong presence in nineteen parties across 'greater Europe'. It had 198 MPs in the 1989–94 session, and currently has 200, as against the EPP's 163 (now 148), and the Liberal Reformists 46 (now 44).[14]

Fortified by the effects of the end of Communism in eastern Europe, and the 1980s attrition of the further left in France, Britain, Spain and Italy, the Socialist group suffered among larger states only in Germany, in the unique circumstances of reunification.[15] Yet unlike the EPP, which has elements of ingrained self- interest amounting at times to collective identity, the Socialists are more of an umbrella group for factions engaged in a wider struggle. Even when confronted by what seemed to be an 'Anglo-Saxon capitalist revanche' in the 1990–93 recession,[16] it was capable of being disrupted by external events such as the Gulf War, when the Labour Party and PDS voted one way, PSI and PSOE another.

Ever since the 1920s, the space on the left of social democracy has remained an area of ambiguity, to which elements in all its constituent Socialist parties might revert depending on domestic pressures. But at the top, unity prevails and the group's leaders meet, as their counterparts do in the DC/EPP conclave, before each European Summit, seeing themselves as the means to construct the first transnational party, the only one yet to fulfil Maastricht's aspirations.[17]

The EPP (formerly Christian Democrat group) on the other hand, is poorly articulated in the Parliament but well-grounded in terms of organization and funding. Having failed, in 1990–91, to acquire the French UDF, as proposed by Giscard, it is unlikely to gain the allegiance of the substantial Gaullist party, even after the 1995 French presidential elections, because the UDF may think again; it has also had problems with attracting Fianna Fáil, since the EPP is already the site chosen by its domestic rivals, Fine Gael. Forza Italia's position is as yet uncertain – more so in 1995 than when it was in government. The German CDU predominates, especially since the collapse of Christian Democracy in Italy, and this ensures its non-confessional outlook – although that path was actually explored first in the merger in the Netherlands between Catholics and Protestants to form the CDA in the 1970s.

Protestant reformism (in British, Dutch or Danish terms) has long coexisted with the defence of certain forms of welfare capitalism and state activism moderated by a lay Catholic concept of subsidiarity and corporatist relations between employers and employed.[18] The EPP has succeeded so far in combining these without surrendering the defence of national identity and culture to the further right. In the late 1980s and 1990s, Helmut Kohl, Wilfried Martens (Belgium) and Ruud Lubbers (Netherlands) gave it a technocratic managerial aspect, which other parties, notably Spain's Partido Popular (J. M. Aznar) have followed. To this model, Wolfgang Schiessel (Austria) and Carl Bildt (Sweden) are likely to accommodate. The EPP stands out against narrow interpretations of national interest – hence the problem for Britain's anti-federalist Tory minority – and asked Portugal's CDS to leave when its leaders turned against Maastricht and campaigned for a referendum.

The 1995 accession tilt towards northern states seems likely to confirm these characteristics permanently, just as the return of former Communists to power under social democratic labels in Poland, Hungary and much of eastern Europe apart from the Czech Republic may, when these are eventually admitted, prejudice coherence in the Socialist group. The EPP group will gain if the Spanish PP becomes a government, while there is still a possibility that the Italian DC's regrouping, under another name and with new faces, may, in alliance with the centre-left, recapture the electoral ground. British Conservatives, goaded by the Christian Democrats' support for a more federal programme for 1996, might also ease out of the EPP into renewed association with the Gaullists or the EDU, now restyled the European Democratic Alliance.

The Liberal group's continued decline, due to poor organization and the fact that roughly 70% of the votes taken in the Parliament reveal an ideological basis for the divisions, suggest that there is a slow, if irregular trend towards bi-polarity.[19] The evolution of the Rainbow group reinforces this proposition, since that has developed from a would-be red-green coalition between the greens and the further left into one heavily influenced by the more aggressive regions; Catalonia, Scotland's SNP, the Basque provinces, Wales's Plaid Cymru, Sardinia and South Tyrol. (Only in Italy did a highly successful regional party, the Northern League – as part of a right-of-centre government in 1994 – temporarily sit on its own in the European Parliament). The Rainbow group is now much less of a pressure group than it was during the 1980s peak of interest in environmental issues and could perhaps become the parliamentary focus for of the Committee of Regions, given that there are some one hundred and sixty regions, only the most salient of which are ever likely to find parliamentary representation on their own (see chapter 9).

Continued lack of party discipline, absences, cross-voting and the phenomenon of 'non-political' clubs like Altiero Spinelli's Crocodile Club, and Boz Ferranti's Kangaroo Club in the early single market days (see chapter 4) suggest that personal and national affinities still count. Major set-piece debates in plenary sessions on matters like human rights or foreign affairs seem almost detached from party identities, and the low-key style of most debates is remote from the adversarial postures common in national assemblies. The European Parliament may therefore be bi-polar in embryo only, as the Italian system was said to be in the late 1970s. But regular alternation of Presidents since 1989 between EPP and Socialists, to the irritation of other smaller groups, is evidence that a slow current does exist. Much still depends on how the Parliament develops in the 1995–9 session, for where power is, parties soon follow. One subject on which all groups can identify is the aim of increasing their Parliament's status.

Much also depends on the behaviour of MEPs as individuals and on the relations between political groups and their domestic equivalents, as well as between the European Parliament and national parliaments. Some MEPs do not detach themselves from their home contexts, especially in France where dual mandates are common, and where leading figures temporarily out of office rest, waiting for the appropriate moment to return. Some national contingents owe a very direct allegiance to their governments: Spanish Socialists voted in favour of the Moroccan Agreement, against the rest of the Socialist group, because the Gonzalez government insisted that there were substantial commercial and diplomatic advantages to be obtained for Spain.[20]

Since the 1980s, competition for seats has led to a sort of parliamentary Darwinism – the emergence of better candidates, together with the elimination of some of the worst absentee MEPs. Yet many are still not of the same calibre as their national equivalents – or, perhaps better put, not subject to equivalent party disciplines – and those who invest the greater part of their time and interest at Strasbourg are, despite the relatively lavish rewards all of them receive, probably still a minority. There are, as ever, those who address the Assembly and then leave, never doing any detailed work, as well as those prepared to justify what the Parliament does, whatever that may be. Strasbourg can be a hard place for those who live far from the Rhineland, though in fact the Danes, Irish and Greeks are relatively good at attending. But since mainstream national parties usually select their candidates, whatever the actual voting procedure, these are too often chosen either from among lists of the second rate or marginal, local notables or from representatives of interests and producer groups – in some contrast to the national delegations appointed before direct elections began in 1979.

Activists can make a name for themselves by choosing a technical area, like external trade, in which to specialize or by taking up a special or unusual cause.[21] It helps sharpen their commitment if they are Belgian or Irish, or belong to the German SPD, as opposed to Forza Italia or the British Conservative party (for Margaret Thatcher saw MEPs as an inferior class of politician).

But the most obvious consequence of engagement in parliamentary affairs is the attention now given to MEPs by the vast horde of lobbyists representing firms or special interests, which has swollen to Brussels proportions since 1986. (In the case of the tobacco industry, the effort was so great that its excesses ended by creating a strongly adverse reaction.) As the mass of internal market legislation emerged, corporate players discovered that the European Parliament was a dangerous place to ignore, partly because MEPs, though individually weak, were still better than they were at influencing the national media, and partly because other lobbyists were moving ahead in this direction.[22] MEPs also offered a useful path for peak organizations to reach other member states so that, for example, the Danish CBI has at times enlisted Liberal as well as EPP support in order to press home its amendments. Whatever the reason, lobbyists and pressure groups tend to direct themselves to MEPs rather than the party groups, which are favoured more by peak national organizations. The ETUC however is weak, and UNICE focuses more on European Parliament committees.

Lobbyists find it easier, as they do in the US Congress, to win over MEPs than they do officials in the Directorates (as French and German ones discovered in the early 1980s, and Dutch and British ones since). MEPs are habitually eager to be involved with issues, to make their voices heard and, lacking staff back-up, may be prepared to accept the well documented, fully prepared cases on offer. Some are amenable to prepared speeches or help with drafting texts. From the lobbyists' point of view, the case is prepared anyway, almost regardless of cost; what matters is to attract those MEPs with a proven record on the appropriate committee. But these are long-term investments in 'serious and permanent work', as one lobbyist put it. They expend a great deal of effort for an uncertain result, since any multinational corporation would envisage trying to enlist 40–50 MEPs, and approach not only the committee rapporteurs but the majority of its members. Lobbyists have to reciprocate by giving an MEP what he or she needs on other occasions – an implied bargain since 'an MEP with a cause suddenly becomes important . . . and all the world comes to see him.'[23]

Much as it would like to, the Parliament cannot regulate this market any better than the Commission does, given the excesses of over-lobbying in agriculture or the pharmaceuticals and HDTV cases. In 1992, the Galle Report illustrated its dilemma, in wishing on the one hand to be open but on the other to prevent Strasbourg when in session from becoming a captive audience. The fact that this report has not yet been published suggests that there is no consensus, even on opening a register of lobbyists, for in that loose collective the possibilities available to Commission Directorates to privilege some leading players at the expense of others simply do not exist. The numbers of lobbyists fell off, predictably, once the bulk of internal market legislation had been passed, and many American lobbyists partially withdrew. But there is today probably four or five times the number cited by Galle, operating from time to time.

Strasbourg is unlikely closely to resemble the US Congress, if only because it does not have the pork barrel in its own hands. It encompasses greater diversity, whether of political groups' relations to their parent parties or of outlooks on precisely how the European Parliament should now develop. There is no ideal MEP, no Platonic form of representation. One spoke of his 'implicit contract with the public, the country in general, constituents in particular . . . not, essentially, the party', but even this generalization would not hold good for ·those elected from party lists. Meanwhile one former president of a national parliamentary delegation to the 1990 Assizes dismissed them all as 'clerks copying the compromises reached in the 25th hour of Brussels secret conclaves'!

The disparagement openly expressed here constitutes the European Parliament's third constraint, after poor internal organization and the wayward calibre of MEPs. Parliamentarians wish above all to serve in a full second chamber, representing their party as well as their country at EC level. But to do this they would have to surmount a vast wall of national parliamentary jealousy, for which the current incremental process of acquiring powers, even of co-decision, is scarcely sufficient. The meetings of parliamentary representatives which take place under its auspices, such as Speakers' Conferences, or the biennial gatherings of parliamentary scrutiny committees and trans-national assemblies of Foreign Affairs committees, appear to be more interested in coordinating their own work around what is agreed to be best practice than in forming links within the Parliament's ambit. If anything, their tendency is to curb the latter's influence, for national MPs are prone to believe that if the supranational group acquired power it would be at their expense.

Jealously between the two levels of parliamentary professions might conceivably disappear if a truly European public were to emerge, on which supranational party groups could base their programmes, and from which the European Parliament would derive a different kind of legitimacy. Until then, from the point of view of national legislatures, it is an illusion to imagine MEPs can somehow represent on the European stage what remains essentially congeries of like-minded national parties. From the latter point of view, they might do better to serve as delegates, reflecting homewards the actions of other member states and parties. That this occurs seldom is as alarming at home as MEPs' habit of reflecting what they consider 'Europe' to be, for that constitutes another dimension of competition between them.

Therefore, from the point of view of national parties, perhaps the only major use the Parliament has is during periods of opposition, when it serves as a means to circumvent and possibly outwit the ruling party or party coalitions. David Martin, one of the European Parliament's most outspoken Vice-Presidents, has long argued that it is neither fully democratic nor equivalent to national parliaments. What the latter surrendered in the Treaties has not been remedied at Strasbourg. This can be read in two ways: either as a plea for further parliamentary power, or as a precursor to the cynical conclusion that if it had these it might well run counter to the governments which signed the Treaties. Maastricht's attempt to square this circle can only be a stage in an extended process of establishing some sort of accountability of EC institutions to the European Parliament – which is not at all the same thing as European democracy, valuable and necessary though such an aim is.

The gap between the European Parliament and national parliaments may even be widening in some member states: Britain and Denmark come to mind, and possibly Germany at the *länder* level, three member states which rank at the top of the range for being well-informed through their parliamentary scrutiny committees. The important and very necessary scrutiny of EC legislation, in fact, appears to be done better in Britain by the House of Lords than by the Commons. This may imply a general rule about the respective skills and functions of first and second chambers.

The first Parliamentary Assizes, held in Rome in 1990, failed to demonstrate solidarity with the Parliament and were followed by a demand from the Bundestag for greater scrutiny in Bonn of all EC legislation. If that were granted, subsidiarity might grow, but the 'democratic deficit' would be remedied at national not European level, and in conditions of great diversity. For the states with centralized coordinating systems for European affairs, parliaments, such as the French assembly, are weak *vis-à-vis* the government, being in receipt of information but little bargaining power over nationally drafted texts.[24] The assembly has, in fact, recovered and become more active in EU affairs, but the European Parliament remains a rival rather than an ally: only in Italy and Belgium are MEPs seen as the precursors of a new order.

There is nothing the European Parliament can do, for example, to harmonize member states' electoral systems yet, as the Gucht Report 1993 pointed out, proportional systems ought to have become the norm. At present the Parliament stands in front of the ECJ for having failed to draft a uniform procedure for elections as required by the 1957 Treaty. If, in 1996, it were to be given the status of a full second chamber it would be because the governments of the larger member states wished it, for their own reasons. (Conversely, Leon Brittan, then Commissioner for External Economic Relations, recently proposed that a committee of national MPs from all member states should work regularly with the European Parliament 'to reassure voters that power over their lives is not ebbing abroad.')

No EC institution can summon the European public into existence. But its absence can be seen as primary evidence that a democratic deficit exists, even if says little about the explanation. Many American analysts consider the Community and its institutions to be creatures of political elites working in conjunction. But the fact that there is no discernible European public can also be used to explain the phenonema of elitist, bureaucratic reality, which mirrors what ministries and administrations in national capitals do, without providing more than a vestige of European government. Since the Council has some resemblance to a cabinet, and the Commission to a civil service, it is the Parliament that seems odd, even unnatural, in its present form.

During the drafting of the Maastricht Treaty, the way to create a 'peoples' Europe' appeared to lie through defining categories of European citizenship, including local election voting rights. Into the same basket went existing, little-used practices such as the right to petition the Parliament, and for the Parliament in turn to appoint an ombudsman and to set up committees of enquiry. Despite these having come into existence, the European Parliament remains on the margins of media attention and national awareness, condemned

by one member state's interests to meet in Strasbourg, far from
what is generally seen as the centre of European affairs. It is
saddled with hostile stereotypes, complex formal procedures, and a
reputation for laxity and waste which is probably now unfair. After
fifteen years of direct elections it has acquired the status only of an
institution of EC accountability, within limits set by member states
according to their own interests.

Yet there is some evidence that Euro-public awareness is developing. In 1991 (admittedly a year of considerable media interest)
Eurobarometer found that 53% of respondents in the twelve
states felt a sense of European identity, ranging in frequency from
'sometimes' to 'often'. Variations existed nevertheless in the proportion of those 'feeling informed' about the EC, from 46% in the
Netherlands to 22% in Spain. Awareness evidently depended on the
portrayal of the Community in national media, for in 1992 the great
majority knew all about Maastricht (85%) and understood the
internal market (69%) but only half were familiar with the Commission or the Parliament (51% and 55%).[25] During the EC's bad
years, 1992–4, support fell away markedly, the main interest centring
on crime and drugs (89%), followed by defence, social policy and
immigration (77% to 72%). Questions of subsidiarity and Parliamentary representation engaged only half of all respondents, while
the matter of EC citizenship occupied a mere 36%.

One Irish MEP expressed the paradox: 'people are Irish first,
then, a long way behind, citizens of the EC; but there is a feelgood
factor about Europe.'[26] It is almost impossible for any EC institution to remedy the disparity between perception of interest and
identity, despite the vast output of often very well-produced
explanatory literature. The Community's own distribution channels
follow national administrative patterns, rather than those appropriate to a mass European society. Pamphlets reach the schools, at
least secondary ones, but few teachers are qualified to explain them
in their context without the pre-existing support of national media –
which, lacking public demand, have little inducement to do so even
in the most Eurocentric states.[27]

In the sense of changing habits, work patterns, mobility, retirement plans, tourism and travel, forms of European consumer

activity do of course exist.[28] Yet in terms of brand loyalty, national (even nationalistic) forms flourish, illustrating Alain Touraine's paradox that global economic activity can coexist with cultural distinctiveness. Germans continued into the 1990s to drink local beer despite the internal market, though the young may be turning from Tuborg and Pilsen, and to Belgian, French or even Mexican brands. Deutsche Bank has had consciously to educate its customers in the virtues of an EMU in which the deutschmark will eventually disappear.[29] The EC's representative in Milan encounters 'a general fear and a deep scepticism among economic operators at local level', even in the richest part of Italy. Such feelings are also widely reciprocated in Denmark,[30] where opinion polls consistently find 80% opposed to the EC's intrusion into political matters.

The gap between national elites, who play the European game, and their publics is still profound. 'The EC' is seen widely as something outside their governing processes, even when national players make no secret of the advantages they gain from its pluralism.[31] Even when EC institutions meet member states' demands, what is done may well not be seen nationally as what was asked for but as concessions wrung by their governments from a remote Brussels bureaucracy, or as something different from what they think they want. Such misconceptions could perhaps be remedied by national governments if they wished, but such remedies are beyond the range of EC institutions, unless the Commission were already a government and the European Parliament a full parliament.

In retrospect, the original Treaties made assumptions which have not been justified: that the European Parliament would be allowed or encouraged to grow in a certain direction, rather than being directed into a supervisory role; that it would be legitimated by direct elections of a common pattern; and that its growth would be paralleled by a European-wide awareness of its democratic standing. It is hard to avoid the conclusion that, if the original signatories were to draft the Treaties today, they would not institute a Parliament of this kind, but choose the Assizes drawn from national parliaments to be a counterpoint to the Council of Ministers.

II. The European Court of Justice

In contrast to the abortive tripartism of Council, Commission and Parliament, the ECJ achieved more than its Treaty origins led early EEC commentators to expect. As a result, its evolution was controversial, marked by accusations of judicial activism, very different from the generally benign commentaries on the Parliament's aspirations (as distinct from criticism of MEPs' actual behaviour). Three questions need to be put here: does the Court display elements of informal politics? Has it come to resemble a supreme court, part of an evolving state? and has it been, by virtue of its judicial activism, an element in the EC's evolution rather than a neutral arbiter of its problems?

Although the ECJ is named in Maastricht Article 4 as one of the EC's five principal institutions, the Presidents of the Court seem deliberately to have kept a low profile up to the 1970s. This may have been because of the series of highly significant decisions which pushed it into public notice, often incurring member states criticism;[32] nevertheless, its workings are still relatively obscure. It is composed of judges from fifteen member states, which allows for a majority of 8–7.[33] In addition, it is served by six Advocates General of similar quality and legal status, whose function is to consider a case in its context and give an opinion for the court's use, at the conclusion. (In 70–80% of plenary courts these are accepted and in 90% of those in chambers, when four or five judges sit to consider what are normally more technical cases.) Whether the sessions are plenary or in chambers, one judge is elected by the rest as rapporteur to sum up. No minority or dissenting judgments are made public and any voting is disguised by the fiction of unanimity. A bare majority of 8–7 (or 3–2 in chambers) is sufficient but judges always seek a wider consensus if possible. Each one has a cabinet of legal secretary-assistants who prepare summaries and advise him, most of them being experts in legal history.

Four types of action come before the Court: preliminary rulings (*questions préjudicielles*) under Article 177, in which a national court asks for elucidation or interpretation of EC law; enforcement actions (*recours en manquement*) by the Commission or member states under Articles 169 or 93 for breaches of EC law; annulment (*recours en annulation*) under Article 173, where a subordinate law is struck down as incompatible; and action for inactivity (*recours en carence*) under Article 175 to force a Community institution to take action if it has not followed the Treaty's injunctions.

The ECJ's caseload is, and always has been, vast. By the 1970s it had become an anomaly that the Community's highest court should be overloaded with a mixture of landmark and trivial cases. Yet despite repeated requests and one formal complaint, member states in the Council took no action to institute a lower court until faced with the sheer volume of 286 legal instruments embodying the internal market in the late 1980s. Under great pressure from business and industrial organizations, who foresaw delays of years before the single market came into effect, they conceded and set up the Court of First Instance (CFI). Their reasons were less nakedly to do with powersharing than Rasmussen suggested, however: in the Council, member states led by France had never been able to agree on how much delegated powers to give the CFI (France especially was reluctant to allow it to deal with competition cases, because of the hybrid role played by the Conseil de la Concurrence, a half juridical, half administrative institution).

Under Article 168a of the Single European Act, the CFI came into operation by the end of 1989, its scope being restricted to competition, ECSC and staff cases, and the damages claimed under all these three headings. In 1993 its brief was expanded to include all individual and corporate complaints, save in the 'defence of trade' area – this being a good indicator of the political considerations which obtained among member states jealous of their sovereignty. The CFI now has fifteen judges, but no Advocates General; it is highly technical and has shown itself to be an effective instrument especially when sitting in chambers. The ECJ, on the other hand, is still overloaded (the duration of cases being longer than it was a decade ago), and remains ripe for further delegation as a result of the 1996 IGC.[34]

Law is central to all aspects of the Community as enjoined by the Treaties and by every legal instrument since 1957. But it is not at all clear that the ECJ has a duty to create a European constitution, although a few judges, notably Federico Mancini, have argued in this sense.[35] For the majority of them, as for member states, its primary function is to interpret the Treaties, in lieu of a constitution – but, according to the context and the circumstances over time, not on strict precedents. The ECJ is fundamentally a praetorian court in the Roman legal tradition rather than an Anglo-Saxon one (which is clear from the fact that some of what has been 'added', for example human rights connotations and the concept of citizenship, have been enshrined in the later Treaties 1986 and 1991).

The ECJ decided two great issues of principle early on. In *Van Gend vs. Loos* (1963) it established the direct effect of EC law, by giving a Dutch transport firm protection against Dutch customs duty imposed on an imported German product, and indicated that this interpretation would also apply in the case of individuals seeking redress. The concept was extended in 1970 to include Council decisions and Commission Directives, so long as these imposed clear and unconditional obligations on a member state. A citizen of any state could thereafter rely on a national court to conform. Thus the ECJ's desire to redirect most of the routine cases to member states' own courts, the 'jurisdictions de droit commun' in the Community's legal system, was fulfilled, leaving it to them to refer to the precedents for preliminary rulings, and making them apply the law directly. There things rested: no member state should benefit from failure to enforce superior law. In *Foster versus British Gas* (1989) the Court went further, extending the obligation to the states' agencies.

At this stage, no individual plaintiff had won redress, and in *Bourgoin* (1986) one such failed to get beyond the UK's Court of Appeal.[36] But in *Francovich and Bonifaci versus the Italian Government* (1989) the ECJ declared it to be inherent in EC law that a member state is liable to an individual for the damage it causes by infringement or failure to implement the law. Over and above that, a state has an obligation of 'general good will' under Article 5 of the 1957 Treaty which extends not only to the previous categories, but to all EC legislative instruments (*Emmott*, 1990). Unless the latter judgment is modified, the ECJ has overriden the time limits for bringing a case which exist in national legal systems, giving a new and sharp definition to a member state's duties towards its citizens – this quite possibly amounts to a definition of European citizenship in general.

After *Van Gend vs. Loos* came the second principle, the absolute supremacy of EC law, as a result of *Costa versus Enel* (1964) (even if the actual plaintiff lost his claim!) Until then it had not been obvious that the Treaties established supremacy, and for nearly a quarter of a century the French Conseil d'Etat resisted the principle, as the German and Italian constitutional courts did in the 1970s, on the grounds that the fundamental or basic rights guaranteed by EC law were less than those already provided in these member states. In spite of this, in *Nolo vs the Commission* (1973) the ECJ designated fundamental rights as 'constitutional traditions common to the member states' and an 'integral part of the general principles of EC law'.[37]

There it stood, while first the German and Italian constitutional courts, and finally, after a series of cases (see p. 297), the Conseil d'Etat itself accepted the position. In 1974, the *Dassonville* judgment established that a member state was unable by its legislation to introduce a fresh barrier to trade, while in 1991, the *Factortame* judgment against the British government made it unequivocally clear that even the law-giving status of national parliaments was subordinate, with the wording of existing statutes being subject to alteration by the Court in order to make its interpretation coincide with EC law – whatever text the parliament in question had initially adopted. One hundred years of the Diceyan interpretation of British parliamentary sovereignty vanished as that body was reduced to the same level as any other member state parliament – its only vestigial weapon (as for the others) resting on the possibility of a national government deciding to secede from the Community.[38]

Demonstrating that the lesson had been learned, and that the British courts had willingly accepted it, the House of Lords ruled in the *Equal Opportunities* case (1994) that aspects of a 1978 Employment Protection Act were incompatible with EC law – thereby not only strengthening the rights of women to equal treatment but making itself effectively a constitutional court, comparable to those in Germany and Italy. It should be added that *Factortame* came at the end of a series of cases where the ECJ habitually took the view that member states have no jurisdiction over the high seas without the Commission's prior approval (but not of course the sea bed and resources such as oil), which some have taken to imply that the high seas are EC territory and consequently an indication of EC statehood.[39]

The ECJ cannot initiate; it can only rule on the cases brought before it, which explains the haphazard ways in which fundamentals have so far been elucidated. In this process, national courts' requests for preliminary rulings (in which the ECJ interprets the law but does not rule on a national law's conformity with it, as it does in enforcement actions), originally introduced to ensure that all states interpreted the law in the same way, have developed into a regular interchange between member states and the EC dimension. Typically, a court will ask for guidance before determining a case and take account of the response; but on many occasions, the ECJ takes the chance to redraft the questions put to it so as to highlight what it considers to be the key issues. This practice steadily increased during the 1980s, reaching a peak in the early 1990s, indicating that all member states now accept both the practice and the value of EC judgments.[40] In that sense, the ECJ has become, in the sphere of EC law, a de facto supreme court whose dicta then irradiate the member states' own legal systems.

The bulk of its work however comes with the direct process of complaint by EC institutions, states, firms or individuals. At the highest level for example, the Commission had to renegotiate the European Economic Agreements with EFTA countries because the first set were held incompatible, since EC judges would have had to interpret the law under two separate jurisdictions (see p. 258, note 43). At a slightly lower, but equally significant level, the Court has since 1992 ensured the freedom of movement in the internal market, enforced competition policy, and pronounced finally on equal pay. Perhaps because of its increasingly salient role and the attention paid by commentators to ambiguities or 'grey areas', where informal mechanisms flourish, there has recently been another growth of questions about its rights, status and activism.

In its external relations, the Court has a natural affinity with the Commission, being co-guardian of the Treaties. It also has a vestigial tension *vis-à-vis* the Council, for obvious reasons. It has generally been favourable to the Parliament (*Isoglucose* and *Chernobyl* 1990 in which the judgment recognized the European Parliament's rights and was included, almost verbatim, as Maastricht Article 173); but it is also quite capable of judging it at fault. Through enforcement proceedings, it has sought always to ensure respect for EC law and its fair and equal application, but it would never bargain with member states, as the Commission does to ensure full compliance over time. Since Maastricht, it has had the power to fine a member state, but no case has yet been tried which would bring the enormous practical difficulties of this into focus.

For all these reasons, member states naturally choose judges of high quality and reputation. The standard reply to questions about partiality on grounds of national affinity, or attempts to manipulate 'their' nationals is that these problems rarely occur.[41] The Court is, nevertheless, the sum of fifteen judges' individual training and personality, evolved in different legal systems. There is no observable trend of bias, though it is sometimes alleged that a protectionist majority exists, favourable to anti-dumping measures against non-EC competitors. A few, rather distant instances, when member state governments have tried to bring pressure to bear, tend to reinforce the modern picture of the Court as standing above crass interference.[42] But the German government complained recently that the Court's preliminary rulings were giving too much protection to migrant workers, both EC Italians and non-EC Turks, and hinted that amendments might be put forward to Article 177 at the 1996 IGC.

This is not to say that other Community institutions do not have a complicated, subtle network of links with the Court. Though neither could be accused of using it in any crude sense, both the Commission and the Council have a sharp interest in how it operates, whether for or against their interests. To a very general extent, for example, the Commission has means to ensure that only the complaints (*mises en demeure*) it most wants heard by the Court actually reach it: out of every hundred, sixty are dealt with via member state responses. Of the forty which reach the stage of Commission warning (*avis motivé*), only four in any year come to the ECJ, given the multiple means available for brokerage at the second stage. But according to at least two judges, the Commission has made surprisingly little use of this informal power.

There is no formal way for the Commission to test out its proposals on the Court (it being for the Legal Service to provide it with such advice), and even if there were informal ones the judges would be unlikely to respond, other than in open court. But since legality is central to all aspects of the Community, if the college or any Commissioner were brought on complaint, it would benefit their case if they could show that they had been guided by appropriate legal advice. (The Legal Service has to act for the EC as a whole, but has no direct access to the Court, save on procedural matters. Its officials' primary responsibility is for the Commission's proper conduct in accordance with the law, and they stand in the firing line if a Commissioner is arraigned. Judges have no natural sympathy for them, nor can they distinguish between the Service as an agency and the Commission as principal).

From the Commission's point of view however, the Court has value as a card in its tactical game with governments, firms or agencies, so long as the latter in turn do not react by recourse to the law (as the Milk Marketing Board did against Commissioner Tugendhat in 1982). A Commission threat to go beyond the *avis motive* is to be taken seriously, even if it is already 'known' that the great proportion of threats turn out later to have been merely gestures. The ECJ constitutes an ally of far greater value in the long term than the Parliament, for with it the Commission has an organic identity of interest, because of its creativity and dedication to shared EC ideals of integration and the defence of the Treaties.[43]

It could be argued that they also share the view that there is too much hastily contrived legislation, put forward less by the Commission on its own than at the urging of the Council and increasingly the Parliament; certainly too many derogations allowed to backsliding member states. But below the level of generalization, there is little common ground to build on. Neither would the college try, given the value represented by a deeply respected Court whose decision no member state has ever rejected (even though some have evaded the consequences), which any injudicious hint of collusion would prejudice. For this reason, the Commission sometimes gives its full backing to a test case, as if the Court were a Supreme Court on the US model, to win an exemplary judgment.

Over the whole period of EC history, the Court has rarely found categorically against the Commission. But there have been landmark cases in which it has referred back matters to the Commission or the Council because they are essentially political and touch on a member state's *amour propre* or willingness to push an issue to the limit (the *Bachmann* case, for instance)[44]; even if, like the first banking Directive, it is an integral element in the internal market. (The Directive covered secrecy in banking supervision, but on preliminary ruling appeared to the Court to be insufficiently precise, so that the Commission had to produce a revised text, the second Directive). Again in the insurance area, in a judgment in December 1989 under Article 100A between the Commission and the Netherlands on one side and Germany, France and Italy on the other, the Court's answer forced the Commission to introduce consumer protection for financial services against its will, and delayed the internal market in that respect by eighteen months.

Since about 1990, the Court has seemed to become more critical of the Commission. In 1991 the Commission negotiated a competition agreement with the United States as part of its increasing body of external agreements. A number of member states trying to cut back on its scope in trade and industrial policy, headed by France and Britain, took this to the ECJ and won on the grounds that the agreement ought first to have been put to the Council. The judgment, however, does not indicate any desire by the Court to hold a balance between them, though the states in question evidently hoped that it might impair the Commission's capacity to represent the whole EC in GATT/WTO negotiations; but it does emphasize its part as referee in the unending struggle over the margins of power.

Between the Court and the Council, the ground is more heavily mined, because of member states' inevitable suspicion about where this 'creativity and originality' may lead. The formal position is entirely clear, but informally the ECJ, like any other court, tends to maximize its jurisdiction. It is not a supreme court, of the US kind at least, and the differences outrank the similarities. But it is supreme in the sphere of EC law, and it invariably outranks national courts. If member states follow its rulings, they do so firstly because of the weight the Court has built up since 1957 and secondly because their own status is at risk should they not.

Manoeuvring begins where competences and practicalities conflict. Member states and the Council withheld anti-dumping legislation from the CFI because the ECJ had already extended and then consolidated enactments put forward by the Commission and because some of them – France, Spain and Greece in particular – feared that the CFI might further extend this, via technicalities, to create what for them would have been a harsher regulatory regime.

No state would now seek directly to influence the Court; at most, it would discreetly ask advice before supporting or attacking another member state's case. Jacques Lang, French culture minister, is known to have invited judges to lunch during the 'Net Book Agreement' negotiations, to explain the agreement's great cultural importance. Such *tentatives* are not *per se* improper, and in any case the Quai d'Orsay refused him permission to plead the case in person. Judges are too senior, too near the end of their careers, too well off, and with academic reputations at stake, to fall for easy blandishments.

Court procedures offer more scope to bring informal influence to bear. Under the rules, member states can take part to argue the significance of a case from their national standpoints. In any reference to the Court or CFI, all the documents are sent to their equivalent of the British treasury solicitor. A range of states, other than the ones in the dock, can thus argue what amounts to a defence (c.f., *Defrenne II*, a case of sex discrimination involving a Sabena air hostess, where Britain and Ireland were both keenly concerned to limit the risk of having to match equal pay retrospectively). The Court duly ruled – as the US Supreme Court probably would have done – that the EC law had direct effect, but that damages should run only from the date of judgement. (Likewise in *Brown-Topska*, a case of racial discrimination.) Again when the British government, having lost its case for refusing visas to Scientologists in the House of Lords (*Van Duyn* case 1973–4), turned to the ECJ, arguing that exclusion was a matter of public policy, the Court probably took account of the 1975 referendum results on UK membership, when it allowed the government to win. But then it had no enforcement powers; today the result might be different.

In some cases member states are indisputably in error, as the UK was over *Factortame*. But in others, they can argue that the Treaties are not coherent, since one Article may contradict another. That more such defences have not surfaced may be explained by the fact that in most of them, concerning existing legislation, such a defence would run counter to their own interests. They do, however, vigorously support complaints by firms, being a formidable weapon against another member state which could otherwise, in its own courts, prevent any such action. Thus the ECJ's jurisprudence has extended this practice especially where Articles 90 and 92–94 operate (c.f., complaints against the French postal service and Eléctricité de France about its subsidies for engineering subsidiaries).

There is also a possibility that undertakings given in the Council of Ministers at an earlier stage may be regarded as binding on the political level, even if they are not sanctioned in law: in this category comes the British government's agreement made in 1985 as part of the SEA IGC. This solemn and binding agreement exempts Britain from abandoning internal market border controls (passport requirements), as required by the Treaty signed in 1986. Yet a case was underway in 1995, drawing vigorous support from the Parliament, designed to test that sort of agreement. The outcome will demonstrate how sensitive judges are to pre-existing, non-statutory qualifications when the enforcement of EU law is at issue.

It is hard to find instances where the Council's collective behaviour has been modified by ECJ rulings, though the very contentious 1970 one on transport policy , which was long resisted by Germany, may fit (see chapter 3). The point was substantiated in

1987 in the field of aviation, which had not been mentioned specifically in the Treaties. But all member states have had to react in their own ways to the protection given to individuals (*Francovich*) in recent years: in the German insurance case (1986), the ECJ made clear that the person needed protection, not against risk but against the German company which insured him, because the policy's conditions were so hedged about as to make it near-useless. Governments across the EC cannot ignore the implication of cases like *Titiager Jute* – where the chairman of a company whose shares had been suspended on the London Stock Exchange, having lost all rounds up to and including the House of Lords, was refused leave to appeal to the ECJ (the Stock Exchange's fear, and its argument, being that the Court might espouse individual European shareholder's rights, to the detriment of British Stock Exchange good practice).

Judges 'direct themselves' in trying a case according to their understanding of the law, their professional training, and their working lifetime's experience of what is appropriate. Quite apart from minute variations in each one's 'canons of construction', the range of systems from which they are appointed extends from the Anglo-Saxon tradition of total implementation and precisely formulated texts to the Italian one of general indications, accompanied by elements of interpretation suited to specific conditions.

It was only as a result of a scrics of cases 1989–90, starting with *Nicolo*, that the French Conseil d'Etat set out, in its 1992 report, its own final account of the long evolution of the integration of EC law in France: this signified both that its last objections had been withdrawn and that a need existed for better training of French lawyers in EC law. This in spite of evidence that French law had had a long and pervasive influence on the development of EC law, whatever the Conseil's earlier fears (expressed in its 1982 report) that the latter was badly conceived according to alien, Anglo-Saxon categories. Not only is French habitually used in ECJ proceedings, but the Court exhibits, like the Conseil d'Etat, '*une jurisprudence prétorienne, audacieuse, fondée sur quelques décisions de principe soigneusement pesées*'.[45]

Not all French lawyers would yet agree. But it does seem that the ECJ has been able to draw out what is best or most appropriate in different national traditions, for example, the doctrine of legal expectation from Germany,[46] or the use of oral process from English law. In a range of celebrated cases including *Heylens* (1987) relating to member state administrative acts, *Nolo* (1974) and *Francovich*, the ECJ has reaffirmed that Community institutions' acts must respect fundamental principles inherent in all member states' systems. National experts of course have their own inputs, mainly in the form of specialized texts say on VAT or product responsibility, insurance risks, or rights of domicile.

New laws follow in a mixture of traditions which has now become the Community's own tradition. But it is worth noting a second time that member states would not allow the Commission at Maastricht to establish a hierarchy of legal norms, even though that already exists in France, Germany and Britain. The subject was included only as a declaration appropriate for the 1996 IGC to pick up, part of the great overhanging wave of the subsidiarity debate, which is likely also to involve the ECJ's own competences.

If the existence of conflict between European law and distinct national legal traditions or trust in the highest national courts can now be seen as a problem of the past, the criteria for judicial appointments are still a present matter, being highly informal and diverse. Member state choices are approved in virtually all cases; but the means by which the names are selected may include political affinity (in Germany and Belgium, a coalition rota exists), horse-trading (in Italy, Spain and Greece), and simple convenience (in Britain, where the Lord Chancellor apparently asks among a select few who would be prepared to go to Luxembourg). It is hardly surprising that, as one said, 'there are differences among judges due to nationality, because each one inevitably sees cases in his own way. But during a case, a "community atmosphere" develops and permeates the judgment.'[47]

In the last resort, the Court and its judges alone carry responsibility for EU law, as well as its primacy and direct application, because the Treaties, unlike other international agreements, confer supranational powers and hence make the Court an essential element of a sort of state. Whatever else it may be, the EU is a *rechtstaat*, a formulation which ensures that it has a political infrastructure which in turn reinforces the *Rechtsstaat*. Since this tends to induce common patterns of behaviour as well as law, the element of actual statehood is self-perpetuating and dynamic. Member states acting together in an IGC could reduce the ECJ's competences, but not eliminate this innate tendency which works always – albeit haphazardly – to diminish their singularity.

The Court however has margins of interpretation which inhibit it from direct confrontation with member states – as when it found the Irish government liable neither to fund the provision of information about abortion nor to change its legislation, but nevertheless ruled that it could not impose restrictions on an individual's right to travel, and to have access to information about clinics outside the Republic where an abortion might be performed (Crotty case).[48] Its inner standard is to pursue the largest possible measure of consensus in the judgments, even if only a bare majority suffices. The Treaty is only a framework; the Court has to fill in gaps by asking what was the Treaty's intent 'and how do we answer the question in the light of what the Treaty *is* [author emphasis] setting out to do . . . so the Court begins by trying to ask itself "what is the purpose?" and then "what is the context?" and from that it leads on to its interpretation . . . the ECJ is more willing to part from the literal words than would be a (British) common law court.'[49] It has a purposive technique, defined by another British judge as 'a solution that makes things work rather than brings things to a halt'.[50]

Low-key as it still aims to be, even at times to play down the significance of its judgments so as not to arouse opposition until much later, the ECJ is in that sense activist. Its members recognize their need to keep in touch with the legal spheres beyond Luxembourg, and beyond the opinions of the Advocates General and their legal secretaries, among academic commentators and reporters of cases. Judges will also discreetly propagate debate – not about their judgments but the deep questions which underlie them – in seminars which they can attend as observers; or they can conduct debate through the columns of the law journals (many of them being professors of law in their own right) and bodies like the Avvocatura di Stato and the Law Society, in a style pioneered by Judge Kutscher, President of the Court 1976–80, who was tireless in lecturing and speaking in member states.

The Court can be flexible, can alter its procedures with the consent of all parties to save time, can act with great expedition and give priority to important preliminary rulings. It can and sometimes does temper the wind, not on principles but in immediate aspects of its judgments (as when it allowed DG3 to investigate IBM's European business practices, or those of Hoechst in 1989, but set limits on their means of inquisition). There can be no plea bargaining, but mitigating circumstances are borne in mind: the Court does not set fines (and has indeed unsuccessfully asked the Commission to set down a clear tariff for them) but it might well mitigate fines' enforcement if this were likely to cause bankruptcy or heavy unemployment in a member state. An exemplary punishment on the other hand would ignore such considerations. In the Polypropylene cartel case (1983) when the fines on the cartel totalled 50 million ecus, ICI's share was 10 million; in 1986–7, the CFI reduced this, in recognition of ICI's cooperative response to compliance procedures, and did so again in the PVC and LDC cases, ICI having already withdrawn from the cartel.[51]

The Court relies on member state courts for enforcement, in effect on the force for compliance built up since 1958 by states who have vested their credit and convenience in the process. It may deplore how slow that is, how prone to compromises, how the accumulation of enforcement judgments weakens respect for the law itself (for example in Italy, the only member state to have had more than ten such judgments to comply with an earlier ruling made against it). 'But if the Court were told that a member state was about to comply, then it might adjourn or postpone the case, rather than slap it down.'[52]

But an apparent tendency to avoid confrontation worries some judges. The Court has at least not been prone to accept the excuse that a member state's parliament has not yet got round to it, ever since the *Leonesco* case in the late 1960s. Meanwhile the most promising avenue for the enforcement of laws which member states' governments dislike may lie not in the Commission's stratagems but via individuals' actions for damages, as in *Francovich*. It takes time but no member state is likely to stand out when monetary penalties, paid to its own or other citizens, are involved. Informal mechanisms exist even here, as they do in all the Community's interstices. Lawyers practising in the EC's courts know accurately where they are, and use them, or play on their availability in preparing their cases.

It is much harder, especially for a non-lawyer, to be categorical about whether the Court has become a supreme court, part of an emerging Community statehood. Some of the early landmark cases were argued from a philosophical as well as from a legal standpoint: Advocate General Marcel le Grange added this dimension to his brilliant exposition in *Costa versus Enel* (1964). Though modern reasoning is always legal in form, this underlying tendency, characteristic of a supreme court, has not entirely disappeared. Secondly, the ECJ's readiness to take account of contexts and circumstances, following trends as they develop rather than sticking strictly to precedent, is akin to the classic US Supreme Court model.

But opinions differ. Though in the great cases it may appear similar to the US model, the ECJ's jurisdiction is more limited and its procedures different. For example, unlike the US Supreme Court, it cannot reject cases: it must hear them and decide, if the Community is to continue its momentum as a contractual undertaking between member states. There is no parallel with the Supreme Court's role in relation to the US states, for member states are not federated. Yet it does strongly resemble the Supreme Court as Judge Marshall envisaged it in the late-eighteenth century, and the closer the EC moves towards statehood, the closer the parallel grows.

On the third question, whether the Court is a participant in the EC's evolution or a neutral arbiter, Rasmussen's argument about judicial activism still has validity, even though the decline in numbers of landmark cases suggests that it is less activist than in the recent past. It is certainly not a sort of 'fifth column', dedicated to undermining member states' sovereignty, as has sometimes been alleged. But it does act in support of what the Commission ought to do; that is, to reaffirm the Treaties which member states have signed and pledged themselves to follow. Judges opposed to federalism (who are probably in a substantial majority) endorse that. The increased power and competence provided by the Maastricht Treaty could, equally, be withdrawn by the next Treaty: there may be an 'iron law' by which a court extends its jurisdiction, but there is no law of incremental build-up in the texts themselves. Legal texts do have a tendency to advance integration cumulatively, an *effet utile*, but this is a political factor whose dynamic does not derive from the Court.

Yet the tendency to activism, properly defined, runs counter to the post-revolutionary tradition in France, and an older way in Britain dating from the mid-seventeenth century, that political momentum draws its dynamism from an increasingly democratic political system, not from its judiciary. The argument that by ratifying the Treaties member states have conceded not merely the powers they understood at the time to be at issue but the powers subsequently declared by the Court (or rather the judges sitting at that time) to be a consequence, remains a major political difficulty – even when a member state's own highest courts accept that this is a necessary consequence. Put in that way, the 'problem of judicial activism' is sometimes a way for member states' governments to evade responsibility for the actions of their predecessors, and their inevitably more limited understanding of what the EC was at that stage of its development. Judges, literally, have no choice but to interpret the Treaty factually and that, in itself (as in *Kramer* (1975) or *Isoglucose*) embodies consequences which were not necessarily obvious at an earlier stage.

The potential for new landmark cases is always there. In a 1992 judgement, Sir Thomas Bingham, Master of the Rolls, imagined the ECJ as 'supplying flesh to a spare and loosely constructed skeleton . . . the choice between submissions may turn not on purely legal (in the British sense) considerations, but on a broader view of what the orderly development of the Community requires.' That broader view may impel the Court to emphasize certain issues or areas of concern, for example in its reformulation of the questions put in preliminary rulings, about say environmental law or human rights. In the past, Green party supporters have been able to hail it as a Court of Appeal against what they saw as brutalist member states, when in fact it has done no more than decide whether governments have gone through the proper procedures.

What heightened such perceptions in cases like the M3 Winchester Bypass, or the Danish glass bottles case in 1986[53] was that the Commission (or rather DG11) appeared to be pushing hard and winning. EC institutions are often at fault, because their lengthy compromises make the law less than clear, just as member states, when they agree regulations between them in very general terms because the political atmosphere is highly-charged, leave wide scope for interpretation which the Court cannot deny to a plaintiff who comes before it.

Judges are well aware of these extra dimensions to their work. Their primary duty is to the Treaties, and only secondarily to the EC's development, yet their margins for manoeuvre favour the work of the Commission and the Council when these two work together.[54] *Cassis de Dijon* (1978) was accepted as 'saving the EC', even when the facts were simple. But the Commission and the Council diverged afterwards on the consequences of that judgment, with its exemptions, because in acting as a safeguard for a member state's fundamental national interests by recognizing the right to exemption under Article 30, the Court allowed scope for factious interplay – and indeed for itself to come back to revise it at a much later date (*Keck*, November 1993). Yet to have ruled otherwise in 1979 would have been construed as far more politically active.

The argument has other implications. Just as the ECJ and CFI now utilize oral procedures from Anglo-Saxon traditions, often with salutary results, so the style of reasoning in the highest English courts has begun slowly to alter. In this area of law, the House of Lords shows itself more purposive, perhaps more activist, and certainly less subservient to the British state than was the case in the first seventy years of this century and perhaps since the early eighteenth century. The process of irradiating member states' legal systems operates at many levels, from the appointment of a magistrate as EC referendaire, who takes back with him an acquaintance with how things are done in Luxembourg, to the wide dissemination of concepts of human rights or the concept of proportionality of remedy to offence.[55] The Union des Avocats Européen, whose annual assembly is held in Luxembourg, aspires to become a European bar with a membership enrolled directly, not through national federations.

Cases likely to reach the Court in the near future, such as Greece's breach of EU law in closing its border with Macedonia, may be highly contentious but do not raise complex points of law. But in future, hard questions about rights, such as employment entitlements under one national system but claimed in another, will certainly emerge. The degree to which the Social Protocol is justiciable may add even worse ones. But the principal unsettled question concerns subsidiarity, with vast philosophical implications, unless member states pre-empt it with their own Treaty texts in 1996. It may not even be justiciable until that happens, unless a national court were to refer upwards the plea of an individual that he was being dealt with at a level detrimental to his case. Member states are more likely to act first, rather than risk the ECJ determining the principles in a matter of such political significance.

9

The Regions

The idea that the region could constitute a legitimate focus for political order had greater impact among the defeated powers after the Second World War than it had, say, in France, while in Britain it had virtually no significance. In what was to become West Germany, recognition that *Land* government would be the way for Germans to demonstrate that they could be trusted with self-government was later extended as the building blocks of the federal state, until it constituted a fundamental part of the Basic Law. So it did in Italy's Constitution of 1949; but, because of the prolonged Cold War and the hostility between the Communist party and the Christian Democrat-dominated governing majority, it was only in the mid–1970s, and the era of Helsinki, that Italian regional governments established themselves with any degree of autonomy. Meanwhile, in Spain after Franco's death, the evolution, in the Constitution of 1978, of seventeen 'autonomous communities' over and above the existing provinces offered an answer to separatism and to the chronic problem of distinct ethnic and historic identities in a supposedly unitary state.

Not until the widespread introduction of regional planning in the 1960s did the economic aspect of regionality across Europe begin to coincide with these political implications. During the EEC's first two decades, the regional question was put indirectly, as a matter of improving poor and backward areas, primarily the Italian Mezzogiorno, through judicious use of the EEC's structural funds. What member states did on their own did not lead to a general policy or model, so that by the time of the 1970s' economic crisis a series of quite distinct political experiments existed.

A British Labour government tinkered with devolution in the late 1970s, primarily to bolster its narrow parliamentary majority, but failed; the subsequent Thatcher governments turned devolution back on itself and vigorously asserted the state's central authority. Belgium, on the other hand, for ethnic and economic reasons, moved steadily towards a federalism so extensive as to leave the state itself in a vestigial position by 1990. The first Mitterrand administration in France began in 1982 to superimpose a regional administrative map on the old geography of departments, using the Deferre Law but without abolishing departments or reducing the power and centralizing force of the prefets, appointed to administer regions by the Ministry of the Interior. Ireland and Denmark remained unmoved, perhaps like Luxembourg considering themselves too small. Greece and Portugal followed suit (despite the latter's brush with civil war in 1974–5), although by 1990 the Portuguese government was planning an administrative division into three regions.

Substantial increases in the Regional Development Funds, contingent upon the internal market and the enormous potential commercial opportunities opening up in the late 1980s, changed this minor, rather distant game altogether, bringing in a great and increasing number of players. Whether or not the wilder hopes attached to regionality, either as the test case for subsidiarity or as the basis for experiments by an EU developmental state were justified is still debatable, as is the significance of that odd speculative creature, the Committee of Regions, to which Maastricht gave birth. But it is clear that certain regions prospered in this context, used it to assert their status and to form links with each other which continue to be attractive to the industrial and financial players.

So much imprecision hangs about the Committee of Regions that it could be argued that the twelve member states simply followed an old EU tradition of trying out an attractive idea in a loosely worded text, then retired to see what would happen. The Treaty's texts offered no definition of what a region was, or how such a Committee should be chosen. The signatories may have followed earlier experience in 1957, when their predecessors had constituted Ecosoc in order to join together the social partners in a forum with some resemblance to early 1930s' concepts of the 'industrial parliament'.

At that time, and in the context of far-ranging, quasi-corporatist experimentation in Austria and Sweden (as well as Germany, Italy and France), it could be assumed that the incorporation of labour and industrial representation into political processes would be fruitful, leading to broader consensus about a nation's macro-economic direction. Born mid-way between the strikes of autumn 1947, which showed that the Cold War had reached the industrial arena, and the 'hot summers' of 1968–9 in Germany, France and Italy, Ecosoc operated for a time in a benign climate. Swedish and Austrian experiments in corporate intermediation appeared to work well, while German *mitbestimmung* and France's more limited concertation mixed with planning even influenced Britain in the early 1960s, although the NEDC which was set up in 1962 failed to implant the real virtues of either in an alien administrative system. Ireland, Italy, the Netherlands and Belgium developed their own variants and Spain embarked on a similar approach in the Moncloa Pacts of 1977.

Whether Ecosoc ever established itself as more than a discussion forum where capital and labour could find each other, launch their prepared papers and mature a certain sense of interdependence, is open to argument. It might have been stillborn, in terms of becoming a full forum for players in the game. But some analysts have suggested that its usefulness outlived the long post-War boom, and that until the mid–1970s Ecosoc helped to preserve a sort of political equivalence between industry and trade unions, whatever the latter's erosion at national levels during the severe recession of 1974–6.[1] Others claim that the oil shock in 1973 and the twin-peak recession that followed, with only partial remission in the late 1970s, revealed concertation to have been an illusion.

Trade union federations had not established powers or influence comparable with employers' organizations. Neither were the achievements of social democracy in the post-War era to survive the late 1970s and 1980s unscathed in any member state. That being so, Ecosoc (like NEDC in Britain) became a shell resounding only to sterile conflict. It was possible perhaps until the late 1970s for national trade union federations to envisage the Commission itself as being on their side, a state of affairs more hopeful than in some member states, but thereafter even that vanished, leaving Ecosoc as a framework for largely ritual encounters, a sounding box apt only to magnify the few legislative ameliorations which a not-unfavourable Commission was still prepared to back.

Blame rested in three main areas; partly with the global context, because trades unions had lost influence and members in virtually every European country in this decade; partly with the peak organization ETUC, which had until then had no means centrally to confront the endemic weaknesses that federations faced at member state level; and partly with Ecosoc itself, an overlarge body of 189 members including consumer and environmental groups, scientists and educationalists, with small appetite for detailed or analytical work, prone to generalized statements and publications at the rate of up to 200 a year. Council Ministers rarely read any of this output except on the few occasions when Ecosoc touched a new and relevant subject like immigration or working-class xenophobia. Ecosoc's existence tended therefore to be justified on the grounds that the players could still find each other there and that its reports gave an indication to EU policy-makers of where consensus might lie: 'maybe it does not really serve anything but it is nevertheless better to have their conclusions in the same direction as one's own position.'²

Ecosoc certainly served as a vehicle for the Commission to propagate the Social Charter directives in the period 1985–9 and was active in the genesis of Maastricht's Social Protocol. But it had no initiating force, so that the trade union federations which had an effect on the outcome used their influence variously with the Commission or their own governments, whose outlooks determined which (if any) of Vasso Papandreou's forty-nine Directives would survive. On the other hand, Ecosoc seems to have been restored to some of its earlier significance after 1992 with the appearance of a more carefully calculated body of social legislation associated with Padraig Flynn and DG5, at a time of a deep common preoccupation with unprecedented levels of unemployment. That the December 1993 White Paper was able to include strikingly market-oriented language about labour markets, as well as neo-Keynesian schemes for employment creation, despite the protests *inter alia* of German and Spanish trade union leaders, suggests that Ecosoc had facilitated a mood of gloomy realism on both sides.

Member states have treated Ecosoc as a theatre where they can run worthy themes which may later be appropriate for the national stage – such as Mitterrand's 'social Europe', and the 1994 protests made in France about 'social dumping' when Hoover transferred 250 jobs from France to its plant in Britain. Certain union federations such as Force Ouvrière in France have found it a valuable forum to put specific questions about, say, the legal requirements for unemployment insurance which obtain in different member states, as a way of exposing the backward ones. Otherwise, much of its time is spent haggling over posts and the *juste retour*. While it is important still in Italy, Spain and Portugal for employers to be seen to talk to unions, this is something quite unnecessary in Northern Europe, given the institutional arrangements which already exist; the whole case has been inapplicable in Britain since about 1983.

The Dutch still take Ecosoc seriously and send good representatives on both sides, if only to inject their own forward-looking ideas and to demonstrate the virtues of small states – unlike Germany or France, where employers have long been reluctant to send experts at all, unless specifically asked. All this is light years away from the cooperation discussed at Val Duchesse meetings ten years ago. In the remoter past, the European Parliament feared Ecosoc as a rival, but it is now completely in Strasbourg's shade, a condition unlikely to be remedied by the entry of EFTA countries where concertation has been endangered at least since 1991.

Insofar as pressures exist to renew or reform Ecosoc, they come from the governments of Germany, Italy and Belgium and Spanish trade union federations; but the essential labour market compromises on wages and conditions of work can only be made first at national level, leaving to a revived ETUC the task of arguing a common denominator later on. Until those earlier compromises are made, banners inscribed with 'Charter 2000' remain gestures. It is not obvious that such compromises can be made outside the four member states mentioned above. Meanwhile, a fear spreads, particularly among trade union federations of the left, that instead, it will be the leading regions which will refocus the industrial triangle and draw into it the missing dimension of financial institutions, thus eroding what is left of Ecosoc.[3]

If Ecosoc did not succeed in thirty years in concentrating the social partners' energies for the Community's benefit, what chance has the Committee of Regions? The Maastricht text prescribed that it should have the same number of representatives and should make the same grandiose attempt to incorporate every relevant interest, whether or not comparable or competent to act. Since its institution is so recent and its proceedings have hardly begun, comment about the Committee itself is premature: what appeared initially to be insuperable problems such as the rivalry between legally denominated regions and municipalities, or the conflict between election and nomination by governments, may turn out to be only teething troubles. Its first three sessions suggest that the organizational impediments are not insuperable. The greater question is whether EU institutions, chiefly the Commission, can infuse it with influence, or whether power can be derived only from below. The Ecosoc case since 1973 suggests that a strong Commission, directed by a clear-sighted President, can do the former but within strict limits dictated by member states. Since the very existence of regions implies a threat to any nation state which has not formally chosen the federal model, there is no reason to assume this case will be easier.

Judgment depends on the answers to four questions: what did the EU intend (or rather what aspects of the Commission's intentions survived Maastricht)? What currently exists? What do the leading player-regions desire? and, What chance have others of taking part usefully in this evolving game? The players have quite different desiderata, depending on their level, and regions differ in every aspect from size to ethos. But where resources, authority and status, devolution or subsidiarity are concerned, every member state has a notable interest in what may emerge.

I. What did the Commission seek?

The thirty-year history of the Regional Development Fund (RDF) suggests that the original EEC aspiration that the Six's regions could reach more or less equivalent stages of development, apart from the Mezzogiorno, vanished around the time of the 1973 extension. Any hope that the CAP surplus would aid the European Investment Bank and the European Social Fund in redistributing resources had evidently already been lost during the 'empty chair' crisis. Of the three new entrants, Ireland qualified in its entirety for the ERDF, which had been reformed and extended as a result of enlargement, on grounds of high unemployment and retarded economic development, while Britain was in due course to receive more than its strict due as an negotiated means of offsetting its onerous budget contributions. By 1980, the system rested on two understandings: that the Commission would coordinate member states' schemes for development, but that these would be proposed, carried out and supervised by national governments themselves. The extent of Commission initiative was thus limited to 10–15% by volume of funds. Yet it was still hoped (for example in the McDougall report) that, given enough time, imbalances could be redressed and the periphery brought up to the standards of rich countries at the core.

The early 1980s brought in Greece, another country eligible as a whole but one which, unlike Ireland, aggressively sought under the first Pasok government to increase its already disproportionate share. Greece's share reached 13% by 1983; but the potential take-up by large areas of Spain and all of Portugal except the Lisbon region seemed very much more likely to prejudice the existing proportion of shares of funds unless the ERDF were vastly increased.[4] Given the open threat that the coming Single European Market would work to the detriment of deprived regions unless offset by very much larger contributions, the first two Delors budgets aimed to double the fund, but also to appease the largest contributors, Germany and Britain, by making the system more centrally accountable and organizing it more efficiently. Already, however, the regional question had moved on from the initial premise about redistribution to cover not only the rich/poor antithesis, but the core/peripheral and central/regional ones, together with the problem of differing kinds of regions, including declining industrial heartlands such as Lorraine, Pas de Calais, Wallonia, Strathclyde, and South Wales.

The integrated Mediterranean programme which was evolved in 1985 as a means to make Spain's and Portugal's entry palatable to Italy, France and Greece, and to give the chance of greater eligibility to France's southern rural areas (and Corsica), provided the model: the British budget settlement, together with British and German expectations from the internal market, and Jacques Delors's sense that a socially unbalanced EC could never progress beyond mere economism, completed the 1985–86 conjunction.[5] Unfortunately, rather than diminishing, regional disparities were at that time actually growing after the unsettled decade, despite evidence on behalf of the ERDF that growth had quickened in the periphery itself.[6] To remedy this problem of differentials, and to offset the predicted result that the internal market would initially benefit larger, northern states most, Article 23 of the Single Act was drafted to deal with economic and social cohesion; the Commission's 1992 report also pointed to reform of the structural funds as a tool to promote more rapid regional development. In effect, the EC had committed itself to remedying or at least off-setting backwardness, a concept susceptible to many interpretations.

In 1988, as part of Delors II, the funds of the RDF and the European Social Fund were coordinated and doubled from 30 to 60 billion ecus for 1989–93. Spending focused on those regions below 75% of the EC's average GDP, on the principle that 'aggravated imbalances' could prejudice the internal market and perhaps vitiate the EC's entire future.[7] Although blocked for a time by Margaret Thatcher (because of the problem of reforming agricultural expenditure), this part of the package was finally concluded thanks to Delors and Kohl at the Brussels Special Summit February 1988.

Unlike the Marshall Plan, with which Delors rather extravagantly compared it, this second beginning led to a new round of claims; for

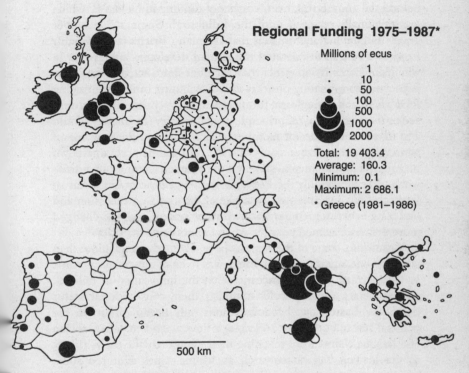

Regional Funding 1975–1987*

Millions of ecus

1
10
50
100
500
1000
2000

Total: 19 403.4
Average: 160.3
Minimum: 0.1
Maximum: 2 686.1

* Greece (1981–1986)

500 km

Note: Since 1988, the basis of calculation has altered to an extent which precludes continuity

FIGURE 9.1

since the internal market had been acknowledged as likely to hurt less-developed regions, it was clear to them that EMU would damage them (and the poor peripheral states of which they formed part) much more. A second bargain, comparable to the 1985 one, lay behind the 1991 IGCs, over 'cohesion' funding in Delors II, which was not finally resolved until the Edinburgh Summit, December 1992. Without that it is unlikely that Germany, Britain (and probably France) would have tolerated the system developed after 1988, in which the Commission rather than member states acted as the prime agency for coordinating projects and distributing funds. In bringing RDF, ESF and agricultural funds into a single conspectus, buttressed by the original 1970s' principle of *additionality* (EC money should add to, not substitute for member state funds) and the new one of *partnership* with member states, the EC took on the preliminaries of becoming a developmental state. Of the planned Community framework agreements, only the Portuguese five-year programme has so far been fully implemented, because of the 1990–93 recession and bickering between member states. But the system itself has changed more than had seemed possible when Delors came to power.[8]

Meanwhile, some of the regions have taken advantage more than others. None, apart from Catalonia, was to be as outspoken as some of the German *Länder*, concerned that the implication of political and monetary union would diminish their constitutional status under the Basic Law. French regions only began to stir, in the political sense, in the late 1980s, at a time when Catalan, Galician and Basque claims were reaching their climax. By the early–1990s, as the leading half-dozen such as Rhône-Alpes acquired some regional consciousness, the Spanish regions seemed to have scaled down their more extreme ambitions. Meanwhile seismic disturbances in the Italian political system had brought into existence a new force, the Northern League, based on Piedmont and Lombardy, to challenge the Christian Democrat-dominated south.

When, in 1985, a number of well-defined areas formed the Association of European Regions (ARE), the Commission gave it moral support, seeing it as the precursor of a more formal 'third level' organization. But ARE turned out to be too divided and unwieldy (since it included regions outside the EC), so the Commission developed the idea of a representative body more influenced by the views of German *Länder*, notably Bavaria and North Rhine-Westfalia, until it became part of the June 1991 package. The Commission's final paper for the IGC in October 1991 proposed the Committee of Regions as a body suitable to advise both Commission and Council, and in this form it was inserted as a codicil to political union.

The Commission college, led by its President, had been the main progenitor; the detailed work being done by DG16. Until then, even the most salient regions had contributed little, and the issue had not caused problems between member states and the Commission, even though the balance of initiative between the college and DG16 had not been finally settled. But on the hard issues of the regional budget, and who should draft the rules, member states were certainly not agreed among themselves. DG16's evolution had taken place largely in the shadows and as the result of several years' work begun in the 1970s by one British Commissioner, George Thomson, and continued after 1985 by another, Bruce Millan, both of whom (being Scottish), had had experience of the last Labour government's industrial strategy and the Scottish Development Authority. It seems likely that Delors was sceptical of Millan's work, because of its empirical bent and the overlap of different approaches implied in fostering both regions and urban centres. He certainly preferred that responsibility for the politically sensitive subject of cohesion funding should remain within the Secretariat rather than relinquishing it to DG16 in 1991. But regional dreams swelled with the increase in actual funds, and contributed incrementally to building up the thesis which viewed the EC as a developmental state. The Commission should not just manage the RDF but use it consciously to redistribute wealth and projects, and to counter the adverse aspects of the internal market. DG16, which allocated the funds but managed only part of them, should become the sponsor of the regions in the manner long adopted for industry by DG3.

But in 1988–90 the disparities between regions were still growing, while the funds remained relatively tiny and the time extremely limited. DG16's responsibility for selection forced it to limit its role to sponsoring structural adjustment among the most deprived – those lying below the line of 75% of the average EU GDP (Objective One) and more recently, areas with less than 8 inhabitants per square kilometre (Objective Six).[9] What was done comprised providing information about how they could fit best into the RDF plan, and selecting the best process for such schemes for co-financing as would promote EU integration.

Seen from above, DG16's responsibilities were not unlike many national regional assistance schemes, aimed at the physical infrastructure, education and training, services, and small businesses, but there existed a secondary agenda, to broach the public/private divide, to open up politically backward regions like Epirus, Tras os Montes, Galicia, or Calabria, and to promote local democracy over and above the closed, often almost eighteenth-century elites which still predominated in such places. At a deeper level still, the agenda pointed to a definition of subsidiarity from the base upwards, through engaging regions in the EU, though this was not argued openly, for fear it would be misinterpreted as tending to the detriment of nation states.

Time being short, the early months after Delors II were devoted to eliciting, approving and coordinating the schemes under the five objectives. DG16 had to deal with the diversity of member states, ranging from France (which reserved its rights over its own schemes), to Portugal and Greece (which initially had no schemes of their own). Britain's government refused to entertain the concept of regions at all.[10] Without putting them in any order of priority, DG16's five working rules appear to have been: bringing the most backward closer to the mean; redressing imbalances generally in the EU and also in member states themselves; providing help to member states to accommodate the problems of having backward regions (for example in Italy to offset protests by the rich north against having to support the Mezzogiorno),[11] and finally to define subsidiarity. There being no possible models for general use, the minimum prescription was that all member states, even Britain, should evolve regions, as Portugal, Ireland and Greece then began to do.

Thus the Committee of Regions itself came into being at Maastricht without a model, for while the idea commanded wide assent, no one was prepared to be dogmatic about its place, powers or priorities. As one official put it, 'it has rights now, but no status or power . . . if successful, it will develop its own terms of reference'.[12] Like Ecosoc, it was intended less as an administrative organ and more as a two-way channel to keep the EC aware of this dimension, propagating to the regions what EC institutions, rather than member states, wished them to hear. As for the funds, the aim shifted a little, from remedying physical to human resource deficiencies. But officials remained aware of how limited their prescriptive powers were, how much they still needed member states' acquiescence, and how the democratizing process had to remain subordinate to what national governments themselves wished to occur.[13]

In the event, during the Maastricht IGC, member states added confusion to what was already imprecise by increasing the Committee representation from the Commission's original figure of 150 to 189, in order to provide for alternative deputies (which reduced the commitment of the originals) and, worse, to allow attendance by representatives of municipalities or local authorities if selected. The Commission had preferred universal election, but member states allowed themselves their own method of choice; thus the first British contingent in 1994, for example, was entirely nominated by the government (only a vote in the House of Commons in 1993 compelled them to make the selection from among *elected* members of local authorities). How the Committee should choose a chairman and officers, and when, where and how often it should meet, were questions left open to delegates when they arrived. They were to have no power of decision or legislation, but like Ecosoc only the right to be consulted (and strictly only where the Maastricht Treaty prescribed).[14]

As the Delors III financial package suffered delays and detractions which undermined the assumption that the ERD Fund would rise exponentially, what followed suggests that member states again disposed of whatever the Commission proposed. That the financial provision scraped through at Edinburgh in 1992, in spite of a dedicated onslaught by Norman Lamont and the UK Treasury, must be ascribed to Spain's urgent advocacy on behalf of cohesion, and to Kohl's weary acceptance that the survival of

Maastricht itself was worth the price that Germany would have to pay. In probably the last budget likely to produce such largesse, the RD Fund achieved its increase on the back of an entirely separate campaign about cohesion. Whether the sums will be sufficient in future to continue to support 75% regions at the level they were in 1993, is already doubtful; on the other hand, the Commission achieved a responsibility which to some extent bypassed the central authorities in member states, thus indirectly promoting what Germany, Spain and the Benelux members also wished for, the greater extension of regionalism as a principle in itself.

Many problems, linked to representation and function, remained. After six months of preparations, a conference of carefully chosen regional and municipal representatives, called by DG16 in Brussels in December 1992, had failed to achieve agreed results, partly for lack of knowledge or understanding, partly because officials were sent who were lower in the ranking order than had been invited, and because cities or regions were unwilling to commit themselves to a new venture in advance. As far as function is concerned, the EU's area of initiative still comprised only 10% of the RD Fund, and this had to include inter-regional development. The vast bulk of schemes still cover what member states would probably wish to do in any case, had they the money. To make operational what the Commission would *like* to do needs far more, even if its desiderata did not cover a range that included some barely credible objectives in cross-border development.

Optimists, among them Jordi Pujol, the Catalan prime minister, who shortly afterwards became chairman of the Committee of Regions, argued that if the Committee attracted able enough representatives, keen to make a reputation, it would, like the Parliament, gradually acquire substantive influence, in the same way used by agricultural representatives who had achieved recognition in the 1960s as if each one had represented his member state as a whole. But in 1994 Ministers in the Council predictably played down the whole institution.[15] It may well be that for them the Committee's value is 'psychological, to show public opinion that the Committee cares about this predicament and is an interlocutor . . .'[16] Regions, after all, in whatever part of Europe, even where they are only just coming into existence (as in Greece or Portugal), appreciate being seen as part of a greater whole.

There is currently a tendency towards giving regions a political dimension (which touches the United Kingdom, the last bastion of the unitary state, whether its government acknowledges it or not – in Northern Ireland, and increasingly Scotland). The questions for 1996 will most likely be whether to create a fourth tier for municipalities (as the stronger regions would wish), or to keep the present uneasy balance between them; whether the system can be extended to eastern Europe, as it clearly can to the new entrants like Austria and Sweden which already possess regions; and whether the defining level for Objective One areas can be raised generally above 75% (and not just in special cases such as Scotland's Highlands and Islands, which was allowed this status (at 77%) by informal agreement).

But whatever else happens, and however far some regions manage to interpret the political element *vis-à-vis* their nation states, the Commission is unlikely to seek to reform political practice in any member state, as it were, from below. Officials at the Commission are forthright: 'We are not in the business of offsetting regional inadequacies to the detriment of member states.'[7] Much of what has been done in the last two years has been to satisfy national needs through improving regional infrastructures, say in Northern Ireland, and financial services, such as the creation of centres to broaden regional capital bases and bolster their stock exchanges, particularly in Barcelona, Turin, Lyons, Bilbao and Stuttgart. One way of putting it is to say that the regions constitute a political economy, a set of market places in their own right, organized but not conducted by the Commission, in which member states conform, voluntarily but under a certain pressure from below. That pressure, which varies in each case, can be shaped to a limited extent by the Commission insofar as it is able to define the concept of best practice in the European polity. Regionalism implies a double devolution, from member state to sub-state and from EU to region.

The founding members of ARE could not agree because each one wanted something different. German *Länder*, for example, sought from Maastricht the same right of direct access to the Council of

Ministers that Belgian regions had earlier obtained (effectively by substituting Flemish or Walloon ministers for national ones.)[18] But regional demands have accumulated incrementally since then, and attract fresh exponents. Dutch, Belgian, French and Italian, as well as Spanish regions now seek to increase their cross-border contacts, where these have economic returns in the Rhineland, the Alps or Pyrenees, through Commission schemes such as Interreg, Recite (1991), and Ouverture (linking regions and cities). Some of these fit with current political reality, as well as history going back to the Holy Roman Empire; others, like the schemes mooted for the borders of Spain and Portugal, Northern Greece, and Sardinia-Corsica, do not.

But what is tangible and what are dreams? Some 1989 agglomerations, from the point of view of transport infrastructure, technology transfer, or human skills, still make excellent sense in 1995. The 'Golden Banana', though predictable to any reader of Braudel's *Mediterranean World at the Time of Philip II*, may be a less obvious candidate for the late 1990s. But in any case these are all powered by the richer regions, whose search for economies of scale and the elusive concept of synergy is quite distinct from DG16's concerns with the poorer end of the range.

Where member states dictate the terms, that is in the case of roughly 85% of regional aid (by volume), national distinctions persist as they did when governments chose their representatives on the Committee of Regions. The German government holds to its long-established federal model; the Spanish one, however, tries to counterbalance autonomous communities' aspirations. French governments, which have been mildy opposed to setting up the Committee, play down any idea that regions are more than an administrative convenience: if the Commission, or DG16 officials meet in a French region, it is normally in the company of the relevant prefect, the local head of the state administration. The Scottish Office in Britain might well agree with the EU coordinating official in Madrid who, having defined decentralization as the way to diminish separatism without impairing national unity, added 'Europe and the regions without nation states will be a complete disaster because there will not be adequate means of integrating the EU itself.'[19]

A cynic might argue that if there were no regional funds, this European dimension would not have been called into existence. But at the Commission's end of the spectrum, two assumptions are habitually made: first, that there *is* a regional dimension, vigorous enough to be given a voice but so variable as to demand harmonization through institutional practice; second, that the political and economic integration of the Community itself depends on achieving harmonization. That Delors emphasized the socio-political significance if disunity were allowed to fester, in his speech to the Parliament in 1985, does not in itself signify federalism even if he implied it; regionality may also be the only plane in which subsidiarity can, in practice, be defined. The devil lies in the detail, for example in considering how regions should relate to municipalities, and how one or other or both might acquire formal links to the Parliament, giving all 160-odd regions formally what only the most advanced now obtain informally.

No one has yet been bold enough to advance a single definition of a region, and the Commission has rarely (if ever) intervened on behalf of a region against the interest of its member state. Yet some regions are undoubtedly exploited by their national authorities, and might welcome redress, if it came in constitutionally admissible ways. Other are condemned to uses which, given wider choice, they might reject; yet others, given any foreseeable level of aid, will still remain wilderness areas, mere tourist dependencies. Transfer payments will continue ad infinitum, but so long as they increase no faster than member states permit, there can be no hope of bringing assisted areas up to the levels of the rich core, as the McDougall Committee argued in 1977. Delors pointed out that the continued existence of economic and social disparities implies that true political union will be restricted to more favoured regions and member state capitals. But where redistribution touches political resources the Committee of Regions is unlikely to be able to help.

II. Regions as they are

Any selection among the variety of European regions can only be arbitrary – to re-use an old academic joke, what you cannot compare, contrast. The aim here has been to take one region in each of the five largest member states, which is economically and politically self-defined, and also active in the regional political market: Scotland and Catalonia (two ancient kingdoms, each with a distinct language and traditions), Baden-Württemberg, Rhône-Alpes and Emilia-Romagna (three recent creations, of 1949 and 1977 respectively). Each has at least one major city, though Scotland has two, Glasgow being the centre of Strathclyde (which, because of its size, could serve as a region in itself). All these bulked large in national plans for regional development in the 1960s and 1970s, and all, compared with others in their nation state, have been activist in the period since.

The same distinction between centralized and decentralized states applies as in chapter 7, with the exception that in this respect Spain's system is decentralized. In the former category, central state agencies for controlling regional development, such as DATAR in France and the Scottish Development Agency (SDA) in Britain, coexist with local centres of power which are vehicles both for extracting regional grants and benefits and mobilizing party votes. It can be argued that since the late 1970s, the French or British state has paid over the odds in transfers to local authorities in order to retain substantive control, and marginalize any separatist elements. But in Germany and Italy and, after 1978, in Spain, the boundaries were legally delimited: the area where informal brokerage could grow up remained correspondingly small – though wider in the Spanish case because the innovation of autonomous communities took time to settle down.[20]

The substate is most clearly demarcated in Germany, for each *Land*, as a sub-nation, has its own political system, administrative competence, and what in practice (certainly in Bavaria) amounts to dual citizenship. *Länder* are not merely reactive but have the power to initiate, largely because central government, being usually in coalition, has to bargain for their cooperation. *Länder* representatives on the Bundesbank Council often outweigh the president and the officials in their influence. Since the EC began involving itself in educational and cultural affairs and aroused suspicion that basic rights were being eroded, the view has grown up in some *Länder* (and not only Bavaria) that something similar to the safeguards of the Basic Law ought to be extended to become the regional pattern for the EU as a whole, to which over a long period all others – even unitary states – should conform (as their currencies would in the Bundesbank-preferred way to EMU). Thus the third tier (and with it Bavarian, Basque or Scottish economic and political institutions) would be legally ensconced within the European superstate, whatever the cost to non-federal nation states.

Many citizens living within historic regions of what are at present unitary states accept the importance of *Heimatgefühl* (belonging to a location) as against *Zugehörigkeitsgefühl* (belonging to a state). Some might concede that the *Länder* have a justification for fears that the latter drains the former of representation in local issues, from schools to policing. But the balance in each country between central and local administration is the product of its entire modern history and is not something to be reassigned lightly, as the Italian case demonstrates: Rome conceded full implementation of the 1949 Constitution only during the disputes of 1975–7, and in practice kept down regional administrations thereafter, at least until the mid-1980s. London (by Scottish accounts) steadily drained what still remained of Scottish institutions during the 1980s, and (in probable breach of the 1707 Treaty of Union) tried out the highly unpopular poll tax one year in advance of its introduction in England.

As Sidney Tarrow has pointed out in his study of local politics in France and Italy, the extent of regional power depends less on formal quantities than on local elites and their informal influence with the centre, via the political parties and trade unions. The result, the tentacles of *clientilismo* in Italy, *caciquismo* in Spain, and similar networks of corruption in Mitterrand's France, has been exposed since the late 1980s by the downfall of a steadily increasing number of ministers and state officials. Something similar has occurred at times in Scottish and Welsh local government. Yet these are the inevitable results of the evolution of mass party systems within specific late nineteenth- and twentieth-century contexts, compounded in the French and Italian cases by the more recent experiences of Vichy and Mussolini's state, the Resistance and, later, the influx of *pieds-noir* from Algeria to France in the 1960s. No region can evolve in the abstract and the circumstances in which *Länder* emerged in 1945–9, or autonomous communities in 1978, cannot occur elsewhere. Belgium is likely to remain a unique model, whereas in Portugal, the Netherlands, and possibly Greece, regions may have strict historic limits. If they emerge at all in Ireland and England they are likely to follow the French pattern and that of several Spanish regions – that is, of administrative convenience – which will also limit the power of industrial and financial players to gain advantage through appealing to regional identity.

Of these five regions, four manifestly belong in the European core (three of them being already linked in the so-called 'Four Motors' group, see p. 744, note 48). The same four remained stable even in the 1990–93 recession. None of them needs technical or other transfers to enable them to go their own way, only (arguably) liberal economic treatment. Scotland, on the other hand, is geographically peripheral and suffers from a declining industrial base, despite having a strong financial sector and a recently acquired high technology component – which seems to refute the received wisdom that foreign direct investment goes where labour is cheap and where the weather is warm. Unlike the others, which have the Rhineland or Pyrenean link (Catalonia, Roussillon, and Midi-Pyrénées),[21] Scotland has (and can have) no neighbourhood linkages except with a vaguely defined English North, and possibly with Northern Ireland – though in the information technology era that should be no inhibition to its manufacturing or financial services.

What follows is an attempt to assess not economic performance but how the region (or hypothetical region, because Scotland has as yet no distinct political status)[22] behaves as a political entrepreneur in the market already described. For example, how far can a region act on its own? How far does it depend not only on the central state's acquiescence, but on an understanding or concordat between the public and private sectors? And in so acting, does the initiative come from the region as a whole or from its cities and metropolitan regions, as if they were, like mediaeval city-states, agencies for fundamental economic innovation? Some argue that the 'urban region', served by air, motorway and high-speed rail transport networks (of which

Economic activity in Europe's regions, by sector

Regional Composition	Scotland	Catalonia	Rhône-Alpes
Agriculture	Lowlands only Fisheries	Strong. Mainly small farms	Small farms
Industry			
large	Declining (steel. coal, shipbuilding)	Car production (VW, Séat, Nissan), pharmaceuticals, metals, textiles, chemicals	Chemicals (Rhône-Poulenc) (Solvay), pharmaceuticals, high-tech
SMEs	Strong - high-tech	Very strong	Strong-mainly supply
Energy	Coal, hydro, oil	Hydro	Hydro, Nuclear(2)
Finance	Banking, (Royal Bank, Bank of Scotland), Stock Exchange	Some local savings banks	Crédit Lyonnais
Services	Research (university led) tourism	Research (university led) tourism winter sports	Research (university and industry), tourism winter sports

Regional Composition	Baden-Württemberg	Emilia-Romagna
Agriculture	Declining	Strong
Industry		
large	Cars (Mercedes), chemicals (Bosch), computers (IBM)	Chemicals textiles Food Industry
SMEs	Large very strong medium sector in metal industries and textiles	Very strong
Energy	None	None
Finance	Small	Small Local savings banks
Services	Research (university and industry), tourism	Some research but no university-industry link; tourism strong services to SMEs

FIGURE 9.2

Barcelona still lacks the latter) is today the most effective spatial unit of competition.[23] (This was the view assiduously propagated by Glasgow in order to forestall the Conservative government's abolition of Strathclyde urban region.) Stuttgart, Barcelona, Lyons, Glasgow and Bologna have all been in the top sixty among economically active European cities in every decade since 1971; in respect of performance, all have been above the predicted mean; and each has reached the top twenty-five in at least one of the three decades.[24]

SCOTLAND[25]

Scotland, not being a region in its own right but an integral part of the United Kingdom, has no formal representation other than in the London Cabinet through the Scottish secretary and the Scottish Office, and in Brussels as part of British representation. It has, of course, its own MEPs, some of whom sit on the Parliament's Regional Intergroup, and it has observers who attend the EU's Regional Political Committee (now the Committee for Development and Reconversion of Regions) for discussion on the allocation of RD funds. Strathclyde was a founder member of ARE and both Glasgow and Edinburgh are represented on the Council of European Municipalities (CEEMR).

Though apparently low in the Cabinet pecking order, the Scottish secretary possesses considerable informal power over UK budget dispositions – above that of the Welsh or Northern Irish secretaries – as the percentage annually granted over the English level of capital allocation indicates.[26] The Scottish Office is also partly responsible for the important resources of North Sea oil and gas, and fisheries. The secretary of state's influence is thus significant at national level but minimal at that of the EU, where he attends the Council of Ministers only rarely and in a specialist capacity. Central government and the Cabinet Office European Secretariat have in fact been successful in pursuing Scottish interests, more so perhaps than might have been expected if the Conservative administration had not been afraid of the implications of their minority status in that part of Britain. But down the scale, the work of the Scottish Development Agency and the HIDB (as well as the Scottish Office and central government) can be recognized in the award of Objective 2 status for the decayed industrial areas of Strathclyde and, in 1994, of Objective I for the status Highlands and Islands.

Highlands and Islands Enterprise and Scottish Enterprise emerged out of the old HIDB and the Scottish Development Agency in 1991, largely in response to the Scottish CBI's request, in order to prepare Scotland to gain maximum advantage from the internal market. There remain tensions however, between these two organizations and elected local authorities (over high-speed rail links for example). Strathclyde, a huge urban but also rural region, found it expedient to set up its own Brussels office to pursue better its interests there. Thus the domestic politics of what Brigid Laffan calls 'grantsmanship' are reflected on the EU stage.

But the regional players acquired a sort of unity on the issue of additionality in opposing the British Treasury (backed by the Scottish Office), which held to the doctrine that the Community funds should not be matched by national equivalents. In the late 1980s, that position lost Scotland substantial amounts of EC money. The argument has however since been modified; and the Scottish Office now admits the agencies' and local authorities' right of direct lobbying in Brussels as long as it is concerned only with grants or resources and remains 'non-political'.[27] Central government's *tutelle* remained, for example, when the Scottish Office asked for a controlling interest in the private sector body Scotland Europa (a business and professional creation intended to proselytize for foreign investment and joint ventures), in order to eliminate what ministers regarded as the anti-Conservative, anti-London elements likely to arise from local business and the Scottish TUC.[28] There is therefore no clear agreement between the players on who speaks for Scotland; rather there exists only a sort of continuous informal competition.

Community money helps to irrigate the Scottish economy but does not necessarily increase local players' bargaining power *vis-à-vis* London, at least so long as central government maintains its formal monopoly. What has been envisaged by the Northern Ireland 'framework agreement' suggests that devolution has returned to the political calendar for the first time since 1979, but the current battle lines between the Conservative and Labour parties make it unlikely to be applied to Scotland before the next elections. Meanwhile the fear of scaring off corporate investment after a deep recession keeps Strathclyde and other economic centres quiet. In the interim the Scottish Office, spurred by Scottish Enterprise and Scottish Financial Enterprise, does appear to work rather more on behalf of, though still far from being a lobby *for*, Scotland than was the case ten years ago.

The fear of losing foreign investment has substance, given the impact of the Scottish National party's successes earlier in the 1980s, at a time when both Labour and the SNP were hostile to the EC. Both changed substantially in the early 1990s, though the SNP still denigrated the Council of Regions as a stratagem to buy off its claim for independence. The Labour party, which has by far the majority of Scottish MPs, now evidently accepts that Scotland has a distinct future within the EU, even if its attitude to Scotland's status within the UK is more nuanced. Both parties may have been influenced by continental European developments, the experience of German *Länder* activity and the political fragmentation of Belgium. Labour has also undergone a process of modernization which is not as complete north of the border as in England. But in Scotland the EU is now almost universally accepted, often with the corollary that it may be possible in Brussels to redress the imbalance with London, in order to free Scotland more from the whims of English government and to ensure greater respect for the differences embodied in Scottish political and cultural traditions.[29] That awareness gives rise to powerful tensions which, when taken in conjunction with the imbalance of parliamentary seats, rises in some sections of public opinion to outright hostility to the Union.

In terms of decision-making, roughly two-thirds of the Scottish economy is fully integrated into England, with the head offices of most larger firms being now in London. The long decline of the staple industries in the 1950s is now probably complete, but the process of adjustment to it, which produced a steadily increasing export orientation in the 1970s (so that 60% of trade now lies with the EU), is not. North Sea oil production has been falling since 1990, and hi-tech electronics, though strongly implanted by IBM,

Honeywell, Mitsubushi and Motorola, remain (like that sector in any European country) vulnerable to loss of competitiveness.

The only home-grown sector is the financial one; the Glasgow Stock Exchange being a unit of London that handles 20% of all UK business. The banks, led by the Bank of Scotland and the Royal Bank, now manage total funds of around £160 million. Financial institutions provide 15% of Scottish GDP and employ 10% of the work-force. So far, according to the interviews here, there appears to be a consensus that the sector has been adequately represented by London and the British Bankers' Association, but Edinburgh's bid against Lyons for some of the EMI's devolved functions may have arisen partly as a gesture of protest against London, because of its insensitivity to Scottish interests. Where local markets are concerned, links have been easy to foster, for example with Bavarian banks and the Banco de Santander. The Scots are increasingly interested in spreading fund management and life insurance, and involving themselves (for example) with mortgage business in Italy. However, like their regional organization, Scottish Financial Enterprise, the financial sector has so far been largely reactive (possibly because of a lack of capital, other than investors' deposits), reserving its main thrust for North America.

Conclusions about Scotland and the internal market reached by the Europa Institute in 1991 are probably still valid: that the economy in general, including the hi-tech area (which depends on global factors), is vulnerable during the restructuring process; that competition will continue to increase, but that there will be new chances for SMEs; that inter-regional cooperation may be possible, and that the peculiar Scots mixture of business and local authority initiative may offer the best way to continue economic regeneration in the more distant future.[30]

As an economic judgment rather than a statement about the politics of autonomy, other matters – agriculture, transport, fisheries and the structural funds – are probably best coped with by the Scottish Office in Edinburgh. But politics will not be left out, as the small, culturally homogenous, tightly knit Scottish political elite knows. Whatever the future of devolution or a Scottish parliament, the fact that since 1994 England has been divided administratively under ten regional directors, covering the spheres of employment, trade and industry, transport and the environment, indicates that regionality is no longer a taboo subject. Scotland's future lies not in making further inroads on the ERD Funds but in securing a better division of the policy-making process.[31] Though Scottish entrepreneurs can be found active in most parts of the world, the business start-up rate by Scots at home was still lower in the decade 1983–93 than in the rest of Britain, apart from the North of England, partly because of lack of access to finance – which a 1994 Bank of Scotland-Scottish Enterprise initiative may help to remedy.[32]

CATALONIA

The history of Spain, as Ortega y Gasset argued in *La Redención de las Provincias* (1927), is the history of its regions. But the seventeen 'autonomous communities' finally constituted in 1983 were not the forty-nine provinces of the nineteenth century, nor the historic entities – save Catalonia, the Basque country and Galicia. Rather they were the best set of local identities which could be composed as an antithesis to Franco's and his generals' cry that Spain was *una, grande y libre*. Many layers of earlier regions and nationalities were subsumed after his death, as the new 1978 Constitution put it, 'under the inseparable unity of the Spanish nation, the common and individual fatherland of all Spanish subjects'.

The aim was to extend self-governing status to all Spain's regions, not merely the historic ones with their ancient grievances against the central power. A measure of power was to be delegated without losing either the state's coherence or the allegiance of very different regions such as Andalucia, Castilla and Aragon. Thus the Catalan statute (1979) gave competence to the parliament (the Generalitat), across fields ranging from cultural affairs, tourism and education to industry, agriculture and trade. Some are shared with Madrid, others vested in the departments and *consellers* or regional ministers. Only one major change has occurred since 1980 in a long period of coalition government between conservative nationalist parties, Convergencia i Unio, headed by Jordi Pujol: an external relations deputy was appointed in 1992, with some of the status of a regional foreign secretary.

Leaving aside vestigial Basque separatism, today's principal tensions in Spain arise from Basque and Catalan desires for distinct representation in the national parliament's Second Chamber, as if it were a Bundesrat, and from the disparity between these two regions and Galicia on one hand, and on the other, confused areas like La Rioja or Cantabria which lack any community identity. But there are two particular complaints, one about central government's financial arrangements with the regions, the other about their lack of direct representation in Brussels. Catalonia after all produces nearly 20% of Spain's GDP, 38% of its industrial exports, and has 13% of its population, in an economy larger than those of Portugal or Ireland, and nearly equal to that of Greece. So far it has been in Madrid's interest, as in London's or Paris's, to restrain the historic regions and allow the rest to evolve over time. But because of the Socialist government's precarious majority since 1993, the more aggressive ones, notably Catalonia whose Convergence and Union votes delivered by Pujol are essential, have been permitted to conduct rather more of their own affairs than the formalities permit.

This has had a clear impact on the course of Catalan politics. Pujol, the master of activist regional gestures in the 1980s, has used his party's fortuitous influence cautiously, evidently hoping to gain incrementally ground that can later be formalized.[33] In 1993, but only for a two-year period, the Gonzalez government conceded its long-standing claim for the region to be allowed to spend 15% of Spanish income tax gathered in the regions.[33A] When Catalonia opened what is in effect a trade office in Buenos Aires, or when the Catalan lobby presses in Brussels, Stuttgart, or Berlin for trading advantages, it does so for form's sake under the aegis of the Spanish embassy, and 'the central government neither fosters nor resents the outcome'.[34] But the formality barely appeases the fears of several member states that the Committee of Regions (whose chair Pujol took) would become not a forum for regions but a vehicle for regions acting as autonomous, probably divergent spokesmen for their member states.[35] Such a rivalry has already grown between Barcelona and Sevilla, which has been since 1989 the Gonzalez government's 'favoured son'.

This is not a path which EU institutions wish to tread because these are not quarrels in which they have any *locus standi*. The ECJ in 1992 confirmed (*vis-à-vis* Spain's Constitutional Tribunal) that the Maastricht Treaty serves as a basic law to ensure the rights of member states to distribute and regulate power between their centres and their regions.[36] Since 1993, the Madrid government has also been careful to play down or even reverse the *de haut en bas* approach in order to foster a more genuine two-way political relationship, which has since eroded Catalan opposition (and undercut the vestigial appeal of Basque terrorism). But the government's EU policy coordinating process still barely takes regional views into account, even when Convergence and Union MPs form part of the governing coalition, and Catalan ministers feel strongly that their case is underplayed in Brussels.

Claims for independence, and cries against Spain's 'fiscal pillage' are now heard only from the margin, the left-wing party, Esquerra Republicana; the position of Initiativa per Catalonia, which seeks greater fiscal autonomy, is more widely shared in the generalitat. Catalan mainstream parties join up in the European Parliament with the Socialist group or EPP. As far as the business players are concerned, ideological argument now focuses on whether SMEs should seek competitive advantage, as the centre-right Catalan government desires, or the locally sponsored development advocated by Socialists and Social Democrats. The sense of Catalan national identity remains absolute; even the employers confederation declares 'we want to defend the interests of our associates . . . and the identity of our region', which would be an unlikely war cry for the Scottish CBI.[37] It is therefore not surprising that Catalonia has had least input of all the 'Four Motors', yet the region has established a powerful influence on the whole Pyrenees 'Euro-region', which gives a modern framework (Catalonia, Roussillon, Midi-Pyrénées) for the ancient kingdom.

Barcelona itself has productive links with Lyons, Milan and Frankfurt as part of the 'European cities cycle', but the differences between Catalan regional and Spanish national ministers should not be exaggerated. They tend to agree on how to address problem areas such as SMEs or financial services' modernization. They also concur on the value of Spain's autonomous community model as a European exemplar, possessing as it does full democratic characteristics comparable to German *Länder* and Belgian regions, as part of a superior tier, boldly distinguished from the rest on the Committee of Regions.[38] In this sense, the Spanish government has assimilated the *Länder* example, as it has done with other Community phenomena in the long process of adjustment to European criteria.

The Catalan employers' confederation (FTN) makes good use of the Spanish national CEOE office in Brussels, as do the main sectoral organizations such as FEIQUE (chemicals) and CON-FEMETAL, which are subsections of national bodies – themselves in turn often run by Catalans. The region as a whole is served by Patronat Catala Pro Europa, an offshoot of the generalitat, whose President is Jordi Pujol. PCPE is a well-developed lobby for overall Catalan interests which acts as the informal representative of the Catalan government in Brussels. An organization tantamount to an embassy naturally provoked the Madrid government when it was first set up, but after a series of heated polemics the Gonzalez government, dependent on Catalan votes, has made an accommodation which involves regular meetings with the Spanish representative in Brussels. PCPE does not seek official status and is not formally recognized by the EU (though it is by the Belgian government). On the other hand, it maintains the direct contacts, outside Spain's permanent representation but tolerated by the Foreign Ministry, with EU institutions and organizations, which was the original intention.[39] Needless to say, since the Patronat links industrial sectors to the EU in the game of regional and research funding, it is popular both with employers' organizations and Catalan businessmen.

SMEs are served (well by all accounts) by PIMEC which in turn links to the central European body, to EUROMNI in Brussels.[40] This compares closely with the situation in Emilia-Romagna, another region where SMEs predominate, and where added-value is the key to economic activity.[41] As in the latter region and in Scotland, finance for SMEs presents a perennial problem, only partly soluble by the savings movement of which the Caixa de Pensión is the largest, ranking third in size among all Spanish banks. Catalonia invites foreign direct investment and obtains about one-third of Spain's total, yet many of its smaller entrepreneurs only thinly veil their suspicion that Catalan savings are pillaged by foreign or Spanish institutions. During the June 1993 election, Catalan and Basque parties asked for their Caixas to be given status as sub-central banks but, bearing in mind that the two held between them 40% of Spain's total reserves, Madrid demurred. In contrast, Catalan offshoots of trade union federations have only a limited hand-hold in Brussels, of infrequent value.

For detailed influence, Catalan industrial and other players tend to concentrate on Spanish officials in Brussels and the Directorates, rather than the European Parliament. As part of its extended bargain with Pujol, the Spanish government offered Catalonia the right to address the Commission directly on ERD Funds, if he in turn helped through the 1994–5 budget. Looking ahead to 1996's IGC, Catalan ministers seek to formalize the gains in influence with Madrid made since 1993 in ways that were not possible at the time of Maastricht. Central government sometimes appears to be on the defensive. The External Relations Ministry has tried to coordinate what Catalans do, for example by associating itself with Pujol's programme of visits, hoping to contain the appearance of separate identity. But the next election could reverse the balance, were the conservative 'espãno-lista' political party to form a government; lacking formal standing, Catalonia's 'external relations' remain vulnerable, even when it concerns economic advantage such as the trade mission to China or Catalan attempts to repair the 'Spanish deficit' in Latin America.[42]

EMILIA-ROMAGNA

Commentators on Mediterranean regions tend to put Catalonia in the category of regions which have achieved a significant degree of control over their European representation, largely through leverage with the Spanish central government. Emilia-Romagna has similar economic and social characteristics: it is rich in human capital and small entrepreneurs, well supplied with migrant labour from a much poorer south, with strong local savings banks, and the dense social and cultural networks with which Machiavelli was familiar in the sixteenth century.[43] In both, there exists a hierarchy of entre-preneurs' associations, differentiated by industrial sectors, club associations, and institutions such as the local stock exchange and chambers of commerce. SMEs in both tend to be family-owned concerns, less concerned with their share capital values than their long-term interests in employing a contented, highly skilled workforce.

It would be tempting to argue that the density of these institutional webs explains the undoubted effectiveness of their political and industrial economies, yet there can be no question that Emilia-Romagna has so far failed to achieve Catalonia's degree of political salience in the Community. This has nothing to do with its not being a member of the 'Four Motors' (as is neighbouring Lombardy); if anything, Emilia-Romagna is rather more effective at playing the EU game, as is Tuscany (which benefited considerably from its 'favoured son', Commissioner Vanni d'Archirafi's tenure of office). (Indeed, the representatives of Baden-Württemberg and Rhône-Alpes in Brussels are beginning to look to Emilia-Romagna in preference to Lombardy, with whose administration they have become disillusioned). Neither is it because its natural regional economy is somehow defective. It has 3.5 million inhabitants (1.14% of the EU's population) but a GDP equal to 1.55% of the EU's.

The main reason for Emilia-Romagna's political weakness in the EU, like that of other Italian regions, lies quite simply in the refusal of the central bureaucracy and political parties to make effective their formal powers. In contrast to Catalonia, where considerable power has been devolved from the central government to the regional government, Emilia-Romagna is subjected to greater constitutional constraints over autonomous regional decision-making and is further constrained by a lack of fiscal autonomy (with central government transfers constituting 80% of the regional budget). For example, it was only in 1993 that the strict prohibition on external representations by the regions under Italian law was relaxed.

A further reason for the lack of influence at the European institutional level can be traced to the socio-economic structure of Emilia-Romagna, in which the role of the SME is dominant. Economically, this suits a region which has more than 300,000 enterprises and seems to fit well with Emilia-Romagna's social traditions. For a long time in the post-War era, it favoured local alliances, each being congeries of small firms trying to extract largesse through their bearing on central government – in effect creating an informal bargaining regime, whose success inhibited other, more party political demands. The Emilia-Romagna model has been studied and copied elsewhere (in Denmark, for example) and is still considered to be an example of social and economic cohesion where economic players act in harmony with political and social forces.[44]

By the late 1990s, however, it seemed that this self-regulating, almost spontaneous mixture of community and market was becoming less effective in what had previously been unquestioned: inducing SMEs to adjust to external competition. A mixture of forces contributed to the changing competitive conditions in Italy during this period, including a significant increase in the cost of labour and capital (disproportionately affecting the competitive position of SMEs as compared with large-scale enterprises), and the implementation by central government of a largely ineffective competitive strategy in the late 1980s which prejudiced the position of the SMEs.[45] These forces, together with the implementation of the Single Market Act, influenced the SMEs to adjust to a new competitive landscape. Central to this adjustment was the role of the association and services centres for SMEs – organized at both the sectoral level and geographic level.[46]

The historical restriction on Emilia-Romagna's SMEs directly lobbying in Brussels contrasts with Catalonia, which has maintained a representative office there since 1978. It is interesting to note that ASTER (Agency for Technological Development of the Region Emilia-Romagna), was only able to establish its Brussels representative office in 1993 in order to support the interests of several hundred SMEs and the regional institutions through enhanced involvement in EU programmes. While the representative office was thinly staffed during this initial period of operation (particularly in comparison to the representative office in Catalonia, which operates with a staff of fifteen), it has nonetheless served to help set in position SMEs from the region on Community programmes (on a project-specific basis) as well as trying to influence higher level policy-making. Nevertheless in 1995 Emilia-Romagna was still the only region to have achieved this level of representation and the only one to have a working relationship with a German *Land* (Hessen).

In relation to the European Commission, the major areas of interest for ASTER (as well as the Region Emilia-Romagna) are DGs 12, 13, 16 and 23. As far as DG16 is concerned (which maintains control over regional policies), Emilia-Romagna is eligible for Objective 2 and 5B Structural Funds (similar to Catalonia). As a player, Emilia-Romagna has a record of implementing Structural Fund projects, particularly in the area of training and agriculture. However unlike Catalonia, which has been able to exercise its leverage over Madrid in tapping into Structural Funds, Emilia-Romagna – as well as the rest of Italy's regions – has been confronted by a persistent bottleneck in Rome with the management and disbursement of money emanating from Brussels. For example, Emilia-Romagna is only now receiving money under the European Social Fund (ESF) which should have been allocated in 1993.

The region cannot act alone to remedy this problem, even though it is the regional authorities who are in the best position to coordinate the different sectors. The existing structures predominantly follow the formal patterns perpetuated by Brussels; but in contrast with Catalonia, where informal politics and lobbying in Brussels is part of a long-term strategy, the filters maintained in Rome tend to subtract value from the process rather than add to it.[47]

RHÔNE-ALPES

In the Commission's study of the 'Four Motors' in 1991, this initiative was seen as 'the most far-reaching model of inter-regional cooperation in Europe to date', one which presaged great things to come.[48] Yet for all the media interest in cross-border activity, the 'Four Motors' began as a Baden-Württemberg initiative, and its principal effective outcome, research and technological cooperation, has been restricted to Rhône-Alpes. The Commission did not put the crucial question, whether the cooperation advanced what had already been in all four separately, but instead took for granted that this would be the case, possibly because initial inquiries suggested that investing firms were inclined to raise their sights to the inter-regional level. It was assumed that innovation would follow, given the prevalence of vigorous large, medium and small firms already established in hi-tech fields.

But actual cases, mainly of university-based research (for example in fibre optics), revealed less synergy than dissimilarities between academic communities. Diversity tended not to work in favour of innovation beyond the level of student exchanges, and although the regional governments had some influence as trend-setters, the main lessons were that cross-border cooperation worked best between regions which were as directly complementary as Rhône-Alpes and Baden-Württemberg.

Regional consciousness and identity are not yet generally well implanted in France among the twenty-two creations of the 1980s. But the Deferre system which set out relations between the regionally elected territorial unit, the prefet, and the Interior Ministry has been in most cases fully internalized now. Since 1986, direct elections have been the rule, to the regional council or parliament, where industrial and agricultural organizations meet. But this council has to obtain leave before applying for any RD Fund grant under Objectives 2 or 5b (the only ones which apply to France). The line of policy responsibility still extends from the prefet (the Ministry of the Interior's representative, appointed by the minister) or his Secretary General to Brussels; DATAR still has its *tutelle* and the Minister the final say. No substantial inroad has been made on the central state. Nor have genuine regional identities evolved a recipe where they existed earlier, as in Brittany. But this has not prevented the growth of former local centres of power into coteries of political influence. In spite of central supervision, a large number of regional politicians from the south have been involved in corruption cases arising mainly out of public works contracts in the last decade, including the mayors of Lyon, Marseilles and Grenoble.

The most developed regions, of which Rhône-Alpes probably comes second after Ile de France, can of course lobby the Commission and the Parliament; in the case of Rhône-Alpes, informal networks seem to be favoured, being furthest removed from the prefet's and Paris's control, as well as being faster and more efficient than the formal system. With 10% of French GDP, Rhône-Alpes has a track record of success stories and a reputation for independence. Yet compared to Scotland or Catalonia, Rhône-Alpes is hard to define as an entity. It contains three major cities – Lyon, Grenoble and St Etienne – of over 300,000 people. Of its work-force, 30% are in industries which have a strong export component and a favourable trade balance. Unemployment runs at least 1% below the French average, despite Rhône-Alpes's earlier dependence on the endangered steel, textiles and metalwork industries. (The turnabout came earlier than most of France with Manufrance's bankruptcy in 1979). Rhône-Alpes is as about as prosperous as any region can be in France today.[49]

Yet its political development only began in the 1980s, influenced substantially by the fact that Giscard's prime minister, Raymond Barre, sat as deputy for the Rhône. Out of the RPR's youth wing came a series of dynamic regional politicians (some later indicted on corruption charges) whose rise paralleled the development of an infrastructure which made Lyon the crossroads of south-central Europe. As in Strathclyde, the surge of successful conversion operations could be ascribed to public-private partnership, like Bologna, development took shape in proliferating SMEs, especially around Grenoble. The link with Baden-Württemberg helped; by 1991 Grenoble University business park contained 120 companies, operating mainly in computer software, chemicals and biomedical research.

Heavy industry (earth-moving and electrical engineering) tended to be located around St Etienne, whose take-off and conversion owed much to central state help and Objective 2 funds. Lyon followed suit but notably became a centre for services and banking, headed by Crédit Agricole, once Crédit Lyonnais had been nationalized in 1981, oriented especially towards SMEs. When the financial boom ended abruptly in 1988, the Lyons stock exchange was centralized in Paris. Crédit Lyonnais's later travails ensured that it would never revert to being a regional concern. Nevertheless, Lyons became host to a range of foreign banks and can be compared with Edinburgh and Amsterdam, and perhaps even Zürich.

The largest firms are chemicals (Rhône-Poulenc) and pharmaceuticals (Institut Merieux) or agro-food complexes. Yet the future seems to lie in service industries; Rhône-Alpes's tourism ranks second after Paris and before the Côte d'Azur. SMEs holds 26% of the total. Unlike Scotland, Rhône-Alpes is exceptionally modern, economically well-balanced and decentralized – a model for French regions' aspirations.[50] Together with Pas de Calais and Nord, it has its own Brussels office, yet its officials acknowledge that this a political matter, set up mainly to bypass a still offhand Permanent Representation, and is not economically efficient.[51] Building on Barre's legacy, however, Rhône-Alpes's lobbying among Commission officials is claimed to have been effective, in some contrast to Emilia-Romagna, apart from SMEs. The region won entry to the Integrated Mediterranean Programme even though it has little agriculture and is not noticeably Mediterranean!

Rhône-Alpes's attempt to develop 'external relations' began in 1976 with a campaign in Frankfurt to present itself as an access route to the warm south, and Lyon as being a tertiary 'centre of decision'. Enterprise Rhône-Alpes took up this work in the 1980s, *inter alia* to develop the region as a winter sports utopia. Direct 'city partnerships' have since developed with Frankfurt and Turin.

Yet in spite of all this activity, what Rhône-Alpes does depends to a significant extent on Paris and on its own prefet's brief, so that it comes closer in the end to the Scottish rather than the Catalan example. The prefet is crucial to how the regional plan is developed, either on RDF matters or questions of political and territorial planning. 'Europe of the regions is an illusion, a dangerous one' according to one central official. The view is that Rhône-Alpes cannot take decisions on its own, and that if it lobbies Brussels it runs the risk of infringing the state's carefully guarded competence. It is personal interest which drives them, in the same official's words, to bypass the state's *tutelle*: 'they should be *content* [author emphasis] to bargain with the Prefet . . . because the strength of regions lies in national solidarity.'[52]

BADEN-WÜRTTEMBERG

Baden-Württemberg is as well situated in the heart of Europe as Rhône-Alpes, on the north-south axis, close to Switzerland, with easy access to Vienna, Budapest or Prague. Constructed in 1949 under the Basic Law it is, unlike Bavaria, not an historic state with an ancient monarchy but a mixed region, a third of whose population and half of its industry is heavily concentrated around three urban regions: Stuttgart, Mannheim, and Friedrichshafen. Activity is concentrated in very highly technical fields – machine tools, electronics, computer software – and services such as planning, consultancy and marketing. Hard hit as its exports were in the early 1990s recession, these remain internationally competitive, as the recoveries of Daimler-Benz, AEG, and Deutsche Aerospace demonstrate.

During the post-War boom, Baden-Württemberg's producers extended their trading scope more than most West German companies outside the EEC, so that by 1988 half its exports went world-wide. It has retained a commitment to free trade and liberal policy exceptional even in the Federal Republic, sharing the view of three of the other four regions considered here that 'Fortress Europe' would be more damaging than any recession. But that does not exclude judicious industrial support: the *land* government has cooperated readily, for example with long-term investment programmes implemented by Daimler-Benz, Bosch, Siemens, and helped to fund the micro systems essential for machine tool competitiveness.[53]

The region's budget is vast by comparison with the others: 194 billion French francs in 1992 as against Lombardy's 129 billion, Catalonia's 56 billion, and Rhône-Alpes's 4.4 billion.[54] It has also been fortunate in its regional government. Lothar Späth, CDU prime minister for much of the 1980s, used the evidence provided by his contacts with a Japanese region in his advocacy of cooperation with Rhône-Alpes in the scientific, university-based programmes of research which constitute the 'Four Motors' only real innovation. Synergy worked, to the extent that two-way traffic has become a matter of routine, hardly worth remarking upon.[55]

The Basic Law gives *Länder* no rights to their own foreign policy. But some of their external activities are informally regarded as *Nebenaussenpolitik*, and under this category Späth was also primarily responsible for Baden-Württemberg's 'external relations' in Japan and Canada, though he failed in an ambitious attempt to get the 'Four Motors' a place at the Rio Environment Summit. When he was succeeded in 1992 by Erwin Teufel (also of the CDU), some of this investment tapered off. However, it was renewed in 1993 in China, Iran and Mexico, on a bi-partisan basis with the SPD.

Efforts like this take time and are complex for local associations like Chambers of Commerce to manage. Yet Baden-Württemberg has also made links with the relatively poor central region of Portugal, and currently plans development aid projects in the Third World.[56] Giant firms such as Daimler-Benz of course have their own external relations departments and need no assistance in Bonn or with the German Permanent Representation or the Commission. For them, as for Rhône-Poulenc, the regional base is of small consequence save where EU research funds are concerned. But for the *Mittelstand* of SMEs, whatever their supplier links to large companies, the *Land* is their world, its state regulatory structures and its institutions theirs.[57] At this level, large and small interests do also, occasionally, coincide: both contested the Commission's attempts to liberalize energy supply and in 1992 formed an organization of local users to defend the status quo.

The financial sector is closer in scope to Edinburgh and Lyon than Barcelona or Bologna. Baden-Württemberg has too small a base for the internal market operations of Germany's three huge banks, Deutsche, Dresdner, and Commerzbank. These maintain branches available to several contiguous regions, from which they can make available investment facilities, say in Luxembourg, free of German withholding tax. The region's own smaller banks have to follow suit and cooperate outside, say with Crédit Mutuel (France). Extensions to Spain and Scotland, on lines already established by Bavaria, are envisaged.[58]

The Basic Law of 1949 reserved to the (West) German state the right to transfer sovereignty to intergovernmental institutions, a right reiterated by the Constitutional Court when it finally pronounced the Single European Act acceptable in 1986. Consequently, the more the EU expands its scope, the more *Länder* governments, and their publics feel they will suffer as their weight in the Bundesrat is imperceptibly diminished. What the federal government concedes as part of inter-state bargains cannot later be repaired; and Baden-Württemberg has followed North Rhine-Westfalia and Bavaria in protesting, ever since the Single European Act became law. Since Maastricht, complaints that the social dimension (education and training) is at risk have reached a crescendo.[59]

The argument, perfected by the time that the Court ruled on the Maastricht Treaty in 1992, has been that the *Länder*'s powers should be increased in the Bundesrat by giving them a share in the scrutiny of EU law, and by physical representation in the Council of Ministers; also informally, by allowing them greater leverage in bargaining with Bonn – assuming that all sixteen of them, east and west, can agree. Baden-Württemberg now has its own office in Brussels, just as Bavaria has had since 1987 when the *Bund-Länder* pact' first permitted it. According to this thesis, subsidiarity is to be decided by the *Länder*: the EU's third stage has to be built partly from below.

There is undoubtedly a business element in this agenda, particularly if the *Land* pattern of managerial sub-states were to be utilized as a Community exemplar, because Baden-Württemberg's export-oriented industries would gain hugely if regions of this type were to become the European convention, even if not the legal norm. Just as the 'Four Motors' turned out to have been a device which allowed participants to discover what substantive grounds existed for making new linkages, so these *tentatives* can be seen as an informal way of probing, in order to find out what might, across all-Europe, serve as the next competitive ground for political and economic change – remembering that several of Baden-Württemberg's more effective economic links already encompass central and eastern Europe.

No single model is likely to bind Europe's regions in the years after 1996. Whatever other purpose the Committee of Regions has, it is not intended to design one. Their current diversity is matched only by differences in what member states will allow them to become, and the inherent conflict between denominated regions, urban areas or city-states is likely to limit many grandiose aggregations to lines on the map.[60] The quickest way to encourage misunderstanding is to transpose regional examples from one national reality to the next; and the quickest way of alienating public opinion from Brussels is to try to shape their definition inside the national context and its always-delicate balance of power. Brussels would be seen as intruding into what is essentially national identity. The German tendency to do so arises firstly from the fact that the *Länder* have so far failed to reform their system in a way that accommodates regions to Brussels and secondly because the political balance of party power gives the SPD leeway only via the *Länder*, so they always stand as the champions of regionality, versus the CDU, in their own political self-interest.

Nevertheless, maps do offer useful patterns, mosaics perhaps rather than developmental shapes. In assessing what current regional alliances and players' strategies amount to, it is not enough to add up linkages, or to count offices in Brussels, or to designate border areas which have economic ties as inter-regions. One must ask what effective networks have been established, and whether the formal effect achieves something beyond what member states would have done anyway, such as the Lyon-Turin motorway – or indeed whether it ought more properly to be construed as a state aid.

Much of the energy expended on hypothesizing these links since the SEA came into force could better have been applied to questions such as differential telecoms pricing. Much regional aid is also very hard work, like the links between SMEs in Picardy and East Anglia, where finding a true partner requires extraordinary serendipity.[61] According to Netherlands' officials, the Dutch regions which profit most are not necessarily the most deserving. Even the choice of representatives for the Committee of Regions produces internal rivalries and inter-state conflicts: lawsuits were actually threatened in 1994 by some member states against Germany and Belgium which both excluded urban regions. Denmark, where the Ministry of the Interior simply nominated twelve members of the prefecture, on the assumption that Denmark constituted a single indivisible region, turned the system on its head and perpetuated central government patronage at the expense of city mayors (see figure 9.2, p. 403).[62]

If one leaves aside the whole matter of funding weaker regions (which except in specific and unusual cases like Northern Ireland is at best likely only to retard an inevitably widening disparity between Europe's economic core and its periphery), the implication seems clear: those regions or urban centres that start early and work hardest will inherit what the EU is to become in the truly profitable fields of research, transport and energy. This says nothing about their precise legal status, for Scotland probably does not need a regional assembly to achieve this (though, given trends in London, it would almost certainly benefit from it, if only in intangible ways and perhaps through an increase in external investors' confidence).[63]

But regional competences are part of the argument for the majority of member states, as the Emilia-Romagna case, contrasted with that of Catalonia, indicates. The prime criterion for effective performance is the balance of a thriving mixed economy and the political ability evident in Baden-Württemberg and Rhône-Alpes to invest the most important economic decisions with a regional component, whether or not they are taken in the end by the central state administration. Few regions apart from the richer core at present aspire to that; many evidently never can. The disparities grow all the time: Catalonia's intake of foreign funds runs at between 50–100% above the Spanish average (despite the deep recession in the car industry there in 1991–3).

All local players can try to build networks, hoping to gain useful transfers of technology, or best-practice examples, or to increase their managerial skills. But those that already have advantages gain most. As Emilia-Romagna demonstrates, the scale of regional markets matters greatly, probably more than transport links, which tend either to follow markets or to become state-owned white elephants in the guise of social services, such as the Madrid-Seville high-speed rail link and many of the domestic air routes served by Olympic, TAP, Iberia and Air France.

On the evidence of the cases set out here, some sort of public private cooperation seems essential to regional success. Yet not all the member state governments which ought to be concerned specifically promote it. Existing links may signify various patterns of thinking and a distinction ought to be made between effective networks and intellectual policy fashions: there is no substance in the *soi-disant* 'Atlantic arc' save peripherality and a certain Commission interest in redefining deprivation. It is at least possible that what a region does can change its own member state's agenda, but rather more likely that it will shift the Commission's. (On the other hand one Portuguese official sees himself not as representing Portugal in Brussels, but Brussels in Portugal.)

Meanwhile, over time inhabitants of a region come to identify with even recent constructions. Surveys in the 1950s revealed that the majority of West Germans disliked the *Länder* innovation, but forty-five years on they have come to respect and admire them, while differentiating themselves by their (not necessarily historic) characteristics.

This is not to say that only what exists physically is real, and that the Commission and DG16 formulate policy in a vacuum. The Community's regional policy cannot, for the social and political reasons urged by Delors in 1985, be written off. Yet 90% of Objective 2 money goes to regions in the activist category, who presented themselves with particular skill during the cohesion arguments under the Portuguese and British Presidencies in 1991 and 1992. Most of the existing research and hi-technology schemes like ESPRIT and EUREKA privilege the advanced regions and the better firms or universities, in the Davignon tradition. Even STAR, SPRINT and the other programmes aimed at SMEs work best in regions like Emilia-Romagna and Catalonia. DG23 has so far failed to formulate a coherent and widely acceptable policy for giving SMEs a better chance of survival as mini-big businesses in a highly competitive environment, partly because they do not appear to wish for what is offered, partly because there is as yet no means of generalizing from known evidence about the cultures of successful industrial districts, beyond the level of banality.

It would be possible simply to ask the best exemplars what they most want, on the assumption that only those who meet the preconditions of success can give regionality an efficient meaning. *Länder* representatives might respond 'that the future Europe will grow from its regions and from the willingness of their inhabitants to think and act as Europeans on the basis of their regional consciousness'.[64] They would also, on existing evidence, exclude any municipalities or urban regions from the charmed circle. Conversely, French regions and the embryonic administrative divisions in England might not welcome what amounts to federalism from below (for which only Belgium and possibly Italy and Spain possess the preconditions). Whereas successive Bavarian prime ministers, from Franz-Josef Strauss to Edmund Stoiber, have incanted 'the necessity of regions' ('we are of course German, and we are especially

European, but above all Bavarian'), deeply contrary views exist even among Bavarians;[65] and whereas Jordi Pujol has relentlessly pursued Third Chamber status for the Committee of Regions, the conditions for a European-wide conjuncture of interests, like those in which *Länder* and Spain's autonomous communities were originally formed, simply do not exist.

Instead there is diversity, not only of geography, culture and economics, but of opinions about the very concept of regionality, which remains as wide as its nineteenth- and early twentieth-century precursors. Danish and Dutch governments object to the Belgian claims for regional access to the Council of Ministers because there is no law to say that smaller states – who constitute a more mixed group than larger ones – should agree on basic principles. On what basis, then, might regions be given a voice as sub-member states to speak about their undoubted concerns in the face, say, of North African migration or the admission of applicant states from eastern Europe?[66] They have of course one overriding economic reason: Pujol quoted Gianni Agnelli's declaration that what interests Fiat is to be involved in every strong region and in the future of whole markets. On that basis one could study the importance of local linkages between firms, SMEs, industrial districts, banks, labour markets, and local agriculture ('the TGV has done for Languedoc what the Rocket did for Lancashire').

Yet although Strathclyde has been claimed 'as a model of how a local authority should interface with DG16',[67] not all linkages create networks, and networks themselves are not made effective simply because their boundaries fit well with regional ones. It is quite possible that the most effective future networks will develop in areas such as student exchange and employee or management training, rather than in productive processes. Larger firms and MNCs tend to avoid the regional political marketplace altogether, except where the ERD Funds, chiefly under Objectives 2 and 5b, come into play. Thus Thomson, the French MNC, is deeply interested in the EC's Periphera Programme but, to take another case, Rhône-Poulenc recognizes for itself no greater regional consequence than 'being a company from Rhône-Alpes'. Fiat and the other Italian giants may be special cases.[68]

The Commission (or rather DGs16 and 23), might argue in favour of extending Europe's competitiveness to as many of the regions as possible, chiefly via the SMEs. But as Ash Amin has argued, the total EU effort, including that of DG23, is far less than what large firms in the EU do already, for their own variety of commercial reasons, and it is this trend that benefits more from the internal market.[69] Here the Emilia-Romagna example is crucial. If large firms were to remodel their sub-units as self-supporting entities in industrial districts or urban regions, they could indeed assist the process, yet it is rarely in their interest to do so. Where they have, the experience has not necessarily been rewarding. IBM, for instance, was until recently the largest business in Scotland and tied itself informally to many RD Fund projects, which assisted its claim to be acting on behalf of Scotland, but this has been affected badly by its European-wide decline.[70] At present, the only answer to the other developmental question – How could the multinationals be attracted to increase investment in *backward* regions? – lies with member state governments and the incentives they offer, which all too often slip into the category of state aids.[71] European Union trade and competition policy actively promotes greater rationalization and concentration in the various European cores so that any disparity with the economic periphery requires even more heroic counter-measures. In the end the regional problem becomes, like all others, a matter of players of different orders, and their distribution of power and interests. Apart from the ameliorating but relatively minor effects of structural spending, the Commission's effective work, like the foundation of the Committee of Regions, has served to bring the regional question more out into the open, and to give it a formulation which at least encourages the players, ranging from member states to firms and banks, to accept that regional disparity is a problem in which they all ought to share.

In that sense, the *Länder*'s overweening response is not unwelcome in Brussels, because since Germany is the largest player it has the most to gain from the preferred solution. But the tension with other member states which this sort of argument rouses, in France, Britain, Denmark, Ireland, or Greece, can only be resolved at the top, not by an ill-defined body formed in the Ecosoc mould. Solutions will emerge between the Council of Ministers and the Commission, if at all, partly shaped by what giant firms do; just as answers will emerge at the same member state level to other related problems such as tourism dependency, the purchase of retirement homes, and the development of leisure amenities in environmentally sensitive areas.

Logically, subsidiarity ought to be defined at this level. In the Danish and Dutch political systems it is already a way of life. One Commissioner suggested that 'regional policy might bring the EU nearer to the citizen' so long as Brussels was seen to consult regions, rather than try to dictate what they did.[72] But could it do so elsewhere, given the competing interests of both ends of the regional spectrum, rich and poor, in what would not be a level at all were it not given such a generic title? All member states have to compound these differences in their domestic contexts, but tend usually to offset the advantages of modernization in the chosen, advanced areas by offering the marginal ones subsidies of many sorts, sops which foster complex mixtures of dependency and resentment. So it could be left as a member state problem, if it were not for the Commission's aspiration to introduce fuller social and political integration.

As a matter of political theory, a third level of European government ought to be possible. If present trends continue, it may have to be made possible, if the EU is to grow towards political integration. Yet at present, in any discussion of Commission policy, it is the regional dimension which exposes most tensions. The Committee of Regions could only develop influence once existing disparities of election, criteria of representation, and the role of municipalities had been resolved. That member states would not in the process insist on their own preferences and delay the outcome is not credible: after all, 85–90% of RD funding at present passes through their control. If it is not permanently to resemble Ecosoc and remain at the mercy of forces outside its control, the Committee of Regions must work informally, fostering an evolutionary plan for many years. Yet if it did, during that time the stronger regions would increase their dominance. There is already evidence that lesser-endowed regions, even some fully autonomous communities in Spain like Andalucia and Castilla, have already lost interest. In the interim, subsidiarity may yet be defined by regions such as those cited here, a proposition which appears to form common ground between European conservatives and social democrats (though not yet British Conservatives), as political fashion dictates the virtues of community in suitably sized packages. Member states after all pay Danegeld to their own regions already, and would pay more if the Regional Development Funds did not exist.

The regional level may therefore offer for study a post-modern variable geometry. Yet the sub-nationalisms which flourish in Catalonia, Scotland and some German *Länder* relate to the wider crises of identity which have affected all member states, including the new entrants, since the shape of wider Europe changed dramatically in 1989. The last time this occurred on so wide a scale in Europe was in 1917–21. The regional issue may therefore possess another dimension, as a theatre where what is unacceptable in national terms may be played out and at the same time contained, allowing the nationalisms which divided all Europe in the past to evolve this time in less destructive forms. It may be possible, even desirable, to let nationalist maelstroms run out their life in the context of regional diversity, in Epirus and Greek Macedonia, as much as the Basque country or Northern Ireland, rather than to skew politics and parties of member states as they once did.

PART THREE

PLAYERS

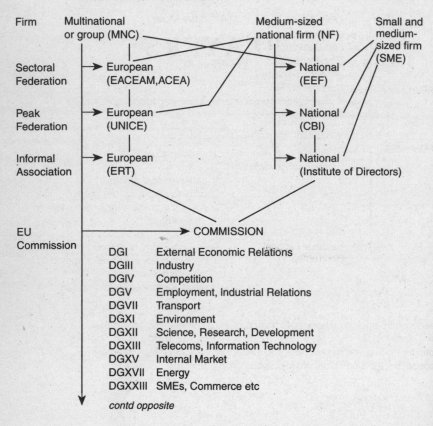

Firms and their lines of access to EU and National Institutions

Firm	Multinational or group (MNC)	Medium-sized national firm (NF)	Small and medium-sized firm (SME)
Sectoral Federation	European (EACEAM,ACEA)	National (EEF)	
Peak Federation	European (UNICE)	National (CBI)	
Informal Association	European (ERT)	National (Institute of Directors)	

EU Commission → COMMISSION

DGI	External Economic Relations
DGIII	Industry
DGIV	Competition
DGV	Employment, Industrial Relations
DGVII	Transport
DGXI	Environment
DGXII	Science, Research, Development
DGXIII	Telecoms, Information Technology
DGXV	Internal Market
DGXVII	Energy
DGXXIII	SMEs, Commerce etc

contd opposite

FIGURE 10.1

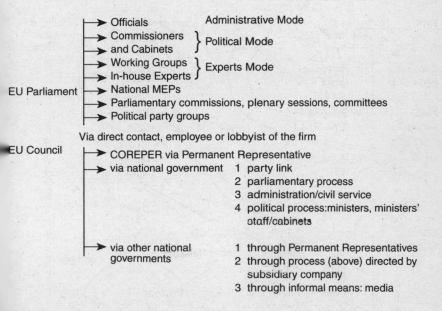

EU Parliament

- Officials   Administrative Mode
- Commissioners
- and Cabinets   } Political Mode
- Working Groups   } Experts Mode
- In-house Experts
- National MEPs
- Parliamentary commissions, plenary sessions, committees
- Political party groups

Via direct contact, employee or lobbyist of the firm

EU Council

- COREPER via Permanent Representative
- via national government
  1. party link
  2. parliamentary process
  3. administration/civil service
  4. political process:ministers, ministers' staff/cabinets
- via other national governments
  1. through Permanent Representatives
  2. through process (above) directed by subsidiary company
  3. through informal means: media

Feedback from each of these to Commissioners, cabinets, and sometimes MEPs

Note: for obvious reasons of time, resources, and their peripheral character, Ecosoc and the Committee of Regions do not figure here.

Player's Links to Decision-Makers
I. Multinational Corporations

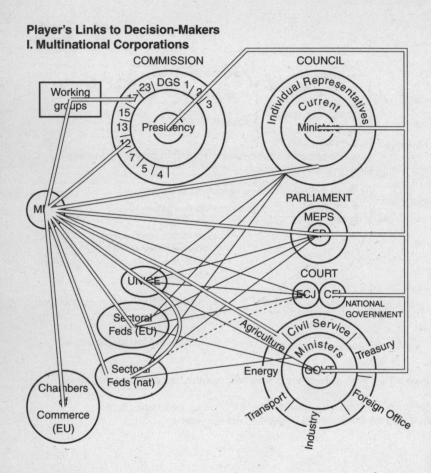

FIGURE 10.2

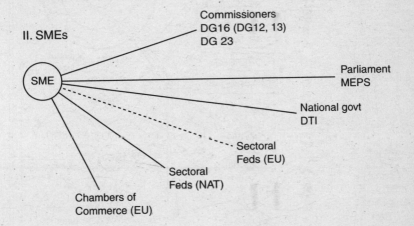

II. SMEs

SME

Commissioners
DG16 (DG12, 13)
DG 23

Parliament
MEPS

National govt
DTI

Sectoral
Feds (EU)

Sectoral
Feds (NAT)

Chambers of
Commerce (EU)

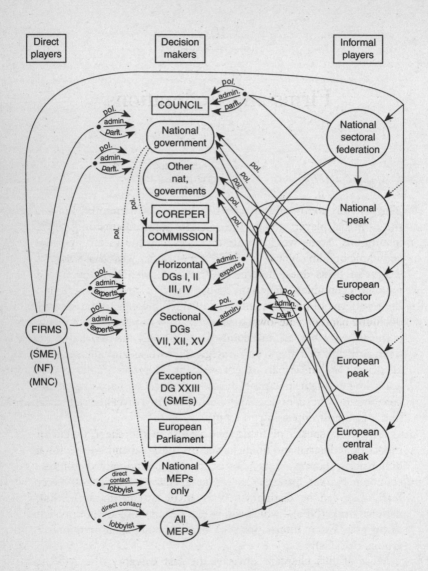

FIGURE 10.3

Firms and Federations

I.   The Firm

The firm has no formal status in the European Community, but it is the principal player outside the arena of governments and public institutions. Some would argue that it is also the most important economic building block. What it does, or rather what the collective weight of firms does, determines the performance of the fifteen national economies, their currencies, their balances of trade and their patterns of employment. Yet unless it belongs to the steadily declining band of state-owned concerns, it is responsible not in any political way, but to its family owners only or shareholders, financiers and managers. Its strategies, networks and alliances are all private and informal, except when it addresses public bodies according to established procedures. It is therefore hard to generalize about how 'it' operates. Above all, the firm's diversity is so great that it is almost impossible to typify.

When one speaks of firms, one is lost in the sheer weight of numbers, industrial and financial sectors, national and international dimensions. However, as players in the Community's political-economic market, 'firms' *do* have general characteristics. At the very least, they can be distinguished as small and medium (SMEs), national firms (NFs) – which can in fact be large but are not present to any great extent internationally – or multinational corporations or groups (MNCs).

Most of this chapter concerns the last category, the MNCs, whose activities have by far the greatest impact and which are rather easier to examine than the national range. The extent of their strategies, and the direct and indirect access they all have to European and national institutions, can be expressed in diagrams sufficiently well to give some idea about the multiplicity of options open to a firm's managers, no matter what industry or sector it operates in. Even the small firm has an interest, which may only be capable of being expressed narrowly, through a Chamber of Commerce to a single national government department; but their activity makes it part of an immensely complex whole. Nothing in the European Union is as monolithic as it seems, no decision or choice is free from the competition between players of different orders, at every stage and level. It may at present be impossible to quantify what firms do (compared to governments' weight in this game), but that is no reason to exclude them from the analysis.

Unlike the players discussed so far, the firm not only has a wide range of choices between different kinds of action but an equally wide one about how 'European' it will be; how the EU side of its activity will be internalized in, say, a legal department or department of government relations; how directly its main board will be involved, and whether it will deal with the EU from its head-quarters at a distance or from a Brussels office. The firm is far more free to change its mind, at the dictates of markets or individual managers, than are other institutional players. It can more easily increase or diminish its EU commitments (many firms reduced their lobbying efforts once the bulk of internal market legislation had been passed), and it can quickly change its strategies either as a result of its own domestic politics or reappraisal of the outside world. In this sense, the firm is theoretically a free agent, although in fact its choices are very much more heavily determined by economic factors and market patterns, shifting competitive advantage and changes among its leading personalities than are the players in governments and EU institutions.

Being, for reasons of market survival, a rapid-response player (unless it is state-owned or sheltered by long-term investors from the consequence of short-term market reactions), the firm does not typically behave according to well-known, formal rules (other than the requirements of national, European and international law). Subject to no single model of behaviour, the rules of its game are likely to be in the form of conventions, based on assumptions shared among competitors about what is negotiable – such rules being policed either on a self-regulating basis or by quasi-formal groups. As a general rule, however, the larger it is, the more likely the firm is to define its own interests as having an EU dimension, as well as global, national and sub-national ones. These are unlikely always to be complementary. Most of the firms considered here have, as a matter of historical adaptation, derived their EU strategies from the patterns long since evolved in their interplay between their own national governments and the international or global economy. 'Europe' is an important part of their legal political and economic context, but that does not automatically make them *European*.

Figure 10.1 sets out the access routes open to the three categories of firms. (It is irrelevant whether they operate in manufacturing, services, or the financial sectors). Figure 10.2 is an attempt at a (necessarily impressionistic) assessment of what reliance is put typically by MNCs and SMEs on the various access channels, and the degree of concern displayed by them towards different EU institutions, NFs being too diverse to reduce to a single chart. Figure 10.3 expresses the links between direct players, decision-makers and indirect players.

These should not be taken as categoric, because every firm is distinct. Its ethos and sense of identity, its managerial style, its workforce, location, competitive advantage, as well as its political skills and networks with federations and governments, all affect the intensity and frequency with which it utilizes the range.

According to a 1988 UN study, there are perhaps 20,000 trans-national firms world-wide, owning roughly 100,000 subsidiaries. But it is not clear how many of these can truly be considered as TNCs,[1] rather than multinationals (MNCs) with a national home base, operating in what is now a global context; so the term MNC is therefore used in preference. The surge of mergers and takeovers, whose third great twentieth-century wave began in the late 1960s and revived again in the 1980s, raised substantial questions about the private government of such firms and what is commonly seen as the privatization of the state. But privatization's future is now limited in a way not foreseeable in the late 1980s, even if it still has a substantial way to go in most European member states. The future of the EU market seems now to lie not in continuous deregulation, but rather in a mixture of deregulation and reregulation, where a substantial number of privatized monopolies will survive.

The European firm is not an untrammelled force, but is generally regulated both at the EU level and in the state where its main base lies. What Joseph Schumpeter called 'capitalism's creative gale' has often undermined the giant overstretched firm (IBM, which saw itself as pre-eminently a European firm, being a case in point). Nevertheless, tensions inherent in the internal market and within industrial and financial sectors, as well as between firms and member states, complicate enormously the Commission's attempts to shape the behaviour of all of them in a higher European interest. The fact that the internal market is not yet (1995) fully in place argues that firms and EU institutions which had wanted it to be in place on the set date, 1 January 1993, had shown themselves weaker than member states, concerned for their own self-interest.

Member states had been in favour of the Single European Act in 1985–6, but not necessarily for the same reasons. Their enthusiasm sometimes wilted once the details became clear, in the long trough leading up to the Hannover Summit 1988. Even after that, particularly in the confused period after Maastricht, some of them defended their sheltered sectors or state-owned companies; others, for reasons of national administrative convenience, delayed the implementation or enforcement of parts of the SEM legislation. The actual picture in 1993, when the internal market in theory came into effect, was more complicated than had been envisaged by the makers (or assessed by the first generation of text books).

Firms' attitudes, at least among MNCs, changed radically during the 1980s, to a greater extent than they had at the time of the first transformation which had been inspired in the early 1970s by the accession of Britain, with its traditions of firms' direct access to public institutions and more developed patterns of informal game-play. Until the mid-1980s, they had generally restricted their interest to competition law and relied on the confluence of national federations and governments to influence the rest of the EC's law-making process. But from then on, the largest and most far-sighted, some of whose heads had joined the ERT or who, if American, belonged to the European Committee of AmCham, tended to take the lead at both points of the compass of influence, in Brussels and in member state capitals. National firms and SMEs generally lagged behind, unless the formal machinery caught them up, as it did in Germany; but for MNCs the tidal wave of legislation demanded a highly expert approach and a novel level of lobbying intensity in Strasbourg and Luxembourg as well as in Brussels.

The larger firms and more coherent sectoral federations had the singular advantage that, unlike the Commission or member state administrations, they knew precisely how their industries worked. Those who would set out the rules and solve policy problems had first to consult, inform themselves and understand, because the MNCs in any sector were invariably in some degree of competition with each other, or wished to hide their collusion. Commission officials needed effective European-wide federations to help achieve a level of general consensus of which, with few exceptions, purely national federations were incapable. Even after the laws had been drafted, passed and implemented, this more structured framework continued because every one of the players had a close interest in how policy was subsequently developed and how the law was in practice to be enforced.

Firms did not change their nature as the internal market came into effect, but the more active ones' behaviour changed, apparently irrevocably, and the volume of active players increased dramatically, as can be gauged simply by the sheer numbers who set up new offices in Brussels after about 1988. At the same time, European sectoral federations in industries which were most at risk from American and Japanese competition, adjusted to these conditions, in some cases by radical reform (see p. 463 *et seq*). Qualitative as well as quantitative adjustments filtered down, reaching the national firm level, at least in Northern Europe, by the early 1990s.

Tensions arose between a firm's behaviour in the national-international context, and how it should react during and after the early 1990s recession in the European one, if its balanced commercial strategy was to complement the patterns of adjustment sought by member state governments, and if it was to position itself to take advantage of the coming deregulation and market liberalization. Full strategic involvement in the Community (which had very rarely been the case for MNCs apart from particular firms such as Fiat before the 1980s), was internalized and universalized.

The European Economic Area, which came into effect in 1993, comprised 380 million people (including most EFTA countries) and covered 40% of world trade. From about 1990, fears that the emergence of this block – and the North American counterpart NAFTA – would produce a more protection-ridden pattern of world trade, seemed for a time to be justified by delays in the GATT-Uruguay round, caused largely by disputes between the United States and the European Union. Sensing a renewed wave of American and Japanese investment inside the Community, including the arrival of fresh players from Taiwan and South Korea, European MNCs took no chances: just in case the internal market should be delayed or frustrated by some governments, or the GATT round not concluded, they and their representative federations, in threatened sectors such as cars, electronics and textiles, worked towards a series of defensive measures which would extend current protection and be phased out only when the Commission had established a congenial trading regime for the future.

Some of their attempts to balance the new economic regime in their own favour are discussed in the next two chapters. In general political terms, this activity gave industrial sectors both a global and a European identity, but at different times and with very specific outcomes for each firm – just as the Multi-Fibre Agreement differed from restrictive agreements elsewhere. But what federations (and the peak organization UNICE, representing each member state's Confederation of Industries) did has to be seen not as autonomous but as the sum of what their members required. That outcome was then transmitted centrally to Brussels and the Commission, and via each national network to Permanent Representatives and MEPs.

How far firms' calculations and attempts to exercise influence affected the Committee's industrial, financial and trade policy as a whole in this recent period, as distinct from SEM legislation up to 1992, can as yet only be guessed at. But since the investment packages implanted by MNCs, grouping research, knowledge, design, management and marketing (which rapidly developing states like Spain desired so much in the 1980s), were ahead of the generality of the economies that welcomed them, the possibility of influence by inward investors even in a country like Britain cannot be excluded.

On the other hand, while a member state government's interest in the national economy may generally coincide with what MNCs would like to see in the *European* context, in political terms their interests are more likely to conflict. Labour law, conditions of work and welfare are obvious cases. Firms may not seek this, but by investing, say, where social welfare costs are lower, they take predictable advantage and stimulate resentments and competition between member states, who may be formally sovereign but out of self-interest allow their sovereignty to be exploited.

From the firm's point of view, prudent management balances its networks of influence between the national government and European institutions. For all their vast variety of outlooks and modes of action, MNCs operate a continuous politics of minimizing risks, whether these be the obvious market ones – exchange rates, foreign competition, labour costs or advances in technology – or political ones to do with regulation, company law and taxation. What then transpires in the EU may be rather more shaped by these arrangements than it is in member states themselves. But so long as member states retain competence to manage their own macro-economic circumstances and, perhaps to a lesser extent, their own systems of welfare, education and training, industrial and trade policy, their relationships with the firms which have a base or investment in them will be a potential cause of dispute with EU institutions which claim overall responsibility for setting the policy framework. Even where the Commission has competence, governments are likely to react strongly to cross-border acquisitions, as well as to direct investment by American, Japanese and south-east Asian companies.

The argument about who uses whom, among member states and multinationals, is far too wide and theoretical to consider here. But recent events in the EMS have demonstrated how international flows of capital may weaken member states' capacity, especially the lesser ones, to resist having global, non-governmental patterns forced on them. In attempting to regulate highly technical, rapidly changing markets such as those in financial derivatives, governments are especially prone to rely on market players to police them or to help them write the rules. But European states are not puny players: they can renew themselves, just as the largest multinationals may decay. Political contexts can be reformed and the interplay between large firms and governments is unlikely to be resolved finally in favour of one or the other in the foreseeable future. Regulation will remain a bargained process, at both levels.

MNCs are not caricatures, seeking political dominion. They want a congenial political context as much as a benign legal one. They tend to behave collectively and defensively, hoping to minimize large risks whether or not in collusion with others, and in areas like the transfer of technology to less-developed countries, they have to contend with problems of the political reaction and media exposure. What can be done in eastern Europe (see p. 651) is not acceptable in the Community, because member states have a vested interest in maintaining each other's practical sovereignty. No player or group of players is exempt from these constraints, not even financial institutions in their choice of lending patterns when, for example, the banks who lend to chemical companies can be held responsible for the environmental hazards to which the borrower's products may give rise.

Intelligence, in the sense of what a firm's managers need to know about Community conditions, extends therefore beyond the obviously relevant officials in say, DG3, 12 or 13, to include the governments of the major states, and the forward plans of the next President state in the Troika. Whether this is called research or intelligence gathering, the substance is political not economic, and analysis will focus on several levels of behaviour, in the Directorates, the college, Coreper, the Parliament, and the Council of Ministers.

Firms have always needed lawyers, from the earliest days of a law-based Community. At national level, MNCs have in the post-War era always needed persons of influence or with access, whether they are styled consultants or lobbyists – the latter being now held in sufficient disrepute for many firms to deny the term altogether.[2] (*Lobbying* is of course what everyone in the game seems to do.) But since the mid-1980s, the quantity and usage of both have altered. The lawyer's role has become more specialized, while lobbyists have developed self-regulating rules and even codes of conduct, as they too aspire to professional status. Both services are now offered to firms on a variety of terms, ranging from temporary links and contracts for single cases or campaigns to longer term ones where monitoring and rapid reaction to EU events is required.

SMEs are unlikely ever to require such specialist services; national firms may do if they are severely disadvantaged by a contradiction between different national practices, as British brewers are penalized by the cross-Channel traffic in beer sold at the far lower French or Belgian levels of excise duty. But many larger NFs and all MNCs will employ their own corporate, taxation or intellectual property legal specialists, who are likely also to manage their government and EU affairs departments (that is, to act as political consultants). Lawyers help the firm to understand EU law, they find alternative interpretations to argue with Brussels, or provide a reasoned case to amend the law. But few except the giant firm can employ enough people to cover all the specialisms needed in the Community arena: hence the growth of the giant law firm offering what is, in effect, a one-stop shop.

Lobbyists are different from lawyers, if only because it is impossible to be an amateur lawyer, whereas there are, as yet, no finals exams in political persuasion and the art of the possible. Although larger firms in western Europe – NFs or MNCs – had all evolved means of access to deal with national governments at different times (later in Europe than in the United States or Britain but universally by the early post-War period), few of them had adequate expertise for dealing with the flood of internal market legislation and the consequential growth of industrial adjustment policy. The effort had to be increased further once the Maastricht Treaty had extended the Parliament's powers of amendment.

In these conditions, lobbyists flourished, set up firms with offices in Brussels and Strasbourg, and developed the arts of persuasion into something approaching a social science. Since it was clear, given the overload from which officials and ministers suffer, that any prizes would go to those who made a good, detailed, *concise* case to the right person at the earliest possible moment, sufficient to convince him or her that the correct answer was the one that best fitted the client, a sort of corporate Darwinism rapidly separated the most effective lobbying firms from the rest. As in nature, the necessities of survival produced abuses and excesses, notably in the tobacco industry's lobbying of MEPs – followed by a reaction, and attempts by both the Commission and the Parliament to regulate this ebullient, rapidly mutating market place.

After more than a decade of evolutionary experience, the lobby market now offers a firm a complex set of choices, priced in effect like firms of lawyers according to a complex formula made up of the quality of what is offered and the client's capacity to pay. The best firms are politically acute, formidably well-connected to the decision-makers, maintain a full intelligence-gathering and analytical capacity and a roll-call of distinguished subscribers.[3] These can alternately monitor long-term developments or mobilize an emergency case against, say, a hostile takeover bid over a weekend. They can handle media presentations, approach and be welcomed by MEPs, know precisely how long to stay on the telephone to a busy official, and advise management when half a loaf is better than no bread. Success may be measured in amendments to the law, but is more likely to consist of getting a better deal for the client at no long-term risk to his credibility.

The firm's ideal is to maintain its permanent advisory service in-house, with recourse to outside specialisms only when necessary. It will rely as far as possible on EU sectoral federations, for reasons of cost, the subscription being very much less than the price of the lobbyist; and informally the Commission has made it clear that its officials prefer to deal with a single agency on behalf of a whole industrial sector, rather than the chaotic diversity of competing firms, particularly when heightened by lobbyists. Federations 'have already come to a compromise'.[4]

Over more than a decade, as a result, practice has affected all those with an EU interest, often in imperceptible ways, even among firms from political cultures which were initially resistant to the idea of adversarial persuasion, such as Germany, the Netherlands and Denmark. (In Germany, as Beate Kohler-Koch has shown, lobbying is seen as a natural but regulated outcome of complex formalized processes of consultation which were originally established as an intrinsic part of the post-War German estate. The Verbände, for example, supply the largest percentage of technical experts on Commission working groups.[5]) They use a novel terminology and imbibe legal and political precepts, possibly even values; they have come to conceive of Europeanness as a desirable addition to or modification of the firm's ethos and identity. In the process, very indirectly, British or Italian or Korean or Hungarian firms assist in the process of transforming both the Community's institutions and their own national governments.

The process is from most points of view mutual and certainly irresistible. But it is detrimental to those who lack the resources to play. SMEs can refer to their Chambers of Commerce, or to national confederations which usually possess a special section devoted to their interests, and national departments of industry. But NFs often fall between, needing more attention than SMEs yet unable to play the full Community game. They may suffer accordingly, except where their base is in a member state with a suitable formal consultation/negotiating framework, such as Germany.

Without a massive sample of hundreds of firms, taking a range of representative views in each, there can be no average, no Weberian 'ideal type' of how 'the firm' behaves as a European player. What is offered here is merely a survey of relevant views from among MNCs, Federations and peak organizations' executives operating in the EU, who were willing to be interviewed. It excludes smaller firms, because of their extreme differentiation and because these have found it impossible to establish more than a minimal *juste retour* at the European level, even with their ostensible 'sponsor' DG23 (despite the often-argued view that the German model of Handwerk, like that of *Länder*, is suitable for the whole Community).

(This view is not shared, for example, in Catalonia or Emilia-Romagna, where supplier-user relations differ, and attitudes to flexible specialization diverge widely from German diversified quality production.)[6]

During the last seven years, patterns of national firms' behaviour as players in the EU have grown to resemble each other more than in the 1980s, partly as a response to the internal market, partly to the politicization of industrial and trade policy by member state governments during the 1990s recession. Europe's specific circumstances have evidently accentuated an evolution that might have been expected in any case from changes in the global environment.[7] But national styles still survive, in firms' designation of priorities, types of lobbying networks, and their ultimate recourses when their interests are directly threatened. Otherwise much of the activity is by way of an insurance policy, a gesture to competitors and a source of inside information.

1. German firms, for example, have created more direct links to Brussels than in the past, beyond the structural networks of consultation and influence provided by federations, *land* and federal government. According to the *Ressortprinzip*, private firms had long been represented in Bonn. But the internal market's enormous accelerator effect left German MNCs dissatisfied, not with the system's ability to act as a filter in Germany but with Bonn's competence in Brussels when set against those of Paris, London or the Hague. Since 1986 there has been both a transposition of activity and a decline in the status and power of the Ministry of Economics *vis-à-vis* the Foreign Ministry and the *Länder* demands. Given the resulting discord, and the widespread feeling that German Commission officials were unresponsive and German MEPs out of the context, MNCs had to resort, in areas of conflict on major issues, first to the Chancellery informally and second to Brussels on a much more incisive basis than before. This latter drive also included direct corporate membership of European-wide federations, for car and chemicals firms, and in due course probably for others.

In perhaps 70% of cases, it is still true that German MNCs use the national federation or the European one indifferently according to the issue. But they now regard it as essential to have regular contact with Commission officials; according to one executive, 'it is useless to meet a Director General if the lower levels are not on one's side.' On political issues, and whenever they risk being isolated, there is stronger cause than in the past to act alone. As the stakes for the firm rose, and as officials not just Commissioners were seen to be active participants in policy-making, the search for contacts and individual influence accelerated – a process which fed on itself, once it was seen to produce results relatively cheaply and without rousing political controversy.[8] It also offered German MNCs a means to contact other member state representatives or national officials, giving a broader base to the effervescence of joint ventures and cross-border mergers which has become a leitmotif of the 1990s, particularly in the financial sector (for example, the operations of Deutsche Bank or Allianz Insurance).

Coincidentally, firms' search for a distinct, individuated network has run parallel with German unification and the quest for a redefined national identity inside the Community. This does not mean that the traditional system operating since the War has been eroded: government and MNCs still on occasion form a common front on major issues affecting industry, such as the proposed energy tax which the industrial federations and car manufacturers agreed to support, in return for a government scheme of incentives – but only if it were made a European-wide requirement.[9]

Firms' individual reasons for seeking influence depend on their own particular circumstances. German or EU federations may be inadequate to represent them in their capacity as 'European technology enterprises'. Yet this does not mean that they see themselves as having gained a European identity, or even that their managements seek to irradiate the firm with a European ethos: the Brussels office is likely to be a strictly utilitarian adjunct, part of its external relations, in one case at least 'responsible for translating what the Commission says into the German mode'. Most of its work will lie in providing information to ensure that the parent firm is not wrong-footed, and monitoring EU trends; those interviewed suggest that less than one-third consists of seeking influence for particular projects. The proportion of direct influence sought, as against the use of federations, varies widely.

Direct influence will count where immediate commercial advantage is concerned, such as linking the firm with the EU's hi-tech research and trade programmes through Phare in eastern Europe; rather less when massed ranks are required to bring influence to bear on the process of fixing norms and standards. The short-lived, extremely expensive, and in the end counter-productive onslaught on MEPs by tobacco companies in January 1992 has become a by-word on how not to employ lobbyists. Some major companies chose not to have Brussels offices at all, relying on the European sectoral federation to do the work. This outlook is practicable so long as the federation, say in chemicals or pharmaceuticals, works effectively on its members' behalf, but would not be possible in the car or electronics industries.

Resources assigned to the European dimension depend entirely on a firm's involvement and the balance between its national, European and international interests. BASF, the chemicals corporation, reckoned that 160 of its employees were concerned with EU affairs in 1993, in comparison to ICI which had 100 in the EU public affairs department before the company's division into ICI and Zeneca. While numbers obviously give an indication of a firm's interest or commitment, the modes chosen to seek influence are entirely idiosyncratic: a firm like Carlsberg or Distillers may as easily operate from its home base, if the informal diplomatic links can be kept in being in this economical way. The Brussels office – which in 1987 Wyn Grant estimated might cost a firm £100,000 a year (probably £200,000 in 1994) – might represent no more than a costly gesture, a declaration of intent, or a way of signifying to competitors that no possible mode of access has been ignored, just as the choice between using a firm's representative or a lobbyist may relate to perceptions about the place where influence is sought.

Brussels is clearly the most important centre, the Parliament being the arena for putting up amendments, counter-proposals and what often amounts to spoiling operations. Few German firms cultivate more than a handful of MEPs, selected according to committee or party membership; one executive regards the European Parliament's political networks as being 'good only for the photograph album'. The largest firms are well able to conduct their own informal diplomacy, but there is a danger, despite the fall-off in mergers in the early 1990s recession, that efficient medium-sized companies will be swallowed up by larger ones. These frequently claim that government should act to protect the existing balance and the stability and autonomy of efficient firms against corporate raiders, in the interests of industrial producers as a whole.[10] Medium-sized firms – a much neglected field of study – are likely to collaborate in this, especially in sheltered markets threatened by liberalization or foreign investment. Resistances, constituting a sort of protectionism, may therefore extend to a defence of habitual German positions such as stock exchange quotation and accountancy practices. MNCs and medium firms, to say nothing of the well organized SMEs, tend therefore to cooperate to preserve the existing multiplicity of networks, so long as each has its own adequate safeguards, such as access to the chancellor, to the Commission or to Coreper, where the *Ressortprinzip* fails to satisfy their needs.

2. If there is a French model for influence, it could be summed up by a DG3 official's comment noting Pechiney's mastery of the art of influence, 'technically perfect dossiers, not too partisan, containing the complete case, ready for argument'. Long used to working in Brussels, though by no means always from a Brussels base, French MNCs almost universally focus on the need always to have an answer for the Commission when asked, and the political requirement to be seen as expert in the field but non-adversarial in tone. Publicity and media intervention politicize discussions, create antagonisms and risk spoiling what is invariably a long-term game – which is of course a political standpoint in its own right.

The MNCs and larger French companies which watched the internal market's evolution after 1988 with a mixture of fear and hope – hope for new markets and commercial freedoms, fear of unfavourable norms, foreign imports and 'social dumping' – have established sufficient direct links to the EU's institutions to be certain of how and where decisions are made. But there is still a tendency, while analysing the information which flows back from Brussels, not to act at the earliest moment but to wait until the drift of Commission policy becomes clear, so that time and money are not wasted on what may turn out to be unimportant or blind alley initiatives. While this worked well in the 1980s, it is now beginning to be seen that British firms have a facility for getting in earlier, often assisted by the UK Representation.

There are French MNCs, especially those with defence links like Thomson, which maintain an exceptionally wide range of links on a permanent basis, with Strasbourg committees as well as several Commission Directorates.[11] Others affirm a need 'to bathe in the Brussels culture', which would be hard to detect on British or German boards, however deeply they have implanted the European dimension. MNCs' executives appear to put more weight on being aware of what informal think-tanks and groupings of individuals do in Brussels, as part of the processes of inserting their own employees as experts on Commission working groups; but they need to work out exactly the same balance as any other firm between the EU chain of influence and the national one.

National links to their key ministries, the Matignon and the Elysée, remain as fundamental as they are for their German equivalents in Bonn. In the last resort, for a firm which is still recognizably a French one, influence over its own government is what matters. Brussels also has the disadvantage of containing too great a mixture of nationalities and professions for long-term influence easily to become rooted. What matters, according to a Paris-based lawyer, is the quality of the interlocutors, not the mere status of 'who you know'. The cost is also a major consideration. Compagnie Générale des Eaux representatives used to commute from Paris to Brussels in the late 1980s until an EU office was set up in 1993. Much effort was required to persuade the main board that this expense was justified, for 'it is long-term work, and takes a long while to show the sort of results that convince'.

Like their German counterparts, French firms often find it necessary to decode for the main board what is said in Brussels. This is not a matter of language but of discourses, and applies to all nationalities. Yet the importance of being in the long-term game is never in doubt. However much expense and effort are criticized, 'the chief executive who telephones Jacques Delors at the last moment, as he could in France, simply has not understood anything.' Alcatal-Alsthom, for example, sees itself as having escaped the problems of Bull and Thomson in the consumer electronics and semiconductor fields, by attuning itself expertly to Commission policy in telecoms and research projects, before the French government's turnabout in 1989.

While there is no French model, any more than there is a German model, French firms appeared to be modifying their strategies for influence in the last years of Mitterrand's Presidency, in order to rely slightly less on the state and rather more on their EU networks. The sense of competition, notably from British firms, and novel ideas from German ones, probably explains the tendency. There has been some recognition that they allowed their techniques to become backward in the protected political environment of the 1980s. Their networks relied too often on outdated political contacts or personal acquaintance with high officials, however professional the dossiers and legal backup.[12] Even professional bodies are not all represented in Brussels, and the Patronat (CNPF) maintains only a small office. This outlook is changing in the 1990s, but less markedly than in Germany; the British method of direct links to officials, using UK Representation, is believed to be more efficient and less likely to oversaturate Commission officials.[13]

3. In the nature of national rivalries, these observations are seldom reciprocated among British firms whose managers tend to complain of unfair continental practices and inadequate support from the Whitehall machine, whose defence of British interests is inevitably couched in a more complex, nuanced definition of what those interests are. Yet their networking skills are sufficiently distinctive, being closer in kind to the conventions built up for access to the British government since before the First World War, from those in France and Germany, which have been created since the Second. Like them, however, the balance in the search for influence between London and Brussels provides a permanent strategic dilemma.

A major British firm such as ICI is likely to have direct links to twice as many Westminster MPs as Strasbourg MEPs, but in Brussels, at any given time, ICI maintains up to 150 monitoring programmes on EU affairs, ranging from the establishment of norms to the technicalities of intellectual property legislation. Whether the cost impact of ever-more demanding EU regulations is contested directly or via the sector federation or the home government, depends on the industry's capacity to organize its own sector: in the majority of cases, an MNC will use both its own resources and those of the European federation, but in different ways to achieve a single end.[14] ICI is prepared to fight alone wherever its direct interests are at risk, as it did on the high price of electricity in Britain after privatization, and again when it helped to defeat a hostile bid from Hanson in May 1991 by arguing, with DG4 and European Parliament backing in Brussels, that this was not in the interests of the European-wide industry. If it wanted only to complain, it would probably rely on the federation to carry the can. ICI is careful about balances, not only between compliance with the Commission and defending its own interests but in behaving so as not to impair its aura of responsibility in the chemicals' Federation collective.

In complete contrast, GEC appears to have been reactive towards the European Union, rarely seeking to influence the Commission. Changes in the international environment and the question of mergers have at times brought the Commission into its focus, but GEC still has no office, no specific contacts, and a point of view in which Brussels remains 'peripheral'. Although this is not typical, many of the CBI's members only began to alter their decision-making processes in the later 1980s, despite the CBI's early and prolonged involvement in the European industrial project, including EMS and EMU. Their degree of physical presence in Brussels therefore remained small and specifically oriented – for example Glaxo's concern with EU regulation of the drugs industry. Distillers in the case of Scotch whisky and Guinness in the case of differential rates of excise tax on alcohol, defended themselves very directly, and from that basis the merged firm has developed a network for broad campaigns with French and German producers, including alliances with Grand Metropolitan and Allied Lyons, and links to the relevant member state governments. Despite having many MPs, and perhaps the European Parliament itself on its side, Guinness had to concede its main campaign in Brussels on discriminatory taxation; and Distillers lost its battle to preserve the duty free market after the year 2000.

Few British companies have deliberately assumed a European profile. Paradoxically, ICL's takeover by a Japanese company is generally explained by the attractions to an outsider investor of its decision to assume a high European profile, and to specialize in products of adaptable software and services for a wide range of member state governments and public bodies, and electronics industry partners in the Esprit consortium. But its mode of lobbying retains something which can be seen as 'Anglo-Saxon': it has excellent relations with the research-oriented DGs, is influential in DG3 and DG4 and also stood up, without suffering political damage, against DG13's desire to provide a sheltered Euro-telecoms regime.

4. Sketchy as this is, the outlines of French, German and British approaches to political persuasion can at least be distinguished from each other, if only by the way that executives of one set of national firms describe each other's methods. There may also be a fourth, Mediterranean mode. But if so, the exemplars are Portugal and Ireland, states whose governments have a primary interest in supporting their firms in winning whatever benefits the Community has to offer, from research programmes to funds for regional development. The suggestion is that Spanish firms tend to follow French examples, both in their mode of operation in Brussels and in the sort of assistance they seek from the Spanish state.

A number of Spanish firms have evidently been touched by the consequences of too close involvement with government – political interference, personal ambition and corruption – as have some of their Italian and French counterparts. Spain's domestic conditions in the mid-1990s, ravaged more by recession even than those of other member states, encouraged both MNCs and NFs to rely on the federations, the CEOE, and the Spanish Permanent Representation. All of them have suffered since 1990 from high interest rates and an overvalued currency in the ERM, and from high energy costs and exceptional labour market rigidities. This familiar litany is seen as remediable at the Brussels end only if the Madrid government continues its defence of Spanish firms and if the EU takes up more seriously the 1993 White Paper's proposals to regenerate industry and employment.

In practice, Spanish firms do not on the whole derive great help from their federations or from CEOE, leaving government to fill the gap (as the Industry Ministry itself laments).[15] Yet those, by their own reckoning, get little more help from government than does say the French CNPF or Italian Confindustria, because the Spanish government's EU coordinating system keeps all transactions under its own control.

5. Italian firms on the other hand, lacking continuous governmental backing over several decades, have developed a unique private enterprise system for influencing EU institutions, whose results have demonstrably benefited Italian MNCs rather than NFs or SMEs. The dense web of influence built up since the 1960s by firms like Fiat, Olivetti and the state concerns headed by IRI (the financial holding which includes Finmeccanica, Alitalia, Ilva, Stet, Finsiel, at least until long-postponed privatization arrives) includes every aspect of Community life and stretches out to the EU's eastern European programmes.

Giants such as Fiat have of course benefited from state assistance in the past, for example in the trade-off with Germany which ensured backing for Opel's new car plant in East Germany, in return for German support of Fiat's 65 billion ecu greenfield development at Malfi in Southern Italy. As a long-established competitor in Brussels, Fiat has an almost unparalleled range of networks which it can supplement by *actes gratuites* such as organizing conferences on urban transport pollution or restoration of the Palazzo Grassi in Venice. One of Fiat's more spectacular successes was to win a differential for car emissions tests as between high and low powered vehicles (having a strong interest in the latter) – only to see the European Parliament tighten up on that also.

Fiat, with its close links to the highest political circles in Rome, may be a unique case. Olivetti has habitually preferred to find out what the Commission's aims are, then to try to fit in with them rather than persuade it to change course. It presents itself as EU-compatible, one of the few MNCs able and willing to help the Commission to achieve whatever it wants as a matter of mutual bencfit. (This has in turn benefited its strategic research partners Groupe Bull and Siemens.) Others, such as the troubled agro-chemicals firm Ferruzzi, have generally relied on national federations' influence; even IRI, despite the vast extent of its holdings, has mainly required information from its Brussels office rather than advocacy. Its links with the majority of Directorates are close enough for it to have served as a useful interlocutor on behalf of the Italian state as far as the Commission is concerned; but it took so long to establish this presence that the returns are still barely visible.[16] IRI shares one characteristic with other Italian MNCs in relative decline such as Ilva (steel), Pirelli (tyres) and Olivetti; for all their size they remain Italian companies and show no sign of wishing to acquire a genuinely European identity. These have less lobbying power outside Italy than their public presence might suggest.

Lower down the scale, it seems probable that Italian firms have missed out on participating in several EU research and high-technology programmes and they still lack institutional access to the markets of eastern Europe. It is the research community's perception that other member states offer better networks and support, for want of which Italian firms and institutes have turned to private consultancies.[17]

6. Amongst smaller states, van Schendelen's evidence is that, at the informal level, Belgian, like French firms, maintain a very close identity of interest with their government: in Denmark, the state has a strong interest in building industrial coalitions on the grounds of economic and political cohesion. Within that general steer, Danish MNCs like Carlsberg go their own individual way. Conversely, in the Netherlands, companies have to rely on their own resources, much as they do in Britain.

Thus Philips' (NL) central office in Eindhoven is small, but crucial to corporate coordination of subsidiaries in France, Germany and elsewhere. Long-established contacts exist with virtually all the Directorates but are matched by the reliance of each component on its member state's Permanent Representation. Characteristic of the Netherlands' style, this sometimes makes it hard to decide whether to go direct to Brussels, or to use the relevant federation or UNICE. Much depends on the strength of the message and whether Philips wants it delivered neat or collectively packaged; knowing that on any major matter the Commission will in any case come to it, directly or via working groups. Philips presents itself as 'reliable, serious and constructive' towards the EU, never as difficult or specifically Dutch – and this sense feels akin to Eriksson (Sweden) and Nokia, following the concept of 'European identity'.

How well this mode can operate for a Dutch company was demonstrated by Shell Europe's response to the Shetland oil spillage in January 1993. Seeing that disaster would precipitate a European argument about tanker safety, the main board formulated a detailed paper in two weeks, prior to the European Parliament and Council debates, which the Commission, Council and MEPs received at the end of the same month. Since this was the only substantive paper then in front of the Council, the points were incorporated in the Commission's own paper – to which of course Shell was delighted to respond. When the main discussions took place on the European Parliament's Transport Committee in November, Shell Europe was the only firm to be invited to attend. On the other hand, Shell was much less successful over the Brent Spar oil rig disposal in 1995.

Firms are active players – invariably so at the MNC end of the spectrum – but not necessarily as their top priority all the time. They have a myriad range of ways to intervene or display their multiple identities, or to seek to exercise influence, and their campaigns resemble those of trench warfare of the First World War: long periods of low-key surveillance and monitoring followed by intensely fought battles, resulting in what are usually marginal gains.

Their conventions of behaviour are not merely appendages of the political market (as neo-classical economists might assert) but a substantive, even primary, force in it. This is not just a matter of lobbying (which ranks as one among several choices of strategy but tends to be over-emphasized by analysts approaching the question from the Brussels or Strasbourg end). Some firms choose to lobby while others, mindful of the disadvantages (such as the high costs, loss of direct control, exposure to misrepresentation and political risk), prefer to make their own alliances, and rely on their own networks; many do both according to need. As a general rule, the larger the firm, the greater the range of options and the more likely it is to rely on its own resources. SMEs can barely imagine such richness of choice.

But few firms wish to stand entirely alone. For a variety of reasons they also make alliances by sector – cars or chemicals, or if based outside the EU's country of origin, in the EC Committee of AmCham, as Japanese firms do in JAMA.[18] The conventions and rules of these associations are based on a mixture of commonalty, national and sectoral identity and the requirements of whichever EU context the association seeks to operate within. Whether in a highly concentrated sector like pharmaceuticals, or one as diverse as consumer electronics, patterns are therefore likely to resemble those already established by what firms do in relation to their national federations and national governments. MNCs' mutations from national to European champions do not necessarily involve significant ruptures with the recent past.

Nevertheless, the fact that virtually all MNCs belong to sectoral peak associations whose role it is to defend their (common) interest through creating a consensus on what that interest might be, leads to an element of analytical distortion, in that it is easier to discuss them collectively as 'chemical companies joined in EACEM' than to see them as distinct entities, even though the firm is usually the predominant influence, and the collective element small. It is certainly easier from the Commission's angle to measure the influence of a collective rather than a single firm, given that officials themselves tend to give priority to the association: being a representative body, it is easier to deal with than its chaos of competing members.

It is an error therefore, derived from a Brussels-centred outlook, to assume that firms that choose to play in the EU arena make themselves prisoners of that game, subject to a sort of regulation by EU institutions which would tend always to reduce the volume and diversity of their exchanges. Firms do not of course rule; they cannot abrogate a member state's sovereignty or the Commission's competences. But they need not act as subservient players unless it suits their managements to do so. That may have been the form taken in the early stages of the political market, when national governments could rely on firms' and federations' corporate bias to work in their favour; in Britain from the 1920s and 1930s up to the early 1970s, in France and Germany until the early 1980s. Since then, with its multipolar frame of reference, the MNC has generally become a global player, which can choose to exert itself in the EU dimension if it wishes. Even state firms and holding companies in the sheltered fields of civil aviation, telecoms or energy are now aware that this future impends.

The giant firms then hold influence. Influence is not the same thing as power but it does include holding part of the initiative, particularly when a firm's influence is maximized collectively in an efficient European federation. Both aspects were facilitated by the internal market, and the vested interests the Commission and member states had in it, which worked on the one hand to attract the firm but on the other gave the firm some indirect control over how the market's legal formulation and its informal construction would develop.

Entry to the EU game imposes a sense of interdependence. Where information exchange transactions with Commission officials (which comprise the largest single part of firms' activity) are concerned, even commercial firms have to accept an element of shared interest, akin to the EU altruism displayed by political players, which makes them that much more acceptable in officials' eyes. Commercial players are not equal, but from the Commission's standpoint their status is equivalent in the business of negotiating benefits and politically marketable trade-offs unless proved otherwise; and if they are accepted as permanent, they are rarely (if ever) denied access. It was an official of the French Trésor who pointed out the necessity 'never to beat anyone completely, but to give something to each participant in the game'.[19]

The same applies to sectoral federations whose justification to their own members is that they are accepted as worthy interlocutors by the bodies they seek to influence (influence, as claimed on their own estimates, being what ensures federations' future membership subscriptions). The mutations required of associations by what is essentially collaboration with the other side constitute their passport to a share in the functions of EC institutions, as in the purely national political market and, insofar as it exists, EU statehood.

On the other side, the Commission cannot cut itself off, being if anything more dependent on the expertise and detailed information about industries that firms provide than member states are in their own national spheres. But it is intrinsically harder to achieve policy unity across fifteen national economies. None of the Directorates concerned (that is those which actually deal with outside players: industry, competition, employment, transport, research, financial institutions) has enough officials or accumulated expertise to assess fully the problems of industries and markets before enunciating policy; neither do they have a member state government's unique political mandate to do so in a single national territory. Preliminary assessments and informal negotiations with firms about what exists, and what may be acceptable, give policies a better chance of success at chefs du cabinet and college level and, again, when Commissioners meet the other main channel of influence via member states in the Council, who are likely to object if their individual concerns have not been defused earlier, via the Commission route.

The process is open, well understood, discreetly conducted but unsecret. It is very widely seen as something without which EU institutions, rooted as they are in consensus politics, could not and should not proceed. The Commission in any case is bound to ask what will be acceptable to a hierarchy of majorities from chefs du cabinet up through the college to the Council. Officials have therefore to conduct their own complex diplomacy with firms and sectoral organizations without relinquishing their formal, if fictitious, autonomy. They have to contain and discipline the flux of firms seeking influence, without excluding any which really matter, without giving away so much as to lose the assent of others which are competitors, and without prejudicing the end product, a consensually agreed law or policy.

Numbers of competitors for influence however are so great, and have increased so dauntingly since the mid-1980s, that it suits officials to deal with federations in the first instance. It is normally easier to rely on the association to bring its members to a sense of collective advantage, albeit at the lowest common denominator, just as it is for any national government wishing to do the same thing. Afterwards, by referring to selected firms' representatives, officials can try to check that a sector's apparent consent actually represents the sum of its members' intentions, and whether rivalries have indeed been composed.[20] Directorates and officials can thus privilege certain interlocutors, the best regulated or most efficient federations (as measured in Brussels), yet can also constrain them by taking second options from selected leading members as they choose. This in turn not only shapes how many federations behave but induces among firms firstly a greater sense of collective action than might otherwise be the case and secondly a tendency always to keep open their private and singular networks, just in case the collective fails to produce what they most want.

In this game of exchange transactions, it can be almost impossible to work out who is using whom, even in apparently clear cases, as when firms' experts are nominated to serve on Commission working groups.[21] The answer may depend on the respondent's point of view about what is at stake. As one executive put it, 'it is necessary to convince the official dealing with the case at the Commission that one's employee is the expert in the field and would substantially contribute to the quality of the outcome.' Yet there is no necessary correlation between the numbers engaged and their success. The fact that dossiers are begun by individual, relatively junior Directorate officials who may then have to deal with senior executives of MNCs, says more about the transaction than the outcome.

Ideally, both sides' 'self-interest' coincides: both take home obvious gains, including the improvements made in recent years to the European federations themselves. But although a poorly articulated or divided federation creates delays, the Commission cannot ignore the realities of what exists; neither can it ignore a disaffected giant firm, of the size of Dresdner Bank, Crédit Lyonnais, Barclays, or Banesto in the financial sector; Bayer, Glaxo, or Rhône-Poulenc among chemicals companies.[22]

The balance of advantage ought not to be estimated by the relative numbers of policy initiatives which emanate from member states, Commissioners or firms. Few proposals come from the fedcrations and even fewer from individual firms (though some of those from member states may originate with them, having been transmitted via their national networking). Influence ought not to be measured only by identifiable proposals, any more than by the number of experts implanted or lobbyists employed. The firm's long-term influence may be directed towards creating an attitude of mind among officials, a predisposition towards a certain technology, or fuel, or standard, or even a recognition of one firm's status *vis-à-vis* another. In the EU's multilateral political community, goods are neither equivalent nor all traded on the same stall.

Apart from the question of who uses whom, it is worth asking whether the sum of these informal diplomacies inhibits the Commission or strengthens it *vis-à-vis* the Council and the Parliament. Again there are difficulties with published evidence: it is not in any firm's or federation's interest to claim too much, certainly not in public, nor in officials' interests to admit leverage of any sort. It is also, without a documentary base, intrinsically impossible for an outsider to adjudicate. On the basis of interviews, it appears that firms and federations reckon that no DGs can ignore their views for fear of having their opposition revived among MEPs and on the Council, and possibly also in Commissioners' Cabinets. If they are incorporated, the Commission's power is correspondingly increased at the Council level. Equally, officials claim that their views are ultimately in control both of the initiative – to which firms only respond – and the actual usage of their information.

Yet in a discourse of ten or fifteen years, the lines between become blurred. It suits everyone to have the basic issues sorted out as far as possible before interpretations or information set progressively harder, the further appraisals move up the ladder. In this sense, the exchange transaction serves to establish informal A points, in the manner of Coreper, which will normally not be challenged later. But this applies only to particular Directorates whose remit is open to commercial and industrial arguments, and which see their roles as seeking optimal (i.e., agreed) solutions to problems which are jointly defined. Where a sector performs badly or has reneged on earlier agreements, as in the reorganization of steel, textiles, and shipbuilding, the Commission may be far more prescriptive; but in areas where both sides have conformed, like pharmaceuticals or chemicals, much less.

For firms, such cooperation may imply a better deal than can be obtained, *seriatim*, with member state governments. Even in the late 1960s, Michel Debré, the French foreign minister, was to be found criticizing the appointment of firms' experts to Commission working groups, not because they gained commercial leverage but because they tended to deprive member states of sovereignty. At that time he was not wrong, through by the 1980s the language already seemed archaic. 'In the length and extreme technicality of these discussions, there is a language created between the participating experts, and ministers responsible are simply unable to follow the details. Once a proposition is made, it is extremely difficult to modify, because the Commission will refer to the working group conclusions. Technicality and language mean that the decision cannot easily be controlled [by member states] and the length of time means that few ministers are in power so long and thus cannot really influence its evolution.'[23]

The Commission has, in any case, its own transnational strategies. It could, for example on car emissions, fight one battle against the industry via Denmark, a member state with no car manufacturing capacity but with exceptionally high environmental standards which could be used to ratchet up the prescribed final norm. But the Commission in the end showed itself, if anything, subservient to the car and petrol industries' viewpoints to the exclusion of alternative and available technologies for the reduction of air pollution.

Whether the Commission in fact exercises its formal autonomy sufficiently to balance competing interests is something on which member states themselves can adjudicate later in the Council of Ministers. There is at present no abstract European interest which all players could acknowledge, and in that sense EU institutions cannot be held to constitute a proto-European state. Officials tend to set their sights lower: according to one Director General, the Commission's job is to be a broker to protect minorities from oppression by majorities ' . . .to champion the small firm, minority or member state cause and to ensure diversity',[24] that is, to fulfil the Treaty's aims of harmonizing economic opportunity and behaviour. Officials in all the Directorates with a sponsoring role and some others, even DG4, conceive of a guardianship mandate, according to which policies' effects but not their principles are tempered towards weaker participants on grounds of socio-economic coherence.[25]

The vast increase in these transactions since the 1970s has not only extended the Commission's engagement with the outside world but gone some way to justifying its claims to be more open and consensual than the member states grouped in the Council. The open, relatively unsecret role of policy mediator and policy-monger, even if neither is impartial nor democratic, now constitutes a large part of its Community legitimacy because it is what essential players need. It also reflects what member state governments do, but admit much less frequently in their own territorial contexts. Without this, arguably, one whole sector of the EU would revert to a Hobbesian war of each against all and the Commission itself would fragment, as one Directorate competed with another.[26]

These networks indicate to both Commission and member states what is generally acceptable, even if the process is not and cannot be made transparent. (Other than the publication of more Green Papers, transparency is a red herring here, for it suits neither side, and could be implemented only if everything were formalized, thus vitiating the entire purpose of the exchange. Transparency has been in practice transposed to the Parliamentary level.)[27] As one DG4 official put it, 'the Commission is a complex institution with a variety of missions and special interests. It is a guardian of the Treaties, but it also has a political responsibility, and every decision has to take account of the whole institution.'[28]

II. *Federations*

Whether membership is compulsory, as in Germany, or voluntary, as in Britain, all federations exist to provide a forum where firms or financial institutions which individually compete with each other can discuss matters affecting them all, and formulate policies either for their own use or to help them adjust to the outside world. National ones are made up of firms which self-evidently share an industrial and political culture. But even with that advantage, it is hard to get beyond the lowest common denominator, unless the body as a whole is internally disciplined – usually by a few dominant firms – or in the German case by a legal and customary framework which ensures access to *Land* and central government.

European federations have no such common culture but instead must blend the corporate interests and idiosyncrasies of fifteen sets of members. Whereas the national ones were formed in the context of the slowly evolving political relationships with governments and trade unions (and to a lesser extent the banking sector), often as long ago as the 1890s, the European federation has grown up much more recently to meet the needs of a Community which is itself still in evolution. National governments have known for nearly a century what they wanted of trade and employers' associations, and how they could best utilize their corporate bias to broker settlements with industrial sectors and a myriad individual firms. But European institutions competing among themselves are not agreed, as a national government is, on the shape of industrial trade and financial policies, even when these are contingent on the internal market.

This is only to say that the 'European federation' is not a standard quantity. What its politics will be depends partly on its membership, whether drawn only from national federations or including giant individual firms in their own right; on how many of the latter dominate each sector's political market, and how effectively these collectives relate to their principal interlocutor, the Commission. From the members' point of view, they exist to do what firms on their own could not: to bring the maximum influence to bear on the Directorates or, at a later stage, the Parliament, and to complement what national federations do in their own capitals. From the Commission side, they are the best perhaps the only way to aggregate a collective viewpoint amongst firms who are often triply antagonistic through competition on industrial, national and even ideological levels.

MNCs' claims to direct membership complicate the issue for

some European federations, although not for the Commission, which welcomes their inclusion. Their intention is usually to free themselves from the constraints of national forums, especially if, as with the German Verbände, a substantial formal role is given to smaller players in the industry. In effect MNCs may be able to break out of an imposed regime, which may be more democratic than they wish, to form a more congenial political cartel which allows them to control the high-level bridge to EU institutions. That some national federations resent this advantage is clear: the German VDA (car industry federation) is aware of the Commission's 'strong preference for talking to European federations',[29] and concludes that what the latter hears is not the true cross-section of opinion in the industry but only the voice of MNCs. As a general rule, resolution of intra-sectoral conflicts takes place at this sectoral level and if not in national then in European federations; it certainly does not take place in the over- arching bodies such as UNICE which many officials regard as 'too gentlemanly' in its search for consensus.[30]

Brokerage at this level does not necessarily produce a harmonious result, as the car industry federation's saga (see p. 471) demonstrates. But the fact that it usually occurs in this way, and that the tendency is to move from informality to gradually more structured relationships with the Commission, suggests that the collective behaviour of giant firms has generally been successful since the 1980s in establishing in the Community the same sort of processes, on an even wider range, that are available in the modern nation state. The existence of what should properly be called an industrial system may then indicate that the EU has acquired another important element of informal statehood.

European federations should be clearly distinguished from other players such as the ERT or EEG, whose members are drawn as individuals from many sectors, and whose proselytizing activity covers a broader range of issues. For all its influence at certain historical points, ERT does not have the function of concerting sectoral policy, nor directly negotiating with specialist departments in the Commission.[31]

They are also different from the highly effective, closely integrated associations of firms which originally operated from national bases outside the Community, but in the case of the American Chamber of Commerce (AmCham) have very much become European concerns since the 1960s. AmCham's European Committee, which in 1993 contained eighty MNCs of the standing of ITT, IBM, General Electric, General Motors, Colegate Palmolive, and their European subsidiaries, has always been a notable player with a long history of success, ranging from combating the Vredeling Directive to advancing telecoms deregulation.

AmCham's experience has not been directly replicated elsewhere, for Japanese companies have in general chosen to join the European federations, for example EACEM, when they were allowed to, although in some sectors such as automobiles they maintain their own organization JAMA, and EIAJ for consumer electronics. But the Japanese have no over-arching body; neither have the Korean *chaebols*, Samsung and Daewoo, which spectacularly, perhaps injudiciously, entered the European markets in the 1990s. Whichever way they chose, for most purposes American companies with a European base have become European, and the same appears to be becoming the case with Japanese ones, given their promotion of European managers and adoption of European techniques in this political sphere. But to some eyes, in France especially, even the long-settled Americans are still too aggressive, too 'Anglo-Saxon' in their lobbying techniques to count as proper Europeans.

A list of European federations is otiose without some form of evaluation. From the point of view of both sides in the bargaining process, their political significance lies in the efficiency of the exchange transaction, and on that basis they can very broadly be categorized as coherent/centralized or less-coherent/competitive. Although Commission officials retain freedom to sift what they offer and to go behind their backs to individual firms, they naturally prefer ones which come with solutions rather than problems and do not behave like warring samurai.[32]

In assessing European federations, CEFIC representing chemicals firms and EFPIA the pharmaceuticals industry may be taken to characterize the coherent, Commission-preferred model; EACEM (consumer electronics) ORGALIME (telecoms) and ACEA (automobiles) the competitive, less-coherent ones.

CEFIC (CHEMICALS)

The collective diplomacy of a handful of giant firms is not intrinsically different from the way in which Dupont, ICI and IG Farben operated in the interwar years; IG Farben's post-War break-up into Hoechst, BASF and Bayer has served mainly to increase the German weighting. All were predisposed to cartels, at least until the Commission's insistence and tough competition policy in the late 1980s; all envisaged the EU as a single market well in advance of 1986. Each has close links with its member state on every major Commission policy from mergers and joint ventures to external trade.

Up to 1985, national federations predominated, but in that year, prior to the Single European Act, John Harvey-Jones of ICI, with German support, instituted firms' direct membership of CEFIC, including American companies. CEFIC then became the basis for a diplomacy extending far beyond the EC into 'wider Europe', former communist states and Turkey. Its aims have been to safeguard the EU's liberal trade regime and to retain the maximum power to regulate themselves. CEFIC cannot direct its members, but relies on peer group pressure to keep the wayward ones in line – most of whom prefer in any case to keep disagreements private and to shun publicity. So far, the federation has hung together (and collectivity has been reinforced by public and environmental groups' hostility to chemicals companies in general). It is well served by a large staff and array of committees and working groups, and is one of the very few federations which is careful to cultivate close links with all the Permanent Representatives and the Council.

It is hardly surprising, therefore, that DG3 officials welcome the result: 'Industry and the players are the best judges . . . which fits the current ethos of non-interventionism.'[33] Although they approach the multinationals like ICI at least as often as the national federations, the industry as a whole is seen, in typical sponsorship terms, as a good ally, somewhat prone to protectionism, which needs political protection against the media exposure and prejudice which flourish, for example, in the European Parliament. From such a basis of mutual understanding, it is easy to construct a thesis about living together in order to ameliorate external political realities. Officials normally (and normatively) talk only to CEFIC on general policy planning. National federations, even in Germany, are subsumed in this pattern, but it is not pretended that the MNCs concerned are European, rather 'international, with a European focus'.[34]

EFPIA (PHARMACEUTICALS)

In this very technical area of highly concentrated firms, negotiated settlements habitually take place at both national and EU level, in a framework of regulation which is policed on both levels by self-regulating players acting in a sort of policy partnership with member states and the European Union. From the Commission's point of view, it is the giant firm that matters, not the federation, which is expected to shape itself to members' requirements. Six MNCs predominate – two German, two British, one French, one Italian – in a multinational governance which happens to fit the EU context of supervision and codes of practice. EFPIA was created specifically by these six to bargain with the EC's institutions over the precise forms of regulation and self-regulation compatible for example with the Commission's drug information policy, harmonization, pricing or patent law.

There can be no better example of how the giants can collectively formulate for the Community a European interest, ranging from testing drugs to pricing or control of marketing authorization. EFPIA has been successful in every case, firstly because the Commission cannot envisage acting without them and, secondly, because of the enormous technical capacity it has to put its members' case efficiently, often against American and Japanese competitors. Here at least, Eurocorporatism, benefiting giant firms at the expense of smaller national ones, has manifestly overtaken member state sovereignty, for EFPIA has become an agency in its own right, its weight beyond the sum of the individual firms which compose it.[35]

EACEM (CONSUMER ELECTRONICS)

As Alan Cawson has argued,[36] the European firms which were still producers in this area in the 1970s first fragmented and then largely capitulated to American and Japanese competition. EACEM's original, long-standing intention has therefore been to mobilize a European front to face increased foreign competition. Yet this industry is one (unlike pharmaceuticals) where coordination is difficult save amongst medium-sized national firms. A hypothetical European policy may be aimed at deciding how the industry should evolve, but the firms themselves have constantly been undermined by global competition. For lack of firms' own competitiveness, the federation's strength has been limited, despite its MNCs' monopoly power (for which the federation serves as a veil) and despite the support of member state governments, employing a series of protective devices to limit foreign penetration.

After the loss of its own producer base during the 1980s, Britain's openness to foreign investment led to Japanese producers' dominance by 1987. France tried to protect Thomson with quotas and restrictions on foreign investment. The leading German firms, Grundig and Siemens, merged defensively with Philips, Thomson or Nokia (Finland). Meanwhile Japanese firms won virtually the entire market in VHS and entered EACEM as European producers, thus helping to transform an association of ever-fewer MNCs into an EU-wide group of giants, each with its own national federation. Of the latter, only the German ZVEI, which in response to Bonn's professed trade liberalism deplores what the others do, stands out as more than a postbox between firms and their national governments.[37]

EACEM's main function was to give cover for the operations of Philips and Thomson, and other producers' requests for indirect support, in order to maintain a European presence *vis-à-vis* the Japanese producers. The latter, now that they were association members, had to concur for the sake of keeping their long-term political low profile, because their principal interest (expressed through EIAJ, based in Dusseldorf since 1962), has been to seek a

Japanese presence on the EU's sponsored research projects – until now without success.

Sectoral governance in electronics implies a tacit agreement not to compete *à l'outrance*, which is currently facilitated by Japanese firms' connivance in a strange ritual whereby they 'complain of anti-dumping by themselves'. Each European firm retains some peer group influence over what others do, and the majority still enjoy some support from member state governments who share their preoccupation with national producers. But as the HDTV case illustrates (see chapter 12), it now appears that Japanese producers are abandoning the good behaviour which once ensured their entry in favour of steadily rising producer demands. Whether EACEM can maximize its influence at each level in order to nullify this latest danger is unclear.

ORGALIME (TELECOMS)

Until the late 1980s, national federations dominated this sector, but with the era of liberalization inspired first in the United States, then in Britain, came a slow erosion of extensive public control, and the cartelization of the equipment and services markets. New technology and aggressive competition in privatized systems spurred a continuing revolution in which consumer demand matched the novel politics of deregulation. Led by the German ZVEI, the national federations began a process of mergers which culminated around 1990 with the creation of a pyramid linking a much smaller number in each member state to the European apex, ORGALIME. Despite this administrative rationalization, much of the original cartel mentality survived and has been, if anything, reinforced by the inclusion of former EFTA members.

In a producer-dominated organization, no firm below the stature of MNC appears to have influence and the pyramid, though plural, positively discourages pluralism. Insofar as firms compete in the political market, they do so in a form prescribed informally by their own governments. Commission officials have little say, given member states' resistance to the general policy of deregulation and liberal trade. Commercial competition, with the exception of already-privatized systems such as British Telecom, is still limited by the political balance of advantage, and although this will presumably no longer be the case in the late 1990s when full liberalization has taken place, the highly structured proposals for alliances made *inter alia* by France Télécom, Deutsche Telekom, Telefonica and SIP suggest that advantage will continue to lie in firms' own networks, backed by government interests, of which the national federations and ORGALIME are merely collective representations.

ACEA (CAR PRODUCERS)

By any reckoning, ACEA is a special case, because those member states which have national producers retain a lively interest not only in their competitiveness but in their status as European champions. (Their combined resistance to Japanese competition is considered in chapter 12.) Two separate European federations existed in the Community's middle years, CLCA (a group of seven national federations) and CCMC (formed in 1972 of the main individual producers, concerned then above all with American competition). These two successfully negotiated a voluntary restrictive agreement with Japan in 1981, but cooperation between them ceased when Japanese producers became members of the more politically salient CCMC. In the era of the GATT Uruguay round and the internal market, car producers' ill-assorted, fitfully antagonistic forums degenerated, making it hard for the many Directorates with an interest in this sector to deal with them comfortably,[38] not least because the producers in CCMC exploited this interest, with the effect of confusing the Commission if not actually dividing it.[39] Sectoral unity was further prejudiced by the behaviour of car firms' chairmen, some of whom had political ambitions, all of whom were portrayed in the media as 'heroes of industry'. Prima donnas of the early 1990s like Kurt Hahn (VW), Jacques Calvet (PSA, Peugeot Citröen), Gianni Agnelli (Fiat), and Raymond Levy (Renault) were always able to call on a Director General in person to obtain satisfaction,[40] unlike their British counterparts who had watched the dismemberment of British Leyland and the recovery of Rover only as a smaller player in the 1980s. Neither CLCA nor CCMC, overwhelmed by the internal market, was able to accommodate the bewildering new situation in which Japanese producers ensconced in Britain became, as American ones Ford and General Motors had long been, EU producers.

Habituated as they were to bargaining directly in Brussels, using their national federations rather than the European ones as a suitable cover for what was in effect member states' game-play, the producers suddenly found the Commission unreceptive, since the main outcome of the internal market was its need for a more efficient European federation with whom to negotiate. Yet the producers' alliances had become so entrenched and hostile that neither side could reach an accommodation. The technical issue was clear enough: with the advent of the single market and the Commission's monopoly of foreign commercial policy, national import restrictions, mainly on Japanese cars, had to be abolished. No one imagined that this would happen immediately. But if a period of transition were to be negotiated (necessarily on an informal basis, since the legal position of Article 113 of the SEA was clear), the Commission as sole negotiator with Japan had to have a federation with which the twelve relevant Directorates could do business, free of the interference of member state governments.

In these circumstances, in 1990, CCMC collapsed under the clear threat that if they did not find an alternative the Commission would arrange a voluntary export restraint deal itself. In effect, the heads of the major producers reformed it under the new title of ACEA, excluding PSA (Peugeot-Citröen), whose eccentric chairman Jacques Calvet sought by a de Gaulle-style veto to prevent the Commission from negotiating a general settlement. Since its refoundation in February 1991, ACEA has permitted American companies, but not Japanese ones, to have individual membership. This new format[41] has so far been able to work with the Commission, for the first time in a decade; and it took part in the second agreement with Japan (see p. 575).

ACEA now operates closer to what can be seen as the European federation form, the umbrella concept of the 'general benefit of manufacturers', which is apparently a matter of relief in Brussels.[42] It is headed by the five activist producers – Ford, Renault, Fiat, VW, and Daimler-Benz – who normally set the agenda, helped by the introduction of majority voting. In this way, what is to be the European interest is devised, according to the collective interest of a still-beleaguered group. It helps that the Japanese agreement has been settled, though the terminal date is still uncertain, and that ACEA can concentrate on slightly less divisive issues of traffic management, transport pollution, and recycling of used vehicles – where media exposure and hostility induce a certain sense of collective identity. The giants still have their private networks and routes to Brussels, but there is some evidence that smaller producers have vested more political capital in ACEA since 1992.[43]

III. Banking and Financial Services

Because there is no intrinsic difference between the *political* behaviour of firms in the various financial and service sectors and those in industry, there is no need to do more than focus on their leading characteristics. The financial players across Europe, apart from central bankers, became aware surprisingly late in the day how the internal market was likely to affect them. With a handful of exceptions, banks, insurance companies and stock exchanges took little part in the agitation for the single market and in most member states: the time lag between the Act in 1986 and active awareness could be measured in years rather than months.[44] In mitigation, it can be argued that each financial market was already adjusting to massive changes which had been occurring since the early 1980s in the global climate of regulation and supervision, and to equally vast technological changes which initially benefited the centres in the triangle London, New York and Tokyo rather than those of continental Europe. A disposition in continental Europe to divide the world into European and Anglo-Saxon varieties of financial behaviour long predated the Single European Act. But differences between these markets and within them on national lines also related to the different policies of member state governments and their central banks, acting as supervisors and regulators.

After the mid-1980s, financial players had to adjust to a Commission-led set of proposals intended to extend to all financial markets the freedoms of establishment, offer of services and capital mobility. These implied a common regulatory regime or regimes for each, within an overall policy of modernizing backward areas to ensure their harmonization and competitiveness *vis-à-vis* the outside world. As was the case with the various sectors of industry and services, markets differed widely. In the financial sphere, some were so technically complex, so driven by technology and globalization as to preclude the evolution of a distinct EU regime. Other issues, such as the survival of only a small number of stock exchanges, raised similar problems to those faced by industry of managed adjustment within the limits that member states could permit.

Lack of technical knowledge in financial restructuring of banks, valuation of assets, fiduciary principles, or the definition of large and small risks and accountability, would have forced Commission officials to engage closely with financial players when working out what was to be done, even if the policy-making period after 1988 had not coincided with a major world recession and the over-exposure or failure of significant institutions such as BCCI, Banesto, and Crédit Lyonnais. In a quite different way from industry, the categories within which policy was discussed were decided either between central bankers in Basel, acting in conjunction with their national Treasuries, or by the professional advisers to both sides, financial players and the Commission.[45]

The variety of firms makes generalization almost impossible; investment banks, facing true international competition, have to be distinguished from commercial or retail banks, still largely integrated into their national contexts, however much they had already engaged in what were usually seen as foreign markets by 1990. This was certainly true for French, Italian, Belgian and Spanish banks, though less so for British and German ones, and less again for particular giants like Deutsche, Dresdner, Barclays, NatWest and Crédit Lyonnais. Not until the mid-1990s did predominantly national or regional banks like the Bank of Scotland or Banco de Santander conceive of Europe as their market.

The Commission's concerns expressed themselves *seriatim* and usually as reactions to external events, depending only partly on their plans predating the Single Act. Since it was officials' and Commissioners' habit to work with the grain, the choice of instruments depended more on which sectors were being or had already been opened up by international competition and deregulation. Banking supervision, capital ratios and the whole range of investment services had priority: insurance markets and stock exchanges were to come later. But this agenda was always liable to be disrupted by a major court case at the ECJ, or a world-wide scandal such as BCCI, or consumer groups' outcry against high rates of charges for banks' cross-border transactions.

Generally, the Commission (mainly DG15), preferred the sector organizations such as the European Banking Federation (FBE) to handle the negotiations. Those which were well integrated, harmonious and able to deal with American and Japanese competitors, performed well, not least because it was in the interest of every government, Treasury and Central Bank that they should. Indeed, on many of the key legislative items, member states habitually acted as brokers through their representatives on the Committee of Central Bank Governors (though not in Germany), sometimes with the assistance of the Bank of International Settlements, during the five years after 1988. This ensured a degree of liberalization and modernization on one hand, while exercising restraint on the Commission from going (as they measured it) 'too far'.

These comfortable arrangements were increasingly prejudiced from two different aspects. Firstly, in all the markets, players had to confront deep differences of practice, commercial judgment and the national legal environment between different traditions, such as between German 'universal banks' and the Anglo-Saxon tradition of segmented services. Secondly, although DG15 retained responsibility for producing the legal texts, DG4, the centre of competition activity, also had a substantial interest. DG15 had already run up against several member states on the questions of insurance regulation and banks' 'single passports'. The trend in competition law (set by the ECJ, as DG4 wished, in the *Flemish Travel Agencies* case 1987) put all pre-existing restrictive agreements at risk and allowed DG4 to examine long-ignored cartels such as banks' interest rates, or their cross-border charges. But whether it did so or not depended on the political conjuncture at the time; in effect, whether the Commission could persuade a majority of member states that the time was right.[46]

Cross-border mergers between financial institutions also brought governments into the arena of competition and merger law. But because of the absence of intensive concentration, and the failure of many cross-border banking mergers attempted since the early 1990s,[47] the considerations which caused so much conflict between DG4 and particular member states in industrial corporate behaviour have not occurred. Member states appear to have contented themselves with indirect lines of defence, in protecting their very divergent financial market practices, until the process of adjustment has been completed; and this probably explains why the FBE has been more mistrustful of Commission initiatives than Europe's industrial federations, which have had to live with officials and Directorates much longer.[48]

Of course the long trend is towards complete liberalization, to which insurance and stock markets must succumb, as banks have done, for global reasons. As one Paribas respondent said, 'the closed protective market has vanished', leaving only vestiges in local markets.[49] Merchant, clearing or investment banks, whatever their chosen centres (London being substantially higher in the pecking order than Paris or Frankfurt), reorganized themselves circa 1988 to meet the challenges of information technology and global competition. Some chose to specialize, say, in private banking or capital markets, others, such as Dresdner Bank, to confront the great question of how to become a truly universal bank, and follow Deutsche Bank's lead in Britain, Italy and Spain (but eschewing the Crédit Lyonnais pattern) because medium-sized investment banks cannot survive in the current economic environment.[50] Deutsche Bank has been trying to buy a French bank for the last fifteen years and has been refused entry subtly by the French banks and authorities, although they own Morgan Grenfell in London and the Banco Italo-Americano in Italy. Dresdner was also rumoured to want to buy a genuine investment bank in London: in summer 1995, it made an offer for Kleinwort Benson.

The Commission's job was not to interfere with this induced adjustment but to ensure that all its facets were subjected to Single

European Market legal and supervisory regimes and to try to harmonize it (in the sense that backward sectors and local financial institutions should benefit and follow suit, rather than suffer the terminal consequences of immediate and unrestricted competition). In this sense, whereas national banks and their federations acted in pure self-interest with their own survival in mind, member govern-. ments, and in particular their Treasuries and Central Banks sought to maintain sufficient control to guarantee that the outcome would suit their own financial traditions and legal systems.

This was easier in some countries than in others. Despite their size in the FBE, French banks belonging to the national federation ABF have until now had a relatively weak voice, partly for lack of political focus, partly because of being – broadly speaking – under government *tutelle*. As a result, they have tended to rely heavily for support and advice on the Paris Trésor. The cataclysmic over-expansion of Crédit Lyonnais revealed in 1995 how government interference could lead them wide of the market; yet only Paribas, Indo-Suez and BNP are privatized. French banks still often use lobbyists, but there is no 'club atmosphere' among them as there is in Britain, and no concerted strategies as there are in Germany. As one French executive put it, 'The British and the Germans are beyond measure more serious than the French, who could be compared with Asterix and Obelix before the Roman armies!'[51]

This judgment is borne out by the fact that German and British banks appear resigned to a very slow erosion of other continental member states' barriers to takeovers, or the opening up of insurance markets, and assume that London markets' continued competitiveness (for example, in attracting one-third of the entire EU's Forex business) is a better solvent of protectionism than lobbying officials who mostly share their free trade concerns but are hamstrung by the Council of Ministers.

What the leading banks – Deutsche and Dresdner, Barclays and NatWest (not Lloyds, an early innovator in the 1970s which had largely withdrawn from EC markets, or Midland which restricted itself to those in wholesale banking) – do through their direct links with national permanent representations and DG15, in preference to national banking federations,[52] shapes the Commission's policy as much as does the legislative framework. A division by size and function between the largest banks acting alone, those grouped in strategic alliances, and the regional or specialized players such as Paribas, BHF and CCF, appears to be coming into effect as the result not of EU policy but of what the players themselves have judged appropriate. Deutsche Bank has certainly reoriented itself within the EC free market tradition set by Hermann Abs, standing ahead of its German counterparts.[53]

Germany's smaller and private banks, on the other hand, suffer under an overprotective state regime which threatens to make them uncompetitive. Partly because of its all-embracing formal role, the German Bankers Federation appears weak, isolated in the FBE, and late to establish itself in Brussels.[54] These conditions are similar to those which compelled industrial leaders to break out of the existing formal framework, even if that still adequately balances the small against the large in Germany itself. The three leading banks – Deutsche, Dresdner and Commerzbank – have all developed a full European array of direct representation and informal influence at all levels in Brussels. As with insurance firms, where the national federation (HGDV) works best for medium-sized national companies, the leaders find their own ways on issues such as consumer protection, liability and the regulatory regime for financial conglomerates. The German domestic structure of representation is so different from those of other member states that on these issues the German state is frequently in a minority[55] and risks remaining at a disadvantage *vis-à-vis* others, France or Italy or Spain, which are changing much faster. Competition with Luxembourg (which enables depositors to avoid German withholding tax) is often cited. From this dilemma, only the big three banks can easily escape, and then only if they transfer part of their centre of gravity outside Germany itself.

In these circumstances, it is not surprising that the view that British players 'seem almost instinctively to understand the importance of the Commission in this field', is widely shared in Brussels, as is the opinion that it can be explained by the superior advocacy of British legal and accountancy firms. Anglo-Saxon methods are suspected of having much to do with relative success and French ones with the relative lack of it among French banks.[56]

In Italy, in contrast to London where liberalization began in 1969–70, banks laboured until 1989 under the state's political control, 'a culture of administration, with the Banca d'Italia running monetary policy by telephone', accompanied by a regime of exceedingly high interest rates which, far from being vulnerable to competition, allowed foreign banks to take advantage of it and rebuild their profits in Italy.

The larger Italian banks such as Credito Italiano, Banca Commerciale and Banca di Roma have had representatives in Brussels for years and have been joined by others such as Monte dei Paschi di Siena. Even smaller regional banks have their own representatives, with the aim of monitoring EU activity and gleaning information which will enable them to act as intermediaries between the Commission and the national administration.[57] In Spain, on the other hand, where the Central Bank played a stronger liberalizing and active modernizing role *vis-à-vis* both finance and industry than did the Banca d'Italia, a small number of banks emerged as modernizers in the 1980s, headed by the Banco Bilbao-Vizcaya (headed by Sanchez Asiain) and Banco Popular. Some Catalan and Basque savings banks also took a leading local part.

Liberalization began after the banking crisis of 1978, in the most radical form adopted by any Mediterranean state[58] and swept away the remnants of Franco's obsolete, over-regulated and dilatory banking system. Foreign banks surged in. Over a period of ten years, culminating with the liberalization of interest rates and bank commissions in 1987, the Central Bank's intervention slowly tapered off: the ratio of compulsory deposits held by the Banco de España fell from 17% in 1990 to 2% by early 1995. On the debit side, the process had severe side effects. How much of the scandals associated principally with Banesto is due to laxity of supervision and how much to the opportunities for individuals, even high up in the Central Bank itself, to enrich themselves from a still not wholly reformed political system, is unclear; but the Spanish experience suggests that very rapid market evolution can only be contained, as it was in Britain, within a highly developed structure where informal conventions complement the formal processes and rules.

With the exceptions of Britain, Germany and the Netherlands, national financial sector federations are generally lacking in independence, formalized and attuned primarily to the requirements of their member state governments. None of the federations has offices in Brussels because, in the opinion of one French member, this would have led to competition between them dangerous to their fragile harmony in the FBE.[59] In smaller states such as Ireland, Portugal and Greece, the national federation's role is barely more than that of an intermediary between domestic, often nationalistic and usually protectionist outlooks. The British Bankers Association, in contrast, sees itself as an interpreter of the banking interest, in conjunction with the Bank of England and the Treasury, as to how the national sector, secure already in the paths of self-regulation, can be kept competitive. Larger banks among its 327 members, however, reserve their own freedom of action just as much as do their German counterparts.[60]

This cleavage between national sectors which have reacted most quickly to global developments and the freedom of the internal market and those which have not, seems to likely in the future to inhibit the phenomenon of 'continental alliances' against London. Most of those interviewed here admitted that British financial institutions still perform better, save on mergers and takeovers where German, French and Italian ones run level. But since clients have to go to London and speak English, some argue that the British err, and forget that in the end 'all business is local'.[61] Much depends on the future direction adopted by American banks and Japanese finance houses such as Nomura, which began in 1993–4 to scale down their operations in London in order to relocate in Germany. Looking into a confused future, it seems that only two forecasts can be made: that concertation would continue among financial institutions, thus reducing the national federations ultimately to shadows; and that the largest German players, though fully international, would retain a German identity, unlike their

British counterparts; therefore the German representational system could continue to have real political meaning.

The European Banking Federation's recent history has, not surprisingly, been ravaged as a result, by conflicts between its national federation members whose natural tendency is to go their own rival ways in secrecy. But it has also been affected by the Commission's attempts to harmonize the banking regimes without unduly exposing whole sectors in the more backward member states to penetration by American and Japanese competitors or to takeovers by the European giants. On the FBE's admission, roughly three-quarters of its members accept the Commission's right to do this in the interest of the European Union and its citizens, but a quarter do not. DG15 has therefore to work with the majority in order both to define the Community's optimum policy and limit the dissidents' capacity to prevent it.[62]

The FBE, a body which in the 1950s and 1960s had been ill-articulated, meeting only rarely in a Brussels office lent by the Belgian Bankers Association, grew around the time of British entry in the 1970s, but remained reactive, not least because before 1985 the Commission produced only one Directive on Banking. The coming of the internal market changed everything, bringing clashes between FBE and Commission over the second Directive, at a time of intensive competition between banks at national federation level. In drafting the SEA White Paper, Arthur Cockfield and DG15 seemed determined to flush out and modernize long-sheltered protected zones, in the interest of European industry and finance; the FBE could either react or see the banking interest overridden. But it was only able to win the consent of a majority of its member federations by constructing an argument that cooperation with the Commission was the only way to get legislation acceptable to them all.

The Commission needed the banking sector's expertise, but was itself divided between DG3's desire to oversee an increase in bank mergers, the better to face external competition, and DG4's concern that the results would concentrate market share too much, which were expressed in the Société Générale de Belgique case.

The fact that Delors emphasized, largely for political reasons, systemic abuses such as the high costs of cross-border money transfers, and the Eurocard case, together with DG4's attempt to turn consumers' associations against them, created deep hostility. Meanwhile the Commission's refusal to prescribe equally severe regulatory treatment for banks and 'non-banks' put the FBE at a disadvantage, seen by its members as unable to exercise effective influence on an issue of overriding importance to bank members (who regarded themselves as labouring under a substantial disadvantage).

The larger banks and bankers associations turned to their central banks (as they had done in the wake of the 1974 liquidity crisis). Governors responded, being sensitive to the national interests involved, and their intervention (being directed against the non-banks based in their own national territories) appears to have weighed heavily with DG15 and the college when making revisions to the second Bank Directive.

Credit belonged chiefly to Central Banks, but the affair helped to re-establish the FBE, which subsequently developed a rather more cerebral form of argument in the late 1980s, based on deeply researched dossiers, in order to re-establish itself as an acceptable coadjutor in DG15's requirements. From 1988 the FBE included representatives from the EFTA countries, then negotiating the European Economic Area, and from 1992 the four 'Visegrad' applicants in eastern Europe. It became clear that it worked best when trying to influence early stages of broad framework legislation, rather than later, at the stage of detailed texts which only aroused old internal rivalries – and in this sense *did* shape the Commission's technical approach. But it was also responsible, after a long British rearguard action, for resolving an old internal dispute between the largest banks as international competitors, and member state banking federations over the second Directive's reciprocity Clauses directed against American banks.[63] Later on, the FBE became a minor interlocutor during the Maastricht-EMU IGC, which raised its status as an expert negotiator *vis-à-vis* the Governors' Committee (for neither Cockfield nor Cecchini had examined the costs of a common currency).

The FBE's connection with member state governments, Central Bankers in Basel and officials in Brussels, and its enhanced capacity to assemble an agreed view, slowly overcame its earlier handicap that nothing could be decided without the consent of the largest national federations. It became trusted in Brussels to the point that individual large banks could reduce their offices' role to technical matters; in such a highly political arena, this could only have been achieved by a demonstration that it really did have influence, not by any assertion of FBE 'leadership'.

Whether its current status will suffice to keep all the rival entities in some sort of harmony as the internal market is actually implemented is another matter. The FBE was able to be helpful in resolving differences in deposit protection between financial centres (near-unlimited in Germany, £100,000 limit in Italy, only £15,000 in Britain) at 20,000 ecus; but at a level which some members regarded as capitulation to the City of London. These are much more important matters than cultural or national differentials because the public interest in regulating financial markets and ensuring their global competitiveness extends far beyond the EC. But national self-interest and the interests of the largest banks still clash; it is the pace of technological change that has brought DG15 into closer alignment with DGs 2, 4 and 13, which now pool their expertise and their links with the national federations and the FBE, thus contributing in the mid-1990s to an interchange which is 'quasi-collegial, quasi-competitive, but never hostile'.[64]

The national federations in the insurance sector are still too diverse to permit such a game to be played out on the EU table, though DG15, speaking for the Commission, would like to be able to do so. Instead, it consults with the principal players, whatever their country of origin.[65] The Federation of Stock Exchanges is in a different position, for its members have experienced attrition for nearly a decade, since Big Bang occurred in the City of London in 1983. Falling numbers of exchanges, especially in member states' peripheries, have ensured that the European Federation cannot possibly move faster than member state governments themselves permit, even if it wished them to integrate more effectively, in the pattern set by Glasgow and Lyons stock exchanges, which are now both parts of integrated national systems.

Instead, disparities actually increased during the 1990s recession, for each German *Land* still possesses its own stock exchange, effectively as part of the local banking system (even if these are now slowly being squeezed out by the three largest, Frankfurt, Düsseldorf and Munich). Elsewhere, in France, Italy, Spain and Belgium, the state remains the regulator, disposed to protect its own, for example by objections to the 1991 cross-border stockbroker draft Directive which would have given firms licensed to trade in securities in one state a passport to do so in the rest. The Commission's Investment Services Directive left regulation to member states. Meanwhile, the exchanges themselves have become commercial bodies, competing internationally for business, while still defending an element of national territory.[66] In the long term this can work only in favour of London, Paris and Frankfurt, the more that cross-border dealing occurs on London's SEAQ International or among international bond dealers.

The Stock Exchanges Federation resembles ACEA, being reconstructed in response to global requirements, whatever weaker or discontented members might wish. On its own, it is incapable of facing the international question of what a member state-based stock exchange is for: the number of stock exchanges is in long-term decline unless each one can attract trading in worldwide stocks. It is not the Commission which imposes a regime of international efficiency and lower costs, but another triangle, that of London, New York and Tokyo. Hence the Federation has no choice but to cooperate with the Commission, to induce modernization by whatever means are possible and acceptable to member states. The alternative is extinction, because whatever member states do to defend their own, there can be no cartel or subsidies solutions, given the 'grey market' on the fringes.

In their arcane complexity and speed of technological change, the financial sectors differ generically from industrial ones. Large players also have a recourse to Central Banks and member state governments which is rarely available to industrial and commercial firms, except in favoured sectors such as defence and among state holdings. National federations are therefore likely to be congenitally weak compared to giant banks or institutions on one hand and European federations on the other, who have some leverage in Basel as well as Brussels, and in the Groups of Five or Ten as well as the European Union.

There is no strict equivalence between markets, or between the bargaining powers of federations which represent their players. Only the FBE has achieved something close to bargaining rights with the Commission; in the stock exchange arena, the game lies almost entirely between member states and Commission. What will evolve in the insurance market and among the as yet unexplored area of building societies and pension funds is not yet clear.

More even than the industrial and service sectors, finance is an international arena, and it is impossible for a member state or even the Commission to isolate a given geographical area within a distinct regulatory or protective cocoon. Players themselves know this, and insofar as they do not accept it – like the stock exchanges in Bremen, Stuttgart or Hamburg – are likely already to be in secular decline, if not on the verge of extinction. The vestigial efforts of member state governments to hold back the tide, however, can be read in the ways in which some, including large member states, choose to define the conjuncture differently, using an Anglo-Saxon versus Continental stereotype, which tends only to postpone the need for remedial action.

Because these markets clear faster and are intrinsically more efficient than industrial ones, there is no natural Commission claim to supervision, other than ensuring that the weak or backward sectors adjust as quickly as they can. Harmonization has become a matter for discussion between Commission and players, almost as equals, according to what fits both the Community and the international requirements. In this sense, the Treaties are interpreted in a rather different context from the one envisaged by their signatories.

* * *

IV. European Confederations

Peak organizations, such as CBI, Patronat, Confindustria, or TUC and trade union confederations, which exist at national level in each member state to represent the whole industrial or labour market to their governments and the outside world, replicate themselves in the European Union because on certain issues these confederations need a single coordinating body. In almost all respects save one, they have similar characteristics, the exception being that they address not a state government sovereign within its territory but a complex of EU authorities: the Commission, the Council, and the Parliament of nationally elected MEPs.

A cynic would find evidence to assert that, just as the national bodies emerged in the early part of the twentieth century as post boxes suited to the purposes of infinitely more powerful industrial employers or trade union federations, so UNICE, the confederation representing industry, has proved itself to be a mere instrument in the service of its national confederations and subordinate as a European player to the sectoral federations. This is to ignore its capacity for brokerage between all fifteen members and the fact that it operates much more at the level of COREPER and the Council than the sectoral federations do, and generally more frequently among MEPs.

The national bodies on both sides of industry all at some point in their evolution crossed a threshold to become significant political players in their own right, usually during great national crises such as the First World War when their state governments needed them to mobilize industry or manpower. Their interwar histories ranged from bare survival or extinction under dictatorships to the evolution of tripartite forms of sharing in the state's curtilage. Nevertheless, in the post–1945 world, an element of triangular or quadripartite corporate bargaining developed in all European states west of the Iron Curtain, much of which survived the 1980s reaction against 'corporatism'.

It might therefore have been expected that such a pattern would develop in the EEC arena and until the mid-1970s there was sufficient evidence for academic commentators such as Ernest Haas to argue the case. But the long – almost continuous – decline of trade union power which followed the mid–1970s crisis ended one aspect of such speculation and insofar as the argument resurfaced later it took the form of distinguishing a different antithesis, between the interests of industry and financial capital. Policy choices lay between EU support for industrial adjustment on one hand, and management of the EMS and progress to EMU via member states'. Treasury-imposed performance criteria on the other. Neo-Keynesian advocates of managed industrial adjustment thus confronted Treasuries and Central Bankers committed to reducing public sector budgets and member states' rates of inflation.

This long-running engagement between industry and the financial sector since the mid–1980s explains why no over-arching body has emerged in Europe to represent the two, just as proposals for a Confederation of British Business failed in the 1960s.[67] But neither this nor the more obvious incompatibility of both industry and finance with trade union movements, accounts for the differential weighting which distinguishes the influence in Europe of UNICE from that of the ETUC.

Despite support from the EU, financially and via Ecosoc, the trade union side has always suffered from lack of resources, and more recently from declining membership – implantation now being as low as 10% in France and Spain compared with Britain (42%), Germany (34%), Italy (40%) and Belgium (53%). It suffers from the inflexibility endemic in a set of organizations still ultimately dependent on perceptions of class rather than financial advantage. Riven for so long by Cold War political cleavages between Social Democrats, Socialists and Communists, trade union confederations have not, until very recently, learned to work together in France, Italy and Spain, while their dependence elsewhere on parties of the left limits their possible courses of action, a handicap which no longer has a mirror effect on industrial and financial organizations *vis-à-vis* parties of the right even in Italy and Spain.

Created in 1973 as a coordinating mechanism for powerful member state confederations, ETUC has usually tended to react to what UNICE does – the reverse of the position at national level.

Moreover what ETUC gained by association with 'social Europe' in 1988–91 seems to have been undermined even by the Commission and well-disposed member states such as the Netherlands, Germany, Belgium and Ireland, once the debate on the part played by wages and the social costs of labour began, with the 1993 White Paper on unemployment and the price of growth.

As a body hoping to wield influence on every issue relating to labour, ETUC has been disadvantaged since the mid–1980s. Despite the Commission's support, and the fact that in the more extended battle over the European Companies Statute it had the backing of Delors, it experienced many losses (notably of the entire Papandreou programme) despite seeing the Eleven accept the Social Protocol. The most its leaders can hope for at present is that there will be, in the end, a recompense because even in Britain, which opted out, many MNCs (including some in AmCham) are in fact now willing to accept not only the Protocol's spirit but to follow the majority of member states in subscribing voluntarily to the detailed legislation (such as the Works Council Directive, finally passed in September 1994) arising from it, thus following the general trend, the pattern of their subsidiaries, and their own predictions about a future Labour government.[68]

Even if trades union confederations had not wilted, in conjunction with the deterioration of influence in national bargaining, ETUC would have been affected by the informal downgrading of Ecosoc and a change in the Commission itself which (with the exception of DG5, labour and industrial relations) has come 'to view the social question only as a result of the economic and industrial dynamics of a free market'.[69] The mechanics by which they were mobilized behind the Social Protocol differ in each case, but for all ETUC officials' claims to have initiated the process, the main momentum evidently came from the Commission, chiefly from Delors and Karel Van Miert.[70]

ETUC's lack of influence, when compared with UNICE, does not of course reflect the relative weighting of its members in their own countries. But most if not all of those were put severely on the defensive, not only during the 1991–3 recession but since, because of high rates of unemployment in member states where their leaderships had previously been politically powerful, such as Ireland, Spain and Portugal. The innate difficulties of reaching agreement between national confederations divided on political and ideological lines, continued to confound their efforts,[71] because at this level the once powerful Communist influence has not entirely disappeared. CGT in France still remains outside ETUC. ETUC became for the first time a truly European body at its seventh congress in 1991, as a result of an initiative by Italy's CGIL; but in that debate the British, Netherlands, French, Irish and Danish representatives opposed giving it powers to act on members' behalf. Worse, perhaps, it still depends substantially on DGB support which, given the post-German unification configuration of the EU, may turn out to be a pervasive disadvantage where other national peak organizations are concerned.

National industrial confederations, of course, vary just as greatly in influence with their own governments (and consequently with Brussels) for historical and socio-economic reasons, and their relative advantage to a large extent determines how each will act on European issues, either as an adjunct to its government or independently. Generally speaking, in states like France where state ownership of large individual firms is widespread, the Patronat is relatively weak, a condition partially remedied by the emergence of AGREF (an association of the CEOs or chairmen of French private MNCs and financial institutions with a shared interest in company and competition law, taxation, and labour market issues);[72] but in federal ones such as Germany, the Netherlands and Belgium, is well ensconced and influential. Spain is an exception to the latter, but the CEOE's weakness may be taken as evidence that in the area of the direction of EU affairs, Spain is actually highly centralized. Ireland's IBEC, though of recent foundation, exhibits strong corporatist tendencies, as is to be expected, given the tri- or quadripartite system established in Dublin.

Confindustria's isolation from government (like that of the Portuguese CIP and Greek SEV) can also be associated with the Italian government's choice of system for coordination.[73] In Britain it is clear that the CBI lost effective access to the Thatcher governments in 1980–81, recovered somewhat during the passage of the SEA, and subsequently extended its range well beyond Whitehall and the UK Permanent Representative to assert its representativity on behalf of a Britain increasingly at odds with continental approaches to the Social Protocol, but whose national interests it believed were in fact were well served by some of the EU's industrial or trade policies.[74]

None of the national confederations excluded itself from the EU's mid-1980s regeneration and the internal market. But the intensity of their advocacy varied and some, like the CNPF in 1984, entered the campaign surprisingly late – because of the mixed feelings felt among the Patronat's members at the likely impact of liberalization on sheltered sectors of French industry. The CBI's earlier enthusiasm waned but then revived with the establishment of a Brussels office in 1981. Yet several of its largest members, such as GEC and Rolls Royce, claimed to be still relying on their own networks, even after the introduction of the internal market.

Other differences run between the national organizations. Whereas most member state's CBIs cover the whole range of trade associations and employers' organizations, and have separate sections responsible for SMEs, Germany and Denmark (and Ireland until 1992) retain an earlier form where each is represented separately in Germany by BDA, BDI and ZDH.[75] Such distinctions make it even harder for UNICE to obtain a collective German view, the process of national filtration and compromise being left in these cases until very late in the day; this encourages German MNCs to act on their own rather than be trammelled. On the other hand, now that the bulk of internal market legislation has been passed, there is less need for the Commission to have all fifteen national confederations in line, leaving more space in the mid-1990s for UNICE's more bureaucratic brokerage.[76]

All firms or federations have ultimately a choice of how to divide their lobbying efforts between national and EU networks. UNICE is inevitably part of the national channel because its members' composition dictates it, even though MNCs or bodies like ERT and AGREF can easily approach it directly if they wish. It rarely seeks to influence Commission policy at the level where MNCs or sectoral federations operate and it is therefore only on the most general questions such as implementing internal market legislation that a Director General or Commissioner would need it (or similar bodies such as SOPA in agriculture, or Eurochambres linking all the Chambers of Commerce associations). UNICE's efforts are channelled towards COREPER and the Council of Ministers, as befits a trans-sectoral group lobbying the collective of member states.

Like most national peak organizations since 1973, these have become administrative complexes, kinds of civil services engaged on long-term projects which require continuity, a developed ethos and a measure of publicity directed at the hypothetical European electorate which sectoral federations normally shun.[77]

But UNICE has only fitted in with this mode of activity in the last decade. Set up by the six original member states' confederations in 1958, it slipped for many years into being the mirror image of the trade union federations, a pattern in which, in the Val Duchesse talks, it aimed (like Ecosoc) at creating a climate of harmony between what were assumed to be compatible social partners. Pushed by some of the national bodies in the mid-1980s,[78] influenced by what was going on outside, most pointedly by demands from the future Commission President Jacques Delors, UNICE conducted its own internal review late in 1984 which led to a substantial reorganization and the appointment of a gifted animator, Zygmunt Tyszkiewicz, as Director General the following year. By 1992 it had a strong secretariat, five main policy working groups (with sub groups open to individual firms) and 50 specialized working groups. It now has a membership of 32 federations in 22 countries of 'wider Europe', and, though bureaucratic, clearly serves as a powerhouse for industry as well as a civil service and think-tank. On the organizational side, it has transformed itself remarkably quickly, with high quality staff (many of whom are graduates of the College of Europe), able to respond to the Commission's requests for consultation, say, over international transport networks or industrial competitiveness while the 1993 White Paper was being constructed.

UNICE provides services to its members but has no power to coopt or bind them. Like the CBI or BDA it can only argue, inform and plead in its regular position papers. Its capacity to deliver any sort of bargain or unanimity to EU institutions depends strictly on the lowest common denominator of agreement among the thirty-two members – the weakest of whom have no hesitation is using the parity of esteem among unequals which UNICE membership assures. It tends therefore invariably to wait – for eighteen months in the case of EMU – for its members to come into line, moved by global or national factors. Some areas remain untouchable over decades, as CAP has been for the French CNPF. Like any such body, it works best when threatened from outside, as its members felt themselves to be by the Vredeling Directive.[79]

In the decade after Vredeling, UNICE acquired a sort of vicarious credit by association with the Single European Act's signature in 1986. It probably did help to make more coherent and public the several powerful industrial voices of that time, since sectoral federations took little part in the campaign, and it undoubtedly helped to familiarize EFTA countries' companies and national federations with the Community and its workings prior to their accession negotiations. Later on, it sometimes became salient in defence of sectoral interests, for example in the case of pharmaceuticals companies 'social acceptability' when marketing their drugs, circa 1990. But it found itself gravely divided by British and American outright opposition to the Social Chapter during the Maastricht IGCs the following year.

Officials often play down UNICE's presumed status, pointing out that unlike ETUC it receives no EU funding (though those funds are in fact intended to redress an imbalance of power adverse to trade unions). Since the mid–1980s, it has deliberately presented itself not as a neocorporatist partner of the Commission – that being part of an earlier unpopular past – but as a friendly and critical ally. Its principal advantage, *vis-à-vis* the sectoral federations, is that EU institutions can never actually ignore it, conferring by default a semi-formalized right of access at all times and on most levels of EU activity except to the Council itself.

Its most valuable function from the point of view of the EU as a whole may however have been that, at the time of Vredeling in 1980–82, just before the EC became a global player by virtue of controlling Europe's internal market environment, it offered a sort of informal association to AmCham (and the Europe-America Council composed of its main European members' CEOs), a situation which could conceivably be repeated in the future for the Japanese and those which may be formed by other Asian competitors. Since it contains within itself both the national confederations which defend free trade and those prone to protectionism, UNICE in fact became in the 1980s and early 1990s a sort of guarantor of the internal market and GATT, an assurance that the xenophobia of Jean-Jacques Servan-Schreiber's *Le Défi Americain* (1967) would, if it recurred, at least be restrained.

The multiple variety of forms of behaviour, networks and perceptions touched on in this chapter may not amount to a negotiated order, but it certainly constitutes a system, albeit a more flexible and indeterminate one than exists in most of the member states. Europe is both a marketplace characterized by pluralistic bargaining and the place where special-interest coalitions flourish. That the two are not incompatible is due to the fact that even the largest MNCs need alliances, with member states on one hand and from within their own sectors on the other, frequently across national borders. The existence of national and European peak organizations corresponds to this structural diversity, as part of an informal division of labour, allowing them to evolve consensus, measures of self-defence, common practice, and pooled resources in the massive task of shifting an entrenched Community in their favour. These are not corporatist bodies and have no power as such to deliver their members' assent (unless they have been given it first) and they lack the quasi-moral claim of UNICE to define a superior European interest in the industrial economy.

The competing players are governed by informal rules or conventions which form, at the core, a matrix of political bargaining between willing if often adversarial players. The self-interest of all of them in continuing this game has proved sufficiently strong to prevent reversion to bi-lateral negotiations. It helps to avoid hostility, uncertainty and failure in the Community's political market because it allows the non-governmental players to operate in several dimensions at the same time, at will. This is peculiarly appropriate to players lacking the sovereignty of member state governments, who cannot evade the political consequences of being economically implicated in the game.

The logic to this is called in German *Allgemeinverbindlichkeit*: bargains are made and generalized in each sector. In each case, there are principal, secondary and even tertiary agents, whose cumulative actions give rise to precedents, whose accumulation comes then to stand, conventionally or contractually, as a sort of quasi-public law with precedents but no texts. This existed from the EU's beginning, but the advent of the internal market has enormously increased the number of would-be players, and the possibilities for entry of a much greater range of small and medium as well as large companies than could have been envisaged in the more obviously corporate 1960s and 1970s. At the same time, earlier distinctions between government and non-governmental organizations, public and private sectors, which once seemed obvious, have become blurred to the point at which some of the former behave in their national interest as if they were private and most of the latter assume at least the veil of public and/or European interest.

From the Commission's point of view – an exposed, often lonely position, especially when confronted by a suspicious or hostile Council of Ministers – there is an overriding need to get politics right in terms of what is best for European markets operating in the international economy. No one player should be left out if it would contribute to making a better, more harmonious whole. Like its industrial policy, the Commission's framework of reference is biased towards negotiated adjustments rather than abrupt free-market terminations. Who uses whom is not a question therefore that elicits clear-cut answers.

European Union institutions nearly always prefer to consult or make informal bargains with federations, on the assumption that much of the processes of elimination has already taken place under this aegis; hence the surrender of some firms' sovereignty begins before the Commission is involved, just as the Commission's informal surrenders begin with officials' acknowledgement that they are not, and never can be, wholly competent in such matters. Because neither side, nor any of their many facets, can admit formally that this occurs, the view about open but informal dialogue expressed in the Sutherland Report is likely to prevail, whether or not a 'structured' one is formally endorsed.

It is unfortunately the case that convenient as this system is it leads Commissioners and officials usually to listen to the same players, to privilege the larger, more salient, better resourced firms at the expense of national ones and SMEs. Despite their attempts to broaden the basis of consultation and to study by means of 'impact fiches' assessments of the consequence of every Commission decision, the problem of isolation in the midst of pluralism remains. But that was true of departmental officials in national games also.

In the European context, a firm's range of options extends far more widely than in the national one but over a similar spectrum, from pure self-interest to acknowledgement that a common, usually sectoral, interest exists, out of which a European interest can be quarried – generally in some sort of association with the Commission. (Unlike European confederations, firms are too brutally constituted, too close to commercial motivation, to acknowledge the force of presenting this 'higher interest' as European *altruism*). If agreements can be achieved on all three levels, firm, national federation and European federation, they are likely to command substantially more recognition in Brussels. A member state's support may facilitate this outcome, and its disengagement will not necessarily prejudice it. But the diversity of firms' behaviour and the fluidity and protean nature of their options is so great that it is often difficult for them as informal political players, even via their European federations, to judge what is successful. Confronted by problems of understanding multiple causes, and the lack of a historical-documentary memory in most firms and federations where 'people are too busy to talk' and there are no archivists, analysts may not be able to view the whole, even in retrospect. Meanwhile, to outsiders, the greater accessibility of peak organizations' records tends to over-emphasize what the latter do, while obscuring the far larger part played by firms themselves.

Sectoral federations, on the other hand, work most efficiently when they can define member firms' broader interests in a language which compels general acquiescence, one that is often partly learned from the Commission: it is a language about the internal market itself, the danger of uncompetitiveness, the interdependence of trade and industrial policy, the balance between profitability and workers' contentment. In this sense, they are more powerful forces for symbiosis in the political marketplace than they could ever be in the economic one, for the chairmen and managing directors even of the MNCs cannot always understand the external balance of power, nor see how their total activity meshes with the EU's external politics.

But have firms become more European in themselves, not just in their political behaviour, since the mid-1980s? The European game has, if anything, increased two older sets of tensions; *within* the firm, between structural economic requirements and the different demands of the European or international context, and *between* the firm and the governments which once defended it as a national champion, but now have to contest with fourteen others and the Commission whether or not to treat them as European champions. It is the Commission, secure in the potential favour of two sets of potential benefactors, which seems best able to play one against the other, but which must always watch, at its back, competitors on the international stage, and the potentially contrary activity of what used to count as 'their own' political authorities.

As for their identity, it is probably still true to see the great majority of firms, financial institutions, and sectoral organizations (including trade union federations) as retaining their national identity, however much their patterns of behaviour and affinity have become international and European. Few, if any, MNCs' political economies proclaim them to be true transnationals. But circumstances since the 1970s have compelled them to act as if they were. Quickening trends after 1973-4 certainly enhanced their specifically European focus, as was evident in their willingness to take part in Commission strategies or stratagems such as ESPRIT, the steel cartel, the various adjustment programmes and, above all, the introduction of the internal market. (Maastricht, EMU and political integration have to be seen as separate and, for non-governmental organizations, far less significant factors.) But for lack of detailed evidence, no valid generalizations can be made about the spread of a European mentality; too much depends on the thousands of senior executives and middle-range managers who staff them, live and work in Europe, but retire to a particular country, town or village.

This is not ultimately a physical matter of setting up offices or of commuting to Brussels and Strasbourg, as Ernest Haas imagined it thirty years ago, but a metaphysical one, for firms are networks of consciously constructed affinity or identity. Business or finance are not monoliths but conceptual areas, where changing patterns of work and skills have caused older categories of differentiation between theoretical enemies to become blurred. The majority of white-collar trades unionists can conceive of themselves today as professional workers rather than producers or wage slaves. Car spares manufacturers, dealers and insurers may have more in common than between manufacturers of small urban vehicles and those of high performance tourers. Given the range of services, even the broad distinctions used here, of industrial and financial players, may already be out of date.

The game has become so structured that the category of MNCs who are well resourced, and continually engaged on a broad front, might be separated from other interest groups as well as lobbyists, the latter being the twentieth-century equivalent of Renaissance mercenaries who work for whatever client hires them. Such firms exist independently of the EU's integration process but operate in it because it is in their interest to do so. In turn, their play stimulates integration and also shapes it, for they have their own interest in defining the European outcome.

In the formal sense, this argument diminishes the EU's apparent statehood. Yet the fact that this political market exists, and shows no signs of diminishing, can also be construed as evidence that the EU shares in what all nation states possess, a congruence between formal and informal systems which is evidence of organic maturity – even if the resulting statehood may be of a different order from theirs.

11

Players in Action

The immense changes in the European Community forecast by the internal market ensured that virtually all large companies and financial institutions would seek to participate in its political evolution as a matter of course, even if they did not necessarily – or at all – acquire a distinctly European identity. During the decade after 1986 they evolved their own means to become more effective players in the European game, and many of them set up offices in Brussels. Wherever European affairs had not already been reflected in their internal politics and the disposition of their senior executives, a new balance developed between their existing international outlook and the requirements of the specific European environment.

At the same time, the configuration of the Commission, to which large firms most often addressed themselves, continued a change which had begun some years earlier. The components of a Community industrial policy, based on research, adjustment and technology transfer, came into closer alignment with competition policy, as the latter developed during the 1980s. Competition policy had always been important and competition cases had been responsible for many of the ECJ's early landmark judgments (which in turn helped to build up the Court's reputation). But in the context of the internal market, Article 90 and the powers against monopolies were essential elements of liberalization, and continued to be so in the fields of telecoms and energy supply.

A vigorous competition policy came to be seen as a security against reversion to protection or defensive activity, as firms attempted to insulate themselves from the new internal market challenges by informal cartels, concentration, and increased dependence on state financing. As a result, DG4 (competition) became much more salient in what was often seen as a highly political manner. Three notable Commissioners in a row, Frans Andriessen (Netherlands), Peter Sutherland (Ireland), and Leon Brittan (Britain) gave DG4 a consistent direction, aided by a further series of ECJ judgments which defined how competition law, as laid down in the Treaties, should be interpreted and applied thirty years on.

Since competition policy has a longer history than the exchange rate mechanism (ERM), it may appear eccentric to bring the two together in a single chapter. But from the point of view of industrial and financial players seeking to influence EU institutions, it serves to show how the Commission began to evolve connections between the previously fragmented areas of competition, industrial policy, trade and macro-economic policies, on which a more general aim of regenerating the European economy might be based.

The decisions taken by member states participating in the ERM, circa 1987, to move to a more rigid framework of exchange rates as the precursor to monetary union (EMU) brought into play central bankers acting as a collective, who had, until then, acted individually (as their governors of national central banks). In that capacity they had always had an interest in the performance of their national industrial and service sectors, though not often to the same extent as in the performance of their financial ones. This interest had surfaced twice within recent memory; during the recessions and government recovery operations of 1974–6 and 1981–3, and was to recur in what for most member states was the more severe recession of 1991–3. The fact that the genesis of EMU drew them together as a planning and policy-making group, however, began to alter their relations not only with all twelve finance ministers in Ecofin, but with their own finance ministries and their own governments, partly as a result of the increased confidence which the governors of banks in smaller states and more recent entrant countries acquired, and partly because one major requirement of EMU was to be a steady increase in their independence.

Both developments had been forecast in the Single European Act. Yet the way they occurred was not inevitable. Individual Commissioners and officials of the Commission acted as interpreters of the EC's higher interest, so that the outcome – the place of competition in Commission policy, and the future design of EMU – was defined in terms of current policy needs, not simply by reference to existing legal texts. The EU's higher interest in practice became equated with what the competition between players – member states as well as the Commission, and firms as well as member states – allowed. The process is easier to see in contentious cases examined here, which is not to say that the great majority of cases did not conform strictly to the law, only that where discretion and bargaining intruded and grey informal areas opened up, the Commission would confront firms which were very often backed by their member states.

I. *Competition Policy*

The three main elements of EU competition policy – monopoly and anti-trust activity, merger regulation and policy towards state aids – fall under DG4. A basic tension has always existed between that and the other DGs responsible for industry, research, regional policy or SMEs. However, the intensity of rivalry between them has altered as the form and application of competition policy has changed since the 1950s.

Anti-trust activity, originally based on concepts evolved in the United States in the late nineteenth century, was applied from the ECSC period onwards in the context of a more general aim of preventing a recurrence of 1930s German companies' dominance in steel, coal, chemicals and engineering. In the 1960s it was assumed that, as a result of the Common Market's evolution, competition would gradually pervade Europe. But policy was actually implemented in the 1970s in such a way as to allow the EEC to create both a protective regime for textiles and a means to rationalize member states' steel industries under cover of emergency cartels. Because member states argued their need to mitigate the social and economic consequences of rationalization at every turn, it became clear that without a distinct structural policy earlier Community aspirations would be permanently stultified.

Except in the cases of air and sea freight transport, the Commission had power to interpret Articles 85 and 86 of the Treaty and therefore, in theory, to provide an antidote. Firms had by law to notify it of restrictive agreements and the Commission had evolved criteria for assessing restrictive practices (which were regarded as acceptable so long as they produced directly technological or economic progress, and did not disadvantage consumers and users or lead to the domination of more than a limited percentage of the market). The regulations of the 1960s were conceived as part of a policy opposed to price fixing and market sharing, production quotas, vertical distribution agreements and collective exclusive dealing. But DG4's incremental progress up to 1974 was partly inhibited by DG3's support for industry during the two-headed recession which lasted until about 1983.

Meanwhile questions came into play which tended to set the Commission in opposition to member states. Long-established national competition agencies such as the German Bundeskartellamt (BKartA), and the British Monopolies and Mergers Commission (MMC) had developed their own codes of practice and precedents for dealing with specifically national markets. The BKartA in particular asserted these as best practice when it came to dealing with the single European market. So initially did the French Conseil de la Concurrence, which was established in 1986, but did not for some time acquire the same status as a decision-maker. In Italy, in contrast, the competition and anti-trust authority AGCM lacked both power and status. Defining the European market, and where in particular cases the relevant distinction lay between that and the national market, inevitably caused DG4 problems in crucial years after 1986.

In the second area, attempts in 1973, after years of discussion, to extend Article 86 to merger regulation (although given some assistance by the ECJ's judgment in the *Continental Can* case that it should apply if the merger left the remaining competitors 'dependent on the dominant undertaking with regard to market behaviour') ran into two serious difficulties. Firstly, in *Continental Can* the Commission's actual decision was annulled (even though the principle stood as far as the future was concerned), revealing how much harder it was to *prove* such a case in the European rather than a national context; secondly and more conclusively, that member states in the Council (egged on by UNICE and the national confederations of industry) were not then willing to make the transfer of sovereignty that would have permitted DG4 to have central regulatory powers.[1] For another decade, DG4 had to be content with the existing notification process which in effect allowed it to delay certain mergers for up to a year – so long as it was not overruled by the Council in 'priority areas' such as aerospace.

The vast majority of cases which have affected companies' decisions since the 1960s are anti-trust ones, such as the current Atlas joint venture in telecoms. But Article 85 can also allow a concern with the much smaller number of merger cases. Here the Commission established, with the authority of the Council, exemptions either for certain forms of cooperation or for whole sectors of industry such as automobile distribution, know-how licensing, or insurance. Thus a systematic policy has developed, which favours certain sorts of cooperation and which is flexible (in that it can be adapted as industrial circumstances – and indeed industrial policies – change). The evolution of exemptions policy, the politics of block exemptions, and the Commission's habit of producing 'non-agreements' to prevent these becoming general and therefore subject to investigation by DG4, amounts to a distinct sub-species of informal politics.

DG3 had made the running when the arguments about industrial restructuring policy first evolved in the 1970s, for DG4 was held back both by its lack of a policy framework, and by member states' own policing powers and agencies. Cases at that time could be prolonged almost indefinitely: the Netherlands cement cartel case lasted for eight years from 1964, and most others until the early 1980s took up to three years. When Andriessen tried to bring forward a system of merger regulation again in 1981, his efforts were rejected by the Council since they were judged to give too much power to the Commission. Only four member states – West

Germany, the Netherlands, Belgium and Luxembourg – lined up on that occasion with the Commission, against France, Britain, Italy and the rest. Mergers had already acquired a high, usually nationalistic, political profile.

But the passage to the Single European Act altered the terms of argument, forcing them all to accept the need for a single central authority rather than twelve separate ones. Member states themselves, usually under strong pressures from industrial players who needed a centrally policed system free of national arbitrariness, altered their views. In the French case, this was because the Kartellamt turned down a merger between Thomson and Grundig. Edith Cresson as a result took up the argument and passed it on to President Mitterrand. Nevertheless, Cresson lost her argument over the exemption clause for mergers under 85(3) and German practice predominated.

Hotly debated from the mid-1980s onwards, the Merger Control Regulation finally emerged in December 1989, providing powers for DG4 to vet all mergers above a certain limit [2] The outcome was closer to German competition law and Kartellamt practice, together with that of Britain and the Netherlands, than the French Conseil de la Concurrence or Mediterranean countries' agencies which habitually took account of industrial, social and regional criteria. Starting in September 1990, DG4 considered sixty mergers in the first year and vetoed one. But the tone was already set in Sutherland's time, for example with the BA–British Caledonian merger, which was allowed in March 1988 so long as Commission requirements about Gatwick routes were observed.

The third area – state aids to private companies as well as state-owned ones (see pp. 519–25) – became virtually a national *chasse gardée* after the empty chair crisis and the Luxembourg compromise. In the 1970s, DG4 had been reduced to asking for information and could do little more than plan policy in the abstract, given the way that member states flagrantly disregarded the rules and rulings, especially where declining industries such as steel, shipbuilding and textiles were concerned. As a result of the revival of confidence inside DG4 after 1981, however, it felt able to attack the highly sensitive area of member states' illegal subsidies. While

DG4 had forbidden only twenty-one instances in the decade before 1981, it added fourteen in the next four years.[3]

The fact that, until about 1981, DG4 had remained a low-key operator restricted by the political weight of member states did not prevent it from being the target of their criticism, designed to limit its powers permanently. Then and again later, it was accused of operating directly under the Treaty, out of the control of the Council of Ministers, and that it was the instigator, prosecutor *and* judge in the cases it did pursue. Associations and federations pointed up the evidence that its regime bore much harder on companies than on governments. (In fact it bore rather harder on American and Japanese companies than their European counterparts – forcing AmCham's EC members and JAMA into diversionary strategies.)

It seemed to DG4 officials that competition policy was least effective where it was most needed – to deal with abuses of market power by state monopolies and public undertakings, and in the highly-contentious field of state aids. But with help from the ECJ, which frequently interpreted the law so as to give the Commission the greatest possible scope for intervention,[4] DG4 was transformed in the mid-1980s. Spurred by their own would-be European champions and industry ministries which understood best the internal market's implications, member state governments also shifted ground. The Cecchini Report (see p. 146), after all, spoke of gains in the internal market's coming 'climate of competition' reaching 200 billion ecus. Under Sutherland, and even more under Brittan, DG4 was enabled to become assertive, particularly in using Articles 90 and 93 more vigorously against monopolies and state aids.

Yet as Sutherland feared, the more the role of policeman and judge was extended, the more flexible and subtle became companies' and member states' defensive responses where the outcome was something different from what they wanted. A wave of mergers flooded through in 1988–90 before the Merger Regulation took effect, and before the Merger Task Force which was to implement it was ready.[5] State aids in the car and airline industries actually rose at this time, even before the recession. On Sutherland's 1986 figures, aids in agriculture, transport, coal and steel amounted to a stifling of competition equivalent to 3% of the EC's GNP, the worst-performing member states by volume being Italy, West Germany, France, Britain and Belgium.[6]

Thereafter that line-up changed as the volume of state aids, first in Britain then in Germany, tapered off. But the number of serious, even flagrant cases did not diminish. They remained roughly stable in France, and rose in Italy (ENI, IRI, Finmeccanica) and Spain (Hunosa) while one or two notable cases such as the Dutch aid to Fokker in 1989 slipped through with Commission agreement. Even though both volume and number fell substantially in Germany, aid continued to flow to what were often deviously categorized regional support schemes, while the Commission appears to have avoided investigation of aids to former East Germany for political reasons connected with the problem of reunification, except when forced to do so by the complaints of other member states, as in the case of steel subsidies in 1994 (see p. 573).

But DG4's new outlook (initiated by Frans Andriessen's orders to steel companies in the early 1980s to repay the money in flagrant cases) was finally established in the *Boussac* case, when Sutherland ordered the French textiles firm to repay 338 million out of 600 million French francs. In the *Denfil* case 1987, the ECJ blocked another loophole by ruling that the onus lay on a company to check as against earlier warnings rather than rely on a defence that they had received state aid in good faith.

During Leon Brittan's tenure as Commissioner, 1989–92, these stakes were increased, and not only by the large size of the fines imposed to deter MNCs whose cartels DG4 uncovered. Brittan was probably no more adversarial than his predecessor, and enjoyed the same 'favourable constituency' in Germany, Britain and the Netherlands. Like Sutherland, he was also independent of his own government in a way that few Commissioners easily achieve. On the other hand, when he encountered the old functional rivalry with DG3, sponsor of industry, he now ran up against the formidable defensive power of Martin Bangemann. Behind Bangemann stood the German industrial lobbies, and the Kartellamt, jealous of its national scope. Worse, the difficult merger and state aids cases arose mainly in France and Italy and stimulated serious opposition to him in the college from Commissioners sympathetic to the position of states like these, keeping their nationalized industries afloat, usually with the supporting argument that the aids were intended to prepare them for privatization once the time was ripe. It became normal to expect the college to have to take at least one vote, very often with Delors on the other side. This changed in the later merger cases, once the test case of Alenia–de Havilland had been won, when it became clear that the Commission's powers were being extended in a way that Delors could approve generally, whatever the effect of particular cases on particular member states.

Brittan was fortunate in being well served, not only by his officials, but by the new Merger Task Force, an elite investigatory body enjoying something close to autonomy,[7] and in the fact that some Commissioners could be persuaded to change sides in the higher EC interest. Pandolfi stood with him for example in the de Havilland case, when Bangemann referred to DG4 as 'the Ayatollahs of competition'. Bangemann also never fought a case to the finish, being content to make his point, but then either to conform or abstain. Brittan's strongest weapon lay in the internal market logic which had inspired member states' change of heart, and in the cumulative process of establishing evidence about how markets actually worked. That DG4 argued against monopoly power not from free market dogma but from proof – that it inhibited the competitiveness which all the players had accepted since 1984 was Europe's main defence against the USA and Japan – worked in its long-term favour.

DG4 had also built up a system of surveillance, using amongst its many sources the financial columns of national newspapers for evidence of abuses. Its officials let companies know that complaints would be welcomed, thus enlisting the injured parties against the abusers, and in a number of cases they managed also to enlist the interest of national media, often against their own governments' interest, by providing more details of restrictive prices or price fixing than their journalists could obtain at home. It is fair to add that the policy of tempering rigour to circumstances, once the principle had been decided (from which poor member states, peripheral regions and SMEs tended to benefit, because of the 'lesser disturbing effect' of their malpractices) tended to work in DG4's favour, outside the four largest member states.[8]

A framework of rules had been established in the monopolies and anti-trust areas long before 1988. Further precedents were gradually evolved in the area of mergers,[9] for example in defining a doctrine of 'joint dominance of a market' (Nestlé–Perrier). Great advances also took place in these years in the financial sector, as restrictive practices were removed or given notice in banking, insurance and stock markets, following internal market legislation. But apart from signal victories over telecoms equipment supply (despite a French challenge at the ECJ) and state information technology monopolies (vital for the markets in videotics, electronic mail, fax, and computer banking), Brittan made only tentative progress in the telecoms area (see chapter 12) and virtually none with national energy or postal monopolies, despite the development of remailing to take advantage of some member states' substantially lower charges. The questions of certain states acting as producer-regulators, of French régies, the Greek tobacco monopoly and Spanish oil, all falling under Article 37, remained for his successor, Karel van Miert.

Where member states' interests are directly involved, all cases have a higher policy content than a legal one. DG4's procedures are in any case quasi-judicial, with elements of discretion and substantial openings for negotiation and compromise. Discretion appears as an element in most legal processes, although at times its proportion is so small as to resemble the quantities in homeopathic medicine. But in DG4's hands, as authorized by the Commission college, it can be considerable, not only in the obvious sense of taking external, economic or social considerations into account, if safeguarding the principle allows, but in considering whether or not to prosecute and under which headings. It can be depicted from outside as (and may in fact be) a force either for justice or injustice (or indeed both), because it can both advance an important principle and modify the law on which it is based.[10]

There are inevitably doubts on political grounds about the eventual line-up of Commissioners in the college, whatever DG4 decides, because in this area above all they tend to submit to national sympathies. It was natural that governments should involve themselves on behalf of what were still regarded as national champions or key industries in this way in the 1980s; less likely, but possible, that their resistances would diminish individually and collectively in the Council of Ministers, once the internal market began to come into effect in the early 1990s. (This point is important when considering the French government's reaction to DG4's conduct in 1990–91.) For a time, however, the 1991–3 recession encouraged resistance, especially on state aids, and masked what can now be seen as an underlying trend. In that sense, DG4 was working with the grain over a long period, and the larger member states were themselves gradually adjusting, forcing smaller, poorer ones to follow suit. (But they did so while arguing loudly for coherence funding or derogations, and not necessarily at a speed dictated by the Commission).

But that did not imply that in the interim member states would not exploit divisions among DG4 officials,[11] nor that the national agencies would necessarily approve of DG4's leading role, its methods such as dawn raids, the greater informal power which accrued to the Commission as a result of its successes, or of the steady mutation from informal compromises to rules and conventions. Thus the German BMWi argued, with support from the Kartellamt's president so closely aligned as to suggest possible collusion, that national agencies' scope for regulating EC competition and merger law should be increased (as if competition policy could embody subsidiarity) and that a new European competition institution should be set up as a more neutral arbiter to handle the EC's routine work, leaving only cases of European importance to DG4. This *Ordnungspolitische Grundsatzabteilung*, it was claimed by French and Italian as well as German agencies,[12] was the proper way to curb the Commission, exclude informal or highly political elements from DG4's judgment, and enhance subsidiarity in a formal, structured way.[13]

In a wide and complicated field where large commercial interests predominate, member states cannot be excluded, resulting in the briefing of top legal firms at great expense. Lobbying by firms and member states in competition areas habitually involves the most senior Commission officials and their Commissioners, not usually with the aim of changing existing law but to influence how the procedures will be implemented, and their outcomes.[14] Pressures are, if anything, increased because the college is the last resort, and because the Commissioner or Director General instructs officials how they should treat a case. Meanwhile member states can use the information which DG4 is bound in law to make public, to make their own prior dispositions or to try to prevent DG4 using informal processes such as 'comfort letters' which permit companies to go ahead – on the grounds that this preempts both the college and the Council's rights.[15]

DG4's inevitable exposure to political pressures had been demonstrated earlier, but it was the landmark merger cases, such as de Havilland and Nestlé–Perrier, and Renault's state aid repayment, which encouraged both the industrial lobbies and the Italian and French government protests at its supposedly high-handed role. (The British government was content to see this occur – until it encountered the same process in the BAe–Rover case.) But these were exceptions, whatever seemed to be the case at the time, and the French reaction can be explained by developments in the politics of national monopolies, not only concerning Renault's future but the state interests in Air France, France Télécom, Bull, Electricité de France, Aérospatiale and Thomson.

In the great majority of cases there is far more cooperation between the Commission and national agencies, amounting to a continued – if informal – dialogue both on individual cases and general principles which extends to expert meetings where member state representatives (and in some French cases, the company representatives) can attend. Member state competition agencies also talk to each other, usually through the medium of position papers, and to the Commission whenever the consultative committees meet, as well during the hearings on individual cases. This many-layered process, inspired both nationally among the 'group of four' (Germany, France, Britain and Spain) and by the transfer of lawyers between national agencies and DG4, as well as by the

Commission itself, helps to create the intellectual climate in which competition law is exercised.[16]

Even if the notable cases are seen as exceptions, being naturally politicized, large grey areas remain. In merger cases there is what may be called a prenotification period, when lawyers habitually negotiate with DG4 officials, often before their clients' contracts are signed, seeking to discover what modifications ought prudently to be made. Something equally informal occurs with exemptions under Articles 85 and 86 (as seemed to have occurred in the Yves St Laurent and Shipping Insurance cases). Preliminary, informal opinions then become part of both sides' later formal arguments.

The whole arena of research and development, joint ventures and strategic alliances can be considered as a grey area in itself. If, say, Thomson, a French firm with subsidiaries in the United States and Germany, embarks on a joint venture in Italy, the elements of a European matter are also inextricably an international one. The emergence of new competitors, whose national affiliation changes with the development of their European or cross-border subsidiaries, the speed of technological change, and the sheer complexity of research itself, mean that all companies will seek to share the cost and risks. Whether cooperation is judged good or bad depends on a decision on whether the outcome fosters or inhibits competition in the European, not the world market; technically, this may be hard for Commission officials to do, but has not so far been demonstrated to be impossible. (Van Miert has cited, as a typical case, the Philips-Thomson-Sogun joint venture to produce liquid crystal display services – a trinational high-tech response to Japanese competition.)

DG4's judgment that a joint venture is 'an instrument to partition markets or to foreclose markets for third parties',[17] must never be seen as arbitrary, or it becomes instantly vulnerable to the objections so often made by national agencies, whose own case law and practice largely excludes arbitrariness. But in the end it may come down to intangibles, to matters of judgment about what the basic aim of the venture is, and whether its outcome will still permit *effective* competition.

There is probably no alternative to the slow build-up of precedents, criteria and rules within the decision-making networks informally composed of DG4 and national agencies. This has produced the useful device of block exemptions where the parties control less than 20% of the EU market. Again, it is the notable exemptions, such as Alcatel-Espace–ANT's ten year exemption for satellite research, allowed under the criterion of long-term technical progress, or Olivetti–Canon's project for copiers, or Continental–Michelin's one for safety tyres, which cause repercussions among competitors. Brittan could be said to have instilled a realistic rather than a theoretical approach, which has so far been continued under van Miert,[18] whose flexibility and discretion disturb the adherents of German legal principles, even if the system of competition law as a whole owes most to the Kartellamt example. Like most examples of Commission practice, the story stays open: but among the players, companies – if not necessarily member states – do admit that they have an interest in the existence of 'a regulatory authority that can look after the genuine interests of European industry, the European consumer, and indeed the European economy as a whole'.[19]

As one German former Commissioner put it, the first thing is to get a decision; for if there is no negotiation, no compromise, the best elements of what constitute a wider industrial policy may be lost.[20] Compromise is preferable to force, because DG4 'is not permanently anti-industry', it has a duty only to shape how firms and industries behave. One result of this has been the acceptance that there is a deeper unity between DG3 and DG4, whatever the surface rifts, which became explicit through a growing congruence between Bangemann and Brittan, to which Delors himself eventually conformed. There are firms' executives (in this case of a German chemicals company) honest enough to admit 'it's a game and we lost', and part of the competition policy game is for DG4 to emulate Machiavelli's exemplary punishment and deter the rest, but without crippling effect. The severest fine for monopoly behaviour has been that imposed on TetraPak, a Swedish firm found to have abused its dominant share in specialized packaging, to have excluded competition and indulged in predatory pricing, and restrictive practices – for which the fine amounted to 75 million ecus. The penalty has since been exceeded in the case of the cement cartel, headed by Ciments Français, the only member firm in the cartel to have failed to negotiate with DG4 at the beginning.[21] But what the Commission called 'the number, gravity and long duration of [TetraPak's] infringements' indicates the importance it attached to the penalty. Yet member states will not allow the Commission to extend its scope: despite three years of argument, there is no sign that the merger thresholds will be lowered, as DG4 has requested, in order for it to acquire jurisdiction over perhaps a hundred cases a year rather than sixty.

Neither is one member state likely to give up its national agency's power to forbid another nation's merger, whatever the impact of Merger Regulation Article 9.[22] Yet the general tendency across the Community is for these newer aspects of competition law to settle down at a much higher level of acceptance than existed in the 1980s. The quality of legal argument and of the legal personnel concerned has also risen significantly in the last decade. Taken together with the process of irradiation which goes on all the time informally between the Commission and national agencies, and the interchange of experts, it seems likely that all governmental players and all institutions are tending towards a mean. Concertation and harmonization are being implemented, from below as well as above.

A series of notable cases make the main points; but it should be borne in mind that such dramatic instances are unlikely to recur, and certainly not in similar numbers.

CARTELS

A. Chemicals Companies

In 1983, a dawn raid by DG4 discovered evidence of a polypropylene cartel, similar to that which had operated for much the same reasons (overproduction of bulk chemicals) in the dyestuffs industry in the 1960s. The earlier fine had been small, amounting only to 50,000 ecus, but in 1983 the Commission decided to set an example and levelled total fines on the major chemicals companies concerned of 50 million ecus. ICI, which at once withdrew, had its share of the fine, 10 million ecus, reduced by the Court of First

Instance because of its compliance and cooperative attitude. A further dawn raid in 1986 exposed a cartel among PVC and LDP producers; once again ICI's share of the fines was reduced because it had ceased to be a member (and this was later cancelled due to procedural irregularities). The next case, over the soda ash cartel, produced fines on the cartel of 7 million ecus under Article 85 and 10 million under 86. The moral is not so easy to read: compliant firms which adjust their behaviour appeared to benefit as the Commission would like to think – but it can be argued that others (such as Hoechst which resisted a German court order and then took the Commission to the ECJ and lost) merely pay a tithe of their profits from longer-continued malpractice. Indeed they may never pay: DG4 has lost a series of cases in the European Court of Justice because of failures to follow the proper procedures in the case against the chemicals cartel, and the appeals continue.

B. Shipping Companies

Maritime traders, whose shipping 'conferences' had originally escaped because they were alleged to provide beneficial integrated services, were included in DG4's scope by decision of the Council in 1987, but were given block exemption because of the intense competition prevailing in a sector with substantial spare capacity, even in the boom years. Nevertheless, because of the 1972 Unctad Code, which was intended to benefit Third World shipping lines, two cases came up in 1992: Boloré (a French West African shipping company) and the SIWA cartel, involving French, German, Dutch and Belgian companies engaged in shipping and air transport to central Africa. Boloré was fined 31 million ecus, despite its political connections and avid lobbying of members of the then French government; SIWA escaped, probably because its four member states intervened much more widely.

C. Financial Cartels

Although the Commission can decide only on the cases which come to DG4 by complaint, the fact that complaints are welcomed, or can be provoked, suggest that there could in practice be an element of choice about which type of abuse to concentrate on. Whether this is in fact so, the 1980s cases in the financial sector seem to have diverted DG4 into issues of payments cards, restrictive practices and cross-border transfer costs, mostly to the benefit of consumer interests, and away from the crucial banks cartel whose management of interest rates affected all industrial borrowers. This was partly because the banks claimed that interest rates were governed by national monetary policy, but mainly because of the high political content involved in taking on so large an interest. Four sets of negotiations did take place in 1986–9 with the Irish, Belgian, Italian, and Dutch banks, all of which agreed merely to consider the question. Nothing more happened until DG4 reopened the file in 1990. By 1992 investigations showed that there had indeed been a cartel in the 1980s, but that it had virtually disappeared as a result of financial deregulation, so that there was little use proceeding with the case.

MERGERS

The merger landmark cases rested on what were ultimately questions of definition, such as; was there evidence of interdependence between national markets so that a fair chance existed of competition continuing in the EU as a whole? Was the European market always the relevant one, or were there circumstances (such as heavy transport costs) where the main consideration should be the national one? And was there evidence of concentration in the world market – indeed did such a world market exist? In putting such questions, DG4 had to rely on wider expertise and the help of other Directorates, whom in turn plaintiffs and complainants naturally sought to influence. DG4 also had to be careful that its inevitable lack of transparency (being judge in its own cases) should not be interpreted by the Court of First Instance as a cover for high-handedness or irregular procedures, which the aggrieved parties always tend to allege.

A. *Magnetti Morelli (1990–91)*

This merger involved a subsidiary of Fiat, manufacturing heavy-duty starter batteries. The merger would have given the new entity over 60% of the French market. Fiat, using former Italian ministers as ambassadors, lobbyied DG4 strongly at the highest level, arguing that the test should be the EC market, in which the two companies would hold only 22%. DG4 responded that, because of the transport costs, it was the French market which should count. In the end, partly because Brittan was not sure of college support, a compromise allowed the merger to go ahead, so long as Fiat sold off 65% of its French holding in the merger.

In a contrast which shows how results of a consistent principle may in practice be inconsistent, Bosch-Varta (1991), also in the batteries sector, was cleared when Varta made advance concessions in the German market.[23] The Mannesman-Boge and the Renault–Volvo mergers (the latter eventually failing because of Swedish share-holders' opposition) raised similar considerations but were allowed, as was Unilever's takeover of Sepal in 1994, despite the impact on the French market in frozen food: this suggests either that the Magnetti Morelli case ought to be seen as an exception, or that the van Miert regime had become more politically modulated than Brittan's.

B. *Dupont and ICI*

Dupont and ICI, both world leaders in chemicals, agreed to merge their nylon fibre production in 1992. DG3 fought for this merger, against strong opposition from the Merger Task Force; in the end, with only minor conditions, it went ahead. The case showed that significant concentration could be acceptable to DG4, if it contributed to an industry's attempt to eliminate overcapacity.[24] For once, DG3 and DG4 saw eye to eye, but not until there had been vigorous lobbying, especially on ICI's part, both of Commissioners and of the British minister, Michael Heseltine. What was negotiable during a deep recession, however, might not have been acceptable during a boom, especially if it had not coincided with the uneasy period in Britain after the first Danish referendum and before the House of Commons gave its long-delayed approval to the Maastricht Treaty.

C. *Aérospatiale–Alenia–de Havilland*

In this case of May 1991, where Aérospatiale (France) and Alenia (Italy) wanted to take over the Canadian aeroplane constructor de

Havilland, the Commission for the first time since the existence of the Merger Regulation prohibited a major takeover. The interdiction caused a strong reaction in public opinion in France, with widespread and hostile media coverage, the Commission being accused of anti-French attitudes, of excessive liberalism and a lack of any kind of sensitivity to the EU's industrial policy.

Aérospatiale Alenia ranked number two in the world market for small and medium turbo-prop passenger aircraft. Acquisition of de Havilland, the number one, would have substantially reinforced this position, giving the group 67% of the EU market – in competition primarily with Boeing and McDonnell-Douglas – a matter that was ostensibly in line with the EU's current industrial policy. But it was the 50% world market share which mattered more, given the context of continuing and difficult GATT Uruguay Round negotiations with the United States.

The circumstances were far from being as simple as the French media later suggested. The takeover was hardly a French national cause, for Alenia was also a state-owned company, in this case Italian, and the companies themselves promoted their case badly, failing even to coordinate their approach. Aérospatiale seems to have been ignorant of EC rules and to have taken Commission approval for granted. Industrial logic was also less sound than it appeared: some of Aérospatiale's competitors privately forecast that it would be swamped by the cost of de Havilland's restructuring.[25]

Whatever was said publicly, the French government did not fully support the merger. In particular, the Trésor judged it too costly in relation to its benefits, a view which in due course filtered through to DG4. The two companies also made no efforts to negotiate or reach a compromise but brazened it out to the end. (It should be added that Aérospatiale's chairman was subsequently replaced and the company's promotion techniques were radically revised.) Finally, DG3 seems not to have involved itself early enough, and then to have taken a confrontational position on the assumption that the industrial policy argument would win through. Bangemann fought it all the way and gave a press conference to emphasize the urgency of industrial policy – but he abstained during the vote, and

DG3 officials now admit that this case taught them to think through DG4's processes as well as their own.

Nevertheless, given the timing, the size of the companies involved, and the way the defence rested on French national chauvinism, it was not easy for DG4. But its officials with French nationality contacted their counterparts in the SGCI and thus learned what the Trésor (which had responsibility for Aérospatiale as a nationalized company) really thought. Despite this, and the issue of a warning from both governments, the companies resisted change, even in the tripartite meetings with the Commission which were called by DG4.

The lack of French government opposition sufficed to confirm DG4's judgment, allowing Brittan to assume that a majority could be won in the college. In the event, six votes swung in his favour in the days between the chefs du cabinet meeting and the college, enough to give him a two-thirds majority, for once with the support of Delors.[26] Success should be ascribed to the careful way DG4 argued its case, which ensured also that the companies did not appeal. Yet it is possible that had the two managements acted otherwise the result might have been different. In the Mannesman-Hoesch case, though an entity was created with over 50% market share in Germany, DG4 accepted that dominance was unlikely, because the German market opens only slowly;[27] and in the Magnetti Alcatal and Accor cases, different combinations or disinvestments were found acceptable.

The media outrage over de Havilland took the Brussels players by surprise, for there was really no case to allege that DG4 was selling out to American producers, already secure in their support from the US defence industry. Yet the occasion exacerbated the protectionist campaign, which affected both DG4's future conduct and the tone of later GATT negotiations. This may have been the first instance of cleavage between the EU centre and member state public opinion during the Maastricht period. Yet in the longer term the de Havilland case proved to be a triumph for empirical investigation of markets, since many officials had not actually *known* what the right answer should be. In retrospect, it can be seen as a landmark in the decline of not only national but European champions and in the evolution of a more balanced trade and industry policy, as well as a stage in the slow death of the defence industry's political leverage over European governments.

D. Nestlé–Perrier

This highly complicated bid raised an important point of legal principle: did the existing law recognize the concept of a *collective* monopoly (oligopoly) or duopoly? When the merger regulation was being negotiated in 1989, the German government, strongly supported by the Kartellamt, had argued that it should, but a majority of other member states rejected the idea, the British government being especially opposed on the grounds that to include it would be to increase the Commission's power. In the end, to DG4's discomfiture, the regulation did not mention duopoly.

An unusual number of interests were involved. Nestlé, one of the largest food and drink companies in Europe (but not in the EC) made a bid for the mineral water producer Perrier, a bid which was not entirely friendly but which derived from a defensive manoeuvre inspired by BSN, a large food and drink company, to prevent the Agnelli family increasing its stake in Perrier, as it had already done in BSN. Part of the agreement in this alliance was that Volvic and others among Perrier's spring waters should be sold to BSM, thus making BSN the largest mineral water producer in France.

The two companies assumed that, since duopoly was excluded from the Merger Regulation and since the case was likely to be dealt with by the French authorities, there would be no problem after notification. But the French government did not wish to have to take a decision which might go against France's apparent national interest, and in due course DG4 decided to open the case, since it raised serious doubts about the merger's compatibility with competition principles, if not the letter of the law. Since Leon Brittan believed that unless the Commission were able to take account of duopoly it could not properly regulate the effects of mergers, the question then became whether the Commission could interpret the law as it stood to that effect, as the Merger Task Force hoped.

The Commission had argued a rather similar position in the Italian Flat Glass case, but under Articles 85 and 86, and had been partly disallowed by the ECJ; so in the immensely complicated arguments which ensued, DG4 took care to move gently and not risk a similar legal challenge. For once, DG3 and DG4 stood together on the proposition that Nestlé and BSN, though individually controlling only about a third of the French mineral market, together would hold two-thirds. The German government reiterated its 1989 arguments and was joined somewhat surprisingly by the French government, whose main motive seems to have been to exclude the Agnellis; the British refused even to acknowledge the possibility of such a construction.

As the political battle developed parallel to the legal one, DG4 was made aware that it would be unwise to risk a further public outcry in France by vetoing the merger before the French referendum on Maastricht. At the same time, Nestlé let DG4 officials know that, unless a compromise were made, it would at once appeal, putting the putative interpretation once again at risk before the ECJ. Between them, DG4 and the players agreed informally to admit the principle but to approve this one merger, subject to only mild conditions: that is, the Commission would require Perrier to sell its mineral waters to a competitor (in the end to Cadbury-Schweppes).

In politically sensitive cases, such stratagems are not uncommon. DG4 won the principle – at least for a time;[28] Nestlé–Perrier obtained the commercial advantages they had sought. But the case had wider repercussions, for it showed not only how member states and companies use each occasion to influence interpretation according to their own interests but how an established legal text could be renegotiated by administrative-judicial process to enshrine in Community law a principle which had been *excluded* when the Regulation passed the Council of Ministers. Nestlé–Perrier gained in the short term, but all other companies found their margins of manoeuvre curtailed thereafter, as the German government and the Kartellamt had originally desired.

STATE AIDS

State aids are intrinsically contrary to the Treaties wherever they distort competition; the criterion being that no market player would have invested a similar amount under the same conditions. Aids are defined as being any direct or indirect financial advantage granted by the state, whether it is at national, regional, or local government level (the latter two categories of course constituting a grey area subject to conflict insofar as regional aid not coming under the Structural Funds can in some cases be construed as giving unfair competitive advantage). The list extends to state-run companies and even independent national bodies such as development agencies. Since they are by nature illegal, such sums, once identified, have to be repaid in their entirety. Failure by governments or agencies to notify the Commission, and a firm's acceptance of aid money in good faith, are not acceptable excuses. The ECJ has made all recipients aware that they too have a duty to notify.

Once the amount of illegal aid is proclaimed, there is no further room for manoeuvre, so companies and governments will try to convince the Commission beforehand either that the market would have advanced the money (or part of it) had an attempt been made, or that the sums were given for purposes which would otherwise legitimate it, such as privatization or restructuring under Commission industrial policy. A substantial field for informal bargaining is thus opened up. Even so, a member state's support is no guarantee of success – or secrecy, because although aids are formally a matter for donor, recipient and the Commission, news leaks out, usually via notices in the *Official Journal*, so that other member states are likely to intervene to uphold their own interests, as the German government argued in front of the ECJ against Belgian payments to the textile industry. Indeed in the Crédit Lyonnais case, the complaints against French government largesse came from French banking competitors.

In investigating systematically the practice of giving aid without notification, and in judging whether assistance which has been notified amounts to aid, the Commission (or rather DG4, followed by the college), has wide discretion. But under Article 93 (2) it is bound to consult with all relevant players, including third parties, and to give adequate reasons for its decision. In some sensitive cases where the Commission is in outright conflict with a national government, member states have been able to get away with dubious subsidies, for what appear to be eminently political reasons.

The behaviour of the Italian governments towards its state-owned steel industry is a recent, flagrant case; that of the German government towards former East German industry, which appears to have been modulated by Delors's close affinity with Chancellor Kohl, more understandable. Since there is no formal set of rules, as there is with the Merger Regulation, the game depends in the first instance on member states playing fair and notifying, and in the second on building up a body of precedents from which to argue in future. Member states' own mutual jealousy helps to police the system: in 1991 the French government challenged the Italian and Spanish governments over their aids to their steel industries, as the German government did in 1993–4; and British Airways has challenged aids to Air France on several occasions, most recently in 1994–5. To put it mildly, these campaigns and complaints have excavated more doubt about questionable matters and illicit behaviour, and caused more offence that any other in the range of competition.

Naturally, in the late 1980s when privatization became a fashionable remedy for the problems of state-owned (usually bankrupt) industries all across Europe, competitors and members which had already gone further down that road were likely to challenge cases where aid was used as a means to improve the stock market flotation prospects of what would otherwise have been difficult (if not impossible) businesses to sell without extracting the profitable elements alone. Even in 1995, the majority of all cases are contested, in politically charged circumstances, often by Commissioners speaking very directly about 'the country they know best'. But the early 1990s recession, which curtailed most of the more important privatizations in France and Italy, made things worse, because new aids had to be provided just to see them through. Unfortunately for the governments concerned, the justification that the money was a one-off transaction, prior to privatization, had often been used up in earlier rounds, so that when the next set of demands came in 1993–5, the cases had to be made *de novo*.

In March 1989, before the French parliamentary elections, the Chirac government made an arrangement with the Commission under which 12 billion French francs were accepted as a legitimate precursor to shutting down 25% of the Renault's capacity by 1990, to be followed by privatization. Unfortunately the next (Socialist) government of Rocard was not prepared to push the legislation through parliament, nor to cut the work force as required. The Commission then brought the case.

Just as de Havilland became a cause célèbre, whatever the intrinsic merits of the Commission's action, the atypical case of Renault's 1991 aid aroused intense feelings. There appears to have been an element of exemplary punishment: DG4's 'prejudice in principle against aids' had been heightened during the first year of Leon Brittan's tenure, and his slight sympathy with poorer struggling member states like Portugal or Greece certainly did not extend to France, Italy and Spain. Renault thus became a test case, not least because the money, having been given in one lump sum to a state-owned company (rather than to a private one in small amounts), was easily recoverable.

French governments had until then habitually ignored the Commission's notification requirements (as they had in the horse racing case, see p. 240 fn 27), despite protests from Sutherland and later Brittan. But when Elizabeth Guigou became Secretary General of SGCI and adviser to Mitterrand, she realized that the circumstances were changing and that France must follow; it should reduce its hostility to DG4 or risk some isolation and, at that point very importantly, serious disagreements with the newly reunited Germany. The initiative, in seeking to explain France's position better and negotiate a solution acceptable in France, thus came from Paris; but being over-laid in the public imagination by the dramatic tenor of the Renault affair was ignored by the media, which tended in retrospect to judge that DG4 had tried to bring France to heel.[29]

Raymond Levy, Renault's chairman, argued that Renault had been committed, as much as the French government, to push through the restructuring. What was not said, and manifestly could not be said, was that this strategy involved large-scale redundancies in what still the heartland of CGT, the Communist trade union confederation, as one precursor to opening the entire French car industry to foreign competitors. In the context of rapidly evolving

French policy, the authorities saw no reason why Britain alone should benefit from direct investment by Japanese producers, given that these already operated in France in the electronics industry. If the underlying game was a national one, to use the Commission and the company to do what French public opinion would never permit, it may explain the behaviour not only of PSA and Jacques Calvet but of ACEA in the VER negotiations with Japan which followed in 1991–2 (see p. 575).

DG4 had no choice but to accept the challenge as it stood, hoping perhaps over the period 1990–91 to develop a *modus vivendi* with the French administration which would not run counter to the Commission's wider industrial policy. Brittan saw himself, and apparently was seen, as a 'partner-adversary who has never put France in a really difficult situation, where irremediable political or economic national interests are endangered. He has a talent for blowing up affairs and then applying pressure on the member state infringing Treaty rules.'[30] Nearer the surface, however, the Renault case was fought out to the limit, with interventions by President Mitterrand himself and Rocard to Commissioners other than Brittan, and by Raymond Levy in person, in order to put the argument that Renault's 12 billion francs had been given for capital provision and research and development.

In the end, DG4 judged that between 50–60% should be categorized as illegal aid, the type of aid being acceptable but the amount excessive. Brittan offered the French a deal: if the case went to the college, it was likely that the sum would be set at 8 billion but if Renault settled in advance, 6 billion would suffice.[31] A compromise was accepted, but rancour exploded in the press, as it had with de Havilland.

More recently, aids cases have clustered in the steel and civil airlines sectors, for obvious reasons (steel is considered in chapter 12). But DG4's intention has been to move on, to two newer and even more sensitive areas: subsidies for exports, and incentives to foreign concerns to make inward investments, both of which are likely, if pursued wholeheartedly, to encounter severe opposition in Britain and Germany as well as in France, Italy and Spain. As far as 'older' categories are concerned, the procedures are now more or less established:[32] any informal bargaining takes place at the beginning, before notification, where efforts are made to render the aid acceptable to the Commission. Since the mere possibility that DG4 will open a case is now a severe deterrent, member states have tended to reduce or modify aids, to make them closer to competitive market conditions, rather than run the risk of a head-on contest.[33]

The Boussac case (see above), that of BAe–Rover and the £350 million sweeteners paid to Alfa Romeo before its sale to Fiat (which had to be repaid in June 1990) can thus been seen as 'old' cases.[34] BAe had bought the UK government's share in Rover – one of the few potentially profitable remaining elements of British Leyland – on the strength of a promise to write off Rover's accumulated debts, and to provide £800 million of new capital. In 1988 the Commission approved this as a once-and-for-all transaction. But then secret 'sweeteners' were added by the DTI, amounting to £44 million, which were judged illegal by the Commission in June 1990.

The investigation was handled by DG4 and the British government, without the third parties, and without keeping BAe-Rover informed, on the grounds that the company was not a party to the illegal transaction. When the repayment was ordered, the British government started High Court proceedings against the company, and BAe–Rover applied for a stay of execution, arguing that the £44 million was not aids but part of the original contract. In February 1992, the ECJ overruled the Commission on the grounds that the company's rightful opportunity to contest the original judgment had been denied. At once the Commission responded: the aids still being illegal, they would re-open the process, and moreover would require repayment of interest on the principal since the affair began in 1990, not 1992, the date of judgment.

Intense bargaining now took place on two levels, that of the government–DTI and the company. Finally the Commission, after what seems to have been a considerable internal struggle, settled for a moratorium and demanded the £44 million with interest only from the ECJ date of 1992. The case made it clear that the Commission takes no account of national tax regimes (putting companies in double jeopardy) and also that the British government would not seek to mitigate the penalty once it had been decided, despite the fact that the then DTI minister, Lord Young, may have been at fault in not succeeding in getting a definitive answer from the Commission in his discussion about the 'sweeteners' at the time.[35] From the company's point of view, it had been let down by both authorities, yet it had no choice but to pay. The Commission congratulated itself that it had given a lesson not only to all companies but to a government which had played riskily and amateurishly. More important for the future, it had succeeded in keeping third parties out of the game, the better to concentrate on the donor and the aid.

After steel, aids to national airlines constitute the longest running battle in this arena. Yet these are also 'old' cases, and the aids are only part of a wider struggle in the liberalization of one of the last bastions of national protection, in which DG4 was never a major player until the Commission's deal with the European carriers, to reduce their air fares in stages, contingent on establishing the internal market. Negotiated between 1987 and 1992, this agreement on fares provided for full liberalization over nine years Britain, followed by the Netherlands and Germany, had clearly set the pace, BA having been privatized in 1987. but at that time, state aid barely concerned the Commission, which directed itself more to pricing and then to mergers. British Airways thus escaped with its privatization related state aids intact, thanks to its skilful diplomacy during the primary stages. Nearly a decade later, Air France was to be criticized severely for failing to do the same.

More recent aids cases have been argued out in a very different political and economic context, characterized by large numbers of dirty tricks, vigorous feints and counter-attacks by different players. The state-owned lines, headed by Air France, objected for example to KLM's attempt to take over or make arrangements with its competitors, and to the allegedly preferential treatment given by DG4 to the BA–Dan Air, and BA–TAT mergers, contrasting it with the treatment of Air France's proposed mergers with UTA–Air Inter, and with Sabena.[36] As far as the sums are concerned, the Commission has so far allowed very large tranches of aid despite DG4's efforts to insist that member states should not be allowed to top up earlier sums simply because of the recession or strike action by employees against threats of redundancy (Air France in 1993, Iberia in 1994).[37] To that, Air France replied in 1992 that theirs was not 'aid' but a 'complex montage' essential for future privatization. Van Miert, responsible for DG7 (transport) at that time, accepted the case. Brittan did not; which may explain DG4's current line, under Brittan's successor van Miert,[38] at a time when recovery began to restore modest profits to the ailing airlines, sufficient perhaps for the mirage of privatization to become a reality.

Of course member states have considerable leverage in any field believed to be central to national interest where, for political reasons, the option of bankruptcy is simply not available. Groupe Bull, the collapsing computer concern, is a case in point; DG4 found French government aid on two occasions in 1993 to have been illegal and attempted, in January 1994, to forestall another tranche which it held to be unjustified in the absence of substantial restructuring (the French government aim being in fact to keep Bull out of the hands of its Japanese competitor NEC).

But in 1992–3, pressure from French Euro-sceptics in Paris, many of them in or close to the Balladur government, was intense; so it is not surprising that DG4 took some care to avoid direct confrontation – and with the governments of Belgium, Portugal, Spain and Greece, for similar reasons.

Trade union activism, at a time when the Commission was showing itself sensitive to historically high unemployment figures, added another dimension in the college. For a time at least, it became easier for beleaguered member states successfully to invoke exemptions for their state-owned industries on the grounds of national exigency or compatibility under Article 93.

What amounts to collective bargaining between nation states is probably only possible in recessionary times and at the governmental-Commission college level where Commissioners seek to establish customary patterns, not to win pyrrhic battles.[39] (It is simply not open to corporate or regional players to act in this way in ordinary competition cases, as they lack both the knowledge and the influence governments possess with rival Directorates and with other Commissioners.) Most of the other state aid loopholes have now been closed. A member state cannot get away with claiming prior notification, if the Commission can prove to the contrary; neither can it extend the approved framework without permission.[40] It is possible, on the other hand, that they may in future be able to argue the importance of environmental considerations, when public utilities like water or electricity supply are privatized and provided with grants to cope with pollution.

But the ECJ has established the principle that, even if a national law does not permit reimbursement, it is still the state's responsibility to change the law in order to restore a properly constituted field of competition. The van Miert-Andreatta agreement, made in July 1993, embodies an Italian government undertaking to reduce state participation in public enterprises, and no longer to give full debt guarantees (as is required under Italian law from a sole share-holder). Whether such an agreement between a Commissioner and a member state is enforceable or justiciable remains to be seen.[41] DG4 has also on occasion tried to restrict the scope of regional aid to wealthier regions, with Germany, rather than the Mediterranean periphery, in mind as a test case. But many lesser state and regional aids slip through, either because they are not notified or detected or because they are distributed in ways and amounts which vitiate the effectiveness of repayment orders.

One other area of informal negotiation concerns the penalties imposed; not for state aids which, being illegal, are automatically repayable in full, but for offences under Articles 85 and 86 which include refusal to provide information and the provision of false or incomplete data. Penalties range from a minimum of 1000 ecus to a maximum of 1 million ecus, or 10% of a company's turnover: the current record having recently been set in the cement cartel case (November 1994), whose fines totalled £200 million. For the Commission, the seriousness of the offence and the length of time it lasted are the main criteria, determined according to the circum-stances of each case.

Those hardest hit, like traffic offenders, will always complain that penalties are arbitrary, and that they have been singled out. Since there is no clear official policy on penalties – and cannot be, given the singular circumstances of each offence – the Commission is to some extent vulnerable to such accusations. Whether it is open to negotiation on the amount before announcing the fine is likely to depend on whether the principle or the deterrent effect is more important. Most companies propose obedience to the principle in future, having gained by non-observance in the past. The ICI case (see p. 512) is instructive, for it shows that the Commission and the ECJ have relatively long memories and require strict performance if reductions or waivers are to be made.

Where a company resists on procedural grounds, for reasons of natural justice, or simply because the time for haggling has passed, the ECJ is their only recourse. Leaving aside procedural irregularities, penalties tend to be imposed more often where the informal bargaining process has failed, or where an industry or a company has established a long pattern of disregard for competition rules. The soda ash cartel offers a clear example – as does Tippex GmbH (judgment February 1990) – even though the soda ash fines were eventually struck out for procedural reasons. Whether or not the firms are in the end forced to pay is not in fact the main sanction; the possibility of fines, and the notoriety, shareholders' protests, and government disfavour which are likely to ensue encourage firms to cooperate as early as possible and to present their case in good faith – and furthermore, in accordance with commercial self-interest, to inform on others once their own offence has been discovered.[42]

Possibilities for informal bargaining occur throughout the arena of competition law but are rarely seen clearly through the distorting medium of national newspapers and television, which tend to focus on hard cases or what individual Commissioners do (for example, whether van Miert had 'gone soft' on airlines in 1993–4). Given that DG4's stringent enforcement of an ever-expanding area dates only from the mid–1980s, it is not surprising that progress should have been made via landmark cases with political implications, or that the Commission should frequently prefer to establish principles, even at the risk of not pressing home the immediate lesson. The game is a long one, in which there will no doubt always be a tendency to hit hardest at the more powerful offenders, and to mitigate the law's rigours for smaller national firms, especially those based in poorer regions.

The impression of draconian justice, which may have had temporary justification in 1990–91, is misguided. In the EC's 22nd Competition Report 1992, Commissioner van Miert emphasized the need in a recession to take account of social, economic and political mitigating circumstances – and the importance of encouraging subsidiarity. These principles, and the Report itself, had been in draft during Brittan's tenure as Commissioner.[43] There may well have been a particular focus on France in these years, but this occurred because the French government was prepared for it to be so, being either hostile to the plaintiffs (Aérospatiale–Alenia) or uncertain how best to proceed (Renault) That the media picture suited the French governments *vis-à-vis* their own electorate, and that the companies' chief executives Bernard Attali and Raymond Levy played openly to that gallery,[44] is not of course in doubt. But any conclusion that DG4 shaped French state behaviour, based on the observation that France's annual rate of infringements fell from ten or twelve cases a year before 1990 to two or three a year afterwards, is unjustified; had DG4 had such powers, it would surely have used them against Italy whose infringements still run at twelve to fifteen a year.

II. Managing the ERM

As an elite within an elite, central bankers are secretive by nature as well as circumstances and accustomed to dealing with each other on professional not political terms (in the conclaves of Basel, the Bank of International Settlements, or the Group of Ten); they constitute a *noyau* of players whose operations are little studied outside the financial press, and are rarely compared with member state players whose currencies they guard, or the industrial ones whose behaviour they frequently seek to control. Yet like the others, they are players in a game whose outcome affects all, on every level, especially the interplay of the Commission, the Monetary Committee and member states' finance ministers on the Council.

It is significantly easier to examine what central bankers do in their own nation states, how they and their institutions relate to Treasuries and Finance Ministries, what part they have in the control of domestic money supply or supervision of banks and financial institutions. Their archives are closed to very recent research, but most now cooperate in the writing of their histories. Practitioners of elite oral history can occasionally discern more recent disagreements between Central Banks and national governments, in say Germany or Britain in 1980–81.[45] (In the German case, the rupture went so far that the government in Bonn considered taking a loan from Saudi Arabia while waiting for the Bundesbank to make its choice between its two grand responsibilities of supporting the currency and supporting the government's economic policy. In the British instance, the Bank of England strove unofficially and informally to push down interest rates sufficiently to mitigate the worst side-effects on industry of an over-rigid monetary stance – and succeeded in part, by manipulating the Treasury bill rate, but at a substantial political price.)

Similar histories could be constructed, in which Central Banks played a role as guardians of the currency and the probity of national economic policy at variance with what governments, preoccupied with political or ideological considerations, considered appropriate. The most obvious is the Banca d'Italia's long post-War struggle to reform the appalling laxity of fiscal stance of over forty successive governments, and their politically corrupt dealings evident in the last ten years. Since 1977 the Banco de España, has played a rather similar role, seeking a sound anti-inflationary policy but without the Banca d'Italia's advantage of providing its government with two prime ministers in a matter of two years.

But this is not the normal habit of central bankers in the EU, firstly because they are formally subordinate to Treasury ministers on the Monetary Committee, and are not present except as advisers on Ecofin; secondly because until monetary union (EMU) became a matter of practical politics, the Committee of Governors which meets in Basel occupied the greyest of areas between Community institutions, the Bank of International Settlements (BIS), and the truly international fora, ranging from the Group of Five to the

Group of Ten. The first occasion when they became overtly concerned as players was in 1989, when member states set up the Delors Committee to write the rules of the future European Central Bank which would administer EMU.

But any suggestion that member states called their central bank governors' collective European force into existence ignores two other dimensions: firstly, the long change of emphasis in all states, in which political priorities shifted during the 1980s from the goals of the post-War settlements, full employment and universal welfare systems, to concern with inflation (in which Central Banks were actors on the international and European as well as national levels); and secondly, the changing format in which the European Monetary System's exchange rate mechanism (ERM) was managed. The former needs no amplification; the latter is crucial here, because the EMS is an agreement made between Central Banks, managed collectively by them, in association with the Community/European Union. When the alignment of currency rates in the ERM is changed, Ecofin meets not as a Council of Ministers but as the twelve (now fifteen) finance ministers of the member states. Hence it can be said that 'informal cooperation is part of the ERM itself – the players *are* the central bankers.'[46]

Although it has been argued that the EMS represented a basic step towards a regional currency bloc,[47] this was not how things seemed to the system's originators in 1979. Articles 67–69 and 104–109 of the Treaties provide for nothing beyond a Monetary Committee to coordinate member states' monetary policies, not to provide a common one. But in default of a dollar standard, after the break-up of the Bretton Woods arrangements in 1971–2, and during the 1970s exchange rate crises, an assumption developed in the Commission that a mechanism linking member states' exchange rates might provide a substitute. This search led, via the Snake, to the EMS as an alternative to an insulated regional system, in whose origins member states (led by Schmidt and Giscard), the Commission (urged on by Roy Jenkins), and central bankers as advisers on the technicalities, all cooperated.

As the underlying reasons for having an EMS changed during the next ten years, so did the role of the progenitors, with central bankers coming to fulfil a role similar to that which they had played before 1914 in managing as well as implementing the Gold Standard. However, whereas central bankers can be seen as a sort of managerial class, united by their technical knowledge and professional ethos, member states divided in two broadly ideological camps. As early as 1972–3, in the wake of the Werner Committee's recommendations that the EEC should complete monetary union within a decade, France and Germany were reading different meanings into the EMU concept.[48] Meanwhile, some member states and one EFTA country had aligned their currencies – the Dutch guilder, the Austrian schilling, and the Danish krone – to the deutschmark.

Put at its simplest, in the highly inflationary period after 1974, the Commission never gave up on EMU, and central bankers never gave up on monetary policy as the essential discipline for all member states. It was not possible to envisage EMU until the right conditions existed throughout the Community, so that nothing could be advanced formally until the general abolition of exchange controls, which was established in 1988 but not completed until 1990 (with extensions for three of the poorer member states). But there existed much earlier possibilities for shaping *how* in practice EMU could be introduced – hence the various stages of the ERM, discussed in chapter 4. Crucially, after 1987, under the influence of the French government, member states edged the ERM into strict narrow bands, and away from the regular realignments of its 'classic period' in the previous four years, so that it would become the 'glide path' along which member states were intended to converge, ready for the finality of EMU, after which currencies would be locked irrevocably together.

EMU was, in the estimation of most Commission economists and the majority of member states which signed the SEA in 1986, a necessary consequence of the Single European Act, even though it appeared tangentially in the text, to appease British and Danish sensibilities. But at that stage the correct path to EMU, the nature of its regime, and the shape of the European Central Bank were still unclear: hence the Delors Committee's deliberations, the elaboration of three stages, and the EMU IGC at Maastricht, which ran in parallel with, Political Union in order to satisfy Germany's deep worries that other governments would, even after Monetary Union, find ways to renege or slide back in the face of domestic, political or economic pressures.

In that movement after 1987, the Commission (eager for full harmonization and common monetary policy as recommended by the Padoa-Schioppa Report) and the Governors' Committee worked together, whatever individuals' various reservations; as did the central bankers of member states like Britain and Spain, which were not then members of the ERM. Despite often serious doubts, Karl-Otto Pöhl (Bundesbank president) and Robin Leigh-Pemberton (Bank of England governor) signed the Delors Report on the assumption that there would be time for all member state economies and currencies eventually to converge. (Pöhl retracted later and publicly admitted his faith in EMU and the Delors Report to have been misguided.)

It was the later addition of a strict timetable, and Spanish entry in the broad plus-or-minus 6% band (which had been forced on the Banco de España by its own government, largely to meet French pressures prior to the Mitterrand–Kohl declaration in April 1990), followed by the start of stage two of EMU and convergence criteria in 1991, which brought these doubts and reservations into play. Until then, central bankers' judgements about the precise modalities required for EMU had not been so clouded, as were those of finance ministers, by political considerations. Nothing that member state governments did after the Madrid Summit in 1989 was to remove central bankers' doubts about the possibility that, in a crisis, politicians in a system related to the ecu (which is a basket of currencies) rather than the DM would revert to claims of national sovereignty and fiscal autonomy, thus reintroducing the 'inconsistent quartet'.

The history of the two disruptive crises of 1992 and 1993 follows, but needs to be supplemented both by contemporary comment (for the crises were to some extent matters of public perception) and some elaboration of the players' own state of mind, because it was their concepts which underpinned the ERM system – differing interpretations between central bankers and national administrators being sources of weakness every time the system came under external threat.

Stage two of EMU had begun in 1991, despite the onset of recession, and politics had already intruded at Maastricht. The planned European Central Bank was not instituted (as the Delors Committee had recommended); rather a European Monetary Institute was created which, finally lodged in Frankfurt, found itself informally overshadowed by the Bundesbank, despite the appointment as chairman of Alexandre Lamfalussy, the French former head of the BIS. Nevertheless, it was assumed that the convergence process would soon operate and that member states would be forced by it to adjust their performance on inflation, interest rates, public debt ratios and budget deficits: an assumption so strong that in the United States it was taken for granted by financial institutions. Any breakdown would thus imply immense opportunities for speculators in the currency markets.

Then came German reunification and the consequences of exchanging deutschmarks for ostmarks at a parity of one to one, which turned out to be just as disastrous as Karl-Otto Pöhl had forecast. The Bundesbank pushed interest rates higher during 1991–2 to counter the overshoot in German money supply, exposing the other eleven member states to a severer recession than would have been the case had it not been for the absurdity of an anchor currency country having the highest rate of inflation of any in the ERM narrow bands. It may be that for their own reasons a majority of the Bundesbank Council wished either to unpin the ERM or return its management to the 'classic period' rules; if so, what seemed valid to them in domestic terms was perceived from outside as a conspiracy from which the rest of Europe was to suffer during the next two and a half years.

The more complaints by member states to the German government accentuated the difference between Bonn and Frankfurt, the more Helmut Schlesinger, the Bundesbank's president, upheld the tradition of stubborn independence set by his predecessors. Those currencies whose interest rates rose highest, the peseta (which had, since its entry in 1989, remained in the 6% band) and the lira became obvious targets for medium-term speculation, particularly by the huge American-managed funds. However, in spite of the omens, a brief period of calm occurred early in 1992, during which Portugal's escudo came into the ERM and, against the odds, the Conservative party won the British general election. Meanwhile, because of the peseta's paradoxical behaviour, the French administration began to suspect that the convergence process, or 'competitive disinflation' might not work out as planned. Yet there was evidence that the French franc might be becoming at last the joint anchor currency, a development that aroused tensions in Germany, as the franc briefly rose above the deutschmark in the narrow band.

After the first Danish referendum, and through the summer of 1992, dismay spread, fanned by the narrowness of the result in France, Maastricht's difficult passage in Britain, and Germany's enforced delay pending the Constitutional Court's judgment. Political uncertainty prejudiced the ERM's management into 1993, exacerbating a flight from the weaker currencies, lira, peseta, escudo and finally sterling. Governments responded differently: the new Amato government in Italy raised interest rates, with serious repercussions on the budget deficit and the fiscal package of reforms amounting to 30 trillion lira which had been prepared in July. In Spain, and contrary to the Central Bank's advice, Carlos Solchaga, the finance minister, appeared willing to devalue the peseta sharply,[49] both to help industry and to finance the government's spending excesses in the three previous years. The peseta fell below the bottom end of the narrow band.

Meanwhile on 16 July, the Bundesbank again raised its rate, with the direct result that speculative pressures moved against sterling, the Swedish krone and the Finnish markka. With the Monetary Committee riven by disagreements, member states took their own courses; in Britain, Norman Lamont boldly raised interest rates to defend sterling in a gesture with profound political effects on the Thatcherite Euro-sceptic faction in the Conservative Party. Given the increasing flow from the lira into deutschmarks, the Bundesbank invoked the 'Emminger letter', protesting against the way that the ERM's automatic support mechanism forced it to bail out the weaker currencies.

In late August and September, member state governments and Central Banks tried to find the means to escape the external pressures, which were due very largely to currency market operators betting on the near-certainty of enforced realignment, whatever the presumed new rules operating in the ERM under Stage One of EMU. Negotiations took place in a severely disunited Monetary Committee, chaired by Jean-Claude Trichet, a French former head of the Trésor and representative of the Ministry of Economics and Finance at Maastricht. Central Banks other than the Bundesbank were, in this case, all to some extent under their government's command. Almost the entire non-German European press blamed the Bundesbank, but it would be more accurate to say that, in each case, governments' self-interest vied with their vestigial awareness that the ERM must not be allowed to collapse in an enforced realignment like that of 1983.

Although Schlesinger took little part in efforts to negotiate a *general* realignment (which was in any case ruled out by the Monetary Committee on 28 August),[50] his deputy, Hans Tietmeyer did, being closer by background and temperament to the German government position and that of the finance state secretary H. Köhler. These two, with Trichet, attempted to negotiate a realignment at least of the lira (Spain having apparently opted to devalue), an arrangement which was undermined when Italian leaks to the press about a deutschmark rate cut induced the Bundesbank Council actually to raise it by a quarter per cent. The start of the switchback ride began on 5/6 September, when the Bundesbank came under intense political pressure to mitigate its stance, as the finance ministers were actually meeting in Bath under the British Presidency.

All the deep rifts were now clear, not only between the Bundesbank and the twelve member state governments (including that of Germany), but between central bankers and their own governments, especially in countries with the highest interest rates. Schlesinger himself contributed to the debacle by an ill-judged comment on 15 September, published two days later in *Handelsblatt*, that devaluation of the lira had not gone far enough and that sterling was now also at risk, a comment which, at British ministers' request, he later – too late – denied having made.

Yet the Bundesbank can hardly be portrayed as the only villain, given that it did offer the elements of a realignment, involving sterling (which was now shown to be heavily over-valued when it entered the ERM), to the Monetary Committee chairman Trichet, who appears to have kept quiet about it for his own or French state reasons, largely to do with France's coming referendum. (The offer was not made directly to the Bank of England, because the Monetary Committee has responsibility for realignments, and Trichet was trusted to pursue it: that this did not happen is a measure of how mistrustful that body had become, and how the ERM's rigidity now blocked all forms of brokerage.)[51]

Black Wednesday followed on 16 September. The pound and the lira left the ERM, after what the *Financial Times* highlighted as an unprecedented flight from sterling involving the biggest action ever mounted by a Central Bank in its defence (at a cost later estimated by some authorities at £15 billion, by the *Economist* at \$15–20 billion). The peseta and the Irish punt followed sterling and the lira downwards but without actually leaving the ERM.

The simplest conclusion is also the most obvious. Given the external pressures on the weaker currencies during the recession, the long-sought convergence process became unattainable, save at a price which was politically quite unacceptable. The failure of certain countries to converge (Italy, Spain, Belgium and Ireland being in the forefront) in turn increased the likelihood of devaluations, from which not only speculators but Asian and southeast Asian Central Banks operating in currency markets stood to make vast sums of money. (One American fund alone, managed by George Soros, recouped £1 billion from sterling's devaluation.) Yet for manifestly political reasons, the option of managed devaluation or a general realignment had been ruled out by finance ministers and their governments, over the heads of at least four or five of the major state Central Banks.

Stability was not restored and, having tested the ERM partners' resolve, currency market operators read the narrow French referendum majority as a portent and set themselves to repeat their coup – this time against the French franc. That was to touch the ERM's heart, for if the Bundesbank had been prepared to see sterling as well as the other weaker currencies go down, there had been no question (save perhaps in Schlesinger's mind) that it was essential, on sound economic as well political grounds, to maintain the *franc fort*. Some talk of a deutschmark–French franc union and the reintroduction of something close to capital controls in Paris made the point explicit. Meanwhile very steep rises in interest rates in Spain, Portugal and Ireland (almost to Italian levels), together with the restoration of capital controls in Spain (which the Commission promptly declared illegal), emphasized the existence of a 'continental defence'. Retrospectively, Britain was widely and unfairly blamed for having engineered the collapse, from which it had by then self- evidently benefited in terms of lower interest rates and a revival in the economy which was envied by Industry Ministries across the whole EU. Currency disturbances continued in the autumn, imperilling the Danish krone, and finally bringing down the Swedish krone and the Finnish markka. Spain devalued again, and Italy's finance minister virtually withdrew from the Monetary Committee.

Speculative attacks on the French franc in November brought government intervention and a climate of acute unease to the French banking system. But at last, thanks to a Bundesbank reappraisal and the efforts of Tietmeyer and Köhler, German interest rates began to fall, allowing Ireland, Spain and Portugal to go ahead, as planned at Hannover in 1988, with the abolition of exchange controls. But the turnaround did not start until February 1993, when the Danish krone, with Bundesbank help, rejoined the deutschmark core; before that, the Belgian franc had tumbled and the punt had almost fallen out of the ERM.

Assistance to Denmark exposed the deutchsmark itself to speculators for the first time, and Schlesinger now admitted to doubts about even the deutschmark–French franc relationship. The ERM's slow recovery up to May 1993 was hedged about with political pressures, arising from the crippling rates now in force also in France. In Spain, the economic consequences of ERM management brought widespread protests and in Lisbon it triggered the resignation of the Bank of Portugal's deputy governor – for the reappraisal which all central bankers were now making of the previous six months' events brought them into conflict with what the larger member state governments still wanted from the ERM.

On 22 May, in a report to Ecofin, the Committee of Governors proposed that in the light of recent experience, the EU should agree to more frequent realignments. Concerned more about the spectre of 'competitive devaluation' eroding the glidepath, Ecofin Ministers refused.[52] That this did not cause more trouble may have been due in part to the Balladur government's public reiteration of faith in France's existing policy and partly at least to further interest rate falls in Germany, which by June finally achieved what amounted to the general devaluation of all currencies save Denmark's against the deutschmark, which the Monetary Committee had rejected nine months earlier.

But the game had not ended. In June, the newly appointed, politically inexperienced French finance minister, Edmond Alphandéry, repeated Lamont's unhappy attempt to coerce the Bundesbank into a faster pattern of interest rate reductions, provoking a confrontation which culminated on 30 July in a set piece battle between the French and the German representatives in Ecofin – at which the French side suggested that imbalances in the ERM could only be cured if the deutschmark itself withdrew. Since the outcome would have been an ERM of one, and since the next day the Banque de France had to spend the unprecedented amount of between £25 and £30 billion defending the franc, the politicians' bluff was at last called. Chancellor Kohl averred that the deutschmark might indeed withdraw, but proposed instead a regime of wider bands of plus-or-minus 15%, instead of 2.5%. In the end, Frankfurt sided with Bonn to preserve the Bundesbank's independence in the long term,[53] and the glidepath thesis was surrendered in order to preserve the Franco-German link. But France's six-year-long attempt to corral the deutschmark and institute EMU on French terms broke down.

After Black Wednesday, the press in each member state had picked over the reasons and lessons of what was generally seen (except in Britain) as a disaster. In France,[54] the tenor had been that something so serious, which questioned the fundamental power of national institutions and the French state itself to control France's external environment, coming after a period of apparent tranquillity, could only be explained by the actions of external speculators, and secondly by disaffection in the ERM stemming from the City of London. Commentators gave credit to the authorities for their sustained defence of the franc, which had been and still was necessary to give it credibility *vis-à-vis* the deutschmark; and also credit to the Bundesbank for its support of France under the Nyborg Agreement. Yet they also evinced fears similar to those before 1987, of Bundesbank domination and the likelihood that a two-speed Europe would ensue, detracting from the intentions set out in the Kohl–Mitterrand declaration. Overall, the mood remained self-congratulatory, even in a hard morose autumn, on the grounds that France had done what it had said it would and what Britain had failed to do, and therefore had deserved German backing.

The Spanish press blamed the same culprits, but included its own government, targeting Solchaga's austerity programme. According to *El País*, the crisis had destroyed confidence not only in the peseta but in Spain's passage to the status of a major European power.[55] Later articles in October castigated the two-speed thesis and averred that Spain's national dignity required it to stay in the ERM, and in the premier league, even at the price then being paid. The Italian press at first accepted the explanation set out by Carlo Ciampi, governor of the Banca d'Italia, to the Senate Treasury Commission on 24 September: that the blame rested equally on member states' delays in convergence, on fears connected with the French referendum, on divergence among member states' governments, and on the speculators. But few followed his defence of continued ERM membership when it involved interest rates over 20%, and Carlo de Benedetti was only the first, most prominent, industrialist to ask why Italian industries should die, so that Germany could fund its reunification.[56]

Two schools contested the crisis's interpretation in Germany. The first argued that the problem arose because the deutschmark had had to carry all the other currencies, whose member states should properly bear responsibility for the outcome; the second, that it was due to governments and central bankers who had collectively failed to answer the question about realignment originally put by Karl-Otto Pöhl. Politicians therefore, having tried to fix exchange rates, had forced the Bundesbank to react by encouraging the core of currencies to evolve instead.[57] As far as individual member states were concerned, Kohl himself angrily rejected Norman Lamont's criticisms of the Bundesbank, but Helmut Schmidt defended Britain and argued that the Bundesbank should have been more diplomatic: all players should have realized 'that monetary policy is foreign policy'.[58]

Financial institutions universally sided with the Bundesbank, but some press commentators criticized the German government's apparent lack of European solidarity and its insistence afterwards that the 'German view' had triumphed. Tietmeyer's talk of concentric circles was welcomed or deplored according to whichever commentator spoke; however, in the late autumn, a general tone emerged in the serious press that the essentials now were to preserve stability, above all in the deutschmark, secondarily in the core group, which now comprised the French franc, and the Belgian, Danish and Dutch currencies.

By that stage, the French government's insistence on fixed parities had come into question, prefiguring Schlesinger's later publicly expressed doubts. The view that no German government could risk all that the DM's stability implied, accompanied by an insistence that the developing European Monetary Institute (EMI) should conform to Bundesbank experience during its early years, was expressed with increasing force during 1993. Public opinion focused on threats to the DM and informed opinion in Germany followed Bonn ministers' awareness of the dilemma, that national self-interest ought to follow Europe's interest, but that other member states could not admit this to be case if Germany were the defining power. In re-establishing the earlier argument for a transition to EMU only through the core currencies, an intellectual argument for broad bands was already being made.

After the second crisis in July 1993, similar comments were voiced in all four major member states. But in Britain, being out of range, blame was now put far more widely on the ERM's inflexibility, so that the denouement was depicted as inevitable. Since the

ERM infrastructure survived under the broad band regime, and since central bankers' management of the system continued to work well, commentators in 1993–4 tended to congratulate those who had held it together at a cost far less than had been experienced during the fluctuations caused by the dollar's rise and fall in the 1980s. Competitive devaluations had been prevented, and a process induced in which interest rates would fall rapidly, minimizing the worst protests in France – though not in Italy and Spain. Observing the effects of the guilder and Danish krone being in the core group, Belgian newspapers complained about being excluded by market pressures and condemned to higher interest rates. The stage was thus set for a novel sort of convergence, and for currency pacts, initially between the French and Belgian francs, but subsequently including the escudo and the lira.[59]

That press comment frequently differed from the deductions made by central bankers is hardly surprising. Opinions among the latter had always been closely grouped, disagreements arising over technical rather than philosophical questions. Technical differences of opinion can have substantial conceptual consequences. But any attempt to categorize what a leading Central Bank stood for risks becoming a travesty: it should be emphasized that what follows is based on a limited number of interviews taken in 1993–4, supplemented by outside comment from each country's financial press.

For the *Banque de France*, moving in 1994 into the first stages of genuine independence from the Trésor, the most significant change was that central bankers' role in managing the EU's monetary policy had grown to the point at which the Committee of Governors resembled a Council of Ministers, in managing the ERM.[60] The process would continue as long as only those member states committed to EMU were admitted or readmitted; in practice this view excluded Italy, and probably Spain and Britain, which were all likely to 'bring politics back in'. Surveying the previous decade, the main conclusion appeared to be that the roles of banking and industry had become so interrelated that, in default of a clear political lead in many member states, the Central Bank players had to face up to the 'inconsistent quartet' argument on their own and ensure that their politicians and national publics drew the right deduction: that is, in favour of convergence policies, and particularly the establishment of an institution other than the Bundesbank (in effect the EMI), to offset Germany's increasing *political* weight in the Community.[61]

Since July 1993, the tactics have altered but the underlying strategy remains. France's independent central bank, led now by Jean-Claude Trichet, still under the Chirac presidency (as of June 1995) pursues the aim of monetary cooperation and the *franc fort*, even if the EMI's role has been curtailed, and despite the price of high interest rates, budget deficits, persistent high unemployment and postponement of the privatization programme. Independent as it now is, the Bank still follows government policy at a deep level. As one minister put it: 'the heart of Maastricht is the single currency: Jacques Rueff, signing the 1957 Treaty, declared "Europe is a single money or it is nothing". That comes before political union which is a long process, not a short one.'[62]

From the *Bundesbank*'s point of view, Tietmeyer's leadership, which has been far more carefully nuanced to take account of both German government policy and the events of July 1993, appears to have removed the technical and many of the principled objections to EMU, given that, from Frankfurt, completion of the third stage looks likely to be delayed and restricted – as had always been the Bundesbank's intention – to the DM-related core group of currencies. The Bundesbank directorate still however insists as a minimum on the convergence criteria provided by Maastricht Article 236, which safeguards Germany's economic sovereignty, as against the EU's 'common interest'.[63] On the other hand, the ERM appears now to have largely been purged of the political elements responsible for the double crisis. The place of central bankers has been clarified and simplified, and the tension between the Bundesbank and its own government (as well as other member states' governments), has been greatly reduced.

Nevertheless, this balance is more one of exhaustion than principle. Bonn's insistence on political union remains a necessary corollary of EMU because there appears to be no other way to compel member state governments not merely to bring about the conditions for convergence on which EMU entry depends but to behave in such a way as to ensure that they hold their economies there for the long-term.[64] Until EPU arrives, the DM core remains of greater significance than the progress of the other member states towards EMU; and the EMI is not yet accepted as an agency capable of superseding the Bundesbank. Better for the present to keep the ERM in good order.[65] Neither are other central banks accepted as equals: Karl-Otto Pöhl made this clear in 1989 when he insisted to the Delors Committee that the ECB Council should be composed not only of the twelve, now fifteen Governors, but six members from its Directorate representing 'the common European interest'.

The *Bank of England* was evidently not independent enough to have impressed its own views on the British government about sterling's proper rate on entering the ERM, nor about a general revaluation in September 1992: neither could it choose its preferences between the French government and Bundesbank way to EMU, because of the government's formulation that what was wanted was a common, not a single, currency. Nevertheless, its opinion favoured France in one aspect; that EMU should be a Community matter, not something constructed around a DM core. If not, Leigh-Pemberton could hardly have signed the Delors Report. Despite the Bank's steadily growing authority, even autonomy in the mid–1990s, in current political circumstances where, against the fervent opposition of the Euro-sceptics, even the chancellor can do little more than keep alive the option of at some point rejoining the ERM, there can be no public Bank of England view on what EMU might amount to. The indications are that, as before, the Bank would emphasize the importance for any currency bloc of free trade and open markets as against the appearance of an exclusive, primarily political club, prone to protective trading.[66]

For the *Banca d'Italia*, the main emphasis in 1994, as after Black Wednesday, was on the domestic scene. The earlier double intention, to stand midway between France and Germany, and to help reform Italy's public finances through the convergence process[67] has, temporarily at least, been set aside until Italy has rebuilt a functioning political system. Such were the gains from devaluation in September 1992 that the Bank was also forced temporarily to give up its attempt to return to the ERM: *faute de mieux*, Italy took the British road.

The bank remains a principled public actor, whose then Governor, Carlo Ciampi, became prime minister in 1993–4 and took the reform campaign further than had previously seemed possible[68] – only to see it submerged in a wave of populist revulsion against all Italy's institutions. Its stance could perhaps be described as in the tradition of Mazzini's concept of *risorgimento*, at odds with much of Italy's twentieth-century political development. During 1994 (like the Bank of England in the 1980s) it was at odds with the Berlusconi government, which tried to gerrymander its directorate, but grew more in sympathy with its successor, given Lamberto Dini's attempts to bring the budget under control. But it remains to some extent dissociated from other governors representing countries with a much stronger sense of national identity. So long as Italian governments let the lira take the strain of their failure to reform Italy's public finances, this isolation, even alienation, is likely to continue.[69]

The *Banco de España* has had to concede to its government on many occasions since the peseta's ERM entry, including the September 1992 devaluation. But even though Spain's policy mix in 1990 was wrong and the peseta was over-valued, and despite the severe devaluation early in 1995, the Bank still prizes membership of the ERM, and seeks an eventual return to the 6% band, and to EMU's third stage. Above all, the main prize is that firm monetary policy and fulfilment of the convergence criteria are 'an absolute need for Spain'.[70] Yet the price has been abnormally high – much worse than in France – and the Bank itself has suffered by becoming seen as hostile not only to the labour movement but to industry as well. 'Trying to create the conditions for the country to modernize itself', requires the imposition of a discipline which could more easily be applied by the Bundesbank, to whose independence the current governor, Angel Rojo, freed to some extent from the Finance Ministry's direct authority in January 1994, evidently aspires.

The *Netherlands Bank*, which is largely independent, accepted the glidepath thesis after 1987 but attempted, unsuccessfully, as part of the Dutch Presidency's draft at Maastricht, to strengthen the proposed EMI, making it closer to the original European Central

Bank intention. On monetary policy, and hence management of the ERM, it has normally stood with, and sometimes served as a stalking horse for, the Bundesbank.[71] As far as convergence criteria are concerned, these are seen as commitments that every member state should have made long ago: in practice, and because several have so far failed to live up to these standards, the present way to EMU lies through the core group of currencies.

The equally independent *Belgian Central Bank* has habitually played a role as mediator and broker in the Governors' Committee, seeing success at ERM management as the only way, in political terms, to induce Belgians themselves to accept the convergence process by reducing the over-arching volume of the EU's largest per capita public debt. There appears to be no other way to ease the present difficulties where, despite the Bundesbank's extensive help in pegging the Belgian franc to the deutschmark, it cannot enter the core group because of its massive budget deficit, so that interest rates remain materially higher than in Holland or Denmark.

In *Denmark*, after hesitations to do with national and central bank independence, Hoffmeyer, the long-serving Central Bank governor, eventually sided with the rest of the Governors' Committee in 1989–90, and signed the Delors Report. The Bank then used the Committee's arguments to try to convince Danish public about EMU.[72] Yet resistance from Danish public opinion led the government to seek its opt-out from EMU at Edinburgh in 1992, though its commitment to the ERM and to membership of the currency core group remain.

Like those of *Portugal* and *Greece*, *Ireland's Central Bank* lives too much in the Finance Ministry's shadow to take any large part in ERM management; yet the fact that a small nation finds itself participating even in a minor way gives it some weight in Irish politics against governments and ministers who habitually shun fiscal reform and would normally let the punt and the reserves take the strain in crises.[73] But sterling's withdrawal from the ERM has worked seriously to its disadvantage, inhibiting the governor from arguing against devaluation. Consequently the link the Bank has striven to make in the last fifteen years between the ERM, entry to EMU, fiscal reform, and remedying Ireland's EU dependency, has been hard to sustain. The lesson has probably not yet been implanted, as it has in Portugal, that smaller states unattached to the core are of marginal importance to the major players.

Among the governors' *noyau*, the status of individual Governors depends not on national prestige or ambition but on economic size and the maintenance of a stable currency. Since the really important things are said less in full meetings than as informal asides, the interests of smaller member states tend to be overlooked. That they are categorized according to the prevailing arguments among larger players reflects the likelihood that some of them will inevitably be relegated to the second tier as that develops in the run-up to EMU. Yet for a time it seemed as if it might have been otherwise. Once the mood of *morosité* which followed July 1993 had lifted there was a chance that, in 1993–4, the majority of currencies would stay in or near the narrow bands, and not need to take refuge in the wider plus-or-minus 15% ones.[74] Since then, the whole system was thrown back into disarray in March 1995. But because the impetus for the current crisis was an external one, brought about by the Mexican crisis and the dollar's remorseless decline, it is likely that the Community players' basic assumptions have not changed: only the short-term position of certain member states has moved, notably Spain, Portugal and possibly France, depending on the Chirac presidency.

Central Banks follow their national governments on some occasions, competing, for example, on where to site the EMI.[75] But governors or their alternates in Basel usually dispute where the real European interest lies, for example over the disposition of monetary aggregates, or over the Commission's right to borrow for infrastructure investment (claimed in its 1993 White Paper), or over EMI's current role in enhancing cooperation between Central Banks. (France, Belgium and Italy opposed Germany and Britain on this, making it impossible for the EMI Council, needing a two-thirds majority, to decide.) Single member state interests still intrude as they did when Pedro Solbes, Spain's finance minister, argued at Ecofin in February 1994 in favour of excluding EFTA entrants from the convergence criteria, since they were much nearer the targets than Mediterranean states, who would therefore be disadvantaged. But the German finance minister, opposing this, spoke for the Ecofin majority (and all the Committee of Governors) in arguing that those who could enter on the due date should do so, and that the majority should not wait for those who would postpone until they were ready.

As of early 1995, the wide bands came to be seen as a successful experiment, not only for those currencies which actually maintained themselves in the old narrow range but even for sterling which, from September 1992 until March 1995, held closer to the deutschmark than when discreetly shadowing it during Nigel Lawson's time as chancellor of the exchequer in the mid-1980s. Capital controls were not generally reintroduced in the crisis of 1992–3, thanks partly to the efforts of DG15 and partly to the Belgian Presidency in the second half of 1993, which induced Spain, Portugal and Greece to surrender them. Despite the recession, convergence, as prescribed by Ecofin following Article 103 (2) of Maastricht, came about substantially faster than had been predicted in the late 1980s and more than could have been expected without the ERM.

The crisis of August 1993 and its aftermath also appeared to have stabilized relations between the Bundesbank and the Bonn government, at a time when Helmut Kohl, secure in his re-election for a final term, was likely to subordinate lesser considerations to the central question of Germany's identity within the enlarging union. France benefited indirectly, for its early preoccupation with corralling the deutschmark diminished once the Basel/Nyborg accords were seen to have worked as intended. At the end of 1994, French interest rates had fallen almost to German levels.

But since the end of 1994 the gap between the virtuous states and the backsliders has widened; there are fewer of the former and more of the latter seem to be dropping back.[76] The timescale to EMU may now retain merit only as a talisman since, despite what finance ministers may say in public, it has ceased to be a means of prediction.

Nevertheless, despite the great volume of protests by industries in all member states before the recession finally lifted, and by the French right ever since, the convergence argument still stood at the end of 1994, which in itself was a vindication of the path agreed six years earlier. At the time of writing (1995), what is at issue, since the glidepath thesis' demise, and can hardly be settled before the 1996 IGC, is how the leap from the present system to EMU – if indeed it takes place – is to be achieved.[77] (Technical delays to do with the design of banknotes and the production of sufficient ecu coins – assuming that this is what they will be called – already presage more serious delays between the launch of EMU and circulation of the new money; in which period some governments may find it very hard to convince their publics that exchange rules are already permanently locked.)

On the other hand, the ERM – still EMU's harbinger – has survived and witnessed the introduction of greater Central Bank independence in France, Spain and Portugal, refuting for the moment predictions about the 'inconsistent quartet'. All three member states are still in the ERM and so far the British government has sustained its anti-inflationary policies. Leaving aside altogether the special case of Greece, only Italy flounders, the sorry exception until it resolves its political crisis. But there is no point in trying to forecast whether all of them will continue to do so, given the social and economic domestic tensions which boil up underneath, most recently during the French presidential election campaign as a result of Jacques Chirac's promises about unemployment policy.

Functionally and temperamentally, central bankers tend to form a collective which at the tail end of two inflationary decades was always likely to find itself in disagreement with political elites, both in member states and across the EU. They were also likely to be criticized for their collective role by their own national financial players.[78] Their role should not be overestimated, being restricted at Community level very largely to monetary policy, preparations for EMU, and ERM management; they are also subject to a matrix of forces, which includes the advice of DG2 and the influence of the Commission President.[79] For all their growing independence from member state governments, Britain included, ensured under the Maastricht Treaty, they are still in the last resort responsible to their member state governments' requirements on economic policy, as well as for their own national supervisory duties. Not until a genuine ECB exists will the primordial transfers of national sovereignty to a European monetary agency be complete. But as one of them put it, in relation to the European stage, 'central bankers do think long-term and with great clarity, and free of the public and political dimension . . . governments have countervailing powers over them, and central bankers in practice very rarely take the lead. But they do have a basic ethic and an influence in shaping the medium and long-term view of other institutions and the political class as a whole, who have to live with the public and democracy.'[80]

Shaping the EMS gave the twelve Central Banks a novel European focus, and managing the ERM has provided an experience comparable to what the CAP has been for agriculture ministers, which the Central Banks of Austria, Finland and Sweden have been able to witness at very close quarters. This is not to say that unelected governors have acquired ministerial status, only that as makers of monetary policy (in most cases) they are not just experts but have an influence on political matters. Thus the Governors' Committee (subordinate as it still is to the Monetary Committee and Ecofin) has developed some of the characteristics of a Council of Ministers. Given that much of the political impetus drained out of the ERM in August 1993, it is fair to argue that since then central bankers have been left by their governments to do the things for which as technical experts they ought to be responsible, leaving the political decisions about EMU's timetable and the convergence criteria to finance ministers and governments. This is, in practice, the European face of their administrative independence in the management of monetary policy, and has built up steadily, uninterrupted by ERM crises, since the Delors Report.

How far then can central bankers be seen as a unique set of players on all three levels – national, European and international? They constitute an elite of a peculiar kind, and it is not surprising that some of the most heavily contested areas of comitology procedure are to be found in the Governors' and the Alternates' Committees, the specialist subcommittees on banking supervision, or the *groupes de contacte*, where member states and Commission work out their endless rivalries.[81] Yet neither the Monetary Committee nor Ecofin finance ministers are competent to judge such technicalities. Both must, *faute de mieux*, rely on the Central Bank experts and their advice, even on substantive questions such as the definition of monetary aggregates and the instruments and operating procedures of the future single monetary policy.[82]

That the central bankers have become such a group is due to a large extent to the Commission search, first for EMS and then for EMU in which, like King Arthur's knights questing for the Holy Grail, they learned to behave as a collective in defining what the long interests of the European Community should be. Having achieved part of this aim through the Community's instrument, the Delors Committee, the Committee of Governors then developed into a body which increasingly took on a life of its own, with only a very informal steer from the Commission.[83]

But this does not mean that the weight of political factors and national interests has been lifted altogether. The convergence criteria are defined in nominal terms, not real ones (a concept which allows Ireland to appear better off than it would otherwise be). This is not yet a question which appears to have been raised in Franco-German discussions, but it has been by the British government, which has suggested the inclusion, for example, of unemployment levels as a real, easily measurable index of performance in an industrial economy. Needless to say, the strongest opposition to that proposal has come from those with the highest rates, headed by Spain. But the point is not necessarily a factious one and might even attract support from German and Netherlands politicians.

What has frequently been raised, only to be rebutted by the Bundesbank directorate, is a soft interpretation of the Maastricht language used to define the convergence criteria. Phrases such as 'come close to' or 'at a satisfactory pace', offer space for political argument which has already been used by Belgian and Irish authorities and occasionally in France. Such arguments might be admissible where the latter is concerned but could too easily (from the point of view of defenders of the DM) be extended to Spain or Portugal. They recur however in another form whenever the single currency is discussed, because the ecu, representing a basket of currencies weak and strong, is unattractive to those directly linked to the DM having depreciated 15% between 1992 and 1995.

Yet since the DM has become, with the yen, the global market's preferred hard currency as the dollar softens, it is progressively more difficult for all the others to conform. During periods of crisis, realignments such as those of Sweden and Italy in January 1995, or Spain and Portugal in March, make it very much harder for these countries afterwards to achieve the convergence criteria. The question then arises of whether governments will take precedence over Central Banks and install EMU as a political configuration, finally to break the power of currency markets to undo patient years of long work by economics ministries, while massaging the actual way the criteria are defined. The appointment as a Bundesbank director of Peter Schmidhuber, a former Commissioner, and the recent speeches made by Tietmeyer, suggest that a climactic struggle over this has not been discounted in Germany.

Herein lies a danger, for member states as much as for the Commission. Central Banks are guardians of national currencies and of the putative European currency and constitute an essential component of any modern state. But like other guardians such as the armed services or judges responsible for the law itself, they have necessarily a singular vision, ill-attuned to the plural politics of the Council of Ministers. They have also been powerless to prevent the random damage to national economies caused by movements in global currency markets. The same question therefore applies to the Community as to any nation state, when the issues are too complex for the political class to decide, and experts draw up the rules or definitions: if the two disagree, who is to judge on the ultimate national (or European) interest? (The point is similar to the British government's dilemma in 1925, whether or not to return to the Gold Standard, and at what parity). The Treaties leave no doubt that the ECJ is the final arbiter of European law, as well as its Court of Appeal; so will central bankers on the ECB's directorate be arbiters on the even more complex, less easily determined questions of monetary policy, once the ECB has been instituted. But in the remaining years before that comes about, who decides, who rules? Whose mode of transition will emerge and will it be triumphant for intellectual or political reasons?

This chapter describes not only the games of different players but their progress towards a double regulatory regime. By incorporating competition policy as a means of macro-economic adjustment, as is argued in chapter 12, the Commission has come to be more than just a European Kartellamt. Meanwhile central bankers, on their way to controlling the EU's monetary policy, are moving towards a similar position as regards Europe's macro-economy. It follows that these two rather disparate institutions may acquire more real power to shape players' economic behaviour than either national or corporate players had bargained for at the time they so enthusiastically approved the Single European Act.

This is to assume that if and when EMU occurs it is accompanied by progress towards political union, a conjunction which ought not to be taken for granted before the end of the 1996–7 IGC. It also assumes that the tensions over monetary union which evidently exist between member states and the Commission are replicated at the level of the Governors' Committee, whose members individually represent their member states but who collectively define what the Community's interest is in this sphere. There is no intrinsic reason why such a person cannot, wearing different hats, fulfil the two roles; nor, once monetary union has taken place, why convergence should not occur between the European interest and those of member states. The high degree of informality in Central Bank practice may even facilitate it.[84]

But will they – or can they – be trusted to abandon nationality, as members of the ECB's Governing Council, with its eventual supranational powers? So argue the Euro-sceptics in several member states, who see governments' control of fiscal policy rather than the currency symbol itself as the principal element of national sovereignty. Yet this end is contingent on what was agreed in the Single European Act and in the nature of the activity they have been engaged in since 1986. Given that member states disagree among themselves far more than central bankers normally will, there is no other way to achieve the truly level playing field, as the Delors

Committee argued. But it is not, and cannot be a matter of political democracy, as the Dutch authorities warned in September 1991, when the pursuit of EMU by France and Germany was allowed finally to hijack and politicize the ERM.[85] Whatever the formal position about accountability, which provides for the Central Banks of France, Spain or Italy, and even the Bundesbank, to report their transactions to their parliaments, an independent Central Bank is not in *practice* accountable except to ministers who define where key national economic interests lie. Even the Bundesbank is in the last resort subject only to the chancellor's political authority. Will such distant, inevitably indirect accountability, especially if it is transposed to the European Parliament, be acceptable to national electorates whose governments have relinquished authority over money supply, with all the dramatic consequences, which will only become apparent in some future recession, at times of monetary stringency?

EMU and the creation of an ECB could also lead, even in the preliminary stages, not only to increasing political power for central bankers and a regime of deflation comparable to those in Europe after 1921, and in the developed world generally after 1931, but to the entrenched dominance of giant firms.[86] Changes imposed largely by French and German governments on the way that the ERM has been managed have made these two political outcomes more likely. Monetary union as a principle and the ECB in its current form were not intrinsically related, because the 'inconsistent quartet' argument relates primarily to the period of nearly fixed exchange rates which occurred once the ERM became rigid around 1987; this coupling came about as a result of the French government's insistence on a particular form of EMU, to which the German government's response was that this could be accepted only in the context of Political Union.

Much still depends on whether the underlying assumptions in the Kohl–Mitterrand agreement, exemplified at Maastricht, survive the 1996 IGC, because it is still economically practicable to decouple EMU and EPU and restore the ERM to its status quo before 1987. Whether it is *politically* possible depends on outcomes which at the time of writing are uncertain: the French government responses under its new president, Chirac, and the manner in which Germany continues to rediscover its long-lost full nationhood. In the way that EMU is defined at present, what is involved is not just a substantial cession of fifteen member states' sovereignty but, potentially, abrogation of much of the Keynesian revolution – to the detriment of their real economies and perhaps of the democratic ordering of all their societies.

Policy–Making: Industry and Trade

Competition law and management of the ERM gives the Community's institutions two of their main weapons to regulate European markets. But the industrial policy area which lies in between was not so easily approached, having grown up piecemeal until it met the countervailing force of free market doctrine in the 1980s. The synoptic approach to European industry which many signatories of the SEA and the Commission expected to follow 1986 was impeded because it became too difficult for governments to admit to interventionism – even though, in their still-regulated economies, it continued to thrive.

The contrasts between member state governments' assumptions about industrial policy are substantial, even when looking only at France and Germany. Although throughout the late 1980s the Commission attempted to broaden the basis so that a coherent policy towards industry should complement competition policy, the internal market, and trade policy (and the handful of import regimes in cars, bananas and so on, which were to survive 1992) together with the social and regional dimensions, no complete definition of European industrial policy has emerged. But Article 130 of the Maastricht Treaty did imply that competitiveness could be improved in four main ways: encouraging firms' own structural adjustment, improving the economic environment, particularly for SMEs, stimulating cooperation and research funding, and exploiting more effectively research and development possibilities.

These ought properly to be called specific policies aimed at various types of industrial problems. Given the exiguous nature of Community funds and instruments, even this much could hardly be implemented before the internal market's completion. The Commission's regulatory powers were self-evidently greater than its financial ones, at a time of budgetary stringency. But its officials had also to overcome a thirty-year legacy in the lack of coordination between its different sectoral aims, which had built up partly due to the divisions and rivalries between Directorates, and partly due to patterns established by dominant MNCs and federations in certain sectors, skilfully backed by their national authorities.

Conversely, the fact that policy towards industry had not been set firmly in a particular mould allowed for an element of flexibility before and during the early 1990s recession which was surprising in so structured an organization – even if some of the actual decisions seemed surprising, perhaps bizarre. Adaptiveness remains an important key to whatever success the Community has had, in most cases by agreement with the industries concerned. Nevertheless, without the Single European Act, and the crucial emphasis on liberalization and competitiveness, as well as managed adjustment, it is hard to imagine that even a proto-industrial policy could have been assembled.

There is no intention here either to tell its history or evaluate its outcome (given the massive literature in economic and political science); only to examine how the various players affected what was done, and how the current policy was developed. In retrospect, the Single Act was a unique event, constructed during a period of constructive transition which is unlikely to be repeated. Given the expectations aroused, the SEA produced a policy-making matrix in which large, especially multinational, enterprises had greater leverage in the European context than they did in their own member states, because in Brussels they and their peak organizations were increasingly united (as member states were not) and had very direct access to the roots of policy-making which were not easily available to governments.

Firms will naturally always seek a world safe for their operations. But insofar as they have combined or made alliances over quite long periods to form a common interest (altruism is too high a word to use in commercial circumstances), and since they began to discover that this entitled them to a better hearing than the mere assertion of self-interest, they committed themselves in the European context to a number of collaborative approaches. This happened particularly where what would otherwise have been the costs of vast investment in research or adjustment might be offset through Community-inspired research projects or structural funds. Immediately available advantage was thus added to the natural tendency of companies and their managements to form monopolies, noted half a century earlier by Joseph Schumpeter. A predisposition grew up to react to Commission blandishments, just as Commission officials were already predisposed by their function, acquaintance and knowledge of a dossier to listen to companies' requests.

Early instances of this political complementarity, such as the steel cartel and Esprit programme, brought into focus the outlines of a more general cooperation (some would call it collaboration) in which the primary layer of bargaining was to be accompanied by a second, more elevated one where the Commission's longer aims of harmonization or modernization could be advanced. Firms might be drawn in by silken ties, there being no other means for the Commission to induce them to conform except to work on their self-interest. Legislation was too blunt an instrument to offer scope for incentives and depended in any case on their member states' consent, so that it was reserved for shaping the framework of regulation.

On that slender basis, the Commission could envisage a policy towards industry capable of fostering a range of associated aims: increasing competitiveness in the face of foreign threats to European markets; holding the Union together (the poor periphery as well as the richer core, labour as well as capital); and preventing multinational corporations from rigging markets to the detriment of competition and consumers. It might also sustain an argument about the EU's public ideals against the hordes of private interests, with the mordant American (or British) alternatives of the 1980s in mind.

All this was easier because, by the late 1980s, expectations about the single market were evidently altering players' political behaviour. The SEA created an informal area where bargaining could profitably take place, which survived the traumas and reverses on the public political level following the Maastricht Treaty. The SEA also enabled the Commission, so often outplayed by member states, to give rather more leadership in the common good, because firms and financial institutions had discovered their own interest in that good. That their perceptions might as a result diverge more than in the past from member states' interests (even their own governments') may not at first have been realized, but it soon became an ingenious weapon in the Commission's hands to constrain backward or resistant governments, if only because none of the active players wanted a return to the 1970s and the era of 'warring states'.

The field is enormous, covering all industry and services. Within the Commission it is a main concern of DGs 1, 2, 4, 7, 12, 13, 16 and 23, but above all, of DG3. Yet there was no obvious orchestra which Delors could conduct; the score in 1986 was already nearly thirty years old, scratched out and reorchestrated, a palimpsest by many hands, whose themes only occasionally complemented each other. Some of the players could agree on nothing more than that discordance should continue, waiting for their own chance to assert a particular harmony. Yet something did emerge as a medium-term result of the Single Act whose accretions in the late 1980s ensured that the connections between research, development, competition policy and trade remain worthwhile.

I. *Industry Policy*

The Commission's fundamental assumptions about markets are tinged with a Hobbesian view. As in any long-established state, they are not seen as free-standing, natural and inevitable, but linked to politics and societies; they conflict, and often work to the detriment of wider public interests unless restrained by law, convention and social habits. For the same reasons which underpin them in nation states, market rules need to be harmonized to ensure at least formal, legal equality for all players, and the essentials which nation states provide: a stable currency, a legal framework, citizenship and property rights, defence of individuals and proper enforcement of the rules. Within or below that, however, at the informal level, the scope for bargaining is much greater than in nation states because of the EU's uncertain and novel statehood; so that what ought properly to be described as a system, if not a negotiated order occupies a more distinctive part of the Community's civil society.

It is a truism that the majority of Commission initiatives arise from member states themselves, players acting through their states, or as legacies from past enactments. Not more than 10–15% originate in the Commission, though these are, in fact, usually the larger items. Much would be done anyway by the member states investing in research or regions, even if the Commission did not exist. Neither do the funds made available under the widest definition of industrial policy, from the Ortoli facility in 1977 onwards, amount to very much compared to what is provided from member states' budgets. But that is not the whole point, since the latter have increasingly agreed to act together in order to reduce the high or politically unacceptable costs of modernizing and adjusting to world conditions, and since firms appreciate the value of a European base, a legal economic and political market context governed by EU rules.

Large firms had long determined something of the outcome: first, being mostly MNCs, they were only partly constrained by what 'their' state wanted in any given circumstances and hence, in making their investment decisions, acted with considerable freedom; second, because the Commission had always chosen to implement industrial policy from the top down, using larger firms and financial institutions' knowledge, experience and practice. Naturally, this led to collaboration as well as cooperation, and a degree of mutual conformity, from which more independent players and CEOs often distanced themselves, and which contrasted at first with the whole pattern of market diversity implied by the single market.

At least until the late 1980s, the Community did not have an industry policy, as that had been understood in post-War France, Sweden or Japan; only a set of ill-assorted sectoral initiatives, buttressed by research projects. This was the predictable outcome of a series of negotiated policies and compromises, gradually broadening over time, in which echoes survived of an initial EEC premise that harmonization would lead to integration – as one of the 1957 signatories, van der Groeben, had declared to the European Parliament, during the 'empty chair' crisis in June 1964. Industry policy before the single market amounted to no more than the slow accumulation of precedents and norms, with particular activity in declining sectors such as shipbuilding, textiles, or steel.

Whatever synoptic vision built up, chiefly in 1972 at the Paris Summit, about ending barriers to trade, opening up public procurement to competition, and restructuring decaying industries, while maintaining the social wage in a full-employment Europe, vanished with the mid-1970s crisis and the onset of increasing mass structural unemployment in the 1980s. Success came to mean crisis resolution, whether in shipbuilding, steel or via the international multifibre agreement (MFA) for textiles. The shipbuilding measures patently failed in the face of eastern European and Asian competition, but the steel cartel appeared successful for a time because, after many fluctuations, it cemented agreement between Germany, France and Italy under ECSC arrangements and curtailed state aids down to 1986.[1]

Until the Single European Act, the legal basis for industrial policies, and the interpretation built on them, remained sectoral, and subject to member states' dispositions. Change occurred slowly, in long cycles modulated by the vagaries of different governments' interpretation and implementation, and could sometimes barely be distinguished from what they would have done in any case. On the other hand, the developing body of informal conventions about *how* things were done tended always to draw together the industrial players who took part, subjecting them to an element of long-term conditioning. The same effects can be detected in the crisis cartels, many of the research projects, some regional policy, and the trade arrangements (quotas or voluntary export restraints (VERS)) that were negotiated with Japan. Given the support provided by the European Investment Bank (EIB) which, though formally independent, became in effect an EC institution, industrial policy acquired a certain financial backing, which was also the post–1990 role of the Recovery and Development Bank (EBRD) in eastern Europe.[2]

On the eve of internal market legislation in 1983, one commentator described the policy environment as 'both competitive and disaggregated'.[3] Contemporary experience suggested that it was easier for a firm to negotiate protective arrangements than to restructure, and that any genuine restructuring could only be achieved collectively, during a period of expansion. It was hardly surprising that British policy diverged during the 1980s, under the Thatcher governments, or that privatization came to be seen as a alternative to the illusion of managed adjustment.[4]

During the decade after 1983, and the French reappraisal which took place sporadically, down to the present time, the EC's industrial policy deepened, widened and intensified, thanks to the work of officials in DG3 and the implants created by two of the EU's most successful Commissioners, Etienne Davignon, who rebuilt DG3's interest in the generality of industry, trade and technology after Altiero Spinelli's legacy had been fragmented during the 1970s; and Arthur Cockfield, author of the 1985 White Paper. DG3 was diverted after the SEA into the minutiae of internal market legislation (losing direct contact with industrial representatives save in the restructuring cases of steel and car production). But it was reconstituted in 1988 under Martin Bangemann, on the basis that industrial policy should no longer be confined to sectors but made horizontal, with the aim of cross-fertilizing industry as a whole, and linking up with trade, research and structural funding.[5]

As the 1990 Commission Paper on industrial policy pointed out, purely sectoral policies had become protectionist deadends. The future was to lie with what was styled 'advanced markets', where competition, trade and industry policy would complement each other, in which DGs 1, 3 and 4 would become 'unavoidable partners'; for example, in the first Framework Programme to improve Portugal's industrial base in 1988–93, and in negotiating the car VER with Japan as a short-term expedient to soften the transition to liberal trade. Links between Directorates were in fact strengthened as DG1 (external trade) came under pressure from the industrial lobbies for anti-dumping relief against Japan. The reallocation of duties, which cost DG3 oversight of the internal market, put in its place research and technology; so that what became a quadrumvirate – (Brittan (DG1a), Bangemann (DG3), Karel van Miert (DG4), and Henning Christophersen (DG2) – took responsibility for the entire range from Esprit to trade, competition to the macro-economic context.

Out of it also came the EU's growth initiative, adopted at the Edinburgh Summit in 1992 and set out in detail in the December 1993 White Paper. This was a much more political document which, tailored to the deep recession, construed structural change in terms of radical alterations in the labour market. But the liberalizing tone displayed in the favour shown towards increasing flexibility of wages and industrial relations practice (the result of long-term forecasts made by the *celulle de prospective*, written up by DG3's central economic team) caused such dissent in the college that, for public consumption it had to be tempered by guidelines written with trade unionists, particularly in Germany and Spain, in mind.[6]

In spite of the liberal, 'advanced market' tone of all Commission documents on industrial policy in this period, and the efforts to take account of outside or uncommitted views, the fact that sectoral demands did resurface in the 1991–3 recession wherever commercial and industrial interests pressed hardest, suggests that logical reorganization of responsibilities within the Commission had been insufficient to break the links between officials and the industries whose behaviour they sought to shape.[7] It should also be said that the onus for change fell primarily on trade unions at a time of very high unemployment. Yet this is only to say that in hard times the EU turns inwards protectively, towards what has become 'its own'; and in these circumstances, capital always does better than labour.

During the 1993 White Paper's gestation, and the whole of 1994, while its proposals were being renegotiated among member states, the combination of research, industrial and trade policy continued to influence bargaining in the Uruguay GATT round (finally signed at the end of 1993), the opening up of public procurement, slow liberalization of telecoms and national airlines, and the introduction of new standard-setting institutions. Whether the Commission, or the firms which crowded in to take advantage, contributed most to accelerating these consequences of the internal market is as

..batable as is the argument about responsibility for its origins. Each used the other, as well as their purely national routes – the stance on GATT of AGREF, representing the largest private concerns in France, and the evolution of an environmental policy towards transport being cases in point.[8] Nevertheless, with its focus on general policy beyond the single market's market orientation, and the particular neo-Keynesian emphasis of the 1993 White Paper, the Commission evidently tried to take on aspects of the developmental state.

Predictably, this policy mixture tended to favour the large companies (who had helped to construct it), requiring DG23 to respond by constructing a synoptic plan for SMEs, in order to improve the position of weaker players. Whether the Community could in fact counterbalance market forces, police them adequately and sustain the effort over time, are questions beyond the scope of this chapter, even if it were possible to measure the evidence at a time of very rapid economic change and political upheaval.[9] In political terms, Social and Christian Democratic parties appear to have become deeply concerned with unemployment and the problems of growth just when the neo-liberal impulse began to falter, even in Britain. In all member states, public opinion on these two issues has since become an important factor conditioning the EU's direction, assisted for the first time since the 1960s by vigorous campaigns mounted from the European Parliament; and the Commission has in turn responded, in a mood of public humility, emphasizing the virtues of empowering member states' courts or agencies,[10] and extending decentralization in the name of subsidiarity.

Whether these recent trends will divert the underlying aims of industrial policy, and establish it as a means to further the general good of European civil society, is entirely uncertain. All that can be hazarded here is that large firms and players will continue to shape the process. Insofar as it is coordinated, adjustment policy will be enacted according to the triangular balance of power between Commission, member states and private sector players. From that point of view, progress to EMU is a contingent not a primary issue, whatever financial interests or central bankers acting for a segment of the national interest think and do. How the Commission's basic aims – to enhance technology, improve competitiveness and make labour markets more flexible – are construed will depend on which of the players takes priority.

At its face value, the agenda expressed in the Commission Paper 'Industrial policy in an open and competitive Europe', published in November 1990,[11] required selective promotion of the trio, competition, technology and trade. 'Industrial policy cannot be seen as independent and isolated, but as the sum of all the other [policies] that exist.' It was assumed that the instruments of policy would take account of players' informed opinion in the opening bargaining system, for the Commission can never know enough, especially in the highly technical, rapidly changing markets covered by DG15. The Commission did not seek overtly to interfere, only to remove obstacles to trade; but the document assumed that once the field became freer, the players would have to adjust and the impetus would encourage the use of new techniques and best practice.

It was intended that research and development should no longer be constrained by the earlier protective patterns. Proliferation of programmes to meet special needs would serve to redirect the cooperation exemplified in Esprit and Eureka as markets and players required. The Commission answered the problem of lack of funds, caused by the politically sensitive approaches of member governments to the EC budget, by arguing that many research and development programmes could efficiently be organized and funded on a national level, with the added virtue of subsidiarity. It also favoured transnational cooperation between research institutes and the exchange of personnel, to say nothing of concern for environmental research.

Being in principle inclined to welcome virtuous statements, member states were apt to accept the need for European-wide cooperation, even in the traditionally sensitive field of military technology (although some difficulties remained, demonstrated for example, in the problems of the European jet fighter programme). That cooperation was more likely to benefit larger companies situated in the EU's geographical core, and within that certain obvious sectors such as consumer electronics, telecoms, aerospace, pharmaceuticals or chemicals, could be read either as an advantage or not, depending on the observer's point of view.[12]

Because companies' networks remain sectoral, largely autonomous, and are therefore vertically assimilated into Commission policy-making, such a policy tends to promote a sort of oligarchic pluralism in which the overview is not preordained but derives from the game itself at any given moment. The ERT's 1992 manifesto *Reshaping Europe* puts this quite plainly. But the circle cannot be squared so easily, for industrial advantage does not fit naturally with social or environmental objectives. Commission White Papers have of course a declaratory intent, and aim to mobilize public as well as industrial consensus. But neither they nor the supposedly neutral agencies (even the standard-setting bodies CEN and CENELEC which are subjected to another level of influence) are above the game. Directors General really have no other means to disseminate knowledge about what they desire and are not averse to drawing power 'from below' to remedy an imbalance 'higher up'. Even so, press and television are more likely to react to an angry motor manufacturer CEO such as Jacques Calvet than to a Commission White Paper.

Making policy in this way is a very different matter from German or Dutch, French or British governmental processes. National administrations share values in ways absent in a polyglot Commission bureaucracy, where ideas and schemes tend to originate at relatively low levels and to flow upwards seeking political approval.[13] Member states still guard what they define as important national interests, for example in refusing to allow the Commission to lower the Merger Regulation thresholds (which they had themselves raised in the Council, when the Merger Regulation was approved in 1989). In 1990, a good year, 293 Standards were approved, but in mid-1993 over a thousand more immediately relevant to the internal market and the free movement of goods were stuck in CEN and CENELEC, despite industrial players' complaints, because of disputes between the Commission and the Council.

Establishment of norms is of course a national, European, and international game and in the Community context dates back many years.[14] Member states and firms have their own dilemmas; whether to strive to delay matters in CEN and CENELEC in order to give themselves time to adjust to the extra costs involved in product redesign, or to jump in quickly, hoping at a higher immediate cost to establish a larger market share (the American solution, which assumes that the dilatory firms will not subsequently retain enough political power to alter or bend the rules). But even in the context of the public procurement Directive, whose principles had long been established in the Single European Act, the governments of Spain, Portugal and Greece were still seeking derogations as late as 1993. Worse, since it tended to bind the future, member states with less of a case for leniency, such as France and Italy, were undermining the rules in advance by granting 'option contracts' to state-owned or national champions up to the year 2000, on the pretext of 'ensuring security of supply and financial confidence'.

It would have been surprising if the internal market's long-term consequences had not been the object of trilateral competition, so radical were the effects on the Community and its values. Whatever the detailed implications, the underlying philosophy tends to be interpreted in one of two ways, corresponding to Michel Albert's distinction between Anglo-Saxon, neo-liberal capitalism, and a more managed, protective Rhineland capitalism (which he considers best suited to European conditions – though he admits it is in fact 'unfortunately regressing').[15] Conflicts of ethics and philosophies merge with and heighten real conflicts of interest between the players. Since no external force or agency can separate the two levels (as might happen in a single nation state), industrial policy remains a prisoner of the past, even while the new forms of European capitalism develop and, for this purpose, once-foreign American and Japanese players become Europeanized.

The rivalries between innovative and sheltered undertakings, between and among firms, states and agencies, cannot be simplified, but are likely to be bedevilled by political and social considerations to a higher degree than occurs in national circumstances. Since the underlying trends suggest that it is large firms and large states which determine the outcomes, there is something to be said for the Commission's view that it is better to make incremental gains which take their arguments into account and leave the wider principles to be resolved by political market forces at the point where member states, community and global markets intersect.

Once again, however, there is a price: the Commission may declare a policy, but conformity rests with the players, unaccountable as they are in the ordinary democratic sense; and barely at all with the European Parliament or national parliaments, which are seen at all points in the triangular game as irrelevant, if not incompetent.[16] (Article 100a purports to include the Parliament on questions of standards as well as internal market legislation; but the European Parliament does not actually become a player unless it is lobbied by either corporate interests or environmental and consumer groups. On the other hand, if that does happen, its unpredictable energy can be lethal for a Commission proposal.)

Debates about how to ensure that the Commission, acting as regulator, can avoid being coerced or captured by member states and players, and how the rules can be applied equally among players of different status, at varying stages of evolution, tend to come from outside, as outcomes of academic, parliamentary or media comment. The Commission habitually relies on such voices in order to develop that part of a long strategy which aspires to a European public accountability. But it is an extremely indirect strategy, in which member states themselves sporadically connive, the paradox being that their governments are occasionally content to be told what to do, when they cannot act on their own for domestic political or electoral reasons.

The 1993 White Paper stands a little apart from the generality of industrial policy, being attuned to a long recession and the unprecedented level of 11% unemployment (17 million people across the Community), which hit hardest Spain, the state which had done more to readjust in the shortest time than any other. Originating in the Commission Presidency, being the joint brainchild of Delors and the *cellule de prospective's* 1991–2 inquiries into 'Europe 2000', its initial aim was to answer a set of questions not only about growth and jobs but about how to remedy the imbalance of capital and labour, how to relegitimize the Commission and the process of integration after Maastricht. Taken up by member states during the British Presidency at Edinburgh, it acquired an extra momentum as a vehicle for trade union claims mediated through DG5's Green Paper, which was presented by Padraig Flynn with the intention of 'enabling everyone to consider social Europe in the future'.[17]

The Copenhagen Summit failed to rally to this cry but gave enough support to the economic ideas for the Commission to prepare a White Paper which the Belgian Presidency then took up as its flagship proposal. Since the pattern of unemployment revealed a substantial structural element, the White Paper propounded neo-Keynesian solutions which would have been equally appropriate in the 1930s: creation of new jobs to take account of rising population figures up to the year 2000, increases in each state's spending on research and training, and the controversial recommendations on how to reduce labour costs.

'Growth, competitiveness and employment: the challenges and paths to the twenty-first century', was too heterodox in its origin, too oriented towards certain sectors and regional or local plans, to be taken as typical of industrial policy in the 1990s. Its claim that the Commission should be given substantial borrowing powers from the EIB for public works, mainly in the transport infrastructure, (though of respectable 1930s' parentage) ran head on into German, British and later Spanish fears that an eight billion ecu convertible bond issue could only exaggerate the Commission's pretensions to be a government beyond the Treaty's legal limits, which might prejudice member states' own credit ratings for international borrowing. Even the 'new realism' about labour costs and flexibility in labour markets, liberalizing of the state-owned energy, postal services and telecoms monopolies, and the social emphasis on taxing pollution rather than human capital (while extending education and training to prevent youth unemployment increasing further), set member states against each other, roughly on the Anglo-Saxon–Rhineland antithesis.

Thatcherite as some of the language appeared to be (and was read as such by German and Spanish trade unionists), the White Paper's underlying intention was probably to help the outgoing

Commission set the Community's agenda under Delors's successor down to the next IGC in 1996. It caused controversy right through 1994 for that reason. But it also offered substantial backing to the industrial policy themes since, unlike its 1990 precursor, it contained a synoptic plan, and applied it in detail to policy areas which had become salient in the years since the Single European Act.

The emphasis on transport mattered most, given the Commission's long concern with trans-European networks and gaps or 'missing links' in the hypothetical high-speed railway system, which had been drawn up to compete effectively with air and road transport between European capital cities (see figure 12.1).

Such schemes had structural and regional implications because their financing relied heavily on additionality (member states, regions and local authorities co-financing with the Community–EIB). The Commission's high-level Transport Group report in December 1990 had scheduled fifteen key link schemes, at a putative cost of 10 billion ecus, with 5 billion more for the rolling stock.[18] The 1993 plans, for new links suitable for 250 kph trains or upgrading existing ones such as Belfast, Dublin, Holyhead, Crewe, with an extension to Cork, to take 200 kph ones, were relaunched at the Corfu Summit July 1994.

At this point, the White Paper's proposals came back into the loop of industrial policy, for the lines included trans-Alpine schemes contingent on Austrian entry, and connections to Lisbon and Berlin, as well as the Irish network. At his last summit as President of the Commission at Essen in December 1994, Delors pleaded for a further 1.2 billion ecus beyond the sums already allocated, to ensure Austria's and Sweden's better integration. The Commission's vision thus spanned integration, regional policy, transport, public procurement, investment, modernization, and technological advance.[19]

Huge problems remained, ranging from the difference of gauge between Spain and the rest of Europe (one of Franco's more debilitating legacies to modern Spain), to the existence of three distinct types of locomotive; French, German, and Italian. The consortium of state railway companies – a mini-Council of Minis-

Delors' £45bn transport projects

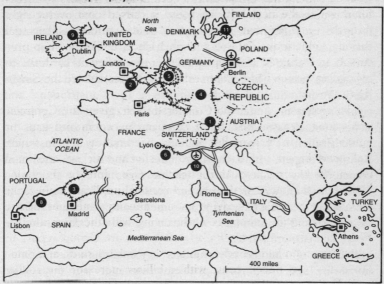

The first phase

1. High-speed north-south rail line. Part of a project to open up a corridor from Berlin to Greece through Italy. Includes a 35-mile rail tunnel through the Alps to help take lorries off the roads.
2. High-speed Paris, Brussels, Cologne, Amsterdam, London rail links, including the Chunnel.
3. High speed rail line linking Spain and Portugal to the French network and joining the Atlantic to the Mediterranean, including 750 miles of new line.
4. High speed rail line linking Paris through eastern France to Germany, completing the east-west axis.
5. Rail and road links between Rotterdam, Hamburg and Karlsruhe, connecting Germany's industrial centres with the principal European port.
6. High-speed rail line from Lyon–Turin for passenger and freight-improved rail links through the Alps. For technical reasons very expensive.
7. Motorway through Greece: the backbone for a motorway system crucial to Greek development. Will connect Greece and Albania, Bulgaria, Macedonia and Turkey.
8. Motorway linking Lisbon to Spanish and French networks via Valladolid. A toll system could encourage the private sector to invest.
9. Improved rail links between Cork, Dublin, Belfast, Larne and Stranraer.
10. Improve Malpensa Airport, Milan to become the hub of northern Italy enabling the concentration of intercontinental and EU flights.
11. Road and rail links from Malmö to Copenhagen, including a bridge across the Oresund

KEY

Railways

++++++ 1st phase   —·—·— 2nd phase

——— Motorways   ═══ Under
                                       ·········· construction

FIGURE 12.1

ters – represented in the Federation of European Railways (CER) – often contrasts with the uneasy blend, in UNIFE, of producers of locomotives, rolling stock, equipment and instruments. Any idea that it might be possible to run an Irish or a Greek train from Athens to Dublin is wholly utopian. Yet the prospects for builders of electric motors, like Alsthom, Asea-Brown Boverie, Siemens AEG-Westinghouse, Ansaldo and Breda, or of instruments and signalling systems under the Commission's framework programme 1992–6 (which associates DGs 3, 7, 12 and 13) are immense, as the modernization of Denmark's railways has already demonstrated. Railways compete with each other in design and technology, not in commerce like airlines. As the leading firms and the federation UNIFE well know, it is the players' consortium which counts, the prize being the great national procurement contracts like Madrid to Barcelona, and the standards whose choice will determine who the future competitors will be.[20]

Because of national governments' opposition to Commission borrowing, and the intrinsic problems associated with large-scale transport links, the Commission also concentrated on plans to improve energy supply which it put to the Essen Summit. The ten schemes depended more on deregulation than finance and had some clear regional implications, including links between Italy and Greece, Spain and Portugal and, possibly more significant, between the Community and Algeria and Morocco, to the south, and Poland, Belorussia, and Russia to the east.

II. Cases

Specific industrial policies can be highlighted briefly under three categories: those where the Davignon tradition of managed adjustment survives (steel, cars, consumer electronics, chemicals and pharmaceuticals); those where liberalization is creeping in (telecoms and financial services, banking, stock exchanges and insurance) and the supportive policies aimed at labour and SMEs.

TRADITIONAL

Despite the assumptions that industrial policy would be directed at 'advanced markets' across the European scene, the allocation of research funds has habitually benefited national champions in the process of becoming European ones, particularly in the case of defence-related industries such as Thomson, GEC, CGEE or Messerschmidt. Indeed it can be argued that Esprit, Race and Eureka have both interventionist and protectionist effects, and are thus naturally at odds with the internal market's primary aims.[21] The case of steel over-production after 1992, in which three member states defended their support of research and development programmes in the existing plants' over-capacity for social or political reasons, illustrates how even more archaic *raison d'état* can frustrate the European ideal.

A. Steel

In theory, the era of state subsidies had ended in 1986 (see note 1). But when the late 1980s boom ended, steel demand stagnated, followed by a slump in prices, so that a further round of restructuring became inevitable. Over-production worsened when, naively, Czechoslovak and Polish producers tried to take advantage of the newly extended European Economic Area by increasing production for the European market, as if the agreements they had just signed with the EU were unlikely to be interpreted as they stood. The Commission's plans, published in November 1992, were condemned as inadequate by the ESCS's Advisory Committee, heavily under the influence of the producer companies. The peak organization, Eurofer, called for a 'manifest crisis' declaration and production quotas. Italy, Germany (because of the factories in former East Germany) and Spain were also not prepared to envisage unemployment on the scale which massive capacity cuts would create.

In the ensuing negotiations, member states were set against each other and, in the German and Italian cases, state-owned or state-supported companies were set against private ones. Much depended on what incentives the Commission felt able to give to offset the social and redevelopment costs. Initially, in January 1993, it offered 240 million ecus over three years, accompanied by measures to inhibit subsidies for plants due for closure. Quotas would be provided to hold back Russian and eastern European imports, together with anti-dumping duties on those from the United States, in default of the multilateral agreements which the Commission had failed to negotiate in 1991–2.

Precise levels of aid were also authorized for plants in former East Germany (Eko-Stahl and Klöckner), southern Italy (Ilva) and Spain (Siderurgia Nacional). These negotiations involved not only DG4 but DG5, given the likelihood that 70–100,000 jobs would be lost. Unfortunately, Commissioner Flynn's attempts to cover these from the Social Fund were frustrated by the Edinburgh 1992 budget limits. Even worse, the German government, fearful for its unification programme,[22] declared the Italian and Spanish deals to be invalid. Italy in turn rejected van Miert's deal and Spain followed suit, knowing that any agreement on the German case required their support.

Meanwhile the independent producers (EISA) urged van Miert, Bangemann and Brittan to stand fast. So contentious did the game become that later stages had to be handled by a neutral Commission, whose chairman Fernand Braun, a former Director General, confronted not only Eurofer but indirectly the three member states themselves. Within the Commission, it appears that Delors was favourable to the German case for political reasons, but not to the others. By July 1993 it seemed that not only the restructuring plan but the internal market in steel was itself threatened.[23]

In November, the entire deal fell apart when France, Britain, Denmark and Luxembourg refused to let the Eko-Stahl part proceed unilaterally. Matters worsened during the winter as Germany's attitude hardened and the Italian government's dilatoriness and evasiveness attracted media blame. A whole series of contingent closure agreements with private producers, and trade agreements with Russia, Ukraine and Kazakhstan were delayed. Heightening the stakes, Eurofer threatened to appeal to the ECJ against any Commission plan. A revised Commission proposal for reductions of 19 million tonnes was then endangered by DG4's precipitate announcement of fines on the private producers, including British Steel, for collusion in pricing steel beams during the late 1980s, which looked as if it were an attempt to blackmail them into acceptance, or at least into curtailing their demand for a crisis cartel. In the end, the Commission was first forced to extend its deadline and then to accept failure. At the end of 1994, van Miert reduced the demand for closures to 11 million tons and allowed the three member states' subsidies to go ahead, because of the impact on unemployment.

Failure may have been preferable to a 'corrupt bargain' – legitimating aids in return for an arbitrary level of capacity reduction. This at any rate was the British, Dutch, French and Danish view, all of whose governments had viewed with great distaste Commission negotiations with the three interested member states which excluded them, in addition to all the private producers. But the college would have evidently have preferred the deal rather than achieving the principle, as a negotiated way of bringing order to the least-productive state-owned companies. The outcome exposed multiple layers of naked self-interest and political expediency, the very reverse of an 'advanced market'.

B. Car Production[24]

Few industries have a higher political profile and few have so many suppliers. Across Europe, car production in 1991 employed 1.5 million people directly, a further one million in components manufacture, and another 7 million indirectly. Yet the producers, sited in less than half the member states, are badly organized and often antagonistic,[25] except when facing up to Japanese penetration. When supported by their member states, on the other hand, car producers can form substantial blocking minorities, so that harmonization of tyres, lighting, windscreens or vehicle testing certificates has in most cases been delayed for up to ten years. In the case of manufacturers' pricing structures and exclusive dealerships, the European car producers (still grouped, until 1991, in CCMC) were able to trade price differentials for a block exemption of distribution networks in 1985, in technical breach of Article 85.[26]

Subsidies retained a high level of political visibility and in 1992 the Commission allowed state aid to the Opel factory in former East Germany as a trade-off for acquiescence in much larger aid to a Fiat plant in the Mezzogiorno. But already by 1990, Japanese producers, having taken advantage of their American competitors' failure to defend the US home market before moving to establish bridgeheads in the United Kingdom, appeared ready to widen their productive base in the Community. National producers in France (where Article 115 did not actually apply), Spain and Italy, who had enjoyed quota restrictions (dating back in the Italian case to an agreement with Japan in 1954) feared that, with the loss of Article 115 protection once the internal market had been established, their long-sheltered domestic sectors would be ravaged. The political influence wielded by Fiat (68% of whose production was sold inside Italy), Renault (49% in France), and PSA–Peugeot-Citröen (45% in France) found ready backing from governments as the 1990s recession set in. Even in Germany, ostensibly committed to free trade, it is said on circumstantial evidence that Count Lambsdorf, then economics minister, had secretly negotiated a 15% quota on Japanese cars as early as 1982.[27]

The Commission therefore had no obvious incentive to make a clean cut once the internal market took effect in 1993. Although Article 115 would disappear, its effects would not immediately be disapplied, nor would the 10.3% external tariff be withdrawn; neither would the European quotas be abolished, since the French and Italian producers had only begun to react with the passing of the Single European Act 1985–6.[28] But the producers' demands for total reciprocity went far beyond any likely Japanese concessions or interpretation of the Single European Act acceptable to the Commission. If the Commission were to be empowered to negotiate a new, interim trade agreement with Japan (and producers could hardly do so without national backing, which would seriously have endangered the Commission's competence), the producers would have to be brought into line first. Yet the governments most concerned were united only in their disapproval of what French and Italian producers regarded as the British Trojan horse. In France, Edith Cresson proved a vigorous opponent of any measure of

Japanese inward investment. The German government, despite its free-trade stance, was lukewarm (even though VW had already had to face up to Japanese competition on its own in the small car market).

The game developed on three quite separate levels. But the Commission for once provided the momentum, between 1988 and 1990, using the fact that the majority of the divided producers, driven largely by Raymond Levy of Renault (who later became ACEA's President, with von Kuhnheim of BMW as Chief Executive Officer, bolstered by the active presence of Ford and General Motors),[29] did not wish to be dragooned by Jacques Calvet of PSA, preferring the negotiations with Japan to be handled centrally rather than bilaterally by governments, among which only the French and Italian could agree. At one critical point, in September 1990, Bangemann himself negotiated with Agnelli and Carl Hahn (VW), deliberately excluding Calvet. This did not immediately presage the break up of CCMS, which made a last attempt to patch up its united front; but very soon afterwards ACEA was formed without PSA. It seems clear than Bangemann precipitated this outcome and may deliberately have fostered it.

Despite the fact that Fiat's very survival was at stake, Gianni Agnelli switched horses at the last moment, as did the Spanish offshoot, Séat. In the end, the French government, which had initially intended to oppose what Cresson regarded as British 'transplants' (with the help of Italy, Spain, Portugal and Greece), and German companies, unsure of their own government's stance,[30] followed Renault's lead, sensing that the Commission, with that united front, might get the best deal possible for up to ten years. Almost fortuitously the field of trade negotiation was opened up again to the Commission which had barely ventured into this arena since 1982.

Until that point, DGs 2, 4, 12 and 13 had envisaged the internal market as an indirect regulator able to induce car producers to modernize themselves to meet external competition.[31] The Commission was now enabled to ask for a VER from Japan, which would give time for them to adjust: five years being the limit proposed by the Commission, ten by the producers. This had the extra merit that it did not prejudice the internal market unduly, or alienate France; but it did affect the GATT Uruguay round (which included VERs). The problem was that, although VERs had existed for many years, even in Britain (SMMT's agreement with JAMA), any new one required legal embodiment – unless the Japanese authorities imposed an export cartel on their own producers.

In the light of the GATT negotiations and divisions on free trade/protection lines inside the college, the formal solution was one which the Commission could not promote. Neither would member states allow the Commission to have a free hand in any informal bargaining with Japanese authorities. In the end, the highly secret negotiations were conducted jointly by DGs 1 and 3 with MITI in Japan; the most concerned member states' foreign, trade and industry ministers being continually engaged. Some parts of the VER's multiple text, agreed in July 1991, have never been published, and aspects of it are still open to different interpretations, mainly by the French government. PSA indeed went on to negotiate a separate VER with Nissan and Toyota regarding British-produced cars. But it appears to consist of a 15% VER, running for a period of seven years up to 1999, after which GATT rules will obtain.

Since such an agreement is necessarily informal, and since VERs are in any case a 'grey area' within GATT, it is possible that the rules of this engagement may be altered before 1999, if EU car producers show signs of failing to adjust in time. What the Japanese government would then do probably depends on how far producers like Nissan, Honda or Mazda in the EU had been accepted by ACEA and the Commission as European under the rules of origin; space for a secondary game has already opened up. But it would also depend on what happens in eastern Europe, where VW has already taken over the Czech producer Skoda, and where components production for German and Italian factories is well-developed.[32]

In comparison with the steel settlement, this solution is relatively liberal. Of more importance here, the outcome was determined first by what the industry could agree on (or be forced to agree on), and second by what the Commission could persuade Japan to accept. Trade and industry policy rode hand in hand, on the comforting assumption that a period of managed change would induce competitiveness without tears.[33] To arguments that the negotiations and the VER agreement were technically illegal and highly ambiguous, officials reply that no other combination could have produced a mutually acceptable answer[34] – and that, with the new balance of forces between producers and member states, harmonization and standardization will proceed faster in future.

Whether the industry can adjust in time is another matter. Fiat has adjusted well since 1990, its car sales in Italy falling from 68% to 35% in mid-1995, the remainder going 25% to EU countries, 40% world-wide. Mercedes currently plans to raise from 10% to 24% the proportion of cars built outside Germany. But adjustment has meant redundancies at home (20,000 in PSA alone) and the transfer of production beyond the EU. Since 1992, the proposed Renault–Volvo merger (or takeover, from the French point of view) has failed, due to Swedish shareholders' opposition, and other producers have entered a range of joint ventures in Brazil, Argentina, India, China and Indonesia which presage immense numbers of redundancies in the European Union – a notable case of social dumping of their own national workforces by producers. Nor is it certain that industry policy will retain its protective tinge as the Commission turns again to uncover the last closed areas, in removing the block exemption on distribution networks and harmonizing taxation differentials.[35]

C. Consumer Electronics

Japanese competition made itself felt in consumer electronics more than a decade earlier than in the automobile industry. When its impact was first felt in the 1970s, Philips was still the only pan-European producer, the rest relying on distinct national markets distinguished by traditions and consumer preferences. By the mid-1980s, everything had changed, as Japanese quality and efficiency either swamped local firms (in Britain) or forced them to merge (in Germany), despite the quotas negotiated by many member states. Only Philips, Thomson and Nokia (Finland) had sufficient capacity to develop a strategy for video recorders.[36]

Philips/Grundig developed a VCR technology (V2000) to

counter Sony's Betamax and JVC's VHS systems (licensed to Philips's other European competitors). Despite support from member governments and the Commission, Philips lost money and market share in an episode that can be read as an important stage in the protracted death of national champions. As a result, companies' forms of defence shifted from purely national measures, such as France's celebrated funnelling of all VCR imports through a single customs post in Poitiers, to European ones. Davignon negotiated a VER with MITI in 1981 to last three years, to be followed by a 14% tariff on Japanese imports – a rate nearly twice the EC's average.

That VER proved to be an unfortunate protection, for the floor price allowed Japanese producers to make a great deal of money at the EC consumers' expense, while at the same time investing heavily and setting up production facilities, even in France. A new round of producer coalitions ensued, influenced by the state-owned French company Thomson's expansion in Germany, Britain and the USA. Philips restructured itself and Nokia expanded into Sweden, Germany and France. At the end of the 1980s these three confronted eight Japanese firms, all with EC headquarters.

The wave of concentration occurred among MNCs as a result of global competition and technological diffusion rather than EC industrial policy. But the European trio retained many protective devices which the Japanese attempted to counter by joining the industry's national federations and EACEM, if not as full members then as extraordinary ones. All of them nevertheless continued to act as cloaks of legitimacy for what the large European producers did. But at the same time, a process of assimilation began, led by Sony, in which Japanese firms started to turn themselves into insiders, in order to penetrate Europe's vast, heavily protected telecoms markets and the EU's research programmes.

The high definition TV project (HDTV), grew out of the Commission's research programme Eureka in 1986, which was intended to preempt Japan and the United States by establishing by 1990 an analogue standard of line definition (EU95) good enough to be accepted by the international broadcasting standards authorities. The potential profits and the technological gains appeared substantially to justify the investment. The only alternative was to wait and then license whatever alternative the Japanese chose to produce, because the United States had its own HDTV standard, though broadcasters showed no desire to use it. An analogue system, later styled HDMac or D2Mac, was to be produced in collaboration between Philips, Thomson (which in due course swallowed Thorn-EMI) and Bosch.

The whole effort depended on a single assumption: that consumers would pay the price for HDTV on wide screens, in the years before a digital standard – almost inevitably an American one – came into effect around the year 2000. Strongly influenced by French government backing for Thomson, DG13 promoted the necessary Directive in favour of the Mac standard, despite warnings from DGs 3 and 4 whose officials strongly opposed the aid about to be given to Thomson. Fatally, the Directive applied only to DBS satellite broadcasting, because Astra (BSB-controlled) already had a UKMac licence. Fatal, because during the development period, Rupert Murdoch's concern Sky, together with Amstrad moved in, using the PAL system on telecom satellites. Once Murdoch had taken over BSB in 1988, PAL undercut the D2Mac project – even though it worked sufficiently well by then for the international authorities to defer their final ultimate choice.

A period of frantic lobbying followed, as the Continental companies, fronted by EACEM, lobbied the Commission and Enrico Pandolfi the Italian Commissioner responsible, in order to modify the 1992 Directive to make it also apply to Astra. Both the French and German governments were drawn in, Mitterrand having intervened personally with Kohl to induce German broadcasters to use HDMac; and the French authorities slyly used the occasion to increase Thomson's subsidy to £400 million, of which only 25% was actually for this project.[37] The Commission had to choose between following what the industry and the Franco-German entente wanted or the interests of at least two million consumers who would be compelled to buy new dishes, having already invested in BSkyB.

Murdoch was not alone on the consumers' side, because American companies had already decided to recoup their lost advantage *vis-à-vis* Japan by completing their own digital system much earlier than expected, in 1995, not 2000: an endeavour paradoxically supported by both Philips and Thomson through their American affiliates. The British government also opposed what it regarded as a supreme waste of EU money.[38] In the end, Pandolfi could do no more than broker a wasteful deal in which the Commission provided a ten-year subsidy to satellite broadcasters to continue with both systems until 2002 – for which the producers would manufacture dual-standard decoders, at an overall cost estimated at £350 million – assuming that this improbable arrangement lasts.

Swayed by the remorseless combination of producer power, thinly veiled by EACEM's claim to be acting in the European interest, and battered from above by the two largest member state governments, the Commission came to a solution which differed in all respects from the US Federal Communications Commission's decision to maintain an open game in the United States without prior favours to any producer group. That the American digital system is most likely to win, commercially, may be a bonus for Philips and Thomson in terms of their American alliances, but not the European viewer, because even though D2Mac and the Japanese HDTV standard work well, they are already obsolescent. Given its close links with the industry, and the historical patterns of political interdependence, the Commission might have found it hard to deal otherwise. But in the same way as the V2000 VCR, consumers had been landed with an expensive dead end whose total cost will amount to roughly £2 billion. There are several morals on offer: the primary one is about the temptation to ignore the public/consumer dimension when creating costly technology without a market.

The HDTV debacle did not of course occur in isolation. Delors, as well as several Commissioners and Directors General, believed that electronics had become a strategic industry for which DG13 should act as sponsor, rather than DG3, whose scepticism had recently became evident in the 1990 paper on industrial policy.[39] But by 1990–91, European producers of semi-conductors such as Bull, Olivetti and Siemens, together with ICL (now owned by Fujitsu), found themselves in a critical position. The merits of industrial policy organized for the benefits of European champion producers experiencing 'sectoral crisis', seemed less obvious, as the *cellule de prospective* and DG4 argued at the time.[40] DG3 in particular wanted to encourage Bull and Thomson to rationalize, on the grounds that no separate European market now existed, and that they should seek world alliances instead, even if these centred outside Europe.[41]

Publicly, the Delors-Kaifu statement in July 1991 made on behalf of the Community and Japanese government seemed to acknowledge this logic: new trade barriers should not be created. Yet only five months earlier, Delors is alleged to have issued a démarche to the college that 'the Community is not, and will not be a free trade zone. It is up to us to make it a European organized space.'[42] This view dominated DG13's paper 'The EU's Electronics and Informatics Industry' (1993), with its presentation of a life or death struggle against the Americans and Japanese.[43]

Yet despite the continued benefits which they evidently drew from such liaisons, the producers themselves seemed even in 1991–2 less interested in remaining European champions than in keeping their European bases afloat until their alliances in the United States became profitable. Evidently for them there would, after 1995, be no 'European organized space'. Since then Bull, having failed to adjust, has drifted steadily downwards and seems likely to fall to a Japanese takeover. Thomson has made itself far less reliant on defence contracts and French government favours. Meanwhile, as digital television crosses the threshold, the Commission has left it to the 180 firms in the Digital Video Broadcasting project to agree on what should be the European standard: a reversion to market logic after the wasted efforts of the early 1990s.

One other point needs to be made about the entry of new players to the game. The HDTV case and its sequel revealed not only the negative power of consumers, but the previously unseen power of broadcasters able to use a variety of satellites, whose directions in world markets the major European producers had to follow in order to survive. As occurred in the video format wars of the early 1980s, software paradoxically led the development of hardware. The game has now changed: DG13 argues that it is necessary to coopt Japanese producers, as Europeans, and even to admit them to future research projects, if the remaining EU suppliers are not to be displaced.[44]

D. Chemicals and Pharmaceuticals

There are no obvious cases here because, many of the biggest and most innovative companies being European, European producers are much less threatened by US or Japanese competition. This sector also has a long tradition of cartelization and international markets (with the exception of medication and the different national insurance systems and the price differentials these cause). Two formidably coordinated European-wide associations, CEFIC and EFPIA, manage their members' consensus so well that the greater part of corporate diplomacy is conducted between them and the relevant Directors General.

DG3 rarely seeks to give a lead, reckoning that these industrial players know best how to survive, competitively, in world markets. Officials' brokerage is usually aimed to resolve intra-industry disputes. In the case where taxes were proposed on CO_2 pollution, DG3's chemical section sought only a 'voluntary commitment' from the producers and subsequently relied heavily on CEFIC documentation when defending their (and the industry's) position at the Rio Summit.[45] Conversely, DG4's prosecution of the various chemicals cartels increased the companies' sense of beleaguered common identity to the point at which DG3 officials sometimes encouraged them to use their national channels to circumvent the college altogether.[46] But the main reason for mutual assistance lies in media and public hostility, and demands for deeper regulation of what are almost invariably depicted as potential polluters.

The wave of mergers, joint ventures and strategic alliances in pharmaceuticals since the mid-1980s suggests that this industry (where it may cost £200 million to develop a single drug which then may not succeed as planned) is moving towards the point of concentration established two decades ago in the chemicals industry. Given the extent of negotiated settlements between the European federation EFPIA (a small but very effective organization)[47] and the sector officials in DG3, member states exercise a close diplomacy with the Community authorities to an extent even greater than in the chemicals industry. EFPIA's eight players (two of which are in Switzerland) are all of world dimensions and collectively are capable of outflanking the Commission, and possibly even the Council, through their influence with member governments: they induced the latter to insert provisions to allow greater self-regulation in the advertising Directive than the Commission had proposed, and to lengthen the time scales in their favour in the 1988 patents Directive.[48]

Nevertheless the European public-interest dimension cannot entirely be ignored. Companies' national outlooks differ in Britain and Germany on one hand, and France and Italy on the other, which may make their united front vulnerable in the impassioned debates when consumers and ecological interests are involved. High as EFPIA ranks on the scale of self-regulation, it cannot insulate itself against public and media outcry, of which the Commission, and member states in their own dimensions, have also to take account. The Commission is by no means a cushion against the outside world, or a veil for industry responses on drug pricing, information control, and marketing techniques. EFPIA's skill however – or rather the collective skills of its members – give a greater advantage in shaping policy for the industry than any other apart from CEFIC. It has reached the stage where it can counter or respond in its own right to Commission policies on, say, price transparency or increasing competition by abolishing market price control mechanisms. Quite apart from influence at national levels, this mutual understanding rests on Commission awareness that the industry has three conditions for survival: a close link between national and world markets, a stable regulatory system which allows long lead times for research and development, and effective mechanisms for transposing technology from laboratory to products.[49] For all three reasons, the Commission is likely to continue to accept that, with certain exceptions, this industry knows best, and that the research-based firms should be privileged in a self-regulating system of private sector governance.[50]

AREAS OF NEW MOMENTUM

American commentators often argue that EU industrial policy is invariably and irredeemably interventionist and protectionist, and must therefore be balanced by a proper competition policy and a strong bent towards deregulation. Overstated as the case usually is, and often based on observations before the internal market came into full effect, it has significant weight, which was used by Leon Brittan both when he was in charge of DG4, and later during the final rounds of GATT negotiations.

It was to be expected that DG4, in full sail after 1988, should place itself at the head of a new onslaught on the state-owned 'natural monopolies' which had successfully resisted change throughout the entire post-War era: telecoms, railways, airlines, postal services, energy generation and supply. These were, naturally, defended by national governments with a series of arguments, firstly about efficiency (which slowly collapsed during the late 1980s in the face of American and then British examples of deregulation, privatization and the introduction of new technology), secondly the social benefits of state subsidies to uneconomic services in remoter or poorer areas (which is still at issue), and thirdly about the ability to provide new investment (where the evidence that the state provides best over the long-term is still strong).

A. Telecoms

The key to DG4's long-delayed liberalizing activity lay in Article 90. In the mid–1980s, Peter Sutherland and a small group of officials in DG4 interpreted Article 90 as an injunction against monopolies pure and simple, and succeeded in linking their view to the internal market's momentum, in spite of a challenge by member states, led by France, at the European Court. Brittan took up the argument, asking not whether he should proceed against the 'natural monopolies' but when: and he began with telecoms, being the area most open to reform, now that telecoms technology had made universal services possible. In 1990 AT and T's 'calling card' operation, for example, gave EU companies and individuals a means to bypass their state telecoms systems and make international calls to the USA for vastly less than the prevailing European prices.

But the member states retained great defensive powers: even though Article 90 in theory gave the Commission power to bypass the Council of Ministers altogether, Brittan was never able to get a college majority prepared to back him in such an epic confrontation.

The Commission therefore chose a more roundabout route. In close consultation with the national authorities, users' associations, standard setting bodies, and the largest equipment manufacturers (grouped in ECTEL), the Commission envisaged complete liberalization of terminal equipment in all new services but, for social and political reasons, did not include the basic infrastructure and services or the telephone network itself.[51] A Green Paper on implementation won approval in the Council in July 1988, leading to a series of directives over the next two years.

If the Commission had expected to undermine resistance by meeting the national and commercial players half-way, they found that opinions had changed by 1990. Directives on open network provision and services ran into densely coordinated opposition in the Council (unlike earlier ones which had met criticism only from Spain and Belgium). No more could be gained this way beyond the Telecoms draft White Paper July 1992 on opening up national telephone services and even this was stalled for two years in the college. The European Parliament voted down a similar Directive in July 1994.

The opening up of gas and electricity supplies, privatized a decade earlier in Britain, failed for similar reasons in 1993, mainly because of disagreements among the Commission Directorates, fostered by national governments. The Commission is still trying to bring Article 90 to bear, but in less advantageous circumstances. It has more recently had to back down on postal services' liberalization, for reasons which go to the heart of European policy-making: the Commission simply does not have the democratic *locus standi*, or the political influence, to reshape deeply held attitudes about the public services in France and Germany, not only among governments and civil servants but public sector work forces and their unions, and, indeed, right across civil society.

Brittan's alternative strategy, to liberalize cross-border communications first, did escape these constraints – for the very practical reason that business needed it – and it will come into force as part of the official process in January 1998. The case has similarities with airlines, where a frontal assault was fiercely resisted by national authorities, forcing the Commission to construct an alliance of suppliers and users to work indirectly to erode entrenched member state defences by skilful use of their own media and public expectations, fostered by changes already taking place in the global market.[52] The 1998 deadline for full Community liberalization, set by the 1990 Directive, whether or not accompanied by privatization (about which the Commission is agnostic), lies a long way ahead for commercial players. But at least they can now plan on an informed basis rather than a speculative one. On the main issue of market advantage, commercial speculation runs wild, as the giant companies scramble for position in the German and Italian telecoms markets – but less successfully in France, where the government stubbornly defended its protectionist public service stance, to the point that AT & T withdrew from its projected takeover of Bull at the end of 1994. More recently, however, France Télécom has been opened up to tender – to the grave disadvantage of Alcatel – possibly as a result of BT's complaints about its joint venture, Atlas, with Deutsche Telekom and Sprint corporation. The game is currently all about access and exclusion before 1998.

Meanwhile in April 1993, van Miert relinquished the idea of liberalizing all EU services in stages over a period of time, in favour of parallel deregulation of both national and cross-border services. Thus no single area or group should be forced to carry an undue burden until the advantages gained in one sector force the rest to concert their own adjustment. Again, he set out what can be seen as a characteristically European solution, the 1998 target date being still comfortably distant, buttressed by safeguards, to be discussed with all interested players, in order to ensure that 'liberalization does not mean deregulation (or a change . . . to an unbridled free-for-all which would risk excluding the weaker members of society from this valuable tool for social integration.'[53]

The language is that of a hypothetical European public and constitutes an implied rebuke to the 'Anglo-Saxon mentality' which in Britain has left only individual regulators, in this case Oftel, to curb corporate greed. It also condemns the giant players' habit of cherry-picking the most profitable business services. In some contrast, and very much in corporate players' favour, the equipment market has been fully opened up, subject only to Commission support for research and technical development. The compromise, which as usual embodies an element of selective assistance, came at the insistence of DG3, in defiance of DG4's basic assumption that, since national monopoly is the worst of all possible obstacles to the internal market, 'corporate Darwinism' is best induced by the Anglo-Saxon model, where companies strive to get into a new game first, followed by their member state governments, leaving the backward ones to adjust as best they can.

Whether the more advanced national systems not yet privatized (like Deutsche Bundespost-Telekom (DBP) whose first privatization sale is not due until 1996) preempt the 1998 target or not, differentiation is likely to grow rapidly, because national regulators are already making decisions in the light of the current business plans of DBP , France Télécom, STET or Telefonica, which have been discussed with finance ministers and guaranteed by the state at borrowing rates well below those available to independent British Telecom. (Their stock exchange price earnings differential may be as great as 10% as against 15–20% for British Telecom.) Some of the current proposals, like Atlas to provide advanced services for global business users, have been attacked by BT (itself involved in a similar venture with an American carrier) as being likely to create a new, more durable monopoly. Yet Portuguese Telecom's privatization has begun; the Spanish government now talks of partial liberalization before 1998, and even France Télécom has an appointment with privatization in the late 1990s, probably coinciding with the second stage of the German system. Today's players include not only the old telecoms corporations (among which both DBP and France Télécom are in technical terms highly advanced) as they prepare for privatization but the American global carriers, suppliers of equipment, and even electricity generators, which are eager to lay high-capacity lines. That a diehard defence could succeed, say by Italian or Greek operators trying to incorporate the alternative infrastructure, seems less and less likely.

Given the political obstacles from governments, and the infighting amongst the other players, the Commission's current schemes, which include deregulation of restrictions on cable TV networks running telecoms services, may be the best answer for business and residential users. But the recent G7 Summit in Brussels witnessed strong pressure from both the European companies and some governments to accelerate the pace of telecoms liberalization if the Community were not to lose its chance of participating in the information super-highway. The global telecoms market is changing so rapidly that the Community's original scheme, with its 1998 date, looks increasingly anachronistic. Modifications are likely to be driven from below, to which both the Commission and the member states will have to respond. This case indicates that governments really are losing their sovereignty on matters once regarded as profound national interests – but to global rather than European forces. Britain could be said to have opted into the global mainstream by privatizing British Telecom; and the British model appears to have the advantage over the Franco-German one. All that the Community can do is to ameliorate the inevitable and indirectly prefer the former. In practice Article 90 has now been defined so as to permit a limited level of monopoly, in deference to a member state's diminishing scope.[54]

B. *Financial Services*

Although the SEA applied to financial services, banks, insurance companies and stock exchanges were generally slow to argue for it or to react to its implications, except in Britain (where deregulation had been completed with Big Bang in the City in October 1986). Because all financial markets were becoming global ones, and because London still handled a larger share of business than any European rival, competition and deregulation were bound to affect every sector of every EC market; but the residues of exchange control[55] and sheltered, protective devices – particularly in insurance – ensured that Commission and Council intervention would be required to achieve parity of harmonization as the internal market developed.

Because technological changes made the provision of new financial services cheap, effective and universal, the Commission could count on having the support of business and consumer demand in all three sectors. The social argument, so effective in defending national monopolies, carried weight only in the area of fraud detection and consumer protection (including insider trading, asset stripping, or anything else to the detriment of shareholders). Fewer conflicts existed between the principle of liberalization and the Commission's concern for gentler macro-economic adjustment; and there was a greater likelihood than in the case of industries that cross-border financial activity would help to erode national or local protective systems.

Unfortunately, the high tide of deregulation which had facilitated the BCCI debacle left an unpleasant flotsam of scandal or mismanagement for the 1990s, including the fall or near-collapse of overblown commercial banks, Banesto, Crédit Lyonnais and later, for rather different reasons, Barings. After an exuberant period of growth, ill-considered mergers and worldwide acquisitions, loans to what became 'sovereign debtors' and a spiral of spreading insurance risks from which Lloyds of London suffered catastrophically, banks and insurance companies had burned their fingers badly. Yet they had invested heavily in what by the 1990s was becoming gross overcapacity, at least in domestic retail markets. Retrenchment and redundancies followed, causing a falling-off in consortium banking and a scaling-back of international business which lasted until 1994–5, which to some extent refuted the optimistic predictions made for financial services in the Cecchini Report.

Of the three sectors, banking caused the least trouble from the Commission's point of view. The second Banking Directive, in 1989, provided a single licence and mutual recognition for banking and securities trading, subject to regulations of minimum capital requirements and supervision. Supplementary provisions dealt with equivalents of supervision, payments systems for large users, and policies to counter money-laundering.

Although there were indications that differing national viewpoints might erect new obstacles during the process of implementation, the way that this and other directives were drafted allowed for diversity of views about the general principles on which the industry would in future develop: the players themselves, in their global environment, would decide on such questions as 'universal banking' or 'bank-assurance'. It seemed that the cultural basis which had up until then encouraged European financial service providers to seek partners with access to local markets would continue,[56] even if

German banks behaved more like British ones where liquidity was concerned, and British ones more like German in seeking equity.[57] This was what the Commission wanted: a homogenized European banking service, with an increasing network of cross-border operations, staffed by chief general managers habituated to Europe whose practice and job mobility would in due course spread to their counterparts in insurance or stock markets.

However, from the point of view of international bond dealers, the Commission seemed 'structuralist': prone to imposing arbitrary rules on the industry for its own political ends or administrative convenience. Officials mitigated some criticisms by their regular consultation with Central Banks, and the largest European banks, Deutsche, Barclays, or Crédit Lyonnais, their national equivalents and the European federation (FBE).[58] It turned out to be much harder to meet governments' regular complaints about the lack of reciprocity shown by American and Japanese banking systems, despite the fact that France, once highly protected, had opened up as least as much as Germany.

As might have been expected, securities traders and investment banks took much longer to adjust than some of the leading retail bankers – Barclays, Citicorp and possibly Crédit Lyonnais in its better days – which had European-wide branch networks (even so, none of these yet provides a full in-house service for cross-border payments, and the services offered are still quite obviously national in character and design).

Competition in financial services between banks, non-banks, near-banks and insurance companies was, of course, foreseen. But in this case competition did not provide an obvious instrument for modernizing the sector as a whole. Although the first, Non-life Assurance Directive passed in 1973, and the first Life one in 1979, insurance lagged behind banking, despite the implications of the fact that the volume of Community pensions income in 1989 amounted to $350 billion (30% of the world's total). The existence of two models, continental and Anglo-Saxon, the former highly regulated, with tied agents and little freedom to design new products, the latter flexible, non-prescriptive and in the hands of independent brokers, presented vastly more obstacles than in banking.[59]

After its second Directive in 1988 on cross-border sales for large risk insurance, the Commission pushed to establish the internal market in commercial insurance, hoping that liberalization would eventually trickle down to the individual holders of domestic policies. But the giant players such as Allianz, Commercial Union, UAP, or Generali themselves compounded the problem of national and local barriers to trade, for insurance companies merged or took each other over avidly in the late 1980s, in expectation of the internal market (often making large losses in the process, through lack of foresight or knowledge of what this concentration was intended to achieve). Although the Commission worked with the European Insurance Federation, the CEA, it represented no more than the lowest common denominator of leading companies and officials found that, unlike CEFIC or EFPIA, they 'had to be careful in using the industry to move member states, for fear of conservative-protectionist supervisory agencies.'[60]

Disagreements between national systems bedevilled attempts to liberalize insurance markets. Although a British mode of defining large risks by the number of employees in a firm was finally adopted, in 1992, it came only after five years' delay caused by the European Federation and the German insurance federations; for similar reasons, the Non-life Directive of 1990 was only agreed on its twentieth draft.[61] It was hardly surprising that the Commission adopted a long strategy, as they had in telecoms, while waiting for technology and global markets themselves to make the running, once the largest insurance companies had rebuilt their profits by the mid-1990s. Siemens' decision to break-out of the very restrictive German market and use American insurers, and the example of self-insurance set by Daimler-Benz, may have been effective solvents of rigid supervisors' attitudes; but in the long run change will be enforced by the problem of ageing societies, with larger numbers of wealthier older citizens with more to insure, at a time in the twenty-first century when no state can afford to cover health and pensions as it does now.

The European insurance area is full of *chasses gardées*, protected by different legal systems and local customs, such as the close relations between Italian banks and insurance companies in selling their products. Insurance comes a long way after banking in DG15 eyes, whose officials are disinclined to attack what they know are protected national enclaves. 'It would be unwise', one said, 'to propose a text disruptive of member state markets.'[62] As some other Directorates do with the industries they sponsor, DG15 relies on national insurance federations and the CEA, and on technical consultants in the working groups provided by the companies themselves. As a result, some technical proposals take at least eighteen months to prepare. On the other hand, if the Commission proposes a text, and looks like pushing it, industry and member states tend to cave in and negotiate – and some governments have recently shown signs of local interests, in the interests of this sector as a whole and its younger professional operators, for example with the third General Directive, covering mass risks, pensions and casualty which passed in July 1994.

But for the marketing of services, and control at national level, where competition lies not in the service but in its narrower range of price and performance, the Commission's aim is no more than minimum harmonization, to bring the worst member states up to the European mean. In the case of the single passport for insurance, now extended from non-life to life policies, the 'Anglo-Dutch' model coexists with the 'continental' one and will do so until (as officials believe) consumers turn naturally to the former; or (as German supervisors believe) the market collapses and requires reregulation.[63] Until events decide between the two contenders, firms make their own dispositions and member states try to keep their public consumers under control, falling behind meanwhile with the internal market schedule.

(At this stage, pension funds did not come into the game, being only fully developed in Britain, Ireland, the Netherlands and Denmark, and to a minor extent in Belgium and Germany. These last two, with Spain, France and Italy, which only legislated in 1992 to allow pension funds to exist, strongly resisted the 1994 Pensions Fund Directive because it would have eroded their governments' captive market in state bonds. Belgium would permit only 15% pension fund investments outside its borders and currency, Portugal and the rest 20%, compared with Britain, the Netherlands, Ireland and Denmark's 60%. The Directive was rejected in June 1994, and the Commission threatened to take eight governments to the European Court.)

A unified securities market in which capital issues could be floated across Europe, and stock exchanges could offer competitive services in every member state, came into existence in the mid–1980s as a by-product of the Single European Act. The Commission hurried through its legislation on unit trusts and mutual recognition in 1985–6, leaving the loose ends to be tidied up later, after Spanish entry and under QMV rules.[64] This was prudent, because none of the items on insider trading, investment services, or declaration of major holdings could have been obtained without QMV, because member states and the stock exchange federation, like the CEA, split roughly on Anglo-Saxon/Code Napoleon lines. Only in 1993 was the legal framework for a single internal market completed, with the European passport for investment firms and capital adequacy requirements. But in this case DG15 found itself more in harmony with the national authorities and central banks than in the insurance sector, able to manoeuvre and make concessions to local demands as part of the doctrine of subsidiarity. It could not prevent intense competition for survival among stock exchanges, particularly in the sixteen German *Länder*, threatened by the dominance of the three largest European markets London, Paris and Frankfurt (which is far from being as developed as a stock market as it is a banking centre)[65] and major regional markets' shift towards uniformity of practice and an international list of quotations.

Here the EU's own institutions are divided. European stock markets cannot for any length of time isolate themselves from this global process, neither can distinctive EU arrangements be put in place when business will inevitably gravitate to those centres where it is most easily done. Yet governments which have not centralized their systems as Britain and France have, still try to defend their own, as do the *Länder*. Following what is still a numerical majority, the Federation of Stock Exchanges prefers to have a European list of all leading equities and government stocks in each centre, to attract external investors and keep as many centres alive as possible. Somehow this is to be provided at the same time as a cross-border wholesale market in securities for professional investors (already provided by London's SEAQ International). Not surprisingly, DG15 appears to be waiting for the market itself to deliver pointers, hoping that one major exchange will emerge in each member state, in which 200–300 blue chip equities and fixed interest stocks can be traded.

The Commission also has ethical problems. Until a single European currency is installed, it is not clear whether it should work for the company whose stocks are traded or for the investing public. Agreement must nevertheless be obtained on the technical matter of a common settlement mechanism, such as Euro 'SA' whose technology is still imperfect. Merely keeping a wide range of exchanges alive, as the majority of member states still desire, is not a means of integration but a defensive tactic likely to end in irreversible decline for most of them. Blocked by the players, the Commission has no easy answer, and so far no obvious means of finding one, since no European interest has emerged to be defined as easily as in the case of banking or insurance.

SUPPORTIVE MECHANISMS

If the Community's language of balance and integration meant anything for industrial policy, it would have involved some element of equilibrium between labour and capital, and between large firms and SMEs. The reality is otherwise, because the Commission is not an instrument well suited either to ensure the defence of weak sectors or to shame the Council into making that a priority.

A. SMEs

SMEs are of such industrial, regional and social diversity that they have no effective voice beyond their member state confederations, except in federal states whose basic laws may permit them to have national representation. Few national confederations give them the weight they enjoy in Germany or, for historic reasons arising from its 1965 merger, in the British CBI. Only in Germany's DIHT do they possess an efficient form of representation capable of leverage in *Länder* capitals and Bonn.[66]

The Directorate which sponsors SMEs is itself relatively weak within the college and has never been endowed with an influential Commissioner, probably because it is of marginal political importance for the ambitious. DG23 officials would prefer all member states with a strong *Handwerk* component to organize it on German lines. But its initiatives have only recently had any measurable effect, so it is not unfair to conclude that, as in many other areas, the Commission is working *with* the grain of events to achieve incremental change, rather than looking for major, quasi-corporatist intervention. DG23 is in any case permeated by SMEs' representatives, and is still 'strongly dependent on the expertise given by the targets it seeks to regulate'.[67] Its action plans concentrate on establishing SMEs' weight in the EU's general culture, through creating a separate budget, cooperative programmes between small firms and attempts to restrain member states from unwarranted micro-regulation. The offices set up in some profusion in regions such as Emilia-Romagna and Catalonia are quite effective in propagating this message; but for reasons explained in chapter 9, they are often stultified by national administrations, so that their effect is less measurable than the sort of local alliances which have grown up in Rhône-Alpes or Baden-Württemberg.

The task might have been easier had DG23 not been so small (100 officials) and low in the pecking order. It has chosen, perhaps correctly in the long run, to propound highly structured solutions, derived from *Länder* experience and German supplier–manufacturer relationships. But these are not themes immediately applicable in more than a handful of the regions where most of Europe's three million SMEs operate. In a large and potentially very important area of industrial policy, it is unfortunate that this office has fallen to a series of undistinguished Commissioners without lasting effect, even in the 1993 White Paper. Too often the 'SMEs' voice' has come to be associated with 'Club Med' demands for grants or derogations.

Yet the sections devoted to SMEs in industrial policy documents, notably the training element, and the *fiches d'impactes*, tracking the results of Commission programmes (in which DG23 and the SME Taskforce have invested their intellectual capital), ought to have made more difference. It is a failure at the college and Commission President's level that policy for SMEs has become a sort of exhortation, aimed with more effect at the big players as if in order to reassure national governments that the Commission has not forgotten. It must be an error, for example, that the socio-economic aspects, vital to SMEs for whom workforce skills represent something much more than merely labour costs, remain in the hands of DG5, while questions about SMEs' industrial location are vested in DGs 16 and 22.[68] Meanwhile SMEs themselves continue, as before, making what use they can of exiguous national networks.

B. Labour

Since the early 1970s, there has been little evidence of what used to be called corporatism, and not much of tripartism save from the trade unions' side. Subjected in the last decade to almost universal decline in density and numbers of members, very high levels of unemployment, the transfer of jobs to countries with lower wages or cheaper welfare systems and the steadily rising inroads on employment of structural changes due to innovations in technology and managerial practice, trade unions have nevertheless managed to develop an intra-European, if not international dimension. It is to their credit that they have found some ways in the EU to confront the recurrence of nightmares their predecessors encountered in the 1890s and 1920s.

ETUC was only formed in 1973, early attempts having foundered on Cold War conflicts. The long slippage began almost immediately, and since then the ETUC has done well to survive and to surmount north–south divisions in Europe, and the ideological arguments between Social and Christian Democrats. Most of the former communist federations, apart from CGT in France, have joined. But despite reforms in 1991, ETUC remains a coordinating body not a supranational organization, poorly endowed in comparison with management and employers' federations or its own confederal members in the larger nation states. It lacks leaders, leadership and unity.

ETUC has a sponsor in DG5 and a public forum in Ecosoc which has not entirely lost weight; but trade union confederations are habitually excluded from the Commission's industry working groups and entirely so from the financial ones. This informal segregation reinforces the innate distinction between the internal market project and what a minority of Commissioners believed to be its alter-ego, the social dimension. One moves with huge kinetic energy, the other is paid lip service but actually backed by only a few member states, notably the Netherlands, Denmark and Greece, whose votes were inadequate for example to defend the European Company Statute, or the forty-seven directives prepared by Vasso Papandreou under the Social Charter.

That some social legislation has been advanced since then, during the post-Maastricht years, owes more to the elasticity of health and safety categories in the Treaties than to Maastricht's Social Protocol, with the exception of rights for part-time workers and pregnant women, the 48-hour week, and the Works Council Directive, the latter applying only to larger companies. By 1993 the Social Protocol was being reinterpreted, firstly as a way for employers and unions to make European-wide agreements on industrial relations, and secondly as the occasion for the Commission to issue very general 'framework directives' which each member state might implement in its own way.

Trades unions themselves, though probably as much responsible for the Protocol's adoption in 1991 as industrialists had been for the Single European Act, were reduced thereafter to pursuing other, bilateral routes in a harsh anti-union climate, seeking joint committees with multinationals, who in the early 1990s showed some signs of reciprocity. The uncompromising equation set out in the 1993 White Paper between restoring flexibility to labour markets and the defence of social priorities, signified how little real help the Commission could offer them, despite the 'days of action' mounted earlier that year; as Delors admitted to the ETUC General Secretary Emilio Gabaglio.[69]

For lack of other choices, ETUC, like its members, has since then taken the struggle to Social Democratic parties and national parliaments, with only limited success in Germany and Britain, and very little indeed in Spain, France or Italy.[70] But it cannot play the role in Brussels that member confederations do with their national governments, because the Commission is not a government. Trade unionists may well regret the faith invested in Mitterrand's and Delors's protestations about social Europe, having discovered that EU institutions are not in fact suitable negotiating partners for players with mass memberships to which they are more or less democratically accountable.[71] But the Commission is not, in that sense, democratic or accountable nor was it intended that it should be. It also notably lacks the sense of struggle against a definable enemy without which classical trades unionism lacks coherence.

Trades unionism is not European in the sense that there has never been a European strike on a European issue, although there are plenty of possible issues such as liberalization of public services and the attached job losses, steel policy, and worker protection through the Social Chapter, in which such a strike might be based. Strikes remain national, intended to embarrass national governments and force them to invoke a national interest in the Council of Ministers. Yet is it is just possible that if those trades unions which have survived the last twenty years were to play their cards differently, in the Community arena and in a manner resembling UNICE, they could recover some of their strategic losses, especially in Germany and France where they still remain a significant force.

III. Trade

The Community's trading patterns, its common external tariff and commercial policy, its arrangements with Third World countries under the Yaoundé and Lomé Agreements, the Association Agreements with eastern Europe, and with Malta, Cyprus, Turkey and North Africa, are closely related to its industrial policy, but have usually been treated as a separate area.[72] Trade is taken last, in this chapter, not because it is of lesser interest (the reverse is true, which explains why Leon Brittan took that portfolio after his time at DG4) but because its concern with nearly all the industrial policy issues – imports and VERs, including cars and consumer electronics, support to EU industries, internal competition and compatibility with GATT – affects the ways in which the three levels of players, Commission, member state governments and firms interact. Trade is in fact one of the best places to observe inter-governmental bargaining and the variety of pressures put on governments and EU institutions to respond to the players outside.

The Commission has a leading role in acting on behalf of the Community in its common commercial policy. This includes GATT negotiations, the trade policy instruments to combat dumping or trade barriers, and the new World Trade Organization's (WTO) management of international trade law. In concert with the Council, it has also a responsibility for negotiations with Asian countries, South America (Mercosur) and the seventy ACP countries which are part of the Fourth Lomé Convention. It regulates for the Community the international trade in financial services, audio-visual and telecom services, maritime transport, and sets the remaining import regimes for Japanese cars, textiles under the MFA, and bananas (see p. 604 fn. 76). Its brief also includes the multilateral steel agreement and bilateral agreements with the main trading countries on public procurement. These obligations are not easily maintained, regarded as they are with some jealousy by member states.

Although the EU has traditionally been seen as an 'instrument for the management of interdependence', it still contained after 1973 wide differences of outlook and trading philosophy between the liberal free trade inclined wing (composed of Britain, the Netherlands, West Germany and Denmark), and the more protectionist states (France, Belgium and Italy), joined in due course by Spain and Portugal, both being substantial textile producers with a strong interest in perpetuating the protective Multifibre Agreement. This basic cleavage was reinforced – and reflected in the contrasting attitudes of DGs 1 (external trade) 3 and 4 – during the mid–1970s crisis and into the 1980s when member governments sought relief from competition in subsidies or anti-dumping duties.

The main elements of trade policy up to the Single European Act reflected the requirements of producers, backed by their governments, in a regime of managed trade wherever sectoral interests were threatened. Member states might shift their ground in certain cases: in the crisis cartel for steel, Britain sided with Germany, when the majority of member states and the Council took the opposite view. The Commission stood out robustly where it could for freer trade, and in defence of GATT (and indirectly, Third World interests).

But in general trade policy tended to be linked by the players to the progress of industrial rationalization – or lack of it. It remained synoptically unplanned because of the lack of a common ground, even when it became obvious that a successful internal market depended on a common external trade policy, if only because of the steady drift towards a potentially triadic world, focused on three great trading blocs in North America, east and south-east Asia, and Europe, which the long delays in negotiating the Uruguay GATT round seemed to encourage.[73] The American accusations of a protectionist Europe reaching for anti-dumping orders and US administrations' demands for reciprocity greatly overstated what was in reality haphazard or reactive, just as it ignored the United States' own protectionist tendencies.

The statement on EU trading policy issued at the Hannover Summit, June 1988, expounded a post-SEA thesis that the EC was open but on conditions. The argument being put in rather clearer terms than earlier gave some justification for Margaret Thatcher's point, in her Bruges speech three months later, that the Community was witnessing a philosophical conflict between British and continental ideologies. Yet she spoke only of member states. The Commission's own study (October 1988) revealed how much the Community would lose if there were indeed such an ideological cleavage, and pledged itself to the success of the forthcoming GATT (Uruguay Round) negotiations. The stand was reinforced by Delors's appointment of Frans Andriessen (Netherlands) to DG1 to replace the protection-minded Belgian, Willi de Clercq. For the next four years, Andriessen was to be part of the policy troika with Brittan and Bangemann.

While United States' policy under Presidents Reagan and Bush veered between fear of the Japanese challenge and desire for a trade war with the EC, the Uruguay round negotiations staggered on, hag-ridden by deep mistrust on the European side (mainly French agricultural producers) about its impact on the CAP. Many of the key points of industrial policy, such as definitions of standards, the use of Article 115 in anti-dumping cases and trade reciprocity contributed to discord between the Community and the American negotiators, led by Carla Hill, who adopted an equally aggressive policy of 'optimism tempered by vigilance'. For many on the American side, the internal market signified the withdrawal of the EU into 'fortress Europe'. Japanese officials, on the other hand, played a far more cautious, low-profile hand, for example seeking access in the car industry while conceding short-term advantage as the VER prescribed, and accepting patiently the countervailing tariff on Japan's electronic products.[74]

It is not self-evident that the EC has become more protectionist in the early 1990s. Instances of anti-dumping had increased in textiles, steel, cement and paper pulp industries in the 1980s, but in response to recession and to a huge accumulation of producer complaints, usually backed by their governments. In contrast, in the period immediately before the SEM began, the French government, among the more protection-minded states, began to alter its stance where several key industries were concerned, including cars, electronics, chemicals and steel. Meanwhile, the USA and Australia turned much more frequently than the EU to the anti-dumping weaponry. It could in fact be argued that the Community's general strategy, that the internal market should be a means of regenerating European industries, was working *avant la lettre*, inducing beneficial changes of behaviour at home, in contrast to the reactive, protection-minded responses abroad, except, significantly, in Japan.

This was not, however, the case in the Community's negotiations with EFTA countries over the European Economic Area (see p. 631), nor with the newly democratic states of eastern Europe. Agreements made with the latter *seemed* to indicate protectiveness, especially in the chemicals industry which enjoyed something close to permanent anti-dumping protection, while the EC's defence of its CAP against Polish and Hungarian food exporters was rivalled in its opposition to free trade only by the French government's opposition to the EC–US Blair House Agreement.

The wars of rhetoric over GATT tended to obscure the Single

Act's longest-term effect, which was to set strict limits to VERs or quotas by removing Article 115 from regular use. The VERs or other restraints negotiated at this time represented an inevitably declining class from which the more far-sighted firms prepared to disengage in advance of the deadlines, thus increasing their comparative advantage over the less acute. Apart from the apparently intractable regime for agricultural products, the worst problems now lay in areas ripe for reciprocity arguments, such as intellectual property and financial services,[75] or the cultural fields where the French authorities, profoundly disturbed about national identity and the protection of the French language, defended quotas on television programmes and films amid assertions that were inevitably nationalistic as well as protective.

Overall, the EU was not driven by a grand protectionist plot, nor was its industrial policy unduly inward-looking. The connection between the two was not susceptible to precise calibrations. But in the cases of steel, textiles, consumer electronics and cars, the language used made it seem so; and the extraordinary case of the 'banana war' added weight to German arguments that the Community's trade measures had been allowed to degenerate.[76] The suspicion of covert protectionism in the Community lingered on as new sources of dissent opened up over the Commission's sole rights to negotiate future anti-dumping measures on behalf of the whole Community. Member states also contested the Commission's Treaty rights to negotiate on their behalf once the World Trade Organization replaced the GATT in 1995, and won ECJ support for their arguments that responsibility should be shared in any new agreements, such as those on intellectual property, tourism and financial services.

The struggles continued. Soon after the GATT round had finally been agreed in December 1993, the Clinton administration put together a new agenda of environmental and labour standards which, in Community terms, amounted to protectionism by another route. They were not in the same category as the demands put by Micky Kantor, the new American trade negotiator, for access to European markets for American films and television programmes but they contributed to a perception that United States' policy had to be seen as 'an aggressive and unilaterally-defined set of trade policies tinged with protectionism . . . with apparent disregard for the multilateral trading system'.[77]

No one could have expected that in the 1993 context, the EU would precipitately have abandoned all trade defences, given the fluctuations of the US dollar and American and Japanese attitudes to reciprocity, especially in banking and intellectual property. More important, particularly for the industrial players, is the path by which the permissible use of Article 115 disappeared for most sectors in January 1993, while the automobile case now diminishes steadily towards the year 2000. That trade barriers have been Europeanized and set on a declining perspective suits the adaptive MNCs, like Thomson, Renault or Bayer, which made their transnational arrangements before 1993. But not all member states have adopted their MNCs' philosophy in a root and branch form,[78] neither are future American and Japanese responses assured.

The 1990 Industry Policy Paper envisaged trade policy as working out according to the recommendations of the *cellule de prospective*: 'sectoral approaches to industrial policy can work during a period but they entail inevitably the risk of delaying structural adjustments and thereby creating job losses in the future. Openness to international trade and respect of rules governing such trade deliver the right signals to the economy and preclude the recourse by the Community to the various types of defensive measures commonly used to protect domestic producers in the furtherance of such policies.'

But it is not easy to assess whether the Community's trade policy has in fact helped to regenerate the industries for which it was intended to provide transitional cover. Some may merely have increased their dividends and exported less, thus failing to adjust.[79] Chemicals and pharmaceuticals appear to have done best under these conditions; petroleum products and computers have probably kept pace; textiles and steel performance has ranged predictably from poor to appalling. Some member states have maintained high levels of effective education, training, and efficient transport infrastructure to complement a stable micro-economy; others have abrogated neo-Keynesian wisdom in order to achieve more flexible labour markets and an impressive rate of foreign inward investment. None has so far combined the two. Average European levels of competitiveness resumed their secular decline in the mid-1990s relative to the United States and the economies of east and south-east Asia.[80]

But the particular sectors, such as cars, which were the focus of Commission plans for industrial adjustment, have restructured to a marked degree: Volkswagen may not be typical but large numbers have been made redundant, while flexible working arrangements have been introduced. In the period extended by the 1991 VER, European car producers, with Fiat well-represented, are rapidly diversifying in eastern Europe and south-east Asia. This may not be as beneficial to the Community as if they had restructured inside the EU and it may well not be sufficient, as the case of computer firms indicates (who, with the exception of Japanese-owned ICL have largely gone under, in spite of ESPRIT and its research derivatives). Even IBM has had to undergo massive restructuring. But the remainder in electronics have made their alliances in order to survive – Siemens-Fujitsu, Olivetti-AT and T-Hitachi, Thomson-JVC – so that the competitive game now lies not between European champions but between corporate multinational networks whose main orientation is the United States. In the later 1990s, the Commission seems more likely therefore to support the EU's element of added value, rather than the life cycle of European producers. Such an outcome would revive at every level disputes with the declining number of member states for whom national ownership still ranks above long-term competitiveness.

In the sense that the large individual firms in industry, services and the financial sectors have made what appear to be appropriate strategic adjustments, completion of the internal market represents modest success for the Community's trade policy. Yet it may be too soon to judge. The EU has only taken on the lineaments of a developmental state in the last ten or twelve years. Development policies take far longer to work than market-oriented ones, and may be seen in the interim as restraints on markets, even if, from a longer perspective, they actually facilitate adjustment. But since most of the EU's adjustment policies have been made acceptable by giving sweeteners to the losers (whether farmers, fishermen or steelworkers), their short-term effects may well be deleterious – which is why some member states accept them privately while continuing to criticize in public.

There is no logical antithesis between inter-governmental and European policies here. But the Commission's hardest choice, acting – if they will allow it – on behalf of fifteen member states in the European interest, is to judge between the economic requirements of competitiveness on one hand and consumers on the other, while not ignoring the implications of total factor analysis where politics and social issues intertwine and acceptability cannot be a single line drawn in the sand between so many conflicting interests.

The new centres for brokerage between firms, peak organizations, member states and Commission, as the internal market works towards the integration of industrial and trade policy, are likely to be the standard-setting bodies, the conjunction of Directorates 1, 3 and 4, and national regulatory or competition agencies. The field of argument extends from industry, strictly defined, into services, health, welfare, culture and the environment. Insofar as they are already enmeshed in the informal process of brokerage and networks which are the subject of this book, EFTA entrants in 1995 stand to gain over those current member states who are less habituated to them, which is no doubt why Austria broke ranks and applied on its own in 1989. The same applies in eastern Europe. But at least the mindless protectionism of the 1970s has disappeared, having been replaced by the disciplines of foreign competition and the search for direct investment.[81]

Commission officials often argue that industrial and trade policy cannot fully be implemented before the arrival of EMU, because industrial policy does not thrive in a void, only in an appropriate macro-economic environment of monetary stability and low interest rates. That EMU and the constraints imposed by an independent central European bank may have protectionist implications has to be accepted as a lesser contingency than the prognosis that they will encourage low interest rates and a sustained supply of direct foreign investment. Whatever the final balance on the Council of Ministers when that decision comes to be taken, such unanimity is much rarer among the non-governmental players: there is no majority there now for a strongly directive industrial policy as practised say in France up to the late 1980s or in Italy today.

Industry policy as expounded by the Commission is less fragmented along sectoral lines than it was even a decade ago. But it does not seem that the outcome will be a clear-cut 'Anglo-Saxon' search for complete liberalization and openness to foreign investors, given the equivocal outcome of much of what was done in Britain in the 1980s. A German type of policy, outwardly liberal but in practice, through informal cooperation, rather more protective of industry so long as it adjusts to foreign competition, is much more likely, with all the implications for 'Rhineland capitalism' that involves.

Industry policy has long been an integral part of Community policy yet, despite its long trajectories since 1957, it is still not fully formed. Evolution depends on the various positions taken up by the larger member states and also the more coherent industrial federations and their MNC members. The former may change, given the vast political and electoral mutations currently at work. EMU may also not be so central a matter: those who shape the pattern of future research and development opportunity may be as influential from the point of view of MNCs as Central Bankers controlling member states' money supply.

The cross-border mergers and alliances currently sought by the Commission do not necessarily produce European champions (except in backward sectors or where national governments interject labour or cultural considerations); rather they foster the internationalization of markets, foreign investment and participation by foreign companies even in 'sheltered areas'. United States' companies hold a place in the top three with those from Britain and France in the number of EU mergers made since 1988. Global concentration is a force against which no protective mode, no industrial policy can stand, now that the EU is a single market.

Industry policy does not therefore necessarily imply defensiveness, and however Commission documents are interpreted in different national contexts, and in the United States and Japan, it is still useful to take them at their face value, given the trilateral brokerage of ideas on which they are usually based, the influence which what may be called the Commission's indicative regulation has had in the past, and the slowly-tightening process of implementation and enforcement of the internal market. It may require historical comparison rather than political-scientific analysis to chart progress, but even though the internal market is far from complete in 1995, the transformation over a decade has been immense. (The more interesting cases today may also be the less dramatic ones: the adjustments of Spain or Belgium rather than those of Britain or Italy.)

The connection between policies for industry, competition and trade has always been clearer to officials, working on interior lines of communication, than to member state politicians. It has usually been in officials' interest to play it down, a lesson reinforced by the post-Maastricht recriminations. But since 1993, the internal market's take-off has brought the linkage into much clearer focus than could have been imagined outside Brussels in 1986, with the support of most industrial and financial players.

Thus it is significant that the Commission now acts as a direct negotiator with the United States not only in respect of the World Trade Organization but DG7's air transport policy, something which in due course affects carriers to Europe from Japan, Korea and south-east Asia. It acts as a broker, informally defining some of the ways that the EU–WTO relationship will evolve, as the Commissioner responsible, Leon Brittan, creates a network of complementary procedures: regular meetings between business leaders as well as officials, to match the permanent secretariat and the parliamentary forums.

On the competition side, what was unthinkable in 1990 has become commonplace, as the Commission pushes to liberalize cross-border energy supply by taking the governments of France, Italy and Spain to court for maintaining import and export monopolies (and those of the Netherlands and Ireland for import ones only). For once, the British government has been delighted to support it (with some *Schadenfreude*) with a 'statement of intervention' to the ECJ. The millennium will not come at once: national monopolies remain, and van Miert is seeking a compromise which would allow both systems to coexist for a time. But there are signs that the internal market's momentum has strengthened the political base of its two chief progenitors, the Commission and the industrial players, whose interests lie in cheaper energy. There may now be less need for the big, blunderbuss Article 90, as the Commission slowly evolves a role as facilitator, for example when permitting Danish electricity companies to make a higher profit so long as those which have already modernized best gain most. Meanwhile, in vetting prices for the coming fibre-optic telecoms network to connect Paris, London, Frankfurt, Milan and Madrid, the Commission is trying to insist on answers to the question why digital circuits in Europe should still cost twice as much as those in the USA.

In reply to the Green Paper on energy policy, the CBI pointed out in July 1994 that the debate about competitiveness risked stagnation because of the inability of fifteen member states and the Commission to agree on what energy policy should be. One answer, derived from the Community's history, is that it should work towards making European suppliers competitive by world standards but in ways which allow the major players to adapt themselves at a pace suited to each one's national context. The other is that of liberalization and freer trade. Debate about negotiated adjustment versus market forces is somewhat older than the Community. But the essential synthesis will no doubt include the connections made by Community institutions, under another name, in 1988–91 between industrial structure, social policy and consumer interests.

It must in any case be fair to conclude that the greater number of public monopolies alive in 1993 will have disappeared by 2000, to the general advantage of European consumers, as bigger and more efficient entities emerge, competing in the internal market. From telecoms to energy supply, postal services to railways, they will have been rationalized by the state or privatized for political as well as economic reasons – *political*, because until now they have been defended solely by member state governments through national networks of influence. But these have become the most heterogeneous, combative, least coordinated elements in the Community, insufficient to protect even their own monopolies against the combined forces of Community institutions, private sector firms and federations acting in their own interests, and with the strong currents of global markets.

There is no reason to assume that the French, Italian or Spanish authorities, to name only large states, would accept this without a counter-attack, even if it were not for the often violent opposition of their trade unions to deregulation. The inter-ministerial working group set up early in 1995 under Christian Stoffaës to study the future of public service industries may be an attempt to produce a new model able to compete with the German one while pushing the British free market alternative towards the periphery. Klaus Hansch, speaking for the European Parliament, has already challenged the Commission's right to use Article 90 to resolve matters of principle such as the future of public utilities. But as Martin Bangemann (DG3) has pointed out, the investment their utilities require, amounting to £120 billion in telecoms alone for the period to 2004, will not be forthcoming unless deregulation takes place.

As in Part Two, Part Three of this book has revealed the endless braid of players' competition to be composed of three principal but unequal strands: Commission, national governments and industrial or financial (and occasionally trades union) players. If the competitive symposium model is used, it can be seen that of the three sets of players, the second is actually the most disparate, for the great majority of MNCs behave in broadly similar ways and for generally similar reasons when they address the EU's institutions. Between them and member states, the gaps have tended to grow and the Commission has tended to stand nearer to the standpoint of MNCs since the Single European Act was signed.

Trilateral networks do not however imply that the nation state is redundant, or that corporatism, as that concept was debated in the 1970s, has returned; they may contain less corporate bias than remains in purely national transactions, because the Community, though centralized in Brussels, is actually based on polycentric pluralism. The Commission's power to 'make' industrial policy, in any more positive sense than setting the agenda and persuading the players to agree on policy texts, is limited by the same basic equation: its powers, whether formal competence or informal persuasion, are to be set against the power of non-cooperation among the various ranks of players who in the last resort will conform only if they see an advantage in doing so. But as far as member states are concerned, the EU's informal governance has steadily grown away from national models, partly because the EU is not an average of twelve or fifteen, but an entity in its own right and partly because member states have already transferred to it enough sovereignty for the Community's political economy to be worth all the other non-governmental players' full and continuous participation.

Since the internal market is perceived by national publics as a purely economic matter (in contrast to the documents signed at Maastricht which are more accurately considered to be political), its long-term governmental and political consequences are more obscure to them than they are to the players themselves. There is in that sense an elite game, conducted largely through informal channels, with results which are positional and rarely capable of precise measurement. What is constructed in this way, however, has a substantial influence on how the European Union develops.

Critics who call this aspect unaccountable or undemocratic are missing the point. In this aspect (more than in most others) the EU is not a mechanism designed for or suited to democracy, neither is it accountable, except to the players themselves, among whom only ministers are elected. As in any nation state, there is no 'natural balance' between capital and labour, nor between the Community's political economy and the European political environment, save what the various players can impose on it. Neither can such balances exist or even be imagined unless the EU became a full state, representing and governing a European public. The EU is as yet a partly formed or imperfect state. But these games nevertheless incline it towards statehood, because all full states incorporated the competitive symposium into their own national political economies long ago.

PART FOUR

STATE WITHOUT
A COUNTRY

Unity and Diversity

At some point, every academic course dealing with the Community asks the question, what is Europe? Where are its boundaries? Is it a unity or a diversity? It was hard, even when there were only the Six, to keep a balance between what was perceived as the centre and the periphery of member states, and it grew more difficult with Nine and then Twelve. But the unity–diversity argument is more complex then mere numbers, touching concepts and behaviour patterns as much as territory and physical standards. As a Belgian former Commissioner put it, 'since the sixties it has become increasingly difficult to resolve specific, apparently technical questions without a general political conception of what Europe should be like. The question is why and on what ground one overcomes one's difficulties and the contradictions of the national objective interests. Thus one makes package deals giving each MS something it needs and making it cede on another point. The biggest package is that balancing industrial and trade policy as against agricultural policy. On the whole the objective interests can then converge. But the package is steadily growing and the balance cannot be held. It is more and more difficult to find an equilibrium, and increasingly, essential policies for the MS are included in the package. It will at one point become necessary to end the disputes in order to fill the political void and let the construction survive.'[1]

The EU would hardly have invested so much effort on harmonization over thirty-five years if greater homogeneity, over and above the gradual globalization of markets, language and technology, had not been seen as a fundamental aim. Yet Jean Monnet did not apparently concern himself with the question of the content of Europe at all, that being something beyond the bounds of speculation.[2] Nearly four decades on, there is an understandably defensive tendency to see the EU as a concrete entity surrounded by 'non-Europe', indicated by the Community's unhappy involvement in the Yugoslav civil wars. But now that the majority of former EFTA countries has joined (with Switzerland a possibility to follow after another referendum in the future), the concept of what the Community is, and what it means to all Europe, is opened up with each proposed extension. Until now the *acquis*, the fundamental legal threshold of entry for new members, has been offset by whatever derogations the existing members are prepared to allow, given the impact of membership requirements on economies only partly able to cope; longer in the case of Greece, Spain and Portugal, minimal, apart from arctic or alpine agriculture, where Austrians and Scandinavians are concerned. But it is already clear, five or six years ahead of serious negotiations with the countries of eastern Europe, that it will be very hard in their case to insist on the entire *acquis communautaire*.

The degree of unity in the Community's still-diverse political economy is a pre-condition to any discussion about whether it possesses a sort of statehood.[3] The question can be put in several ways; as a matter of geography, or economic development, or in terms of political compatibility or social composition. But it can also be argued that since the member states and the other ranks of players share in the informal side of the Community, as their governments self-evidently do in the formal one, this provides a greater momentum for the sort of integration which spans political and economic activity. Because, in their own way, all the fifteen nations possess an informal side, the development of a European analogue is likely to occur not in the form of an average but as a selection of their most efficient practices, compounded by innovations likely to survive international competition. The practices described in Parts Two and Three contribute to integration, albeit in different ways from what the legal texts prescribe.

But the influence of non-governmental players is confined largely to the economic sphere, and is quite distinct from questions about the Community's often incoherent responses since 1985 to external factors and challenges in the areas of foreign policy. Changes in Europe's environment (with which failures are most frequently associated, in global trade, border policing and immigration, as well as defence and foreign policy crises on its borders) have tended to reinforce differences within the Community, leading to just as much cleavage and paralysis in the early 1990s as in the mid–1970s, for the very obvious reason that member states respond differently and the Commission lacks competence to act as initiator.

The Maastricht Treaty finally came into force on 1st November 1993, nearly two years after the contracting parties' agreement, having been ratified by the last member state, Germany, only on 12 October 1993. Its lack of precision, compromises and implied exemptions stored up trouble for the future and the next IGC, but did not in themselves militate against unity. Nevertheless that Treaty contrasted with the Single European Act: it was as if Maastricht had been designed with a multi-speed Europe in mind. As the *Economist* put it; 'when the EC's leaders meet on October 29th to congratulate themselves on seeing the Maastricht Treaty at last ratified, they will be celebrating with relief rather than relish . . . the EC's twelve heads of government have seen its dreams mocked; those for EMU by the markets, those for a common foreign policy by their own divisions over Yugoslavia.'[4]

The Community's worst internal divisions have usually been caused by the eruption of different national interests and occasional systemic failure, rather than by individual events in foreign policy areas. The Community is also very short of practice and, from the point of view of activist member states like France and Britain, is a secondary player whenever American intervention is concerned (as the Gulf War demonstrated in 1990), in spite of the fact that the Community is now an integrated regional economy, comparable to that of North America as a whole. But its coherence should not be assessed from extreme cases. The EMU crises in 1992–3 might profitably be compared with the 1931 pan-European financial collapse (which also involved the United States); and the Yugoslav civil wars with the Spanish civil war – Spain in 1936 being as remote from Europe's core as Yugoslavia was in 1992. Member states have shown themselves capable of working together, particularly in relation to eastern Europe and the former Soviet Union; and while some of the fissures exposed by threats from the south and south-east are serious, some are remediable with time and patience.

I. Divisions

There are four obvious sets of fault lines within the Community: geographical, economic, political and social.

GEOGRAPHICAL

The north–south cleavage, which was evident to the EEC's founders only in the sense that Italy's Mezzogiorno was conceived of as a region requiring intensive care, grew rapidly in the 1980s with the accession of Greece, Spain and Portugal, and later, during the 1990s, with Italy's prolonged relapse from being the 'best European' into incoherence and wasted efforts. Very much more discussion about the Community, at least in the northern world languages of English, French and German, is centred on the role of the north, and what is still in effect the Rhineland core, including Germany, France and the Low Countries. What Italy and Spain do tends to be an adjunct, investigated by regional specialists (who rarely venture into Portugal or Greece) or by their own nationals whose research traditions are somewhat different and whose audiences within Europe are inevitably smaller.

Even in Brussels, it is easy to lump together Greece, Spain and Portugal, along with an Italy which has lost some of its earlier influence and respect; less easy to ask whether these very diverse nations are, beyond the most obvious points, representative of a southern Europe, or Mediterranean world, as if Braudel had concluded his magisterial survey in 1990 rather than 1590. The image of southern Europe as a constraint on the north is of course of northern origin. It draws strength, however, from observations about a wide range of EU activity: it appears to them that southern member states ask for grants, money, and derogations for their

SMEs, northern ones for reduced fiscal burdens, tighter control of (southern) fraud, and less interference by the Commission.

More generally, the northern group is liberal, the Mediterranean one protectionist, a distinction with some resonance among the new entrants, Sweden and Finland on one hand and Austria on the other.[5] According to one German car manufacturing executive, 'the typical German firm is concerned only with its own interests but in "Latin states" the firm regards itself more as a national lobbyist'; according to another, from a chemicals company, the north concerns itself far more with environmental protection and safety standards and checks on the export of chemical weapons.[6] A characteristic comment is that for the north, norms are the minimum on which to build, for the less-developed south they are the maximum to which they aspire. To which a firm from the south might well respond that the costs of adapting to the higher standards of safety or environmental protection are so great as to make even that standard problematic.

These are stereotypes, like the frequently heard assertion that structural and cohesion funds represent the north's subscription to ensure that the south keeps quiet. Southern states could reply that, despite recent reforms, the CAP is still essentially a northern policy, covering agricultural products which can be stored for long periods rather than tomatoes or citrus fruit. Where stereotypes thrive on prejudice and commercial disadvantage, it is hard even to be certain where the dividing line should be drawn. (In many ways, Ireland can be considered as a 'southern' state.) An historical socio-economic fault line runs along the river Tagus dividing northern Iberia from the once-Moorish south. A similar line separates northern France from the Midi; and it was an Italian economist from Bologna who said that, for all the Community's efforts, it had failed to solve the Mezzogiorno's problems – but it had succeeded in liberating the north of Italy from Rome.

Spain's evolution since 1976, its astonishingly rapid economic development up to 1991, and the equally surprising political tenacity of nominally socialist governments confronted with a still-backward welfare infrastructure and labour market, has increased the differentiation from an Italy which was incomparably more 'advanced' than Spain at the time that Franco died. Portugal is not Greece, as each passing year demonstrates; to quote another German observer, 'while Greeks can integrate socially (unlike Turks), they cannot accept majority rulings, not being a mature polity.'[7]

Trading insults is an old game, at least as old as the early nineteenth-century English traveller who remarked, 'the Italians have undoubtedly fine qualities, and possess those essential requisites, intelligence and enterprise which would make them a great nation, if it were not for the wretchedness of their governments.'[8] A rather more important set of questions relates to what the south's identity consists of and whether it possesses priorities and common interests that do not characterize the north. It is true that the Spanish government in particular has documented its concern with the effect of EFTA enlargement and the predicted shift in centre of EU gravity north-eastwards, because it affects Spain adversely; and that its hard bargaining stance finally won a substantial increase in cohesion funds in 1992. But Spain has had to contend in one decade not only with the terms of accession in 1986, but the arrival of the internal market; and its government (unlike that of Britain) still expects to joint EMU on time. That the Spanish people, having been marginalized from the European mainstream for over two centuries, have managed to adapt to this without domestic upheaval is a tribute to both Spain and the Community. The same can fairly be said of Portugal.

To make the north–south argument stick, it would be necessary to prove that southern states habitually resort to certain kinds of stratagems, that they are to be characterized more than northern states by regional problems, and that their relative backwardness influences the sorts of investments which foreign or European sources make. There is evidence for this and evidence against, for example in the regions cited in chapter 9 (though a full assessment is far beyond the scope of this book). But a judgment would be useful in addressing three important issues in the near future. Will the south behave as a homogeneous unit once a two- (or even three-) speed Europe emerges, perhaps formally as well as informally? This seems very unlikely, given the way Spanish and

Portuguese governments have held to their programmes so far. Greece's case is improving, though the point is seldom made in western European media, and Italy's current political–cultural problems are mercifully unique. A rather more interesting question is whether the federal aspects of Spain's and Italy's constitutions will lead them to line up increasingly with Germany and Belgium. There is also a matter which the south did not choose but which geography and Maastricht's third pillar dictate: how these governments should act in regard to the louring problems of near-Europe – or rather the Mahgreb, eastern Mediterranean and Balkans, two-thirds of the immense and sporadically threatening arc stretching from Dakar to Murmansk.

ECONOMIC

The argument in this case is about the core and the periphery. Neither is a clear concept, and the core can be represented in a variety of ways. At one end of the spectrum stand the historic centres of Europe (the Rhineland, Ile de France, the city states of northern Italy and the Mediterranean littoral from Genoa to Barcelona); at the other, the urban–region clusters and transport networks of the late twentieth century. They are not entirely contiguous but preconceptions about their strengths and needs continue to structure the Commission's array of Directorates, all except the countervailing ones concerned with the various kinds of peripheries; DG16 with its regions, DG23 with its SMEs and tourist dependencies.

Within the core itself, preconceptions accrue to particular standpoints. There may be no more overall logic to the 'north Mediterranean Banana' than there is to the 'Gaelic–Atlantic Arc' on the periphery, but several sorts of logic combine in the assertion that a lozenge with its points in East Anglia, Paris, Hannover and Milan constitutes the EU's heartland. One Spanish Foreign Ministry official observed that this was an 'old' core of France, Germany and Benelux, with which the other member states always have to make an effort, because it fits easily together and the Commission takes it as a marker. To this, governments on the periphery can react only in two ways; in Spain and Italy by adapting to the mean, or in Britain (up to now) by differentiating itself from it.[9]

Yet in the information technology era the core and periphery may both be illusions, a compound put together by economic geographers unable to keep up with the speed of investment flows and the mobility of highly skilled individuals. 'It is in the interests of states to diffuse investment and infrastructure, and therefore in the EU's interest also,' declared a French central banker. 'But equally, there is no "logic of the periphery"; what matters is stability in that periphery.'[10]

POLITICAL

The distinctions between small and large states have always been the most obvious. Yet even in 1957, two of the Six, the Netherlands (14.9 million population) and Belgium (9.9 million) represented a sort of middle ground (the semi-small), to be joined later, not by Spain (a major state) but by Greece (10 million) and Portugal (10.3 million), together with Sweden (8.5 million). Measurement by GDP per head of population, on the other hand, which corresponds to the Community's declared aims, immediately reverses the pecking order (see figure 13.1).

The important distinction is not size or wealth or even history (few small nations have not had their 'fast, fierce hour and sweet') but effectiveness as political players in the European Union. This may be measured by the equation constituting weight in the Council of Ministers: the force of national EU affairs coordination combined with the efficiency of Permanent Representation and the influence of national corporate players. To that should be added the relative advantage some large states possess, or the means that smaller states habitually use to make themselves heard over and beyond their normal 'entitlement'.

One Italian Central Bank observer defined effectiveness as the product of size, of a sound economy (measured by long-term bond yield) and good government and public institutions. The latter element, at least, suggests that a table could be drawn up not of the Commission's management deficit – which is how the spotlight is usually directed – but of member states' deficiencies in their political economies, in which case, according to the same source,

GDP per head of population amongst EU countries, 1990 [3] **(not including Luxembourg and before the full effect of Germany reunification)**

Ranking	Country	GDP per head ($)	Population (millions)
1	Finland	26,070	5.0
2	Sweden	23,680	8.5
3	Germany	22,730	64.1
4	Denmark	22,090	5.1
5	France	19,480	56.3
6	Austria	19,240	7.7
7	Netherlands	17,330	14.9
8	Italy	16,850	57.6
9	United Kingdom	16,070	57.4
10	Belgium	15,440	9.9
11	Spain	10,920	38.9
12	Ireland	9,550	3.5
13	Greece	6,000	10.0
14	Portugal	4,890	10.3

FIGURE 13.1

the list would start with France, Britain and then Germany.[11] The two aspects may be more closely connected than seemed likely to an earlier generation of policy studies.

Small states tend to use the Presidency to show the world they are in charge. In the past, large ones scarcely needed to, unless their incompetence had already been widely demonstrated; but this may be changing in the light of pressures to change the voting rules and the Presidency's rotation. Small ones have to make alliances more often, and bargain for large ones' support, whether to advance their own schemes or to frustrate what the Commission is trying to do. Small ones also rely more on the member state they follow in the Troika, and on Commission proposals.[12]

The resources that middling or smaller states possess owe almost everything to the innate qualities of their political economies. Some, like Ireland, have natural allies or find allies naturally. The Netherlands has not, because its obvious choice, Germany, is not yet acceptable to Dutch public opinion, despite the existence of an active but anguished public debate. The answer is therefore 'to use one's position wisely, to have intensive contacts with all, and lobby for Dutch specific interests. The remedy is to know as best one can the partner's problems and deficiencies, as well as its possibilities, and to ask only what is feasible. Hidden agendas are of very limited use because one knows the partners too well, and they are found out too quickly.'[13] Yet the Netherlands has rated as an effective player ever since the Beyen Plan, possibly because of its governments' long-standing hostility to de Gaulle's vision of *l'Europe des patries*, according to which small states always do badly.[14]

Because they have been overridden in the past, smaller states often hang together, especially where the accession of new states is concerned. But the theoretical majority comprising Belgium, the Netherlands, Luxembourg, Denmark, Ireland, Portugal and Greece, which could outweigh the Franco-German entente, has never been formulated. There is no real 'tyranny of the small', save in their steadfast addiction to existing voting ratios in the Council and the Parliament. Their 'natural allies' appear to change according to the issue; for example, on trade issues Ireland's allies are often Britain and Germany; on cohesion, Portugal and Greece. Denmark lines up with Britain, Germany and the Netherlands on free trade, and with France on agriculture, but maintains a prickly stand-off position on most other matters. Up at least to the time of Maastricht, both Ireland and Denmark habitually saw the Commission as the guardian of small states and sought to increase its power.[15] Greece has not, but it is the only member state with three vulnerable borders, affected by nearly all the quarrels in near-Europe (chiefly of course the Balkan conflicts but also the results of domestic problems in Yugoslav Macedonia, Albania and Turkey).

Yet size does convey a kind of status. In the Governors' Committee in Basel and on the Monetary Committee Central Bank representatives from small states 'do not frustrate those of large ones by speaking up often, so that when they do have something to say, they are listened to'.[16] For the same reason, the Irish Prime Minister Garret Fitzgerald intervened on behalf of the Erasmus scheme for cross-border student placements by an appeal direct to Chirac and Genscher in 1985: 'both were astonished; together they took action to remedy the situation.'[17]

Small states can play on large ones' need for temporary allies, as Britain needed Ireland to frustrate the Social Charter Directives. Some can ratchet up the bidding in the standards game because their own standards are higher, say on CO_2 pollution, as Denmark (not a car-producing nation) did in order to benefit Danish con- sumers and their environment.[18] By such alliances and stratagems, small states preserve their identity and maximize their potential.

SOCIAL

Member states who use referenda could legitimately accuse those who do not of lacking an important element of mature democracy. The way that countries' political systems link government and their elites with the people (as citizens, electors, workers or consumers) says as much about unity or lack of it as do the means that governments and elites use to educate their publics in what 'Europe' ought to mean. But if one takes a different disciplinary focus, the three most important social cleavages in the twenty-first century are already those between a numerically declining working population and the increasing numbers of pensioners, especially those, mainly women, reaching extreme old age; between the highly educated and the low achievers; and between those in work and the unemployed.

But this can also be expressed as an argument about growing homogeneity between member states, which share similar patterns: falling birth rates, ageing populations, divorce, single parenthood, education, gender patterns at home, workplace and leisure, and enjoy ever-more standardized forms of food, drink and entertainment. Austria and the nordic entrants fall into the same pattern. But by 2010 the EU will almost certainly include central eastern and south-eastern nations which are socially very different. The tensions that will come with the entry of Poland (38 millions), the Czech Republic (10.3 millions), Hungary (10.3 millions), and possibly Slovakia (5.3 millions), to say nothing of the three Baltic States (7.9 millions), Romania (23.2 millions), Bulgaria (8.9 millions) or Turkey

(59.9 millions), all of whose population pyramids will still then resemble those of the older western Europe of 1960, are self evident.

A lawyer describing the growth of unity within Europe might emphasize the declining numbers of clashes between legal systems, although he would have to emphasize how the remnants of national particularism survive: Danish or Channel Islands' insistence on citizenship qualifications for property ownership for example, or (more important to business) the French interpretation of national origin of a company from its ownership, whereas in Germany or Britain it depends on where it is registered. But a social geographer would indicate other points of difference; the unending spread of urban centres, some of them virtual city states, leaving endlessly declining rural areas (in France, for example, where even in 1958, 24% of the population was still employed in agriculture), increasingly protected but also isolated, amounting in some instances to the status of guarded wilderness, open to the ravages of tourism, leisure and retirement homes.[19]

Michel Albert's distinction between different sorts of capitalism, his main concern being with the Anglo-Saxon and Rhineland varieties, was referred to earlier. The argument can be extended to differentiate attitudes among member states' political elites to free trade and protection, to management training, promotion, industrial policy, technology transfer, accountancy practices or foreign direct investment. From there it is only a logical step to arguing that a two-speed Europe existed from the moment of Britain's entry, with its long transition period and the possibilities of exemption or opt-out which culminated in 1991.[20]

Conversely, and not only to justify the supposedly Anglo-Saxon point of view, it should be said that without the margins of manoeuvre, the grey informal areas of bargaining and interpretation for which the British players have been responsible, probably more than any other national group, the Community would have made less progress than it has, even under the QMV rules of the internal market. Certainly German players find informal political practices undemocratic and distasteful, except when strictly necessary. At the

Ageing Populations and Falling Birthrates in Industrialized Countries

Ageing population

Percentage over 65
☐ 1990 ▨ 2010 ■ 2040

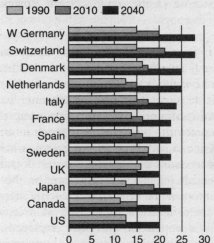

W Germany
Switzerland
Denmark
Netherlands
Italy
France
Spain
Sweden
UK
Japan
Canada
US

0   5   10   15   20   25   30

Falling birthrates

Number of children per woman
■ 1991 ☐ 1960

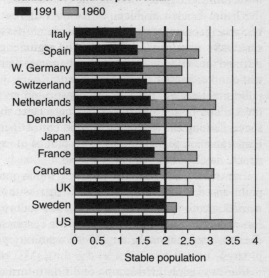

Italy
Spain
W. Germany
Switzerland
Netherlands
Denmark
Japan
France
Canada
UK
Sweden
US

0   0.5   1   1.5   2   2.5   3   3.5   4

Stable population

FIGURE 13.2

risk of caricature, the British style has habitually been to move at the slowest pace with legislation but then to implement it promptly and enforce it thoroughly – from the standpoint of British public opinion, often too punctiliously.[21] Whether this represents greater progress towards integration than more hasty legislation, implemented late and listlessly enforced by some member states, is at least open to argument. It is the latter rather than the former which leads the EU into a de facto multi-speed engagement, because the more lax members do not have the willpower or tenacity to catch up, so that de facto becomes de jure in all but name – an outcome intensely objectionable to lawyers and those member states guided either by the German system of institutions or the Napoleonic state.

The remedy for this in recent years has been to evolve a whole range of informal practices such as *réunions pacquets*, to erect a staged formula for compliance which only as a last resort turns to the European Court. Directorates and Commissioners use the law 'only in a very limited number of cases . . . more and more, the process is one of dialogue . . . to enforce implementation without using the infraction procedure.'[22] Within the Commission at least, facing up to the hydra-headed problem of member states' dilatoriness, it has become 'an essential part of subsidiarity . . . not to use the law unless absolutely necessary', but rather to induce governments which infringe the law to face up to the dilemma of being part of the Union without recognizing their objections.[23]

Informal politics have always constituted an important sector of the EU's polity and always will, bearing a large share of responsibility for facilitating the outcomes desired by competing member states, corporations, and institutions. This part of the system has created a dense, flexible, self-regulated but ambiguously defined network of conventions and behaviour patterns which positively facilitates a multi-speed Community. (It also facilitates informal alliances and smaller groups with no official status, who meet for their own reasons – such as the congregation of Christian Democrats whose decisions did much to undermine the British position in Rome in 1988; see p. 167.)

One answer to the dilemma of diversity and different speeds lies in the game between a variety of players which feeds on, constantly modifies, and regenerates the informal part of the system. The game is itself a unity, because all players who achieve entry (that is, not all would-be players), of whatever size, status or power, share in the whole. The Community's incoherence and incompetencies may be remedied or reformed in practice because it suits the players to do so; factionalism is offset by tactical or strategic alliances; carping, derogation, or infractions are remedied by peer-group pressures, and the subtle interplay of Commission officials, media and informers. Even the outright obduracy of a de Gaulle or a Thatcher is eroded or avoided in the end, as a stream eventually finds its way past any natural obstacle.

But this evolution of greater unity through informal means is circumscribed. Member states which take part in much wider games than the internal market retain formal power, as does the Commission where it has competence. Legal texts may be reinterpreted and evaded, but the law has so far remained supreme. Corporate players have usually restricted their operations to the political economy (although this may now be changing, because peak organizations have reached a point where they have to be heard on all aspects of policy if they are to reflect their members' confederations' international requirements – a point which the CBI's predecessors and the TUC had attained in Britain during the Second World War). The game described here also has few cultural, philosophical or religious overtones and few points of contact with nationalism, except insofar as politicians give it national or nationalistic meanings. It is primarily an economic one, where economic interests predominate, which is why its political product, informal bargaining, is seen particularly in Germany as something reprehensible, by nature akin to the (isolated) British view of what the Community ought to be.

That the substance is economic and not endowed with cultural or philosophical overtones also makes the EU hard to accept for many of its citizens, no matter where they live, and leaves it open to criticism for being a technocracy, a mere bureaucracy. The Anglo-Saxon (or Nordic) component is certainly part of the reason that the European Union's ideological dimension, or variants of it, divide along north–south lines. This suggests, with Alain Touraine, that the late twentieth century witnesses convergence in the political economy and divergence in many social and most cultural spheres.[24]

The extent of this phenomenon may not have been evident in 1957, though it seems to have informed de Gaulle's thinking on both occasions when he considered and rejected Britain's application for entry. It has certainly been prominent since Britain's entry and is currently displayed in the differing processes of privatization and the behaviour of public utilities. Several, predominantly southern, member states believe it can only increase now that three rich, particularist, ecologically demanding, northern members have been admitted. It makes the next extension in central and eastern Europe and the Mediterranean, even in its narrowest form, very much more problematic because that will incorporate states whose previous political, economic and social history and cultural formations have been different at most points from the present fifteen members since the early seventeenth century;[25] whose ability to take on all the *acquis* at once, even with massive derogations, is uncertain; and whose preference, if the choice were open, would most likely be to follow Spanish and Portuguese experience and align their economies first, with their social arrangements following well behind.

II. *Applicants*

At each successive extension, the argument has been heard that the Community will not be able to assimilate the newcomers without making radical institutional reforms, affecting tenure of the Presidency, voting in the Council (both qualified majority and the size of minority blocking votes), the number and functions of Commissioners, comitology and procedures in Coreper. so far the nightmare that new member states would remain undigested, creating political and ideological tensions, has not occurred, although some observers regard the admission of Greece – and in a different way, of Britain – as significant errors. Both have in fact become markedly more European, despite their governments' frequently rebarbative behaviour. But the Community – or rather

France acting *vice* a certain idea of Europe – delayed the entry first of Britain then of Spain (and inevitably of Portugal), in the latter case by six years, not only out of self-interest but because of concerns that the two larger states among them could not adapt sufficiently quickly. Similar scepticism already exists about the two largest current applicants, Poland and Turkey. While Austria, Finland and Sweden were already habituated to the networks of informal politics which facilitated their admission, the same is less true for those in central and eastern Europe and in the eastern Mediterranean.

Had Britain behaved otherwise in 1955–7, had the EEC been less suspicious, more binding links might have been made in the short period before de Gaulle came to power with the countries which chose, *faute de mieux*, to form EFTA in the late 1950s. But after the mid–1960s this possibility was sharply curtailed. Austria had already considered applying but could not do so in the 1950s and 1960s; Finland was too constrained by its Soviet neighbour, and Sweden by its neutrality; Norway voted against in 1972. But on most indices, other than the essential political commitment, these countries could have joined at any time. The Austrian schilling has had a fixed link to the deutschmark, for example, for over twenty years; and the standards of hygiene, health, welfare and environmental protection of all of them have remained well above EC norms.

For varying reasons, but above all because they feared isolation in world markets, EFTA members started negotiations for a European Economic Area with the EC in 1984. Despite the overtures made by Delors at the time, and the lead shown by Norway's prime minister Gro-Harlem Brundtland, these took five difficult years and seared many of the EFTA negotiators. (It was an Austrian who remarked that Brussels was a bazaar, with everything up for trade.) Nevertheless, they began to modify their statutes to conform with Community legislation so that, as the Edinburgh Summit accepted in December 1992, they had by then already installed at least 60% of the *acquis*. All were to be net contributors to the budget, and most fulfilled the criteria for EMU convergence at that point. Indeed the negotiations for membership, which lasted a mere fourteen months to March 1994, turned out to be far easier and more friendly than the earlier ones had been for the European Economic Area.

The Economic Area (EEA), delayed by a judgment of the ECJ (see p. 258), did not come into effect until the end of 1993, by which time it was something of a sideshow, affecting in the longer term only Norway (which rejected actual membership in November 1994) and Iceland, since Switzerland had voted in a referendum in 1992 against participating in the EEA. The key negotiations took place between December 1992 and March 1993, yet neither the fact that they began nor the outcome was inevitable. On the EFTA side were issues of great substance, which had been responsible for the initial divergence in the 1950s: foreign policy (and neutrality in the Austrian, Finnish and Swedish cases), alpine or arctic agriculture, the rural environment, monetary union, regions and subsidiarity. In turn the Community negotiators could not make the concessions that their own northern member states among them might have favoured, because of Mediterranean countries' concern with cohesion and structural requirements,[26] and the traumas already associated with CAP reform and 'sensitive' exports of steel, textiles, paper and cement.

None of these proved insuperable. To French demands that Austria and Sweden formally relinquish neutrality, the two replied that they could accept the CFSP framework and would abandon neutrality when satisfied that it could protect them (a compromise which left on the table the possibility of future cleavage within CFSP between the militarily active states Britain and France, and the majority). The Community – or rather the Council – gave an unofficial undertaking to reconsider its environmental standards in 1999, by which time the Eftans understood, or hoped, that the EU would have advanced to their level. But the problem of alpine and arctic agriculture got not no further than the award of a new category of support, Objective 6, and the chance to deal with it as a matter of land occupancy rather than agricultural production was lost. The burden instead fell on agricultural subsidies, while Austria's contentious transit agreement, limiting lorry traffic between Germany and Italy across the Alps, was extended until 2001.

Negotiations were made easier than in the case of Spain and Portugal, because the applicants had had informal access to Community institutions since the EEA negotiations began. After

Austria made the first bid in 1989, this was extended to the Presidential Troika; an indication of how greatly the majority of states wished them to succeed. More of a church wedding after long cohabitation than a bartered marriage, the enlargement seemed as a result to offer only benefits – increased revenue, remission after the gloomy post-Maastricht atmosphere, and an incursion of members with proven records on implementation, enforcement and the repression of fraud. Hence the sticking points, even on the use of *snuss*, Swedish chewing tobacco, were massaged away relatively quickly (all but that of Norwegian fisheries). In the event, the deals were adequate to produce narrow referenda majorities: in Austria on 12 June (66.4% to 33.6%), in Finland on 16 October (57% to 43%) and Sweden on 13 November (52.2% to 46.9%), but not Norway on 28 November (52.5% against).[27] But these votes say little about the degree of political, economic or ideological compatibility which underpinned the negotiations, or the informal links which had already facilitated the process of assimilation.

AUSTRIA AND SWEDEN[28]

Austria had drawn back from applying for membership in the late 1950s partly because, only four years after withdrawal from military occupation, the Soviet Union still held what amounted to a veto on its external policy, and partly because the Socialist government feared to join what appeared to many of its activists to be a capitalist club. The latter opinion survived for nearly twenty-five years, despite a change among the political elite, until Bruno Kreisky's fall in the early 1980s swept away Austria's deliberate isolation and a foreign policy which had been oriented towards the Middle East and the Third World. But through all that time, the Christian Democrats (ÖVP)[29] and the business, industrial and financial elites defended a more outward-looking version of Austria and took part in the activities of the European Democratic Union.

Long-denied contradictions between Austria's pattern of slow economic growth, the high costs of concertation with the social partners, and the high level of its citizens' expectations broke out during the 1980s. Contented, sober, rather self-righteous, the country had done well in the 1970s, almost alone in Europe; so that the EC came to appear distant and unattractive. But the mood changed even before the Single European Act and altered more rapidly after it, stimulated by scandals in various state-owned industries and heavy budget deficits which debilitated the Socialist party. The political right revived, eager for Austria to enter the EC as a full member, in preference to the European Economic Area, if possible before other EFTA members.

At that stage, neutrality and Austria's sense of particular identity seemed to preclude full membership. But a broadly based working group, set up by the Vranitsky coalition government in 1987, concluded that Austria must nevertheless be part of the internal market. The government therefore broke EFTA ranks and applied in July 1989, several months ahead of the transformation of eastern Europe which threatened to take control of the future out of Austrian hands. Beside the overriding economic imperative, on which the political elite and the majority of *Länder* representatives on the working party were agreed, neutrality, the alpine ecology, and the potential threat to national identity took second place. This did not, however, imply public unanimity, for the old Socialist opposition was soon joined by a new nationalist right, ably led by Jörg Haider of the Freedom Party, who played skilfully on manifest divisions between informed opinion, and what large numbers of less-informed voters felt to be the case, in a country where local interests predominate.

A similar assessment could be made of Sweden, whose government had begun to make the reappraisal rather earlier (because of its industries' global orientation) and was disconcerted to be so forestalled. Sweden had been isolated from the European political mainstream for very much longer, since the Napoleonic war when it split from Denmark. It had kept out of all subsequent nineteenth- and twentieth-century wars – but like Finland and unlike Austria, since 1945 had maintained its own effective modern defence force.

Neutrality and self-imposed detachment kept Sweden out of the Messina conference. But as the economic heavyweight in EFTA, over 50% of whose goods went to export and 75% of those to the EEC, Sweden experienced the change earlier than Austria; a debate about EEC membership ran through the 1960s, and the government almost applied for entry in 1971. Various free trade agreements with the EEC followed. The internal debate swelled in the early 1980s, partly as a result of Gyllenhammer's leadership of the ERT, and the government decided that it was imperative to share in the internal market; but not as a member, only as part of the EEA. Not until 1989, but before the Warsaw Pact dissolved, did the debate about membership start, opening up at the same time the possibility for Sweden to reappraise its entire foreign policy and neutrality.

Sweden had already been convulsed by change. A new-right politics had emerged in 1976 and broken the Social Democrats' forty-year monopoly. The government of Carl Bildt, from 1991 to 1994, introduced liberalization and deregulation but failed to apply radical reform to Sweden's welfare state or its labour market and public sector, despite the pervasive and deep economic crisis after 1989. A country which could have met the EMU convergence criteria when these were first proposed had acquired a budget deficit of 14% of GDP by 1993, and was to devalue the krone twice during the ERM's convulsions.

Depending on the observer's political standpoint, this crisis can be blamed on the overblown public sector or the speculative financial and property boom which collapsed in 1990. Voter resistance to paying the price, and divisions in public opinion after the EU application had been made in June 1991, encouraged the appearance of a nationalist party called New Democracy; so that opposition based largely on the urban–rural divide and strongholds in the far north and west, though ill-organized, came close to overturning the negotiated EU terms of entry during the referendum, despite the overwhelming range of elite opinion, including trade unions, in support of the terms.

Although Sweden had already undergone much of the required transition, including adoption of a great part of the Single Act and its four freedoms, it had its own problems and reservations. In the vast Nörrland, regional support schemes were more favourable than anything that the EU could offer (though agricultural reform there had already begun). The government had no intention of relinquishing free trade with the three Baltic states, with whom it had fostered more extensive links than those under the EC's auspices between Germany and Poland. It had stricter rules about the environment; public opinion seemed unwilling to tolerate unemployment levels of 10% for any length of time; and despite the crisis Swedish public institutions appeared to be wedded to concepts of welfare, equality, local communities, and openness, with which few European member states could compare.

Swedish negotiators, like their Austrian counterparts, had found themselves ill-at-ease during the long EEA negotiations fearing, correctly, that they were being exploited by masters of rules and conventions in which they could not take part. Opposition leaders exploited this gulf of practice, as they did the greater one between their capital cities and remoter regions. Whether in the Austrian Vorarlberg or the Swedish Nörrland, arguments that these countries could rest safely within the EEA, while serving as motors – Austria for the former Austro-Hungarian imperial lands, or Sweden for the Baltic region, Belarus and northern Russia – still appeared plausible alternatives.[30]

In terms of the impact on national economic geography and industrial identity, Austria's application was a harder case to argue than Sweden's, since the latter possessed a more liberalized international environment with a broader range of multinational corporations. Sweden's particularism had already suffered severely, whereas Austria still appeared to enjoy the 'Biedermeier complex', a certain level of introspective self-satisfaction married to an understandable distrust of the hard choices posed by EU membership. Given public anxieties about change, it was not surprising that the political, industrial and other elites, who saw clearly that the transformation of eastern Europe made Austria's 'third way' untenable, focused on the narrow questions of entry not the implications for national identity. Yet it was these which the new nationalist right of Jörg Haider took up, in its newspaper *Täglich Alles*, emphasizing the impact on clean Austrian air, food and tranquillity.[31] Haider's party had greater electoral success than Wachtmeister's New Democracy in Sweden, though the impact in the referendum may have been similar, since both argued continually that on this issue government was out of line with the people.[32]

Yet, as in Sweden, no clear image of the new national identity emerged. The Austrian government had its own conception of the future as the power house of technology, investment and transport infrastructure for a great swathe of eastern Europe (15,000 joint Austrian–Hungarian ventures had been set up by 1993). With more than a tinge of irredentism, Alois Mock, the foreign minister, had concerted with Hans-Dietrich Genscher the recognition of Croatia, at least partly as a means to stop the flood of refugees from former Yugoslavia; yet for historical reasons Austria was precluded from direct involvement there or in Bosnia. De Michelis's initiative, the dream of a *pentagonale* not unlike the old Austro-Hungarian empire, tempted some intellectuals as a possible counter to German dominance in central Europe; but in practice Austrians found themselves threatened by eastern European imports and potentially challenged by the dynamism and rising productivity of Hungarian labour.[33] Germany, so long the anchor, seemed to be over-committed. The answer therefore had to lie in the Community.

Austria's geography made its role as entrepôt on the north–south and east–west transits inevitable. Equally, its sheltered industries, high costs of labour, and over-protected state sector would have been threatened in any case by developments in the global economy, as the government understood when making the 1989 application. Textiles, cement, paper industries and food processing, and virtually all state enterprises, would have suffered restructuring and unemployment unless the Austrian National Bank's hard monetary policy had been abandoned. But no party conceived of breaking the schilling-deutschmark link.

Not having suffered the same economic crisis, Austria might not have felt the same economic constraints as Sweden, whatever its political imperative. Rigidities in industry, characterized by large numbers of SMEs and few firms of MNC status, were greater than in Sweden, and trade unions were resistant to change. Much of Austria's financial sector had been liberalized by 1994 but insurance was still sheltered, bank services remained over-priced and restrictive, and banks themselves, encumbered by an accumulation of debt in foreign business, feared exposure to takeovers. Such fears fuelled a still lively debate about the export of capital and failure of domestic investment. In Sweden, on the other hand, banking and the stock market had been thoroughly liberalized to OECD standards by 1990, and the prohibition on alien shareholdings lifted in 1993. Swedish banks formed links with others in Britain, Germany, France and Luxembourg.

Both countries' Central Banks enjoyed similar levels of autonomy, and similar, informal 'anteroom' facilities in Basel at the Monday meetings of Central Bank governors.[34] But the Riksbank's industrial policy ethos has been more in favour of openness and competition (ever since the abolition of exchange control in the late 1980s) than that of the Austrian National Bank: the takeover of a major Austrian bank is not yet imaginable, but Swedish banks are having radically to restructure as a result of the devastating banking crisis of 1989–92.

In both countries, trade union leaders after contentious arguments espoused the European cause, yet both took care to emphasize the Social Protocol and their role as full social partners, speaking to electorates who may not have realized how ineffective Ecosoc had become. Both emphasized how close they were to the German model of legally backed concertation as a way of warding off the likely impact of the downturn in wages and rising unemployment. Faced with the EU's 1993 White Paper's warnings, both naturally emphasized workers' added value as an argument against wage cutting.

In the run-up to the referenda, pessimistic commentators tended to point up Austria's lack of perspective beyond central Europe, and to Sweden's preoccupation with its nordic identity, to say nothing of the ignorance of EU affairs widely evident across the SME sector. In the event, a majority of Austrians accepted that the transformation wrought in eastern Europe and the Balkans, and Germany's new historic role, made their own once-cherished post-War position untenable. A narrower majority of Swedes admitted that a nation of their size and diversity, committed to liberal trade, could not maintain its unique social and economic stability outside the larger European framework.

These were, at least, the viewpoints of their industrial and financial organizations, even if they disagreed on detail.[35] All the industrial federations and several MNCs took an indirect part in the referenda campaigns, not only in Brussels but in the national capitals of those member states like Spain, France and Portugal which were most opposed to their entry, and one of the leading banks helped the Wallenburg Institute during the EU referendum campaign. Like central bankers, their officials enjoyed a sort of 'ante-room status' in the Commission, usually through the medium of *stagiaires*, who served as informally licensed conduits of information. Their member firms had also long enjoyed access to other member states' administrations: cases exist of these agreeing to defend Swedish interests in Coreper if they coincided with their own.

Like many of their counterparts among EU member states, the Swedish Chamber of Commerce and the two employers' confederations, on which sectoral federations relied almost entirely, cooperated very closely with their governments in the referendum campaign, but became aware during it how weak their effective presence in Brussels had been until then: neither had the direct links to officials in the DGs which the trade union confederation possessed and both found themselves uneasy in domestic polemics, caught between defence of the Social Protocol and evident loss of faith in their own welfare models.[36] Both had used, and continued to use, German and British peak organizations as supporters; both favoured EMU as a long-term guarantee of fiscal probity, a secure macro-economic environment and a disciplined labour market.[37]

It is hard even to guess which of the two countries has to make harder choices now. Austria has to undergo industrial and financial adjustments and an enormous revaluation of national identity and national myths. But the Swedish public has to face what may be a harder choice between restructuring the political economy of its welfare state and opting for the slow track, and out of EMU, from the beginning, a transition over which it is almost impossible for a Social Democratic government to preside. The possibility of a faction in the EU, as the three new entrants join Britain and Denmark in the awkward squad, is a most unwelcome prospect in Brussels; yet this was the interpretation newspapers in France and Belgium gave to their new Commissioners' performances at the European parliamentary hearings in January 1995.

Sweden has already begun to adjust its concept of neutrality through its membership of CSCE and the possibility is that the

WEU may in future be acceptable. Talk of NATO membership is taboo and probably irrelevant, but Sweden has joined NATO's 'Partnership for Peace'. The Yugoslav civil wars, and the fact that a nordic battalion served on the peacekeeping force, have drawn Sweden into Europe's south-eastern border preoccupation, in some contrast to Austria's dilemmas there. For both of them neutrality is beginning to resemble the Cheshire Cat 'which vanished slowly away, leaving behind nothing but the grin'.

Sweden and Austria aspire, like the Netherlands or Belgium, to form part of a growing group of middling EU states, able to keep pace in technology and selected industrial sectors with the leaders; to be part of the core, northern and non-Latin. In their referenda, both demonstrated the importance of having mature, well-organized industrial, labour and financial representatives aligned to their EU counterparts. On the main lines of what should be called 'foreign economic' policy, these interests concur with their governments': embassies in Third World countries are being reduced or closed, new networks set up by Austria in eastern and south-eastern Europe, by Sweden in the Baltic republics and Russia. That these hinterlands overlap with seventeenth- or nineteenth-century empires is slightly more than coincidence, as the routes chosen to connect Communist-era transport systems with those of central and western Europe indicate.

The 'anteroom effect', though very obvious after 1988–9, was not simply an EU gift but it was allowed to operate more successfully in some areas such as central banking than others like agriculture. Much depended on personal or organizational links between different levels of players on each side.[38] The accession process itself revealed not only an underlying Community desire for negotiations to succeed, which had not been universal in the cases of Spain and Portugal, but a shared mental *acquis* about what each sector's interests were for the 1990s.

For their part, the EFTA governments' political elites, and industrial or financial players, wanted entry for political reasons in order to share the power to regulate Europe's future and their own, more than the economic advantages offered by the EEA's incorporation of the internal market. The Twelve wanted them for the contributions which their wealth, standards of living and democratic track record would bring. Linked already over many years, EFTA industrial and financial players had habituated themselves to the European orchestra's tempo and especially in Finland (but not Norway) were only too well aware of what the Soviet Union's disintegration portended if they did not join. Yet the newcomers' presence is not an unqualified advantage, neither does it necessarily increase the Community's unity, whatever it may do for economic integration. These governments won their referenda by expounding the Community as a form of mutual economic benefit society, and denying federalist inclinations. The potential to be a Trojan Horse with a coherent nordic identity exists, even if the recently elected Social Democrats in Sweden and Finland, anxiously trying to defend their national social inheritance, show no signs of introducing major disruptions or divergent philosophies. Neither of these statements could be made about eastern Europe.

CZECH REPUBLIC AND HUNGARY[39]

Until 1989, the Community, for most of its existence, had been a civilian project in an area of the world whose military aspect was held in suspension by the Cold War and its détente-based aftermath. Defence and foreign policy (other than political cooperation), had not seriously entered its agenda; nor had the German question except as a by-product of superpower relationships. The EC had not obviously campaigned for new members but had welcomed Greece, Spain and Portugal when they became democracies, at least partly to forestall any subsequent drift towards Communism during the Euro-Communist period in the late 1970s.

The Soviet Union's disintegration and the Berlin Wall's collapse ended a division of Europe which dated not just from 1949 but from 1917, which reopened questions about south-eastern Europe last settled at the Congress of Berlin. It was not 'an end of history' but the rediscovery of many buried histories across what, in the Kaiserreich, used to be called *MittelEuropa*. From then on, the Community had to reconsider its relations with both Russia and the USA, its own nature as a political and economic organism, and its geographical extent.

EFTA countries had always been 'natural members', even if they chose not to join at the beginning. In 1990 East Germany was accepted as a recovered part of an existing member under the terms of West Germany's 1949 Basic Law, as if it had been a group of *Länder*, not an independent state. But no such understandings or legal formulae could apply to what in the inter-War years had been the 'lands between' Germany and Russia, cut off for forty years by Comecon and the Warsaw Pact, of whom the most likely candidates were the countries calling themselves the Visegrad group: Poland, Czechoslovakia (which split into Czech and Slovak Republics after 1992) and Hungary. These are the closest to the Community in historical ties, and cultural, political and economic evolution.

Although, in the context of what NATO was to become, these countries' strategic status concerned the United States, now that the Cold War had ended, their economic status interested American companies and investors more than the US government. Even before the Yugoslav civil war began, President Bush had indicated that US interests in Europe related more to newly reunited Germany than to Britain, a view reinforced by the Clinton administration, which increasingly viewed the Community as a junior partner rather than a distant ally. This line of reasoning led to a new thesis about the EU's capacity for self-defence or independent foreign policy; there was a recognition that NATO's command structure needed to be modified, together with the transfer of certain tasks to WEU.

An expectation that the former Comecon states would apply to the EU sooner rather than later affected negotiations with the EFTA countries in two ways: it accelerated the process, so that the 'natural core' of Europe would have time to stabilize and reconsider itself; but it also emphasized the barrier to entry. The fact that the *acquis* had not been substantially modified to meet the requirements of Austria, Finland, or Sweden served as a warning to future members not to expect Greek or even Iberian terms in some hypothetical 'larger interest', as had existed in the late 1970s or mid–1980s.

Initially, the Community seemed to have captured change in eastern Europe. In 1989–91, the EU, with 700 billion ecus for agriculture, infrastructure, training, and environmental recovery – and amid exaggerated talk of a new Marshall Plan – made itself broker for a recovery operation in the wake of the Paris Economic Summit, July 1989, by coordinating, with US acquiescence, international relief, food aid and credits first for Poland and Hungary and then for eastern Europe in general. Shortly afterwards it found itself acting as originator or transmission belt for venture capital, know-how technology, training, management and ways to improve access to Western markets. Agreements between the EU and Comecon dating back to the last two years of the Communist era were soon consolidated into Association Agreements, which had economic as well as political connotations of linkage to the West.

Mitterrand and Delors in particular aimed to fit eastern Europe's future into the general scheme of EMU, the 1991 IGC, and the start of political union under the French Presidency. This was before Germany's 1990 elections returned Kohl with a majority, which validated unification and might be interpreted as a licence to use the Community umbrella as a means of extending Germany's narrow economic advantage in middle Europe.[40]

As one result, the European Bank for Reconstruction and Development (EBRD), founded in order to channel direct investment to central and eastern Europe in a synoptic manner, was allowed to acquire a distinctly French tinge, which its first president, Jacques Attali, made no attempt to disguise. (Though allocated to London as part of a complex deal on the siting of Community agencies, EBRD was later to be the subject of a German attempt to relocate it in Frankfurt, possibly with similar competitive aims in mind.) An underlying rivalry of nation states extended beyond control of prestige institutions to the question of which member state would be able most effectively to use EU programmes and investments to establish national advantage for its own industrial and financial players.

The EU's unified front held together despite this and despite the fact that the Spanish government stood out, not in opposition to extending Europe's economic space but in questioning the costs, both to the Community (in particular the CAP) and to its own economy (which risked losing potential investors to an area of extremely cheap, relatively well-educated labour into which large

German investments were already flowing). Yet the Commission's emphasis on central and eastern Europe was not deflected, and the better prepared of these countries moved towards a sort of outer waiting room, less privileged than the EFTA 'ante-room', and thronged with candidates of varying degrees of credibility – among them, Slovenia (the only relatively stable state to emerge from former Yugoslavia), Romania, Bulgaria and the Baltic States. Once the Association Agreements, which contained the beginnings of a political element as well as economic arrangements, were concluded (or in the case of the Czech and Slovak Republics renegotiated after their split), their governments began to prepare claims to entry with varying degrees of *chutzpah* and panic, knowing that they desperately needed at least a guarantee of eventual acceptance if they were to attract the foreign investment and political interest which would help them to construct political and economic stability. How they would be able to control the speed of adjustment, how obviously they would have to submit to processes of conformity designed in the West, was not then clear.

Four distinct clusters of problems clouded all subsequent discussion about the speed of acceptance and the status to be granted to these post-Communist countries which, in EU terminology, had to be grouped together, whatever their markedly different prospects. (It was the four best-prepared states themselves which created the 'Visegrad group', in an effort to differentiate themselves from the rest.) In no particular order, these were: the requirement of a reunited Germany to have member states to its east, so that it should not be on the EU's border given whatever form Russia– Belarus–Ukraine was to take; wider concerns among member states about potential threats of chaos, or waves of migrants not only from eastern Europe but the south-east/Middle East, and southern (North African) frontiers; the fears of Mediterranean member states and certain industrial sectors – agriculture, steel, textiles, or cement – that such new entrants would undercut their own positions (a fear given tangible form when Czechoslovakia and Poland increased their steel exports to the EU just as the recession began); and general uncertainty about the ability even of the Visegrad four to recreate themselves as stable political entities with economies and administrations sufficiently close to the standards of western European liberal democracies.

An inherent conflict between the EU's narrower economic aims, expressed through the Agreements, and its general political outlook towards potential members (in what was only in theory part of 'wider Europe'), accounts for the highly-generalized statements about ultimate entry made at Copenhagen (June 1993) which barely advanced the position sketched out at Edinburgh. Thereafter, each country's evolution took a different path, forcing EU politicians to face up to a diversity greater than they had expected. At the same time, the narrow sectoral interests of commercial players, backed indirectly by their governments, intruded on the EC side – giving the vulnerable eastern European states the impression that a mercantilist Union was eager only to single out for investment the best firms or to buy the few profitable parts of state concerns then being privatized.

From Edinburgh onwards, the British, Danish and German Presidencies were able to ensure that a more generous message predominated until the significant promises made under the German Presidency at the Essen Summit in December 1994. But self-interest appeared to shape the Association Agreements, particularly those made in the second round with the Czech and Slovak Republics. At a time when the deeper problems of economic and political reconversion had already surfaced, this inevitably influenced the way the Visegrad countries defined themselves, especially in their elections of September 1993 and March 1994, in which Poland and Hungary turned from governments with a free market orientation to coalitions under the socialist label, many of whose members had served under the former regime.

Diplomats and Commission officials naturally asked the same questions of these countries as they had, albeit unnecessarily, of the EFTA applicants: how far had their political and social systems, their industrial and financial institutions already adapted to EU conditions in the first three years of freedom from Comecon, the Soviet trading system, and what was the current rate of adaptation? After the initial euphoria, to Western eyes there had been, in 1989–90, a serious slackening in the conversion process, and enormous difficulties surfaced in 1991: problems of privatization, dealing with state monopolies, the massive (and soon-irredeemable) debts within Comecon from the former Soviet Union, and rapidly rising inflation.

By 1993, the leading three, Poland, the Czech Republic and Hungary, seemed to have recovered the initiative. Hungary had enforced a bankruptcy law, Poland had renewed its monetary severity after the Olszewski's government's relaxation, and the Czechs had gone through an unprecedented and apparently successful wave of privatization. Public savings had recovered in all three countries and the bulk of foreign trade had shifted, probably irrevocably, from a bankrupt Comecon to the EU and the rest of the world. Remaining problems appeared to western commentators remediable, given the evident reservoir of entrepreneurial ability, the lead given by the three governments, and the technical resources supplied by the West through programmes such as Phare – so long as the green light of eventual EU entry kept enthusiasm alive.[41]

Three underlying problems stood out: the poor quality of management in general, particularly among those over forty-five who appeared unable to abandon the habits inculcated throughout their working lives under Communism; the limited public tolerance of unemployment and downgraded expectations; and, in Hungary and Slovakia (but much less in Poland and the Czech Republic) the rise of nationalism, anti-western sentiments, and popular dislike of minorities.

But by mid-1994, the time of the Hungarian elections, central and eastern Europe no longer presented the bright uncomplicated face of popular protests and velvet revolutions. Even the Visegrad four seemed to have reverted to national characteristics reminiscent of the 1920s. Hungary, in particular, had accumulated the highest level of debt of any of the former Comecon states, standing at $28 billion by the end of 1994. But it was not open to EU Summits to say such things too outspokenly, for fear of stimulating worse, nor to offer promises only to a selected minority of these states. On the other hand, it was impossible not to give them some grounds for hope, for fear of the national recidivism which rejection might stimulate.

Yugoslavia had poisoned the well and made it immeasurably more difficult to accept that the revival of nationalism, often with implications of border revision, was a phenomenon only to be expected after the mass migrations which had occurred in the previous seventy years; one not necessarily loaded with 1930s or 1900s connotations. Nationalism undeniably existed: it had surfaced in both Austria and Sweden as a by-product of the economic crisis and the referenda, and continued to grow in Austria, even if it died down afterwards in Sweden. The first problem was how to define it; the second, having decided whether it was acceptable or malignant, was how to deal with it, given its far-right repercussions in nearly every EU member state.

One response was to argue for relatively rapid two-stage entry: either economic union first and political union later, or vice versa, depending on the way the problem was assessed: but not until the EU's own institutions had first been reformed to cope with a Europe of eighteen or more member states.[42] In the interim, the overall effect of Association Agreements and the summit declarations was to create a rather vaguer even more informal 'ante-room', in which the links and networks which EU countries needed to take for granted could grow up (for example, between Central Banks or industrial federations which might influence evolution towards a market economy).

For this the Kohl government seems to have taken primary responsibility, with the German Presidency in the second half of 1994 in mind. Few present at Copenhagen imagined that all the central and eastern European representatives would be attending an EU Summit at Essen within 18 months, or that the European Parliament President, Klaus Hänsch, would request their actual *participation* in the 1996 IGC. Yet it was just as easy from an eastern European point of view to decry this progress and portray the EU as dilatory, concerned only to readjust its own procedures, liable therefore to make the same mistakes about central European political systems that France, Britain and Weimar Germany had done in the 1920s. From the same defensive perspective, there were signs that, at the same time, aggressive Western MNCs were cherry-picking the best elements of what had been state-owned industries and leaving the rest and their under-employed workers to rot. A sense of being exploited by an alien EU agenda, which had not been the opinion of more than tiny minority in EFTA countries, pervaded the debate.

It is not perhaps surprising that countries which have had only two relatively short chances since the nineteenth-century world collapsed in 1918 to overcome in their own time the problems of economic and political adjustment, should have hesitated or weakened in an intensely difficult, still widely unpopular and often very painful endeavour to modernize on western terms, without recent experience, at an unprecedented speed. In the West, the existence of a properly functioning, formal decision-making process is the necessary precondition to creating the informal one, designed to render the formal more subtle and acceptable than its legal–constitutional rigour would permit. In eastern European countries after 1989, the formal procedures either did not exist or were not clear or applicable, so that the informal grew out of the earlier system and became midwife to the new-old one.

Under Communism, the informal side had indeed redressed something of the imbalance of legitimacy, but outside the formal process. It had frequently been illegal, always oppositional, and normally a matter of very private enterprise, even in its most collective aspect. Although after 1989 legitimate, formal structures soon came into existence, the complementary patterns of informal behaviour which in the West are taken for granted, could not develop rapidly enough: and in the tense area between public and private life, a variety of behaviours coexisted. This, rather than the survival of former Communist administrators (some of whom have in fact served the new democracies well) may explain the ramifications of nepotism, corruption and criminality which spread widely in the early 1990s.

On the EU side, twelve member states had their own very mixed self-interests, which frequently distorted Community policy. Quite apart from the matter of trade defence against specific eastern European exports, the general balance of trade clearly favoured the Community. As the social costs of converting to a market economy mounted, and as political parties evolved and became genuine mass organizations with roots in popular preferences, alternatives were argued in mitigation. Even in the Czech Republic, the only one of the three to keep its centre-right government in 1994, arguments surfaced like those of the Austrian and Swedish antis, about a middle road and reliance on the development of a 'hinterland' further east. The stress of maintaining democracy and good administration, without falling into a mendicant mode which was likely to offend the EU as much as any economic backsliding, was considerable.

In the two countries under consideration, the Czech Republic and Hungary, it is clear that neither one expects entry before 2000. The Czech government has stepped back a little from its earlier free-market rigour to something closer to one-nation Toryism, with overtones of social peace and political consensus, despite its prime minister, Vaclav Klaus's pledges to cut back on the welfare state: the Hungarian government of Gyula Horn since 1993 has reverted to something approximating to social-democratic planning. It is not hard in Hungary to find evidence of nostalgia for the days of Kadar, and the security of 'goulash communism' with full employment and modest relative prosperity. Hungary's bankruptcy law has not been as widely applied as was initially hoped, for fear of unemployment; and the similar Czech law, passed in 1993, has been tempered by hidden subsidies to the handful of very large state enterprises which have not yet been privatized.[43] State support for export producers survives for the same reason.[44]

Evidence about commercial adaptation, making privatized firms profitable and competitive, is too patchy yet to hazard an answer to the questions of whether the Czech and Hungarian economies are evolving in ways compatible with EU membership. Even the outcome of the privatization process is not clear.[45] By 2000, answers will be easier and in that respect the Community may be right to wait. But what role the EU (and its member states and companies) should play now that the primary phase of lending, technology implantation, management and employee training is over, is not clear either. So far, any pointers have to draw indirectly on the evidence of the EU's general initiatives like Phare, and the lending initiatives of its agencies, the EIB and the EBRD. But although the latter has greatly improved its services since 1993, their aims do not always fit with what individual member states and companies are doing in their own commercial interest. This is hardly surprising, since the EU has never had direct experience of what to do in such a case, its involvement with Lomé countries' development being wholly inappropriate.

The greatest single problem, as it was in East Germany, concerns how to change mentalities – a problem masked in the early days by the appearance of a generation of young entrepreneurs and politicians who seemed miraculously to have escaped the Communist mould, as flowers spring up in the desert after the first rainstorm in forty years. These were not drawn only from the under-40s; the combination of recovered memory from before 1949, and the antibodies which always existed in the Communist era, may account for the small numbers of more senior administrators and entrepreneurs who provided continuity, and who in many cases – grossly overworked and tempted by private sector salaries – run key government departments today.

But there is a significant difference, in eastern European eyes, between recovery after a long interregnum and the imposition of Western solutions, between what remains of national virtues and what can easily be portrayed as carpetbaggers' values. In between there exists a mixed element. In Hungary especially, some of the old elite were able to negotiate the Communist party's protracted funeral in the late 1980s, salt away wealth, and found their own concerns during the transition, re-emerging as part of new, jostling elites, as their predecessors did in Bonn or Rome in the early 1950s.

What might have been salvaged from the past was sometimes destroyed, as Czech economic planning teams were broken up by Jiri Dienstbier and replaced with inexperienced young economists. Meanwhile some of the worst features of the Communist period blighted the future. Neither country had any hope of enforcing the enormous debts due from the former Soviet Union and Comecon trading partners. Hungarian governments made three attempts, all to no avail, to resolve the problems of cross-border and inter-firm indebtedness; the Czechs managed to reschedule the former through the medium of the Consolidation Bank, but the inter-firm debts still drag down those large firms which have not yet been privatized. Both countries have found it hard to re-establish the virtues of public administration, in societies where 'the Ministry' was for two generations regarded as the enemy. At many levels, the habits of Communist bureaucracy have mutated, in a reversal of evolutionary theory, to the Austro-Hungarian rubber stamp.

From the beginning, the Association Agreements conditioned the search for a model to shorten the development process; yet without giving much protection to vulnerable economies, or defining what constituted restructuring, what 'infant industries' were, and what degree of industrial policy and regional transference was legitimate or proper. If industrial and financial restructuring was hard, it was even more difficult to establish a respectable administrative process, an efficient customs system, to coordinate departments, or to restore respect for taxation. When it has been a problem to discover what a ministry is, it was not surprising that real Ministries of Finance, Economy, Trade and Industry take time to resolve their divergent interests or to create informal means to keep rivalries under control. Yet these rivalries were small compared to those between the Visegrad countries' governments and between them and the rest of former Comecon in their eagerness to get into the EU.

Statistics from which to measure management behaviour are either not adequately collected or do not yet exist. Civil servants in Departments of Trade or Industry sense that the generality of managers is still closer to production norms than accounting standards. It seems difficult to induce middle management to think of consumer needs, waste reduction or removal of bottlenecks in production. What occurs inside enterprises which have not been cauterized by association with foreign investors, surfaces in the sectoral federations, and whenever arguments occur about how to carry through the transition, whether to seek outright protection rather than full exposure to the free market, with its consequences of redundancy for managers as well as workers. The proliferation of such organizations in a a free-for-all rivalry inhibits the spread of a reflective management culture: the very idea of long-term managerial strategy has had to be created *ab initio*.

Although it may be unwise to generalize from a limited number of cases, an assertion by the more effective domestic industrial lobbies that the transition should be handled in a way and at a pace commensurate with national sensibilities appears to be increasing. In the case of Tatra, a Czech manufacturer of very heavy lorries, after privatization a US management team with a chief executive officer from Chrysler was imported. This appeared successful in commercial terms, and relatively free of conflict. But in less than two years the three Americans were forced out for alleged failure to put the company right. For reasons which seemed similar, the proposed joint venture between Air France and the Czech airline CSA was broken off and the French share bought back. An important privatization in Hungary of the state's last hotel chain was likewise withdrawn from an American investor at the last moment. The phenomenon naturally is most obvious where real profits are at stake, in the telecoms and oil-refining industries, where Czechs in particular have a strong relative advantage in central Europe.

The problem with selecting particular cases is that it becomes almost impossible to generalize convincingly; yet the industrial sectors' failure, in both the Czech Republic and Hungary, to evolve coherent forms of sector federation representation on the western model inhibits the usual alternative. Unions have better structural access to their governments and to ETUC, but for lack of management organization to argue with have less cause than in the EU to refrain from destructive strikes. Complaints are rife in both countries that management seeks always to reduce the workforce, if necessary by bankruptcy, causing government to intervene. Industrial relations, in fact, barely exist, except as a by-product of a government's electoral presentation – or lack of it – as demonstrated by the near-general strike which met a government attempt to increase the petrol tax in Hungary in 1992. The fact that the Czech government imposes what is in effect a wages freeze through taxation inhibits labour mobility. Paradoxically, those peak organizations which work best are networks representing SMEs; not the larger companies, whose managers either fear speaking out in public or do not know what to say. It is often easier for heads of industry to explain unemployment as a politically inevitable concession to the West, and to portray the EU as an unbending external regulator.

Whatever their public declarations, western companies have often given the impression of wishing to strip out the best lines, say in pharmaceuticals or fine chemicals, whereas governments seek a turnaround in all sectors, even the old state-owned heavy industries.[46] Whether a general turnaround is practicable depends on complex equations to do with assets, management and workforce skills, the overhang of debts, the possibility of restructuring or break-up, the potential to attract foreign investment and joint ventures. The essential element in privatization is not the sale of assets but sales to owners capable of restructuring a firm efficiently. This means, in eastern European circumstances, more than 'downsizing' or 'delayering': in many cases, new chief executives cannot survive without the assent of their managements or workforces. Hungarian and Czech restructuring, according to a very recent survey, has probably been less deep than that in Poland.[47] Instances in the joint ventures – VW-Skoda in car production and Ford-Autopar in car components – indicate that profitable restructuring *can* take place, as it is in Hungary's food processing, consumer electronic, and components industries, but also that the initial advantage of cheap labour is already being eroded, having fallen in Hungary from roughly one-tenth of the European mean in 1990 to one-third in 1994.

Despite the success of both countries in attracting a diversified pattern of foreign investment, which in the Czech Republic amounted to $3.1 billion between 1989 and 1995, the latter has been the recipient mainly of German direct investment, while Hungary has received roughly equal amounts from Germany and Austria. Though predictable, this has had political repercussions. But whereas parts of the Czech economy can be seen as complementary to German needs, much of Hungarian industry already competes with its Austrian counterparts. Both will probably suffer, rather than gain, from Austria's entry to the EU. In another sense of the word investment, Hungary's reservoir of overseas national entrepreneurs has turned out to be less of an advantage than expected, because of their tendency to buy only the best bits from the State Property Agency and to join foreign firms of consultants.

The problems of restructuring are compounded by shortages of capital in still-imperfect markets, and a notable lack of well-presented, credible schemes, the proportion of valid ones, according to Czech and Hungarian banking sources, falling between one in ten and one in twenty. Czech banks, though fully liberalized, and used to self-regulation under Central Bank supervision, do not yet present the full service profile of their European competitors. The inter-bank market in Prague is illiquid, and investment banking, copied from Western models, has been slow to operate.

Nevertheless, this compares well with Hungary, where five of the six main banks are still state owned, and powerful enough to have frustrated the Privatization Ministry in 1992, building on fears that foreign takeovers would lead to dominance in industry followed by heavy unemployment.[48] Nationalist suspicions have not eroded as they were in Seden when the Alien Shareholders Act was recinded. although the insurance field where there was no distinct Hungarian industry, has been taken entirely into foreign hands.[49]

Apart from the privatized Central European Investment Bank (which already finances 15% of Hungarian trade and can syndicate national loans and fund itself more cheaply on the inter-bank markets than the Central Bank can), the rest of the system is deficient by western standards, particularly in the quality of its risk assessment: in 1990 Hungary's banks came near to collapse, and the state's reserves fell to $400 million. The money market is narrow and oligopolistic, with 75% of transactions handled by the state; the state in turn defends Hungarian national interests against foreign entrants in what can be described as 'strategic areas'. This, rather than commercial considerations, tends to determine the level of loan support and makes aspirations to convertibility of the forint implausible.

Security for lending tends in both the Czech Republic and Hungary still to be based on physical assets and real estate, with the less-eligible companies being funded through state-owned sources. Banks still tend to ask for state guarantees for large lending which the government is willing to provide only for very substantial projects, such as the pipeline to Germany or the Czekada tram contract with Brazil. Current lending patterns, quite apart from the debts dating from before 1990, contain more non-performing debts than would be acceptable in any western European country; and the stock markets in Prague and Budapest, though founded on Western principles and active in a small range of securities and blue chip holdings, are potentially exposed – in the former to competition among what are still wholly excessive numbers of funds dealing in privatization shares (the majority of which are likely to fall under the control of banks, whose judgement will then dominate economic evolution), in the latter to a climate of feverish speculation.

Their Central Banks share in the informal 'ante-room' facilities offered in Basel since 1990. But since they differ (the Czech National Bank being refounded on Bundesbank principles, the Hungarian one closer to the proposed ECB model), it is not surprising that their views of the economy and their duties to implement government policy also differ. The HNB allows itself rather more space than the CNB for considerations of industrial policy, unemployment, lack of worker mobility and regional disequilibrium – and since the Hungarian government appears to be heavily involved still in manipulating financial markets, there is some doubt as to whether Hungary could fulfil minimum Community criteria.

Both countries are approaching a turning-point in 1995. Czech monetary policy has so far assisted a firm pattern of growth, held down inflation and produced the appearance of a disciplined transition to a market economy. But very substantial new investments will be needed if the second stage of restructuring industry is to be achieved. Yet the banking system is currently having to make provision for a high and continuing level of non-performing debt and the stock market has been falling since 1994. Without that invest-ment surge, the conditions for structural depression are always present. In Hungary, politically inspired amelioration of the social effects of restructuring combines with increasing state and public sector debts, rising wage costs, and loss of relative advantage to presage the growth of an unsustainable deficit, unless fiscal rigour is restored. Manoeuvres in Gyula Horn's Cabinet over the appoint-ments of bank governor and finance minister in 1994–5, augur badly for Western expectations and the future of open foreign access.

Czech and Hungarian networks have been impressive in diplo-matic terms in Brussels and the larger member state embassies, but there has been some neglect of (or failure to address), those countries most antagonistic to their accession, chiefly France,

Spain, Portugal and Italy. Coordination of efforts towards the European Union, though regarded by governments as vital, has to compete with the continued problems of adjusting to the margins of identity, as old nations learn how to inhabit newly discovered states. This may account for the unreality of expectations on the applicants' side and the caution on the EU's that was evident at the Essen Summit in December 1994. Yet for the first time, under the German Presidency's auspices, member states at Essen made clear what it was that they expected these countries to do: requirements which were repeated by Jacques Santer in his state of the union speech in January 1995. The Community would have to ensure that these countries matched the West's legal and economic standards, in accordance with the *acquis communautaire*. In return, and to help them to that point with some urgency, Commission resources including the Phare programme were to be channelled directly into a 'pre-accession strategy', and a supportive programme of transport network development.

No order of preference was stated but it was recognized that access would be 'individual but clustered'. The phrase allows for more than one interpretation: the Czech Republic and Hungary on their own; the Visegrad group; Visegrad plus Slovenia and Bulgaria; and all former Comecon applicants. Without stating so publicly, it seems most likely that the first choice is the more practicable, given the implications for the CAP of Polish entry. (One estimate is that the Visegrad group's admission would add 63.6 billion ecus to the CAP's cost, if CAP were not reformed.) Voting ratios in the Council provide a second, highly political reason to defer entry until the EU has reformed its own procedures: the Visegrad four could outweigh the 'poor periphery' (Ireland, Spain, Portugal and Greece), while in alliance with it they would have a strong blocking minority. And this says nothing about Cyprus's promised negotiations after the IGC, Malta, or the three Baltic States (whose Association Agreements are still under negotiation). The Essen meeting may have represented some progress on Copenhagen, yet it provided evidently much less than Chancellor Kohl had hoped for when he declared in May 1994 that 'the Baltic Sea is just as much a European one as the Mediterranean'.

Whether a German government could accept the exclusion of Poland in favour of only the Czech Republic and Hungary (and Hungary may in any case fail to meet the EU's criteria) is as uncertain as whether the EU as a whole would be prepared to discriminate in such a manner. Alternatively, entry around 2000 seems to depend on the EU finding ways either to modify the *acquis* by creating a second class of membership, or to structure entry according to an unprecedented timescale. The Greek precedent might be appropriate, except that there is unlikely to be a majority, let alone unanimity, among governments which remember the sort of renegotiations Greece sparked off in 1981 and 1983. In any case, as all the EU's recent studies show (but which DG7 cannot admit to be the case), the CAP has to be fundamentally reformed before these countries can be admitted, if the budget system is not to break down or GATT rules to be contravened.

Meanwhile, as the EU sorts out in 1995–6 whether its priorities on the periphery lie with eastern Europe, Turkey or North Africa (as the French and Spanish governments are now inclined to argue), these old nations/new states continue to evolve in their own ways, each reacting separately to western involvement and intervention. The emergence of a Czech Republic in 1992 restored a Protestant-capitalist tradition, with strong German links and four hundred years of tradition. Hungary, conscious still of the Treaty of Trianon's 'unique act of reprisal', in which it lost one-third of its territory and a quarter of its population, mainly to Slovakia and Rumania in 1918–19, has a more problem-ridden task of establishing national identity in a world turned upside down. The results will depend on national peculiarities and trends, both new and long submerged, in countries which are fortunately neither so far away nor so opaque to western eyes as they were in the 1920s.

TURKEY AND THE MEDITERRANEAN WORLD

The Essen Summit devoted time both to the 'Mediterranean orphans', Cyprus and Malta, and to Turkey, whose application for membership had been frozen for many years but with which a Customs Union was due for negotiation early in 1995. Turkey had not benefited from events in eastern Europe, and despite the public protestations of some member states it was hard to see that any block of support for its eventual membership existed in the EU, given bitter, long-standing Greek opposition, the uneasiness of German governments about the status of Turkish *Gastarbeiter*, and more general European concerns about divided Cyprus and the Turkish army's response to Kurdish insurgency in south-eastern Anatolia.

The view is common in Turkey that its government would have stood a better chance of membership if it had applied in the early 1970s, before Greece did and before the ten years of harsh military rule which estranged it from western Europe and led to the invasion and occupation of northern Cyprus, which was declared illegal by the EU's foreign ministers in November 1983. The formal documents, the 1963 Ankara Treaty and the 1973 Additional Protocol still stand: Article 28 of Ankara declares that Turkey will eventually enter. But from the Fourth Financial Protocol in 1980, all EU development money was blocked by the Greek veto. From Greece's accession until early 1995, the programmes of all Greek governments sought to define Turkey as neither European nor part of the EU's Mediterranean interest.

From the Turkish side such an argument was of course unacceptable, Turkey having been part of the European world since the fourteenth century, and Hittite Anatolia the key centre of Bronze Age civilization. Modern Turkey, created out of the remnants of the Ottoman Empire under Kemal Ataturk in the 1920s, was at least partly modelled on the European nation state, albeit with a strongly authoritarian nationalist tinge; and its governments have attempted to demarcate its eastern borders more decisively than its western one, the implication being that Turkey is not only not Arab but barely Asiatic. As a NATO member of many years standing, they portrayed Turkey up to the end of the Cold War as a defence against Communism. Once NATO became problematic, after 1989, this picture turned to one of being the West's outlying defence against the successive rings of chaos ranging from the Caucasus through Iran and Iraq to Syria, Israel and the Lebanon.

In the period since democracy was restored, none of Turkey's political parties has felt able to launch an accession campaign, the nearest thing to it being the realignment advocated by Turgut Ozal which ensured Turkey's participation, with the United States, Britain and France, Egypt and Saudi Arabia, in the Gulf War. After Ozal's sudden death, Kurdish demands for recognition as a minority and a measure of autonomy were distorted and exacerbated by the PKK's liberation campaign, and the relentless counter-insurgency operations mounted by the Turkish army.

Turkish membership of the Customs Union was due to be concluded in 1995, but the European Parliament rejected a customs union and the Greek government linked the question with Cyprus's negotiations for membership. Since the status of northern Cyprus remained unchanged, Greek objections continued. Nevertheless, from 1992 onwards the Commission's Customs Court had prepared the necessary transitional arrangements, together with technical assistance programmes. Turkey's single duty system began to come in to alignment, together with VAT at 15% in October 1993; so that Turkey was in fact prepared to enter the common tariff in full and to adapt to the new standards, including those on intellectual property, which represented the current *acquis*.

The negotiations began early in 1995, according to plan, with some stimulus from the outgoing German Presidency. The Greek government objected but let it be known that it would lift its veto if a firm timetable were given to Cyprus's membership application. The EU side agreed, and after one more attempt to extract advantage Greece finally withdrew its veto, having won the assurance that negotiation with Cyprus could begin six months after the 1996 IGC ended. In return, Turkey gained not only the Customs Union but the accumulated EU aid built up over nearly twenty years, amounting to $1.2 billion.

This settlement has to be seen in the light of an apparent determination by the ageing prime minister, Andreas Papandreou, to reduce Greece's vulnerability, not only across the Aegean but on the borders with Albania and Yugoslav Macedonia. The Turkish government also needed to demonstrate its credentials as an EU partner, so that Tansu Ciller's government gave an assurance not to intervene in the process of Cypriot reunification: a stance seriously prejudiced by the army's demonstration shortly afterwards of the 'frontier defence' thesis, by assaulting PKK camps in northern Iraq, which caused protests (but not substantive action) from the German government.

Two consequences followed; one minor, the opening of negotiations also with Malta; one major, as the accession focus shifted to the Mediterranean, to the German government's dismay and the delight of the French, increasingly preoccupied with Islamic terrorism and insurgency in Algeria. (Algeria has not so far been included in the Euro-Med Association Agreements under discussion with Morocco and Tunisia, despite proposals from Manuel Marin, Commissioner with responsibility for the Middle East and North Africa, for an increase in EU aid.)

The Customs Union was well received by Turkey's increasingly polarized political parties, in spite of continued opposition by the secular Muslim Welfare Party. Turkey's exporters obtained free access for everything except textiles and clothing but in return the 12.8% tariff had to disappear at a time of 150% inflation. The cost in lost revenue on European imports will be severe and is at present unlikely to be offset by further Community money. In Turkey's current fiscal and banking crisis, the government cannot easily cut its budget or service its debt. Lost revenue can be met only by increasing indirect taxation, at a time when the import surge is likely to hit very many Turkish industries and increase urban unemployment. No one in industry or the financial world, and possibly not even in the Ministry of Finance, has any clear idea of what are the overall costs involved.[50]

The political elite had been divided, but the government argued that the Customs Union was a test case, with many of the implications that NAFTA had for Mexico. Urgency was politically important also, not only in relation to the near and Middle East but to the areas of Turkey's Black Sea cooperation and with the former Soviet Republics of Turkic central Asia, in view of the threat to Islam in Bosnia. At that stage, however, there could be no question of reviving the membership application, in the light of member states' fundamental, if rarely stated objections that Turkey, with a GDP per capita of less than $4000, is still a poor country; a large, populous and regionally extremely diverse secular state with a rapidly growing Islamic party, and a poor record on democracy and human rights (to say nothing of recent, still bitter regional quarrels with Greece, also a NATO and EU country, in the Aegean). Given the option, the EU would certainly prefer Poland, the only other applicant approaching Turkey's size and population.

Yet Turkey's institutions are, strictly speaking, comparable to those of eastern Europe. Its Central Bank takes part in the same meetings in Basel, even if it shares less of the informal discourse.[51] The financial sector has been liberalized and is fully open to foreign concerns, which now include 22 out of 70 banks. The insurance area is no more sheltered than in Italy and Austria, and the capital market appears to function adequately for industrial and SMEs' needs.

However, shortages exist, particularly of skilled administrators. Those engaged on the Customs Union negotiations formed a skilled but small and overworked group. Politics habitually over-rides industrial logic and there are signs that, like some Italian officials before 1993, the Foreign Ministry as well as the State Planning Office sees the EU as an external force, through association with which Turkey can continue the long reforming and modernizing process which dates back to 1923. The example of Italy in the 1970s is not wholly far-fetched.

Turkey is regionally more diverse than any member state, but can claim that, unlike Greece or Ireland, not all its regions would qualify for structural assistance. Its government can deploy the same argument about being a trading and strategic bridge to the Black Sea region, Moldavia and central Asia as can Austria to south-eastern Europe, or Spain and Portugal to Latin America. Its Chambers of Commerce and industrial organizations have net-works on a par with those in Poland. But all that is part of a much larger game, within the Turkish political elite, echoing from the 1920s, as the memory of Kemal's state dims and Kemalism itself decays, defended chiefly and often stringently by the army and the national bureaucracy.[52] Turgut Ozal's death came at the worst of times, leaving Turkey prone to an intractable set of conflicts. Yet as one official put it, 'Turkey has to be seen to fulfil obligations, and to give no handle to the opposition. It cannot be seen to flag or take part in "Arab conflicts", or it will lose its special place in the EU's world outlook.'[53]

The eastern European and the eastern Mediterranean applicants pose questions about what Europe is in a novel and revealing way, and what diversity is permissible within the underlying aims of integration, which was not the case with the accession of Austria, Finland and Sweden. The three constituent elements of any state – its political, economic and socio-cultural space – are normally coterminous. But in the case of the Community, whatever its ultimate boundaries may be these do not necessarily coincide, and the lack of natural congruence causes much more profound dilemmas than the practical, inherently soluble matters of institutional reform. There are also no pointers in the EU's basic legal texts.

Turkey might, for example, enter on political grounds but not on economic or cultural ones; the Ukraine on cultural but not economic and political ones; the Visegrad group and the Baltic States on all three. At present speculation is vacuous, but the questions of space and identity have to be resolved, not only because there are practical matters such as defence, foreign policy and the home and justice pillars of Maastricht which cannot easily be postponed but because they contain an enigma which in the end relates to the EU's inmost dynamics. The EU is a legally constituted body with a fully developed theory of governance; yet how can it resolve problems which are intrinsically those of the state without possessing statehood?

The precursors of European unity, which can be discerned in the Popular Fronts of 1935–7 and the resistances to the Third Reich, were responses to a threat within the confines of wider Europe to what the protagonists believed Europe's identity to be. Even the Cold War response was not entirely to an external one, for the source, the Soviet Union, came within the Europe of 1914. In the sense that all three movements took Europe to be democratic, open and peaceable, the series could be extended back into the nineteenth century to include struggles against autocracy or imperialism, both of which, in their later manifestations, had some influence on the EEC's origins and early evolution. This aspect of the Community's unity and its unique identity may have diminished or become less relevant when the great European ideological divide ended in 1989. But at the same time, what for French and some Benelux leaders had been *le défi américain*, and for most British governments the 'special relationship' also altered – though it is far too early to guess where its latest metamorphosis tends.

It was always likely that in the conditions after 1989 older sources of disunity would revive. Whether they become endemic depends on two sets of factors operating in the 1990s, one external and one internal: how the European periphery develops, and how the various crises of national identity, from which virtually all member states currently suffer, resolve themselves and are resolved within the Community context. Unlike the period before 1989, there is no intrinsic reason why either set of factors should affect the industrial and financial players whose games are international. But what they do in the economic sphere – and increasingly in the political one – gives a definite steer to the Community's evolution and may accentuate the cleavage between political– cultural elements and the political economy, between national life and global markets, which has opened up dramatically since the 1970s.

In spite of what is universally criticized as a failure of EU policy during the Yugoslav civil wars, the current outcome of CFSP appears still to be to keep Europe's south-eastern and southern borders as quiet as possible whilst not disrupting NATO, preparing for some sort of transition to WEU and assimilating the EFTA round of new members. Keeping the borders quiet is a problem with a lineage stretching back to the Roman Empire through the mediaeval and early modern Holy Roman Empire, to say nothing of Napoleon's Empire and the Third Reich. Currently it involves deepening the European Economic Agreements, ratifying the Customs Union with Turkey, and, if statements can be believed, preparing proposals for structural assistance, trade and employment in the countries stretching from Egypt to Morocco. What sort of partnership will develop with Russia and its uncertain neighbours Belarus and the Ukraine is not at present something member state governments like to contemplate in isolation from the United States.

Among the largest states there are considerable and worrying differences of emphasis and substance; on the priorities in eastern and southern Europe and the near or Middle East and about the integration/enlargement equation now that the three EFTA members are on board. More immediately, since the EU is faced (or 'threatened' according to one point of view), with several distinct waves of refugees/migrants, the NAFTA solution – investing deeply in whichever over-populated, less developed country on its periphery currently resembles Mexico – has reached the agenda in a variety of forms, all of which involve the EU acting as a developmental agency beyond its natural borders.

Since the laws affecting refugees have been changed once recently in Germany, and may be tightened up again,[54] and since the French, Spanish and Italian Interior Ministries have strengthened existing constraints, the problem is less one of legal refugees and migrants, more of illegal ones and their habitual counterpoints – crime, drugs and terrorism. Thus the second and third pillars of Maastricht are conjoined.

The arc stretching from Murmansk through 180 degrees of a circle to Casablanca is not of course uniformly threatening; indeed some of its sections, such as the Ukraine, tend to act as two-way valves or intermediate mechanisms to give a sort of insulation in return for irrigation by European prosperity. This is the elemental case for increasing the EU's level of political benevolence both to the Visegrad group (and its neighbours) and to Turkey. It cannot easily be applied to North Africa because the countries of the Mahgreb are irrelevant as a barrier to a sub-Saharan black Africa which presents no threat except via small numbers of illegal immigrants. The *threat* comes from North Africa itself, or rather (at the moment of writing) from Algeria's political seed-bed of fundamentalist Muslim terrorists. Algeria is perhaps the main problem facing Europe after Yugoslavia, one facing France and to some extent Spain, rather than Germany and Austria, and it already mirrors within France the problems Germany has had with Yugoslavia: a common, ill-omened history, a blend of colonial guilt, immigration, social discord and political unrest. Algeria is also, like Mexico, vastly over-populated in relation to any foreseeable availability of work.

Yet the coherence of both sides of the Mediterranean has as respectable an ancestry and socio-cultural history as that between the Balkans and Turkey or Scandinavia and the Baltic States. Europe's capacity and willpower to cut itself off from the former colonial, poor, over-populated, under-employed southern rim of the Mediterranean is however still greater than in the case of Turkey, and certainly greater than in eastern Europe, which may be the true 'second circle'. That this appears to recreate an ancient religious divide between Christianity and Islam may be coincidental, yet it inevitably arouses suspicions even in Turkey, let alone Egypt and Algeria.

Egypt's 2.5% per annum increase in births and Algeria's 3% point up the demographic challenge, especially given that Islamic theology resists birth control. Algeria's problem of unemployment, agricultural neglect, illiteracy, import substitution, low technical base and vast debts, represents only the worst case. Tunisia, Morocco and Libya are politically fragile and ethnically as well as socially divided. The government of France, and increasingly those of Spain and Italy, point to various remedies: redefining debts, cooperation and aid programmes, a Mediterranean investment bank, even – timidly so far – opening European markets to Mahgreb agriculture. Any one of these would increase discord in the Community and none may be possible before a fuller reform of the CAP than any that has so far occurred.[55]

Paradoxically, media, public and governments appear to concentrate more readily on problems of the third circle, in Russia's Caucasian periphery, and the Middle East or black Africa. Yet 4% of Germany's population is Turkish and 10% of France's originates from the Mahgreb. The detritus of seventy-five years since 1914, beginning with the expulsion of Armenians and Greeks from Asiatic Turkey, continuing with Algeria's expulsion of *pieds-noirs* and *harkis* in 1964, shows no signs of concluding with ethnic cleansing in Bosnia (which is, on most reckonings, within the first circle). It is this external, alien (yet also inner) portent which threatens to divide the Community in an unprecedented way in the near future, opening up a truly appalling picture that greed and xenophobia will enforce new and unwelcome loyalties and alignments. Yet it is only two hundred years since western European travellers and intellectuals admired and took as counterpoints Ottoman and Mameluk civilizations just as they admired Mughal India and the China of Chien Lung.

It is be futile to guess at the outcomes of these long-fermented problems: much easier to concentrate on the relatively straightforward, if discreetly veiled, games and informal politics among consenting European players. The only opinion worth venturing is that none of them will be properly addressed unless it becomes an overriding necessity, like the Iraqi invasion of Kuwait, or the Slovene–Croat–Serbian period of the Yugoslav civil wars – at least until the larger member states have sufficiently resolved their own crises of identity. And that can hardly happen before France's political spectrum has cleared and Germany has sorted out its present dilemmas on further European integration while ensuring the precise ordering of Middle Europe.

Habitually the Community piles all its discontents and hopes on to the agenda of the next IGC. No conceivable IGC in 1996, spread over any number of months, could address all this. Debates will run on into the next century, concurrently with the development (or not, as the case may be) of a tripartite division of the world between three massive trading blocs. The EU as such has very little power to affect events in the second circle, let alone the third.

But assuming that cultural diversity can coexist with economic globalization, the Community's fifteen member states have the firm and world-powerful basis of a nearly-completed internal market and a share of 38.3% (1994) of world trade. Whether or not the outstanding two Maastricht pillars are brought within the Community's full scope is unlikely to increase its quantum of influence in the world. Political union might, though that is not the ostensible reason for pursuing it. But the antithesis need not be between widening and deepening, only between aspects of both, though to put it in that way requires some argument about the EU's quality of statehood *vis-à-vis* its national members' aspirations.

The momentum of integration has expanded or diminished over thirty-five years, according to the rhythms of growth and recession, political euphoria and gloom. As the machine expands, it booms out messages about federalism, as it contracts it breathes the words subsidiarity and proportionality. Similar if slower cycles accompanied the creation of European nation states in the sixteenth and seventeenth centuries. The only true *acquis* is what affects permanently the behaviour of every player from member states to the individual firm or association and ultimately the individual citizen of Europe. How much of the behavioural change, however, is wrought by forces within the EU and how much is a response to events and impulses outside will be hard, even in thirty years, for historians to decide.

Some of the causes of the EU's disunity are obvious; yet of physical or conceptual, geographical or commercial differences, disagreements of internal or external origin, none has so far halted its evolution. But in qualitative as well as quantitative terms, the Single European Act and the chain of events which began in 1989 (to which Maastricht was only an indirect response) distinguish the EU's second era from its first.

Rather less obviously, a tension grew up after 1989 between maintaining the momentum of integration renewed by the internal market and the Maastricht Treaty and the effects on member state behaviour of manifestations of nationalism, from which none of the twelve nor the EFTA and eastern European applicants was exempted. If the national and European archives opened up in thirty years' time reveal that some of the participants at Maastricht understood this, it will be too late to congratulate the progenitors. Yet precisely because in 1994 they were already in late middle or old age (that is, taking Helmut Kohl, Jacques Delors and François Mitterrand to be the principals), and had experienced the Second World War and sought to explain its origins, they may have foreseen how what they tried to do might serve to prevent a repetition of the damage done in the closing years of the nineteenth century: to contain extreme forms of nationalism and the conflicts which were to divide Europe utterly between 1911 and 1919.

14

Conclusion

I.

Orchestrate has two meanings; one formal and precise – to arrange a score for the instruments in a orchestra; the other, informal – to fix or to arrange for things to happen in the order one desires. This book's title is meant to convey both meanings, because the orchestra described here has no conductor (but at least two main contenders for the job), and no composer's score (save what each set of instruments, strings, woodwind or brass, tries to play). Yet there is a common convention that they should play a certain sort of music, according to one notation, with the ultimate aim of creating harmony. Each successive movement of the continuing symphony has its origin and variations in the one before.

In the formal and legal sense, this of course is unacceptable. The Treaties lay down what has been agreed by the sovereign players and what therefore will be. But that is a higher fiction: in the gaps between what the law says and what actually takes place, between the public version of how authority operates and the reality, lie the processes described here. The gap is largest at the most fundamental level, between the grandiose aims constantly referred to in a rhetoric which is as particular as Aristotelian logic or mediaeval religious disputation, and the incremental progress – in the *general* direction of those aims – achieved on the ground. The contrast between Commission aims, set annually by its President to the Parliament, and what follows in the next twelve months demonstrates the point: Jacques Santer's desire, expressed in January 1995, to bring the CFSP and Interior Ministry pillars of

Maastricht within the Commission's competence, is unlikely to be fulfilled this year or at the next IGC.

From an historian's point of view, it is hard to see that the European Union has any predetermined end. It is a political system without a prime mover, a proto-state without a constitution and, though it had an initial sort of 'big bang', it is also grounded in so recent a past that there is no space for myth, only historical argument about the conditions which caused it to be born. There is no misty pre-history whose supposed traditions might hypothesize a social contract. For all the efforts of federalists, functionalists, neofunctionalists and interdependence theorists to assign primacy to a single process, no single theory commands general assent.

I have no intention of trying to add to their number. The most a contemporary historian can do is to show how the Community's diverse union was built by individuals and like-minded groups, serving their own, national, regional or commercial interests in particular circumstances, as part of the general evolution of Europe in a wider world. What has occurred, after all, is an illustration not so much of the Tower of Babel (whose builders had a plan but irreconcilable workforces) as of Engels's dictum that the product of many separate wills is something that none of them specifically willed.

The Community is the product as much of discontinuities and accident (what Maitland called the troughs and hollows of history) as of constructive waves in the rare periods of consensus. There is no point in seeking a generic title to describe something which one set of analysts sees as a framework for managed relations among member states and another as a hybrid authority of a novel kind. Since it outgrew the early 1970s assumption that there was a profound link between what the Six governments wanted and 'Rhineland capitalism', the Community has not fitted accurately any of the traditional descriptive categories for Europe. (In that sense, as de Gaulle suspected, Britain's entry has complicated matters, not simplified them.)

What is observed depends on the analyst's standpoint and discipline, whether legal, political, economic or historical (or a mixture of all of them). There is of course a broad substratum of agreement that the Community is more than a regime but less than a full political system.¹ Although its *acquis* builds up steadily, it is not a true community and its institutions have constantly to renegotiate large areas of their authority if the *acquis* is to be fully binding – that is, to be *internalized* in patterns of thought and behaviour.

Interpretation and implementation of the Community's enactments vary between governments. What is a necessary and therefore acceptable delay for one may be seen as unconscionable indolence by another. Interpretation of the law, 'how things are done', being still largely a matter for member states' governments, depends partly on their domestic players' needs and their contrary responses to the threats or opportunities which exist outside the EU. Descriptions by practitioners or analysts tend to confirm that 'the EU is what you see'; like Weber's rationality, the *acquis*' stable crust covers a vast molten magma of diversity, if not irrationality.

In a lecture in 1991, following Hegel's *Es gibt keinen Staat in Europa*, Etienne Balibar declared, 'we have to ask ourselves what this Europe means and what it will signify tomorrow . . . Europe is not something which is "constructed" at a slower or faster pace, with greater or less ease: it is a historical problem without any pre-established solutions.'² One former British chancellor of the exchequer called it, 'a constellation of interests. Ministers have power on major issues, but lose this *vis-à-vis* the incremental force of institutions whose individual members have great influence.' A Spanish central banker put it differently; 'a conglomerate of states with services in common . . . a consortium, like a public work, united for this project only'.³

The Community can be defined as a common economy, a common governing culture, or a shared administrative structure. Some observers compare it with cities or city states, in rivalry with each other, from the middle ages to the seventeenth century. Others portray it as the offshoot of a certain sort of capitalism, Rhineland as opposed to Anglo-Saxon or Japanese. That it is distinct and probably unique is rarely in dispute. At the risk of caricature, its limits range from the religious (the 1891 papal encyclical, *De Rerum Novarum* with the present pope's centenary reiteration in 1991 that Europeans are 'a people' not 'peoples'), to the pop culture of Eurodisney outside Paris, open to all Europeans as 'citizens of a new world'.

Not surprisingly, this Community has not given rise to what President Mitterrand once called a *théorie des ensembles*. It has too many identities, national, regional, local; perhaps for that reason it missed what in retrospect was its greatest chance to rationalize itself between 1989 and 1992 while Russia was weak and the United States euphoric, settling instead for the limited terms, brokered by governments, of the Maastricht Treaty of Union, thereby laying itself open to Margaret Thatcher's taunt that, 'there is no substitute for the national state.'[4] In the only legal pronouncement yet made on its nature, the German Constitutional Court ruled in 1993 that the Community is a *Staatenverbund*, not a federal *Bundesstaat*, nor a confederal *Staatenbund*. There is no precise English or French equivalent for a term that implies close association dependent on the consent of national entities. Yet in the last resort these control the valve which inflates or deflates the European balloon.

However much historians try to prevent the Chinese walls of different disciplines from becoming impermeable, the problem remains that the confusion of events which is their raw material cannot be mobilized into explanations and theories with the facility of social scientists, armed with an algebraic base. Historians have also been slow to address recent developments in the EU, for the understandable reason that they lack access to its documentation after 1964. In any case, the fact that each category of documents is composed in separate contexts makes a synoptic view laborious. What is recorded by governments and European institutions is very different in kind and quality from the minutes of firms and financial institutions operating in the EU and global contexts. The raw material thus prejudices historians from contributing to often highly theoretical and unempirical debates about political systems. For these reasons, the idea of a competitive symposium, advanced in the Introduction, is used only as a descriptive device.

Nevertheless, there are two main aspects where an historian can contribute insights: firstly, into the behaviour of a great and increasing number of players of different status and power as their games change over time; secondly, into the interplay between the formal and informal aspects of the system, as the two relate to each other in a very different context from that in which the Treaty of Rome was signed in 1957. He or she can also ensure that the system itself is treated as a whole rather than as parts, or the sum of its parts.

Since the EU lacks an unambiguous, clearly defined aim, its history could hardly be teleological. The Treaties have been modified by political practice and court decisions over nearly forty years; there is as much point now in asking about the original signatories' intentions as there is in studying the Philadelphia convention of 1787 and the Federal Papers. (As yet there is no EU school of conservative lawyers, as there is in the United States, who seek to discover an 'original direction' – as if no change had taken place in that union in two hundred years.) The ECJ directs itself not only to the Treaties, of which it is guardian and interpreter but to contemporary circumstances and the political and economic context of the cases which come before it: which allow it also to revise its own earlier judgments.

Because it has been subjected to so many different sorts of analysis, the Community's short past has been forced into several different modes, and confused, even from the narrative point of view. Self-evidently, change and development in the way the EU works have been deeply affected by the economic cycle. But this does not mean that there was always a direct correlation between economic and political activity, even if the political recovery associated with the mid–1980s and the Single European Act appear to dwarf earlier pinnacles of enthusiasm like 1972. Contrary to popular perception, many of the most fruitful ideas (ERM, common foreign policy, harmonization, common trade policy and overseas aid, as well as many key ECJ cases) date from the 1970s. The importance of boom and recession and the responses to the development of global markets lie in the fact that each cycle has had a different impact. As far as the players were concerned, the 1973–5 economic and financial crisis profoundly altered the balance between industrial firms and labour organizations, but produced a mainly defensive, protectionist response. Those of 1980–83 and 1991–3 stimulated all large enterprises and their federations or associations to adjust and become more competitive.

It is easy therefore to assume that the first was a mistaken reaction, the second a correct one, and that in explaining the results for the Community (liberalization even of telecoms, transport and energy, competition policy, research-assisted adjustment, mutual recognition rather than harmonization, financial deregulation, and the abandonment of 'fortress Europe' in favour of the Uruguay round and the WTO) the Single European Act has been crucial. But this produces two related problems for the historian: one concerning the origins of the SEA and the establishment of the internal market; the other connecting these to what went before. The SEA process and the internal market ran in conjunction with a rapid evolution in the world economy and global markets, just as Maastricht took place in the louring context of 1989 events and the reversion of Europe's central and south-eastern borders to the patterns of the 1920s. There is a danger in concentrating on the decade after 1985 as if the heightened tempo since were destined to play for ever. It should be remembered that the leading industrial, commercial and financial organizations were present much earlier and were vigorous players even in the 1960s, and although, as was argued in chapter 4, a very much larger number of them involved themselves deeply in the SEA debate, it was not the case for many that Brussels was the game's centre. Where 'the centre' and 'the periphery' were varied according to the business cycle, players' global strategy and individual chief executives' assessments.

The argument that the SEA and the still-developing internal market have proved a truly significant turning-point must rest on demonstrating changes of behaviour among other players as well as governments, bearing in mind that, even if it can be shown that firms or banks have accustomed themselves to bargaining in Brussels and to negotiating regulatory regimes, so that each one's European affairs section has become a microcosm of what governments now do, the explanation may lie in world not European trends. The evidence here suggests that the tensions *within* firms, depending on whether they aim at national, European or global markets, are in fact essentially similar to those which occur within governments, between one ministry and another *vis-à-vis* European affairs. But since governments no longer react as they did in the

1970s in habitual defence of their national champions, the largest firms and multinationals have been compelled by the twin scourges of foreign competition and domestic liberalization to find their own solutions, often in permanent direct links to Community institutions.

In general, multinationals have accustomed themselves to the new requirements of their political economy. Those that have not tend to be under state control or in sheltered parts of national economies, which are in the future likely to be exposed even in the protective cases such as Austria or Greece. But in the process their older identities and affinities have been abandoned.[5] Put crudely, does BMW's takeover of Rover make it a German firm? Was Rover, given its dependence on Honda, a British firm in the first place? American companies, as Alan Cawson and Peter Holmes have argued, became truly European players because they had to. Insofar as European champions have moved into American markets, they have made themselves international.

Japanese transnational companies act as if they were European, joining sectoral federations, employing European nationals, training future managers through their European subsidiaries, and staying much longer in Europe than observers expected even five years ago. Sharp and Sony act so as to be allowed to take part in European research programmes, no doubt in order to appropriate the result for Japanese global markets (as scholars digest and reinterpret, without obvious plagiarism).

Daimler-Benz, under the direction of Edzard Reuter, claims to be an 'integrated technology corporation'. But is it still a German one? After vast restructuring of its parts, Mercedes, AEG (of which little now remains in the form when it was bought), Daimler-Benz Aerospace (formerly Deutsche Aerospace), DASA, and Fokker (once a Dutch aircraft concern), it is manifestly a global entity with a headquarters in Germany. Whether this and the profound 1990s adjustments of other MNCs contribute a German model to the existing array of French, British, Netherlands, Italian or Spanish models is irrelevant: their transitions are a symbol of the protean revivalism which the SEM/global market contingency has stimulated.

Something similar has occurred amongst public utilities, which are increasingly diversifying into new services and stretching out into global markets beyond the EU's regulatory range. Deutsche Telekom has recently bought a share in Satelindo, the Indonesian equivalent. Siemens and PowerGen have formed a consortium to build a power station in Java, and RWE Energie is deeply involved in South Africa – all this in one month, March 1995. Utilities already privatized, such as British Telecom, stalk the European market, water companies and electricity suppliers buy into each other as MNCs used to in the years preceding the single market.

The gap between MNCs and the national and SME players is probably still widening, although since MNCs generally act as market leaders, medium-sized firms may already be following them, crossing borders and behaving differently in different markets. They have changed the EU's political marketplace, probably ir-reversibly, because all the serious players (which does not include those who work sporadically or only through lobbyists) have engaged themselves permanently, on a large scale and with sub-stantial resources at every level, to the evolution of means of influence over their common regulatory environment. A firm cannot ignore any of these approaches, not because all means are equal or have a commercial or even a viable return, but because their competitors might gain advantage there if not.[6]

This process began before the 1980s, but its manifestations have altered since then. Behaviour has become very much more profes-sional, in a sort of corporate Darwinism[7] so that it is essential for the outsider to study firms both as individual players and as members of sectoral organizations. There is no such thing as the 'typical firm', if indeed there ever was. Players have had to learn to operate in every available sector of the game; this includes those who were often sluggish to see new opportunities in the past, notably in the insurance sector. The ECJ and the Court of First Instance are now prominent features in players' calculations: in turn, judges and attorneys general take account of such players' circumstances in ways which were not observable before the mid–1980s.

Not all links lead to the development of real, lasting networks, but neither are they confined by regional or national borders. Cross-border regional links, for example, in the Low Countries, the Rhine Valley, northern Italy and the south-west Pyrenees have acquired genuine substance in the last five years. Density of networks and complementarity are the determining factors in whether or not groupings such as the 'Four Motors' actually create integrated economic space, as they do with Baden-Württemberg and Rhône-Alpes, though less so where Catalonia and Lombardy are concerned.

This comes 'from below', and is the product of many interrelated aims and activities; it is not in EC institutions' power to create. Networks grow and will grow faster in the 1990s for purely technical reasons, and much faster in commercial and financial spheres than political ones. At the 'top end', central bankers on the Delors Committee demonstrated, in drafting the rules for the future European Central Bank, that they already shared a political as well as a professional ethos.

In this complicated game, the member states are not abstractions, *monstres froids* ordering the play. They are themselves players of great diversity, as their reasons for signing the SEA in 1985–6 demonstrated. To compare their European affairs national coordinating systems, as they really work, rather than as displayed formally in organigrams, is to see fundamental differences between centralized states (France, Britain, Denmark, Spain – despite appearances – and Portugal), decentralized or federal ones (Germany, the Netherlands, Belgium) and ill-organized ones (Italy, Greece). The results of course affect how regions develop, whether they are mere territorial entities as in the case of Rhône-Alpes, or possess elements of informal statehood based partly on historic claims as in Catalonia and Scotland; and whether Permanent Representatives, at the other end of the wedge of influence, open their offices and their own networks to corporate players even beyond their own national base (seeking, for example, as some Greek firms have done through the French office, to gain access to lucrative EC-inspired contracts in francophone Africa).

The Single European Act did not create all this, but its long sequel is largely responsible for the increase in the capacity of member states and economic players to adjust to world changes. Very much as forecast in the early 1980s, the better players' responses enabled them to become more competitive within a unique regulatory regime, whose centre of gravity initially lay within what Michel Albert called Rhineland capitalism but by the 1990s is associated with what the economies of northern Europe, naturally including France, have come generally to represent.

EU governance facilitated this outcome, spurred both by the Commission, which oversaw the SEA's fulfilment, and the leading, usually northern member state governments. Between them, they gave it enough credibility for the players to take the bait. Meanwhile the players themselves had established their own requirements both in Brussels and more importantly in their national capitals, so that they could influence governments to do this in the way that suited them best. The answers to the question of whether in the end the process was supranational or effectively coordinated by national governments must wait for the archives to be opened. For the present, the game was neither closely regulated nor a 'Anglo-Saxon' free-for-all: Community institutions, member states and non-governmental players all shared in what Wolfgang Wessels calls the 'fusion process'.

II.

Informal activities, and the rules and conventions which control them, have a greater impact at the Community level even than in nation states, where political systems have matured over centuries (even if several have been seriously disrupted in the twentieth century). This was true from the beginning, and informal characteristics have become a Community hallmark. But the combination of reduced state effectiveness at the national level, and greatly extended EU policy at the Community one, after the crisis of the 1970s had worked itself out (that is, around the mid-1980s), increased their volume and brought them into greater practical prominence. Informal politics mattered more to the practitioners because so much more was at stake.

Insofar as nation states are concerned, to look at how the

Community functions from this aspect is to follow a well-documented political science path. The problem there is to document patterns on any continuous basis, given the resistance of long-established governmental systems to ceding any authority to commercial players except in an emergency.[8] But the Community is different: the weight of its informal activities derives from its peculiar formal structure and in turn contributes to how that structure works and evolves. Indeed, informality is one consequence of the long Community tradition of setting down markers in legal texts, to be implemented in riper circumstances at a later date. As a general rule, the informal facilitates and complements the formal. But it is not superior: the formal part of the system sets the legal and constitutional framework within which the informal operates, thriving in open systems, permeating authoritarian ones. The two intertwine whenever questions of interpretation and implementation give grounds for discretion or alternative constructions. The formal may supervene to tidy up or discipline the informal, but in turn the informal will find ways of subverting, modifying or even replacing the formal if it ossifies.[9]

If informality had not been available, Jean Monnet could hardly have put together his coalition. In the late 1950s it was however far less explicit and barely publicized. Today it is both visible and very widely disseminated. But substantial difficulties inhibit analysis: social scientists tend to reduce the informal to formal abstractions, and historians to avoid it altogether for lack of proper documentation. Yet it is not hard to show that in complex modern societies formal mechanisms rely on the continual good behaviour of those who take part: political institutions, administrators, publics. In periods of tension, without the informal easements, the formal parts become more rigid or unworkable the more pressures build up. No mechanism is so perfect that it cannot be disturbed by dissidents or outsiders. Yet no mechanism can be designed to alter itself over time, to meet challenges of which the originators can have no conception, unless it possesses informal latitude. As a rough rule, the more formalistic or authoritarian a system, the less this is possible; formality conjoined with the informal has a better chance of importing flexibility and preventing systemic failure.

Any habitual, non-mandatory procedure could be described as informal but such a definition is so wide as to be meaningless. Informal politics is normally policed in some way but is not justiciable. It is more often implied or understood than it is explicit; individual entities or closely knit private groups use it more effectively than do public bodies. The informal is often temporary, and can mutate towards semi-formal institutions such as *réunions pacquets* or 'confessionals' or fully formal procedures such as the comitology rules which were designed to prevent endless haggling every time a new committee was set up. Players cannot fight on all fronts all the time and sometimes voluntarily bind themselves to formality. Self-regulation and plural linkages are encouraged rather than hierarchies of power. Incorporation rather than exclusion is the rule – but mainly for the larger, better organized players. Losers are therefore forced to find other ways to gain access, as trades unions were in the Community after the mid–1970s, embarking on a twenty-year search to avoid exclusion, which the EU's formal attempts to resist proved largely useless.

For those with the size and skill to play, informal politics tends to stabilize and humanize the EU's political market rather than encouraging the pursuit of strictly rational self-interest. To a minimum extent, all players, like member states themselves, must demonstrate an element of altruism (European-mindedness) as well as basic self-interest, not only because they want to be considered by their peers and competitors but to make themselves acceptable to EU institutions and officials. These in turn have some control over those to whom they allow privileged access, thus determining their behaviour to a certain extent.

There is a spectrum and all players can choose between formal and informal modes, and the shades of grey between them. Whether they use the full range depends on their size, needs and aims. Rules and conventions are policed on both sides, with many nuanced penalties for infringement.[10] Inclusion depends on a player's willingness to accept the rules and conventions of its own club or association (in effect, a form of peer-group assessment).

Informal politics exist wherever there are grey areas (and there are many in the Community), from the appointment of a Commission

President to how member state nationals act properly as neutral experts on Commission working groups. As one Swiss bank executive put it, 'the most important things in the EC are never on paper . . . or if they are, they are in documents which don't officially exist'.[11] On the appointment of experts, a French company executive in the car industry noted that, 'the task is to convince the official in charge of the dossier that one's employee is an expert in the field and would add substantially to the proposal's quality'.[12] Whole institutions exist in these interstices, like Ecofin's Economic Policy Committee and the Committee of Central Bankers' Alternates. Informality flourishes in conditions of pluralistic bargaining and interdependence and it increases in geometrical progression with the number of players.

Informality accrues where regulatory competences are less well established, where formal procedures work badly or slowly, and where interdependence requires players to concert policy together – especially when that requirement comes from the Commission, to which they must respond as part of the customary gift exchange (itself the precondition for their continued influence). It flourishes wherever there is ambiguity, experimentation, and the crossing of physical or metaphysical borders.

It is not necessary that it should be covert, though it is usually confidential or discreet and tends to wither with publicity. It is very rarely illicit, because if it were it could not regularly fulfil its prime role. It is natural, empirical, uncertain. Since its essence is to make the formal side more efficient, it requires a measure of trust, a faith in commonalty. For this reason, informal processes work best where there is professional common ground, say among lawyers, central bankers or journalists – unlike the politics of politicians, which tends to divide. Informality assumes reciprocity and trade-offs, though not necessarily in marketable goods, and it flourishes indifferently in both private and public dimensions. It probably could not operate in a technically free market – but political marketplaces are even less likely than economic ones to be free, because human beings are never entirely rational, and are more irrational in the former than the latter.

These propositions apply equally to nation states as traders insofar as their Community membership is concerned. Luxembourg has so far defended its refusal to introduce a withholding tax on bank deposits, against German government protests, by raising each time in Brussels the need for a Commission-wide harmonized policy – which would of course curtail freedom of banking in the enclaves of the Channel Islands and the Dutch West Indies. It was a French government official, not a corporate executive, who observed the need to know which Commission officials dealing with their area had had their promotions blocked; 'then inflate the dossier, give them added value, and build in false bombs that the official can explode without hurting the case.'[13] Another from the Trésor gave his rule, 'never to beat anyone completely but to give something to each participant in the game.'[14]

The EU, as a senior official put it, 'is an open bargaining system: the Commission cannot know the latest trends, and *it would be unwise* [author emphasis] to propose a text disruptive of markets'.[15] Another; 'there has to be latitude for making deals. Total transparency is not necessarily desirable. The EC is composed of fifteen proud nations: there have to be trade-offs.'[16] At the '113 Group' monthly meeting, when Deputy Secretaries lunch together in Brussels, ostensibly with their interpreters, they shop around: 'If you give this much, my Minister might do so and so . . .'.

In the *Discorsi*, Machiavelli accounted for the survival of the Roman republic for over five hundred years by the multiplicity of intermediate mechanisms. Such an argument refers to the foundations of effective power, not, as in *The Prince*, to its mere exercise. When formal politics is heavily contested, informal politics has to produce remedies, if the system is not to ossify; the 'empty chair' crisis led to the Luxembourg Compromise.

Whatever areas member states, officials, or commercial players are engaged in, the antennae developed for informal activity enable them to pick up nuances or deep shifts in their common games more quickly than would otherwise occur; survival demands rapid reaction, serviced by the best (that is, most effective) research and intelligence. Financial players naturally react faster than industrial or labour ones, those in financial derivatives markets fastest of all. Where they fail, as Barings and, more catastrophically, Crédit

Lyonnais did, the penalties are greater. Trying to regulate successively financial services, banking, insurance and stock exchanges, the Commission has in some areas – small risks insurance or the supervision of non-banks – effectively handed over the game to the players. Some matters are beyond the capacity of bureaucrats, judges or politicians.

Informal politics shortens circuits and provides far more alternatives than formal EU institutions can, short as they are of personnel. The history of the Werner period in the early 1970s and the EMS, as well as the SEA's evolution and origins (and especially its implantation), cannot be written without taking it into account. EMU could hardly have been floated without complementary informal politics going back to the conjunction of central bankers working out the rules on the Delors Committee, while exploring how the ERM could become the glidepath to EMU.

Those who know intuitively, who have the resources, who employ the most gifted individuals, do best. Those who come from a flexible administrative tradition such as Britain's may have a greater advantage: the interviews taken for this book show how much British operators are envied. Those who have to refer back to take account of their government's *tutelle* or who rely on national actors and Permanent Representatives probably have less advantage: those who have neither, even less. There is no point in claiming, however, that the system is either representative or democratic; and the 'nice guys' often lose. Yet because hard bargaining is the only way to produce consensus, informal politics serves to diminish the levels of aggression common to all formal, adversarial systems.

III.

A new and many-centred view of Europe does not lead easily to a neat set of conclusions. On the formal side, it is probably correct to argue that the Community's institutions risk paralysis if the current fifteen member states become eighteen or twenty without institutional reform; even if new informal practices were to evolve, such as the Troika, or now-formal ones such as Coreper, which served to overcome rigidities in the past. The argument here however is different: there is no apparent danger of overload in the informal parts of the system (and the fact that the Commission and the Parliament have desisted from trying further to regulate lobbyists' access confirms it). The interplay between the institutions which have competence to make policy and those players who wish to modify it is self-regulating. In that sense, the game is not finite, but extends to every level or terrain, as the front line in the First World War spread within weeks from its Belgian core to a line from the Channel to the Swiss border.[17]

That the informal can expand is not enough: it must be successful, since that is its *raison d'être*. But the reasons for success are rarely understood, and many of the industrial and financial players – and indeed hard-pressed Commission officials – have neither time nor the access to corporate memory which would enable them to analyse why successes have occurred. Commercial organizations' aims, after all, are not always the same as those of politicians and governments who have electorates in mind: confederations of industry for example favour EMU more than most of their governments. There is no ordered hierarchy such as exists in a formal system: the commercial player can tap into any number of member state linkages, at Permanent Representative level or via MEPs. The informal is closer in form to the Internet than to encryption-based computer networks. Influence relates less to the sectors of operation – hi-tech or otherwise – than to the players' skill, determination, or the extent to which each one sees threat or advantage. Choice between direct or indirect lines of approach, national capital or Brussels, depends on the player's perception of what is best, so that the best measure of a member state's coordination apparatus for European Affairs is actually whether their networks are used by the players in preference to others.

All of today's participants engage for the long term: in current global conditions, indirect influence is one of their main options. Success means more than implementation of a particular amendment in a Directive: the aim may be to rely on a process of permeation, acculturation or irradiation with a different point of view. It would be hard to assess, say, whether a point of principle is traded for short-term advantage or not: the outcome may depend on whether the firm concerned or its competitor is most likely to suffer in later years when the principle is eventually enforced. A positional gain may be measured by the fixing of a norm at a level detrimental to those who have not yet installed catalytic converters; by exemption of a process on special grounds; or by setting an environmental standard just high enough to win acceptance from the purists and polluters alike.

Regional and national politics have their own measures of success. Germany's *Länder* have developed a rhetoric of sovereignty, which can be useful in extracting economic subventions which are then doubled up by the federal government under the principle of additionality. Bonn, in turn, used the reconversion of the eastern *Länder* to support requests for structural aid from the Community. Success may be very indirect indeed. Member state governments may submit, without obvious loss of sovereignty, to the Community's rulings, to win what they themselves are unwilling to enforce on their electorates: as in the case of industrial adjustment in France in the 1960s and 1990s or Austria in public utilities reform since its entry in 1995.

The game also induces a process of socialization, habituating players to each other, forcing them to think through other points of view and subsequently live with them. Indeed this Euro-civilizing aspect may come to be seen, looking back from early in the next century, as informal politics' largest contribution to the European Union. But it is not a negotiated order in the neo-corporatist sense, as concertation or *Mitbestimmung* operated in some European countries from the 1950s to the 1980s. The sheer number of players, links and options makes it not only pluralist but polycentric in its pluralism. So many of the commercial players have part of their being outside the Community (as do its member states) that their participation itself transposes one to the other, diminishing their singularity. The EU is shaped by players in the world beyond, more than was possible in the 1970s, by transfusions of habits and novel practices which in the 1990s – unlike the 1970s, when they sought protection – work to diminish the EU's naturally inward-looking tendencies. Players in turn grow accustomed to moving across global–European–national levels of identity. How much they are affected and homogenized is something that can only be tested by studying each one individually.

Between them, the players constitute an unique political market-place – with trade-offs, alliances and cartels – which is a necessary condition for the existence of a modern state. The games here may resemble George Tsibelis's 'nested games', each with its own agenda and procedures, more than they do those in national contexts; this is because the SEA's history (which still continues to evolve, and not only because the internal market is incomplete) affected all industrial, financial and labour markets, and the whole way that the mixed economy in Europe was conceived and policed (and by what sort of regulatory system). The original conception of the internal market's political economy, strictly defined, was then expanded, so as to relate to social affairs, industrial relations, migration and emigration, welfare and the environment. As Wolfgang Hager has put it, 'liberalization beyond a certain threshold requires a functioning polity as a framework,'[18] ground rules to protect individuals and groups, in a European context which contains the past as well as the present and future, even if a European public does not yet exist.

But mundane practice erodes the long vision. 'The Commission does not usually have an ongoing transcendent sense of mission, more often as short-term aims as any national government.' Other motives drive it; 'where the Commission feels it has no control, it will try to formalize its role and status, to get in on the act, suspicious of what member states may do.'[19] Such is the volume of business and the range of issues involved that players gravitate to Brussels as a matter of course, not to a single authority as they would in a national capital but to a mixed polity where bargaining and negotiation are constituent modes.

The sort of induction which this type of market produces is the result of a sense of interdependence married to tangible evidence of mutual advantage. Given the complexity of players which have both structural and functional aims (and whose many-layered understandings are contingent on each other), the European political market is underwritten by the joint Commission-Council struggle to keep a single version of the general interest alive, while taking sufficient account of each player's own version of the European interest for it to stay content. There may be no necessary linkage between economic and political union; progress may never surpass the lowest common denominator of whatever number of players take part. Even a series of state crises, of public debates, budget deficits, or failed expectations may not induce the fundamental reforms on which EMU, EPU, and further extensions are predicated.[20] Neither is it clear that political union, even if it came about, would better harmonize performance.

Nevertheless, there is at least a case for arguing that, insofar as the Commission and Council cooperate, they are able gradually to extend the effective if intangible level of statehood immanent in European institutions. It may be that member states acting from a position of strength deliberately use the internal market as a cover to sell liberalization to their electorates who would have rejected it from a national source if they had known the price; but such diversionary tactics also enhance the future capacity of the body made responsible. The Single European Act contained more than was apparent at the time, as not only Margaret Thatcher but the French government discovered, with what can be described as the end of Colbert's state, circa 1991; but it required the Commission and the ECJ to insist on it in full. Member states have become agents implementing these outcomes, to which they consented in very different circumstances, often in fact in opposition to their own electorates (who may yet resist the harsh medicine, having seen few of the promised benefits, despite the end of the 1990s recession). Europe's statehood has been built up piecemeal, not constructed according to plan.[21]

But what is that statehood? Two impressions, by practitioners, are worth quoting. 'A new type of person leads a new type of state. At a dinner in Basel, fourteen people from twelve nations, speaking two languages without realizing which; this is quite different from the 1930s, the era of Schacht and Norman; more like a meeting of kings before 1914.' 'A state already exists. Environmental law raises the question, whose environment? and what is the European interest? If a game exists, then the state exists and a state interest.

But it is much more diverse than nation states, and in theory reversible . . . the game is also more haphazard than on the national level, which has been structured over a long period.'²²

If a game which is common to all twentieth-century industrial nations exists in the European Union, then the Community's informal statehood must develop further. It also shares, in whole or in part, formal state attributes such as the right to issue and defend the currency, to prescribe and enforce laws, to govern with due authority, and – in embryo only – to defend itself and its members. This is not to deny that at present all these depend to a great extent on member states' approval and execution. In addition, the EU possesses some institutions which are analogous those of the state: Directorates and civil servants, judges and courts, Parliament, competition and fraud detection agencies. Ber Borochev argued about Zionism, decades before Israel came into being, that a state could exist without a country on the basis of ethnic and religious identity, law, custom and historical memory. The EU possesses much of this, based on a mediaeval history, five hundred years more recent than the Jewish kingdom extinguished by the Emperor Titus. Some would call the EU's tendency to vague declarations and imprecise competences mediaeval, in contrast to nineteenth-century clarity of contract law.

But the EU is an Enlightenment, rather than a mediaeval artefact, owing more to the triumph of reason over nature than the reverse. It rests on a legal basis, its texts are legal, lawyers interleave even the informal bargaining, and its court is the only final arbiter. Unlike Borochev's vision, it has no archetype and is subject to no prophecy; neither does it have a sacred homeland – for its territory is extensible at the will of all current members, on conditions which only they can determine.

A national state, in Ralf Dahrendorf's far from pessimistic formulation,²³ is heterogeneous, based on common citizenship and, as opposed to an ethnic nation, can encompass a variety of cultures and even languages. The underlying question is whether this Europe, whose boundaries are likely to expand again at the turn of the century to include for the first time parts of Slavonic Europe, has the courage to make itself more of a nation state. As yet, the strongest advocates of the nation state's primacy are those who would limit the Community's capacity to do so; with reason, since there exists no convincing conceptual replacement for the nation state, short of an international polity.

Were the latter to exist, the individual citizen would be the subject of international law and could obtain redress where basic rights were violated. It may be that over time the ECJ's judgments will contribute to that end. But for the present and the immediate future the EU is a state not only without a country but without a public, because there is no evidence that a European public or public opinion is coming into being as a political phenomenon. What does exist is more of a cultural and consumer identity. Neither do EU institutions demonstrate much interest in creating or educating such a public, although virtually all the players, at all levels, compete by declamation to define what they refer to as the 'European public interest'.

Current debates about the Community emphasize that, whatever descriptive phrase is used, it is a semi-developed political system. But since the Union has no precisely defined end, this is a tautology. Easier to argue is that its informal side can also be creative and that it has elements of statehood which have grown faster since about 1985 than in earlier decades. Yet the Community is also evidently an inter-governmental mechanism for managing economic interdependence;[24] what one Danish observer calls 'efficient cooperation on certain topics, as necessary'.[25]

The view that the EU is a mechanism for modifying what exists in accordance with what its members agree to want over long periods of time is preferable: firstly, as is clear from recent history, member states will not permit otherwise; secondly, the dense richness of material resists any alternative. In its public rhetoric the EU, or its spokesmen, therefore tend to lay down large principles and wait for the texts to fructify, often years later. But at the same time, in the developed world generally, the national state is under a severe process of attrition, eroded by forms of regionalism at one end and weighed down by the power of global markets at the other; both being very much more effective solvents of national singularity than they were during the EEC's infancy. What hopes member states have in the 1990s of managing contemporary Europe's open diversity can only be in tune with what international trade and money markets permit.

This has affected one aspect of the EU's critics since 1991, from Denmark to Britain and back to Austria and Norway. As the ERM crises continue to demonstrate, short of EMU there is not much refuge for currencies; nor does GATT/WTO offer much protection to beleaguered national film and television production companies. Among fifteen states, even the Franco-German entente has less power than formerly. In practice the German CDU proposals for much-enhanced political union and a 'joint Franco-German Presidency' in 1994–5 have come to very little, barely more than the largely academic enthusiasm vested in regionality.

One test of whether the centre of gravity has shifted away from the nation state will come with stage three of EMU, and whether it is presented in the late 1990s as a largely-technical consequence of the Single European Act or as a third pillar in its own right, profoundly curbing member states' sovereignty. Until now, governments have tolerated extensions of the Community's *acquis* because their domestic and international contexts pointed the balance of advantage that way. Like the current state of scholarship on the subject of human evolution, the EU's history is more a matter of fits and starts, conforming to climate and economic geography, than Darwin's grand evolutionary progression.

Yet governments are not always the chief arbiters, whatever the case was at Maastricht. That triumph for the inter-governmental cartel was followed by a reaction, not of the hypothetical European public but national ones. If electorates object, through their votes or by more direct action, as sections of the Italian, Spanish and French publics have on recent occasions, individuals may recapture the sense of making their own history. If, at the time of writing, the Chirac presidency bends to public outcry about wages and unemployment, it will inevitably undermine the *franc fort*, erasing eight years of patient effort, leaving EMU, even on German terms, consigned to a remoter future.

Statehood grows from below as well as from above. So far, it has been the national publics which have been the most notable absentees from the formal system, save at elections for the Parliament, and from the competitive symposium, out of ignorance, indifference, or preoccupation, in Guizot's phrase, with enriching themselves. Were they to become habitual rather than sporadic players, at regional as well as national level, they would change the very nature of the European game in a way similar to the accommodations by nation state polities to the twentieth-century advent of mass society.

But the Community is not a democracy and, in the form which had evolved by the late 1960s, was not meant to be. It was taken for granted in practice by the main players, if not in their public statements, that leadership could be provided only by a European elite drawn from national elites, which would work in relative obscurity, unanswerable to national electorates – platonic guardians of the new commonwealth in constant competition with the governments of the day.

It can be argued that, given the multiple forms of representation which the other players have created for themselves, a broader sort of democracy has grown up since then (without the correlation of a corporative chamber which was fashionable in the 1920s). But the EEC/EC's institutions were never intended to act as arbiters of the democratic balance between players and their interests and governments – except insofar as they had the capacity to bring what officials saw as imbalances to media and national governments' notice in their public language. There is no standard to measure network activity on the Community stage, other than that it contributes to the agreed ends for which the Community exists. At national level, such networks have existed at least since the end of the nineteenth century, and the legitimacy debate has not succeeded in giving them a formal political dimension, other than in fascist regimes where they never actually worked. In member states, and hence in the Community, tri- or quadrilateral bargaining goes on in informal systems which are more or less pluralist and distinct from parliamentary 'politics', although the European Parliament has now entered this area of the game.[26]

Having no higher good than self-interest wrapped in a vague general interest in continuing the process with the least friction, the game among commercial and governmental players is almost impossible to explain, let alone justify to the various publics, and thus is rarely documented. The players being of different orders, status and power, do not naturally work together well in formal contexts, such as development councils or Ecosoc, whose value depends on whether the ultimate decision-makers are minded or not to listen. The substantive criteria for their influence with the same decision-makers are mutual advantage, greater efficiency of transaction and greater harmony. The price is invariably that decisions come no faster than the collectivity of players allows. But since there is as yet no European public, and the Commission is not competent to declare the ultimate interest (beyond giving a coherent view of medium-term projects and desirable additions to the *acquis*),[27] the European interest can only be the sum of all that these players desire, mediated by their competition (which excludes what is not acceptable to the majority that exists on any given issue).

All that the authorities, the Council, the Commission and the Directorates can do to alter the outcome is to temper the wind of competition to the deprived region, the unprivileged minority interest, the weaker or backward power, using the small percentage of member states' total revenue assigned to Community use, half of which is still swallowed up by the Common Agricultural Programme.[28] More significantly, however, they have to decide how to try to regulate the informal sphere, privileging certain players and appeasing certain interests on one hand and enforcing strict competition on the other, in the hope of fostering the political market as well as encouraging economic adaptation. There is neither a Basic Law nor perfect competition in the informal sphere: political problems which national governments cannot or will not treat are reflected backwards onto the Community and the players themselves.

A former British Cabinet minister put it this way: 'There is a democratic deficit and evidence of elite rule. But if you recognize the Community as something unprecedented, not to be compared with national governments (rather than seek, through federalism to make it compatible), it emerges, correctly, as a negotiated area where accountability is to the players, and the test of legitimacy is what the players will accept . . .'.[29] A French central banker put a similar point, but rather differently: 'Europe is a system of law and rights, not yet a political system. Those who claim a right have powerful instruments to make it effective; but the instruments for political action are weak, and there is a dangerous mistrust of them and reliance on juridical action.'[30]

Insofar as the EU's informal politics address the issue of legitimacy, they concentrate on humanizing rather than regulating change, especially in the labour market, so that future social policy is likely to facilitate economic migration and adaptation to enforced change, easing the pain by allowing individuals to carry with them their entitlements, and providing new forms of training. Beyond that there remains the Delors project for aiding the 'socially excluded'; and, in the formal sense, the Maastricht Treaty's clauses enhancing what until 1991 had been very limited categories of citizenship.

That Treaty's intention was that the European Parliament should remedy the widespread perception of democratic deficit. But Delors himself admitted that Europe began as an elitist project in which all that was required was to convince the decision-makers. Even if that 'phase of benign despotism' is now over, it has not been replaced by something remotely resembling parliamentary democracy. During his tenure of office, Delors also declared that he personally was not in favour of opening the Council's debates to public scrutiny: 'if meetings were made public, every participant will speak with journalists in mind. Dynamic *compromises* [author emphasis] will be harder to find.'[31] Despite the numbers of draft constitutions for Europe since the Draft Treaty on Union in 1984, Maastricht itself was negotiated by member governments in secret, according to each one's perception of its national interest. Yet the effects of what has been done since 1985 will affect the social development of all its 370 million inhabitants for the foreseeable future.

A state may conceivably have citizens, even if it lacks territorial identity and public. So far European citizenship has been very limited in scope and construed largely in socio-economic terms – work or mobility. Yet true citizenship is a full system of rights, protection and participation. What exists in 1995 – specific rights to domicile, participation in EU or local elections, petition and recourse – seems to be a parallel citizenship, common to all nationalities but distinct from them, as a person may be Christian but affiliate to any one of many denominations. This appears able to provide only a 'disjointed pluralism . . . characterized by a profound absence of hierarchy and monopoly, among a wide variety of players of different but uncertain status – "rich in civil rights, poor in political rights, and with very little of what T. H. Marshall called 'social rights'"'.[32]

Subsidiarity, the concept which might regulate both the relations between informal players and the rights of individuals at different levels, is foreign to many legal systems but present in almost all federal constitutions. It is embodied in the 1957 Treaty (Article 36.2) and is in theory justiciable (Article 190). Yet it is ill-defined, and the case which would elicit an ECJ judgment has yet to be brought, despite the Single European Act's extension of it to environmental issues. The Commission has prudently not been tempted to try to alter member state basic competences and could probably never do more than assess what was effective or not where non-exclusive competences were concerned. Regions may be the area where practice may exhume some general principles, since it is unlikely that a national court will seek advice on something self-evidently appropriate to a member state's supreme tribunal. If so, the Committee of Regions is a most tentative way of proceeding. But then subsidiarity, if ever justiciable, has a disturbing obverse. It could be the basis of endless spoiling tactics by regions, especially German *Länder* whose subsidiarity is already enshrined in the Basic Law, and possibly – as in Belgium – by ethnic groups.[33]

Individuals, nevertheless, build the European Union, whether acting as members of groups, associations, or commercial interests at one end, or as Community officials at the other.[34] A Commissioner's oath to serve European interests as a whole is not a small matter, and the Commission itself acts as a *noyau*, an enforced community. At all levels, as a certain mutual understanding spreads among them, different players become sucked into a high-level assimilation or *engrenage*,[35] where commonalty or the capacity for joint management may grow up, as the legacy of Pope Gregory VII was translated into the high mediaeval system of government and law, to whose Curia Europeans naturally turned for redress, accepting papal claims to be the 'universal ordinary' or bishop of all.

Put in a rather different way, what Wolfgang Wessels calls 'the state-like political-administrative system' has developed *pari passu* with that of the leading western European states since the Second World War.[36] All have been locked into a condition of increasing interdependency since the collapse of Bretton Woods in 1971–2 and the first oil crisis, but especially since it became clear in the early 1990s that few if any member states could continue to satisfy their publics' expectations of their welfare provision.

All nation states' increasing post-1970 rate of failure, in terms of what governments declare to their electorates they can achieve, goes some way to explain why member states in general unburden themselves onto the Community, in order to achieve, in a coordinated, relatively low cost fashion (for example through the internal market) the adjustment of their economies (and ultimately no doubt their social systems) which they fear to do individually. In this way, indirectly, governments foster the embryo state or 'state in being', hoping that the Community can remedy what in their eyes is an inadmissible want of power, confronted with global forces; the alternative is to present their electorates with evidence of state failure, or a 'new right' withdrawal from the arena entirely. Avid to take up every chance to increase their competence, the EU institutions, led by the Commission, attempt to fulfil twin roles, as scapegoat for them, and *deus ex machina* to help them do what they would, but dare not.

Whether the Community can work in this way is no clearer than is the future of EMU or political union in 1995. The very concept of a 'state without a country' denotes something novel and indeterminate. The Community's statehood has worked up until now; it is relatively efficient (not from the standpoint of the best, but from that of the average). Comparisons of how it is in 1995 with historic models of the nation state, even ones taken from 1957 or 1973, invite a category error; it will be what the players make of it, not what some prime mover declares, like a carpet weaver instructing his children in the proper numbers of knots to make a predetermined pattern, from a paper handed down through family tradition.

Because formal and informal sides have generally complemented each other, and because the result has been adequate to keep the majority of players' interests engaged, the Community has at least kept under control the worst of Europe's problems of economic and social adjustment during the transition from national post-War settlements during the age of global competition which began in the mid-1970s. Whether it can continue to contain the deepest rooted problems in the late 1990s, let alone those of the twenty-first century, defies prediction.

It is possible that the EU's looming crises, the 1996 IGCs' encounter with institutional reform, extension to eastern Europe, CFSP and the interior ministry questions, will turn out to be no graver than the problems of 1974, which seemed insuperable to observers at the end of 1973. There is no reason intrinsic to the EU why the universal crisis of welfare expectancy and ageing populations cannot be mitigated, collectively, over the next decade; structural unemployment may not run on longer than it did in the 1930s. Furthermore the Community may be able to provide the politico-economic context in which the fiscal-political crises in Italy, Belgium and Greece, among long-standing members, and Sweden and Finland among new entrants, can be solved. Put bluntly, one useful function of a political elite is to be able to see a little way into the future and in this case discern what John Gray has called the malady of infinite aspiration, 'the groundless conviction that our species is exempt from the natural constraints that govern every other species of which we have knowledge'.[37]

If this does happen, it will not be because of formulae, federal, confederal or intergovernmental, but because the majority of interests find common cause to support solutions, as they did in the mid-1980s, when the internal market took final shape. It is hard from the standpoint of British political life, a hall with many windows (most of them fitted with mirrors instead of transparent glass), to realize how great a mental, even *psychological* investment has been made by industry, commerce and finance in all the member states, including Britain, in an economic integration accompanied by a liberal regulatory regime, which carries on its back further social and political possibilities to mitigate what would otherwise be unacceptable consequences. Contrary to right-wing fantasies in Britain and the United States, this has the support of American, Japanese, Korean and south-east Asian multinationals' direct investment.

Yet from such sources, in every single member state, come ancestral voices prophesying disaster to the national identity.[38] They have one strong point: it is too easy simply to assert that the cultural dimension can somehow be separated from the political and economic ones, in order to allow the latter to exist in their own dimension. It may also be too simple to think that the symbols of national sovereignty will be enough to mobilize popular consent for the consequences of European integration when their reality has been eviscerated. On the other hand, national identities have to be rediscovered in the wake of the Cold War, the re-formation of middle Europe, and Germany's unification; that elemental problem would be working itself out whatever governments were in power, whatever the EU did, profoundly affecting north–south divisions in Europe and the nature of the Franco-German entente.

In political and economic terms, it is not unreasonable to forecast that, whether or not monetary union comes about in the form prescribed at Maastricht, political authority will centre for the next decade on the hard core of currencies attached to the deutschmark. This, in conjunction with Germany's new natural authority on the Council, presents problems (in no special order) for the Netherlands, Denmark, Britain, Austria and Italy, as well as the most obvious candidate France, whose long dominance of the Union's political evolution is threatened to an unprecedented degree – as the Mitterrand administration's silent response to the 1994 CDU proposals about Europe's future demonstrated.

The Community is at present confronted by several sorts of nationalism in wider Europe, each as likely to prejudice integration as their predecessors were in the 1920s: among political groups, usually on the extreme right, in certain regions, and in an inchoate form among whole publics confused by a search for national identity more unsettling than any which has been experienced in the memory of people younger than ninety. This is the EU's current ideological burden, not class divisions or conflict between rival capitalisms. If the epigraph at the beginning of this book is to have again the resonance that it had during the Enlightenment, if there is to be a European common culture, the EU's institutions have to contain these nationalisms in forms which allow them to develop fruitfully but without the sort of conflicts which have erupted in three great waves since the 1890s.

Europeans have a great twentieth-century reservoir of experience about what not to do. The Community may not be the best possible organization but, like democracy, it is what we have and so far has proved better than any of the alternatives. It is a central argument here that the economic players' involvement and commitment provides it with stability and a safeguard against extremism which should be welcomed not deplored as if it were somehow undemocratic.

The Community is at best slow moving and liable to protectionism, rarely more than the sum of its members' interests; but it has so far been a reasonably efficient vehicle for the things its members require – which is itself a characteristic of successful states. There is already a danger, however, in that member states (and the national media that reflect their preconceptions) tend more than in the past to blame it for what are at best joint failures: the Gulf War, the Yugoslav civil wars, high unemployment. The scapegoat function is a useful tool in the game, but since member states' own networks and responsibilities extend to the heart of it, their fault remains, and in the long run may discredit them and increase disillusion with all political enterprises.

It is in member states' own interests for their creation, the EU, to function well. Whenever it does, the lineaments of its statehood become a little clearer. Their self-interest indicates that because they alone can no longer furnish the prosperity and happiness which their citizens demand, integration should imply the evolution of the European state; the EU, as Alan Milward puts it, is the rescuer of the nation state.[39] Such rescues alter those who are saved.

The game of solving problems in competition and in common will naturally continue. The networks examined here may or may not deepen but they will increase their scope, and become more complex. They will help to open up sheltered areas and in the future reopen ones that have yet to close. As in all political changes, the outer layers of the onion become dry and need peeling away. The fusion of formal and informal will become more subtle and at the same time more exposed to public debate. The informal will be forced to show itself acceptable and even become, perhaps in some as yet unheard-of way, accountable; but only when there is a public informed enough to require it to be so.

NOTES

INTRODUCTION

1. Robert Brenner: *Merchants and Revolution* (Princeton: 1993).
2. Whether the intensity of a firm's effort derives from its long-term commitment to the EU or its prudent policy of taking out political insurance depends on its circumstances at any one time and the availability of rewards or means to shape the legal, regulatory environment. A permanent, influential presence is expensive, time-consuming and requires special skills and personnel.
3. FR79, (GR11), p. 3. 'There is a tendency to progressive convergence as they work together.'
4. FR10, p. 1.
5. I have followed Anthony Seldon's useful classification in *Elite Oral History* (1983) which is still the best survey. But see also Paul Thompson, *The Voice of the Past: The Historian and Oral History* (2nd edn. 1988).

CHAPTER ONE

1. The best textbook surveying the events in this chapter is P. Gerbet, *La Construction de L'Europe* (2nd edn, Paris: 1994). The structure of much of this chapter was derived from a report prepared for the European Commission which was written together with Daniel Barbezat and Wendy Asbeek Brusse and with the assistance of Rik Schreurs.
2. P-H. Spaak, *Combats inachevés*, (2 vols, Paris: 1970/71); J. Monnet, *Mémoires* (Paris: 1976); E. Hirsch, *Ainsi va la vie* (Lausanne: 1988); R. Marjolin, *Le travail d'une vie* (Paris: 1986); C. Pineau and C. Rimbaud, *Le grand pari, l'aventure du traité de Rome* (Paris: 1991); P. Pflimlin, *Mémoires d'une Européen, de la IVe à la Ve Republique* (Paris: 1991); P. Uri, *Penser pour l'action: un fondateur de l'Europe* (Paris: 1991).
3. S. Hoffmann, 'Obstinate or Obsolete? The Fate of the Nation State and the Case of Western Europe' in *Daedalus: Journal of the American Academy of Arts and Sciences*, 95, 3 (1966), pp. 863–915.
4. See introductory chapters in A. S. Milward, *The European Rescue of the Nation State* (London: 1992), and A. S. Milward (ed.), *The Frontiers of National Sovereignty* (London: 1993).
5. For recent surveys, see A. S. Milward, *The Reconstruction of Western Europe, 1945–1951* (London: 2nd edn. 1994) and H. van der Wee, *Prosperity and Upheaval: The World Economy, 1944–1980* (Berkeley: 1987).
6. W. A. Brown, *The United States and the Restoration of World Trade: An Analysis and Appraisal of the ITO Charter and the General Agreement on Tariffs and Trade* (Washington: 1950); R. Gardner, *Sterling–Dollar*

Diplomacy. Anglo-American Collaboration in the Reconstruction of Multilateral Trade (Oxford: 1956).

7. See A. S. Milward, *The Reconstruction of Western Europe, 1945–1951* (London: 1984).

8. The following provide different perspectives on the origins and functioning of the Marshall Plan: A. Carew, *Labour under the Marshall Plan: The politics of productivity and the marketing of management science* (Manchester: 1987); D. W. Ellwood, *Rebuilding Europe: Western Europe, America and Postwar Reconstruction* (London: 1992); M. J. Hogan, *The Marshall Plan: America, Britain, and the Reconstruction of Western Europe, 1947–1952* (New York, Cambridge: 1987); C. L. Mee, *The Marshall Plan: The Launching of the Pax Americana* (New York: 1984); Milward, *The Reconstruction*; I. Wexler, *The Marshall Plan Revisited: The European Recovery Programme in Economic Perspective* (Westport: 1983).

9. J. B. de Long & B. Eichengreen, 'The Marshall Plan: history's most sucessful structural adjustment program' in R. Dornbusch *et al* (eds), *Postwar Economic Reconstruction and Lessons for the East Today* (Cambridge: 1991), pp. 189–230; B. Eichengreen and M. Uzan, 'The Marshall Plan: Economic Effects and Implications for Eastern Europe and the former USSR' in *Economic Policy*, 14 (1991), pp. 13–76; A. S. Milward, 'Was the Marshall Plan Necessary?' in *Diplomatic History*, 13, 2 (1989), pp. 231–53.

10. The 'official' study is J. Kaplan and G. Schleiminger, *The European Payments Union-Financial Diplomacy in the 1950s* (Oxford: 1989). See also M. Dickhaus, 'It is only the provisional that lasts: The European Payments Union' in R. T. Griffiths (ed.), *Explorations in OEEC History* (Paris: 1995); W. Diebold, *Trade and Payments in Western Europe: A Study in Economic Cooperation, 1947–1951* (New York: 1952); B. Eichengreen, *Reconstructing Europe's trade and payments: The European Payments Union* (Manchester: 1993); Milward, *The Reconstruction of Western Europe, 1945–1951*.

11. W. Asbeek Brusse, *West European Tariff Plans 1947–1957: From Study group to Common Market*, EUI Ph.D (Florence: 1991); Brown, *The United States*; W. Diebold, *The End of the ITO* (Princeton: 1952); K. Kock, *International Trade Policy and the GATT, 1947–1967* (Stockholm: 1969).

12. H. Brugmans, *Prophètes et fondateurs de l'Europe* (Bruges: 1974). See also the four volumes in the series by W. Lipgens (ed.), *Documents on the History of European Integration*, (Berlin/New York: 1985–91), as well as the voluminous works on Spinelli and the Italian federalists but especially S. Pistone (ed.), *L'idea dell'unificazione europea dalla prima alla seconda guerra mondiale* (Turin: 1975).

13. See the works of D. Preda, especially, *Sulla Soglia dell' Unione* (Milan: 1994); *Storia di una speranza. La battaglia per la CED e la Federazione Europea nella carte della delegazione italiana (1950–1952)* (Milan: 1990), and 'De Gasperi, Spinelli e l'articolo 38 della CED' in *Il Politico*, 4 (1989).

14. See articles by A. J. Boekestijn and T. E. Mommens in R. T. Griffiths (ed.), *The Netherlands and the Integration of Europe, 1945–1957* (Amsterdam: 1989); A. E. Kersten, *Maken drie kleinen een grote? De politieke invloed van Benelux 1945–1955*

(Bussum: 1982); J. E. Meade (ed.), *Case Studies in European Economic Union: The Mechanics of Integration* (London: 1962); M. Wiesglas, *Benelux. van nabuurstaten tot uniepartners* (Amsterdam, Brussels: 1949).

15. R. T. Griffiths and F. M. B. Lynch, 'L'échec de la "Petite Europe": le Conseil Tripartite, 1944–1948' in *Revue d'Histoire de la Deuxieme guerre mondiale et des Conflicts Contemporains*, 152 (1988), pp. 39–62.

16. P. Guillen, 'Le projet d'union économique entre la France, l'Italie et le Benelux' in R. Poidevin (ed.), *Origins of the European Integration, March 1948–May 1950* (Brussels, Baden-Baden, Paris, Milan: 1986); E. Serra, 'L'union doganale italofrancese e la conferenza di Santa Margherita' in *Italia e Francia, 1946–1954* (Milan: 1989), pp. 73–114.

17. R. T. Griffiths and F. M. B. Lynch, 'L'échec de la "Petite Europe": les negociations Fritalux/Finebel, 1949–1950' in *Revue Historique*, 274 (1985), pp. 159–189; Guillen, 'Le projet d'union économique'.

18. W. Diebold, *The Schuman Plan: A Study in Economic Cooperation, 1950–1959* (New York: 1959); J. Gillingham, *Coal, Steel, and the Rebirth of Europe, 1945–55* (Cambridge, 1991); K. Schwabe (ed.), *The Beginnings of the Schuman-Plan* (Brussels, Paris, Baden-Baden, ilan: 1988); R. Poidevin, *Robert Schuman, homme d'Etat 1886–1963* (Paris: 1986); D. Spierenberg and R. Poidevin, *Histoire de la Communauté européenne du charbon et de l'acier, une expérience supranationale* (Brussels: 1993).

19. For the functioning of the ECSC, see Diebold, *The Schuman Plan*; E. Haas, *The Uniting of Europe. Political, Social*

and Economic Forces, 1950–1957 (Stanford: 1958); Gillingham, *Coal, Steel*; Milward, *The European Rescue*; J-M. Palayret, 'Jean Monnet, la haute Autorité de la CECA face au problème de la reconcentration de la sidérurgie dans la Ruhr (1950–1958)' in *Revue d'Histoire Diplomatique*, (1991), pp. 308–48; Spierenberg and Poidevin, *Histoire*.

20. There is a large literature on this topic but see especially A. Vasori, *Il Patto di Bruxelles (1948): tra integrazione europea e alleanza atlantica* (Rome: 1990).

21. See T. P. Ireland, *Creating the Entangling Alliance: The Origins of the North Atlantic Treaty Organization*, (Westport: 1981); L. S. Kaplan, *The United States and NATO: The Formative Years* (Kentucky UP: 1984); *NATO and the United States: The Enduring Alliance* (Boston, 1988); M. P. Leffler, *A preponderance of power: national security, the Truman administration and the Cold War* (Stanford: 1992); J. Smith (ed.), *The Origins of NATO* (Exeter: 1990).

22. Another area with a huge literature but see P. Guillen, 'Les chefs militaires français: Le réarmement de Allemagne et la CED, 1950–1954' in *Revue d'histoire de la deuxième guerre mondiale*, 33, 129 (1983), pp. 3–33; P. Melandri, 'Les Etats-Unis et le plan Pleven: Octobre 1950 – Juillet 1951' in *Relations Internationales*, 11 (1977), pp. 201–29; R. Poidevin, 'La France devant le problème de la CED: incidences nationales et internationales, été 1951 à été 1953' in *Revue d'histoire de la deuxième guerre mondiale* 33, 129 (1983), pp. 35–57; V. E. Volkmann and W. Schwengler (eds), *Die Europäische Verteidigungsgemeinschaft: Stand und Probleme der*

Forschung (Boppard am Rhein: 1985).

23. A. Clesse, *Le projet de C.E.D. du Plan Pleven au 'crime' du 30 aout: Histoire d'un malentendu européen* (Baden-Baden: 1989); E. Fursdon, *The European Defence Community: A History* (London: 1979); L. Kollner (eds.), *Anfaenge westdeutscher Sicherheitspolitik 1945–1956: Die EVG-Phase* (Munich: 1990); B. Thoss and H. E. Volkmann (eds), *Sicherheits – und Deutschlandpolitik der Bundesrepublik im Maechtesystem der Jahre 1953–1956* (Boppard am Rhein: 1988); Volkmann and Schwengler (eds), *Die Europäische Verteidigungsgemeinschaft*.

24. R. Cardozo, 'The Project for a Political Community (1952–54)' in R. Pryce (ed.), *The Dynamics of European Union* (London, Sydney, New York: 1987), pp. 49–77; R. T. Griffiths, 'Europe's First Constitution: The European Political Community, 1952–1954' in S. Martin (ed.), *The Construction of Europe. Essays in Honour of Emile Noël* (Dordrecht, Boston, London: 1994), pp. 17–39. See also the essays in G. Trausch (ed), *Die Europaeische Integration vom Schuman-Plan bis zu den Vertraegen von Rom* (Baden-Baden, Milan, Paris, Brussels: 1993).

25. R. T. Griffiths, 'The Beyen Plan' in Griffiths (ed.), *The Netherlands and the Integration of Europe, 1945–1957* (Amsterdam: 1990).

26. P. Gerbet, *La naissance du Marché Commun* (Brussels: 1987); H-J. Küsters, *Die Gründung der europäischen Wirtschaftsgemeinschaft* (Baden-Baden: 1982) and articles in E. Serra, *The Relaunching of Europe and the Treaties of Rome* (Milan, Paris, Baden-Baden, Brussels: 1986).

27. P. Weilemann, *Die Anfaenge der Europäische Atomgemeinschaft: zur Gruendungsgeschichte von EURATOM, 1955–957* (Baden-Baden: 1983).

28. Griffiths, 'The Beyen Plan'.

29. Griffiths, *The Netherlands*; Kuesters, *Die Gründung*; Milward, *The European Rescue*; Milward (ed.), *The Frontiers*; Serra, *The Relaunching*.

30. For the UK policy at this time see S. Burgess and E. Edwards, 'The Six plus One: British Policy-making and the question of European economic integration, 1955' in *International Affairs*, 64, 3 (1988), pp. 393–413; R. T. Griffiths, 'La dinamica dell'inertia politica. La partecipazione ed il ritiro del Regno Unito nella conferenza Spaak, 1955–1956' in E. Decleva and A. Magliazza (eds), *Diplomazia e storia delle relazioni internazionali. Studi in onore di Enrico Serra* (Milan: 1991), pp. 677–97; J. W. Young, '"The Parting of the Ways"?: Britain, the Messina Conference and the Spaak Committee, June-December 1955' in M. Dockrill and J. W. Young (eds) *British Foreign Policy, 1945–56* (Basingstoke: 1989), pp. 197–224; Young, *Britain and European Unity, 1945–1992* (London: 1993).

CHAPTER TWO

1. The best textbook surveying the events in this chapter is P. Gerbet, *La Construction de L'Europe* (2nd edn, Paris: 1994).

2. The chapter was written with research assistance from Monika Dickhaus and Stuart Ward.

3. P. du Bois (ed.), *EFTA from Yesterday to Tomorrow* (Geneva: 1987); M. Camps, *Britain and the European Community, 1955–1963* (London:

1964); R. T. Griffiths, 'The Failure of the Wider European Free Trade Area' in *EFTA Bulletin* 3/91 (1991); J. W. Young, *Britain and the Unity of Europe* (London: 1993).

4. Du Bois, *EFTA From Yesterday to Tomorrow*; Camps, *Britain and the European Communities*; R. T. Griffiths, 'The Importance of Fish in the Creation of EFTA' in *EFTA Bulletin* 1/92 (1992).

5. For an outline of EFTA's provisions see V. Curzon, *The Essentials of Economic Integration: Lessons of EFTA Experience* (London: 1974); F. V. Meyer, *The Seven: A Provisional Appraisal of the European Free Trade Association* (London: 1960); G. D. N. Worswick (ed.), *The Free Trade Proposals* (Oxford: 1960).

6. L. Lindberg, *The Political Dynamics of European Economic Integration* (Stanford: 1963).

7. G. Barclay, *Commonwealth or Europe?* (Quebec: 1970).

8. For archive-based studies, see A. Horne, *Macmillan, 1957–1986* (London: 1989); R. T. Griffiths and S. Ward (eds), *Courting the Common Market. The First Membership Applications and the French veto* (London: 1995). For more traditional accounts see, N. Beloff, *The General Says No: Britain's Exclusion from Europe* (London: 1963); Camps, *Britain and the European Community*; W. Jeserich, *Die Konflikt zwischen EWG und EFTA: Ein Kapitel aus Grossbritanniens Europapolitik* (Cologne: 1963); E. Jouve, *Le Général de Gaulle et la construction de l'Europe, 1940–66* (Paris: 1967); K. Kaiser, *EWG und Freihandelszone, England und der Kontinent in der europaeischen Integration* (Leiden: 1963); J. Newhouse, *De Gaulle and the Anglo-Saxons* (London: 1970).

9. See Griffiths and Ward, *Courting the Common Market*; T. Miljan, *The Reluctant Europeans: The Attitudes of the Nordic Countries towards European Integration* (London: 1977).

10. E. Barnavi and S. Friedländer, *La Politique étrangère du général de Gaulle* (Geneva: 1985); S. J. Bodenheimer, *Political Union. A Microcosm of European Politics, 1960–1966* (Leiden: 1967); P. Gerbet, 'The Fouchet Plan' in R. Pryce (ed.), *The Dynamics of European Union* (London: 1987); Jouve, *Le Général de Gaulle*; L. Pattison de Ménil, *Who Speaks for Europe? The Vision of Charles de Gaulle* (London: 1977); A. Silj, *Europe's Political Puzzle: A Study of the Fouchet Negotiations and the 1963 Veto* (Cambridge, Mass.: 1967).

11. For the record, he cited the first Delors Commission as the second example.

12. J. Paxton, *The developing Common Market* (London: 1976); D. Swann, *The Economics of the Common Market* (London: 1970); H. von der Groeben, *Aufbaujahre der Europaeischen Gemeinschaft – Das Ringen um den Gemeinsamen Markt und die Politische Union (1958–1966)* (Baden-Baden: 1982).

13. For the List G problem see T. Rhenish, *Die Deutsche Industrie und die gruendung der Europaeischen Wirtschaftsgemeinschaft*, EUI Ph.D (Florence: 1994).

14. G. P. Casadio, *Transatlantic trade. USA-EEC confrontation in the GATT negotiations* (Dordrecht: 1973); G. Curzon and V. Curzon, 'The Management of trade relations in the GATT' in A. Shonfield (ed.), *International economic relations of the Western world 1959–1971* (London: 1976). K. Kock, *International Trade Policy and the GATT 1947–1967*

(Stockholm: 1969). For the first archive based study, see the article by Y. Alkema in D. Brinkley and R. T. Griffiths (eds), *Kennedy and Europe* (Louisiana: 1995).

15. C. Cosgrove-Twitchett, *Europe and Africa* (Farnborough: 1978); W. Feld, *The European Community in World Affairs* (1976); H. Hasenpflug, 'Ausgestaltung und handelspolitische Wirkungen der EG-Assoziierungs- und Praeferenzpolitik' in T. M. Loch (ed), *Die Assoziierungs- und Praeferenzpolitik der EG* (Bonn: 1974); J. Moss, *The Yaounde Convention 1964–75*, Ph.D (1978).

16. The first archive based study is A. Burger, *Voor Boerenvolk en Vaderland. De vorming van het EEG-landbouwbeleid, 1959–1966* (Amsterdam: 1993). See also, S. Harris (ed.), *The Food and Farm Policies of the European Community* (Chichester: 1983); J. Marsh and C. Ritson, *Agricultural Policy and the Common Market* (London: 1971) and the articles by A. Fearne and C. Saunders in C. Ritson (ed), *The Common Agricultural Policy and the World Economy* (Oxford: 1991).

17. S. Mansholt, 'The promised land for a Community' in C. Barber (ed.), *European Community, Vision and Reality* (London: 1973); OECD, *Agricultural policy of the EEC* (Paris: 1974).

18. T. Josling and S. Harris, 'Europe's Green Money' in *The Three Banks Review* (1976).

19. H. Corbet and D. Robertson, *Europe's Free Trade Area Experiment; EFTA and Economic Integration* (Oxford, New York: 1970); V. Curzon, *The Essentials of Economic Integration: Lessons of EFTA Experience* (London: 1974).

20. D. Allen, 'Managing the Common Market. The Competition Policy' in H. Wallace, W. Wallace and C. Webb (eds), *Policy Making in the European Community* (Chichester: 1977); A. Cairncross (ed.), *Wirtschaftspolitik für Europa* (Munich: 1974); J. Davidow, 'EEC Fact Finding procedures in Competition Cases' in *Common Market Law Review*, 14 (1977); C. Layton, *Cross-Frontier Mergers in Europe* (Bath: 1971); D. Swann and D. L. McLachlan, *Competition policy in the European Community* (London: 1967); W. van Gerven, '12 years EEC competition law' in *Common Market Law Review*, 11 (1974).

21. C. D. Edwards, *Control of Cartels and Monopolies. An international comparison* (New York: 1967).

22. B. Balassa (ed.), *European economic integration* (Amsterdam: 1975); M. Davenport, 'The economic impact of the EEC' in A. Boltho (ed.), *The European economy* (Oxford: 1982); D. G. Mayes, 'The effects of economic integration on trade' in *Journal of Common Market Studies* (1978); W. Sellekaerts, 'How meaningful are empirical studies on trade creation and trade diversion?' in *Weltwirtschaftliches Archiv* (1973); P. J. Verdoorn and A. Schwartz, 'Two alternative estimates of the effects of EEC and EFTA on patterns of trade' in *European Economic Review* (1972).

23. Verdoorn and Schwartz, 'Two Alternative Estimates'; see also W. E. Prewo, 'Integration Effects in the EEC. An attempt at quantification in a general equilibrium framework' in *European Economic Review*, 5 (1974), pp. 379–405.

24. O. Emminger, *DM, Dollar, Waehrungskrisen* (Stuttgart: 1986); D. C. Kruse, *Monetary integration in*

Western Europe. EMU, EMS and beyond (London: 1980); P. Ludlow, *The making of the EMS: a case study of the politics of the EC* (London: 1982); D. Simard, *La France et la remise en cause du système Bretton Woods 1945–71. Colloque Ministère de l'économie, des finances et du budget* (Paris: 1992); B. Tew, *The evolution of the International Monetary System 1945–77* (London: 1977); L. Tsoukalis, *The politics and economics of European monetary integration* (London: 1977).

25. For example: in 1959, P. Wigny proposed an EEC Unit of Account; in 1959 the Parliament proposed a Reserve System; in 1961 the Monetary Committee named centralization of monetary decisions as a step forward and in 1962 the Commission submitted an Action Program for the second stage of the Common Market which also dealt with monetary integration.

26. Young, *Britain and European Unity*; S. George, *An Awkward Partner: Britain in the European Community* (Oxford: 1990); see also W. Brandt, *Aussenpoltik, Deutschlandpolitik, Europapolitik* (Berlin: 1968); C. Franck, 'New ambitions: From the Hague to Paris Summits (1969–72)' in Pryce (ed.), *The Dynamics of Europe*; E. A. Kolodziej, *French international policy under de Gaulle and Pompidou: the politics of grandeur* (Ithaca: 1974).

CHAPTER THREE

1. The Davignon Report (1972), represented a counterpoint, on behalf of smaller member states, to a decade of alliance mechanisms, large member states' jealousy about sovereignty, and an inbuilt tendency to regard economic matters as technical and subordinate, to the obvious detriment of EC institutions. Davignon proposed a non-binding agreement on political cooperation with no new institutions or legal formalities, but one which safeguarded small states against the sort of intergovernmental processes then taking place in the European Council. The informal practice he suggested, that the Council of Foreign Ministers and the Commission should discuss foreign policy issues, got no further until Pompidou had died and Jobert had been replaced as French foreign minister; but as changes in French politics opened up a previously-taboo area, it then grew into semi-formality, achieving genuine cooperation with officials. (c.f. S. Nuttall, *European Political Cooperation* (Oxford: 1992), pp. 45–55.)

2. KM95, p. 3.

3. This, despite George Thomson's efforts to recruit top civil servants, and Heath's promise that it would help rather than hinder their careers.

4. France withdrew its opposition, on condition that member states were left in control of their quotas. (c.f., R. Jenkins, *European Diary* (London: 1989), pp. 57–8). Regional policy was detached from competition, to stand on its own, with Thomson as Commissioner and Renato Ruggiero as Director General.

5. c.f., A. Pijpers *et al*, *European Political Cooperation in the 1980s* (Dordrecht: 1988), pp. 3–48, and S. Nuttall, *European Political Cooperation*, pp. 58–66, 116–17.

6. S. George, *An Awkward Partner: Britain in the European Community* (O.U.I.: 1990).

7. Henry Kissinger produced an alternative 'mutual insurance society' using OECD support funds, and denounced the Ecofin scheme (*Witteveen* II) as selling out to OPEC. (c.f., D. Healey, *The Time of My Life* (London: 1989), pp. 423–6).

8. For the period 1974–1977: Sterling-DM 6.05 to 4.03, Sterling-Dollar 2.34 to 1.75.

9. Demand over the period 1973–83 grew fastest in the areas of information technology, electrical and electronic goods, chemicals and pharmaceuticals; moderately in plastics, transport equipment, food processing, paper and machinery; more slowly in the metal industries, textiles and construction products. In almost every case however it remained weaker in the EC, stronger in the United States and stronger still in Japan (L. T. Katseli, 'The Political Economy of European Integration' in *International Spectator* XXIV (3/4 July-December 1989).

10. Roy Jenkins, Commission President, commented waspishly in 1978, 'the problem of relations with Austria is that they are at once outside the Community and a crossroads of the Community . . . perhaps we could give them some money to build a new autobahn.' (*European Diary*, p. 507).

11. *Viz* the 1975 ruling under Article 228 (1) that EC powers in matters covered by the Common Commercial Policy were exclusive.

12. c.f. Schmidt's speech (Bonn, 12 May 1977), in which he remarked that Jenkins wanted a Commission of twelve potential prime ministers, whereas they should be people 'who could never be Prime Ministers' (quoted in Jenkins's *European Diary*, p. 123). For the European Council,

see Simon Bulmer and Wolfgang Wessels, *The European Council* (Macmillan: 1987).

13. As was suggested in chapter 2, the early integrationists had given great weight to incorporation of organized interest groups. No supranational representation of industry and labour developed however, other than on Ecosoc which had become a largely ritualized forum. Certainly nothing included the financial sectors, apart from a brief period in the early 1970s. But until around 1974 a notional EC-wide tripartism, involving some Directorates and the Commission itself, was seen as a surrogate for the still absent 'European public' involvement. Developed *ad hoc*, with no claim to being based on equality of bargaining power, this system never approached the robustness of Swedish codetermination nor German *mitbestimmung*. Neither did the Commission officials encourage general interchanges, only links in particular policy areas where they needed information or expertise. This social sector thus developed in a similar way to others, where the Commission remedied its inadequacies, and put together agreed packages, *avant la lettre*, in a highly pluralistic arena. But 1973–5 brought such labour discontent, as inflation and unemployment struck together to produce stagflation, that these older arrangements offered no basis afterwards on which to establish an industrial programme for recovery. UNICE had existed since 1958, as had the Conference of Chambers of Commerce, and the BFE had represented banking since 1960; but ETUC was only set up in 1973. It was at this stage an ill-coordinated,

lightly staffed body, with not much greater weight than the sum of its national members. Ecosoc itself was simply not a body in which consensus could be bargained.

14. See W. Streeck & P. Schmitter, 'From National Corporatism to Transnational Pluralism: Organised Interests in the Single European Market' in *Politics and Society* (Vol. 19, No. 2, June 1991), pp. 133–164.

15. H. Wallace, W. Wallace, C. Webb (eds), *Policy-making in the European Community* (2nd edn, Chichester: 1983), p. 89.

16. The first occurred in April 1974 as a military coup by left-wing, middle-ranking officers; the second, as a restoration of civilian government, after a period of rule shared between the Armed Forces Movement and the Communist Party had ended in an abortive uprising in November 1975.

17. Spain had made approaches in 1962 and 1964, and though rebuffed, the technocrats in Franco's later governments did finally gain a rather limited preferential trade agreement in 1970. This benefited Spain more than the EC and hence inhibited further concessions; talks about a new agreement ended abruptly in 1975 in EC disgust at the execution of two ETA and three FRAP members. On Franco's death, 20 November 1975, the new king Juan Carlos pledged Spain to reinstate democracy, political parties and free elections.

18. R. Jenkins, *European Diary*, p. 200.

19. Spain's large agricultural sector threatened other Mediterranean producers, especially in southern France. Both Giscard and later Mitterrand used this to bargain a better CAP deal, in advance of accession,

for France's own farmers, until then less privileged than the grain and beef producers of northern Europe. The issue surfaced again in each election from 1978 to 1981 and spilled over into the fisheries arguments, since Spain's vast fleet amounted to 70% of the EC's total tonnage. (Poaching led to near hostilities between France and Spain in 1984.) Yet the EC's new 200-mile limit had effectively excluded them from most of the Mediterranean and much of the Atlantic. Spain, like Britain in the 1960s, also showed itself unwilling to accept France's pretensions to political leadership in the EC, and strongly resented France's refusal to extradite Basque terrorists, on grounds of political persecution – a dispute not resolved until 1984. Finally, as host to the largest number of Iberian migrant workers, France had no more desire than Germany had with Turkey to find Spanish and Portuguese entitled as citizens of the EC.

20. D. Healey, *The Time of My Life*, pp. 438–9.

21. At this stage, only West Germany and the Netherlands allowed free capital movements.

22. R. Jenkins, *European Diary*, p. 198.

23. The Soviet Union had just installed SS20 missiles in eastern Europe, to German dismay: part of the trade-off turned out to be the promise of Cruise missiles, installed as a counter-measure in NATO bases in Britain and the Netherlands.

24. These details were worked out between Bernard Clapier (Banque de France), and M. Schuman in the German Chancellery, with the Central Bank governors and the EC's Monetary Committee, in a remarkably cooperative atmosphere

among a core of experts insulated from most other aspects of EC politics, which in turn prefigured the Delors Committee 1988 (see p. 171)

25. Although Jenkins could not claim more than an animator's role in EMS, he had materially advanced the position of President, and represented the EC at the first Western Economic Summit, to Giscard's evident displeasure. For Jenkins's view of Giscard's determination to curb the Community's initiating role, see *European Diary*, p. 311.

26. c.f., Giscard's interview with *Der Spiegel*, 1 January 1979, where he spoke of his earlier thoughts about 'a united France in a confederal Europe', led by the European Council and an executive responsible to it, in a permanent inter-governmental partnership.

27. For Dell's account see 'Report of the Three Wise Men' in *Contemporary European History* (March 1994).

28. Britain and Italy were prepared to accept only one per member state, France was not.

29. In this quarrel the French Presidency played a conciliatory role, and won agreement from all the nine except the Netherlands (which continued to defend the Parliament's position) to an informal procedure for resolving such crises in the future.

30. By this time, the Eurocommunists' dream of linking with the Socialist Party's left in France, Spain, Portugal and Italy to form a broad political front had evaporated.

31. This rose from twenty-one in the entire decade 1970–80 to fourteen in the four years after 1981. Yet the Court ruled that DG4 prosecutions were limited by national interest benefits: the difference made by the

Philip Morris case, 1981, lay in the fact that the law was clarified rather than made more stringent.

32. The case itself was not entirely simple: West Germany had excluded Cassis as a fortified wine falling between the wine and spirit categories, under the brandtwein monopoly. The judges may not fully have seen the significance of continued exceptions to their ruling, under Article 30. The *first* principle which the judges declared was that the Treaty recognized the rights of all members to defend their own urgent national needs, but they did not specify whether this was a basic right or a residual one (that is to say, did it precede the Community or was it merely contingent on it?) The ECJ subsequently backtracked on some of the principle in the *Niseme* case, firstly by not recognizing the Commission's own advisory council on food additives, secondly by putting the onus in public health cases on the Commission to prove the product was safe, rather than on the member state (in this instance the Netherlands) to prove it was unsafe. This and other qualifications had long consequences for further proceedings, for example on health and tax fraud, as well as more obvious areas such as environmental protection.

33. The grounds being that the beer had not been prepared according to German specifications, and that the mineral water bubbles helped kill off bacteria. (See ECJ judgment in the beer case, 1 September 1986, a valuable supplement to the Cassis principle of free circulation).

34. c.f., Commission Communication 2 October 1980 on the *Cassis de Dijon* implications (O.J. C256/2).

35. S. Nuttall, *op.cit*, pp. 149–81. In May 1981 France and Germany jointly raised a $6 billion loan bypassing the EC's credit institutions. To Italian and Benelux protests, Germany replied that it was tired of making excessive financial contributions, of Brussels' delays, and of EC chauvinism. While this mood owed much to disillusionment about the results of Germany's 1979 economic altruism, it showed that the 'European motor', as the Franco-German entente was often styled, was as ready as any to revert to 'un-European' behaviour.

36. Faced with the trade imbalance with Japan, the Council of Ministers issued a coded threat in December 1980 to take action if Japanese markets were not opened up to the EC; in May 1981 they focused on the export of cars and voluntary export restraints (VERs).

37. The EC cannot be said to have had an industrial policy in the early days of Customs Union: the first synoptic thinking came only with the Colonna memorandum in 1970, on which no action was taken.

38. The *Continental Can Company* case also revealed how hard it was to prove in law the way a market share operated; and the Court ruled against the Commission. Even the principle had not been established entirely, for as late as 1981 the Council objected to DG4 taking sole initiating powers under Article 86 in such a highly political area.

39. For this, see E. M. Milanesi, 'La Politica Industriale della CE, 1959–90' in *Acquisizioni, Fusioni e Concorrenza* (1992).

40. The ECJ's February 1983 list of offenders put Italy at the top with 29 breaches of obligation, followed by Belgium 6, UK 5, France 4, Ireland 3, West Germany, Denmark and the Netherlands 1 each. On the harmonization side, the EC council in December 1982 set a three-month deadline for 23 Directives on non-tariff barriers, principally in the car industry. It seemed a triumph for the Commission over sectional interests, won by using health, pollution, safety and technical norms. Yet it was frustrated, despite the German Presidency's efforts, because German free traders could not accept the trade-off that France required, i.e., heightened measures against non-EC countries' 'unfair trading'.

41. c.f., J. Pelkmans, L. A. Winters, H. Wallace, *Europe's Domestic Market* (RIIA 1988, Chatham House Paper 43).

42. France, Netherlands, Ireland, Greece, Denmark, Belgium, Ireland and Netherlands again, and Germany.

43. It also involved strengthening the ERM. The franc was to be stabilized in order to suppress inflation and aid fiscal discipline; henceforward, having been in effect a franc-led zone, the ERM would become a DM one.

44. Mitterrand's commitment to integration dated from the 1950s but had always been defined in a very French sense, in which French political leadership and France's interests (e.g., in Africa) were taken for granted. From the Common Programme in 1973 onwards, he had skilfully held a divergent Union of the Left together and could not at first abandon the promises made to CERES and the PCF: hence the two stages of June 1982, when he let Mauroy carry the blame, and

March 1983, when he himself took the lead.

45. Realignments in March and September 1981, January and June 1982, and finally and most contentiously March 1983.

46. c.f., H. Wallace & A. Ridley, 'Europe: the challenge of diversity' (RIIA 1985, Chatham House Paper 29).

47. It had been the rule since 1966 that Treaty of Rome rules applied to new policies unless a member state pleaded the Luxembourg Compromise (a rare occasion); but majority voting obtained where the policy framework had already been set. Over the period, where QMV operated, an informal process developed in which the mere suggestion of a vote was often enough to induce compromise. Conversely, as the British discovered in May 1982, the threat of a veto required careful preparation and construction of minority alliances.

48. In spite of the rebarbative tone of most British communications in this period, EC countries (even Italy, which had a large second generation emigrant population in the Argentine), gave some support to Britain in the 1982 Falklands War.

49. There was a limited number of exceptions, including Ford (Europe) which had had an office in Brussels since 1969 and Fiat which had evolved at the same time a European delegation responsible for the whole corporation, seeing the EC as a better guarantor of a stable environment for itself than Italy alone.

50. CBI archives, European Steering Committee, 1973–84 *passim*. (March 1982 (meeting with Narjes). That the CBI and the City of London had long been pressing for

action on non-tariff barriers and freedom for financial services is corroborated by Margaret Thatcher's memoirs; see *The Downing Street Years* (London: 1993), p. 553.

51. c.f. John Raisman's speeches, CBI Conference, November 1981, November 1983 and the CBI's evidence to the House of Lords Select Committee on the Internal Market (1A 42/82) about the need to enlighten ministers and bureaucracies of all ten member states about the internal market's opportunities, and what use could be made of *Cassis de Dijon*.

52. By the late 1970s, UNICE was seen as bogged down in reactive work, meeting trades unions' demands, or sectional activity such as steel restructuring, and in the fight against the Vredeling Directive.

53. CBI European Committee March 1980: the DTI asked the CBI and the City's EEC Liaison Committee to approach Davignon and Tugendhat, the Commissioners, on behalf of UK industry and financial markets. By December 1982, the CBI had nine separate study groups working on proposals to improve the internal market.

54. By 1982, ETUC claimed to represent 41 million members in nineteen European countries. Its triennial conference in April 1983 at the Hague concentrated on an underlying unemployment figure of 13 million, plus 2 million more but concealed, and forecast a rise to 20 million by 1985. Such views were listened to in the Commission, and by some member states such as Denmark, the Netherlands and West Germany. ETUC's credibility had recovered since 1975, partly because of UNICE's campaign to

kill off the Vredeling Directive, promulgated in 1980, despite support from Ivor Richard, Commissioner for Employment and Social Affairs; partly because it was expected that the EP would vote for it in 1982, with the support of many DC parties, some Liberals, and Socialists and Communists, to say nothing of nine out of ten national ministers of labour (excluding Britain). In the event, with the support of Narjes and Tugendhat, UNICE and affiliated national bodies including American companies and AmCham, succeeded in castrating Vredeling with amendments, so that it emerged from the Parliament after 'the most expensive lobbying campaign in the EC's history', as a mere shadow. Richard came back fiercely, but failed the following year to get his revisions through the Commission college.

55. Mrs Thatcher dissented, with support from Denmark and Greece; they were outvoted, and Geoffrey Howe later persuaded her to make the best of it (c.f., Lord Cockfield '1992 – Bilan d'un Renaissance', paper presented at Brussels 17 December 1992.).

56. Once the twenty-three Directives had been blocked in the Council of Ministers, summer 1982 (see p. 97 n. 40), the log-jam built up steadily. Stasis frustrated firms and officials who, by the end of 1982, had 770 protective devices to investigate and twenty directives on standards deadlocked, all by member states. The Commission's new strategy, based on *Cassis de Dijon*, of liberalization backed up by member states' own technical departments and standards offices (which left the use of Treaty powers under Article 100 only to essential cases and minimum standards), seemed to have been frustrated yet again.

57. See Council Directive, 28 March (83/189/EEC).

58. *The Downing Street Years*, pp. 312–14. Denmark, Greece and Ireland also protested. Later Thatcher realized it had been 'the linguistic skeleton on which so much institutional flesh would grow'. Aided by Conservative MEPs, the EP voted overwhelmingly for the draft Treaty, not so much for the thing itself but to obtain better instruments for future influence. Whether this improved its representativity *vis-à-vis* its electorates is open to doubt: at the second round of direct elections in June 1984, two trends showed themselves: large abstentions, at 40% higher than in 1979; and an anti-government swing among those who did vote (*Economist*, 23 June 1984. With a turnout of only 31%, the UK vote was the lowest by 20%.

59. The CBI was also involved in this planning (European Committee Minutes 1A 137/83); it is not yet clear whether the French and German organizations were.

60. Mitterrand withdrew French co-operation on the budget settlement, probably the better to achieve his *coup de théatre* the following year. Thatcher had failed to entice Kohl by 'an offer' that the new Commission President should be a German (hardly surprising, since it had already been agreed between Bonn and Paris that it should go to the latter); and her aggressive conduct on the second day (*The Downing Street Years*, pp. 336–8) completed the estrangement.

61. According to her memoirs (p. 39), Thatcher even considered withholding Britain's existing payments. Papers were prepared by the Treasury to that effect.

62. The British case was put with vigour and effective backing by officials. Nevertheless only the trade-offs with Germany made a solution possible.

63. Why did Mitterrand change here? Partly as a consequence of his earlier *grand tournant*, the withdrawal of Communist ministers, and the decline of the Socialist left which had contested Spanish entry because of the impact on the smallholders' vote in the south. Mitterrand could stand the loss of Socialist support if it meant further marginalizing the Communists in their decade-long struggle for a majority vote. He also changed partly because of the new Rocard-Delors government's policies: their line on economic policy was similar to that of Germany and the rest of the EC, which wanted accession in order to gain access for German factories to the Spanish market. Thirdly, the sense of a package deal: if the whole log-jam shifted (which was in the interests of French industry, not least because of industrial investment in Spain, whatever the minority of farmers argued), then France should be in the lead and shape the way that the package was put together. (A Sofrès poll in 1983 confirmed that every department in France but one was in favour.) Fourthly, Spain had elected Felipe Gonzalez leader of the PSOE in October 1982: there would never be a better leader for Mitterrand, who shared his problem of an activist left. The Spanish foreign minister, Fernando Morán, spent most of 1983–4 lobbying political leaders in the EC and leant heavily on fellow Socialist administrations, particularly in Italy. Also the Gonzalez government was deeply divided over Spanish entry to NATO: the Nine used the narrow referendum victory and Spain's application for entry in 1983 shrewdly as proof of Spain's political commitment to EC membership, with the implied threat that if the latter were refused public opinion would render the former inoperative – a threat to which Germany and Britain were highly sensitive, in the climate of American-Soviet hostilities.

64. At the threat of which, in February 1984, French customs officers went on strike. Lorry drivers then set up road blocks creating massive traffic jams. On that occasion, the lorry drivers won.

65. Most of the early momentum in the insurance sector came from Britain, seeking to revive a long-dormant article from the 1957 Treaty in order to prise open markets in West Germany. There was strong support from the Commission and the Netherlands; but France and Germany, above all, opposed it. Much was hoped for from the Schleicher case, which reached the Kammergericht in February 1983 but was lost in September and then taken on by the Commission (Tugendhat) and to the ECJ. At that point, the opposition drew back: West Germany would accept if mass risks were excluded, and France followed suit by altering its taxation policy on insurance premiums (formerly a substantive source of revenue).

66. Regional policy was one of the few areas where expansion took place, despite the endless budgetary quar-

rels of a dismal decade. This can be explained by the work of three dedicated Commissioners, themselves drawn from deprived regions, George Thomson, Antonio Giolitti, and Bruce Millan, and DG16 officials keen to create an area for redistribution of funds; secondly by an alliance between Italy, Ireland and Britain, joined later by Greece, and by the principle of additionality, under which EC funds were added to, but not as a replacement for, national funding. Spain and Portugal of course waited eagerly for a share in a much enlarged cake, while MEPs found a novel role. Despite all this, it would hardly have occurred without the eventual consent of the main player, West Germany (whose finance minister argued strongly against), or the interplay of many self-interests ranging from Britain's in Northern Ireland to Belgium's experiment in regionality. The total also remained tiny compared with that going to CAP.

CHAPTER FOUR

1. This could work in two directions: the meetings between Bundeskartellamt and French DGCCRF, later joined by British and Spanish officials in the 'group of four', were intended to prevent loss of national influence as the EC created its own means of control. Their reactions in turn influenced their national governments in the direction of a common policy, which was then refracted through the Council and affected how the Commission itself proceeded.

2. Performance during this period varied according to the country concerned. Inflation rates fell slowly (in the case of Italy and Ireland very slowly) and converged on the German rate, which gave heart to Commission officials planning for eventual economic union and EMU, and offered a largely fortuitous help to governments in dealing with their domestic situations.

3. Nigel Lawson, the chancellor, was almost alone in advocating entry for economic reasons in 1985 (*The View From No. 11* (London: 1992), pp. 484–5.

4. The end product of this reorientation can be seen in the Conseil d'Etat's final acceptance (*Niccolo* judgment, October 1988) of EC legal texts as being in all respects prior to French ones. Until then there had been a series of conflicts between EC laws and Articles 34 and 38 of the French constitution, France being the only EC state which held out on the principle that national courts had a right to adjudicate on EC texts. Had this not happened, all 286 Single Act laws might have ended up at the ECJ.

5. E. Haywood, 'The European Policy of François Mitterrand' in *JCMS* (Vol. 31, No. 2, June 1993), pp. 269–82.

6. *Handelsblatt* interview with Mitterrand (cited in *Agence Europe*, No. 3782), 4 February 1984.

7. S. Bulmer and W. Peterson, *The Federal Republic of Germany and the EC* (London: 1987), p. 13.

8. Speech to the European Parliament, 24 May 1984 in Brussels. France's attitude to QMV may have altered earlier: it had joined the majority in May 1982 in order to override Britain's attempted veto, revealing that the Luxembourg Compromise was not a fixed quantity and depended on a member state acquiring a minimum number of allies.

9. Quoted in R. Jenkins, *European Diary*, p. 123.

10. M. Thatcher, *The Downing Street Years*. N. Lawson, *The View from No. 11* provides a well reasoned counter-point. For a careful analysis of the factors behind the British decision to sign the SEA, see Phil Budden 'The Making of the SEA: the UK and the EC' (unpublished Ph.D thesis: 1994.)

11. *Economist*, 25 December 1982.

12. c.f., M. Thatcher, *The Downing Street Years*, p. 536, with much talk of 'statism and centralism'. When he was Commissioner, Christopher Tugendhat actually sent a memorandum (12 November 1984, paras 12–14) arguing that national sovereignty had long since been eroded and that Britain's effective independence was all that mattered: he was not reappointed but replaced by Leon Brittan.

13. The British Presidency in 1981 pressed hard for deregulation of financial services; something was achieved in stock-exchange harmonization, accountancy rules, product liability and mutual recognition of professional qualifications.

14. N. Lawson, *The View From No. 11*, p. 111. Sterling M3 was tacitly abandoned two years before the public declaration.

15. Ibid, pp. 485–493. See also R. K. Middlemas, *Power, Competition and the State* (Vol.3 London: 1990), chapter 7.

16. I am grateful to Professor Helen Wallace for this insight into the 'Papandreou Effect'.

17. Ireland's exports in 1960 – 75% to the UK, 6% to the EC; in 1981 – 40% UK, 30% EC, mainly to France, Germany and Benelux.

18. EC economic grants and subsidies rose from £36.7m in 1973 to £305m in 1981; social fund £4.1m to £73m; total £4.38m to £551.18m; plus loans (EIB and ECSC) £11.31m to £244.8m. Irish contributions rose from £6.1m to £112.21m. For source see note 19 (below).

19. c.f., P. Keatinge, B. Laffan, R. O'Donnell, 'Weighing up Gains and Losses' in P. Keatinge (ed.), *Ireland and EC Membership Evaluated* (London: 1991), p. 287. FitzGerald had attempted to introduce greater use of QMV in the Irish Presidency in 1974 (see *All in a Life: An Autobiography* (London: 1991) pp. 147–8.)

20. Lise Lyck, *Denmark and EC Membership Evaluated* (London: 1992), chapter 6 *passim*.

21. Pasok absorbed the old centre-left party Mavros and benefited from the monarchy's abolition. A major source of anti-American feeling derived from NATO's failure to prevent the Turkish invasion of Cyprus in 1983, but in fact this long antipathy dated from the civil wars of 1944–9.

22. C. O'Nuallain (ed.), *The Presidency of the EC Council of Ministers* (London: 1985), p. 113.

23. The influential core comprised the prime minister Felipe Gonzalez and the foreign minister Fernando Morán, Pedro Solbes (agriculture) with Calvo Sotelo, a former prime minister, and the Banco de España (playing a similar role to the Banca d' Italia), Sanchez Asiain (Banco Bilbao-Vizcaya), together with Luis Valls, the Catalan head of Banco Popular.

24. Catalan industry and commerce took the lead, aware of the likely impact on Spain's sheltered labour-intensive industries such as textiles and

footwear. Generally CEOE and its members followed government.

25. PT 4, p. 2. Under Salazar and Caetano, insofar as it looked to Europe at all, Portugal had concerned itself more with EFTA than the EC.

26. Public opinion polls at the time of Maastricht showed a clear majority, 54% in favour, 22% against, 24% uncertain. These figures should be read as a commentary on European Union rather than the specifics of Maastricht.

27. Broadly speaking, their views can be represented by three consecutive articles: W. Sandholz and J. Zuysman '1992: Recasting the European Bargain' in *World Politics* (Vol XLII, No. 1, October 1989), pp. 95–128; A. Moravcik, 'Negotiating the SEA; National Interests and Conventional Strategies in the EC' in *International Organisation* (45.1, Winter 1991), pp. 19–56; and Maria Green 'The Politics of Big Business in the Single Market Programme' at EC Studies Association 3rd International Conference, May 1993. The first ascribes changes of outlook to awareness of takeovers in the EC, and Japanese and American market advantage among industrial producers and financial sectors as well as states. 'Structural situations create the choice', and the choices were made by member states, in novel alliance with industrial and commercial elites. The second argues that the primary source 'lies in the interests of the states themselves and the relative power each brings to Brussels' (p. 56); hence industry had no influence except via DG3 and the Commission's plans for technical norms and standards. The ERT could be effective only

when the Ten had agreed to go ahead. In contrast, Maria Green uses a documented study of the ERT to show that it played an important role in promoting the single market concept, notably by defining it as a unified, rather than a mere Common Market. Multinational companies including US firms in the European Committee of AmCham then came rapidly into the forefront, helping to set the agenda and maintain the Delors-Cockfield momentum throughout.

28. Earliest references to abolition of non-tariff barriers of course predate this: c.f., CBI Europe Steering Committee, June 1976 Minutes (but this envisaged UNICE as the lever); March 1977 (via UK rep) and June 1977 (general support for the Davignon programme). Basil de Ferranti's speech to the Parliament (December 1979) marks a turning point, but the CBI as a whole did not commit itself to the internal market until March 1980, in conjunction with the UK government (DTI's) own approach. The CBI paper 'Objectives for the UK Presidency', June 1981 and its Director General's Conference Speech in November set out the full doctrine, followed by evidence to the House of Lords Select Committee, March 1982 (1A 42/82).

29. The best instances are in telematics. After failure of the late 1970s national champions to face up to IBM, Texas, AT&T or Japanese firms' competition in microelectronics, computers and telecoms despite state aids, R & D subsidies and mergers, Davignon's alliance inspired hopes that European cooperation could achieve

what nation states had manifestly failed to do.

30. CBI, July 1984 Review of UNICE.

31. FR24, p. 2.

32. Once established in office, after one collective discussion with Commissioners in June 1985 before the Milan Summit, Delors switched from relying on the ERT as a whole to reliance for advice on selected members, not because they were representative but because of their individual status and quality.

33. The ERT's paper 'Foundations for the Future of European Industry' was given to Davignon for use at Stuttgart.

34. Maria Green, 'Organising Industrial Coalitions', SEI Seminar Paper, Industrial Networks in the EC, October 1994.

35. It still fitted well, for example with President Mitterrand's 'Nouvelle Etape pour l'Europe' (September 1983); c.f., W. Adams and C. Stoffaës (eds.), *French Industrial Policy* (Brookings, Washington: 1986), pp. 136–8. This is not to deprecate ERT's influence on individual states, such as the contacts organized on transport plans between the Italian Transport Ministry and the Fiat and Pirelli groups.

36. The case of ICL may however be typical. Seeing what the internal market would bring, its board set the company to become a pan-European player, making mix-and-match IT components rather than computer mainframes. Lord Soames, its chairman and a former UK ambassador in Paris, chaired the CBI's European Advisory Panel on how British industry could and should adapt to the new conditions, until Sir Michael Butler, Britain's representative in Brussels until then, took over in 1987.

37. *Economist*, 27 June 1987, pp. 79–80. In 1988–9, mergers or takeovers amounted to a total of $60 billion, but not all these succeeded (de Benedetti's attempt to takeover Société Général de Belgique was blocked by Belgian-French cooperation, using Banque de Suez as means to turn SGB into a European development bank with multiple participation).

38. Having helped to defeat Vredeling, the European Committee of AmCham threw itself in 1983 into the internal market campaign, set up a data base, and increased its budget tenfold with the aims of becoming a 'unique and highly competent representative gathering, speaking for European companies of US parentage on the challenge of the 1990s'. Of its 110 corporate members, 15 were then in the top twenty of the *Fortune* list.

39. M. Green, *op. cit* p. 29, quoting interviews with J. Delors.

40. J. Delors, *La France par l'Europe* (Paris: 1988), pp. 47, 50–1.

41. Moravcik, *op.cit*, p. 35.

42. Margaret Thatcher had hoped for a German chairman, to forestall any French leverage. But Dooge handled it well and his Committee's distinguished composition, its highly competent secretariat, and its similarity to the 1955 Spaak Committee, ensured a high level of discussion, at least until half way through, when the German representative came under predictable pressure from the *Länder*, which feared that QMV would erode their prerogatives and privilege the Commission.

43. Howe thought it possible to argue for QMV but without an IGC (i.e., that member states should agree in advance to abstain from using the national veto in specified areas),

because he and Thatcher preferred a convention-bound approach to a rule-based one, and feared that if there were an IGC, it might lead far beyond the single market (c.f. *Europe and the Future* (September 1984)). Later, before Milan, they saw this strategy as a way to preempt the Franco-German line and drafted their own proposals for European Union, only to be upstaged by the proposed Franco-German treaty.

44. M. Thatcher, *The Downing Street Years*, pp. 533, 545, 548–51. See also G. Fitzgerald, *All in a Life: An Autobiography* (London: 1991), pp. 596–7.

45. VC94, p. 3.

46. Cecchini's research indicated, with vast statistical apparatus, that this was so – even if the figures were massaged to produce the result. Delors was persuaded to authorize publication of the whole volume at the same time as the Report. The Commission's complementary report 'The Economics of 1992', on the costs of *not* implementing the single market, may have been even more influential at member state level.

47. 'The internal market will provide the economic context for the regeneration of European industry in both goods and services'; he also spelt out what amounted to a supply side shock, followed by a ripple effect bringing a 4–7% increase in EC GDP, and trade reciprocity with Japan and the United States, over and above the once-for-all gain of more than 200 million ecus. The price would be adjustment by labour and management, and a stiffened ERM to inhibit devaluation, which would lead on to EMU. (Introduction to the Cecchini Report, UK edition, 1988).

48. KM97, p. 2.

49. That EFTA would be included had been made clear in the 1984 Luxembourg Declaration, which was reiterated by Delors in 1989. The Commission maintained close relations with Swedish, Finnish and Austrian business leaders.

50. Article 100(4), one of the last to be agreed in the new Treaty, did in fact allow member states to keep the veto (article 36 Exigences Importantes) but only after full explanation to the Commission, which then had the right to take the case to the ECJ. Another member state could act in the same way if it felt affected by discrimination or disguised restraints of trade, rather than 'legitimate dergation'. On the wider scale, in July 1987, the Council of Ministers also changed the procedure under which a majority vote could be called. Thereafter, though the point had not been discussed in the Dooge Committee, it appeared that the Luxembourg Compromise was dead. Whether it was or not, had to be tested: Germany did so once in June 1985; no member state has tried since.

51. The EP adopted a subdued tone throughout and relied on Italy's persuasiveness to ward off French opposition, mainly because its members feared precipitating an institutional crisis if they over-used their powers to reject the EC's budget, or to censure the Commission. (It *had* overplayed its hand – albeit quite legitimately – already on the latter by taking action on the Commission's failure to embark on a common transport policy: ECJ May 1985). Instead, the IGC set up a sort of mini-Coreper which allowed the EP to be consulted and its views to be heard, which Luxembourg

pushed through in the teeth of French, Dutch and Danish complaints. Thus the Commission remained free in its leading role, before and during the IGC, to advance the overall package before member states had their full chance in December to coordinate objections or make alliances.

52. M. Thatcher, *The Downing Street Years*, p. 536. She depicted an unholy coalition of Christian Democrats and Socialists 'forcing the pace of integration', in cahoots with the Commission. A new demonology, personified by Delors, began to emerge (c.f., *The Downing Street Years*, p. 708). Nigel Lawson, the chancellor of the exchequer lamented the preamble's inclusion of EMU (*The View From No. 11*, pp. 893–4).

53. In meetings with ETUC at Val Duchesse in 1985–6, Cockfield had tried to persuade trade union leaders to be less negative in their approach to the single market: the Greeks however jumped the gun and frightened the financial-industrial side of the *entente*.

54. *Economist*, 2 July 1988.

55. Led by Davignon and Ortoli, the ERT attempted to condition progress with regular meetings in Brussels and pressure on governments (M. Green, *op.cit*, p. 43); but this in itself hardly explains the Hannover success.

56. Detailed implementation provided a challenge to existing regulatory and professional bodies in each member state. The British Customs and Excise applied four principles: to keep it simple, to reduce the burdens on business, to make reduction of fraud effective, and to have it ready by January 1993. In that sense HM Customs became players, having an effect on negotiations for a framework for indirect tax rates and the system for excise on goods, drink and tobacco, on the principle of destination. Britain developed a model of consultation with DG21's 'listening committee'. Brussels in turn became both a court of appeal and an animator in regard to the problems of interpretation and implementation. These general tendencies led to effective harmonization over time, whatever member states said in their domestic political contexts.

57. MEPs for example discovered that it was Israeli practice to leave Arab-produced citrus fruit destined for export to the EC to deteriorate while Israeli goods were shipped first. Using a threat to refuse to vote for the 260 amending protocols, they forced Cheysson, the pro-Israeli French foreign minister, and the Council of Ministers to give assurances that the EC would not tolerate such discrimination.

58. An *Economist* survey, 9 July 1988, showed that 'financial prices' had fallen in two years by 14% in Italy, 12% in Germany, 10% in France, 7% in the UK.

59. The way opened up in 1987 when the Commission redefined 'large risks' and set lower policy thresholds, above which openness would prevail (see p. 593).

60. *Agence Europe*, 4 December 1992 (No. 5871).

CHAPTER FIVE

1. Cohesion had been at issue since January 1987 when the Commission proposed doubling the Structural Funds in order to offset the com-

parative disadvantage from which
Mediterranean member states were
likely to suffer as a result of the
internal market. Margaret Thatcher
countered with a demand for restructuring the CAP itself. Germany
had then sabotaged the Dutch Presidency's attempt at a settlement later
in the year, partly to assuage
domestic opinion, partly the better to
sort it out according to German
ideas before the Greek Presidency.
The final bargain was, in effect, that
West Germany would carry the costs
as part of a new 'Mediterranean
bargain'; access to the Spanish and
Portuguese markets being the main
prize. France's return, for supporting Germany in February 1988,
came from easier access to the Research Funds for the structural
modernization of its state industry
sector. EC revenues rose from 1%
to 1.2% of member states' GDP.
Thatcher seems to have contented
herself with the hope that EC spending would as a consequence be
better audited and monitored.
2. *The Downing Street Years*, pp. 727,
742–6. 'By the summer of 1988 he
(Delors) had altogether slipped his
leash as a fonctionnaire and become
a fully fledged political spokesman
for federalism.' (p. 792). For her
attempt to entice Mitterrand see pp.
793, 796–8.
3. It is significant that she wholly misinterpreted Kohl's one tactful essay
in reconciliation at Deidesheim in
December 1988 and used the occasion to tell the chancellor how
Germany should conduct its defence
policy. *The Downing Street Years*, pp.
747–8.
4. Delors's speech to the EP, July
1988. To the TUC he declared 'It is
essential to strengthen our control of

our economic and social development, of technology and of our
monetary capacity.' *The Times*, 9
September 1988, p. 4. See also
Nigel Lawson, *The View From No.
11*, p. 907.
5. c.f., EC Annual Report 1986, p. 36.
6. This has been well argued by
Loukas Katzelis in 'The Political
Economy of European Integration:
from Euro Sclerosis to Euro Crpor-
atism' in *The International Spectator*
XXIV (No. 3/4, July–December
1989), especially pp. 189–195.
7. In July 1990, contrary to the usual
practice of including most DG's
desiderata in his annual presentation
to the EP, Delors asked for precise
details of what each wanted, and
held them firmly to it. It was these
items, in coherent order, which he
put forward in January 1991 as the
clear agenda for when the IGCs
began in Luxembourg.
8. EC entry had been approved by a
unanimous vote in the Spanish parliament (the PCE abstaining) and
generally by public opinion, apart
from some Catalan business interests and the small agricultural sector
which felt ignored in the haste to
sign an agreement. The Gonzalez
government intended to make
maximum use of the transition
period. Nevertheless, the Accession
Treaty was seen as a hard bargain,
leaving many problems to be dealt
with, perhaps by renegotiation in the
manner already explored by Greece.
Up to 1990, falling inflation and
energy prices and a flood of new
investment, largely from Germany,
led to the establishment of new
plants such as Volkswagen, and
growth averaging 4.6% p.a. The
government won EC aid for the steel
industry, and regional funding for

the backward agricultural areas of the south and west. But by 1990, even before the recession, structural problems of overheating, 7% inflation, and heavy trade and budget deficits had become endemic. Portugal followed a similar pattern: its difficulties lay in the lack of resources for basic infrastructural improvement, the need to modernize financial services after a severe stock market crash in 1987, and the persistence of very high state borrowing, crowding out small industry and specialized agriculture.

9. *Inter alia*, GEC and Siemens' bid for Plessey, Metal Box's merger with CMB Packaging, ASEA's merger with Brown-Boveri; Deutsche Bank's purchase of Morgan Grenfell, and the CGE-Alsthom/Fiat-Alcatel-Alsthom mergers.

10. The CBI for example acted mainly as a publicist, urging the British government, at its 1987 conference, not to fail to take advantage of the coming single market, though 'too few British companies are aware of the significance'. Council's brief to the EC's Steering Committee, July 1986, had been concerned with reducing state aid to industry, transparency and liberalization, e.g., in the case of cross-border mergers; its general support for what the DTI was doing did not vary in the late 1980s, in the period of 'active dialogue' intended to galvanize British firms. It also accepted the Padoa-Schioppa Report on monetary union (June 1987) and argued for greater coordination of monetary policies – at least until 1991. See also the *Economist* Survey of EC Business Opinion, June 1991.

11. For a British account of this episode, see M. Thatcher, *The Downing Street Years*, pp. 763–5.

12. The thirty-four CSCE conference members signed the Charter of Paris, endorsing German unification together with reductions in NATO and Warsaw Pact forces, on 21 November; thereby ending the Cold War and the major division of Europe – though not the earlier line drawn after the 1917 Bolshevik Revolution. By early 1991, both the Warsaw Pact and Comecon had disintegrated, closely followed by the entire Soviet imperium.

13. Part of what follows is based on discussions with Bernard Connelly, author of a forthcoming study of the EMS. Also M. J. Artis, 'The Maastricht Road to Monetary Union' in *Journal of Common Market Studies* (No.3 September 1992), pp. 289–309.

14. The French finance minister, Edouard Balladur, accepted the logic of force and, by refusing to intervene, forced the unwilling Bundesbank to accept this realignment. K. O. Pöhl however declared that the Bundesbank's reaction was not in future to be taken for granted – each case would be assessed on its merits.

15. Participants agreed at Nyborg (the Nyborg Agreement) in September 1987 to allow any member to borrow in order to intervene, when at the ERM limit, and to delay repayment; the stresses were inevitably felt by the anchor currency, the DM, which had to support weaker currencies from its own reserves; for example in October 1987 and July 1993.

16. Tommaso Padoa-Schioppa, deputy governor of the Bank of Italy, made his report on the 'inconsistent quartet' to the Commission in 1986. He was one of Delors's intellectual mentors and a rapporteur in 1988,

having taking part on the Giscard-Schmidt Committee the previous year. The Bank of Italy had a particular interest in furthering EMU as a deus ex machina to reform Italy's errant public finances.

17. It may be assumed that Pöhl signed because the rules of convergence and ECB independence from politics satisfied the Bundesbank, and because at that stage there was no fixed timetable. Leigh-Pemberton did so partly because of the Bank's own determination to restrain inflation in future, partly because of confusion among ministers: Nigel Lawson later denounced the report as a French-led distraction from the single market (speech, Chatham House, 25 January 1989).

18. N. Lawson, *The View from No. 11*, pp. 928–36.

19. Lawson might have been prepared to accept some sort of stage two, but Thatcher was not (c.f., *The View From No. 11*, pp. 913, 918). But he resigned in 1989, to be followed as chancellor by John Major. Lawson's 'shadowing' had set sterling around the 2.70 DM level, but in summer 1990 it rose to 2.98 DM. Major's intention in going into the narrow band, and at 2.90 DM, was apparently to be able to reduce British interest rates; Thatcher would have prefered the 6% band (*The Downing Street Years*, pp. 723–4). Perhaps the worst policy failure (due to the urgency of preventing the Prime Minister from reneging) was not to consult the other member governments, as ERM conventions required. Most were furious: German and French Ecofin ministers discussed *imposing* an alternative rate on Britain. At this point Britain lost the sympathy which might have assisted

Germany to help sterling out when the final crisis came in September 1992 (see below, p. 537).

20. Remaining hurdles such as appointments to the ECB's Directorate were resolved on the Bundesbank model: Ecofin would appoint to the Directorate, the Council of Ministers only to its Council; while the ECB was only to report to the Parliament, despite a Dutch attempt during the IGC to enforce greater accountability.

21. France was not the only ERM member in this predicament. After a long period of sustained growth, Ireland suffered severe disinflation and 18% unemployment, hence its dependence on EC transfer paymnts.

22. Some Germans argued from their nineteenth-century history that unification dated only from 1871 and the Reichsbank from 1875, whereas the Zollverein began in 1834, and locked-in currency rates developed in 1838.

23. On the budget deficit issue, Britain, Ireland and Portugal stood together; on wages and foreign borrowing Italy, France, Belgium and Spain. Germany and the Netherlands wanted precise rules about 'excessive budget deficits'; Britain and Portugal none; and the northern and Mediterranean states divided over cohesion funds and crisis support measures. At the risk of over-simplifying very complex negotiations, Germany wanted binding rules to inhibit profligate member states from damaging the system or opening it to 'Mediterranean leverage'. So a clause was written in, with Italy's agreement, to limit any *right* to an EC currency rescue, which Spain, led by Carlos Westendorp,

fought hard to offset by the provision of yet larger cohesion funds.

Ecofin's power to refuse loans and to recommend reforms (in what the *Economist* called its 'in-house IMF role') were made subject to QMV. A loan to Greece was actually refused in December 1990, to Delors's fury (see p. 725 n. 7).

24. State Secretary Horst Köhler even issued a rebuke that the Bundesbank was 'not a supergovernment' and should not judge in matters of taxation, state spending and wages. Schlesinger conceded finally on the Maastricht terms, having won most of the Bundesbank's technical points, in November 1991.

25. M. J. Artis, (*art. cit.* fn. 13) p. 309.

26. How long the road would be can be judged from the 1990 position:

Convergence Indicators, 1990

(1) Inflation; (2) Long-term Bond Yields;
(3) Budget Deficit/GDP; (4) Gross Public Debt/GDP

percentages

	(1)	(2)	(3)	(4)
Belgium	3.4	10.1	5.7	127.3
Denmark	2.6	10.6	1.5	66.4
Germany	2.7	8.8	1.9	43.6
Greece	20.4	n.a.	20.4	93.7
Spain	6.7	14.7	4.0	44.5
France	3.4	10.4	1.7	46.6
Ireland	3.3	10.1	3.6	103.0
Italy	6.5	11.9	10.7	98.6
Luxembourg	3.7	n.a.	−4.8	7.3
Netherlands	2.4	9.0	5.3	78.3
Portugal	13.4	11.3	5.8	68.2
UK	9.5	11.1	0.7	42.8

Source, M. J. Artis, *op.cit*, p. 304.

27. For a detailed treatment, see Colchester and Buchan, *op.cit*, pp. 178–190. A Commission Paper on mobility and social issues 'Communication from the Commission concerning its action programme relating to the implementation of the Community Charter of Basic Social Rights for Workers' (COM (189) 568 final), 29 November 1989, was given extra status by the Court of First Instance's approval.

28. CBI European Advisory Committee Minutes September-December 1988. Taking a more cautious line than before, the CBI sought to spin out discussion rather than fight the Charter head on, fearing that with help from Social Democratic governments, ETUC might hamper progress to the single market.

29. It was already obvious from the speed with which Spain's trade surplus had been replaced by a growing deficit as early as 1987, that more regional funds would be required than the 7.9 billion ecus allocated in February 1988, rising to

13.1 billion in 1992. During the IGCs, a new game emerged, as the poorest four, Spain, Portugal, Greece and Ireland discovered that with Italian assistance they could win support for regional representation and larger funds, so long as they avoided pruning existing spending on the Italian Mezzogiorno. Cohesion developed in the same political matrix as structural and regional funds, under the benign authority of DG16 (see chapter 9).

30. Member states' objections (chiefly those of France), to a Court of First Instance were finally withdrawn, so that the Court of Assessors could be appointed in 1989. The ECJ's workload at that time can be gauged by its duties in 1989: 569 letters of formal notice, 227 reasoned opinions, 73 cases heard.

31. The Eureka programme, based partly on microchip technology, was intended primarily for civil use, but had clear military implications and remained barred by the USA from eastern Europe until 1993.

32. c.f., Mitterrand's speech (reported in *Le Monde*, 22 September 1992), where he referred to the waste of years since the French Assembly had rejected EDC. French troops had already by then taken part in the Gulf War, under the American overall command, even if for home consumption their operations remained distinct. Mitterrand's vision encompassed eastern Europe, as if reviving the 1930s Little Entente, within the EC's purview – that 'oasis of stability and success', as he termed it in a speech to the European Parliament in November 1989.

33. *Economist*, 1 December 1990, p. 65.

34. c.f. C. Patten's article in *Marxism Today*, February 1991.

35. Since the Luxembourg Declaration, April 1984, and the long-spun out negotiations for an European Economic Area, the EFTA countries had been approximating their national laws to the EC *acquis*. Each of them, for separate reasons, had come round to the point of considering whether to apply for membership. Austria broke ranks first, and applied to join the EC in March 1989. The others delayed, uncertain about the reactions from their publics: the Swiss and Norwegians in particular feared supranational domination.

36. It is not obvious for example that British negotiators realized at the time the full implications for British sovereignty of the fact that human rights, protected by the European Human Rights Convention, was to become explicitly part of the EC's constitutional law.

37. See David Buchan, *Europe, The Strange Superpower* (Aldershot: 1993).

38. R. Corbett 'The Intergovernmental Conference on Political Union' in *Journal of Common Market Studies* (No.3, September 1992), pp. 271–298.

39. Provided by the case of a minor, refused permission by a lower court to travel abroad to seek an abortion, in the light of the Irish Constitution, despite the fact that she was under age and had been raped.

40. Speech given on his behalf by the French ambassador in London at Chatham House, 26 October 1993.

41. c.f., John Major's article (*Economist* 25 September 1993), aimed at the domestic audience, which gave great offence elsewhere with its comparison of EMU to a rain dance.

42. The Court defined the Community as a union of sovereign states, whose sovereignty has only partly been delegated to the Community's institutions. In particular, the Commission cannot add to its competences on its own account, even on the basis of competences which already exist. The Court argued that the closer the European Union comes to statehood, the more it should be democratically and directly controlled; and it declared that the stages of EMU are not automatic but require ratification by the Bundestag. The Court reinforced its own legal status *vis-à-vis* the European Court of Justice, perhaps for the first time since the Simmenthal case, and indirectly made an assumption about the existence of a hierarchy of norms which did not constitute any part of the Maastricht Treaty.

43. There were some achievements nevertheless: a temporary budget settlement, further increases in structural and cohesion funds (21.3 billion and 1.5 billion ecus in 1993 to 30 billion and 2.6 billion in 1999); and notably the fixing of a target date for EFTA negotiations early in 1993. The nadir of self-interested squabbling came at the Ecofin meeting in September when Norman Lamont put the onus on the Bundesbank to reduce German interest rates. To the other eleven, Britain seemed to abuse the Presidency out of mere self-interest and lost for a time its chance of being in the inner group at 'the heart of Europe'. Inspite of this, Helmut Kohl continued to give help, if only to resolve the Danish problem quickly, and to assist Mitterrand during his second period of cohabitation.

44. *Financial Times*, 23 March 1993, p. 17.

POSTSCRIPT

1. c.f., Commission Report February 1995. Only Denmark, France and the Netherlands scored over 94%, in the middle group, Britain had around 90%; Germany stood at 83%.

2. VC99 (DK p. 3).

CHAPTER SIX

1. 1976 Jenkins, Heath (vetoed by Wilson) and Soames (vetoed by Giscard); 1980 Thorn, Cheysson (unacceptable to Schmidt), Davignon (unacceptable to Giscard). In Britain in 1980 Lord Carrington supported Davignon, as Thatcher did Thorn.

2. There is as yet no authoritative study of the office, neo-functionalist theory and the approach adopted by Ernst Haas having become unfashionable by the mid-1980s. For Delors himself and his system see Charles Grant, *Inside the House that Jacques Built* (London: 1994). For the views of a perceptive insider, see George Ross 'Policy development and the cabinet system in the Delors Commission', unpublished paper, Harvard University, based on a 1991 *stage*, and a case study of industrial policy.

3. KM127, p. 3.

4. G. Ross, *art.cit.*

5. KM127, p. 4.

6. Interview ORTF, 26 February 1992.

7. It appears that Delors telephoned the French PM Rocard to inform him that the case would be discussed in the college. Rocard then lobbied several Commissioners on the

morning of the meeting, something which *was* outside the conventions, and has since been repeated only in the Spanish steel case when Gonzalez instructed both Spanish Commissioners. The Greek loan, following Pasok's first spending burst in 1984–5, was arranged between Papandreou the prime minister and Delors, despite opposition from Trichet, then Chairman of the Monetary Committee. When DG2, supported by the Monetary Committee, reported that Greek performance did not justify the second tranche in 1986, Papandreou brought pressure to bear on Delors, as a result of which Mitterrand and Kohl asked Trichet to concede, and the tranche was approved. (KM56, p. 3).

8. c.f., his criticism, speaking 'for the college and the union', that the British conception that subsidiarity gave a member state an automatic veto over Commission policy 'would paralyse the Community'. *The Times*, 15 October 1992, p. 1.

9. KM129, p. 4 and KM127, pp. 2–3.

10. Comprised in 1991 of nine French nationals and one each from Germany, Britain and the Netherlands.

11. G. Ross, *art.cit*, p. 13.

12. A good case is the *cellule de prospective*, set up in 1989 to make a general overview (which was by then beyond the capacity of chefs du cabinet, for lack of time), in order to advise Delors about issues likely to become prominent, such as migration or the environment. (Even this failed to forecast the reaction of the member state publics to the Maastricht Treaty, which was predicted neither in the college nor the Council.)

13. KM127, p. 4.

14. c.f., the threat by France to end this monopoly during the 1996 IGC made by Alain Lamassoure (*Economist*, 25 June 1994, p. 41).

15. c.f., Emmanuel Butaud 'The Commission' in *Revue des Centres du Pouvoir Européen* (Groupe de Belles Feuilles: 1993) pp. 114–20.

16. Many inevitably reflect periodic domestic preoccupations. It has been easy for France always to send highly qualified Commissioners (Mitterrand in 1992 for instance was able to dally between Edmond Alphandéry and Christiane Scrivener, whom he had earlier dismissed (*Le Monde*, 15 December 1992)). But it is much harder for small states to do so. In the Irish case, there is a marked contrast between two outstanding nominees, Sutherland and McSharry, and a number of party hacks. It suited Dublin to have as Commissioner a personality who is effective in Brussels but would have fitted badly inside the governing coalition (which collapsed in 1994).

17. KM3, p. 1.

18. KM126, p. 3.

19. c.f. d'Archirafi's interview reported in *The European*, 22–25 March 1993, p. 39.

20. Cockfield could not win all the arguments: although Delors was in favour of his policy of harmonizing VAT (on children's clothes and newspapers), the two decisive votes against in the college came from the other British Commissioner and a French one who feared that Cockfield's proposal would discredit the Commission itself in Britain during the 1987 elections.

21. The case of Ripa De Meana, the erratic Environment Commissioner at the time of the Rio Summit 1992,

is instructive. He ignored member state sensibilities wholesale when preparing the EC's energy tax proposals, then condemned France's 'abusive, arbitrary and cynical blackmail', for blocking the establishment of the European environmental agency until the French government received guarantees that the Parliament should remain at Strasbourg. He also took on the British government over the building of motorways at Twyford Down and Oxleas Wood. The gestures were welcomed, especially by Green parties, but the Commissioner lost most of his arguments in the college for lack of detailed preparation.

22. *Economist* 25 March 1989. Table on p. 66. Cabinets are known to take advice from MS Permanent Representatives about the proposals emanating from the Directorates, although this can also be interpreted as part of their function to keep Commissioners widely informed.

23. The system of comitology, adopted in 1987, was intended to regulate those committees lying at the interchange of Commission and the Council. Rivalry now occurs not so much over their function, which is formally delimited, as over which models to choose: the advisory one, which favours Brussels and is normally preferred by the Netherlands, or the inter-governmental one, regularly advocated by Britain and France.

24. In the case of the German-inspired packaging Directive, which most non-German firms wished to dispute, the Commission was content for the industry's peak organization to sort things out for it, keeping as far as possible from the rival claimants.

25. KM20, p. 4.

26. At least until the case has become blatant: DG4 officials and Commissioner Sutherland were unwilling to take on the Pasok government of Greece in 1987–8, despite its repeated failures to live up to promises from its own Ministry of National Economy. Despite Leon Brittan's more vigorous prosecution of contraventions after 1989, it was not until 1992 that the Commission decided to take the subsequent New Democracy government to court, and then mainly to educate the Greek public in what it hoped 1990s' realities should be.

27. The French state since the nineteenth century has aided horseracing with tax advantages. Having abolished these themselves, Britain and others put pressure on France because they regarded the advantage as an unfair commercial practice and not a part of national life. French racing organizations waged a long and successful rearguard action, blocking and lobbying in Paris, Strasbourg and Brussels, giving the government and themselves time to make new dispositions – one of the rare instances of aristocratic influence in late twentieth-century Europe.

28. Five environmental proposals were withdrawn in July 1992, just as John Major's first British Presidency opened.

29. FR16, p. 2.

30. KM93, p. 2.

31. KM126, pp. 4–5.

32. SP30, p. 2; PT4, p. 1.

33. The EU's system of committees and working groups is highly complex, given the heterogeneity and variety of different committees and their respective legal status, budgetary

attribution, competences and composition. Between 1987 and 1993 those committees which acted as consultative mechanisms between the Commission and interest organizations grew quantitatively much less than those committees on which civil servants from member states were represented. This suggests that the 'bureaucratization' of EU processes is primarily due to the involvement of experts from national governments and to a much lesser extent to that of interest organizations in the committee system. Interests groups seem to prefer informal ways to institutionalized forms of collaboration.

34. Nevertheless, in 1993 the ECJ criticized appointments made under pressure from the Italian and Spanish governments in DG14 over the heads of better qualified Dutch and Germans, the clear implication being that the 'national quotas' by which these appointments were justified were contrary to the EC rule that merit should be the main criterion.

35. PT4, p. 1.

36. When the company Solvay was judged to have violated Article 86 in the sodium bicarbonate market by DG4, DG1 refused to alter its mind about Solvay's anti-dumping rights in the same market!

37. Hence DG3's support for the Aerospatial-Alenia attempt to buy de Havilland, and Bangemann's curse on what he called DG4's 'Ayatollahs of competition'.

38. In conducting its process against the state aids given to Air France in Autumn 1992, DG4 was opposed by both DG7 (transport) and DG16 (regions) who accepted the French government's arguments.

39. Various means exist to inhibit or neutralize the lobbies and lobbyists: the Commission can create consultative committees, under the comitology procedure, to regulate their activity; and it can set up seminars, on the same model, where Commission officials or experts can observe without taking part. Both of these tend to regularize and thus regulate informal activity (c.f., the paper on lobby regulation (OJ C63/2 March 1993) which advocated 'an open and structured dialogue between the Commission and interest groups', and presented greater formality of access, for a wider, better-balanced range of players). Given that numbers had increased since 1985 from 3000 to 10,000 lobbyists in over 500 firms in Brussels, it is not surprising that the Commission found them hard to codify, let alone regulate.

40. c.f., Commission decision about restructuring steel, 1994. The cause of DG4's process was that the government's aid was manifestly not aimed at closure of the state steel company Ilva. DG4 objected to DG3's plan to allow aid, correctly as the Legal Services declared, and the college reluctantly accepted – and amended the conditions on state aid so that the carefully constructed compromise plan, which met the objections of the private steel makers, the Bresciani group of producers fell apart.

41. Angry, in late 1992, about a proposed law on guest workers, Chancellor Kohl, being under media and television pressure at home, instructed the German Permanent Representative to make contact direct. The most the Legal Service could do was to avoid a formal meeting and listen informally to the German argument.

42. In the endless struggle over competence, the Legal Service had recently been overwhelmed by the complex procedures for DG11 to make complaints against a member state under Article 169 for failure to enforce EC laws on pollution or the environmental impact of large public works. It may be said to pay a member state to go ahead in such conditions, as the experiences of the worst offenders Greece, then Italy, followed by Spain, seem to prove. There has been a sharp drop in the number of cases actually referred to the ECJ, from 14% of cases in 1989 to 3.7% in 1993. Under a less assertive Presidency than Delors's, and a less engaged Environmental Commissioner, Ioannis Paleokrassis, the tendency to compromise or drop processes, or delay until the project is too far advanced, increased.

43. Because a chapter of five judges drawn from both EC and EFTA might have reached a decision on disputes under the Agreement which would have conflicted with what an EC-only chapter would have done. This might have prejudiced the autonomy of EC law.

44. KM127, p. 4.

45. VC79, p. 4.

46. FR75 (BG2), p. 2.

47. FR57 (NL), p. 2.

48. IT12, p. 3.

49. A BASF survey as early as 1981 showed this to be the norm among German MNCs. A member of one Denmark's largest companies declared 'all big companies think European, as well as internationally . . . business is pro-European and wants the young to be so minded' (VC97 p. 3) and an executive of a French conglomerate added, 'Brussels has become less of an enemy, actually a partner on occasions. It is totally impossible for a company of this size with a rational economic strategy, to ignore it.' (FR27 p. 2).

50. Although the comparison may be only tangential, it is worth noting that in 1993 the Council of Europe conducted a survey of staff attitudes and found 44% entirely agreed and 28% largely agreed on the proposition 'I am a Euro official': but only 8% entirely, 20% largely, thought 'I work for the European ideal' (as against 30% largely not and 24% not at all); while 64% entirely, 29% largely, believed that the future of the European ideal depended on member states. (Council of Europe circular no. 541 25 June 1993, Tables 1.1., 2.1. and 10.4.) Significantly, perhaps, the 1988 Commission survey asked rather different questions, about how staff thought they could get on, and what qualities were required for promotion.

51. FR6, p. 3.

52. The Groupement des Avocats Européens has recently been instituted as a forum with the aim 'to constitute the larger bar of Europe at Luxembourg, a European order of lawyers' (FR82, p. 3). Original, even audacious, given its direct membership outside national legal federations, it is made up mostly of French; a few Germans, a handful of British and a strong Italian interest.

CHAPTER SEVEN

1. The European Council may also constitute a Council of Ministers, not usually to legislate but to resolve particularly intractable problems, or to give legal form to their decisions.

2. The sequence until 1993 followed the first letter of member states' names, in their own language, i.e. Hellas, España. In December 1993 this was modified, mainly to take account of the predicted entry of EFTA countries.

3. The standard text is H. Wallace, W. Wallace, and C. Webb, *Policy-making in the European Community* (Chichester: 1983), chapters 1–4 (but especially chapters 2 and 3).

4. H. Wallace and F. Hayes Renshaw, 'Collective Leadership, Confederal Bargaining, and the Limits of Federal Identity', 2nd ECSA World Conference, Brussels, 5–6 May 1986. There is surprisingly little literature on this most central body other than descriptions of its formal procedures and structures.

5. FR39, p. 1.

6. VC56, p. 6.

7. Lord Howe, Lecture at Nuffield College, Oxford, 30 April 1993.

8. Both Ecofin and the Governors discuss similar topics from the different standpoints of the Treasuries *vis-à-vis* Central Banks. The alternates have space and time for less inhibited, substantive discussion, for example of the monetary conditions in each member state and the ERM's workings.

9. KM42, p. 2.

10. KM93, p. 3.

11. C. Engel & C. Borrmann, *Vom Konsens zur Mehrheitsentscheidung* (Bonn: 1991) and P. Budden & B. Munroe, 'Decision Making, the Council of Ministers' First ECSA conference paper, Washington DC, May 1993.

12. VC46, p. 2.

13. Only a handful of multinationals would habitually refer to other ones, representing their cross-border subsidiaries. Philips for example has a positive interest in not always being seen as a Dutch company.

14. KM95, pp. 1–2.

15. R. Jenkins, *European Diary 1977–81*, p. 74. At that time there were only 25 in the room, as opposed to 198 at Council meetings.

16. The Brussels Summit in June 1987 (when eleven, led by Wilfried Martens, outfaced Britain on the budget question), demonstrated that a European Council majority can impose its views in the end, and helped to set the tone for the Hannover Summit the following year.

17. FR21, p. 3.

18. VC51, p. 4.

19. c.f. The valuable series 'EC Membership Evaluated', published for each member state (Pinter: 1991–4).

20. FR20, p. 2.

21. FR34, p. 4.

22. The article written by John Major for the *Economist* (25 August 1993, pp. 23–7), is significant more for its terminology than its content, e.g. 'malaise in Europe', 'Debate . . . too often conducted in extremes'; 'central vision that alarms so many voters in the applicant countries'; witness also the comparison of reciting the EMU 'mantra' to a rain dance, with 'about the same potency'; 'an historic agenda . . . for Europe's leaders, not its bureaucrats'; finally, 'it is for nations to build Europe, not for Europe to attempt to supersede nations . . . the Treaty of Rome is not a creed, it is an instrument. We must tune it to the times.'

23. The most comprehensive description of France's system is given by Christian Lequesne, 'The Central Political Administrative Apparatus of France and the EC 1981–91' (un-

published Ph.D thesis, Paris: 1993). The most extensive comparison is given in 'Action or Reaction?' (5th Evenstein Colloquium, Kerkrade, October 1987) supplemented by reference to a number of seminar papers such as the IEP Colloquium, 'EC Decision Making', Bonn, 6–7 September 1993 and N. Nugent, *The Government and Politics of the European Community* (Basingstoke: 1991), R. A. W. Rhodes & D. Mack, 'New Directions in the Study of Policy Networks' in *European Journal of Political Research* (Vol. 21, nos. 1.2, 1992), pp. 181–205 and M. P. van Schendelen (ed.), *National Public and Private EC Lobbying* (Aldershot: 1993) which covers many member states in minute detail.

24. Cresson's main legacy were the ministerial European policy groups, GEMs, created because the administration did not initially cooperate with her as an outsider. Formally, these were intended to coordinate the central and local administrative levels, and the industrial and labour market players. Here they had some success, but only at the level of larger firms, not SMEs as she had hoped; and largely through the prefets' agency, acting in the regions on behalf of central power. From Paris, 'Europe of the regions' is seen as a foolhardy Brussels illusion.

25. SGCI is first and foremost the place where the civil service heads meet and try to iron out their differences in order to come up with a coherent national position for France, this being particularly important on dossiers involving several ministries. The Quai as well as the Ministry of Economy and Finance tries its best to avoid the consultation process and both defend their own positions, depending on the political constellation of the moment. SGCI is also the place where the members of the Permanent Representation receive their orders. The regional counterpart, DATAR, serves as the Ministry of the Interior's outpost in what it calls 'territorial units', or regions, the central state in the guise of regional planner.

26. The Brussels office, whatever was intended originally in Paris, now provides substantially more than 'after sales service' (FR29, p. 1). *Inter alia*, it provides French companies with a head start where chances of contracts exist, funded by EC money, in Europe or the Third World. Such are its results in francophone Africa that non-French companies come to it, seeking to set up joint ventures there. Recently it has turned its attention to the Phare programmes in eastern Europe, competing (albeit late in the day) with Germany.

27. FR45, p. 1.

28. The British government is seen in Paris as more efficient because, for example, in the state aids cases it negotiated with DG4 before making notification, so that the aid was likely to be compatible by the time the interpretation came to be made.

29. FR1, p. 1.

30. KM95, p. 2.

31. c.f., Sir Percy Cradock's last dispatch 'Reflections on the State of the Service', noting how professionalism had turned to fatalism or reluctance to say 'no Minister'. The only way to offset this was for EC-related officials to establish trust directly with the prime minister and by-pass Powell as interlocutor, as occurred at Brussels in 1987; but even this became harder

at the end, during German reunification.

32. VC44, pp. 1–2.

33. Ibid., p. 2.

34. c.f., B. G. Bender, 'Whitehall. Central Government and 1992' in *Public Policy and Administration* (Vol.6, no.1, spring 1991), pp. 13–20. See also generally, D. Spence, 'The Role of the Civil Service: the British Case' in S. Mazey and J. Richardson (eds), *Lobbying in the EC* (Oxford: 1993), pp. 47–73.

35. VC50, p. 1.

36. B. G. Bender, *art.cit.* pp. 16–17.

37. SP11, p. 2.

38. SP32, p. 1.

39. SP6, p. 2.

40. PT7, pp. 1–2.

41. PT5, p. 2.

42. In one case in 1971, over preferential tariffs for Third World countries, the BMWi had to disregard powerful arguments put by the BDI that the burden would fall on Germany since the US had not accepted the scheme, because the Bonn government had for years advocated the idea in EC forums.

43. Beate Kohler-Koch, 'German Lobbying in Brussels' (unpublished paper, IFP Seminar, March 1992). See generally S. Bulmer & W. Patterson, *The Federal Republic of Germany and the European Community* (London: 1987), pp. 25–42.

44. The bargaining and eventual settlement of European agencies' location provides a mini-history of the interstate market, notable for a protracted squabble between Britain and Spain over the Medicines Evaluation agency (London having had to cede the Monetary Institute to Frankfurt). Britain won, but Spain in compensation got two agencies: trademarks, and Health and Safety. France had to be content with its guarantee that the Parliament would remain, contrary to all logic, at Strasbourg, but Belgium, in the Presidency, received nothing – this being a poor reward for prime minister Dehaene's leadership.

45. In 1990, the VDA (car producers association) put its proposals on CO_2 emissions directly to Kohl, having found that 'coordination varies according to who writes the German position . . . it is badly done if a project falls between ministers' spheres' (FR77 (GR), p. 4). In contrast to the British case, the chemicals industry 'would like to be closer, but the political world is afraid of being seen as selling out to it'. (ibid)

46. As is argued by Colin Crouch 'Cooperation and Competition in Germany' in C. Crouch and D. Marquand (eds), *Ethics and Markets* (Oxford: 1993), pp. 80–98.

47. Generally, see M. van den Bos, *Dutch EC Policy Making* (London: 1993), chapters 3 & 6.

48. FR60, (NL) p. 3.

49. M. van Schendelen (ed.), *National Public and Private Lobbying in the EC*, chapter 8.

50. VC90, p. 2.

51. J. van Ginderachter, 'The Belgian Federal Model', 2nd ECSA World Conference, Brussels, May 1994.

52. The NESC's report 'A Strategy for the '90s EC, Stability and Social Change' compares Ireland with other small member states facing both adjustment problems and increasing dependency on cohesion funds, needing the external discipline of ERM and EMU.

53. Marco Giuliano, 'Il Processo Decisionale Italiano' in *Polis* (Vol. 6, 1992) pp. 307–42. Generally, D.

Hine, *Governing Italy: the Politics of Bargained Pluralism* (Oxford: 1993).

54. IT24, p. 2, L. Lanzacolo, 'Interest Groups in Italy: From Pressure Activity to Policy Networks' in J. Richardson (ed.), *Pressure Groups* (Oxford: 1993), pp. 113–130.

55. IT9, p. 1.

56. IT22, 23, and 24, p. 2.

57. The standard comparative work is C. O'Nuallain and J. H. Horschett (eds), *The Presidency of the European Council of Ministers: impacts and implication for national governments* (London: 1985); see also G. Edwards & H. Wallace, *The Council of Ministers of the European Community and the President-in-Office* (Federal Trust Paper Chichester: 1975).

58. P. Ludlow, 'The UK Presidency: A view from Brussels' in *JCMS* 31. (No.2, June 1993), pp. 246–67.

59. The fact that the Netherlands proposed something unacceptable to all the eleven can be attributed partly to its deep hostility to the inter-governmentalism rife at Maastricht, partly to misunderstandings in the coordinating process between foreign minister and prime minister. But it may also have had symbolic importance as a gesture to Dutch public opinion.

60. FR32, p. 1; also FR6, p. 3.

61. In 1993, Belgium took a line against airline deregulation, to the fury of BA and Lufthansa, but very congenial to its own state-owned enterprise Sabena, as well as to Air France, Alitalia, TAP, Iberia, and Olympia, all of which were dependent on state help to stave off bankruptcy.

62. For the best general accounts see the essays in R. Picht and W. Wessels (eds), *Motor für Europa?*

(IEP Bonn: 1990), particularly Picht's chapter 1, pp. 33–47.

63. For her account see *The Downing Street Years*, pp. 790–1, 796–8, 813–15.

64. KM113, p. 2.

65. Margaret Thatcher, *The Downing Street Years*, p. 794.

66. R. Morgan, 'Germany in the new Europe' in C. Crouch & D. Marquand (eds), *Towards Greater Europe* (London: 1992), p. 155.

67. KM39, p. 2.

68. In the field of research and development for example (a natural target for high technology cooperation), failures have outweighed successes, even in cases which ought to have been fertile, such as high-speed trains and energy supply or telecoms. The record of Alcatel's German subsidiary, or Alsthom-Boveri stands out as rare examples of what can be done commercially, rather than attempts such as France's Hermes project politically to foster integration. (K. W. Grewlich, *Motor für Europa*, chapter 3, pp. 161–86).

69. Viz, the quarrel begun when Edmond Alphandéry, the inexperienced French finance minister, announced too publicly that he would put pressure on Theodore Waigel and Helmut Schlesinger of the Bundesbank to relax Germany's 'overly restrictive monetary policy', to ease France's domestic economy restraints in August 1993.

70. FR49, p. 2.

71. Reports of the Court of Assessors on fraud provide the occasion for much mutual recrimination, which is sometimes planned in advance (SP31, p. 2).

72. Portugal has even proposed a 'council of small states' able to 'make declarations' later to be adopted as

texts by larger states needing their votes (PT3, p. 2).

73. Where the Commission has competence, for example in the internal market, it can of course do so: c.f., the case of British car prices, where EC policy finally succeeded in achieving gains for British consumers buying direct from the continent, where the British government had failed to move the motor industry despite being in breach of Article 85 (J. Kaye and D. Thompson 'Policy for Industry' in R. Dornbusch and R. Layard (eds), *The Performance of the British Economy* (Oxford: 1987), pp. 180–210. Since 1991, the ECJ has had power to fine a member state, but that has not yet been used. It took three years from the Commission's first letter to Italy about failure to alter its discriminatory Stock exchange rules even to get a case to the Court. In all other spheres, the Commission can regulate behaviour only via laws which they and the Parliament must sanction, or if the Court should develop a new interpretation of what already exists (see chapter 8).

74. Apart from the general statements made variously by German, French and British governments or party political sources, proposals by Kenneth Clarke, Britain's chancellor of the exchequer, that Ecofin should investigate all Commission proposals' impact on member states' finances, had a clear intention of curbing the urban waste water Directive, whose cost has been estimated at £10 billion for England and Wales during the 1990s.

75. FR6, p. 1.

76. Access to Commission documents is a good case in point: the Secretary General had never refused a case in recent years and there had been no complaints. But the Netherlands insisted on 'a code of conduct' as a guide for the public. This produced a surge of applications to see documentation, while the rule itself unsettled the Legal Service's appreciation of the legal basis and poduced delays. The Netherlands challenged this in court. Now, with appeals, the whole process has produced a notable burden. Yet the Council remains as secretive as it ever was.

77. In 1994, the ECJ declared void a Directive on marketing cosmetics because the Commission had not consulted the Scientific Committee, even though it had no statutory duty to do so.

78. *The Times*, 9 October 1992; *Economist*, 14 November 1992, p. 44.

79. Thatcher, *The Downing Street Years*, p. 743.

80. BKartA view expressed in FR68, (GR3) p. 3. This tactic was used not only in steel cases, but to counter the establishment of a VW-Ford factory in Portugal which had gone ahead on just such a comfort letter. Yet the procedure is intrinsically of value and saves a great deal of time.

81. FR55, p. 1.

82. The Commission's initiating role can itself be challenged; in a recent case, in October 1992, the Health Ministers' Council approved a forward programme, ahead of Maastricht ratification, which could have been construed as a form of initiative.

83. On the first occasion, the French government took Commissioner Sutherland to the ECJ, arguing that Article 90 related only to disclosure of information on government relations with national monopolies, not on new legislation. But the ECJ

came down in favour of the Commission, in 1990, as it did in 1991 in the Port of Genoa case.

84. Having settled the GATT Uruguay round at the end of 1993, member states and Commission in 1994 engaged in a dispute over whether the Commission should represent the EU on the new World Trade Organization, the successor to GATT, or member states themselves. Those like Britain and France, which wanted the latter because of their specialities in financial services, intellectual property, etc, argued that these were 'new areas' outside the Commission's and the EU's existing competence. The Commission feared that would break up the whole trade policy front, and took it in February 1994 to the ECJ.

CHAPTER EIGHT

1. The standard accounts of the EP are F. Jacobs, R. Corbett, M. Shackleton, *The European Parliament* (Harlow: 1990), J. V. Louis and D. Waelbroeck (eds), *Le Parlement Européen dans l'évolution institutionelle* (Brussels: 1988); there is also a clear summary in Desmond Dinan, *Ever Closer Union?: an introduction to the European Community* (Basingstoke: 1994), pp. 257–93.

2. See figure 8:2, p. 735.

3. Average of all member states, 1976: 62.5%, 1985: 59%, 1989: 58.5%, 1994: 56.4%. Within these figures, the disparities were enormous, ranging from Belgium and Luxembourg (where voting is compulsory), at 90% average, to Britain and Portugal at 36.4% and 35.7% in 1994.

4. D. Strasser, *The Finances of Europe:*

the budgetary and fiscal law of the European Community (7th edn, Luxembourg: 1991), p. 291.

5. R. Corbett, 'The IGC on Political Union' in *JCMS* (No. 3, September 1992), pp. 271–94, describes the Parliament's part in this, from the Martin Reports at the Rome Assizes onwards. Although a sort of majority existed in favour of co-decision for the adoption of all future legislation, the minority, composed of Britain, Denmark, Ireland and Portugal was sufficient to prevent that outcome, given that both France and the Commission remained lukewarm.

6. Attendance improved markedly in the 1984–9 session compared with the previous one (average 300 MEPs in divisions as against 210); but MEPs from Mediterranean states and France were still notorious for their absence.

7. After some talk of rejecting his nomination on the grounds that his candidature had been masterminded by France and Germany, the Spanish, Greek, Portuguese and Danish delegations tipped the balance in his favour. The inquisition procedure applies also to EC agency appointments such as that of Alexandre Lamfalussy, chairman of the European Monetary Institution, Frankfurt.

8. KM127, p. 6, Senior Commission official, Cabinet Delors.

9. VC41, p. 1.

10. By then the EP was linked to the Commission's computer printout of the internal market progress, under subject headings.

11. FR2, p. 2, French Senator.

12. As part of this mobilization, MEPs received a letter in favour of the EFTA applicants signed by Helmut Kohl and the prime ministers of

Country	Turnout (%)			Electoral system	Seats in EP	Female MEPs in 1989	Pop. per MEP (000s)
	1979	1984	1989				
Belgium	84.9	83.4	81	Proportional representation (PR) list system in 3 constituencies	25	6	403.3
Denmark	47.8	52.4	46.2	PR list system on national basis	16	6	301.8
France	60.7	56.7	48.7	PR list system on national basis	87	17	664.4
Germany	65.7	56.8	62.3	PR list system on federal basis	99	29	818.2
Greece	78.5 (1981)	77.2	79.1	PR list system on national basis	25	0	412
Ireland	53.6	47.6	68.3	Single transferable vote system in 4 constituencies	15	2	240
Italy	84.9	85.9	81	PR list system in 5 constituencies	87	12	654
Luxembourg	88.9	88.8	87.4	PR list system on national basis	6	3	66.7
Netherlands	57.8	50.5	47.2	PR list system on national basis	31	7	496.8
Portugal	–	72.2 (1987)	51.2	PR list system on national basis	25	3	372
Spain	–	68.9 (1987)	54.6	PR list system on national basis	64	11	610.9
UK	32.8	32.6	36.2	First-past-the-post system (PR in N. Ireland)	87	12	669.8

Figure 8:2

Benelux and Greece, indicating that if the extension went through, the EP would be consulted before the 1996 IGC much more than had been the case before Maastricht.

13. After the 1989 electoral disaster in the British European election, the Conservative party applied to join but was refused, thanks to objections by the Netherlands and Ireland's Fine Gael, both of which objected to Margaret Thatcher's views on the EC and the Social Protocol. Under John Major, a sort of opening to Christian Democracy occurred, associated with Chris Patten, and Tory MEPs began to join as individuals. Negotiations for full membership, party to party, began in 1991 but have not yet been completed, since on certain key issues such as Northern Ireland the Major government

has reserved the right to call its MEPs into line, in the same way that the Spanish or French governments do with their Socialist ones. Patten's initiatives with the German CDU lapsed when he left British politics in 1992, but his article in *Marxism Today* (February 1991) is of interest for its discovery of 'the need to find an English rhetoric for what comes so naturally to German Christian Democrats, namely the social market economy'. This link with Christian Democracy was not an option which had been open to Edward Heath in 1973–4 because of the confessional element that was still rife for example in the Italian DC – witness the British attempt in 1978 to create a non-Catholic grouping, the EDU (KM95, p. 3).

14.

	European Socialist Group	200	(198)
	European People's party	148	(163)
	Liberal and Democratic Reformists	46	(44)
	European emocratic Alliance	24	(20)
	Greens	23	(28)
	Left Unity	12	(13)
	Technical Group of the Right	12	(14)
	Rainbow Group	8	(16)
	Independents/Not Attached	96	(21)
	Total	569	(518)

(Totals prior to June 1994 in brackets)

15. It is worth noting that in the majority of member states, these two parties predominate: France, Germany, UK, Spain, Netherlands, Greece, Portugal (Ireland is one odd one out, for historic reasons; Italy is another, because of its continuing political revolution. Denmark, Belgium and Luxembourg are, as always, coalition countries).

16. VC58, p. 1: this is the sense of M. Duverger's article in *Le Monde* (15 April 1993, p. 2), where the Socialist Group's target was stated as being to oppose 'a new savage capitalism on a scale as yet unknown' bringing unemployment, lower wages and salaries, the decline of agricultural and rural values, and shifts of employment to low-welfare countries such as the UK.

17. VC86, (IRL) p. 1.
18. c.f., H. Wilensky, 'Leftism, Catholicism, and Democratic Corporatism' (UCLA Institute of Industrial Relations, 1981). Many of these concepts surfaced in Chris Patten's article (*op.cit*) including 'The importance of the collective and community' and 'the responsibilities which should properly be carried by the state or underpinned by the state'.
19. VC58, p. 2. Former UK party leader.
20. SP18, p. 2; SP27, p. 4.
21. Witness the case of Mary Binotti, Irish MEP, who won a signal victory on behalf of an Irish speech therapist married to a Frenchman but debarred by administrative obfuscation from practising in France, when she persuaded the EP to castigate the Commission for being too soft on backsliding member states in allowing freedom of mobility for professionally qualified people.
22. VC57, p. 3.
23. FR24, p. 5; FR48 (NL), p. 1.
24. Alan Lamassoure, Chairman of the Budget Control Committee in the late 1980s, sought unavailingly to remedy this from the Parliament end.
25. *Eurobarometer* No.38, 1992.
26. VC78 (IRL) p. 2.
27. FR48 (NL3), p. 2, IT18, p. 2.
28. L. Saillard, 'Le Consommateur Européen' in *Belle-Feuilles Revue des Centres de Pouvoir Européens* (Autumn 1992), pp. 124–9.
29. FR67 (GR2), p. 1; FR71 (GR6), p. 1
30. IT18, p. 1, VC94 (DK) p. 1.
31. Wolfgang Hagen, 'Public Interest and Market; Europe's 1992 Project' (Andrew Shonfield Association Paper, September 1988), p. 31.
32. H. Rasmussen, *On Law and Policy in the European Court of Justice: a comparative study in judicial policy-making* (Dordrecht: 1986), which, following American political science treatment of the Supreme Court as a policy-maker, created a model of Treaty interpretation which could be characterized as 'activist'. According to this analysis, the ECJ had been subject to a range of 'policy inputs' or pressures of which the most effective had been the tradition of judicial activism, not only in the ECJ itself but in national courts and parliaments. Thanks to this, the Court had become the focus of pressures, often via academic associations, or the opinions put to it by Advocates General or member states; and negatively through member states' defiance or attempts to curb it, e.g., by delaying for nearly thirty years setting up the Court of First Instance. See also A. Lloyd and A. Winckler (eds), 'La Place du Juge dans la construction communautaire' in *L'Europe en Chantier* (Paris: 1993), pp. 133–42, which examines the perennial suspicions of the judge as policy-maker exhibited by national politicians and left-of-centre parties.
33. Competition intruded even in this area, because the convention when there were twelve, requiring a thirteenth to give a majority, that the thirteenth judge be drawn in rotation from the four largest states, was challenged by Spain in 1988, and only conceded by Italy after much argument.

34.

	1970	1985	1994
Case load per annum	79	433	342 (CFI 399)
Time preliminary rulings	4½ mths	14 mths	18 mths
Time direct actions	6 mths	20 mths	24 mths

The backlog (cases pending) was 527 cases in 1985 and is ECJ519, CFI 438 (April 1995).

35. c.f., F. Mancini, 'The Making of a Constitution for Europe' in Keohane & Hoffman (eds), *The New European Community* (Boulder: 1991), pp. 177–194.

36. In *Bourgoin*, the Appeal Court refused the plea of French turkey producers for damages against the British government, which had prohibited the import of turkeys two months before Christmas on the pretext of danger from Newcastle Disease – though the real cause was probably the repeated activity of French farmers seeking to exclude British lamb, which ceased soon afterwards. Nevertheless Britain was declared in breach of Article 30 by the Court.

37. ECR491, case 4/73.

38. N. Hummings, 'The Sovereignty of Parliament' in Barr European News, E/89E 166 (1990). In 1988, the UK government passed the Merchant Shipping Act to prevent Spanish-owned vessels from registering as British in order to utilize the British fishing quota. The Act had not yet come into effect, when the Spanish complaint against the restrictions reached the House of Lords which (as the High Court and the Appeal Court had also done) implicitly accepted that the supremacy of parliament was a dead letter, but found itself inhibited from declaring so, in confrontation with its own elected government. It indicated however that the Commission could bring the case under Article 169. When the Commission did so, the ECJ ruled that Britain could not legally impose the restrictions requiring 75% ownership by resident UK citizens. (See C221/89 and *The Times* Law Report, 19 May 1989). The British government had been guilty of breaching not only seven Articles but the Treaties themselves, and the law should be 'disapplied', i.e., the Court found a formula without directly overruling the member state Parliament (as it had done in *Costa* and *Simmenthal* (1975.))

39. VC68, p. 4.

40. Germany currently tops the list for requests:

Requests	1991	1992
Germany	52	62
Italy	36	22
Netherlands	17	18
Belgium	19	16
France	29	15
UK	4	15

(Source: Commission 'The Control & Application of EC Law', 10th report, 28 April 1993).

41. Lord MacKenzie-Stuart, 'The EC and the Court of Law', Hamlyn Lectures, 29th series (1977).

42. When the ECJ held in 1967 that the Commission was entitled to negotiate external trade agreements, and that member states had lost this power (Multi-Lateral Treaty in UN Economic Commission for Europe) de Gaulle rang the (French) President of the Court to protest, but without avail. Ten years later, in 1978, in a dispute over the Parliament's powers, President Giscard, at a luncheon called by Roy Jenkins, with Emilio Colombo and the Court's presiding judge Hans Kuscher, portrayed the affair as a 'great constitutional crisis'. Kuscher firmly resisted this testing of the margins of manoeuvre (KM91, p. 3).

43. Judge Mancini has put this in a different way, seeing the Commission as the Court's 'mighty ally on the path of further integration', a view not widely shared by his colleagues. (KM96, KM130, KM131, *passim*).

44. Bachmann, a German living in Belgium found that under Belgian taxation he received no taxation relief on his German pension scheme payments. The Commission, favouring the transport of pensions across borders, argued in Bachmann's favour, but the Court referred instead to the Belgian government's right to maintain its own coherent tax regime. Even though the Commission had pinned its future policy in the insurance market on success, it had to find an alternative method (see chapter 11).

45. M. Pinault, 'The Influence of French Law' in *Belles-Feuilles* (autumn: 1992), pp. 75–84. Pinault referred specifically to the resemb-

lance between the ECJ, the Court of Cassation, and the Conseil d'Etat; and between the Advocate General's function and that of Government Commissioners acting in the Conseil.

46. c.f., ECJ 3 May 1978, case 12/77.

47. KM96, p. 5.

48. c.f., also SPUC *vs.* Grogan 1991 when the Court ruled that because students distributing leaflets with abortion information had not actually been paid to do so, they were not in law providing a service, for which free mobility is prescribed. Had they been paid, it would have been very hard for the Court not to have required the Irish government to back down, as the British government had to in *Factortame*.

49. Lord Slynn in BBC Radio Four 'Analysis' programme, 'The ECJ and its Role' (4 February 1993), transcript page 6.

50. Ibid, p. 7.

51. VC59, p. 1.

52. KM96, p. 6. The current list of member states in default on implementation is, in descending order, Denmark, Britain, France, Germany, Netherlands, Ireland, Luxembourg, Belgium, Spain, Greece, Italy, Portugal.

53. In which the Court ruled (302/86) that the idea of restraints to protect the environment was acceptable an proportionate, but that the actual measures chosen were not.

54. KM96, p. 4.

55. BBC transcript, *loc.cit*, p. 11.

CHAPTER NINE

1. KM55 p. 12

2. FR11 p. 2, French Commission official.

3. SP23, p. 3.

4. It was of course already clear that despite twenty years of the RDF, the Mezzogiorno remained backward and corrupt, whilst some areas of France and Germany had benefited excessively from CAP funds. As the 1972 Wiener Report had forecast, the EEC had failed as a mechanism for managed adjustment, despite extra resources and better agreement on aims. From 1974–84 the Council found itself unable to get agreement between the recipient states and those who paid the most; by which time argument had become embroiled further by the British budget complaint and the dispute between economic liberals and dirigistes.

5. In his speech to the EP, March 1985, Delors referred to the need for social solidarity if north–south political confrontation were not to occur. The regions must be brought into a 'common weal, contributing to the vigour of the European entity.'

6. Commission, 4th Periodic Report on the Regions, 1990.

7. T. Padoa-Schioppa, *Efficiency, Stability and Equity* (Oxford: 1987), pp. 93–102.

8. PT8, pp. 1–2.

9. The six objectives as they stand to day are: Objective (1): areas of deprivation (75%); (2) Decayed industrial regions, unemployment higher than EU average, (also 75%); (3) areas of long-term unemployment, and remobilizing young people in the workforce; (4) adapting workers to industrial change and innovation; (5) adjustment in agriculture and SMEs; (6) sparsely-populated regions (such as Finnmark). Of these (1) provided 64% of the total in 1993, (2) 12.5%, and that part of (5) for SMEs, 2%, specifically allocated to regions.

10. The government did however set up ten regional administrations in April 1994, which the Labour opposition has since hailed as precursors of regional government (*Economist*, 29 April 1995, p. 36).

11. From the Commission's point of view, the difficulty with the Northern League was its apparent vindictiveness towards the south, which not only threatened Italy's integrity but made it harder than ever to reach the areas in greatest need.

12. KM29, p. 2.

13. KM155, pp. 1–6 generally.

14. The Committee of Regions: Method of choice by each member state, 1993–4.

Country	No. of Seats	Criterion
Belgium	12	5 seats for Flemish region, 2 for Walloon region, 2 for Brussels, 2 for Walloon community, 1 for German-speaking community.
Denmark	9	4 seats for counties, 4 to municipalities, 1 to Copenhagen
Germany	24	*Länder* choice, but 3 seats reserved to municipalities
Greece	12	All nominated by government, of whom 8 mayors and 4 state officials

(Continued)

Country	No. of Seats	Criterion
Spain	21	1 seat each for 17 autonomous communities, 4 for local authorities
France	24	Balanced choice between 22 regions, departments and communes, allowing 8 for each level
Ireland	9	All nominated by government.
Italy	24	12 seats for regions, 5 for provinces, 7 for communes
Luxembourg	6	Government choice from local authority nominees
Netherlands	12	6 seats to municipalities (mayors), 6 to provinces
Portugal	12	Government nominations for 10 mainland seats and 2 for Madeira and Azores
U.K.	24	Government nomination from local authority elected representatives, in proportion 14 England, 5 Scotland, 3 Wales, 2 Northern Ireland

(Source: Commission, 25 October, 1993)

Note: Protests against the non-elected members by the more virtuous appeared likely for a time to bring the Committee in front of the ECJ.

15. KM12, p. 2.
16. VC26, p. 2.
17. KM127, pp. 5–6.
18. This 'right' grew up informally, having been conceded as a matter of appeasement by Leo Tindemans in 1984 when he gave permission for them to attend the Cultural Affairs Council of Ministers as part of Belgium's 'shared voice'. They did not in fact attend on that occasion, but reclaimed the right later; and German *Länder* in 1989–90 neatly took the same trick.
19. SP20, p. 3; SP22, p. 3.
20. From the moment when the new king, Juan Carlos, unexpectedly referred two days after Franco's death to the 'peculiarities of our peoples' (22 November 1975), a fifteen-year long game developed in which the Spanish state's integrity was protected by making the minimum concessions acceptable to a majority of autonomous communities – which were of very different composition and social or cultural homogeneity.
21. For which see *El Temps*, 'Suplemento Especial', 21 February 1994.
22. Scotland does, however, under the Act of Union, retain its distinct legal system, local government, its schools and universities, and its systems of professional qualification.
23. P. C. Cheshire 'European Integration and Regional Responses', SEM Initiative Working Paper No. 1 NIESR.

See overleaf.

Regional Business Centres

	Bank HQs	Overseas Banks	International cities served by air	Air passengers per year
Barcelona	16	36	40	10.3m
Edinburgh	7	8	102	2.6m
Lyons	4	22	103	3.9m
Stuttgart	11	7	134	4.7m

(Source: Bankers' Almanac World Ranking 1994 and *Aeroport* Magazine)

24. I. Begg and D. Mayer, 'Social and Economic Cohesion among Regions in the 1990s' (NIESR: 1991)

25. Generally, see J. Brand, J. Mitchell, J. Surridge, 'Scottish Identity and the Politics of the EC' (2nd ECSA World Conference, Brussels, May 1994), and S. Mazey & J. Richardson 'The Scottish Experience' in *Lobbying the EC* (Oxford: 1993), pp. 93–120.

26. Gross Domestic Fixed Capital Formation, by purpose of government, per capita (£ per head)

	UK	England	Scotland	Wales	N.Ireland
1980	99.3	92.5	143.0	105.8	139.0
1985	121.0	107.0	175.0	144.4	120.4

Source: CSO
Note: after 1985 the format changed.

27. Treasury opposition was modified in an agreement of February 1992 arranged by Sir John Kerr, Bruce Millan and DG16 in the case of Objective 2 money for redundant coal fields, where 800 million ecus had been held up; this seemed to have modified the Scottish Office's intransigent outlook. But the Treasury/SO still maintained in 1993 that the burden of matching RD funds should be shared between state and local authorities. (*Financial Times*, 24 February 1993, p. 1).

28. Mazey and Richardson, *Lobbying in the EC*, pp. 115–18.

29. c.f., D. McCrone, *Understanding Scotland: The Sociology of a Stateless Nation* (London: 1993).

30. Europa Institute 1991: *The Single Market and the Scottish Economy*. Also VC8, p. 3.

31. VC30, p. 1.

32. *Economist*, 3 September 1994, pp. 26–7.

33. c.f., J. P. Fusi, 'Spanish Regionalism' in RSA lecture, RSA Journal (Vol. CXLII, No. 5452, August–September 1994).

33a. Unlike Navarra and the Basque Country which, for historical reasons, raise about 80% of revenue locally, Catalonia and the other fourteen regions, under the 1980 law, raise only less important taxes, roughly 16% of the total. The rest come from the Spanish central funds: it is from this element that the 15% derives.

34. SP4, p. 1.

35. SP26, p. 2.

36. Constitutional Court, June 1992, Judgment *re* the Sectoral Commission, Madrid, regulation of local implementation of RD Funds. While it was normally for the province to

administer the funds, Community norms were duty bound to conform with the Spanish Constitution and could not override it.

37. SP1, p. 1.
38. SP20, pp. 1–2.
39. SP33 p. 2, SP34.
40. SP8, p. 1, SP17, pp. 1–3.
41. ICEM report, *Catalonia 2010*, which speaks of 40,000 SMEs, mostly family owned.
42. SP7, p. 2; SP6, p. 1–3. *El Pais*, 18 January 1993, p. 15, 23 January, p. 20, and *El Periodico*, 12 January, p. 14.
43. R. Putman, R. Leonardi, R. Nanetti in *Making Democracy Work* (Princeton: 1993), argue that the existence of a strong civic culture, based on Bologna, was the principal determinant over several centuries. c.f., also Leonardo Parri, 'Politichi Locali per l'innovazione Tecnologica: Roma ed Emilia-Romagna' in *Stato e Mercato*, pp. 77–115, who posits the phenomenon of 'private interest governments' as a sub-state evolution, in which what matters most are not party affiliations, but social networks, alliances and links with regional public authorities. In the latter arena matters of regulation, intervention, resource allocation and the SME regime are argued out. See also *Il Sole 24 Ore* survey of 65 industrial districts in Emilia-Romagna in *Gioelli, Bambole, Coltelli* (1992), which concluded that a district is created by a small industry with similar or complementary products, and economies of scale *between* firms, unique to this region.
44. IT 1, p. 2; *Financial Times*, 28 July 1995, p. 7.
45. *Il Sole 24 Ore*, 12 October 1991, p. 7.
46. The service centres (organized according to sector) dated back to the 1970s, in terms of their impact on

serving the interest of SMEs. For example, in 1973 a regional financial holding was created, ERVET, on which sectoral as well as horizontal service centres still depend. Several of the service centres established under ERVET include CITER (textiles), CESMA (agricultural machinery), SVEX (export industry) and ASTER (the Agency for Technological Development).

47. IT7, p. 23; IT22, p. 1.
48. Commission Combined Study, Stefan Kuhlmann (ed.), Final report for DG12 and the Commission, September 1991. The Four Motors initiative began in September 1988 as a medium to facilitate long-term political collaboration between similar regions. No new institutions were envisaged, apart from three-monthly meetings of the four prime ministers. The essence lay in research and technology cooperation.
49. This picture is taken from a range of articles in *Le Monde, Figaro, Libération, La Croix, Les Echos* and *Le Nouveau Journal*, together with *Financial Times* Reports and the Economic Intelligence Report on Rhône-Alpes No. 2165. But see also J-B Laurencin, *L'Europe, L'Avenir de Rhône-Alpes* (Grenoble: 1991) and M. Dunford, *Rhône-Alpes in the 1990s* (*Economist* Intelligence Unit, London: 1992).
50. Paris EC Information Bureau 1992. *Le Monde*, 3 November 1992.
51. FR47, p. 1.
52. FR18, p. 3.
53. *Süddeutsche Zeitung*, 19 January 1993, p. 22.
54. Rhône-Alpes Conseil Regional Report 1993.
55. GR1, pp. 1–2.
56. GR15, pp. 1–3.
57. GR13, p. 3.

58. GR4, p. 2.
59. c.f., F. Algieri, O. Schmuck, W. Wessels, *Die Landtage in Europäischen Integrationsprozess nach Maastricht* (Düsseldorf: 1992).
60. An Association du Grand Sud has existed since 1986 to serve the Mediterranean littoral, for example, and more recently an Association du Grand Est – both remain to be proved.
61. FR51, pp. 1–2.
62. VC109, (DK) p. 3; VC113, (DK) p. 5.
63. Scotland's future appears now to depend far more on what happens in Northern Ireland than on Labour party promises of what may happen after the next election, or Conservative denials that autonomy should ever be allowed. Ireland has almost been the catalyst for devolution in the past, in 1919, and any restoration of Stormont would bring the aborted Scottish parliament of 1978–9 back into play.
64. IEP Bonn, February 1991 Project, 'Regions in the EC', final report by *Länder*, State and Senate Chancellories, p. 2.
65. KM2, p. 4, as against KM113, p. 3.
66. c.f., Pujol's lecture, 'El Poder Regional y la nueva Europa' (Complutense University Madrid, 18 July 1993).
67. VC34, p. 1.
68. FR64, p. 2; FR55, p. 1.
69. Ash Amin, 'Big Firms Versus the Regions in the SEM' (SEM Initiative NIESR Working Paper No.2).
70. VC5, p. 2.
71. Objective 2 support for naval construction in the early 1990s produced aid to Hamburg, one of Germany's richest cities.
72. SP34, p. 2; PT8, pp. 1–2.

CHAPTER TEN

1. Very few companies pass the tests of having over 50% of their activity outside the home base and of indifferently transposing themselves across frontiers (G. Hofstede, *Culture's Consequences* (Newbury Park: 1984), pp. 391–6). IBM probably passes these tests but Siemens, whose productive trading patterns and corporate behaviour are indeed transnational (but whose legal format and ownership is German, and hence protected from takeover) and whose managerial direction is German but on a global scale, does not.
2. FR27, p. 2. Lawyers, in contrast, are not generally seen as lobbyists, even when engaged in lobbying (FR55, p. 2). The literature on lobbying is growing rapidly; e.g., B. Vever, *Pratiquer l'Europe: stratégies et réseaux* (Eyroles: 1992) and A. B. Philip, *Pressure Groups in the EC* (UACES: 1985) which merely lists lobbies. More convincing analyses are to be found in M. Chameu, J. Nonon & M. Clamen, *L'Europe et ses couloirs* (Paris: 1991) and D-C Prévost-Testart *Le Lobbying ou L'Echequirer des Pouvoirs* (Paris: 1993) which describe how lobbying works and what are its requirements.
3. As of 1992–3 among Brussels lobbyists, there were 12 major firms, roughly 100 consultants, and several hundred part-time or minor firms. 25 firms could be considered serious players (KM134, *passim*). See also B. Kohler-Koch (1994), p. 174, where the numbers are estimated to have grown fourfold in the years 1985–90. Charges in 1990 were, in one firm's case, £500 per month for simple monitoring, £1500 for per

month for full monitoring – identifying new issues and giving advice – £3–5000 a month for a primary service, making contacts and running a campaign on a daily basis, and for a 24-hour service, upwards of £10,000 per month.

4. FR49, p. 1. Some French industrial observers argue that it is better not to act directly at all except when the firm's immediate interest is at stake (FR56, p. 1). This view is usually put as a contrast to the 'Anglo-Saxon' stereotype, whose adversarial technique is assumed to be an attempt to influence everything (FR44, p. 1).

5. M. Strauch, *Lobbying, Wirtschaft und Politik in Wechsel* (Frankfurt: 1993).

6. Generally, see M. V. Schendelen, *National and Public and Private EC Lobbying*; J. Greenwood, J. R. Grote & K. Ronit, *Organised interests in the EC* (London: 1993), chapters 1, 6 & 8; S. Mazey & J. Richardson, *Lobbying in the EC*; J. M. Stopford & S. Strange, *Rival States, Rival Firms* (Cambridge: 1991); and for the financial sector, A. Mullineux (ed.), *European Banking* (Oxford: 1992)

7. That may have more to do with the outlook of DG23's Director General, Heinrich von Moltke, than opinion generally in the Community. Certainly this would be disputed by the CBI's small firms sector and by PIMEC, the Catalan association which sees Madrid as interested only in MNCs (SP17, p. 2). It would however be possible to contrast the minimal influence of the Italian organizations CGIA and CNA even in Rome, let alone Brussels, with that of German HWKs and IHKs in the *Länder* and DHKT in Bonn, which is undeniable. Membership of the Italian bodies is patchy, rarely passing 30% except in Emilia-

Romagna; that of the German ones runs close to 100%.

8. C. Siebert, E. Swindlund, *Nation state and interdependence: interaction models in the EC trade policy* (IEP Bonn: 1988).

9. *Handelsblatt*, 6 August 1992, p. 19.

10. H. Weiss (BDI President), lecture to the Royal Society of Arts, 23 June 1992 (RSA Journal, CXL No. 5434), p. 753.

11. Prior to the 1989 statement on semiconductors, Thomson was one of Commissioner Pandolfi's three main interlocutors at DG13, together with Philips and Siemens. The level of its influence can be seen from two instances. When the Russian air traffic control system was up for renewal in 1993–4, Thomson was able to arrange a meeting between the Russian delegation and the EU Commissioner, Karel van Miert. DG1 also assisted Thomson to buy a bankrupt US missile producer, with the cooperation of two other Commissioners, arguing that the takeover secured the EU's interest in inhibiting American discrimination.

12. *Le Monde*, Lobbying supplement, 3 November 1992.

13. E. Bertaud 'Lobbying in the EC', Groupe des Belles-Feuilles Supplement, March 1990.

14. VC48, p. 3.

15. SP11, SP28.

16. An IRI internal paper 'Thirty Years of Italian Industry in Brussels' (Summer 1992) provides interesting documentation to explain why the Italian government has failed to cultivate EU institutions. Blame apparently lies partly with the choice of appointments (too many failed politicians) and partly with failure to sponsor firms on a continuous basis because of departmental rivalries in

Rome. Industrial incentives for large as well as small companies have encouraged both to operate inside Italy in preference to seeking to implant themselves in other member states, whilst EC-supported research and development funds have habitually been diverted to political ends. IRI set out to remedy this in Brussels and, with its EC partners, claimed some success – but only up to 1989. Thereafter Italy was increasingly left behind, isolated in a history of warring national champions left over from the Davignon era of the early 1980s. In the end, IRI has had to fight the campaign for a new EU-oriented industrial policy in Italy, with as yet uncertain results.

17. IT6, pp. 1–2; IT9, p. 2.
18. Japanese firms' recent long-term stategy appeared to have been very much more conciliatory than were American companies in the 1950s and 1960s: to show permanent commitment and sensitivity to European sensibilities, to lie low, avoid quick or dramatic profits, refrain from killing off rivals while they withered or mutated, and to become insiders through the transfer of technology and the use of non-Japanese managers. At 6% of the EU's foreign direct investment, the Japanese share was still small compared to that of the US in 1991; but it is now rising steadily. Current strategy still appears to focus on partnerships which suit member states' own needs in manufacturing, not services, and on allowing autonomy to existing establishments. Fears of a more aggressive stance may not be justified (Sir Leslie Fielding, 'Japanese Investment in the EC' (EUI Confer-

ence, Europe and Japan, Florence, June 1992)).
19. FR33, p. 3.
20. This very necessary stage usually involves testing opinion among the more activist members of a sectoral organization. Passive firms, smaller firms, above all SMEs, tend to be left out of such secondary diplomacies, despite attempts on other levels by DG16 or 23 to galvanize the latter (PT4 p. 2; SP30, p. 1).
21. In an attempt to offset corporate leverage, these experts are seconded to the Commission and paid by them. Yet they form a majority on the over 250 working parties which advise the DGs, and from which many technical initiatives emerge. This inevitably colours the early stages of policy-making. The majority of firms' executives interviewed here saw this as an important element in creating patterns of long-term influence, only partly offset by the DGs' other resort, to academic experts.
22. When DG15 was preparing the Banking Fraud Legislation in 1990, Barclays drafted amendments to the proposals for supervision, data protection and electronic fraud. These were checked with the Home Office in London, the British Bankers' Association and the European Bankers' Federation, but initially met little response among DG15 officials in Brussels, possibly because the British Treasury disagreed with them. Barclays then went to the Director General, where the response was such that the amendments were largely incorporated in the final proposal.
23. FR24, p. 1.
24. VC25, p. 2.
25. Thus DG4 might shade competition

rules for SMEs' collaborative agreements, because of their 'lesser distorting effect' (KM126, p. 5). Over the 1992 Insurance Directive, on risk concentration, DG15 and the Commission supported a French government plea to exempt the small mutual associations which are a feature of the French system, on such grounds, even though this came very late in the day; and won despite opposition in the Council from at least three member states.

26. 'Talking to the EC: Consultation, lobbying, and openness' (*Forum Europe* Conference, 15 June 1993).

27. The Galle Report on lobby regulation whose authors set out (April 1993), as a minimum, to register all lobbyists in the Parliament, has not been published because of inherent difficulties, compounded by players' own lobbying, especially AmCham, British firms and some Permanent Representatives which did not want 'their' firms' competitive advantage curtailed. Galle was in fact an attempt by MEPs to capture the initiative, and run a cordon sanitaire around Strasbourg to prevent the lobbyists with the most wealthy clients driving out the rest; and also to inhibit MEPs from the pernicious practice of picking up their dossiers in an undiscriminating way. In contrast the Commission's proposals (Official Journal C63/2, 5 February 1993) for 'an open and structured dialogue between the Commission and interests groups', aimed differently, at defining their relations, mainly to prevent disputes between national and EU federations, or where non-representative bodies like ERT intervene; also to exclude corruption and insure the rights of information and openness guaran-

teed by Maastricht. The aim was to add formal rules to conventions governing access, encouraging the widest number of effective players to participate. This too has been found to be ineffective however because of the numbers and because of the difficulty of formalizing the informal, except where it suits both sides to do so.

28. FR11, p. 1.
29. FR78, p. 2; GR10, p. 1.
30. VC23, p. 2.
31. For a full account of the ERT and EEG see Maria Green-Cowles 'The Politics of Big Business in the EC' (Unpublished Open university Ph.D thesis, 1994).
32. FR7, p. 6.
33. KM26, p. 1.
34. It is worth noting that the German chemical federation, VCI, opened its own Brussels office in 1993 to increase its weight in CEFIC *vis-à-vis* Britain and France, and to serve as a more suitable filter for information for German members less used to Brussels concepts (FR77 (GR9), p. 4). In contrast, Spain's members in FEIQUE, which rank 5th by volume in the EC, suffer from low technology and investment and a poor export record. This appears to affect their political bargaining power adversely (SP8, p. 2).
35. Greenwood, Grote and Ronit, p. 96. VC124, p. 3.
36. See A. Cawson *et al*, *Hostile Brothers: Competition and Closure in the European Electronics Industry* (Oxford: 1989), especially chapter 4.
37. FR80, (GR12), p. 1.
38. S. Mazey & J. Richardson, *Lobbying in the EC*, chapters 7 & 8.
39. KM33, pp. 1–2. This was the case especially in the area of employment (DG5) given the numbers employed

in car production across the EU and their high concentration in certain towns such as Wolfsburg (VW) and the VW/SEAT plant in Catalonia.

40. KM35, p. 3.

41. ACEA now comprises BMW*, Daimler-Benz*, Renault*, and Fiat* (which both changed sides at the last moment), MAN, Porsche, VW*, Rover Group, Rolls Royce, DAF-Volvo, General Motors*, Ford, AB-Volvo*, Saab-Scania. (Those starred maintain a Brussels office, a factor which argues some element of EU irradiation).

42. KM108, p. 2.

43. A. McLaughlin, G. Jordan, W. Maloney 'Corporate Lobbying in the EC' in _JCMS_ (Vol. 31, No. 2, June 1993), pp. 191–211.

44. CBI Committee minutes, _passim_, 1983–6. VC60, p. 3. The _Economist_ Special report, European Financial Centres No. 5 (March 1991), points out however that this defect was to a large extent remedied by the Bank of England's close contact in the 1980s, despite Britain being excluded from the ERM, e.g., in the ecu banking business, as applied to Treasury Bills and interest rate futures.

45. G. Lanciano 'The Italian Banking System and European Integration: A supervisory perspective' Banco Populari de Bergama, 9th International Seminar, June 1992; P. Lagayette 'International and External Control of Market Opportunities' in _La Revue Banquaire_, No. 486, September 1988; D. M. Nuti 'The Role of the Banking Sector in the Process of Privatisation' (DG15 Economic Paper No. 98, November 1992).

46. The former had up to the mid–1980s been a far greater impediment to liberal policy, yet it was only challenged once the cartel was ceasing to

hold together; the latter appears still to be almost invulnerable, given the banks' argument that if charges were reduced, the transmission of small amounts would become so uneconomic they would cease.

47. AMRO-ABN – and the Société Générale de Belgique. Only Barclays and CitiBank appear successful. Cooperation agreements and takeovers such as Deutsche of Morgan Grenfell are of course another matter.

48. KM13, p. 2. French and British banking federations hold roughly 20% each in FBE, followed by the German BDB which rarely takes the initiative but defends the interests of German banks in depth; then by Belgium, the Netherlands and Italy.

49. FR30, p. 1.

50. FR66, (GR3), p. 3.

51. FR36, p. 1.

52. VC65, p. 1.

53. FR67, (GR), p. 1.

54. The role of the German Bankers Federation (BDB) is formally to concert policy for all the sector – in the first instance with Bonn, secondly with the FBE. Informally however, the larger members habitually have recourse to the BMWi and the state secretary for the economy, and increasingly to Brussels. (GR8, p. 2; FR76 (GR8), p. 1).

55. FR76 (GR8), p. 2.

56. FR20, p. 3. The quotation is from FR10, p. 1 (DG2 official).

57. IT17, p. 2.

58. The Bank of Spain pursued a monetarist policy in the period after Franco 1977–88, (as it has again since the crisis of 1990), in order to meet two consecutive challenges: EC entry and ERM entry in 1989. As far as financial institutions are

concerned, the banking crisis of 1978 provided the starting point. It took ten years to create a fully liberalized regime covering commercial banks, financial institutions, cooperative and savings banks together with building societies. Very little liberalization has been achieved so far in the insurance sector. Portuguese banks, nationalized during the 1974–5 revolution, were only privatized in the early 1990s. By 1993 the number of foreign banks in Lisbon had risen to forty (as against fourteen in 1984); but the majority of Portuguese banks still retain their old links to industrial conglomerates (PT6, p. 2).

59. FR13, pp. 1–2.
60. VC72, pp. 1–2.
61. Speech by Jorn Badenhoop, Brussels Banking Seminar, 27 March 1992.
62. KM115, p. 1–2; VC72, p. 3.
63. KM115, *passim*; S. Mazey & J. Richardson, *op.cit*, pp. 90–91. American banks at this time used European advisers, and deliberately presented themselves as 'European entities'.
64. KM115, p. 5.
65. Mazey & Richardson, *op.cit*, pp. 88–9. Allianz (Germany) is the largest player, with Britain's Prudential Royal Insurance, Italy's Generali and France's AP and AXA being not far behind.
66. Exchanges which were reformed or reformed themselves in 1992 include Milan as well as Frankfurt and Paris. As of June 1993, the twelve member states still possessed thirty-two stock exchanges and twenty-two futures and options markets. In addition to the big three or four, Amsterdam and Madrid still aspire to international status, while

in former East Germany, Leipzig hoped to reopen (*Economist*, 19 June 1993, p. 19). Regional exchanges in Germany have resisted concentration in Frankfurt, however, and have complained strongly against German MNCs such as BASF, which aim to de-list their stocks in order to focus on Frankfurt. Deutsche Bank, acting for BASF, has been accused of orchestrating a campaign to strip them of their trading functions and reduce them to information and advisory centres (*European*, 8 December 1994).

67. Yet a British Business Bureau under the CBI's umbrella, funded by the City as well as industrial federations, has proved a useful vehicle for cooperation on behalf of British federations unwilling to set up their own direct networks in Brussels. Similar arrangements were made in Germany and France in 1988.
68. *Handelsblatt*, 6 August 1992, gives a list of those which had declared their hand in mid–1992.
69. FR53, p. . The only major instance where the Commission asked all national organizations for their assistance (comparable to its requests to sectoral federations and firms), seems to have been in preparing the Commission Presidency's *cellule de prospective* 1993 study, 'The EC challenge after 1992', in conjunction with the twelve member states' national research institutions, McKinsey & Co., and the ERT.
70. VC23, p. 2; SP9, pp. 2–3; IT6, p. 2. Delors' speech at the TUC conference in September 1988 was itself a landmark in that organization's turnabout which ended decades of hostility to the EU concept. The three French federations (FO, CFDT and CGT) claimed credit for

reinvigorating Mitterrand's enthusiasm for 'social Europe' during 1990. The TUC took rather longer to react, but helped to form the Labour party's stance during the Maastricht debates in Britain in early 1992. For the TUC's more recent approximation to the 1993 White Paper, see David Lea, 'European Framework Agreements – a trade union opportunity' in *Journal, International Centre for Trade Union Rights* (1994). This is not far from the argument put since 1992 by the German DGB (itself largely responsible for creating ETUC and then funding its operation in the 1970s), which has been applied in detail (as in Germany by most sectoral trade unions), to safety, conditions of employment and the shaping of industrial policy (GR5, p. 2; GR14, p.2).

71. SP15, p. 3; SP19, p. 3. The majority of trade union confederations have set up their own Brussels offices (the TUC as recently as 1993). The patterns of strikes aimed at preventing factory closures or changes of work practice in Italy, France, Spain, Belgium and Germany during 1993–4, does not augur well.

72. AGREF resembles a one-nation ERT and is equally activist, in detail, on most Commission policies in these fields, being especially critical of the European Company Statute. Though very influential in Paris, it rarely relies on French governments to intervene; it has had good access to Commissioners and Delors himself, operating with great discretion, 'so that nothing appears in the press because that would make it impossible for the Commission to take up the subject directly, sometimes at all.' (FR25, p. 1; FR37, p. 5).

73. Confindustria's officials are well aware of being isolated, even mistrusted, in Brussels through association with the Italian government. They try where possible therefore to stand with CNPF, CBI or the German associations (IT2, pp. 2–3), and use the partly-owned magazine *Il Sole: 24 Ore* with sales of 300,000), 'to lay down the broad lines of its policy, through the editorials and presentation of news' (KM36, p. 2).

74. CBI EC Steering Committee, 4 April 1988, and especially June and December 1988. c.f., also S. Mazey & J. Richardson, *op.cit.* chapter 11. Something similar happened in the Danish CDI because of business criticism of the high costs of EU social policy (VC80, (DK), p. 2).

75. These three campaigned together, for example for admission of the EFTA applicants in 192–3 (*VWD Europa*, 9 December 1992, p. 8).

76. It is noticeable that both BDI and BDA work by consensus over the long term and in accordance with post-War conceptions of West German balance. Coordination occurs in Bonn and the Verbände tend to follow very closely the German government line on all external questions to do, for example, with reunification (GR5 & GR6). c.f. also the 'Forum of German Industry' organized by DIHT (Association of Chambers) and other leading industrial interest groups in 1992, where a German industrial front was mobilized in support of Maastricht, the single market and extension of the European Union to EFTA applicants (GR2, p. 1–2). According to a Dutch observer, the German organizations hesitated for many years before flexing their

muscles in this way – as the CBI and Netherlands VNO habitually do – but this restraint has now ended (FR60 (NL5), p. 5).

77. For example, for simplification of the European trademarks system in a minimum of languages (*Agence Europe*, 11 November 1992, No. 5855), and in defence of GATT and liberal trade (ibid, 1 January 1993).

78. CBI EC Steering Committee minutes; as early as June 1976, the CBI was arguing that UNICE should be the means to give a new impetus to the EC and to counter the excessive demands of trade union federations. Although the CBI's belief in UNICE tapered off in some disillusionment, it was renewed in 1984 prior to UNICE's reconstruction, in which CBI members, including Lord Pennock, played a large part (Mazey and Richardson, p. 204).

79. On that occasion, AmCham's EC Committee and the CBI took the lead successfully, but the Directive's emasculation owed more to UNICE's national members working individually on their own governments in order to reach Coreper and the Council. Governments in turn used UNICE's unanimity to deflect hostility of their own trade union movements and publics (CBI European Committee minutes, September 1980).

CHAPTER ELEVEN

1. Wallace, Wallace & Webb, *EC Policy Making*, 2nd edn, chapter 7 pp. 225–9.

2. World-wide turnover of both parties combined of 5 billion ecus, European turnover of 250 million ecus, or more than 60% of national market share.

3. The *Philip Morris* case can be considered a landmark because the ECJ's use of Article 85 (rather than 86 which had served in the *Continental Can* case) extended policy in theory even to minor mergers. It moved UNICE to protest that the Council rather than the Court should sort out such fundamentally important economic questons.

4. Wallace, Wallace and Webb, p. 214.

5. According to Commission figures, (20th Report on Competition Policy), 117 mergers occurred in 1986–7, and 90 joint ventures, 159 and 129 in 1988–89, and 180 and 156 in 1989–90. A decline ensued, probably due to the recession. The incidence was highest in computers, electronics, chemicals, the automotive and aerospace sectors. In terms of acquisitions, 70–75% of these took place in Germany, France, Britain, Netherlands, and Italy; in terms of targets, in Germany, France, Britain, Italy and Spain.

6. The subsidy league

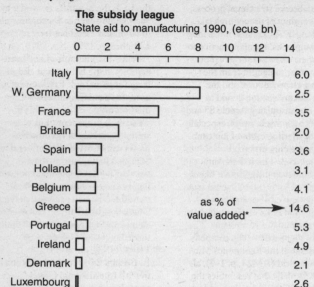

The subsidy league
State aid to manufacturing 1990, (ecus bn)

Italy	6.0
W. Germany	2.5
France	3.5
Britain	2.0
Spain	3.6
Holland	3.1
Belgium	4.1
Greece	as % of value added* → 14.6
Portugal	5.3
Ireland	4.9
Denmark	2.1
Luxembourg	2.6

* 1986–90 annual average

Figure 11:6

7. VC29, *passim*.

8. Brittan was evidently much more sympathetic to ill-requited efforts to liberalize by the Spanish competition section in the Economics Ministry, in the teeth of government support for Spanish state holdings, than he was to West German aid to East Germany, or Italian aid to the Mezzogiorno (KM24, pp. 1–3).

9. The rules were of course contained in the Merger Regulations which prescribed compulsory notification, followed by a month's period before declaring the majority of cases acceptable. For those requiring investigation (roughly 10% in any year), DG4 had powers to ask for information during the next four months, before authorizing or vetoing the merger. Penalties for infringement could be inflicted – up to 10% of annual turnover – and companies could appeal against the judgment to the ECJ.

10. Keith Hawkins (ed.), *The Uses of Discretion* (Oxford: 1994). House of Lords Select Committee on EC, First Report 1993–4, 'Enforcement of Commission Competition Rules' (HMSO 1993), Recommendations 157–58.

11. Several of the interviews point to a generic difference between an 'Anglo-Saxon' section in DG4 which is habitually flexible, open to

negotiation, and a 'German' one, keen to observe strict legal process, whose conduct of procedures takes much longer. As a result, it has long been companies' regular practice to notify their cases as mergers if possible, in order to benefit from the four-month procedure; and the 'Anglo-Saxon' section is said to connive by disguising Article 85 and 86 cases with this in mind, especially where borderline cases of joint subsidiaries are concerned.

12. IT14, pp. 1–2. The Italian Anti-Trust Authority prides itself, like the Banca D'Italia, on standing out from a largely protectionist Italian government; and in its methods seeks to model itself on the Kartellamt. The same might be said of the competition section in the Economics Ministry in Madrid (KM24, p. 1–3), although formally that resembles the French DGCCRF, being part of the state administration.

13. *Handelsblatt*, 5 October 1992, p. 3; also 4 January 1993, for the President's speech. The Commission responded in February 1993 with a Communication, intended to codify some of DG4's informal practices and thus undermine the German criticisms.

14. FR68 (GR3), pp. 1–3, former Kartellamt official.

15. Comfort letters have the effect of allowing the parties in a case to proceed, on the understanding that their case has been approved. In the VW–Ford joint venture for instance, where aid (accompanied by a comfort letter) was allowed in July 1991 to build a challenger to the Matra–Renault Espace, in Portugal under the first framework programme; both Matra and Renault objected. Their first request for an

emergency ruling was rejected by the ECJ; the plaintiffs revived it by complaining against Portuguese aid of 97 billion escudos (*Agence Europe*, 13 February 1993, No. 5919) on the grounds that this subsidized overcapacity in the EU market and distorted regional aid. In the end, DG4 accepted a compromise; the Commission would never use this instance as a precedent, thus constraining its long-term informal power quite severely. In effect, DG4 admitted that it had issued the comfort letter too soon: a comfort letter has no status in EC law and therefore its existence is no defence. The firms, with French and German tacit support, thus forced DG4 into formality (FR68 (GR3), p. 3).

16. FR68 (GR3), pp. 1–3.

17. L. Brittan, 25 May 1992; Speech to the 6th International Cartel Conference, Berlin.

18. As van Miert put it, policy 'is necessarily evolutionary in nature and must respond to the changing European and world economic social and political climate if it is to remain relevant and vital.' Rules should be based on 'as broad a consensus of the participants as possible.' Speech to the European Parliament (*Agence Europe*, 22 February 1993, No. 5925); also speech to the RIIA, 11 May 1993.

19. L. Brittan speech, *op.cit*. Also KM 126, pp. 1–3, *passim*.

20. KM20, pp. 3–4.

21. Ciments Français has complained to the ECJ that it was singled out for unusual punishment. The other members of the cement cartel were two Belgian companies, and Blue Circle Industries (Britain), who have also appealed on the grounds that they were refused access to some of

DG4's evidence against them: a landmark defence which has nothing to do with the merits of the case. (*Agence Europe*, 3 December 1992, No. 5870).

22. Witness the Spanish and Italian protests against DG4's handling of a Proctor and Gamble–Lines joint agreement. As a result, during the thirty days between publication of DG4's consent in the *Official Journal* and final approval, the decision was rescinded by the college (IT14, p. 1).

23. KM35, pp. 2–3. In both cases, DG3 argued against DG4 on the grounds that national markets were no more than 'historic legacies' (KM27, p. 1).

24. KM26, pp. 2–3; VC 29, pp. 2–3.

25. In 1991, the Aerospace Industrial Association (ECNA) was still a loose organization, run on a low budget. Companies habitually represented themselves and let each other get on with their own deals: BAe for example only opposed this merger later, when DG4 pointed out the implications. Subsequently, however, when ECNA woke up, the larger companies instituted a controlling group, including BAe and Fokker, better able to represent the Association on all issues including GATT.

26. FR1, p. 2, former SGCI official.

27. *Nord-Europa*, 13 November 1992, p. 4.

28. At the end of 1993, van Miert rejected, on similar grounds, a merger between Mannesmann Vallource and Ilva's stainless steel tubes interests; but his decision was rejected by the college in January 1994, in a split vote 8/8, thanks to Delors's abstention. The current position is therefore unclear.

29. Nevertheless, a judgment of 21 November 1991 (case C–354/90) by the ECJ established that the Conseil d'État's role was confined to protecting the rights of individuals while the Commission undertook its investigation, not to reviewing the substance of the case: this may be seen as a final stage in the long process discussed earlier, by which French authorities came to accept the ECJ's exclusive and superior jurisdiction.

30. FR1, p. 2, former SGCI official.

31. KM126, p. 2. It is claimed that the Delors cabinet forewarned Rocard, whose ministers in turn contacted several Commissioners, something which would not have occurred in any member state other than Spain (KM57, pp. 3–4).

32. c.f., Commission's First Survey on State Aids to Industry (1989). The 1992 Survey suggests that DG4 requires clear proof of positive effect, social benefits, restructuring or modernization, and is generally opposed to the retention of the sectoral status quo, even in the classic cases of shipbuilding, steel, synthetic fibres and car production. The same is likely to apply in future to aids to the financial sector, and to cross-subsidies in postal services and telecoms.

33. FR1, pp. 2–3; FR11, *passim*.

34. In the Boussac instance, the French government had failed to notify.

35. Lord Young, *The Enterprise Years: a Businessman in the Cabinet* (London: 1990), pp. 296–302 and 326.

36. *Agence Europe*, 3 December 1992, No. 5870.

37. In 1991 to Air France and Sabena, in 1992 to Air France and Iberia, in 1993 TAP and Olympic and Aer Lingus. The sums involved are vast,

Air France being taken to the ECJ early in 1995 over the Commission's approval of a £2.3bn subsidy, at a time when Spain approached the Commission for approval of £650m for Iberia, despite acceptance of £1bn in 1992. A further £2.4bn, contingent on Air France's restructuring was still at issue after the company had decided to cancel many of its outstanding aircraft orders.

38. FR1, p. 2.

39. The complicated negotiations over state aids for Fiat's greenfield plant at Melfi in the Italian Mezzogiorno, were based partly on a trade-off with German aid to East Germany (see p. 576), partly on the argument that intensity of development in a region as deprived as Basilicata matched the extent of state aid in the total aid (30%) (*Agence Europe*, 13 February 1993, No. 5919).

40 Spain v. the Commission (C–312/90), Italy v. the Commission (C–47/91); judgments of 30 June 1992.

41. *Agence Europe*, 29 July 1993, p. 10; 14 October 1993, p. 14, No. 6085.

42. Luc Gyselen 'The Commission's fining policy in competition cases', paper presented to seminar on competition law, University of Leiden, November 1992, especially pp. 15–18. The shipping firm Boloré for example (see above, p. 513) withdrew from all Conference cartels, not only the West African ones, as an indication of good behaviour.

43. *Agence Europe*, 20 May 1993, No. 5984.

44. *Agence Europe*, 16 November 1992, No. 5858.

45. BIS: *Eight European Central Banks* (London: 1963); E. Kennedy, *The Bundesbank: Germany's Central Bank in the International System* (London:

1991); A. Mullineux (ed), *European Banking* (Oxford: 1992); N. Thygesen and D. Gros, *European Monetary Integration* (London: 1992). Of particular value is M. Deane and R. Pringle, *The Central Banks* (London: 1994).

46. FR2, p. 3, French former foreign minister. As if in emulation of their influence, Ecofin has recently set up an Economic Policy Committee, junior to but not subordinate to the Monetary Committee, in order to be able to discuss monetary policy in an environment free of 'politics' – and of Central Bank Governors.

47. Loukas Tsoukalis, *The New European Economy* (Oxford: 1991), pp. 67–78.

48. The EMS's origins go back to the December 1969 Hague Summit, when Georges Pompidou and Willi Brandt advocated monetary union; at which stage it could already be seen that West Germany was concerned with the EC's overall economic health, France with its monetary stability. Despite this evident divergence, the Werner Committee in 1972 recommended monetary union within ten years.

49. The Bank of Spain colluded, against its will, in a governmental operation to lower the peseta by reducing interest rates because the Gonzalez government wished to show support to France (and also to Britain, where sterling was coming under pressure).

50. For a good contemporary account of these events see *Sunday Times*, 6 December 1992, pp. 1–2. It is not clear who among finance ministers called for a general realignment, or whether this public rejection represented the views of both the Bundesbank and Trichet himself. As late as the Bath Ecofin meeting 5/6 Sep-

tember, the Dutch Finance Ministry was still pushing the Bundesbank to change its mind, but Schlesinger refused (KM25, p. 6).

51. KM 39, pp. 1–2. Above all, the Monetary Committee did not discuss what the correct rates ought to be, because to do so would be to imply that a realignment was desirable, thus throwing doubt on the whole glidepath thesis. (Such discussion had ceased to be possible roughly at the time of sterling's ERM entry, when Trichet had only hinted that DM 2.95 was too high, while de Larosière (Bank of France) and Ciampi (Bank of Italy) indicated it might be too low.) The Bank of England may have wished for a sterling devaluation but was inhibited by Lamont, the chancellor; the lifeline of a joint arrangement between sterling and lira, offered by Amato on 13 September, was tacitly rejected or ignored by the British government.

52. In public, this episode provoked further recrimination against Britain and the ERM's devaluers, and Kohl's phrase about 'provoking turbulence to torpedo the process of EMU' was reiterated by Delors and Raymond Barre.

53. The most likely explanation is that since Tietmeyer, the Bundesbank's number two, supported Kohl's argument that Germany's post-unification pattern of evolution within the EU required a Franco-German entente, Schlesinger for reasons of German self-interest accepted the wider bands as a precondition for the continuance of ERM and eventual EMU/EPU. It is said that Tietmeyer gave a guarantee that when he succeeded as Bundesbank president, he would initiate sharper interest rate cuts. But for that concession, France, Belgium and Denmark would probably have cut their rates, in unison, and *forced* a deutschmark revaluation or a German rate cut, thus severely damaging the Bundesbank's prestige (KM111, p. 2.). Tietmeyer however, was aware that the recession in Germany would require such cuts in any case in the second half of 1993.

54. Summary, based on articles in *Le Monde, Quotidien de Paris, L'Exprés, Figaro, le Point*.

55. *El País*, 27 September 1992, *et seq.*

56. *La Repubblica*, 19 September 1992. For Ciampi's later argument, directed against Franco-German hegemony, see *Corriere della Sera*, 23 October 1992.

57. For the first interpretation see *Handelsblatt*, 18 September 1992, p. 2; for the second, *Handelsblatt*, 22 September 1992, p. 11.

58. *Die Zeit*, 9 October 1992, p. 1.

59. *Economist*, 7 August 1993, p. 24.

60. FR19, pp. 1–2; KM15, p. 4.

61. KM15, p. 3.

62. Lecture, CERI Paris, April 1992.

63. KM18, p. 1, Bundesbank former deputy director.

64. In July 1994, deeply sensitive to any likelihood of derogation from the convergence rules, the Bundesbank directorate attempted, through sympathetic members of the Bundestag, to block a Commission proposal to give special treatment to Ireland. In the same month, Tietmeyer accused the British government of conducting an 'inexact and risky' anti-inflationary policy.

65. H. Schlesinger, 31 January 1992, speech to Stockholm School of Economics, p. 21.

66. KM41, p. 3. Leigh-Pemberton was careful to distinguish between convergence criteria as the essential

pre-history for EMU, and EPU as a separate matter (speech to the English Speaking Union, 22 November 1990). Two years later, in a more nuanced address at Green College, Oxford (13 February 1992), he expressed considerable scepticism about the convergence thesis, and portrayed EMU as a means to complete the internal market – but with possible prejudicial effects on freer trade. It is worth adding that the Scottish banks are in general more outspoken in support of the way ERM is managed, and favour EMU, since they object strongly to the inconvenience and expense of doing business in twelve currencies plagued by fluctuations in rates (VC8, p. 3).

67. KM37, p. 1.

68. In the Paolo Boffi lecture (Milan, 22 October 1991), Carlo Ciampi declared that convergence was the only way forward: 'a commitment to economic self-discipline, above all to price stability'.

69. The case of Italy's balance of payments loan, agreed by the Council of Ministers June 1993, is instructive. The Monetary Committee consented, despite arguments by DG2 that Italy's three year budget targets lacked credibility. 'Compensation for the recession' emerged as an argument which finance ministers and Delors would accept, to keep Italy within the convergence programme. Nevertheless, thanks to the tough line argued by DG2, and Henning Christophersen the Commissioner, Italy had to accept the imposition of a significant degree of external financial discipline.

70. KM22, p. 3.

71. FR72 (NL8), pp. 1–2.

72. VC95 (DK), p. 3.

73. VC75 (IRL), p. 3.

74. VC96, p. 2.

75. The French government appears to have wanted it to go to Luxembourg or Bonn, in preference to Frankfurt. Apart from Frankfurt, the only other serious contender was Amsterdam, despite all Britain's advocacy of London (KM111, p. 2). The deciding factor may have been the German argument that to put it in Frankfurt, almost in the shadow of the Bundesbank, was the only means of convincing German public opinion to accept the deutschmark's eventual demise.

76. See table over, figure 11:76

77. G. Bishop 'Is there a rapid route to an EMU of the few?', UACES conference on *EMS in the 90s*, June 1993. In early December 1994, Henning Christophersen forecast that EMU would be achieved in 1998–9, but not by a restoration of the narrow bands; rates were more likely to be fixed at the central one existing on the starting date. There seems no doubt that the technical problems of transition to a single currency can be solved before then. But convergence of the eight member state currencies needed as a minimum for the transition is most uncertain, as is the Maastricht date of 1996 for the EMI to finalize its proposals. Substantial difficulties still exist (mid-1995) between the Bundesbank and other Central Banks, for example over the need for compulsory bank reserves, and how far the EMI is to prefigure the eventual ECB.

78. Member state banking systems habitually complain that they are excluded from the Governors' detailed plans for EMU's third stage for payment systems or harmonization

Converging towards union? (1993 figures)				
	Inflation rate%	Budget balance % of GDP	Debt % of GDP	Long-term interest rate %
	1993 average*	1993	1993	1993 average
Germany	4.1	−3.4	45.0	6.6
France	2.1	−5.9	39.2	7.0
Italy	4.3	−10.0	108.0	10.1
Britain	1.6	−7.6	47.3	7.7
Spain	4.7	−7.2	48.8	10.8
Holland	2.2	−4.0	79.7	6.5
Belgium	2.7	−7.4	131.9	7.3
Denmark	1.3	−4.4	73.4	7.5
Portugal	6.7	−8.9	63.5	8.7
Greece	14.7	−15.4	106.7	23.9
Ireland	1.6	−3.0	91.6	8.2
Luxembourg	3.5	−2.5	7.3	7.5
Potential EU members (as of 1993)				
Sweden	4.5	−13.0	53.0	8.8
Austria	3.7	−4.5	56.6	6.8
Norway	2.3	−3.4	43.3	7.2
Finland	2.2	−10.8	37.0	8.9

*Latest 12 months
Source European Commission; OECD; National statistics, Deutsche Bank Research

Figure 11:76

(Source: *Economist*, 15 January 1994, p. 80.)

rules. Yet they need to know what is going to happen, several years ahead, to plan how to conform in the least costly, most efficient way. Not unreasonably, they wish to be party to what is said in the small working groups attached to the Governors' Committee and Committee of Alternates where 'discussion is pragmatic, practical, with little politics or ideology, and connected to the real world' (KM37 p. 3).

79. These are not necessarily weighty interlocutors, however, as was demonstrated when the British government asked Ecofin in mid-September 1992 for a general suspension of the ERM. Delors was eventually persuaded to make a similar proposal to the Monetary Committee. In both forums, the majority refused – a decision which would almost certainly have been different had it been left to the Governors' Committee alone.

80. KM18, p. 6.

81. KM40, p. 2.

82. The five technical but still major areas for EMI study are currently, statistics, payment systems, the type of European banknote, accounting issues, and the establishment of information systems. The costs to all fifteen banking systems of the transition are expected to be prodigious.

83. KM91, p. 3, former President of the Commission. The same point was argued in a study prepared for the EP by Stefan Collignan and the Association for Monetary Union in Europe, July 1993, which advocated a renewed ERM drive to EMU 'based on voluntary cooperation between formerly autonomous and politically independent central banks' (p. 32); see also Central Bank Governors Annual Report, 1992 as summarized by *Agence Europe*, 21 April 1993 No. 1831.

84. I. Harden 'Sovereignty and the Eurofed' in *Political Quarterly*, October 1990, pp. 402–13.

85. KM111, p. 3. When the Commission's Paris office asked Sofres in 1992 for an opinion poll on why the French public thought EMU mattered, the great majority (78%) of respondents answered that it would enable the EU to stand up to the dollar and the yen; an equal number feared that it would ensconce the deutschmark in a dominant position.

86. Ash Amin and Michael Dietrich, *Towards a New Europe? Structural Changes in the European Economy* (Aldershot: 1991), chapter 8.

CHAPTER TWELVE

1. By 1980, steel capacity utilization had fallen from its 1974 peak of 85% to 55% in the face of competition from the Asian producers, Brazil and above all, Japan. Yet because of the impact on employment, member states were not prepared to close factories or rationalize their industries. The West German government opposed the Commission declaring 'manifest crisis' under ECSC Article 58, arguing that member states should in fact re-

structure, no matter what the cost. After a long enquiry, the Commission had adopted the Davignon plan in 1977 (under Article 61) which allowed price fixing, voluntary quotas and bilateral agreements with foreign producers. Extended in 1978 and 1981, it worked well with Japan and the United States, despite West German, Italian and British complaints, not least because it allowed the producers (Eurofer) and trade unions a voice in the arrangements. Consequently it protected employment, but failed to reduce capacity sufficiently, and barely touched state subsidies. During the early 1980s recession, it was renegotiated by a coalition of France, Britain, Luxembourg, Belgium and the Netherlands, against German and Italian opposition, under a 'manifest crisis' with mandatory quotas (October 1980). Despite a more rapid fall in capacity from 792,000 tons in 1975 to 600,000 tons in 1980, the next stage divided Eurofer, ranging the more efficient producers in Germany and Britain (soon to be privatized) and Italy (the Bresciani group) against state-owned sectors elsewhere. The Commission intervened, decisively, threatening to remove Article 58 cover unless the Council of Ministers agreed to abandon state aids – which it did in June 1981, supposedly with effect from 1986.

2. Though dogged for some years by controversy about its surprising lethargy in actually lending to the intended recipients (which was exacerbated by the flamboyant style of its first president, Jacques Attali, and accusations later that it existed only to serve French interests), the EBRD under its second president,

Jacques de Larosière, did useful, under-rated work in eastern Europe in the early 1990s. Its involvement in the Slovakian nuclear project at Mochavce has, however, recently revived criticism about its political motivation.

3. W. Wallace, H. Wallace & W. Webb, *Policymaking in the EC*, pp. 65, 288. See also E. M. Milanesi, 'La Politica Industriale della CE' in *Nomisma Review* (December 1992), pp. 11–59.

4. Britain also had no equivalent of CLORA, the French group of ten state research institutes, working together as a team in Brussels, and integrated both with the SGCI and French universities to prepare dossiers on new areas of research. CLORA's effects, like those of its German counterpart, can be read in the near-monopoly maintained by French and German scientific terminology in Community transactions.

5. KM107, pp. 1–5, DG3 Director General.

6. KM126, pp. 3–4, former Commissioner.

7. KM31, p.2; KM126, p. 4.

8. DG7's Green Paper 'The Impact of Transport on the Environment' (Com (92) 46), was produced after long consultation with hauliers, drivers unions, freight firms and shippers associations (A. Young, 'Public and private interests in the EU', SEI Paper (October 1994), p. 8) This gave it a somewhat one-sided tendency.

9. Ash Amin and Michael Dietrich, *Towards a New Europe? Structural Changes in the European Economy*, offers an illuminating discussion of these questions and the contemporary debates among economists.

10. For example, in the wake of the ECJ's 1986 judgment on minimum harmonization, DG15's preparation of the banking capital and liquidity directive set general rules but left it to member states to apply their own detailed requirements on solvency of financial institutions.

11. COM (90), 556.

12. As is set out by M. Alcouffe, *L'Europe Industrielle* (2 vols. Paris: 1992), vol. 1, chapter 1, pp. 17–31. See also Mark Aspinwall 'Policy integration and highly mobile investment: EC shipping policy' (ECSA/Ford Foundation Paper 1993) who argues that in this area, Commission policy has been shaped by the systemic power of firms to disinvest into flags of convenience if they do not obtain what they want.

13. VC22, *passim*.

14. CEN (the European committee for standards/norms) and CENELEC (covering electrical norms) were constituted from existing national bodies and remained heterogeneous and slower to work than the national ones. Attempts to speed up the process by making sectoral entities led to unwieldy agglomerations, some of over 200 members, only a handful of whom took part in the voluntary, densely bargained drafting processes. Standards drafting is an essential adjunct to the internal market, but both CEN and CENELEC produce only a fraction of what is done by the national agencies in Germany, Britain and France (Schreiber (1991), pp. 102–3).

15. Wolfgang Hager, 'Public Interests and the Market: Europe's 1992 project' (Paper for Andrew Shonfield Association Seminar, September 1988). M. Albert, 'Which Capitalism for Europe?'

(Seminar in European micro-economics, Forward Studies Group, December 1992).

16. This applies even when they and their growing environmental groups achieve successes, say against the car producers, on catalytic conver-ters for small cars, or over the pharmaceuticals campaign attempts to modify the Commission's adver-tising Directive in 1992.

17. *Agence Europe*, 22–23 March 1993, No. 5945, reporting ETUC's General Secretary Emilio Gabaglio.

18. Com (89) 564 (Final) aimed to provide firstly the means of separat-ing railway operations from the track and infrastructure, secondly management independence and commercial running, thirdly com-mercial accounting and an end to subsidies, and fourthly, cross-border services with free access to the networks.

19. KM28, pp. 1–4.

20. VC121, pp. 1–3, D. Hollings *et al*, 'European Railways prospects for long distance passenger services in the 1990s' (*Economist* Intelligence Unit Paper, October 1991).

21. Margaret Sharp, 'The Single Market and European Policies for Advanced Technologies' (*Political Quarterly* Special Issue, *Beyond the Single Market*, October 1990). For a more outspoken American view-point, overtly hostile to Delors, see George Ross, 'Sliding into Indust-rial Policy: Inside the European Commission' in *French Politics and Society* (11.3., Winter 1993). Ross argued that for Delors there was 'no such thing as a pure market', only an organized framework (ordnung-spolitik) with a social dimension, offsetting the rigours of competi-tion.

22. Eko-Stahl's restructuring, according to the German authorities, was to involve *increasing* production by 835,000 tonnes; if not, it would not be saved. The unemployment impact on Eisenhuttenstadt would be very severe, and the Kohl govern-ment's policies for Brandenburg could not be implemented.

23. *Agence Europe*, 7 July 1993 No. 6016.

24. For this sector, see A. Smith & A. J. Venables, 'Automobiles' in G. C. Hufbauer (ed.), *Europe 1992: An American Perspective* (Brookings Inst. 1993), chapter 3; see also M. Mason, 'Europe's Response to the Japanese Automotive Challenge' in *JCMS* (Vol.32, No.4, December 1994).

25. The most obvious case is that of catalytic converters, long fitted as standard in Germany, thanks to the environmental lobby's efforts. German producers solidly backed DG3 in supporting their European-wide introduction, to the detriment of French, British and Italian manu-facturers.

26. R. Dornbusch and R. Layard, *Per-formance of the British Economy* (Oxford: 1987), pp. 197–8.

27. A. Smith and A. J. Venables, art cit, pp. 125–6; T. Gaudillot, *La Dernière Bataille de L'Automobile Européen* (Paris: 1992). KM33, p. 1. French authorities rejected a proposal by Mazda to set up in Angers, despite support from the mayor, even though in the electronics industry Japanese producers were already well established in France.

28. Renault is the most notable case. Facing bankruptcy in 1982 had it not been for the government *regie*, Renault was turned round by Raymond Levy after 1985 using the threat of foreign competition. In the

former heartland of the PCF trade union CGT, Levy forced the workforce to accept 40,000 redundancies, huge increases in productivity, and a range of new models and concepts such as the Espace – which went far to justify French state aid, despite the prosecution by DG4 detailed in chapter 11.

29. M. McLaughlin & G. Jordan, 'The Car Industry' in S. Mazey and J. Richardson, *Lobbying in the EC*, pp. 112–159.

30. FR20, pp. 1–2.

31. KM30, p. 13; KM33, pp. 1–4.

32. P. Holmes and A. Smith, 'Trade, Competition and Industry Policy for Cars' (SEI paper October 1994). The EU has already refused to allow Poland to allocate its existing quotas to EU firms promising to invest in domestic production.

33. Commission communication to the car industry, 8 May 1992, pp. 18–19.

34. KM35, p. 3; KM11, p. 3.

35. M. Bangemann, memorandum on competition and prospects for the European automotive industry, quoted in *Agence Europe*, 25 February 1994, No. 1972.

36. Alan Cawson *et al, Hostile Brothers: Competition and Closure in the European Electronics Industry* (Oxford: 1990), and Greenwood, Grote and Ronit, *Organized Interests in the EC*, pp. 101–17.

37. Greenwood, Grote and Ronit, p. 115.

38. VC69, pp. 1–4.

39. G. Ross, 'Sidling in to Industrial Policy' in *French Politics and Society* (11.3. Winter 1993). KM107, *passim*.

40. Guy de Jonquières, *Financial Times*, 22 October 1990, for what seems to be the earliest public critique of this outcome of Esprit.

41. KM32, pp. 1–4; KM107, pp. 2–3.

42. G. Ross, *art.cit*, p. 39.

43. Com SEC (9) 1 565 Final 3, April 1993.

44. Alan Cawson, 'Large Firms as Political Actors' (SEI Seminar Paper, October 1994).

45. KM26, pp. 1–4.

46. IT21, pp. 1–2; FR77 (GR9), p. 3. German members are more prone to using these: conversely Ferruzzi normally follows the CEFIC line.

47. EFPIA comprises six large players, each of world status, and two others based in Switzerland. Hoechst (6), Bayer (12), Smith Kline Beecham (2), Rhône-Poulenc (14), Famitalia, and Roche (9), Ciby-Geigy (4), Sandoz (13) (1992 world rankings).

48. VC124, *passim*.

49. Sir Geoffrey Owen, 'The British Pharmaceutical and Chemicals Industries' (FMI paper, 17 March 1993), p. 33.

50. Greenwood, Grote and Ronit, pp. 78–79.

51. Greenwood, Grote and Ronit, pp. 43–60, 62–64. H. Ungerer and N. Costello, *Telecommunications in Europe* (Luxembourg: 1988) p. 261.

52. Alcatel, now the largest telecoms equipment supplier in the EU and number two in the world, provided an instance, like Thomson in electronics, of how a national player, having escaped state control and mutated into a transnational one, could bring such influence to bear, as it were from within the national commercial culture, which it fostered by lobbying the Commission for a rule of reciprocity with Japan (*Financial Times*, 16 January 1990, 25 April 1991) hoping to create for itself a partnership with France Télécom. But by 1995, this strategy had run into deep trouble, leaving

Alcatel exposed. Siemens has tried to follow suit, with stringent criticisms of Deutsche Bundespost's resistance to deregulation, exploiting the German government's publicly professed liberalization sentiments.

53. Van Miert quoted in *Agence Europe*, 22 April 1993, No. 1832.

54. c.f., the Belgian postal monopoly case where, in answer to a request for guidance from a Belgian court, the ECJ ruled that monopoly in the core service was admissible as a 'general economic aim', whereas in supplementary or improved services it was not.

55. Abolished in Spain and Ireland 1992. Greece and Portugal have a derogation until 1995.

56. VC8, p. 1.

57. Manfred Weber, 'Banks in the Internal Market: Positions and Expectations' in *Europäische Zeitung* (January 1993). The subsequent patterns of acquisition by Deutsche Bank, Dresdner, and Commerzbank, particularly that of Deutsche in London, and the lack of expansion in universal banking, indicate just how carefully strategic planning has been implemented.

58. VC57, p. 2; SP21, p. 2. The Bank of England and SIB for example were able to win amendments to the Investment Services Directive, November 1988.

59. GR9, pp. 1–2. German supervisors worried about the supervision of international financial conglomerates to German standards, and about how conflicts of supervision competence between major players' cross-border offices could be resolved.

60. KM53, p. 3.

61. The CEA originally proposed a figure of 2000 for the number of employees, dropped quickly to 1000,

and finally settled for 500, a figure which the Commission had already persuaded the Council to accept. Denmark, Ireland, Italy and Luxembourg only accepted this figure in January 1993, nearly a year after Belgium, France, Germany, Spain, and Portugal.

62. KM48, p. 3. An attempt by DG15 to harmonize the law on insurance contracts and individual responsibility was blocked 6–6 in the Council in 1985. An ECJ judgment in 1986 subsequently provided that, in lieu of harmonization, a member state might retain its own laws so long as they satisfied the criteria of proportionality, non-discrimination and the 'general good', with no duplication of protection. As far as DG15 is concerned, this position is likely to remain.

63. KM53, p. 2; VC63, pp. 2–3. German government consultation with existing insurers in Germany is so widespread that the national players invariably have time either to ban a new product from outside or to copy it before it comes on the market; see P. E. Hunt, 'Effects of 1992 on the Insurance Industry in Britain and Germany' (NIESR Discussion Paper, No. 18), p. 11. German concern about the lack of consumer protection, on the other hand, forced the Commission to rewrite its 1989 proposals for the single market in insurance, and delayed the outcome to mid–1994.

64. KM52, pp. 1–2.

65. Only 660 companies are currently listed in Germany with a capitalization equivalent to 29% of GDP; 726 (31%) in Paris; 1,865 (117%) in London.

66. Jürgen Grote, 'Small Firms in the EC' in Greenwood, Grote and Ronit

(eds), pp. 119–67, gives an excellent detailed portrait of this diversity.

67. ibid. p. 163.

68. VC67, pp. 1–4, IOD Official, London. An Anglo-German Society study of SMEs perceived 'a major mismatch between the emphasis of policy at EU and national level, and what SME owners think that policy should be'. Cross-border search programmes, for example, appear to potential partners to be geared more towards EU integration than market logic.

69. *Agence Europe*, 2 April 1993; *ibid*, June 1993 No. 5998, for a report on the Copenhagen Conference where the only specific response to a debate on 'social exclusion in Europe' was a repetition of the call for jobs originally set out in the ERT's report 'Employment Policies in Europe for the 1990s', November 1989.

70. In the wake of withdrawals by foreign investors in Spain's car and electromechanical industries, Luis Martinez, minister of labour, introduced proposals for a new model of industrial relations law, mainly to increase employers' powers to hire and fire. Yet at over 3 million, unemployment had just touched 23%, the highest in Spain's modern history, well before the end of a recession which had hit late and was to ease well after the EU average. In spite of this, the Gonzalez government held to its tight monetary policy, determined to attract foreign investment again when the cycle turned.

71. Hans W. Platzer, *Gewerkschaftspolitik ohne Grenzen?* (Bonn: 1991); C. G. A. Bryant, 'Europe and the European Community 1992' in *Sociology* (Vol. 25 2, 1991), pp. 189–207.

72. Wallace, Wallace & Webb, chapter 10; Colchester & Buchan, chapter 15.

73. Josef Esser, 'Transnational Corporatism in a Trilateral World' (Andrew Shonfield Association Paper, March 1991). For the specifically free trade point of view, see C. Egan and P. McKiernan, *Inside Fortress Europe* (*Economist* Intelligence Unit, 1993) and J. P. Hayes, *Making Trade Policy in the European Community* (Basingstoke: 1993).

74. V. N. Balasubramanyam and D. Greenaway, 'Economic Integration and FDI: Japanese investment in the EC' in *JCMS* (No. 2, June 1992), pp. 175–193. Japan became the fastest growing source of FDI in the EC, with benign effects on the latter's comparative advantage and some additional impetus to integration, which was offset at the national level by competition between member states over where it should be located.

75. Initially the United States offered only 'US nationals treatment' in response to EC demands for full reciprocity. In the Montreal Arrangement, 1988–89, the EC settled for 'national treatment that gives effective access' (Colchester and Buchan, pp. 204–5).

76. The banana war originated in 1957 when, on Adenauer's instructions, the German delegation in Rome claimed and won the duty-free import of (large) 'dollar bananas' from Latin America, over and above the protected imports of (smaller) African and West Indian ones. This privilege was shared in practice only with Belgium and the Netherlands, and later Denmark and Ireland, since the other member states drew either on their former colonies (ACP

bananas) or their sources in Cyprus, the Canaries, Madeira, and the Caribbean (EC bananas). Up to 1992, imports stood at 20% ACP, 30% EC, 50% dollar bananas. But this system could not survive the internal market's abolition of frontiers, for ACP and EC bananas could not compete under a free trade regime with Latin American plantation cultures.

After months of deadlock, the Agricultural Council adopted, by a narrow majority, a new import regime in February 1993, but only because the Danish Presidency changed sides at the last moment. The quota for dollar bananas was set at 2 million tons, subject to a 20% duty ($144 per ton) but a swingeing $1200 above that limit. ACP producers got 857,000 tons and EC ones 854,000, both duty free. Spurred by public anger, the German authorities protested and were joined by Belgium and the Netherlands, whose governments claimed that their ports of entry would suffer. (All these ignored the rapid rise of dollar banana imports which had preceded the 1993 settlement.) Finally, Germany appealed to the ECJ, citing evasions of the CAP, GATT, and the proportionality principle.

The matter was settled in a masterpiece of informal politics, in which the Community agreed 'to take note' of these legal objections, but went ahead with the quotas, before signature of the GATT accord. The principal sufferers, other than the German public, appear to have been the giant American fruit corporations Chiquita and Del Monte. But much later, in January 1995, the German Supreme Court ruled on a plea by the importers, Atlanta, that importers' basic rights had been infringed by the new quotas; allowing these subsequently to demand a higher ratio. This judgment apparently conflicts directly with the ECJ's judgment upholding their legality. If it comes to the ECJ again, however, the Court might well withdraw from its earlier, maximalist defence of the protectionist position, rather than risk a major state's non-compliance.

77. Patrick Low, *Trading Free: the GATT and US Trade Policy* (New York: 1993), p. 244.

78. During the Council discussion in May 1993 about reinforcing the EU trade instruments, for example, the free traders – Germany, Britain, Netherlands, Denmark and Luxembourg – found themselves once again in opposition to the majority who wished to strengthen these instruments against what a French document described as the 'impressive arsenal of American unilateralism'. The Commission, needless to say, took up a position in between the two (*Agence Europe*, 15 May 1993, No. 5981 and 19 November 1992, No. 1860).

79. cf., D. Mayes, *The External Implications of European Integration* (New York: 1993), p. 61. The decline in the index of European trade specialization suggests that this is so, especially where firms are still state supported.

80. Walter Eltis, 'The Reestablishment of Economic Competitiveness' in *International Bank Credit Analyst* (No.32, No.9, 1994).

81. Peter Holmes, 'Trade, Competition and Technology Policy in the EC' (Paper for NWO–ERC Conference, November 1991).

CHAPTER THIRTEEN

1. FR75, p. 1.
2. William Wallace, 'From the twelve to the twenty four' in C. Crouch & D. Marquand (eds), *Towards Greater Europe?* (Oxford: 1992), p. 40.
3. Academic studies of the Community have on the whole avoided this question of statehood. After the first period ended in the mid–1970s, when integration was the primary research topic, very large numbers of investigations (mainly by political scientists and economists), took place into policy-making and institutions. These currently focus on whether the EU's institutions can cope with a body of fifteen, possibly twenty members; whether member states have the will or capacity to reform the system, and whether the unity of Maastricht's three pillars can actually be implemented. As was always implied, this endeavour requires the cooperation of all the social sciences, not just economics, law and politics, but including history and political economy: R. Harrison, 'Europe a Challenge to the Social Sciences' in *International Social Science Journal* (131.1992), pp. 3–22; H. Wallace, 'European Government in Turbulent Times' in *JCMS* (31.1993), pp. 292–303; D. Mayes, 'The Future Research Agenda' in S. Bulmer and A. Scott (eds), *Economic and Political Integration in Europe* (Oxford: 1994), pp. 265–72; B. Laffan and R. O'Donnell, 'Economy, Society and Politics in the EC: a framework for analysis' ECSA Paper (Washington: May 1993).
4. *Economist*, 23 October 1993, p. 15.
5. VC92, p. 1.
6. GR13, p. 3; FR69 (GR4), p. 1.
7. KM20, p. 7.
8. Henry Sass, *A Journey to Rome and Naples in 1817* (London: 1818).
9. SP22, p. 2.
10. KM15, p. 7.
11. KM37, p. 4. For a discussion of the Commission's effective performance see Les Metcalfe, 'Reducing the European Management Deficit' SEI/ESRC Workshop 'Regulating Europe' February 1994.
12. KM57, pp. 1–2, Official of Commission Presidency Cabinet.
13. FR57 (NL4), pp. 3–4.
14. FR65 (NL8), p. 2.
15. VC75, p. 2; VC76, p. 3; VC95 (DK), p. 2. Ireland won its claimed share of cohesion funds in 1992 at Edinburgh partly by playing the 'good member state card' and emerged with no less success than Spain.
16. VC87, p. 1.
17. VC81, p. 2.
18. VC99 (DK), p. 2
19. c.f., I. B. F. Kormoss, *La Notion géographique de l'Europe à travers les siècles* (College of Europe: 1992).
20. FR2, p. 1.
21. The text governing the treatment of carcasses in slaughter houses translates as 'nettoyer' in French, 'clean' in Britain. In France this is correctly interpreted as 'wipe clean' (with a cloth); in Britain as 'wash', with a high pressure hose, contrary to all good butchering and culinary practice. The effect of over-zealous interpretation of Community instructions on slaughter-houses in the decline of the British meat trade, and in particular in lamb production, is now well documented; the role in this of the largest retailers, and their influence on the Ministry of Agriculture remains unclear.
22. KM6, pp. 1–2; KM110, pp. 1–5.

23. It has become habitual to point to Italy and Greece as the worst-off member states. But as Marco Giuliani points out in 'Italy and its EC politics: a different equilibrium' ('EC Decision-Making', IFP Seminar, September 1993), the Italian case is not as bad as is often alleged.

24. A. Touraine, *Critique of Modernity* (Oxford: 1995), Part II, chap. 3.

25. In 1919, that is within living memory, the Czech Republic was created and the Austro-Hungarian Empire dissolved, leaving a truncated Austrian state and a Hungary denuded, by the Treaty of Trianon, of almost half its territory and a third of its Magyar population. Similarly, the modern Turkish state dates only from 1923.

26. Even when Switzerland withdrew from the EEA, Spain increased its claims on the grounds that the Spanish share from future budgets had been diminished by the absence of a large net contributor.

27. How much the 'No' votes profited from Britain's equivocation in an attempt to hold the size of the blocking minority at its existing level is not clear. At the very least, the display of Council divisions and member states' self-interest damaged the arguments for entry.

28. For logistical reasons, only two countries were chosen in the EFTA group, and also only two in central and eastern Europe. The Finnish case is near enough to the Swedish one for some of the deductions about players' linkages to apply. (See the chapter on Finland in C. Crouch and D. Marquand (eds.) *Towards a Greater Europe?*, pp. 118–29.) The assessments in Austria and Sweden are based mainly on interviews conducted in April and November 1993.

29. There was no post-War resemblance to Franco's Spain, nor to Italy, since the Catholic church had lost the habit of political interference during the Nazi era; but some of the lay Catholic–business links can be compared, including the influence of Opus Dei.

30. KM106, pp. 1–2.

31. The transit of heavy goods lorries between Germany and Italy provided the main case of exhaust and noise pollution in the Vorarlberg/Brenner area. Austria had imposed a nighttime ban on lorries, and after German and Italian hauliers' retaliation, signed a three year transit agreement limiting numbers according to the levels of noise and exhaust emissions, with the eventual aim of reducing traffic volume by 40% by 2003 and diverting the rest to rail. Switzerland's withdrawal from the EEA in 1992 made the case for renewing this agreement after 1995 a highly contentious part of the accession agreements: it was finally agreed to extend it to 2001. East–West transit raised rather fewer problems, because Austria planned in any case to upgrade to 160 kph standard the railway lines to Prague, Vienna and Budapest, with improvements on the routes to Bratislava and the Adriatic ports of Riyeka and Koper.

32. KM89, p. 3.

33. Apart from the 'sensitive' industries, finished exports from Austria of materials from Hungary or Czechoslovakia suffered severe tariff disadvantages. Hungarian and Czech tourism also began to compete for a share of Austria's richer tourist market.

34. These were ampler than the facilities offered to Spain's and Portugal's Central Bank governors before 1986 and included the Monday 'teatime'

meetings with EU governors and the Bank of International Settlements, the services of an unofficial technical information bureau, and briefings from the Governors' Committee Secretariat. Personal and informal links with the four large member states Central Banks supported the 'cooperative monetary policy' of the EEA, even before that came into effect; but in January 1993, Trichet still refused 'information status' *vis-à-vis* the Monetary Committee.

35. KM104, p. 1. The case of the Renault–Volvo merger suggests that Swedish shareholders shared Austrian fears about the predatory nature of EU cross-border transactions and the cultural implications for what is Sweden's largest company. This fear did not extend to the ASEA Brown Boveri merger, from which Sweden has obviously gained, as it is likely to do also from the movement of companies out of Norway after the adverse referendum there in December 1994.

36. KM99, p. 3.

37. KM90, p. 4.

38. KM88, p. 3.

39. Again, for logistical reasons, it was possible to examine only two countries in central and eastern Europe. These assessments are based on interviews conducted in March and April 1993.

40. c.f., Delors's speech, Bruges, 17 October 1989; Mitterrand's to the European Parliament 25 October 1989.

41. For a characteristic view, early in 1993, see the *Economist* Survey of eastern Europe, 13 March 1993.

42. FR77 (GR9), p. 6; FR80 (GR12), p. 4.

43. Privatization in the Czech Republic occurred in two stages: the greater number of enterprises, through the coupon system, by 1993; the rest, either companies with legal problems consequent on the Czech–Slovak split, or those like Skoda-Pilzn, encumbered with non-performing debts from Russia or former Comecon partners, were scheduled for February 1995. The success of privatization, as far as the economic performance of enterprises is concerned, is offset by the fact that the bulk of them are owned by funds of varying stability and expertise, many of which have not performed as well as the leaders. Four hundred of these existed in 1993, 600 in 1995. Since the greater part are owned ultimately by the banks, much industrial ownership may in effect end up with them, so that the outcome will not be a broadly distributed share ownership but one more narrowly concentrated in financial institutions than in most EU member states.

44. KM82, p. 3. Both governments had liberalized virtually all foreign trade by 1993, having resisted domestic demands for protection. Yet having expected a 'soft EU response' for their admittedly provocative 'sensitive exports', they were taken aback by the quotas, and the EU's unwillingness to accept mitigating arguments about inexperience (KM79, p. 1).

45. R. Frydman and A. Rapaczynski, *Privatization in Eastern Europe: Is the State Withering Away?* (Budapest: 1994).

46. In the restructuring of the giant, effectively bankrupt Skoda-Pilzn by Czech Commercial Bank and Investment Bank, Siemens entered the game for the railways section, Westinghouse for nuclear electric.

Despite the fact that the concern was loaded with pre–1990 debts, the government tried to prevent cherry-picking with some success. Nevertheless, rationalized and slimmed down by an industrialist from the previous era, Lubomir Soudik, with the use of £700m of EBRD money, Skoda-Pilzn was turned round to profitability. The Czech way involved, however, intricate deals with government and Czech banks which have left the company's share price in considerable obscurity, while its debts remain startlingly high.

47. *Economist*, 20 October 1994, pp. 29–30.

48. The old guard in government won an important battle in 1992 over loan consolidation against the Central Bank: the latter wanted market players to buy up deeply discounted corporate debts and to use the chance to restructure the firms concerned: the former preferred to prop up employment, with the 1994 elections in mind.

49. A case which justified this was General Electric's take-over of Tungsram, in order to use its Hungarian name, logo and distribution network. One such instance can offset many better experiences such as Suzuki, Opel, and United Biscuit's cross-border operations.

50. The only picture of the consequences for industry comes from private research institutions (KM121, *passim*). State-owned industries are likely to do worst, and the Customs Union was therefore supported more by the Chambers of Commerce than by industrial federations. Agriculture, food processing, textiles and state-owned cement firms will suffer most, the best forecast of bankruptcies being between

10–15%. Electronics, private textiles firms, car components and pharmaceuticals seem likely to survive, while consumer durables and contracting (in which Turkish firms already compete for international projects) may do well.

51. KM117, p. 1.

52. When a group of Kurdish MPs had their parliamentary privilege removed so that they could be tried and sentenced for up to 15 years in prison for offences connected with Kurdish autonomy, in autumn 1993, President Mitterrand sent a personal protest to all European heads of government.

53. KM121, p. 2.

54. Rights of the *Aussiedler* have also been limited, and Germany has paid the Russian government to care for as many as possible of the Volga Germans in situ.

55. The 1995 proposal of Manuel Marin, the Spanish Commissioner with responsibility for the Middle East and North Africa, was for an increase in aid to 5.5 billion ecus accompanied by further technological cooperation and trade. This was substantial enough to have aroused opposition from Germany, Denmark and the Netherlands. The settlement (June 1995) was for a *minimum* of 1.24 bn ecus a year for four years for central and eastern Europe, 700m a year for the Mahgreb.

CHAPTER FOURTEEN

1. Wallace, Wallace & Webb, p. 409.

2. Quoted in the *London Review of Books*, 25 Feb 1993, p. 6.

3. KM92, p. 4; KM (SP) 23, p. 3.

4. Interview in *The European*, 21–24 August 1992.

5. R. Reich, 'Who is Us?' in *Harvard Business Review* (January–February, 1990), pp. 53–64.

6. It is sometimes argued that players are more concerned with relative than with collective advantage. In the more coherent industrial sectors like chemicals and pharmaceuticals or railway locomotives, this is not so and may not even be true for the less coherent, such as motorcars and consumer electronics, firstly because it is almost impossible for a large firm not to play in the EU market and secondly because the extensive range of modes available ensures that relative advantage can be defended on other levels – for example by utilizing group pressures on those perceived as playing only for their own interests, or deprecating what they do to Commission officials in order to ensure their partial exclusion or downgrading (c.f., ACEA and Peugeot-Citroën).

7. Certain individual professions also do well, notably lawyers. But the important distinction may not be their professional orientation or their national affinities but whether, for example, lawyers come from a working or an academic background.

8. c.f., Phillipe Schmitter and G. Lembruch (eds), *Trends towards corporatist intermediation* (London: 1979); S. Tarrow, P. Katzenstein & L. Graziano, *Territorial Politics in Industrial Nations* (Prager: 1978), Peter Hall, *Governing the Economy: the politics of state intervention in Britain and France* (Cambridge: 1986).

9. This could, perhaps, be built up into a theory of different varieties of pluralism evolving in post-mediaeval states. The absence of revolution in Britain since 1688 has often been attributed to a surfeit of informal

mechanisms; the prevalence of regular upheavals in twentieth-century France to a system which, though highly formalized, is vested in an informal elite which largely excludes, or gives only conditional access to the same players who in Britain enjoy sustained informal access. Hence the events in France of 1934, 1936, 1958 and 1968.

10. One should distinguish between *external rules*, which have formal, even legal embodiment, *internal rules*, which are akin to a firm's articles of association and are agreed jointly within a sectoral association or federation of associations, *conventions*, which are established over time, by acquiescence (compliance with them being enforced by peer-group pressure) and *habits*, which condition the behaviour of players (but have no penalties attached) and are possessed by all associative groups.

11. FR70 (GR7), p. 1.

12. FR24, p. 1.

13. FR38, p. 2.

14. FR33, p. 3.

15. KM49, p. 3.

16. VC2, p. 2.

17. In the pharmaceuticals field for example, 'the Commission has to listen to all consumers (not just the drugs companies and EFPIA) such as member states on social security issues, and patients and doctors who have their own European representation' (VC124, p. 2).

18. W. Hager, 'Public interest and the Market: Europe's 1992 project' (Andrew Shonfield Association Paper, September 1988), p. 1.

19. VC60, p. 1.

20. I have in mind the situation in which a government's defence of the national interest is made to approxi-

mate to the need to strike a deal in the European context, because member states' governments on their own cannot fulfil their publics' expectations. Necessity (electoral or economic) forces them to act so, and the competitive symposium ensures, firstly that they can do so collectively rather than alone, and secondly that they can treat the EU institutions as a neutral arbiter, yet also blame them as scapegoat if things then go wrong.

21. Because of the failure in 1991 to install a 'hierarchy of norms' there is as yet no graduated pyramid of competences, such as exists in federal or confederal systems; only competences which are extended or not according to the circumstances of the time and member states' own view of their interests. Accountability in fact is to member state governments not to Parliament. Significantly, current plans for reform focus on voting in the Council of Ministers, reforming the college (with fewer Commissioners and perhaps fewer Commission powers), and ending what some French politicians refer to as 'the tyranny of small states'.

22. KM18, p. 5; KM20, p. 7.

23. Ralf Dahrendorf, 'Die Zukunft des Nationalstaates', MERKUR, *Deutsche Zeitschrift für Europäisches Denken*, No.9/10, 48th year (Stuttgart: 1994).

24. A. Moravcsik (1993), p. 30.

25. VC98 (DK), p. 3.

26. The bulk of European law, apart from the Code of Human Rights, tends to define people by economic criteria as workers or consumers. It is only in systems which are still immature that political *parties* represent producer interests; like the Peasant parties in central and eastern Europe, or the current 'bureaucratic corporatism' in Russia.

27. It does not have what the German portmanteau word *Inkompetenzkompensationskompetenz* seeks to describe.

28. And not always then: in Germany, the large banks are opposed to the introduction of money market funds. Small banks would prefer to have them, but the regulatory authorities refuse, and the Commission is currently unwilling to act, so small banks must go to foreign markets where and if these exist (FR76 (GR8), p. 3).

29. KM93, pp. 4–5.

30. KM15, p. 2.

31. Quoted in the *Independent*, 13 October 1992.

32. W. Streeck & P. Schmitter, 'From national corporatism to transnational pluralism' in *Politics and Society* (129, No.2, 1991), p. 164.

33. Delors himself admitted in 1991, 'frequently, I have the impression that subsidiarity is a fig leaf to conceal unwillingness to honour commitments which have already been endorsed.' *Subsidiarity; the Challenge of Change* (EIPA, Maastricht 1991), pp. 7–19.

34. From an historian's perspective, it appears significant that one quality peculiar to the EU is that so far elements of national sovereignty have been transposed without seriously rupturing member states' historic identities, and without requiring more rewriting of the actual histories that are taught in schools, in a European sense, than was involved for example writing them in a feminist sense. It will be harder to write a *peoples'* history for Europe, firstly because of citizenship tradi-

tions which in Germany derive from rights regardless of territory, but in France from residence in a territory, and in Britain from subjection under a crown; secondly because of the way that European institutions have been constructed by political elites; c.f., R. Brubaker, *Citizenship and Nationhood in France and Germany* (Cambridge, Massachusetts: 1992). Spain grants citizenship after two years' residence to inhabitants of its former colonies, Denmark lowers its residence requirements from 7 to 2 years for Nordic applicants.

35. c.f., Emile Noël, *Working Together: the Institutions of the EC* (Luxembourg: 1994).

36. W. Wessels, 'The Search for an Optimal Strategy of the New Europe' in *International Affairs* (1994.3), pp. 445–57.

37. John Gray, *Beyond the New Right:*

markets, *Government and the Environment* (London: 1993), p. 138.

38. As Linda Colley has pointed out in *Britons* (New Haven: 1992), it would have been absurd until the mid-sixteenth century even to ask the question whether England, Scotland or Ireland were a part of Europe. Another hundred to two hundred years were needed before the idea of England/Britain as a distinctive nation emerged: that idea coalesced in the face of the Napoleonic transformation of Europe, and was then adapted successively by what became the world's first industrial power, and by the later nineteenth-century imperial power. Britain's twentieth-century history can be read as a prolonged elegy in redefinition.

39. A. S. Milward, *The European Rescue of the Nation State* (London: 1992).

INDEX

accessions to the EC 89, 100, 616, 624, 630, 682
Britain/Denmark/Ireland 69, 73–4; EFTA states 146, 189, 198, 199, 203, 204, 221, 243, 352, 492, 547–8, 607, 616, 620, 631–42, 717n, 723n, 724n, 736n, 750n; and geographical divisions 618; Greece/Spain/Portugal 85–6, 641; Parliament and 352, 353, 356; and QMV 279; RDF and 86, 389; *see also* applicants
accountability
of central banks 554, 721n; of EC 199, 361, 568, 600, 612, 691, 770n
ACEA 467, 471–3, 484, 523, 577, 578
Acheson, Dean 15, 25
Action Committee for a United States of Europe 31, 68, 105
additionality 405, 570, 684, 742n
Adenauer, Konrad 34, 38, 40, 44, 117, 323, 764n
Adonnino report 108, 110
aeronautics/aerospace industry 83, 96, 565
Aerospatiale merger 515–18, 529
Africa 115, 228
former colonies 50–1, 75, 133, 134, 664; Francophone 228, 730n; North, EC relations with 75, 82, 657, 664; shipping cartels 513
Agency for Regional Technological Development (ASTER) 414, 415, 743n
Agnelli, Gianni 222, 425, 471, 577
AGREF 103, 137, 296, 489, 490, 564, 750n
Agricultural Council 270, 277, 281, 285, 764n
agriculture 4, 14, 179, 615

arctic/alpine 632; British 41; Commissioner for 228; EFTA and 39; Franco-German wheat agreement 29; French 29, 168, 626; green pool negotiations 29; Irish 128; over-lobbying in 359; post-War 5, 6, 7; Spanish 86, 707n; surpluses 53, 54; White Paper and 145; *see also* Common Agricultural Policy
aid 7–13, 50–1, 75, 659, 660, 672, 769n
Alcatel 588, 762n
Algeria 660, 664–5
Alphandéry, Edmond 539, 725n, 732n
altruism xvii, 322, 458, 495, 557, 679
American Chamber of Commerce
European Committee 140, 439, 457, 488
and DG4 504; EC representation 137; and internal market debate 716n; MNCs and 466, 715n; and monetary union 164; UNICE and 492; and Vredeling Directive 104, 105, 181, 711n
Andreotti, Giulio 144, 167–9
Andriessen, Frans 221, 232
on collegiality 220; as competition Commissioner 231, 249, 499; as external affairs Commissioner 163, 602; merger regulations 502; and state aids 505
Ankara Treaty 658
anteroom effect 637–8, 640, 647, 655
anti-dumping orders 56, 370, 373, 562, 574, 601, 602–4
anti-trust policy
cartels 97; DG4 and 500; in German tradition 250, 500; Italian Anti-Trust Authority 753n; and media 350
applicants

Austria/Sweden 633–41; French opposition to 40–2, 67–8, 629–30, 655; Turkey/Mediterranean 657–61; Visegrad group 203, 327, 482, 616, 625, 631, 641–57; *see also* accessions
Archirafi, Vanni d' 229, 413
army, European 25–7
Association Agreements 600
  Euro-Med 353, 642; east European 643–5, 647, 650, 656
Association of European Regions (ARE) 392, 397, 404
Athens Summit (1983) 106–7, 131
Atlas 588, 589
Attali, Jacques 166, 296, 643, 759n
Austria 766n
  application 259, 570, 607, 616, 631–2, 633–42, 723n; central bank 550, 637–8; and collapse of Communism 165; corporatism 385; currency alignment 532; and EC 75, 706n, 717n; economy 637; EEA member 205, 636; EFTA member 38, 82, 181, 631–2; and ERM 689; federations 638–9; firms 674; isolationism 633; liberalism of 619; nationalism in 636, 647; public utilities 684; referendum 633, 636, 640; and regional development 397; relations with eastern Europe 636–7, 640, 653, 767n; society in 625
Austrian National Bank 550, 637–8
automobile industry xix, 447, 601, 605
  catalytic converter row 760–1n; emissions legislation 454, 462, 731n; federations 103, 40, 446, 448, 465, 467, 471–3; German 761n; industrial policy in 575–9; 710n; Italian 454; Japanese 164, 471–2, 562, 575–9, 601; joint ventures 653; mergers 514–15, 579; protectionism 604; in recession 79; restructuring 606; state aids 505, 522–3, 524, 576; VERs 577–9, 601, 603, 606
aviation 375, 586
  airline liberalization 321, 525, 563,

587–8, 732n; and competition policy 501, 502, 503; DG7 and 609; joint ventures 652; mergers 506, 515–18, 525; state aids 332, 505, 521, 523, 525–6, 754–5n

Baden-Württemberg 400, 415, 417, 423, 597, 676
  case study 418–21, Fig 9.2
BAe-Rover takeover 524–5
Balladur, Edouard 171, 205, 291, 327, 337, 527, 539, 720n
Baltic States 625, 635, 640, 644, 656, 662, 665
'banana war' 604, 764n
Banca d'Italia 316, 479, 554, 720n
  and EMS/EMU 87, 123, 173, 317; and ERM 544–5; isolation of 545; relations with government 530, 545, 753n
Banco de España 479, 554, 749n
  and EMU 173, 533; and ERM 535, 545, 755n; relations with government 132, 177, 530, 549
Bangemann, Martin 156, 202, 221, 602, 727n
  and car industry 577, 761n; as industry Commissioner 163, 248, 324, 516, 562, 563; on public utilities 611; relations with DG4 232, 505, 511, 727n; and steel industry 574
Bank of England 87, 120, 121, 748n, 762n
  defence of sterling 537; and ECB 172, 721n; and EMU 533, 544; and ERM 544; relations with government 530, 544, 545, 756n
Bank of International Settlements 475, 529, 530, 767n
Bank of Portugal 538
banking/banks xv, 210, 770n
  American 480, 482; in applicant states 637–8, 653–4; British 477–8, 479, 480, 592; cartels 250, 514; and competition rules 507; cross-border activity 591–2; debtors' crisis 94, 135, 479; DG4 and 250; Directives 135, 149, 372,

481–2, 591, 759n; diversity in 474;
EC representation 478–9, 673;
failures 474, 591, 681–2;
federations 135, 473–85, 748n;
French 418, 477; German 420–1,
477–8, 592, 762n; harmonization
681; industrial policy for 591–2;
and internal market 135, 252, 473,
590; Italian 123, 316, 479; lending
patterns 442; liberalization of 476;
lobbyists 477; in Luxembourg 127;
mergers 476, 748n; and monetary
union 150; Portuguese 749n; relations with central banks 482, 757n;
relations with Commission 481–2,
590–1, 746–7n; relations with
federations 464; relations with government 313; Scottish 407, 408,
474, 757n; Spanish 412, 474, 479;
supervision committees 550; *see
also* central banks
Banque de France 219, 295, 554, 707n
defence of franc 539; and EMS 87;
and EMU 173, 177; and ERM
297, 542–3; relations with Bundesbank 328; relations with government 542–3, 549
Baron Enrique, Chair of Foreign Affairs
Committee 352, 353
Barre, Raymond 198, 201, 417, 418,
756n
Barre Report 64; Plan Barre 80, 88,
99, 137
BASF 448, 749n
Bavaria 418, 420, 425
Belgian Central Bank 546
Belgium
and airline deregulation 321, 732n;
attitudes to EC 126, 192, 261; as
Benelux state 17–18; and Beyen
Plan 31; central bank *see* Belgian
Central Bank; and CFSP 191; and
Commission 227, 232, 240;
common market negotiations 33;
and competition policy 503; and
convergence 551; coordination
process 313–14; corporatism in
385; EC Presidencies 126, 147,
151, 204, 320, 321, 322, 548, 569;

and ECJ 738n; economy 88, 95,
546; and Ecosoc 387; ECSC membership 1, 17; and EMU 147, 166,
173, 177; and enlargement of EC
45, 86; and EPC 28; and ERM 113,
170, 537, 542, 546; and European
Parliament 238, 341, 343, 361; federalism in 126, 384; financial sector
150, 484, 514; firms 455; and
FRITALUX 19–20; industry 22,
126; and Interior Ministry issues
194; and internal market 126; and
legislation 126; Maastricht ratification 199; MEPs 358, 735n; ministries 313; monetary policy 66; peak
organizations 489; Permanent Representatives 284, 314; postal
monopoly 762n; post-colonial
status 51; public opinion in 314,
320; and regionality 425; regions
188, 398, 402, 741n; and Single
European Act 148; and state aids
505, 520; trade 126; trade unions
487; and veto powers 90
Benelux 329
attitude to EC 198, 322; Commissioners 229; creation of 17; defence
pact members 24; in DM zone 67;
ECSC membership 1, 17, 21, 23;
EEC-effect on trade 61; European
agenda of 29; favour integration
101; France and 18–19;
FRITALUX 19–20; political party
consensus 91; and protectionism
37; and regionalism 396; Schengen
Agreement 186; and tariffs 14; *see
also* Belgium; Luxembourg; Net-
herlands
Bérégovoy, Pierre 166, 176, 200, 239
Berlusconi government, Italy 206, 545
Beyen, Jan Willem 27
Beyen Plan 28, 31–3, 125, 624
Bildt, Carl 356, 635
Blair House Agreement 168, 603
Boloré 513, 755n
Bonn Declaration (1961) 44
borders see frontiers
Brandt, Willi 65, 79, 329, 755n
Braun, Fernand 106, 138, 574

Bretton Woods system 5, 62, 65, 76, 87, 323, 531, 694
Britain *see* United Kingdom
British Bankers' Association 407, 480
British Telecom (BT) 588, 589, 590, 675
Brittan, Leon 221, 224, 602, 714n, 726n
 at DG1 243, 362, 563, 600, 609; at DG4 163, 218, 228, 231, 249, 499, 505–7, 511, 529, 586, 752n; GATT negotiations 337, 586; and industrial policy 206, 586; and internal market 121, 141; and mergers 515, 517, 518; Parliament proposal 362; relations with Bangemann 232, 505–6; relations with member states 522, 523; and state aids 504, 522, 523, 526; and state monopolies 586, 587; and steel industry 574
Brunner, Manfred 202, 228
Brussels Pact (1948) 24
Brussels Special Summit (1988) 390
budget 642
 crises 93, 101, 107; Delors II 163, 189; disputes 183, 191, 203; French support withdrawn 711n; German contribution 117; Parliament and 52, 91, 342; post-1992 cycle 169; reform 107; settlement 156, 719n, 724n; system strengthened 85; UK contributions 75, 83, 93, 100, 102, 105, 107, 112, 120, 121
Bulgaria 625, 644, 656
Bull 526, 582–3, 588
Bundesbank 554
 attitude to ECB 172, 178, 721n; and convergence 551; Council 400, 534, 536; Directorate 543, 551, 756n; and EMU 87–9, 119, 157, 158, 176, 177, 543–4, 552; and ERM 113, 170, 171, 174, 534, 535–7, 541, 543–4, 720n, 755n, 756n; interest rate policy 306, 534–6, 539; relations with Bonn 174, 175, 179, 530, 543, 548, 722n; relations with central banks 328, 540, 544; relations with

member states 536, 543, 756n; and revaluation 66
Bundeskartellamt 501, 511
 industrial policy of 118; and mergers 503, 518, 519; relations with Directorates 505, 508
Bush, George 140, 159, 190, 326, 642
bureaucracy 334, 350, 629
Butler, Sir Michael 177, 716n

Callaghan, James 81, 88
Calvet, Jacques 471, 472, 523, 566, 577
capitalism
 Anglo-Saxon/Rhineland 567, 669, 670, 677; capital and labour 596; member states attitudes towards 626
cars *see* automobile industry
cartels 467, 470, 499, 512–14
 anti-trust 97; banking 250, 514; cement 502, 512, 527, 753n; chemicals 378, 512–13, 584; crisis 83, 94, 95, 97, 120, 248, 500, 561, 575; ECSC prohibition on 22; EFTA and 55; in financial sector 475, 513–14; of MNCs 505; registration of 57–8; shipping companies 513, 755n; soda ash 528; steel 83, 97, 248, 496, 500, 558, 575, 602; textiles 81
Carter, Jimmy 88, 94
Catalonia 392, 400, 415, 423, 424, 446, 597, 676, 714–15n
 case study 408–12, Fig 9.2
CCMC 471–2, 575, 577
Cecchini, Paolo 106, 482
 Cecchini Report 146, 150, 152, 350, 504, 591, 717n
CEFIC 466, 467–8, 584–5
cellule de prospective
 Delors and 204, 221, 225, 725n; and industrial policy 583; studies 568, 749n; and trade policy 605; and White Paper (1993) 563, 568;
cement industry 502, 512, 527, 603, 753n
CENELEC 566–7, 760n
central banks xvi, 61–2, 65, 78, 529–31

accountability 554; of applicant states 637–8, 654–5, 660–1, 767n; attitudes to ECB 172; Central Bankers Committee 156, 171–2; Central Bankers Report 179; collective action by 499; Commission compared with 338; Committee of Alternates 336, 547, 550, 680, 758n; Committee of Governors 63, 87, 148, 270, 277–8, 344, 475, 482, 530, 533, 539, 542, 546, 547, 548, 550, 551, 553, 624, 638, 708n, 729n, 758n; cooperation between 87; EC role of 530–1, 549; and Ecofin 499, 530, 539; and EMS 87–8, 119, 344, 531–2, 550, 551; and EMU 87–9, 135, 173, 499, 530, 533, 551, 554, 758n; and ERM 120, 169, 529–55; and financial sector liberalization 477; and inflation 531; informal politics in 547, 553; and internal market 135; and monetary policy 530–2; policy-making by 474; political ethos of 676; relations with banks 482, 757n; relations with Commission 336, 533, 551; relations with DG2 247, 549; relations with EEA 767n; relations with financial sector 473, 484, 499, 549, 592, 757–8n; relations with governments 177, 499, 529, 530, 536, 537, 538, 542–7, 548, 549–50, 552; relations with industry 103, 499, 529, 545; relations with member states 531; relations with Parliament 344; singular vision of 552; small/large state representatives 624; under Maastricht Treaty 549; within nation state 530; *see also* European Central Bank; and under individual banks
Centre Européen des Normes (CEN) 131, 566–7, 760n
CEOE 133, 411, 453–4, 489, 715n
CGIL 181, 489
CGT 489, 522, 598, 750n
Chambers of Commerce 420, 436, 445, 491, 639, 661

see also American Chamber of Commerce
chemical industry xviii, 460, 462
cartels 378, 512–13, 584; collaboration in 566; federations 103, 446, 448, 452, 584–5, 747n; industrial policy 584–5; mergers 515; protectionism 603; regeneration of 605
Cheysson, Claude 228, 724n
Chirac, Jacques 79, 80, 151, 206, 327, 521, 549, 555, 625, 689
Christian Democrats 355, 356, 564, 628, 633, 736n
Christophersen, Henning 334, 563, 757n
Ciampi, Carlo 173, 540, 545, 756n, 757n
citizenship, European 194, 692–3
diverse traditions of 773n; ECJ and 367, 368; Parliament and 184, 362–4
civil service 256, 260–1, 276
British 75, 120, 189, 245, 300, 705n; committee representation 727n; French 293; Greek 306; Irish 314
CLCA 471
Clinton, Bill 326, 604, 642
CNPF *see* Patronat
coal industry 1, 17, 21–4
European Coal and Steel Community 1, 17, 21–4
Cockfield, Arthur 93, 105, 156, 222, 228, 230, 231, 482, 725n
Delors and 218, 221; and ETUC 718n; and industrial policy 562; and SEA White Paper 142–3, 144, 145–6, 148, 150, 151, 235, 248, 265, 481
co-decision 195, 347, 349, 353, Fig 8.3
cohesion 156, 306, 390, 395–6, 424, 723n
see also structural cohesion
Cohesion Fund 169, 173, 183, 224, 508, 724n
Council's acceptance of 322; IGCs on 392; Ireland and 314, 765n; and north/south divide 619; Secretariat responsibility for 220, 221,

253, 393; Spain and 177, 204, 280, 303, 620

Cold War 7, 24, 193, 383, 487, 641, 662, 720n

Colombo, Emilio 90, 123, 739n

Colombo-Genscher initiative 102, 118

colonies 50–1, 75, 664

Colonna Report 98, 709n

Comecon
agreements with 82, 643; debts 183, 646; applicants 642–6; instability of 94; relations with EC 116; trade with 114; US trade embargo 96

Comité des Sages 89–90

comitology system 336, 348–9, 679, 726n, 727n
in advisory committees 335; in central banks 550; in Commission 237; in Coreper 282; and enlargement 630

Committee of Central Bank Governors see central banks

Committee for European Economic Cooperation (CEEC) 8, 19

Committee of Permanent Representatives (Coreper) 83, 160, 277, 280–5, 682
and enlargement 630; negotiating process in 273; relations with Commission 281, 283; relations with Council of Ministers 269–70, 281; relations with federations 467, 486, 491; relations with firms 284, 442, 449, 638–9; relations with governments 283, 308; relations with Parliament 351; role of 101, 266–7, 269–70, 272, 274, 281, 283, Fig 7.1; *see also* Permanent Representatives

Committee of Regions 399, 411, 422, 425, 426, 693
appointment procedure 395, 398, 422–3, 741n; formal/informal aspects of 209, 428; member states' view of 396, 409, 428; under Maastricht Treaty 180, 211, 254, 384, 388, 393, 394–5; and Rainbow MEPs 357; *see also* regi-

onal policy; regions

committees 243, 726–7n
Commission use of 335; Council of Ministers 269–70; Ecofin 277–8; Parliamentary 349, 352; *see also* comitology system

Common Agricultural Policy (CAP) 35, 38, 39, 550
and cohesion 156, 718–19n; Commission role in 226, 265; and enlargement of EC 86, 656–7, 707n; farm prices dispute 93, 100, 107; financing of 53, 156, 691; France and 49, 492; fraud in 264; and GATT negotiations 603; green exchange rates 54, 65; Hague agreement on 68; Monetary Compensation Amounts 54, 81, 107; negotiations 52–4; and north/south divide 619; protectionism in 603; reform of 90, 100, 101, 107–8, 112, 148, 203, 665; surplus 389; UK and 120; US and 96

Common Foreign and Security Policy (CFSP) 277, 672, 695
aims of 663; applicants and 632; Commission and 668; Coreper and 270; Council and 267; and defence 192–3, 197; France and 158–9, 166, 187–8, 326; German support for 166, 187, 326; and Maastricht Treaty 162, 191–3; Parliament and 348, 353; Presidency's role in 192; UK and 190

Communism 641, 646, 650
communist federations 598; communist parties 91, 354, 356, 489, 708n; in Hungary 650; informal politics under 648

company law 83, 84

competition 601
between Comecon countries 651; between Directorates 500, 505, 557; in financial sector 592; between firms 436, 439, 451, 464, 469, 558, 565, 567; foreign 607; in industrial sector 567; between institutions 348, 349–50; between MEPs 360; in ECJ 737n; and in-

formal politics 691; inter-state 331, 643, 764n; regional 388, 409, 422; in trade 372, 576–83

competition policy 55–9, 500–29, 563, 585, 673, 691

Brittan and Delors and 218, 231; CFI and 366; Commission and 55–9, 206, 498, 500–1, 553, 609; Competition Reports 529; Directorate *see* DG4; ECJ and 96, 224, 369, 475, 498–9; European institution proposal 508; firms interest in 438; France and 240, 297; Germany and 113, 280; and industrial policy 562; Italy and 317; lobbying on 509; loss of momentum 204; member states and 97, 329, 334, 508; national agencies 501, 508, 509–11, 512, 607; and national interest 234; penalties 527–8; and regions 426; and single market 154, 155, 241, 498–9; and White Paper 145, 146; *see also* cartels; mergers; state aids

competitive symposium xii, xvi, 611–12, 671, 770n

in civil service 260; Commission as 141; public and 690

competitiveness 471, 672

and energy policy 610; industrial policy and 557, 558, 565, 569, 606–7

computer industry 606

concertation 385–7, 684

Conciliation Committees 353

Confederation of British Business 487

Confederation of British Industry (CBI) 103, 486, 710n

and Dekker Report 104, 139; and EMU 173, 720n; and energy policy 610; European Advisory Committee/Panel 716n, 722n; European involvement 452, 489–90; European Steering Committee 104, 720n; and internal market 104, 121, 490, 710n, 711n, 715n, 720n; loss of influence 121; relations with government 103, 137, 489, 720n; Scottish 405; SME sector 254,

597, 745n; and Social Charter 722n; and UNICE 751n; and Vredeling 104

Confederation of Danish Industries 130

confederations *see* peak organizations

Conference on Security and Cooperation in Europe (CSCE) 69, 76, 127, 167, 321, 639, 720n

Confindustria 103, 123, 137, 254, 316, 454, 486, 489, 750n

Conseil de la Concurrence 366, 501, 503

Conseil d'Etat 297, 368, 375, 754n

Conservative Party (UK) 198

attitude to EC 74, 121, 299; and budget 93; CDU links 189; election victory 535; and EMS 114; *Europe and the Future* 120; and European Parliament 90; Eurosceptics 159, 189, 202, 535, 544; MEPs 176, 354, 356, 358, 736n; parliamentary dilemma of 201–2; and regions 404, 428; and Vredeling 104

constitution 367, 692, 723n

consultation procedure Fig 8.1, 8.2

consumer electronics *see* electronics

consumerism, European 363–4

convergence *see* Economic and Monetary Union

Convergence and Union coalition (Catalonia) 408–10

coordination *see* national coordination

Copenhagen Summits (1974) 285; (1982) 105, 129, 143; (1993) 569, 645, 763n

core/periphery divisions 621–2

Corfu Summit (1994) 206, 215, 287, 321, 328, 570

corporate players *see* firms; industry

corporatism 385, 468, 486, 598, 611, 684

Council of Europe 16, 728n

Council of European Municipalities (CEEMR) 404

Council of Foreign Ministers 266, 277, 705n

Council of Ministers 270–80

and CAP 52, 53, 100, 107; chair of 267, 272, 729n; changes majority voting procedure 717n; and competition policy 502, 508; confidentiality of 267, 275, 319; consultation by 277, 349; creation of EMS 87–8, 169; decisions 268; and defence policy 192–3; Delors and 224; ECJ ruling on 92; and Ecosoc 386; and enlargement of EC 85–6; and European Council 728–30n; Franco-German entente and 327; and industrial policy 566; and Interior Ministry issues 194; and internal market 105, 140–1, 143, 711n; legislative process 267–9, 273, Fig 7.1; and Maastricht 191, 192; mediating role of 274; and member states 211, 266–7, 270–80; and Monetary Fund 89; and monetary policy 64; negotiating process 214, 273–4; and policy changes 82; public opinion and 273; QMV in 269, 278–9, 622, 630, 656, Fig 7.2, 7.3; regional representation 421, 425; relations with Commission 85–6, 89–90, 210, 214, 215, 257, 266–7, 275, 278, 338, 347, 459, 566, 586–7; relations with Committee of Regions 396; relations with Coreper 269–70, 281; relations with ECJ 370, 373–5; relations with federations 467, 486, 491; relations with financial sector 590; relations with industry 277, 442; relations with Parliament 91, 92, 102, 266–7, 276, 340–1, 342–3, 347–50, 353; relations with regions 397–8, 404, 427, 741n; role of 266–7, 270, 287; Secretariat 269–70, 272, 274, 286; and state monopolies 586–7; and statehood 686; and subsidies 57; and trade 47–8, 140, 601; and UK budget question 105

Court of Assessors 255, 723n, 732n
Court of Auditors 85, 264, 342
Court of First Instance (CFI) 381, 675 and anti-dumping legislation 373; competition cases 378, 513, 514; Legal Service and 257; member states and 366, 373, 723n, 737n;

proposed 145; set up 366
courts, national 365, 367–9, 381
Craxi, Bettino 144, 145, 146, 167
Crédit Lyonnais 417, 474, 477, 591, 592
Cresson, Edith 191, 200, 295, 503, 576–7, 730n
crime 163, 184, 186, 188
cultural affairs 194, 400, 604, 607, 629
currency 689
    alignment 66, 86–8, 532; common 544; convertibility 61, 65; cooperation 78–9; crisis (1973) 67, 76; ecu 88, 173; Eurodollar market 62; flotation of 66–7, 76, 79; hard ecu proposal 168, 177–8; markets 204, 552; pacts 542; single 112, 116, 157, 169, 172–3, 196, 481, 549, 551, 596, 757n; 'Snake' 66, 76, 79, 82, 83, 87, 531; speculation 534–7, 540; *see also* Economic and Monetary Union; Exchange Rate Mechanism; monetary policy
customs union 19–20, 33
    Beyen Plan 28, 31–2; and CAP 52; documentary standardization 108, 112; in EEC 34, 37, 39, 47, 48; EFTA and 39; for and internal market 55, 76; member states' attitudes to 76; with Turkey 657, 659, 660, 661, 663
Cyprus 656, 658–9
Czech National Bank 655
Czechoslovakia/Czech Republic 68, 203, 205, 766n, 767n
    application 625, 641–57; Association Agreement 644, 646; conversion process 644, 646; debt 650; direct investment 653; economy 655; EU networks 655; financial sector 654; industry 573, 578, 644, 652–3, 768n; privatization 649, 767–9n

Daimler-Benz 674
DATAR 400, 416, 730n
Davignon, Etienne 198, 221, 231, 232, 580, 724n
    Davignon Plan 120, 126, 758n; Davignon Report 69, 73, 84, 705n; at DG3 103, 142, 248; and ERT

138, 718n; and industrial policy 96, 562, 572; research initiative 136
de Boissieu, Pierre 188
de Clerq, Willi 352, 602
de Gaulle, Charles 38, 191, 325, 630, 669
 anti-federalism of 40, 42, 45; and applicants 40–2, 67–8, 629–30; concept of Europe 43–4, 624; Directoire concept 89, 101; and ECJ 739n; and Franco-German entente 323; Political Union proposal 43–5; relations with USA 68; view of Commission 338
de Havilland merger 515–18, 522
de Larosière, Jacques 173, 759n
de Michelis, Gianni 193, 316, 637
debtors' crisis 94, 135
decentralization 564
defence industry 485
 Commission and 333; cooperation in 565; French 185, 450; procurement 184; reconstruction of 96; research funding 573
defence policy 158, 641
 Brussels Pact 24; cooperation in 24, 326; de Gaulle's proposals 43–4; European Defence Community 17, 25–8, 185; Franco-British alliance 24; Franco-German proposal 187; French 116, 158; and internal market 184; Maastricht proposals 184–5, 192–3, 197; member states and 193, 329, 617; NATO 24–5; Pleven Plan 25; post-war 24–8; and WEU 642; *see also* Common Foreign and Security Policy
Deferre Law 384, 416
Dehaene, Jean-Luc 206, 215, 313, 328, 731n
Dekker, Wisse 138, 139
 Europe 1990 report 103, 104, 125, 126, 138, 143
Delors, Jacques 599, 756n, 758n
 addresses to Parliament 141, 146, 160–1; attitude to Britain 146, 221; background 217, 219–20; cabinet of 221, 223, 225, 725n; campaign to represent EC 160; chairs

Central Bankers Committee 156, 171–2, 531; and competition policy 506; consultation exercise 110, 137, 141; Delors I 342; Delors II 156, 161–3, 189, 210, 218–19, 220, 342, 390, 392; Delors III 195, 203, 221, 395; and eastern Europe 643; and EEA 631; on elitism 692; and ERT 138, 716n; and financial sector abuses 482; French bias of 220; as French Finance Minister 99, 170, 219; and German reunification 220; grand design of 161–2, 217; and industry 332, 574, 582, 583; on institutional reform 198; and internal market 141–2; and Maastricht Treaty 196, 225; and markets 760n; and media 236; as MEP 219; on political union 399; Presidency of 108, 110, 112, 163, 179, 214, 215, 216–26, 264, 703n; and Regional Fund 389–90; and regional policy 424; relations with Commissioners 220, 233; relations with Council 220, 226; relations with Directorates 161, 233, 234, 244, 250, 393, 517, 719n; relations with Kohl 219, 328, 521; relations with member states 159–61; relations with Parliament 238, 349, 353; relations with peak organizations 491, 750n; relations with Thatcher 121, 158, 215, 220, 718n, 719n; relations with trades unions 488; and social policy 181, 195, 399, 488, 600, 692, 740n, 750n; on subsidiarity 219, 773n; success of 196; think tank 725n; on trade 583; transport projects 570, Fig 12.1; TUC address 159, 719n, 750n; and union plan 116; vision of Europe 141–2, 146; and White Paper (1993) 568
Delors Committee/Report on Monetary Union (1986) 166, 532, 708n, 721n
 and ECB 156, 171–2, 531, 534, 544, 553, 676; and EMU 173, 533, 546, 551, 682
democracy 612, 690

in applicant states 644; democratic deficit 341, 351, 361, 362, 691–2; EMU and 553; European 361, 662; local 394, 395, 411; in member states 625

demography Fig 13.2

Denmark
accession 42, 67, 6,9, 73–4; attitude to Commission 236; attitude to EC 37, 129–30; central bank 546; coordination process 312–13; and Council confidentiality 275; currency 532, 538; defence policy 193; EC affairs in 198; EC Presidencies 129, 151, 203, 229, 645; economy 88, 95, 198; EFTA membership 38; and EMU 168, 173, 198, 532, 546; and ERM 113, 170, 171, 538, 546, 689; and European Parliament 195, 343, 361; financial sector 150; firms 445, 455; Folketing 129, 312; government 129–30, 198; industry 130, 136, 313, 574–5; and Interior Ministry issues 194; and internal market 130, 145, 146; legal system 626; and legislation 92; Maastricht opt-outs 198, 318, 326; Market Committee 312; MEPs 358, 735n; ministries 313; monetary policy 66; opposition to Social Charter 181; and passports 154; peak organizations 358, 489, 490, 750n; Permanent Representatives 284, 312; political parties 129, 198; and pollution standards 625; public opinion in 165, 171, 190, 197–8, 312, 364, 546; referenda 130, 146, 197–8, 202, 203, 204, 312, 535; and regions 384, 413, 422–3, 425; relations with member states 130, 330, 624; and social Europe 599; sovereignty issue 198; and subsidiarity 427

Department of Trade and Industry (DTI) 120
and CBI 137; and Dekker report 139; and SMEs 301; and state aids 524–5

deregulation *see* liberalization

Deutsche Bank 364, 447, 474, 476, 478, 592, 749n

Deutsche Bundespost-Telekom (DBP) 588, 589, 675, 762n

development
developmental state 384, 392, 564, 606; Directorate (DG8) 228; EU as developmental agency 664

devolution 384, 388, 405, 407, 744n

DG1 (External Affairs Directorate) 163, 221, 223, 243, 559, 562, 602
and trade 578, 601, 607

DG1A (Trade Directorate) 223, 243, 249

DG2 (Economy and Finance Directorate) 221, 228, 559
and car industry 577; and economic integration 247; and Greek loan 725n; relations with central banks 247, 549; relations with federations 483

DG3 (Industry Directorate) 163, 221, 228, 247–9, 324, 572, 715n
competence enlarged 142; and consumer electronics 581–3; and financial sector 481; and industrial policy 559, 562, 582, 584; and internal market 105, 223, 248, 562; investigatory role of 378; and mergers 515–17, 519; relations with DG4 232, 248, 293, 501–2, 505, 511, 515, 727n, 754n; relations with federations 103, 467; relations with firms 453; relations with MNCs 136; research and technology competence 563; and telecoms liberalization 589; and trade 578, 601, 607 DG4 (Competition Directorate) 163, 249–51, 332, 499, 559, 562, 583
Anglo Saxon/German practices in 752–3n; and car industry 577; and cartels 512–14, 584; comfort letters 509, 753n; competition policy 500–7, 747n; discretion in 507, 511; and financial sector 475, 481–2, 483; fines imposed 511–13; and HDTV 581; increased powers of 223–4; informal methods of 508,

509–11, 528, 753n; and mergers 146, 249–50, 336, 502–3, 509, 512, 514–19; 753–4n; and monopolies 250–1, 500, 506, 586; relations with Council 709n; relations with DG3 232, 248, 293, 501–2, 505, 511, 515, 727n, 754n; relations with federations 136; relations with firms 452, 453, 510; relations with member states 239, 334, 504, 508, 522, 726n; relations with national agencies 509–10; and state aids 146, 332, 334, 336, 503–4, 520–8; and state monopolies 589; and steel restructuring 574–5; surveillance system 506; and telecoms liberalization 586; and trade 601, 607; use of media 336

DG5 (Employment and Industrial Relations Directorate) 249, 386, 488, 598, 748n
  and ETUC 599; Green Paper 569; industrial policy 574

DG7 (Transport Directorate) 526, 559, 572, 609, 657

DG8 (Development Directorate) 228, 243

DG11 (Environment Directorate) 251, 332, 334, 381, 728n DG12 (Research Directorate) 249, 251, 415, 559
  and car industry 577; and transport policy 572

DG13 (Telecoms Directorate) 244, 249, 251, 415, 453, 483, 559
  and car industry 577; and consumer electronics 581–3; 'The EU's Electronics and Informatics Industry' 583; and transport 572

DG15 (Financial Services Directorate) 246, 565
  and ERM crisis 548; insurance sector measures 594, 762–3n; and internal market 248, 252; relations with banks 478, 482; relations with federations 475, 481, 483, 594; relations with member states 747n; stock exchange measures 595–6

DG16 (Regions Directorate) 252–4, 396, 415, 426, 559, 598, 621, 713n
  and cohesion fund 723n; funding policy 162, 393–4, 742n; Millan as Commissioner 220, 234, 253, 332; responsibility for Regional Fund 180, 252

DG23 (SMEs Directorate) 211, 254–5, 445, 621, 745n
  and industrial policy 559, 564, 597–8; and regions 415, 424, 426; relations with firms 597; weakness of 597

DGB 181, 489, 750n

DIHK 597

Dillon, Douglas 48

Dini, Lamberto 545

Directorates xxv, 214, 242–56
  appointments system 244–5, 727n; compared with ministries 255–6; for consumer affairs 214; and core/ periphery concept 621; Delors and 161, 233, 234, 719n; Directors General 141, 214, 216, 223, 228, 233–4, 242, 244, 255, 566; ethos of 247, 259; French predominance in 245; governments and 232; guardianship mandate of 463, 747n; and impartiality 227; increased specialization of 102; industrial 180; inter-Directorate relations 500, 501, 505, 557, 562, 587; and internal market White Paper 143, 146; and legislation 628; lobbying of 359; and Maastricht agenda 161; officials 242, 244–6, 255, 259–61, 447; relations with Chefs du Cabinets 233–4; relations with Commission President 218, 223, 719n; relations with Commissioners 229, 232, 233, 244, 247, 255; relations with federations 249, 460–1, 464, 467, 471, 475, 584, 479n; relations with financial sector 460, 475, 478, 481, 746–7n; relations with firms 249, 442, 450, 452, 453, 455, 459–61, 467, 471; relations with Legal Service 258; relations with member

states 216, 234, 240, 245–6, 310, 316, 475, 476, 502, 504, 507, 508, 586; relations with Parliament 352; relations with peak organizations 256; relations with regions 415, 426; reorganization of 223, 243; staff shortages in xvii, 244; *see also* DGI, etc.

diversity 615–18, 667, 670

divisions 617–18
  economic 621–2; geographical 101, 127, 186, 203, 328, 618–21, 740n; political 622–5; social 625–30

Dooge Committee 108, 110, 128, 130, 716n, 717n
  and QMV 144; and monetary reform 145

Draft Treaty of Union (1984) 108, 191–2, 195–6, 199, 311, 319, 350, 692, 732n

Dresdner Bank 474, 476, 478

Dublin Summits
  (1979) 93; (1984) 121, 143, 144; (1990) 157, 166

Dunkirk, Treaty of (1947) 24

EACEM 457, 466, 469–70, 580–2

East Germany 650
  accepted into EU 168, 642; aid 505, 521, 684; MEPs 332; steel industry 574, 760n; and West Germany 79, 168, 174, 203

Eastern Europe 154, 241, 618
  applicants 203, 327, 482, 607, 616, 625, 631, 641–57, 695; Association Agreements 643–5, 647, 650; Austria and 636–7, 640; collapse of Soviet Union 165; Communists 356; conversion process 644–5, 648, 650–1; debt 646, 650; DGI and 243; EBRD and 166, 561, 643, 649, 759n; energy links 572; financial sector 653–5; firms 650–2; and foreign policy 184, 185, 723n; Germany and 189, 190, 202, 245, 327, 653; industry 442, 573–4, 578, 651, 761n; and Interior Ministry issues 185; loan and support programmes 183, 224,

448, 642–3, 646, 649, 730n; and regional development 397; trade agreements 191, 600, 603

Economic and Finance Committee (Ecofin) 77, 101, 270, 275, 277–8, 308, 551, 729n, 755n
  Bath meeting 536, 755n; central banks and 499, 530, 539; and Delors Report 173; Economic Policy Committee 76, 277, 680, 755n; and ERM 278, 531, 539, 547–8, 758n; and freedom of capital movements 278; and harmonization of VAT 151; in-house IMF role of 722n; Lamont at 724n; monetary union discussions 87, 147; and UK ERM entry 721n

Economic and Monetary Union (EMU) 105, 188, 696, 713n
  abandoned 70, 76; achievement of 549, 757n; British opposition to 147, 166, 189; Bundesbank and 87–9, 119, 157; central banks and 87–9, 135, 173, 499, 530, 533, 549, 554; Commission and 63, 64, 87, 88, 161, 163, 169, 177–8, 500, 532–3, 705n; convergence 177–8, 203, 532–3, 534–5, 537, 540, 542, 543–6, 547–8, 550, 551–2, 631, 722n, 756n, 757n, 757n; crises 617; Delors Committee on 173, 533, 546, 551, 682; Denmark and 130; disagreement on 147; doubts about 203; Ecofin and 278; effect on regions 392; endorsed by Hague Summit 65, 68, 755n; and ERM 169, 173; favoured by Commission 87; firms and 164; first steps towards 88; Franco-German entente and 325–6; Germany and 147, 157–8, 168, 173, 175, 289, 306, 309, 325, 328, 532, 533, 724n; governments and 175, 533, 552; and industrial policy 607–8; and informal politics 682; and internal market 109, 145, 146; Ireland and 129; Luxembourg and 127; Maastricht Treaty 163,

169–79, 196–7; member states and 87–8, 147, 157–8, 532–3; Netherlands and 125; optimism over 152; and political union 543, 553–4; public opinion on 162, 758n; reinforced 66; and Single European Act 147–8, 150, 153, 154, 169, 532, 718n; and Social Charter 161; and sovereignty 179, 183, 533, 553, 555, 689; stages of 166, 167, 168, 173, 177–8; timetable for 173, 177–8, 548, 550; and trade policy 607; Treaty on 177; two-tier system 547; UK opt-out 178, 195; Werner Report on 65, 69, 87, 532, 755n

Economic and Social Committee (Ecosoc) 75, 180, 254, 385–8, 395, 426, 691, 706–7n
achievements of 386–7; downgrading of 387, 488, 638; formal/informal aspects of 209; as industrial parliament 385–6; Netherlands and 125; reform of 387; and regions 388; relations with ETUC 599; and social policy 386; trades unions and 276, 385–7, 487, 488

Economic Cooperation Agency (ECA) 8–9, 10, 13
economic policy
Commission and 499; coordination of 28, 84; de Gaulle's proposal 43–4; EEC's early years 47–50; EMU 65, 66, 68–70; macro 84, 88, 95, 499, 563; supplyside 161
see also monetary policy
Economic Policy Committee 76, 277, 680, 755n
Economist, The 173, 187, 617, 722n, 729n
economy xxii, 4
crisis of 1973–5 xv, 70, 73, 77–8; crisis of 1981–3 xv, 93–4; crisis of 1990–93 xv; cycles 672; EC as economic entity 629; EC balance of payments 7, 62;
economic divisions 77, 621–2; European, post-War 6–10; GDP of member states Fig 13.1; interest rates 171, 174; recovery 81

Edinburgh Summit (1992) 203–5, 275 and applicants 631, 645; budget limits 574; cohesion issue 304, 392, 395–6; Danish opt-outs agreed 198, 546; Kohl's concessions 326; and siting of Parliament 332, 344; UK at 321; and White Paper (1993) 563, 569
education 161, 194, 400, 569, 605, 625
EFPIA 466, 468, 584–5, 761–2n
Egypt 663, 665
Eisenhower, Dwight D. 30–1
Eko-Stahl 574, 760n
elections
electoral systems 361–2; European Parliament 83, 85, 91, 107, 285, 340–1, 711n, 734n; national 98, 709n; voting rights 194
electronics industry 453
alliances 606; consumer xix, 79, 457, 565, 579–83, 601, 604; federations 440, 448, 466–7, 469–70, 580; HDTV 470, 580–3; restructuring 606; semi-conductors 582–3
elitism 692
Elysée Treaty 116, 323, 327
Emilia-Romagna 400, 423, 424, 426, 446, 597, 745n
case study 412–15, Fig 9.2
Emminger, Otmar 88, 89, 119, 170, 535
employers see firms
employment 569
in car industry 575; Directorate *see* DG5; *see also* unemployment
empty chair crisis 52, 67, 210, 503, 681
energy 78
deregulation of 498, 569, 572, 609–10; Green Paper 610; nuclear 29–31, 33; OECD Conference (1975) 81; policy 77, 82, 101, 423, 572; and regions 572; 9; supply 586, 587, 610; tax 447
enlargement of EC see accessions
environmental policy 146, 184, 206, 329, 607
applicants and 632; Commission/member state clashes 725–6n; Directorate see DG11; ECJ and 380–1; Eco-taxation working group

256; infringements 332; member states and 332, 733n; Parliament and 760n; pollution tax 569, 584; research 565; Rio Summit 420, 584; and state aids 527; subsidiarity in 693; in transport 564, 759n
Erasmus scheme 350, 625
Erhardt, Ludwig 38
Esprit Programme 112, 136, 251, 424, 453, 496, 558, 563, 565, 573, 606, 761n
Essen Summit 304
    and applicants 205, 570, 645, 647, 655–6, 657; ETUC 387, 487–9, 492, 707n, 710–11n, 760n
    coordinating role of 598; East Europe and 652; and Ecosoc 599; and EU industrial policy 598–600; relations with Commission 488; relations with DG5 599; and single market 718n; and Social Charter 181, 488; and social issues 84, 104, 180, 488; weakness of 358, 386, 487, 488
EURATOM 1, 30–1, 46
Eureka programme 251, 424, 565, 573, 580, 723n
Eurobarometer 363
Eurocorporatism 468
Eurodollar market 62
Eurofer 573–4, 758–9n
Europe-America Council 492–3
European Bank for Recovery and Development (EBRD) 166, 561, 643, 649, 759n
European Banking Federation (FBE) 135, 475, 476, 478, 480, 481–3, 485, 592, 748n
European Central Bank (ECB) 88, 148, 157, 169, 198, 532, 534, 757n
    accountability 554, 721n; appointments to 721n; Delors Committee 156, 171–2, 531, 534, 544, 553, 676; Directorate 552; draft statutes 177; Dutch proposals at Maastricht 178; effects on sovereignty 172, 550; Governing Council 553; and national interests 553; and protectionism 607; prototype proposal 171, 172; role in EMU 173

European Coal and Steel Community (ECSC) 1, 17, 21–4, 561
    administrative structure 22–3; defence policy 26; economic impact of 23; effect of Korean War on 25; merger with EEC 46; Monnet in 29
European Commission xxv, 35, 37, 210, 213–65
    access to documents 733n; aims of 213, 668; alliance-building in 232–4; anonymity in 236; borrowing powers 547, 569, 572; bureaucracy in 334; cabinet, President's 217, 221, 222–3, 225; cabinets, Commissioners' 217, 218, 223, 227, 233, 234, 244, 726n; and CFSP 668; cheating in 230; *chefs du cabinet* 233–4; college 141, 195, 204, 214, 215, 216, 220, 222, 224–5, 226–42, 266; comitology system 237, 282, 336, 726n, 727n; commercial policy 601; Commissioners xxxv–xxxix, 195, 214, 220, 221, 223, 226–42, 255–6, 259, 267; compared to government 235; and competition policy 55–9, 206, 498, 500–2, 506, 508, 509; competences of 93, 183, 338, 724n; Customs Court 659; as developmental state 564; and ECB 178; effectiveness of 622; and EMU 63, 64, 87, 88, 161, 163, 169, 177–8, 500, 532–3, 705n; energy policy 572, 609–10; and enlargement of EC 85, 630, 643; Europeanism of 259–64; exemptions policy 502, 511; expansion of 159–60, 161; financial sector policy 590–6, 763n; and foreign policy 50–1, 183, 191, 705n; formal/informal aspects of 209, 242–3, 629; and Free Trade Area 38; General Reports 51; Green Papers 463, 569, 587; and harmonization 93, 149, 558; increased authority of 332, 337; industrial policy 83, 95, 96–7, 98, 101, 161, 180, 498, 556–8, 564–5, 568, 573–5, 576–7, 581–2, 585,

587, 607–11; Industry Policy Paper (1990) 562, 565, 605; informal politics in 215, 223–4, 225; initiatives 53, 82, 89, 91–2, 145, 195, 201, 210, 226, 240, 241–2, 256, 272, 332, 334, 560, Fig 7.1; and internal market 84, 96–7, 101, 106, 140, 153, 154, 333, 717n; and international relations 50–1; and labour issues 84, 104, 182, 706n; legal role of 237, 238, 257, 628; lobbying of 102, 256, 418, 725n, 727n; and Luxembourg Compromise 53; and Maastricht Treaty 163, 194, 196, 197, 204, 225, 236, 337; markets, view of 559; media and 160, 162, 235–6, 240; mediatory role of 463; motivation of 685; national interests in 220, 229–30, 234; negotiating rights 604, 609; personnel 46, 74–5, 112, 214; policy-making process 566; as political elite 259–60; and political union 83, 163, 186, 191, 192; portfolio allocation 228, 243; power-base of 235, 612; Presidency xxxv–xxxix, 141, 195, 214–25, 228, 233, 256, 258, 267, 286, 288, 332, 549, 680, 708n; public perception of 235–6, 241, 260; relations with central banks 336, 533, 551; relations with Coreper 281; relations with Council of Ministers 85–6, 89–90, 210, 214, 215, 257, 266–7, 272, 275, 278, 338, 347, 566, 586–7; relations with Directorates 218, 223, 229, 232–4, 506, 719n; relations with ECJ 91–3, 96, 237, 238, 258, 369, 370–2, 708n, 739n; relations with European Council 183, 226, 233, 235, 238, 241; relations with federations 243, 439, 440, 444, 459–60, 464–5, 466, 468, 471–2, 476, 481–3, 485, 585; relations with financial sector 163, 236, 237, 473–8, 481–2, 484–5, 682; relations with firms 222, 225, 237, 240–1, 438, 441, 442, 444, 447, 449, 452, 454–5, 456,

458–63, 464–5, 494–5, 558, 566; relations with governments 53, 164, 227–31, 235, 240, 333, 339, 526, 559, 595; relations with industry xvii–xviii, 102, 163, 563; relations with interest groups 235, 242–3, 747n; relations with member states 53, 90, 93, 96, 115, 117, 125, 153–4, 160, 163, 179, 210, 214, 216, 217, 218, 219, 226–31, 233, 234, 236, 239–40, 259, 261, 288, 331–9, 340, 397, 501, 512, 564, 568, 569, 604, 609, 693, 725–6n, 733n, 734n; relations with Parliament 90, 227, 233, 235, 238, 340, 344, 347, 349, 353, 717n; relations with peak organizations 138, 237, 457, 492, 710n, 726n, 750n; relations with Presidency 320; relations with regions 83, 180, 388, 389–99, 426–7; relations with small states 623; relations with trades unions 386, 488, 599, 749n; resistance to change 223–4; role of 89, 90, 213, 227, 708n; scapegoat syndrome 236–7, 337–8; Secretariat 215, 221–2, 234, 253, 257; Secretary General 217, 218, 221–2, 244; and Single European Act 105, 141–2, 145–6, 148, 559, 686, 718n; SME policy 596–8; and social policy 181, 488, 706n; and state aids 505; and statehood 686; strategy of 239–40; structure 214; supplyside policies 161; and telecoms liberalization 586–90, 610; and trade 48–50, 140, 149, 161, 372, 499, 577, 601–2, 604–7, 734n, 739n; Transport Group report 570; transport projects 570–2, Fig 12.1; vision of Europe 101, 146, 149, 570; voting procedures 232; White Papers 566, 568–9; *see also* Directorates General
European Companies Statute 182, 239, 488, 599, 750n
European Convention on Human Rights 194, 723n

European Council xxx, 210, 266, 273, 285–8
and Council of Ministers 728–30n; established 82; and European Union 85, 105, 191; and Franco-German entente 323, 327; inter-governmental nature of 267, 275; meetings, listed xl–xli, 166–9; Netherlands and 125; and Parliament 83, 102, 183; public opinion and 273, 276; relations with Commission 183, 226, 287; relations with Coreper 282; role of 89–90, 115, 708n; strengthening of 166; *see also* Inter-Governmental Conferences; Presidency; and under individual summits

European Court of Justice (ECJ) xvi, xxiii, 58, 210, 365–82, 552, 672
activism of 365, 377, 379–80, 737n; Advocates General 365; anti-trust cartel offenders list 709n; appointments 376; *Bachman* case 372, 739n; and 'banana war' 764n; *Cassis de Dijon* case 92–3, 106, 142, 381, 708n, 710n, 711n; Commission before 238, 353, 717n; commitment to integration 82; and Committee of Regions 741; and competition policy 96, 224, 369, 475, 498–9, 503–4, 513, 519, 528; *Continental Can* case 96, 141, 501–2, 709n; and Directorates 249, 586, 727n; and EEA 631; effect of institutional reform on 183, 723n; enforcement 378–9; and environment infringements 332; fines 378; formal/informal aspects of 209; formulation of judgements 672; French influence on 375; and frontier controls 348; German beer ruling 337; and German Constitutional Court 724n; industrial policy issues 574; and insurance sector 762–3n; and Interior Ministry issues 258; and internal market 141, 366; and international polity 688; *Isoglucose* case 342, 370, 380; judges 365, 375–6, 737n; *Kramer* judgment 91–2, 380; and merger regulation 96, 141, 501–2, 751n; *Niseme* case 708n; overloading of 145, 366, 738n; and Parliamentary powers 342; and Pensions Fund Directive 595; *Philip Morris* case 96, 141, 503–4, 708n, 751n; Presidents 365; principle of minimum harmonization 252, 759n; referrals to 728n; relations with Commission 91–3, 96, 237, 238, 337, 370–2, 504, 708n, 733n, 739n; relations with Council of Ministers 275, 370, 373–5; relations with Legal Service 257, 58, 371; relations with member states 317, 365, 366, 369, 370, 372–9, 380, 381–2, 733n, 754n; relations with national courts 365; relations with other players 675; relations with Parliament 102, 362, 370; relations with regions 410; *Roquette* judgment 92; *Simmenthal* judgment 91–2, 724n, 738n; and Single European Act 686; and state aids 503–4, 505, 520, 524–5, 527, 754n; and state monopolies 762n; and subsidiarity 194, 693; as supreme court 369, 372, 373, 379; types of action in 365–6; and wine war 91

European Defence Community (EDC) 25–8, 31
collapse of 28, 185, 723n; Treaty (1952) 17, 26

European Democratic Alliance/Union 356, 633, 736n, Fig 8.4

European Economic Agreements 369, 663

European Economic Area (EEA) 108, 205, 280, 440, 482, 603, 631–2, 723n
Austria in 636; Legal Department's role in 258; and steel imports 573; Sweden in 634, 636

European Enterprise Group (EEG) 139, 465

European Free Trade Association (EFTA)

accessions 146, 189, 198, 199, 203,
204, 221, 243, 352, 492, 547–8,
607, 616, 620, 631–42, 717n,
723n, 724n, 736n, 750n; associate
EC membership of 280; Austria
and 633–4; and collapse of Communism 165; compared with EEC
39, 129; and currency fluctuation
79, 723n; and ERM 547; established 38; European Economic
Agreements 369; and European
Economic Area 108, 205, 258, 603;
membership of FBE 482; Portugal
and 715n; relations with EC 75, 82,
116; removal of tariffs 55, 59–60;
Sweden and 634; and trade distortion 55; trade figures 60; tripartism
in 181; UK and 69
European Insurance Federation (CEA)
593–4, 762n
European Investment Bank 332, 389,
570, 649, 654
 Commission borrowing powers 569;
 and industrial policy 561
European Monetary Fund 76, 88, 89
European Monetary Institute (EMI)
178, 534, 511, 543, 545, 547
 appointments 734n; areas of study
 758n; Council 547; and EMU
 757n; German view of 544; location of 179, 203, 309, 328, 407,
 547, 757n
European Monetary System (EMS)
 central banks and 87–8, 119, 344,
 531–2; creation of 87–8, 169, 531,
 755n; early proposals 87;
 fluctuations 100, 710n;
 Franco-German role in 324, 327;
 Ireland and 128; Italy and 123;
 Jenkins' proposals 87; Kohl and
 309; member states and 87–8, 90,
 441–2, 532; Netherlands and 125;
 Parliament and 344; revaluation
 106; and Single European Act
 147–8; UK and 114
European Parliament (EP) xvi, 210,
340–64, 690
 antipathy towards 91; and appointments 228, 347, 734n; approves

Maastricht Treaty 199; Assizes
184, 191, 195, 343, 350, 361, 364;
bi-polarity trend 356, 357; British
Labour Party and 75; and budget
52, 91; Bureau 352; calibre of
MEPs 357–8; clubs 103, 137, 357;
co-decision powers 195, 347, 349,
353, Fig 8.3; committees 349, 352,
456; consultation procedure Fig
8.1, 8.2; and cooperation 349;
debates 357; Delors and 141, 146,
160–1, 238, 349, 351, 353; and
democratic deficit 692; draft
Treaty of Union 108, 350; and
Ecosoc 387; EFTA admissions
vote 352, 736n; elections 83, 85,
91, 107, 285, 340–1, 711n, 734n;
and EMS/ERM 344; and EMU
166; enlargement of 332; and
European citizenship 362; European Democratic Alliance 736n,
Fig 8.4; European People's Party
grouping 176, 351, 354–6, 736n,
Fig 8.4; and European Union 105,
106, 116, 192, 711n; formal/
informal aspects of 209; French
attitudes towards 83, 91, 116, 143,
188, 297, 332; and human rights
194; and ICGs 184; increased
powers 83, 89, 143, 145, 148, 158,
161, 184, 188, 238, 717–18n; and
industrial policy 568, 760n; initiatory powers 184; and
inter-governmentalism 91, 102;
Italian attitude towards 146, 168;
Liberal and Democratic Reformist
group 354, 356, 736n, Fig 8.4;
lobbying of 348, 352, 358–9, 568;
location of 332, 344, 362; Maastricht provisions 150, 184, 186,
191, 282, 340, 343, 347, 348,
734n; MEPs by member state
735n; monetary proposals 63,
705n; Netherlands and 125; political groupings in 354–7, Fig 8.4;
and political IGC 186, 191; powers
of 342–7; Presidency 351, 357; and
QMV 194; Rainbow Group 357,
736n, Fig 8.4; reallocation of seats

196; Regional Intergroup 404; and regions 91; rejects Customs Union 659; relations with Commission 90, 227, 233, 235, 238, 340, 344, 347, 349, 351, 717n; relations with Coreper 282; relations with Council of Ministers 91, 92, 102, 266–7, 276, 340–1, 342–3, 347–50, 353; relations with Directorates 352; relations with ECJ 102, 370; relations with European Council 83; relations with federations 464, 486; relations with firms 440, 442, 448, 450, 452; relations with governments 352, 357; relations with industry xviii, 103, 468; relations with member states 331, 340, 343, 348, 351, 352, 353, 360, 363; relations with national parliaments 351, 357, 360–2; relations with Permanent Representatives 351; relations with regions 399; reports 83, 352; role of 340–1, Fig 7.1; and SEA 150, 342, 353; Socialist/Social Democrats group 351, 354–6, 736n, Fig 8.4; and telecoms liberalization 587; and Treaty of Rome 35; and unemployment/growth 564; and Vredeling Directive 104, 711n

European Payments Union (EPU) 10–14, 18, 21

European People's Party (EPP) 176, 351, 354–6, 736n, Fig 8.4

European Political Community (EPC) 27–8, 31

European Political Cooperation (EPC) 69, 75

European Recovery Program (ERP) 8–10

European Regional Development Fund (ERDF) see Regional Development Fund

European Round Table (ERT) 103, 104, 123, 439, 490

influence in EC 137, 138–9, 716n; and IGCs 164; and internal market concept 139, 715n; and monetary union 164; 'Rebuilding Confidence' pamphlet 164; relations with Commission 222; *Reshaping Europe* 566; and SEA 718n; and sectoral interests 465; Swedish leadership of 634

European Social Fund see Social Fund

European Socialists Group 351, 354–5, 736n, Fig 8.4

European Union (EU) 197

accepted by Council 85; Parliament and 105, 106; French attitude towards 115; Ireland and 129; reports on 69, 73, 83, 84, 85, 705n; see also Economic and Monetary Union; Maastricht Treaty of European Union; political union

exchange controls 64, 147, 149, 156, 532, 538, 590, 762n

Exchange Rate Mechanism (ERM) 88, 147, 277, 554, 67

Black Wednesday 537, 539; central banks and 120, 169, 529–55; classic phase of 113, 532, 534; and convergence 532; crises in 197, 203, 203, 533–9, 547–8; DG2 and 247; Ecofin and 278, 531; EMU and 169–79, 499; France and 113, 115–16, 158, 169–71, 174, 176, 532, 535, 537; Germany and 169, 202, 534, 535–7; governments and 113, 176, 535–6; industry and 548; informal cooperation in 531; Italy leaves 537; management of 529–55; member states and 113–14, 532, 535, 547; politicization of 553–4; Portuguese entry 535; realignment 536–7, 539, 540, 552, 755–6n; Spanish entry 533; UK and 88–9, 114, 120, 153, 158, 166, 171, 174–5, 203, 220, 278, 299, 537, 538, 714n, 721n

exchange rate policy 62, 64–6, 173

exports 6, 419

EEC-EFTA 60; export credits 322; intra-EEC 60; intra-EFTA 60; levies 81; subsidies 523; voluntary export restraints 95, 140, 561, 562, 577–9, 580, 601, 603–4, 709n

external affairs see international relations

Fabius, Laurent 99, 146
Falklands War 126, 710n
federalism 2, 16–17, 666, 691
    applicant states and 641; in Belgium
    126, 384; British attitude to 16, 40;
    Commission and 196; Delors and
    399; de Gaulle and 40, 42, 44; in
    EC 35, 36, 37, 38, 143; in ECJ
    380; Maastricht and 191, 192, 195;
    Mitterrand's speech on 107, 143;
    and north/south divide 621;
    regions and 188, 425
Federation of Stock Exchanges 483–4,
    595–6
federations 463–97
    in applicant states 638, 651–2;
    bargaining strategy 495–6; effects
    of recession on xv; employers' 133,
    411, 412, 715n; European 439,
    446–8, 452, 460, 463–73; financial
    services 473–85, 593–4; German
    463–4, 465; and industrial policy
    557, 584, 608; informal politics of
    494–5; and internal market 472;
    links with EU 439, 440; national
    464, 465, 469, 472; and policy in-
    itiatives 460–1; relations with
    banking sector 464; relations with
    Commission 243, 439, 440, 444,
    459–60, 464–5, 466, 468, 471–2,
    476, 481–3, 485, 585; relations
    with Coreper 467; relations with
    Council of Ministers 467; relations
    with Directorates 249, 460–1, 464,
    471, 475, 483, 504, 584, 594,
    748n; relations with firms 444;
    relations with government 464,
    469, 470, 731n; relations with Par-
    liament 464; relations with trades
    unions 464; role of 463–4; sectoral
    102–3, 136–7, 457–9, 467–73,
    495–6; and SMEs 445; and
    Vredeling Directive 104; *see also*
    peak organizations
Ferranti, Basil de 137, 357, 715n
Fianna Fáil 354, 355
Fiat 440, 454, 514–15, 577, 579, 606,
    755n
finance, EC

additionality 405, 570, 742n; Directo-
    rate sec DG2; Parliament's role in
    342; *see also* budget
financial institutions xvi, xxv–xxix,
    155, 210, 498, 673, 706n
    in applicant states 637, 653–4, 661;
    Belgian 150, 484; British 120, 135,
    150, 477–9, 480, 590, 714n; Brus-
    sels offices 498; cartels 475,
    513–14; Catalan Caixas 411; com-
    petition 250, 507, 592; and concer-
    tation 388; dominance of 78; ECJ
    and 372; and ERM crisis 541;
    federations 463, 473–85; financial
    services Directorate *see* DG15;
    French 150, 418, 477, 484; German
    150, 309, 420, 477–8, 484;
    harmonization of 150, 474, 477,
    481, 485, 590; and industrial policy
    560, 590–6; informality in 478, 480,
    681–2; and internal market 109,
    135, 150, 252, 372, 473, 590, 593,
    595; Italian 123, 150, 316, 479, 484;
    liberalization of 135, 476, 479, 591,
    593, 673; in Luxembourg 150, 478;
    mergers 447, 476, 481, 593; and
    monetary union 150, 164;
    Portuguese 749n; regional 397;
    relations with central banks 473,
    484, 549, 592, 757–8n; relations
    with Commission 163, 236, 237,
    473–8, 481, 484–5, 592, 682; rela-
    tions with Directorates 460, 478,
    481–2, 746–7n; relations with firms
    442; relations with government 311,
    314, 442, 476, 477, 484, 559, 748n,
    763n; relations with industry 487;
    relations with member states 475–6,
    483, 559, 593; relations with na-
    tional coordinators 301, 309; rela-
    tions with Permanent Represen-
    tatives 478; relations with regions
    384, 402; Scottish 407; and SEA
    143, 150–1, 160, 163–4, 590, 718n;
    Spanish 150, 412, 479, 484, 749n;
    trade by 601; UK and 120, 714n; *see
    also* banking
Fine Gael 355, 736n
Finland

application 259, 631, 640–1, 642; central bank 550; and collapse of Communism 165, 640; currency 535, 538; EEA member 205; liberalism in 619; referendum 633; relations with EC 75, 717n

firms 109, 210, 211, 435–63, 493–7, 498, 622
  access to EU 436, 557, 673–4, Fig 10.1; access to national institutions 436, Fig 10.1; activism of 456; American 58–9, 472; in applicant states 638–9, 645, 649, 650–2; attitude to EC 560; bargaining procedures 493–4; Belgian 455; British 301, 438, 450, 451–3; Brussels offices 262, 448, 450, 497, 498; collaboration between 557–8, 560, 565; company law 83–4, 626; competences of 629; and competition policy 504, 511, 526, 528; competitiveness 471, 557; consultants 442–4; Danish 445, 455; defence measures of 580; Dutch 125, 311, 445, 455–6; and ECJ 374; and Ecosoc 387; and EMU 554; and enlargement 645, 647, 652, 768n; and ERT 138–9; Eurochampions 248, 249, 251, 457, 471, 496, 573, 582, 608, 674; European ethos of 262–3, 426–7, 445, 447, 453, 496–7, 498, 728n; European resources 448; external relations of 420; French 418, 449–51; German 308, 309, 446–9, 619, 674–5; global 674–5; index of commitment of xviii, 699n; individual influence of 139–40; and industrial policy 556, 560, 564, 596; and informal politics xv–xvi, 435, 436–7, 448–9, 461, 493, 628, 683–4; intelligence gathering 442; and internal market 136, 139, 143, 160, 438–40, 449, 458, 467, 496, 606, 715n; investment decisions 560; Irish 453; Italian 122, 123, 316, 454–5, 746n; Japanese 151–2, 453, 457, 466, 746n; legal consultants 442–3, 744n; links to deci-

sion makers Fig 10.2, 10.3; lobbyists 358–9, 436, 443–4, 456, 619; management 84, 646, 651; in Mediterranean states 619; and monetary union 164; national 262, 435, 439, 443, 445–6, Fig 10.1, 10–3; national champions 573, 580; national identity of 674; nationalization 99; north/south divide in 619; oligopolistic tendencies of 112; policy initiatives 460–1; Portuguese 453; privatization of 99, 120, 437–8, 506, 521; relations with Commission 222, 225, 237, 240–1, 438, 441, 442, 447, 449, 452, 454, 456, 458–63, 464, 494–5, 558, 566; relations with Coreper 284, 442, 449, 453, 455, 676, 729n; relations with Council 276; relations with Directorates 249, 442, 450, 452, 453, 455, 459–61, 471, 506, 510; relations with financial sector 442; relations with government 97, 112, 137–8, 164, 436, 439, 441, 442, 443, 447, 450, 451, 452, 453–4, 455, 458, 462, 496, 559, 678; relations with member states 559; relations with national coordinators 296, 301, 303, 308, 313, 730n; relations with Parliament 440, 442, 448, 450, 452; relations with Presidency 442; relations with regions 426, 427; relative v. collective advantage xviii–xix, 769n; resources switched to EC 109; Scottish 408; and SEA 149, 151–2, 163–4, 557; sectoral alliances and networks 457, 566; and Social Charter 181, 222; Spanish 453–4; strategic involvement in EU 440; success of 683; and trade policy 601, 603; trans-national (TNCs) 437, 496, 605, 674, 744n, 762n; working group representation 460, 462, 746n; *see also* federations; industry; multinational corporations; small and medium-sized enterprises

fisheries 81, 85, 93, 163, 707n

FitzGerald, Garret 128, 624, 714n
Flynn, Padraig 234, 386, 569, 574
Fontainebleau Summit (1984) 107–8,
  112, 114, 115, 140, 143, 321, 325
food regulations 92, 708n
foreign policy 94, 158, 641, 642
  of applicant states 640; Commission
  role in 183; Coreper and 270, 285;
  Council of Ministers and 270, 274,
  285; Davignon Report 69, 705n;
  disagreement in 147, 203; ECJ
  ruling on 92; early challenges 46;
  European Political Cooperation 69;
  General Affairs Council 276, 277,
  286; Hallstein Report 39; incoherence of 616–17; and Maastricht
  Treaty 191–2; member states and
  184, 330; and neighbouring states
  663–5; Parliamentary Foreign
  Affairs Committee 352, 353; and
  political union 184–8; Presidency
  and 318; regional 408, 412, 418,
  420; *see also* Common Foreign and
  Security Policy
Forza Italia 355, 358
Fouchet Plan 44–5, 325
'Four Motors' group 254, 402, 410,
  413, 415, 419, 421, 743n
France
  agriculture 29, 168, 626; Assembly
  361, 737n; assessment of membership 289–90; attitudes to EC
  115–17, 188, 190–1, 192, 202, 293,
  322; and Benelux 18; and British
  EC application 40–2, 45, 67–8, 74,
  630; and CAP 52, 90, 156, 289;
  and CFI 366; colonies 50–1; and
  Commission 89–90, 166, 201, 227,
  240, 334, 725n; and competition
  policy 366, 501, 503, 506, 508,
  509, 516–18, 529; Constitutional
  Council 83; and convergence 551;
  coordination process 293–7, 730n;
  corporatism in 385; and Council
  166; cultural quotas 604; currency
  62, 63, 64, 65, 66, 67, 79, 80, 83,
  87, 95, 99, 170, 289, 327–8, 538;
  defence policy 116, 158, 185, 187,
  188, 193, 197; and Delors Presi-

dency 220; dominance under
  threat 696; and EC law 92, 116,
  297, 368, 375, 713n; EC officials
  245, 262; EC Presidencies 89, 90,
  107, 114, 143, 320–1, 325; and
  ECB 178; and ECJ 734, 738n,
  754n; economy 95, 99, 170, 176;
  and Ecosoc 387; ECSC membership 1, 17, 21, 23; EDC proposals
  25–8, 185; and EEC negotiations
  32, 33–4; effectiveness of 623; and
  EMI 757n; Empty Chair policy 52,
  67, 503; and EMU 88, 147, 148,
  157–8, 166, 173, 177, 325–6, 532,
  554; and EPC 28; and EPU 12, 14;
  and ERBD 166, 643, 759n; and
  ERM 113, 115–16, 158, 169–71,
  174, 176, 532, 535, 537–8,
  539–41, 547, 548; and European
  Parliament 83, 91, 116, 166, 188,
  195, 332, 341, 348; European
  project in 115; exchange controls
  64, 156; financial sector 150, 418,
  477, 484, 592; firms 418, 449–51,
  469, 608; and foreign policy 187–8,
  192, 270, 285, 293, 328;
  Franco-German conflict 1, 24, 25,
  28–9, 81, 114, 328, 539;
  Franco-German entente 67–8, 82,
  100, 108, 115, 116, 124, 143, 144,
  156–7, 166–7, 175, 215, 296, 321,
  323–9, 353, 689, 696, 709n;
  Franco-Italian Customs Union 19;
  FRITALUX 19–20; and GATT
  205, 327; and German reunification 165, 325; Giscard Government 79–80; and HDTV Directive
  581; horse-racing tax row 522,
  726n; industrial policy 567, 608,
  684; industry 80, 103, 115, 136,
  137, 417–18, 576, 580; infringements of EC law 240, 529; and
  institutional reform 195, 201; and
  integration 100, 115–16; and Interior Ministry issues 194; and internal market 105, 191; and Japanese
  inward investment 576–7; legal
  system 626; Maastricht ratification
  199, 200–1; media 539–40; MEPs

352, 354–5, 357, 735n; ministries 293–5, 450, 730n; nuclear programme 29–31, 33, 80; and oil crisis 79–80; opposition to free trade area 38; Parliament 197; peak organizations 104, 489; Permanent Representatives 284, 296, 418, 730n; Planning Commission 21; political leadership of 89, 114; political parties 200, 203, 354–5; and political union 157–8, 166, 175, 325; President 296; protectionism 33, 289, 603; public opinion in 165, 186, 188, 190, 200, 323, 516, 689, 758n; referendum 200–1, 276, 535, 537, 540; and Regional Fund 394, 705n; regions 384, 390, 392, 398, 400, 401, 416–19, 425, 730n; relations with Directorates 522–3; relations with Ireland 83, 109; relations with Italy 81, 109; relations with Spain 86, 108, 707n, 712n; relations with UK 24, 41, 67–8, 73, 190; relations with US 617; Schengen Agreement 186; and Single European Act 148, 686; socialism 98, 99; sovereignty question 116, 324; and state aids 236, 289, 505, 521–3, 525–6; state monopolies 587; and steel restructuring 574–5; and subsidiarity 201, 297; and supranationality 27; telecoms 588, 762n; trade 61; trade unions 387, 487, 489; and variable geometry 190; *see also* Rhône-Alpes

France Télécom 588, 589, 762n
Franco-German Economic Council 327
Franco-German entente; see France, Germany
Franco-German Treaty of Friendship and Cooperation 45
Franco-Italian Customs Union 19
fraud
in EC 264, 306, 329, 334, 350; in financial sector 590–1; in Mediterranean states 619
Free Trade Area
British proposal 33, 37–8, 47;

EEC-EFTA 75; with former EEC colonies 51; *see also* European Free Trade Association
FRITALUX 19
frontiers 663
controls 6, 108, 112, 348, 374; and national security 184; policing of 163, 617; Schengen Agreement on 186

Galle Report 359, 747n
Gabaglio, Emilio 599, 760n
Gasperi, Alcide de 17, 27
Gaullists 79–80, 91, 355, 356
GEC 452, 573
General Affairs Council (GAC) 276, 277, 285, 286, 288, 308
General Agreement on Tariffs and Trade (GATT) 5, 39, 46, 168, 179, 205, 263, 329, 493, 586, 601, 689
Commission's role in 372, 602, 734n; Delors and 160; Dillon Round 48–9; French acceptance of 327; Franco-German disputes 328; and intra-European trade 12–13, 14, 47; Kennedy Round 49; Parliament's role in 348; Tokyo Round 90; Uruguay Round 204, 337, 440, 471, 516, 563–4, 578, 602–4, 673; Yaounde and 51
Genscher, Hans-Dietrich 100, 625, 636
and Commission portfolios 228; and EU foreign policy 187; Genscher-Colombo initiative 102, 118; relations with Kohl 157, 326
geographical divisions 618–21
see also north/south divide
German Bankers Federation (BDB) 478, 748n
Germany
assessment of membership 289; attitudes to EC 117–19, 192, 306, 322; authority of 696; and 'banana war' 604, 764n; and Beyen Plan 32, 33; border question 327, 644; and budget 117; Bundestag 308, 361; and CAP 52, 90, 107, 156, 719n;

central bank see Bundesbank; chancellor 308–10; and Commission 90, 226, 227, 334, 569, 724n; and common market negotiations 33; and competition policy 113, 280, 289, 501, 503, 508, 518, 519; Constitutional Court 202, 671, 724n; coordination process 306–10; Coreper representatives 284; currency 63, 64, 65–6, 68, 77, 79; decentralization 118–19; defence policy 119, 185, 193; direct investment in eastern Europe 653; draft Treaty 191; and EC law 368; EC Presidencies 118, 151, 153, 156, 309, 320, 325, 350, 645, 647, 656, 659; and ECB 178; and ECJ 370, 738n; economy 77, 79, 88, 94–5, 100, 118, 174; and Ecosoc 387; ECSC membership 1, 17, 21, 23; and EDC 26; effectiveness of 623; and EMU 147, 157–8, 168, 173, 175, 289, 306, 328, 309, 325, 532, 533, 552, 554, 724n; and EPC 28; and EPU 11–12, 14; and ERM 169, 202, 534, 535, 540–1, 548; and ERP 9; and European Parliament 158, 184, 188, 238, 279, 341, 353–4, 361; federations 463–4, 465, 489, 490, 750–1n; financial sector 150, 309, 420, 477–8, 480–1, 484, 592, 762n, 763n; firms 308, 309, 445, 446–9, 467, 469, 619, 674–5; foreign policy 79, 100, 117, 119, 157, 187, 190, 327, 328; Franco-German conflict 1, 24, 25, 28–9, 81, 114, 328, 539; Franco-German entente 67–8, 82, 100, 108, 115, 116, 124, 143, 144, 156–7, 166–7, 175, 215, 296, 321, 323–9, 353, 689, 696, 709n; and Free Trade Area 38; and FRITALUX 20; governments 118; and HDTV Directive 581; industrial policy 608; industry 4, 20, 79, 117, 118, 136, 137, 151, 306, 419–20, 500, 573–5, 576, 579, 758n, 760n; inflation 534; and informal politics 626, 629; and institutional reform 188; and integration 24, 29, 100, 101, 118; and Interior Ministry issues 194; internal disagreements 156–7; and internal market 151; international relations 79, 323; and Japanese inward investment 577; *länder* (regions) 91, 148, 156, 168, 180, 188, 203, 308, 361, 383, 392–3, 397, 398, 400, 419–22, 424–5, 427, 484, 595, 684, 693, 716n; and legislation 92; lobbying 445; and Maastricht 199, 202–3, 617, 721n; media 202–3, 541; MEPs 355, 358, 735n; ministries 308–9, 446, 508; *mitbestimmung* 385, 684; Modell Deutschland 137; monetary policy 79, 88, 119, 707n; and NATO 25, 28, 326; officials 245, 262; and oil crisis 79; peak organizations 103, 308, 731n; Permanent Representatives 309, 310; political parties 79, 91, 99, 100, 175, 355; and political union 116, 118, 150, 157–8, 166, 175, 187, 188–9, 191, 289, 325–6, 689; public opinion in 186, 188, 202–3, 323, 364, 541, 757n; and QMV 279; rearmament 25–6, 28; and refugees 664, 768n; and Regional Fund 82; and regionalism 396; relations with Italy 109, 143; relations with Spain 330; relations with UK 119, 326; relations with US 63; reunification 157, 158, 165, 168, 174, 175, 176, 196, 220, 279, 296, 306, 325, 326, 327, 355, 447, 534, 540, 574, 641, 643, 684, 720n; revaluation 62, 64, 66, 68, 87; Schengen Agreement 186; scrutiny of EC legislation 361, 421; and Single European Act 148; SMEs 420, 439, 596–7, 763n; sovereignty transfers 421; and state aids 505, 520, 521; state monopolies 587; and subsidiarity 188, 203, 308; substates 400; trade 6, 48, 61, 79; telecoms 588–9,

762n; trades unions 310, 487, 489;
and Turkish *gastarbeiter* 658; *see
also* Baden-Württemberg; East
Germany
Giscard d'Estaing, Valéry 79–80, 82,
100, 115, 201
    and Commission 89, 215, 216, 338,
    708n, 724n; complaints of *lourdeur*
    90; and Council 89, 708n; and ECJ
    739n; European Central Bank
    proposal 171; as Finance Minister
    87; and Franco-German entente
    323–4; and institutional reform 89;
    monetary policy 87, 88, 531;
    reserve unit proposal 63; and
    Spanish EC application 86, 707n
Gonzalez, Felipe 132, 206, 712n, 714n,
    725n
    government of 162, 302, 357, 409,
    411, 719n, 755n, 763n
Gorbachev, Mikhail 109–10, 114, 153,
    157
governments
    British 120; and Commission Presi-
    dency 215; and competition policy
    508, 509; Coreper meetings 266;
    Danish 129; and defence issues
    187; Departments of Industry 106;
    and DGs 232; divisions at Maas-
    tricht 164; Dutch 124; and EC
    enactments 670; and ECJ 82; and
    Ecosoc 387; and EMU 175, 533;
    and ERM 113, 176, 535–6, 540;
    and European Parliament 83;
    formal politics of 616; Greek
    130–1; and harmonization 155; and
    industrial policy 556, 561; inter-
    governmental supremacy 82–3;
    and internal market 97, 105, 106,
    141, 142, 155; Italian 122–3; and
    Maastricht Treaty 162, 164, 178,
    197, 198–9, 201, 721–2n; and poli-
    tical union 163, 189–90, 192; rela-
    tions with central banks 177, 499,
    530, 536, 537, 538, 542–7,
    549–50, 552; relations with Com-
    mission 53, 164, 227–31, 236, 261,
    333, 339, 526, 559; relations with
    Directorates 246; relations with

federations 103, 104, 137–8, 308,
    464, 469, 470, 489, 731n; relations
    with financial sector 311, 314, 442,
    473, 476, 477, 484, 485, 559, 594,
    748n, 763n; relations with firms
    97, 112, 137–8, 164, 436, 439, 441,
    442, 443, 445, 447, 450, 451, 452,
    453–4, 455, 458, 462, 496, 559,
    678; relations with industry 98,
    176; relations with Legal Service
    259; relations with MEPs 352, 357;
    and public opinion 364; relations
    with regions 404–5, 407, 412, 413;
    relations with trades unions 176;
    and SEA 142–9, 152, 154; and
    Social Charter 181; and social di-
    versity 625; Spanish 132; and state
    monopolies 589–90; and trade
    policy 601, 603; unilateral actions
    94, 98; *see also* member states
Greece
    accession 85–6, 90, 130, 616, 618,
    630, 657; anti-Americanism 714n;
    assessment of EC membership
    261; attitudes to EC 130–2, 192,
    322, 630; central bank 546; centrist
    governing philosophy 91, 305–6;
    civil war 7; coordination process
    305–6; court case against 726n;
    devaluation 106; and ECB 178;
    and EMU 173; federations 480,
    489; firms 674, 676; Foreign Min-
    istry 305–6; governments 130–1;
    industry 277; infringements of EC
    law 766n; and Interior Ministry
    issues 194; and internal market
    negotiations 145; loan 220, 722n,
    725n; Maastricht ratification 201;
    and Macedonia 320, 382; as Medi-
    terranean state 620, 621; MEPs
    358, 735n; Pasok government 101,
    107, 130–1, 389, 714n, 726n; Per-
    manent Representatives 284, 306;
    Presidencies 106–7, 131, 149, 151,
    160, 320; public opinion in 131;
    and public procurement Directive
    567; and Regional Fund 107, 162,
    389, 394, 723n; regions 384, 397,
    402; relations with EC 82; relations

with member states 329, 330; relations with Turkey 657–9, 660; and Single European Act 131, 148; as small state 624; and social Europe 599; and Structural Fund 148; talks with Soviet Union 160
Green Papers 463, 569, 587, 610
Green Parties 356, 380, 736n, Fig 8.4
Group of Five (G5) 160, 274, 278, 321, 485, 530
Group of Seven (G7) 167, 171, 274, 278, 321
Louvre Accord 170; relations with Commission 223; and telecoms liberalization 589
Group of Ten 529, 531
growth initiatives 563, 564, 569
Grundig 469, 563, 579
Gucht Report 362
Guigou, Elizabeth 146, 154, 187, 295, 296, 522
Guinness 452–3
Gulf War 193, 617, 659, 666, 697, 723n

Hague Congress (1948) 16
Hague Summit (1969) 65, 68 9, 285, 755n
Hallstein, Walter 216, 218, 220
and customs union 47; first Commission President 38, 46, 90, 214; Hallstein Report 39; opposition to de Gaulle proposals 44; on tariff cuts 47
Hannover Summit (1988) 149–50, 156–7, 162, 309, 320, 325, 350
capital movements agreement 147, 278, 317; and Delors Committee 148; European union agreement 151, 152, 153; informal politics at 286; interest rate agreement 171, 538; trade statement 602
Hansch, Klaus 351, 354, 611, 647
harmonization policy 241, 672
in car industry 575, 579; Colonna Report 98; de Gaulle and 191; EC Council and 233, 709n; ECJ and Commission roles in 92–3, 149, 558; ECJ principle of minimum harmonization 252, 759n; of

economic opportunity 463; of electoral systems 361–2; of financial sector 150, 474, 477, 481, 485, 590, 594, 681; as fundamental aim 615; governments and 155; and integration 561; of laws 83–4, 182; Luxembourg and 127; of markets 559; regional 399; tax 145, 149, 151, 160, 579, 718n, 725n; technical 106, 136; UK and 120
Harvey-Jones, John 138, 467
Haughey, Charles 129, 166
Healey, Denis 81, 87
health and safety 182, 599, 731n
health policy 92, 194, 607, 708n
Heath, Edward 705n, 724n
and British EC application 40, 43, 45, 69, 74; and Christian Democracy 736n; and Foreign Office 299; Government of 73–4; loses 1974 election 74; relations with Pompidou 329
Haider, Jörg 634, 636
Helsinki Accord 69, 76
history
and actor-agency dilemma 3; contemporary xii; of European state 687, 689; 1945–58 1–36; 1958–73 37–70; 1973–83 73–110; 1980–88 111–55; 1988–93 156–205; revisionist 2–3
Hoffman, Paul 10, 14–15
Horn, Gyula 649, 655
House of Lords 368, 374, 381, 738n
Howe, Geoffrey 145, 711n
agricultural prices veto 100; on Council confidentiality 275, 729n; and ERM 158, 174; SEA without IGC proposal 144, 177; supports internal market 121; Stresa proposals 116, 144, 716n
human rights 194, 367, 380, 723n
Hungarian National Bank 655
Hungary
application 203, 205, 625, 641–57; Communist elite 650; conversion process 644, 646; debt 646, 650; direct investment 653; economy 655; elections 645; EU networks

655; financial sector 654; industry 652–3; loan schemes 183, 642; nationalism 646; privatization 652; relations with Austria 636–7, 653, 766n, 767n
Hurd, Douglas 189

IBM 438, 606, 744n
Iceland 75, 632
ICI 467
chemicals cartel case 378, 512–13, 528; Dupont merger 515; EC representation 451–2
ICL 448, 453, 582, 606, 716n
immigration 165, 202, 274, 328, 617, 665
economic migrants 185, 186, 707n; illegal immigrants 186, 664; Parliament and 348; refugees 185–6, 188
imports 6, 8, 13–14, 50, 601
industrial policy 57, 79, 559–600, 709n
British 120; car production 575–9; cases 572–600; chemical industry 584–5; Commission and 83, 95, 96–7, 98, 101, 161, 180, 498–9, 556–8; Commission Paper on (1990) 562, 565, 605; consensus lost 96; consumer electronics industry 579–83; Council of Ministers and 270; as crisis resolution 561; DG4 and 511; early 76, 561; and EMU 607–8; financial sector and 560, 590–6; firms and 556, 560; funding under 560; German view of 118; governments and 556; horizontal 562; industry campaigns for 102; influence of interest groups 102; informal politics in 558, 561; interventionist nature of 585; on labour 598–600; lack of cohesion in 556–7, 559; and Maastricht Treaty 194; member states and 97, 561; of member states 102, 137, 556; pharmaceutical industry 584–5; sectoral 560, 561, 562, 563; on SMEs 596–8, 763n; for steel 573–5; and trade 600–1; and transport policy 570; in UK 74, 113,

137, 562; White Paper (1993) 204, 223, 332, 387, 454, 488, 491, 563, 568–9, 750n
industrial relations 84, 165, 182
draft directives 166; in eastern Europe 652; and Social Protocol 599; Spanish 763n; White Paper (1993) and 563
industry xvii–xviii, 109, 290, 622, 673
in applicant countries 637, 650–3, 660, 768n; British 121; competitiveness of 112; concentration 59; cooperation in 502; decline in 182; Directorate see DG3; Dutch 125; and east European applicants 645; EC 55–9; EC organization of 414; ECJ rulings 92; and Ecosoc 385; effect of recession xv, 77, 79, 94–6; and ERM 548; European confederation see UNICE; as European player 136–7, 715n; French 80, 103, 115, 136, 137, 417–18; German 4, 20, 79, 117, 118, 136, 137, 151, 306, 419–20; inclusion in political process 385; increased demand 706n; industrial policy 102, 154, 155; and internal market 97, 102, 104, 135, 151, 715n; Italian 123; lack of supranational representation 706n; lobbying by 102, 152, 358, 411, 414; loss of competitiveness 79; and monetary union 87; nationalized 506; post-War 4–5; rationalization of 602; regeneration of 101, 161, 603, 605; relations with central banks 103; relations with Commission xvii–xviii, 83, 96–7, 98, 163, 563; relations with Council of Ministers 277; relations with financial sector 487; relations with governments 98, 103, 164, 176, 277, 311, 313, 314, 585; relations with MEPs 103, 358; relations with national coordinators 296, 301, 303, 305, 311, 730n; relations with regions 384, 402, 426; restructuring 83, 96, 97, 204, 332, 502, 561, 562, 573–4, 606, 651–3, 768n; Scottish

402, 406–7; Spanish 132; versus
agriculture 615; and 1993 White
Paper 332; *see also* federations;
firms; peak organizations
inflation 78, 88, 170, 171, 713n
in eastern Europe 645; in Germany
534; in Italy 80; role of central
banks in 531; in UK 80, 81, 171,
706n
informal politics xiii, xiv, xv–xvii, 209,
612, 628, 677–84, 688
in banana war 764n; amongst central
bankers 547, 553; Commission's
use of 230, 231, 233, 238, 240,
242–3, 281, 371, 509; Commission
President's use of 215, 221, 223–4,
225; in Committee of Regions 209,
428; in competition cases 502, 508,
509–11, 527, 528, 691; Council's
use of 101, 277, 278, 350; defined
xv–xvii, 679; DG4's use of 508,
509–11, 753n; and EC legislation
628; and EC statehood 559–60; in
ECJ 370, 371, 373, 379; of EFTA
applicants 632–3; in ERM 531;
Euro-civilizing aspect of 684; in
European Council 286, 287, 318;
federations use of 494–5; financial
sector's use of 478; firms' use of
xv–xvi, 435, 436–7, 448–9, 461,
493; and formal politics 678;
Germany and 626; in government
forums 272; in industrial policy
558, 561; industry and 136; and
integration 616; in legal affairs 258,
687; and legitimacy 692; member
states' use of 209, 288, 331, 616,
626; new applicants and 630–1,
647–8; Parliament's use of 347,
352; peak organizations' use of
137; regions' use of 400, 401, 405,
417; in Social Charter negotiations
182–3; in state aids cases 520, 524;
and statehood 688; in trade 578;
UK and 626; under Communism
648; and unity 628–9
information technology industry 136,
716n
infrastructure 547

regional 180, 253, 397; White Paper
(1993)
institutions, EC 210, 340–82
accountability 199, 361; competition
between 348, 349–50; crisis in 81;
and democracy 690; Dooge Committee on 108, 110, 128, 130, 142,
144, 716n; formal role of 209;
French attitude towards 115, 158;
German attitudes towards 158; increased competencies for 183–4,
188, 194; and informal politics 628;
location of 179, 290, 309, 328, 332,
344, 362, 643, 731n; post-War integration of 15; reform 89, 100,
130, 143–4, 145, 146, 169, 183,
195, 198, 201, 630, 647, 682, 695;
relations with federations 464;
relations with member states 211,
694; of state 687; *see also* under
individual institutions
insurance sector 320, 475, 485, 591,
675
in applicant countries 654; and competition policy 507; Directives
592–4; ECJ and 372, 375, 739n;
federations 483, 593–4; German
478; harmonization of 594; industrial policy for 592–4; and internal
market 135, 150, 252, 473, 590,
593, 712n; Italian 123; liberalization of 593; major players 749n
Integrated Mediterranean Programme
418
integration, European 1–2, 73, 615–16,
666–7
and actor-agency dilemma 3–4; and
American hegemony theory 3; in
Benelux 17; Commission view of
146, 149, 570; Commission's role
in 265; and control of Germany 24,
29; in defence policy 24–7;
economic 1–14, 47–50; in ECSC
21–4; EPC proposal 27–8; France
and 115; Germany and 24, 29, 100,
101, 118; harmonization and 561;
and informal politics 616;
Luxembourg and 127; Mitterrand
and 100, 709n; monetary 62–3, 65,

68–9, 705n; Netherlands and 125; of nuclear programme 29–31; OEEC and 10; political and institutional 15–16, 68–9, 85; popular movements 15–17; and regions 394, 427; relaunched 32; UK antipathy towards 121; US calls for 9–10, 14–15

interest groups
committee representation 243, 727n; Danish 312; industrial 102; informal relations of 243, 727n; organized 706–7n; relations with Commission 235, 242–3, 747n; *see also* lobbyists

Inter-Governmental Conference (IGC) 288
attitudes of firms to 164; planned for 1996 193, 196, 204, 206, 291, 321, 326, 331, 332, 349, 353–4, 366, 370, 376, 382, 412, 549, 553, 554, 647, 666, 695, 725n, 736n; on single market 147; *see also* European Council; and under individual Summits

inter-governmentalism 11, 15, 46, 92, 310, 688, 689
Commission and 140, 241; Coreper and 281, 282; of Council of Ministers 275; Danish antagonism topwards 130; in defence policy 193; during recession 95; Dutch antagonism towards 124, 288; of European Council 267, 275, 287; and European Parliament 91; favoured by Giscard 89, 708n; favoured by UK 154; of Interior Ministry issues 267; as source of national antagonism 288; and sovereignty 421

Interior Ministry issues 267, 329, 695
Commission and 668; Council and 194, 270; East European effect on 185–6; ECJ and 258; IGC on 169, 184; inter-governmental nature of 267; and Maastricht Treaty 163, 188, 192, 194; member states and 194; Parliament and 348

internal market/single market 98, 204–6, 226, 666, 673
Belgium and 126; benefits of 146, 152, 717n; Commission's role in 84, 96–7, 101, 105, 106, 140–3, 146, 226, 717n; and competition 567; consensus on 110, 695; Council and 140–1, 143; and customs union 55; and defence policy 184; delay in xv, 76, 438, 440; Denmark and 130; DG3's role in 105, 142, 248; ECJ and 141, 366, 369; and EMU 109, 145, 146; expanded concept of 685; federations and 472, 490; financial sector and 109, 135, 150, 252, 372, 473, 475, 590, 593, 595, 712n; firms and xv, 136, 139, 143, 160, 438–40, 442, 446, 449, 458, 606, 715n; France and 100, 115, 137; Germany and 137, 309; governments and 97, 105, 106, 141, 142, 147; Group on Operation of 153; and industrial policy 556–7, 607; and industrial regeneration 603; industry and 97, 102, 104, 135, 137, 715n; intergovernmental conference on 109; Italy and 123–4, 236; labour and 135; and liberalization 686; Luxembourg and 127; member states and 97, 98, 135, 142–7, 152, 153, 154, 156, 334, 438; Parliament's role in 568; Portugal and 135; prototype declaration 106; public perception of 612; pursuit of 101; and regions 389, 390, 393, 407; and Social Charter 182; Spain and 133; stasis in 711n; and trade policy 602, 607; trimming back of 334; UK attitude towards 120, 121, 122; *see also* Single European Act

Internal Market Council 105, 106
International Bank for Reconstruction and Development (IBRD) *see* World Bank
International Labour Organization 185
International Monetary Fund (IMF) 5, 10

Committee of Twenty 77, 78; and
Portugal 134; and UK 87
international relations 50–1, 221
Directorate *see* DG1
International Trade Organization (ITO)
5, 12
Intra-European Payments Agreement
(1948) 8
investment 154–5, 419, 570
in eastern Europe 653; by firms 560;
inward 125, 406–7, 412, 423, 441,
522–3, 576–7, 606, 607, 608, 696,
746n, 764n; by member states 560,
586; post-War 6, 8, 9
Investment Services Directive 484,
762n
Ireland
accession 43, 67, 69, 73–4; adjustment difficulties 314, 731n;
agriculture 128; assessment of
membership 261; attitudes to EC
127–9, 192, 262, 322; banks 514;
central bank 546; cohesion funds
314, 765n; and Commission 332;
Commissioners 232, 725n; and
convergence 551; coordination
process 314–15; corporatism in
385; defence policy 193; devaluation 95; EC Presidency 128, 144,
322; and ECJ 377; economy 88,
127; and EMS 128; and EMU 129,
147; and ERM 88, 170, 537, 538,
546, 721n; and European union
101, 129; federations 480, 489;
firms 453; industry 128; and Interior Ministry issues 194; and internal market 147; Maastricht
ratification 128, 199; MEPs 354,
355, 358, 735n, 737n; ministries
314; monetary policy 66; officials
245, 261; and parliamentary co-
decision 195; and passports 154;
Permanent Representatives 284,
317; political parties 128–9, 315,
354, 355, 736n; public opinion in
128, 200; referenda 128, 147, 200;
and Regional Fund 82, 128, 389,
723n; regions 384, 394, 402; relations with France 83, 109, 128,

166; relations with member states
330, 623–5; relations with UK 127,
261, 315; and Single European Act
148; as small state 623; and Social
Chapter 625; as 'southern' state
619; and Structural Fund 148;
subsidies 128, 714n; trade 128,
489, 714n
IRI 454, 455, 745–6n
Islam 659–60, 664–5
Italy
attitudes to EC 122–4, 192, 322; and
Benelux 18; budget row 332; and
CAP 38; central bank *see* Banca
d'Italia; and Commission 227, 240;
and competition policy 501, 503,
506, 508, 509, 529; coordination
process 315–17, 489; corporatism
in 385; currency fluctuations 66,
67, 76, 80, 95, 535, 536; defence
policy 193; deficit 63; disorganization of 316–17, 618; and EC law
368; EC Presidencies 124, 144,
151, 167–8; and ECB 178; and
ECJ 737n, 738n; economic
dualism in 61; and Ecosoc 387;
ECSC membership 1, 17, 21, 23;
and EMS 123; and EMU 88, 147,
173, 177, 203, 542, 720n; and EPC
28; and ERP 170, 171, 534, 535,
537, 544–5, 549, 552; and ERP 9;
and European Parliament 145, 148,
168, 184, 238, 341, 343, 361,
717n; exchange controls abolished
156; federalism in 16–17; financial
sector 123, 150, 316, 479, 484,
514; firms 122, 123, 316, 454–5,
746n; Franco-Italian Customs
Union 19; FRITALUX 19–20;
government 122–3, 315, 746n; industrial policy 567, 608; industry
123, 136, 277, 316, 573–6, 579;
infringements of EC law 92, 122,
240, 332, 378, 529, 733n, 766n;
and Interior Ministry issues 194;
and internal market 123–4, 144,
236; Maastricht ratification 199; as
Mediterranean state 619–21;
MEPs 354, 355, 358, 735n; Mez-

zogiorno 123, 253, 383, 389, 394, 618, 619; ministries 315–16; monetary policy 535; and oil crisis 77, 80; parliament 123, 357; peak organizations 103, 123, 316, 489; as peripheral state 621; Permanent Representatives 284–5; political crisis 316–17, 549; political parties 91, 122, 123, 124, 165, 203, 354–5, 356, 383; and political union 101, 123, 192; public opinion in 123, 186, 190, 316, 364; and Regional Fund 82, 162, 723n; regions 91, 123, 253, 316, 383, 389, 392, 394, 398, 400, 401, 412–15, 618; relations with Commission 316, 317; relations with France 81, 109, 143, 330; relations with Germany 109, 330; relations with member states 316; and Single European Act 148, 149; and Social Charter 181; and Spanish EC application 86; and state aids 505, 521, 527, 755n; telecoms 588; trade 61; trade unions 387, 487; US and 9; *see also* Emilia-Romagna

JAMA 457, 466, 504, 578
Japan
  car industry 164, 523, 562, 575–7, 601, 603, 761n; consumer electronics industry 579–80, 583; economy 77, 81; financial sector 480, 592; firms 151–2, 453, 457, 466, 469–70, 471–2, 504, 674, 746n; at GATT 603; inward investment by 576–7; Japanese as Europeans 580, 583; MITI 578, 580; protectionism 96; trade 79, 87, 95, 603, 709n
Jenkins, Roy 739n
  on Austria 706n; and EMS 87, 216, 324, 531; on European Council 286; Presidency of 90, 215, 221, 351, 708n, 724n; view of Commission 706n
joint ventures 510, 579, 584, 636, 652–3

Kantor, Mickey 604
Karamanlis, Prime Minister 85, 91, 130
Kennedy, John F. 41, 49
Klaus, Vaclav 649
Klepsch, Egon 351
Kohl, Helmut 100, 118, 206
  and Commission Presidency 156; and Council 119; and defence policy 187; and East European applicants 647, 656; and EMU 157, 756n; and EPP 356; and ERM 539, 541, 548; and German reunification 168, 175, 326; leading role of 724n; and Maastricht 195, 310, 318, 326; and national coordination 309–10; and Parliament 184; and political unity 157, 166, 189; and regions 390, 395; relations with Delors 219, 328, 521; relations with Genscher 156–7; relations with Mitterrand 100, 144, 157, 166, 175, 321, 323–9; structural fund concessions 326; 'Treaty of European Unity' 144
Köhler, H. 536, 538
Korean firms 466
Kreisky, Bruno 633
Kreisky Report 181
Kutscher, Hans 378, 739n

labour xviii, 606, 692
  and capital 596; Commission and 84, 104, 182, 706n; costs 569; and Ecosoc 385, 387; effect of economic crisis on xv; in EFTA 181; and internal market 135, 160; inclusion in political process 385; and industrial policy 565, 598–600; law 182; migrant workers 185, 370, 707n; Ministries of 104; Netherlands and 125; and Social Charter 181; and social diversity 625; supranational representation 706n; White Paper (1993) and 563, 569; worker participation 84, 102, 104; *see also* trades unions
Labour Party (UK) 120, 121, 299

attitude to EC 406; governments
80–1; Industrial Strategy 137, 393;
and Maastricht 750n; MEPs 75, 83;
and regions 384, 740n; Scotland
and 406; and Social Protocol 201
Lamassoure, Alain 201, 725n, 737n
Lamfalussy, Alexandre 534, 734n
Lamont, Norman 151, 395, 535, 541,
724n, 756n
Lamoureux, François 218, 221
Lamy, Pascal 218, 223
law, European 155, 211, 687, 692
Belgium and 126; co-decision procedure Fig 8.3; Commission's role
in 237, 238, 257; company 83–4;
constitutional 723n; consultation
procedure Fig 8.1, 8.2; direct effect
established 367; discretion in 507;
faith in undermined 100–1; firms
and 558; formal/informal aspects of
628, 678; France and 116, 297,
713n; generated by SEA 159, 162;
health and safety 182; hierarchy of
legal norms proposal 333, 376; infringements of 231, 239–40, 264,
366, 367, 628, 739n; Italy and 92,
102; Law Reports 258–9; legal consultants 442–3, 744n; legislation
process 267–9, 273, Fig 7.1;
member state diversity 626;
member states and 331, 333,
367–9, 626–8, 670; and national
law 367–8; over-hasty legislation
371; regional basis for 401; scrutiny
of 301, 361, 421; and subsidiarity
628; supremacy of 367–8, 629;
types of legislation 269; UK and
626–8, 630, 766n; *see also* European
Court of Justice
Lawson, Nigel
on Delors Report 721n; and ERM
120, 158, 166, 174, 548, 713n,
721n; and SEA 718n
le Grange, Marcel 379
Lee, Sir Frank 40
Legal Service
and access to documents 733n; of
Commission 215, 217, 221, 237,
257–8, 371, 727–8n; of Council

274; and Presidency 318; relations
with ECJ 257, 258, 371
legislation see law
Leigh-Pemberton, Robin 120, 172, 533,
544, 721n, 756–7n
Levy, Raymond 522, 523, 529, 577,
761n
Liberal and Democratic Reformists
354, 356, 736n, Fig 8.4
liberalization 557, 673
in airline sector 321, 525, 563, 587–8;
in energy supply 498, 569, 572,
609; in financial sector 476, 479,
591, 593; and internal market 686;
policy 238, 334, 420, 498, 608; of
state monopolies 586–8; telecoms
238, 334, 466, 470–1, 498, 563,
586–90, 762n
Lisbon Summit (1992) 203
lobbying xviii, xix, 243, 497, 683,
744–5n
by banks 477; of Commission 102,
152, 256, 727n; in competition
areas 509; of Council 276; of Directorates 359; by federations 490,
581; by firms 358–9, 436, 443–4,
456, 515, 581, 619; by industry
414, 448, 770n; of MEPs 348, 352,
358–9, 448, 568, 747n; of national
coordinators 308; by regions 405,
411, 417, 418; *see also* interest
groups
Lomé Convention 75, 115, 600, 601,
650
Louvre Accord 170
Lubbers, Ruud 168, 192, 195, 356
Luxembourg
attitudes to Europe 126–7, 262, 312;
Benelux country 17–18; and competition policy 503; EC Presidencies 127, 146–7, 151, 169, 191–4,
322; ECSC membership 1, 17; and
EMU 127, 173; and ERM 113;
and European Parliament 184,
341; financial sector 150, 478; and
harmonization 127; and integration
127; and internal market 127;
Maastricht ratification 199; MEPs
735n; monetary policy 66; 'non-

paper' 191, 192, 318; Permanent
Representatives 284; and QMV
279; and regions 384; relations
with Belgium 127; relations with
Netherlands 127; and steel restructuring 574; use of trade-offs
681
Luxembourg Compromise (1966) 52–3,
57, 67, 89, 144, 190, 291–2, 681,
710n
British attempt at 101; effect on
Coreper 281; veto powers 90, 291,
717n
Luxembourg Declaration 717n, 723n
Luxembourg Summit (1985) 142,
144–6, 177, 286

Maastricht Summit (1991)
agenda 154, 164, 191; Commission's
role in 179, 186, 191, 210; Committee of Regions set up 393–5;
concurrent IGCs introduced
167–9, 177; EMU IGC 178, 179,
482, 532–3; government alliances
721–2n; member states and 186–7,
191; Parliament's role in 184, 186,
191, 343, 734n; political IGC 179,
184–6, 191; poor management of
162; regional compromises 148;
and Social Charter 181, 182; UK
and 195
Maastricht Treaty of Union xi, xiv, 226,
671, 673
central banks under 549; citizenship
under 692; Commission and 163,
194, 196, 197, 204, 225; and
defence issues 185, 192–3; differences over 191–2; draft Treaty
108, 191–2, 195–6, 199, 311, 319,
350, 692, 732n; ECJ powers 370,
380; effect on *länder* 421; EMU
section 169–79, 196–7, 543, 548;
and foreign policy 191–2; governments and 197; and industrial
policy 556; industry and 164, 442;
institutional reform 183, 282;
member states and 337; and multi-
speed Europe 617; national
debates on 197–203; opt-outs 178,

183, 189, 195, 198, 201, 202, 310,
318, 326; and Parliamentary
powers 150, 282, 340, 343, 347,
348, 361; and 'people's Europe'
362; players in 195–6; political
parties 341; political union 184–95;
public opinion and 111, 162,
164–5, 186, 189–90, 197–203,
725n 725n; ratification of 197–203,
617; regions 148, 180, 384, 388;
secrecy of negotiations 692; Social
Protocol 180–3, 599; and subsidiarity 258; and unity 617
McDougall Report 84, 389, 399
Macmillan, Harold 39, 40, 41, 45
McSharry, Ray 219, 232, 275n
Madrid Summit (1989) 166, 173, 533
Magnetti Morelli merger 514–15
Major, John
attitude to EC 176, 187, 729n; as
Chancellor of the Exchequer 167,
177; *Economist* article 729n; on
EMU 723n; at Maastricht 178,
183, 195–6; and Maastricht Bill
202, 326; and national coordination 300; opposition to Dehaene
appointment 206, 328; and political
union 189; Presidency of 726n; as
Prime Minister 175–6, 177, 736n;
and UK ERM entry 174, 721n
majority voting 35, 710n
frequency increases 101; Luxembourg Compromise 52–3, 57, 67,
89, 710n; and veto 101, 147, 291,
717n; *see also* qualified majority
voting
Malta 656, 657, 660
management 84, 646, 651
Mancini, Federico 367, 739n
Mansholt, Sicco 46, 216, 232
as Agriculture Commissioner 52, 53,
218; Commission Vice-President
41
Marin, Manuel 163, 220, 243, 660,
769n
markets
advanced 562–3, 573, 575; Commission view of 559; Marshall Plan 7–
10, 390, 642

Martens, Wilfried 356
Martin, David 361
Martin Reports 191, 343
Matutes, Abel 351
Mauroy, Pierre 99, 106, 708n
media 210, 262, 697
  anti-trust proposals 350; on applicant
    states 639; British 121, 264, 299;
    and chemical industry 584–5;
    Commission and 160, 162, 235–6,
    240, 264, 336; DG4 and 336, 506,
    522, 529; and ERM crisis 536,
    539–42; European Council and
    273, 280; and European Par-
    liament 343, 350, 362–3; and
    Franco-German entente 327;
    French 539–40; German 202–3,
    541; Greek 131; and Maastricht
    164, 190, 196, 197, 198; member
    states and 333; and Presidency
    318; Spanish 133, 303, 540
Mediterranean states 116, 329, 335
  applicants 630, 657–61; Commis-
    sioners from 231; corruption in
    220, 619; EC programmes for 102,
    108, 390, 414, 418; and east Euro-
    pean applicants 644; eastern 625,
    631; and enlargement 632; and
    geographical divisions 163,
    618–19; national interests of 187,
    330; North African states 663–5;
    officials from 246; and structural
    funds 719n; *see also* under indi-
    vidual countries
member states xiii, xl–xli, 115–35,
    266–339, 676
  and accessions 67–8, 86, 648; at-
    titudes to EC 263, 270, 289–92;
    694, 697, 770n; and budget 565;
    and car industry 575–8; and CFI
    366; and competition policy 97,
    503–4, 508–9, 512, 518–19, 523,
    753–4n; cooperation and alliances
    323–30, 623–5, 628–9; coordina-
    tion processes 292–317;
    core/periphery 621–2; in Council
    of Ministers 211, 270–80, Fig 7.2,
    7.3; and defence policy 193; delay-
    ing tactics 335; and Delors II

agenda 160, 161–2, 163; disciplin-
  ing of 331; divergences 676; and
  EC institutions 266–70; and EC
  law 331, 333, 367–9, 626–8, 670;
  economic divisions 621–2; and
  Ecosoc 387; effectiveness as
  players 622; and EMS 87–8, 90,
  441–2, 532; and EMU 87–8, 147,
  157–8, 532, 533, 542, 543–4, 553;
  and ERM 113–14, 532, 535, 540,
  547, 757n; and EU statehood 686,
  687; in European Council 285–8,
  290; failure of 694; and foreign
  policy 184, 617; formal/informal
  politics of 629; French view of 89;
  geographical divisions 618–21; and
  industrial policy 97, 102, 137, 556,
  560, 561, 564, 566, 568, 584–5,
  606–8, 611; and informal politics
  209, 288, 331, 616, 628, 677–8,
  680–1, 769n; infringements of
  European law 231, 239–40, 264;
  initiatory role 90, 560; inter-state
  relations 81, 104, 109, 167, 270,
  272, 323–9, 505, 601, 615,
  617–18, 643, 764n; and Interior
  Ministry issues 192, 194; and
  internal market 76, 98, 135, 142–7,
  152, 153, 154, 156, 334, 438; and
  Maastricht Treaty 163, 164,
  186–7, 196, 197–203, 225, 692;
  mediatory role of 463; monetary
  policy of 534; negotiating process
  of 273–4; number of decisions Fig
  7.2; Permanent Representatives
  266, 280–5; political divisions
  622–5; and political union 157–9,
  186, 191–2; populations Fig 7.3;
  Presidency 317–22; and programmes 643; and QMV 194, 241,
  268–9, Fig 7.2; relations with
  central banks 531; relations with
  Commission 53, 96, 153–4, 163,
  210, 214, 216, 218, 219, 226–31,
  234, 236, 239–42, 257, 259, 265,
  288, 331–9, 340, 501, 512, 553,
  568, 569, 572, 601, 604, 609,
  725–6n, 734n; relations with Directorates 216, 234, 240, 245–6,

310, 316, 475, 476, 502, 504, 508, 586; relations with ECJ 317, 365, 366, 369, 370, 372, 373–9, 380, 381–2, 733n; relations with financial sector 475–6, 483, 485, 559, 594, 596, 762n; relations with firms 441, 559, 611; relations with institutions 211, 694; relations with Legal Service 257, 727–8n; relations with Parliament 331, 340–1, 343, 348, 360, 363; relations with regions 388, 395, 398, 399, 409–10, 422, 424, 427–8, 560; and research collaboration 565; rivalries 186–7, 330–9, 441, 521; and SEA 149, 151, 152, 290, 438; small/large states 622–5; social diversity 625–30; and social Europe 599; and sovereignty 612, 684, 773n; and Soviet Union 114; and state aids 503, 520–2, 523–4, 526; and state monopolies 586–8, 590, 610–11; and steel restructuring 573–5; and subsidiarity 693; and telecoms liberalization 586–8, 590; trade-offs between 680–1; and trade policy 601–2, 604; types of 228–9; unilateral actions of 94–5; and unity 615; and White Paper (1993) 563, 569; *see also* Council of Ministers; governments; Inter-Governmental Conferences; and under individual countries

Merger Task Force 250, 256, 504, 506, 515, 518

mergers 164, 437, 449, 504, 514–19, 720n, 751n, 754n

   Commission and 59, 506; in consumer electronics 579; cross-border 59, 181, 239, 447, 476, 608, 767n, 768n; DG4 and 146, 249–50, 336, 502–3, 509, 512, 753–4n; ECJ and 96, 141, 241, 501–2; in electronics sector 606; exemption clauses 502; in financial sector 447, 476, 481, 593, 716n; member states and 503; Merger Regulation 96, 141, 503, 504, 516, 518, 566, 752n; in pharmaceuticals

584; precedents established 507; prenotification period 510; and SEA 140

migration 185, 330, 370, 644, 646, 664, 692, 707n

Milan Summit (1985) 124, 130, 143, 144–5, 301

Millan, Bruce 220, 234, 253, 332, 393, 742n

Mitterrand, François 80, 190, 206, 671

   address to parliament 143; and budget 711n; and Commissioners 228, 275n; commitment to integration 100, 709n; and defence policy 158, 185, 187, 723n; and eastern Europe 643; economic policy 99–100; and ERM 170; European economic entente proposal 183; European project of 116–17, 143; federalism speech 107; and French politics 151; and German reunification 175, 220; government of 98–9, 200; and HDTV Directive 581; industrial regime 113; and Maastricht 195, 200–1; opposition to incremental momentum 101; and QMV 279; re-establishes French leadership 107, 108, 115; and regions 384; relations with Kohl 100, 144, 157, 166, 175, 321, 323–9; and Renault state aids case 523; second term 166; on social Europe 100, 182, 387, 600, 750n; socialist programme 115, 325; and Spanish EC application 86, 707n, 712n; 'Treaty of European Unity' 144; and Turkish Kurds 768n; view of France's role in Europe 116, 325

Mock, Alois 356, 636

Mollet, Guy 33, 34

Monetary Committee 62, 277, 529, 535, 550, 705n, 708n, 767n

   central banks in 87, 530; and DG2 247, 725n; and ERM 536, 537, 539, 755–6n, 758n; Italian withdrawal 538; served by Coreper 277; served by Ecofin 277, 281;

small/large state representatives
624; under Treaties 531
monetary policy 61–7, 7–5n
central banks and 530–2, 549, 552–3;
European Monetary Fund 76;
Franco-German discord 328,
732n; member states and 534;
reform 145; reserve unit proposal
63, 64; single 551; unit of account
adopted 63–4; Werner Committee
65, 69, 87; *see also* Economic and
Monetary Union; European
Monetary System
Monnet, Jean 21, 29, 31, 32, 68, 105,
110, 615, 678
Jean Monnet Committee 138;
Monnet Plan 21
monopolies 558
and competition policy 498; DG4 and
250–1, 500, 506, 586; duopoly
518; fines 511–12; France and 239;
liberalization of 569; media 350–1;
privatized 438; state 56, 251, 504,
507, 509, 586–90, 609–10, 645,
762n
Monopolies and Mergers Commission
(MMC) 501
Morán, Fernando 712n, 714n
Moro, Aldo 80, 91
Morocco 353, 357, 660, 663, 665
Movimento Federalista Europeo 16–17
Multi-Fibre Agreement 81, 440, 561,
601
multinational corporations (MNCs) 58,
102, 109, 151–2, 435–6, 497, 606
access to EU 136, 674, Fig 10.1;
American 466; in applicant states
636, 638; British 452–3, 488;
cartels 505; consultants 442–3; in
consumer electronics 580; Danish
455; and enlargement 647; and
European federations 464–5;
European ethos of 262–3, 447,
728n; French 449–51; German
446–9, 490, 674–5; and industrial
federations 457, 468–70; and industrial policy 557, 558, 608, 611;
informal EC links 136; Italian
454–5; investment decisions 560;

links to decision makers 437,
438–9, Fig 10.2, 10.3; lobbying by
359, 443; national identity of 496;
and regions 426; relations with
Commission 465; relations with
Coreper 284, 729n; relations with
Directorates 467–8; relations with
government 447, 458, 560; relations with member states 441, 493,
611; relations with MEPs xviii,
440; relations with trades unions
599; sectoral alliances 493; and
SEA 557; and Social Protocol 488;
and trade 605
multi-speed Europe 617, 620, 628
Murdoch, Rupert 581

Narjes, Karl-Heinz 103, 106, 138, 140,
142, 711n
Natali, Commissioner 218, 221
nation state 687–90
failure of 694, 697; *see also* member
states; statehood
national coordination xviii, 292–317,
361, 622, 655, 676, 683
national governments *see* governments
national identity xv, 202, 261, 422,
696
British 299, 732n; Catalan 410; crises
428, 663, 666; Danish 312; of east
European states 657; amongst
officials 246, 259–60, 263; of non-
political players 496
national interest 81–2, 95, 291, 617
in Commission 220, 229–30, 234; in
Coreper 282; in Council of Ministers 274, 275, 276, 279; in ECB
553; in ECJ 370; and enlargement
648; in industrial policy 566; and
inter-state relations 331; at Maastricht 187; perceived 3–4; of Presidency 321; SEA and 290; in
working groups 246–7
nationalism xi, 15, 330, 667, 696–7
Austrian 636, 647; British 121; east
European 165, 188, 646; and EC
game 629; and recession 81; and
regionality 428; in Sweden 646–7;
in Turkey 658

Nestlé-Perrier merger 335, 507, 509, 518–19

Netherlands
    attitude to Europe 124–5, 192, 261;
    attitude to former colonies 50;
    banks 514; Benelux country 17–18,
    124; and Beyen Plan 32, 125;
    cement cartel case 502; central
    bank see Netherlands Bank; and
    CFSP 191; and common market
    treaty 35; and Commission 125,
    227, 232, 240; and competition
    policy 503; coordination process
    311–12; corporatism in 385; and
    Council 125, 311; currency align-
    ment 532; decentralization in 311;
    defence policy 125, 193; drugs
    policy 186; and EC institutions
    199; EC Presidencies 124, 151,
    169, 178, 182–3, 188, 192, 322,
    545, 719n; and ECJ 738n;
    economy 95; and Ecosoc 387;
    ECSC membership 1, 17; and
    EDC 26, 27; effectiveness of
    623–4; and EMS 125; and EMU
    125, 147, 173; energy policy 77;
    and EPC 27; and ERM 113,
    545–6, 755n; and European Par-
    liament 125, 184, 341; firms 125,
    311, 445, 455–6; and Free Trade
    Area 38; governments 124; indus-
    try 125, 136, 311; and integration
    125; and inter-governmentalism
    124, 288; and Interior Ministry
    matters 192, 194; and labour 125,
    181; Maastricht Draft Treaty 192,
    195, 196, 199, 311, 319, 732n;
    Maastricht ratification 199; MEPs
    735n; ministries 311; monetary
    policy 65, 66, 707n; peak organ-
    izations 489; Permanent Represen-
    tatives 284, 311; political parties
    355; and political union 45, 125;
    Prime Minister 311; public opinion
    in 125, 199, 732n; and QMV 125;
    and regionality 425; regions 398,
    402, 422; relations with member
    states 311, 623–4; relations with
    Nordic countries 330; revaluation

    63; Schengen Agreement 199; and
    Single European Act 148, 199; as
    medium-sized state 623–4; and
    social Europe 599; and Spanish EC
    application 86; and state aids 505;
    and steel restructuring 575; and
    subsidiarity 427; and tariffs 48;
    trade 125; trades unions 489

Netherlands Bank 173, 545–6

networks xvi, 676
    firms' 457; regional 412–13, 425–6,
    675–6

Neunreither Committee 349

neutrality 632, 634, 635, 639–40

Nicholson Report 137

Noël, Emile 90, 221–2, 229

Nokia 469, 579, 580

North American Free Trade Area
    (NAFTA) 440, 664

North Atlantic Treaty Organisation
    (NATO) 24–5, 44, 98, 271, 321,
    663, 707n
    EU/US partnership in 326; France
    and 185, 187; Germany and 25, 28,
    168; Greece and 86; Military
    Committee 185; Netherlands and
    125; revised role of 193, 642; Spain
    and 101, 712n; Sweden and 640;
    Turkey and 658; UK and 190;
    WEU and 187, 193

north/side divide 101, 163, 203, 328,
    329, 618–21, 629, 696
    Delors on 740n; and funding 619,
    719n; Luxembourg and 127; at
    Maastricht 186

Northern Ireland 397, 402, 405, 422,
    744n

Northern League (Italy) 357, 392

Norway
    application 42, 67, 82, 632; and ERM
    689; free trade agreement with
    EEC 75; member of EFTA 38, 82;
    referendum 82, 205, 631, 633,
    766n;

nuclear programme
    energy 29–31, 33; EURATOM 1,
    30–1; French 29–30, 80; weapons
    29–30, 42, 94, 98, 707n

Nyborg Agreement 541, 548, 720n

Official Journal 241, 333, 520
oil crisis
(1973) 55, 76–81, 109, 694; (1980)
88, 89, 93, 128
Olivetti 454, 582
OPEC 77, 93
ORGALIME 467, 470–1
Organization for Economic Cooperation
and Development (OECD) 77, 78,
81
Organization for European Economic
Cooperation (OEEC) 8, 10, 12, 37,
295
agricultural brief of 29; attempts at
integration 10; Council 11, 14;
Dragon scheme 31; and nuclear
cooperation 31; trade liberalization
scheme 12–13
Ortoli, François-Xavier 75, 76, 81, 138,
216, 718n
Ortoli Initiative 96, 560
Ozal, Turgut 659, 661

Padoa-Schioppa report 172, 316, 533,
720–1n
Pandolfi, Enrico 250, 506, 581–2, 745n
Papandreou, Andreas 101, 107, 130,
166, 659, 725n
Papandreou, Vasso 163, 182, 220, 222,
230, 386, 488, 599
Paris, Treaty of 22
Paris Economic Summit (1989) 224,
643
Paris Summits 281, 285, 561
parliaments, national 599
and EC law 368, 378; and industrial
policy 568; relations with EP 351,
357, 360–2
passport union 83, 154
Patronat (CNPF) 451, 454, 486, 489,
and CAP 492; and internal market
104, 137, 490; relations with Directorates 103
Patronat Catala Pro Europa 411
Patten, Chris 189, 736n, 737n
peak organizations xv, 210
in applicant states 639, 652; attitude
to Europe 262; competences of
629; EC representation 137, 557,

639; and EMU 683; European 103,
486–97; French 104, 489; German
308, 489; industrial 486, 489–90;
informal operations 137; and internal market 104, 164, 490; Italian
103, 123, 316, 489; national 103,
486, 489–90; relations with Commission xvii, 103, 138, 237, 457,
490–1, 492, 600, 710n, 726n, 750n;
relations with Coreper 486, 491;
relations with Council of Ministers
486, 491; relations with Directorates 103, 256, 502; relations with
governments 103, 104, 137–8, 308,
489; relations with MEPs 358; and
SEA 492; sectoral 457; SMEs and
596; trades unions 386, 486–9, 492,
598–600
pensions/pensioners 182, 252, 592, 625
Perissich, Riccardo 106, 248
Permanent Representatives xviii,
xxxv–xl, 622, 682
British 301, 284, 451; Danish 312;
Dutch 455; French 284, 296, 418,
730n; German 309, 310; Greek
306; Italian 123, 317; Portuguese
304; relations with Commission
230, 231, 234, 301, 335, 726n; relations with financial sector 478; relations with firms 296, 304, 310, 440,
676; relations with governments
296, 308; relations with Parliament
351; Spanish 453; *see also* Committee of Permanent Representatives
Phare programme 224, 448, 646, 649,
656, 730n
pharmaceutical industry xviii, 82, 359,
462
and advertising Directive 760n; collaboration in 566; federations 448,
457, 466, 468, 584–5; industrial
policy 584–5; lobbying 770n; regeneration of 605; UNICE and 492
Philips 104, 455–6, 469, 579–82
Pleven Plan 25
Pöhl, Karl-Otto
and ECB 172, 544, 721n; and EMU
173, 533; and ERM realignments
540–1, 720n; protest against cur-

rency swap 174, 534; resignation
175
Poland 126
    application 203, 205, 625, 631, 660;
        conversion process 644, 646; elec-
        tions 645; Germany and 168, 327,
        328; industry 573, 644, 653, 761n;
        loan programme 183, 642; Solid-
        arity 94
political class, European 259–63
political divisions 622–5
political parties 199, 770n
    in applicant states 648, 658, 660;
        concern with unemployment and
        growth 564; development of
        common identity 91; European
        forums 274; in European Par-
        liament 354–7; under Maastricht
        Treaty 341; national, and MEPs
        357, 358, 359–60; pan-European
        354, 360; regional 356–7; relations
        with regions 401, 413; *see also*
        under individual countries
political union 666, 686
    Commission and 235; Denmark and
        130; discussions 43–5, 68–9; effect
        on regions 392, 399; and EMU
        543, 553–4; European Political
        Cooperation 69, 73, 75–6; Franco-
        German entente and 325–6;
        Germany and 116, 151, 157; IGCs
        179; Italy and 123; Maastricht IGC
        162, 163, 184–95; Netherlands and
        125; optimism over 152; political
        cooperation 82, 94, 145, 148, 193;
        political integration 15–17, 146;
        reports on 69, 73, 83, 84, 705n;
        and supranationality 3
Pompidou, Georges 68, 69, 73, 79, 329,
    705n, 755n
popular movements 15–17, 662
Portugal
    accession 85–6, 108, 146, 390, 616,
        618, 630, 720n; attitudes to EC
        133–5, 305, 322; central bank 546,
        549; coordination process 304–5;
        Council of EC Ministers 304;
        council of small states proposal
        733n; defence policy 193; EC

presidency 203, 320; economy 134,
    302; EFTA membership 38, 133;
    and EMU 173; and ERM 535,
    538, 547, 552; and European Par-
    liament 195, 343; federations 480,
    489; financial sector 480, 749n;
    firms 453; five year programme
    248; free trade agreement with
    EEC 75; industry 304, 305, 562;
    and Interior Ministry issues 194;
    and internal market 135; Maas-
    tricht ratification 199–200; as
    Mediterranean state 620–1; MEPs
    352, 735n; and monetary union
    134; Permanent Representatives
    284, 304; political parties 133;
    public opinion in 134, 305, 715n;
    and public procurement Directive
    567; and Regional Fund 219, 389,
    392, 394, 723n; and regions 384,
    397, 402, 420; relations with EC
    82; relations with member states
    330; revolution 85, 707n; trade
    unions 387, 489
postal services 586, 587, 610
Powell, Charles 299, 731n
Prag Report 350
Presidency 317–22
    and European Council 287; and
        enlargement 630; foreign policy
        role 318; joint Franco-German
        689; listing xxxv–xl; parity of
        tenure in 90, 198, 321; relations
        with Council 278, 318; relations
        with firms 442; relations with Par-
        liament 353; role of 192, 274; small
        states and 623; *see also* Troika; and
        under individual member states
privatization 437–8, 610
    in eastern Europe 645–6, 649, 652–3,
        767–9n; and state aids 506, 521–2,
        527; telecoms 589; in UK 99, 120,
        562, 586, 588
protectionism 14, 28, 440, 626
    American 5, 10, 12, 96, 602, 604–5;
        during recession 94, 95, 96, 104,
        709n; in EC 55, 81, 113, 154, 204,
        248, 270, 449, 498, 517, 525,
        602–4, 672, 697; in ECJ 370;

EMU and 607; French 33, 191,
603; in industrial policy 562; Irish
128; in Mediterranean states 619;
Netherlands and 125; relaxation of
37
PSA 576, 577, 578, 579
public
European 688; national 689–90
public opinion xv, 162, 210, 363–4, 689
Austrian 634, 636; Belgian 314, 320;
British xiii, 121, 165, 186, 190,
201, 626; and chemical industry
584–5; Commission and 235–6,
241, 260, 336–7; and Council of
Ministers 273, 276, 280; Danish
165, 171, 190, 197–8, 312, 364;
Dutch 125, 199, 732n; on EMU
549, 758n; European 688; French
165, 175, 186, 188, 190, 200, 323,
516–17, 758n; German 186, 188,
202–3, 323, 364, 541; governments
and 240; Greek 131; on internal
market 612; Irish 128, 200; Italian
123, 186, 190, 316, 364; on Maastricht 111, 162, 164–5, 186,
189–90, 197–203, 725n; on Parliament 350; Portuguese 134, 305,
715n; and regions 422; Scottish
406; on Single European Act 686;
Spanish 133, 186, 303, 719n;
Swedish 635; on unemployment
and growth 564
public procurement 567, 570, 601
public utilities 611, 675, 684
Pujol, Jordi 396, 408–9, 411, 412, 425

quadripartism 486, 749n
qualified majority voting (QMV) 89,
117, 138, 143, 216, 291, 710n
in Council of Ministers 268–9,
278–9, 292, Fig 7.2, 7.3; in
defence issues 192, 193; disagreement on 147; effect on Commission 241; extension of 166,
183–4, 278; and financial sector
measures 595; France and 166,
713–14n; Ireland and 714n; on
Maastricht issues 194; Netherlands
and 125; UK and 121–2, 131, 144,

148, 182, 716n; and veto 291;
weightings 269, 622, Fig 7.2
quotas 12–14, 55, 140
in car industry 576; colonies and
50–1; in consumer electronics
579; cultural 604; intra-EEC 47;
SEA and 604; in steel industry
573–4

Race programme 251, 573
railways 570–2, 586, 610, Fig 12.1
Rainbow Group of MEPs 357, 736n,
Fig 8.4
Reagan, Ronald 94, 96, 99, 113, 140,
159, 171
recession 197, 238, 320, 499, 526, 529,
603, 672
(1974–6) xv, 70, 73, 77, 109, 385,
501; (1984–6) xv, 73, 78, 89,
93–6, 102, 112; (1990–93) xv, 78,
154, 248, 263, 303, 304, 402, 521,
534, 537, 557, 563, 568
referenda 625
Austria 633, 636, 640; Denmark
130, 146, 197–8, 202, 203, 204,
312, 535; Finland 633; France
200, 276, 535, 537, 540; Ireland
128, 147, 199; Norway 82, 631,
633, 766n; Sweden 633, 635, 636,
640; Switzerland 616; UK xiii, 81,
83, 201
Regional Development Fund (RDF,
ERDF) 180, 285, 389–90, 394,
395–6, 416, 739–40n, Fig 9.1
additionality issue 405, 742n; budget
722–3n; Commission and 83, 226,
265; creation of 69, 75, 82, 705n;
DG16 and 252–3; disagreements
over 82; distribution of 84, 107;
and enlargement of EC 86, 389;
extension to rich members 162–3;
firms and 426; Greece and 107,
162, 389, 723n; increases in 112,
384, 389, 390, 396; Ireland and
82, 128, 389, 723n; member state
control of 428; Portugal and 219,
389, 392, 723n; and state aids
520; UK and 75, 82, 389
regional policy 98, 424, 427, 561

Commission and 83, 97, 570; Council and 84; objectives of 394, 397, 740n; regional development plan 253; and Single European Act 145, 148, 253

regionality 384, 396, 397, 408, 425, 689

regions 210, 211, 320, 383-428
   activism of 424; advanced 254, 398, 424, 527; autonomous communities 383, 400, 408, 411, 425, 428; case studies 399-428, Fig 9.2; Commission and 388, 389-99; and competition policy 526; and concertation 388; corruption in 401, 417; cross-border contacts 398, 416, 422, 676; Directorate see DG16; disparity of 393, 425, 427; EC representation 404-5, 409, 411, 414-15, 417, 419, 421, 425; effect of EMU on 392; effect of internal market on 390; 'Four Motors' group 254, 402, 410, 413, 415, 419, 421, 676, 743n; funding *see* Regional Development Fund; Maastricht Treaty and 148, 180, 183, 199, 421; of Mediterranean states 620; political parties 356-7; regional development plan 253; regional politics 684; regional support schemes 505; relations with Council 276, 277; relations with national states 388, 395, 398, 399, 401, 405-6, 409-10, 412, 421, 422, 424, 427-8, 560, 676; relations with Parliament 399; relations with trades unions 180; rivalries between 388, 409, 422; SEA and 421; SMEs in 410-11, 413-15, 417-18, 420, 424, 426, 597; sovereignty of 684; and subsidiarity 254, 384, 388, 394, 399, 421, 427, 428, 693; *see also* Committee of Regions; and under individual states

Renault 576-7, 761n
   state aids case 522-3, 529; Volvo merger 579, 767n

research and development 96, 98, 102, 180, 331, 561, 608, 673

CLORA 759n; collaboration in 556, 558, 565; DG4 and 250, 502, 510; Franco-German cooperation 732n; in industrial policy 556, 560, 562, 565; Japanese and 580, 583; member states investment in 560; programmes 251, 424, 455, 470, 558, 565, 674, 723n; regions and 416, 420, 423, 424, 743n; Research Funds 253, 420, 556, 573, 719n; in steel industry 573; in telecoms 589; White Paper (1993) proposals 569

restrictive business practices 57-8, 501, 506, 511-12, 514

Rueff, Jacques 63, 543

réunions pacquets 149

Rey, Jean 216, 218

Rhône-Alpes 400, 420, 423, 597, 676
   case study 415-19, Fig 9.2

Richardson, Gordon 87, 120

Riksbank 550, 638

Rio Environment Summit 419, 584

Rocard, Michel 522, 523, 724-5n, 754n

Rome, Treaty of (1957) 31, 32, 35-6, 48-9, 186, 672
   on colonies 50; Commission's role under 238, 337; and competition policy 56, 57, 59; and monetary policy 62; recognised by de Gaulle 43; subsidiarity in 693

Rome Summit (1990) 167, 301

Ruhe, Volker 189

Romania 625, 644

Russia 663
   see also Soviet Union

Saar 28-9

Santer, Jacques 205, 214, 218, 226, 236, 264
   allocation of portfolios 228; appointment of 215, 224, 347, 734n; reorganization of DGs 223, 243; state of union speech 656, 668

Scandinavia
   accessions 616, 665; in DM zone 67; and tariffs 14; *see also* under individual countries

Schengen Agreement 108, 186, 192

Schiller, K. 66

Schlesinger, Helmut 179, 534, 536, 538, 541, 722n, 756n
Schmidt, Helmut 79, 82, 99, 100, 118, 119, 198
and Commission 215, 216, 706n, 724n; and ERM 541; and Franco-German entente 323–4; and monetary union 88, 531
Schuman, Robert 17, 19, 27
Schuman Plan 21, 46
science and technology 154, 331, 570
DG3 and 248; effect of recession 95; and industrial policy 76, 8,2, 565; programmes 112, 136, 455, 573, 760n; regions and 424; technology transfers 442
Scotland 397, 400, 401, 402, 423, 676, 744n
and Act of Union 742n; banks 407, 408, 474, 757n; case study 404–8, Fig 9.2; and devolution 423n; EC funding 405, 742n; EC representation 404–5; financial sector 407; Highlands and Islands 397, 404–5; industry 402, 406, 426; and internal market 407; public opinion in 406; relations with UK government 406
Scottish Development Agency 253, 393, 400, 404
Scottish Enterprise 405, 406, 408
Scottish Financial Enterprise 406, 407
Scottish Office/Secretary 398, 404–6, 407
Scrivener, Christiane 151, 160, 725n
Second World War 383
effect on integration 15; post-War boom ends 78; post-War settlement ends 165, 323, 695; reconstruction 4–5, 8, 21
security policy 158, 184
see also Common Foreign and Security Policy; defence policy
self-interest xii, xv, 209, 210, 211, 317, 645, 690
of firms 495, 558; and informal politics 679; of member states 322, 330, 697; *see also* national interest
semi-conductor industry 582–3

Service de Coordination Inter-ministerial (SGCI) 295, 296–7, 517, 522, 730n, 759n
service industries 251, 418, 419
shipbuilding 79, 461
crisis measures 83, 561; state aids 92, 95, 503
shipping company cartels 513, 755n
Siemens 582, 593, 675, 744n, 762n
Single European Act (1986) xi, xiv, 105, 112, 152, 186, 226, 500, 672–3, 686
CFI under 366; Commission's role in 105, 141–2, 145–6, 148, 159, 718n; Commission under 559; and competition policy 503; Denmark and 130; and EMU 147–8, 150, 153, 154, 169, 532, 553, 718n effect on *länder* 421; and European Council 286; financial services and 590, 595; governments and 142–9; Greece and 131; implementation of 149–50; and industrial policy 557, 559; and informal politics 558; Italy and 124; member states and 149, 151, 152, 290, 438; Parliament and 150, 342, 353; preamble 147–8, 718n; ratification of 148, 152; and regional policy 145, 148, 253; timetable for 141, 148–9; UK and 714n; unanimity of support for 330; White Paper (1985) 104, 105, 111, 124, 129, 135, 142–3, 145–6, 159, 218, 235, 481
Single European Market (SEM)/single market see internal market
Slovak Republic (Slovakia) 205, 625, 644–6
Slovenia 644, 656
small and medium-sized enterprises (SMEs) 112, 435–6
access to EU 675, Fig 10.1; in applicant states 638; assistance for 97, 618–19; and competition policy 507; Directorate see DG23; EC schemes 251, 424; federations 596; German 420, 439, 596; and industrial policy 556, 564, 596–8, 763n; links to decision makers 437,

439, 445, Fig 10.2, 10.3; and mergers 449; and regional development plan 253; and regions 410–11, 413–15, 417–18, 420, 424, 426, 597; relations with Commission 746n; relations with Directorates 251, 253–4, 463, 597, 747n; relations with government 301; SME Taskforce 598
small/large states 622–5
Smithsonian Agreement 66
Soames, Lord 67, 716n, 724n
Soares, Mario 85, 134
Social Charter 329
    Commission and 161; Ecosoc and 386; IGC and 169; member states and 599, 625; trades unions and 224
social democrats 99, 385, 564, 599
Social Fund (ESF) 389
    Commission role in 226; doubling of 390; planning stage 75; and steel job losses 574
social policy 97, 155, 184, 692
    Commission and 181, 488, 706n; Commissioner for 163, 166; Ecosoc and 386; and EMU 161; legislation 599; member state diversity 625–30; Mitterrand's social Europe 100, 116, 182, 387, 569, 600, 750n; Parliament's role in 350; Social Action Programme 75, 82; social dimension of internal market 599; UK and 120, 151, 488; and White Paper (1993) 569
Social Protocol 180–3, 195
    conflict over 166, 181–2; ECJ and 382; Ecosoc and 386; and EMU 161; ETUC and 488; first draft 166; and internal market 182; Maastricht Treaty 196; MNCs and 488; Thatcher and 335, 736n; trades unions and 180–1, 599, 638; UK opt-out 201, 202, 310
Socialists
    Austrian 633; French 98, 99, 115, 199, 200, 203, 217; Italian 123; Parliamentary group 351, 354–5, 736n, Fig 8.4

Solchaga, Carlos 173, 303, 535, 540
sovereignty 696
    Commission and 241; ECB and 172, 550; EMU and 179, 183, 533, 553, 555, 689; European Council and 287; firms and 441, 462, 468; French 116, 324; German Constitutional Court ruling on 723n; intergovernmental institutions and 421; *länder* and 684; legal 333, 379; Maastricht and 192; member states transfer of 612; parliamentary 368, 738n; pooling of 15; regional policy and 254; state monopolies and 590; surrender of 1–2, 3, 4, 16–17, 21, 684, 773n; Thatcher's defence of 159; UK and 201, 236, 723n
Soviet Union 618
    British veto loan 167; Cold War 24, 662; collapse of xiv, 153, 163, 165, 202, 641, 720n; CSCE meetings 167; and German reunification 168; Gorbachev 109–10; influence in Austria 633; invasion of Afghanistan 94, 318; member states and 114; nuclear threat 707n; varying responses to 101
Spaak, Paul Henri 33, 34, 44, 45, 313
Spaak Committee/Report 33, 58, 162, 716n
Spain
    accession 85–6, 108, 132, 108, 146, 169, 390, 616, 618, 620, 630, 707n, 712n, 714n, 719n; assessment of membership 290, 719–20n; attitudes to EC 132–3, 192, 302, 303, 322; central bank see Banco de España; and cohesion 395; and cohesion funds 177, 204, 280, 303, 620; and Commission 227, 332, 569; and competition policy 505, 752n, 753n; coordination process 301–4, 410; corporatism in 385; coup attempt 86; currency devaluations 177, 535, 536, 545; death of Franco 85, 408, 707n; defence policy 101, 193, 712n; and EC budget 766n; EC officials 245; EC Presidencies

160, 166, 173, 350; and ECJ
737n; economy 132–3, 199, 302,
304; and EMS/ERM 132, 153,
162, 171, 173–4, 176, 302, 533,
535, 537, 538, 540, 545, 547, 552,
755n; and EMU 173, 203, 542,
620; and European Parliament
348; exchange controls abolished
156; federations 133, 411, 453–4,
489, 715n, 747n; financial sector
150, 412, 479, 484, 749n; firms
453–4; fisheries 707n; government
132, 408–10; industrial relations
763n; industry 132, 303, 411,
573–5, 576; and institutional
reform 195; and Interior Ministry
issues 194; and internal market
133, 302, 620; and Maastricht
186, 199; as major player 162;
media 133, 303, 540; as Mediterranean state 619–20; MEPs
352, 356, 357, 735n; ministers
302–3; opposition to enlargement
620, 643; as peripheral state 621;
Permanent Representatives 453;
and political IGC 191; political
parties 133, 302, 356; public
opinion in 133, 186, 303, 719n;
and public procurement Directive
567; and Regional Fund 389; and
regionalism 396; regions 180, 303,
304, 383, 392, 398, 400, 408–12,
428, 723n, 741–2n; relations with
EC 82; relations with France 86,
330, 707n; relations with Germany
330; and SEA 149; self-interest of
230; and Social Charter 182; and
state aids 521; telecoms 589; trade
unions 387, 412, 487, 489; unemployment 568, 763n; *see also* Catalonia
Späth, Lothar 419–20
Spierenberg 284
  Committee 90, 244, 265
Spinelli, Altiero 16–17, 27, 123, 136,
  248, 357, 562
Spinelli Report 95, 116, 120
Sprint programme 251, 424
Standards 566–7, 572, 684, 760n

agencies 566–7, 607; for HDTV
580–2; member states and 625;
policy 95, 108, 139, 140, 563, 711n;
role of Parliament 568; USA and
603
Star programme 251, 424
state aids 270, 499, 500, 505, 508,
519–28
British 730n; in car industry 505,
522–3, 524, 576; Commission and
95, 141, 231; Commission Surveys
754n; in consumer electronics 581;
defined 520; DG4 and 146, 332,
334, 336, 503–4, 520–7; in eastern
Europe 649; ECJ cases 92, 224,
520; French 220, 236, 293, 522–3,
727n; German 280; league table
752n; notification requirements
520, 522, 527; partisanship in 230;
and regions 422, 426; Spanish 334;
to state monopolies 586; in steel
industry 92, 335, 503, 505, 521,
523, 561, 575; and Treaty of Rome
56, 57
statehood, EC 662, 686–90, 694, 697,
765n
attributes of 687; federations and 459;
formal and informal 497, 560,
686–8; and high seas ruling 369;
imperfection of 612; and industrial
system 465; institutions of 462, 687;
and law 377, 379; member states
and 666, 686, 687; and political
unity 616
steel industry 461, 573, 758–9n
cartels 83, 97, 248, 496, 500, 558, 561,
575, 602; crisis 231, 335, 573,
758–9n; effects of recession 79, 94;
European Coal and Steel Community 1, 17, 21–4; French 80;
industrial policy 573–5; multilateral
agreement 601; post-War 5, 21;
protectionist measures 603, 604;
reconstruction of 96, 605; research
programmes 573; restructuring
plan 573–4, 727n; state aids 92,
335, 503, 505, 521, 523, 561, 575;
US and 96
stock exchanges/markets 474, 475, 749n

and competition policy 507; in eastern
Europe 654; ECJ and 375, 733n;
federation 483–4, 595–6; industrial
policy on 595–6; and internal
market 135, 150, 252, 473, 590,
595; member state/Commission
bargaining 485; New York crash
(1987) 171; regional 397, 407, 418,
484, 595, 749n; stockbroker draft
Directive 484
Stockholm Convention (1960) 38
Strasbourg Summit (1989) 166
Strathclyde 400, 404, 405, 406, 417,
425
Strauss, Franz-Josef 148, 424
Structural Fund 383, 427
Commission and 231, 234, 332;
Eastern *länder* and 684; increased
148, 183, 718–19n, 724n; and industrial policy 558, 562; Ireland
and 148, 234, 332; Italy and 316,
415; Kohl's concessions on 326;
and north/south divide 619,
718–19n; reform of 107, 390; and
state aids 520
structural policy 161, 501
Stuttgart Summit (1983) 106, 140
Declaration on EC Unity 105, 139,
143, 321, 327
subsidies, state *see* state aids
subsidiarity 93, 361, 508, 666, 693
and competition policy 529; and
decentralization 564; Delors on
219, 773n; EC law and 376, 382;
and financial sector 595; France
and 201, 297; *länder* and 188, 203,
308; and legislation 333, 628;
Maastricht Treaty and 194, 195,
258; Parliament's demand for 350;
and regionalism 254, 384, 388,
394, 399, 421, 427, 428; in research and development 565; UK
and 187, 194, 725n
substate 400, 421, 428
supranationality 1–4, 677
abandoned by France 27; compared
with inter-governmental agency
46–7; of Coreper 282; of Council
of Ministers 275; in defence 25; of

ECSC 22; and EEC 35, 37, 67; of
Interior Ministry issues 267; Italian
enthusiasm for 17; in nuclear programme 31
Sutherland, Peter 232, 522, 725n, 726n
before ECJ 733–4n; and competition
policy 206, 231, 249, 499, 503,
504, 505, 586; and internal market
141, 153; Sutherland Report 495
Sweden
application 67, 259, 570, 631,
633–41, 642; attitude to EEC 37,
82; central bank *see* Riksbank; and
collapse of Communism 165;
corporatism in 385; currency 535,
538; economy 635; EEA membership 205, 632, 636; EFTA membership 38, 82, 631–2, 634; and
ERM 552; federations 638–9;
isolation 634; liberalism of 619;
mergers 767n; monetary policy 67;
nationalism 646–7; political parties
635; public opinion in 635; referendum 633, 635, 636, 640;
regions 397, 635; relations with EC
75, 634, 717n
Switzerland
attitude to EEC 37; and EEA 205,
632, 766n; EFTA membership 38;
free trade agreement 75; MNCs
113, 135; referendum 616; and
tariffs 14;

Tacis 224
tariffs
barriers, French 34; coal and steel 23;
Common External Tariff 39, 47–9,
59; dismantling of 55, 59; EEC and
former colonies 50–1; in EFTA 38;
intra-EEC 35, 47–8; reductions
12–14, 31, 47–9; union 19
taxation
Bachmann case 372, 739n; harmonization of 145, 149, 151, 160, 579,
718n, 725n; pollution tax 569, 584;
VAT 106, 151, 160, 335, 725n
technology *see* science and technology
telecoms 250, 580
collaboration in 565; and competition

policy 507; draft White Paper 587; Directorate see DG13; federations 467, 470–1; fibre-optics network 610; Green Paper 587; industrial policy 586–90; investment needs 611; liberalization 238, 334, 466, 470–1, 498, 563, 569, 586–7, 762n; privatization 589; state monopolies 586, 589–90, 610; trade in 601

television, HDTV 580–2, 583

temple model of EU 188, 192, 196, 265

textile industry 79, 81, 440, 461
 crisis cartels 83; ECJ and 503–4; Multi-Fibre Agreement 81, 440, 561, 601; protectionist measures 500, 603, 604; reconstruction of 96, 605; state aids 95, 503, 505, 520

Thatcher, Margaret 94, 139, 142, 671, 724n
 addresses European Parliament 102; attitude to EC 120, 158–9, 736n; blocks RDF increases 390; Bruges speech 159, 602; and budget contribution 93–4, 107, 712n; and Bush 190; and CAP 719n; and Commission 228, 230, 335, 338; conspiracy theory 158; defence of sovereignty 159; and Directorate officials 245; and Dooge Committee 144, 716n; downfall of 167, 175, 189, 190; *The Downing Street Years* 119; and ERM 114, 120, 174, 721n; and European Council 276; and European Union 106, 325, 716n; and Franco-German entente 144, 167, 717n; and German reunification 158, 175, 325, 326; government of 98; industrial policy 562; and internal market 120, 142, 151, 711n; isolation of 159; ministerial disputes 299; opposition to devolution 384; opposition to incremental momentum 101; and QMV 121–2, 131, 145; relations with Delors 121, 158, 215, 220, 718n, 719n; relations with Italy 167; relations with Kohl 711n,

719n; relations with Mitterrand 158, 719n; and Single European Act 145, 148, 300, 686, 718n; and Social Protocol 335, 736n; view of MEPs 358

Thatcherism 78, 98–9, 569

Third World 420, 640
 shipping 513; trade agreements 50–2, 75, 115, 600, 602, 731n

Thomson 450, 469, 503, 573, 579, 580–3, 745n

Thompson, George 393, 705n

Thorn, Gaston 101, 102, 215, 216, 221, 225, 235, 342, 725n

Tietmeyer, Hans 536, 538, 541, 543, 552, 756n

Tindemans, Leo 83, 85, 105, 741n

tobacco industry 444, 448, 507

tourism 194

trade
 barriers, EC 368, 601, 605; bilateral agreements with US 140; Commission and 48–50, 140, 149, 161, 372, 499, 577, 734n, 739n; competition policy 55–9; Council of Ministers and 270; creation and diversion 59–61; Directorate see DG1A; distortions 39, 55–7; eastern European 646, 648, 768n; EEC-effect 59–61; and EMU 607; expansion of 75; and frontier controls 6; global 617, 666; and industrial policy 556, 562, 565, 578, 600–12; international 59, 146, 154; intra-ECSC 23; intra-EEC 47–8, 59–60, 76, 85, 126; intra-European 7, 12–14, 18, 54, 60; member states' attitudes towards 601, 626, 764–5n; national safeguards imposed 81; non-tariff barriers 55, 103, 104, 139, 155, 709n, 715n; peak organizations 308; policy 155, 426, 563, 600–12, 672; post-War relationships 5–7; role of DG1 243; tariffs 12–14, 31, 47–9, 59, 140; trade liberalization scheme 12–13; trading blocs 60–1; US 96, 113, 140, 440; versus agriculture 615; with Africa 50–1, 75; with Japan 561, 576–7

Trades Union Congress (TUC) 159,
486, 719n, 750n
trades unions 210
in applicant states 652; and applications 638; bargaining powers
104; British 75, 120; Brussels representation 750n; and Ecosoc 276,
385–7, 487, 488, 599; effect of
unemployment on 488–9; European confederation *see* ETUC;
French 387; German 310; industrial policy on 598–600; and informal politics 679; internal
market and 160; intra-European
dimension in 598; loss of influence
84, 386, 487; national confederations 486–9, 750n; opposition to deregulation 611; participation in Social Action Programme
75; relations with Commission
386, 488, 599–600, 749n; relations with Council of Ministers
277; relations with federations
464; relations with governments
176, 386; relations with regions
180, 388, 401; and SEA 718n; and
Social Protocol 180–2, 224, 599,
638; and state aids 526; and White
Paper (1993) 387, 563, 569, 599
training 97, 161, 180, 253, 255, 569,
597, 605
transport
Austrian transit agreement 632,
766–7n; Commission and 97, 238,
570–2, 717n; cross-border networks 194; Delors projects Fig
12.1; ECJ and 82, 374; ECSC role
in 29; environmental policy in 564,
759n; ERT influence 716n;
member states and 329, 605; Parliament and 91, 456, 717n;
railways 570–2, Fig 12.1; regions
and 423; Transport Group report
570, 760n; in White Paper (1993)
569, 570
Treaties 211, 213, 668, 672
Amendment Committee 101; Commission's role in 219, 226; ECJ
and 365, 367, 377, 379; Monetary

Committee under 531; Parliament
under 364
Treaty of European Unity
EP draft 108; Kohl/Mitterand proposal 116, 144; *see also* Maastricht
Treaty of European Union
tree image of EU 188, 192
Trichet, Jean-Claude 536, 537, 543,
755n, 756n, 767n
tripartism 84, 125, 181, 182, 314, 486,
598, 706n
Troika 127, 147, 318, 319, 320, 321,
353, 442, 623, 632, 682
Truman Doctrine 7, 24
Tugendhat, Christopher 142, 228, 230,
371, 710n, 711n, 712n, 714n
Tunisia 660, 665
Turkey 664, 665, 766n
application 130, 625, 631, 657–61,
662; Association Agreement held
up 353; invasion of Cyprus 131,
658, 714n; Kurds 658, 768n
two-speed/two-tier Europe 101, 122,
143, 540, 620, 626
and EMU 547
Tyszkiewicz, Zygmunt 491

Ukraine 202, 662, 663, 664
unemployment 78, 104, 161, 181, 182,
185, 205, 303, 387, 695, 697, 710n
in car industry 579; and convergence
551; in eastern Europe 646, 652;
effect on industrial policy 561;
effect on trades unions 488–9, 526;
insurance 387; and social diversity
625; Spanish 568, 763n; in steel
industry 573–5; and White Paper
(1993) 568, 569
UNICE 139, 440, 456, 465, 487,
490–3, 600, 706n
and EMU 492; history of 491; and
internal market 136, 137, 493; level
of operations 486, 490–1; and
merger regulations 751n; relations
with Commission 138; relations
with Coreper 486, 491; relations
with Council of Ministers 486,
491; relations with DG4 502; relations with national federations 103;

relations with Parliament 358, 486;
and SEA 492; and Social Charter
181, 182; and Vredeling Directive
104, 492, 711n, 751n
United Europe Movement 16
United Kingdom xiii
accession 39–42, 45, 63, 67–8, 69,
73–5, 169, 438, 630, 669;
agriculture 41; assessment of
membership 119, 290; attitude to
EC 33, 37, 39, 101, 119–22, 146,
154, 158–9, 176, 192, 262, 322,
630, 695–6; bilateral action 100;
and border controls 348; budget
question 75, 83, 93, 100, 102, 105,
112, 120, 121, 299, 390; Cabinet
Office 299–301, 404; car industry
471, 576, 578; and CAP 120,
299–300; central bank see Bank of
England; civil service 75, 120, 189,
245, 300, 705n; and Commission
121, 154, 158, 217, 226, 227, 236,
264, 334–5, 518, 569; Committee
of regions nominations 395; and
Commonwealth 41, 75; and competition policy 503, 509; and consumer electronics industry 582;
and convergence 551; coordination
process 297–301; currency
fluctuations 64, 66, 67, 76, 535;
defence policy 193; devolution
proposals 384; DTI 120, 137; and
EC legislation 361, 368, 626, 766n;
EC officials 245, 262, 300, 301,
730–1n; EC Presidencies 121, 151,
201, 203, 318, 320, 321, 569, 645,
724n, 726n; and EC trade 113; and
ECB 178; and ECJ 274, 374, 376,
738n; and ECSC 21; effectiveness
of 623; and EFTA 33, 37–8, 41,
69; and EMI 757n; and EMU 147,
148, 166, 168, 173, 176–7, 189,
202, 299, 532, 542, 544; and
energy dispute 609; and EPU 12,
14; and ERM 88–9, 114, 120, 153,
158, 166, 171, 174–5, 203–4, 220,
278, 299, 537, 538, 541, 544, 549,
689, 714n, 721n, 756n, 758n; and
European Parliament 91, 195, 341,

343, 348, 361, 711n; Falklands
War 710n; financial sector 120,
135, 150, 477–9, 480, 590, 592,
714n; firms 301, 438, 450, 451–3,
608; Foreign Office 299; and
foreign policy 184, 190, 192, 270,
274; and Franco-German entente
167, 329; hard ecu proposal 168,
177–8; Heath Government 73–4;
implementation of Directives 269;
industrial policy 74, 113, 137, 562,
586, 608; industry 94, 121, 406–7;
inflation 80, 81, 706n; and informal
politics 626, 682; infringements of
EC law 738n; and Interior Ministry
issues 192, 194; and internal
market 120, 121, 122, 144, 145,
146, 147, 154; isolation of 159,
166, 173, 187, 329; Labour Government 80–1; and labour relations
239; Maastricht opt-outs 178, 183,
189, 195, 198, 202; Maastricht
ratification 198, 201, 204; Macmillan Government 39–41; MEPs
354, 356, 358, 735n; ministries
297–300, monetarism 98, 120; national identity 299, 773n; nationalism 121; NEDC 385, 386; and oil
crisis 77, 80–1; opposition to federalism 16, 192, 195; opposition to
Social Charter 166, 181, 182, 202,
310, 625; opposition to tax
harmonization 151, 160; opposition
to Yaounde 51; Parliament and EC
121, 301, 361, 368; and passports
154; as peripheral state 621; Permanent Representatives 284, 301,
451; political parties 121, 299; and
political union 44–5, 189;
privatization 99, 120, 562, 586,
588, 590; public opinion in xiii,
121, 165, 186, 190, 201, 626; and
QMV 121–2, 131, 144, 194, 278,
279, 292; referendum xiii, 81, 83,
201; and Regional Fund 75, 82,
389, 395; regions 394, 397, 398,
400, 401, 402, 408, 425, 740n;
reintegration of 325; relations with
Denmark 130, 330; relations with

France 24, 190; relations with Germany 119; relations with member states 167, 625; relations with US 7, 159, 190, 617; and Single European Act 148, 152, 278, 300, 374; and social policy 120, 151, 488, 490; and sovereignty 21, 201, 236, 714n, 723n; and state aids 505, 524; and steel restructuring 574–5; and subsidiarity 187, 194, 297, 725n; Thatcherism 78, 98; trade unions 387, 487, 489; and two-speed Europe 626; and veto 291, 710n; welfare system 98; and WEU 28; *see also* Scotland

United States
    aid, post-War 7–13, 20; balance of payments deficit 61, 65, 78; banks 480, 482, 592; competition agreement 372; and continental states 101; economy 77, 81, 99, 171; and EDC 26–7; and EEC monetary policy 63; and European integration 9–10; European influence of 617; federations 492–3; firms 58–9, 472, 504, 608, 642, 674; and GATT 12–13, 48, 603; and German reunification 326; hegemony of 3, 26; industry 581–2, 583; and internal market 603; lobbyists 359; MNCs 76, 113, 136; monetary policy 66, 87; and NATO 24; nuclear policy 30–1; opposition to Yaounde 51; as political model 15; post-War industrial productivity 5; and post-War trade 5–6; protectionism 5, 10, 12, 96, 602, 604–5; Reaganomics 99; relations with EC 39, 46, 77, 642, 662; relations with UK 7, 159, 642; tariffs 49; telecoms industry 589; trade 96, 113, 140, 440, 602, 604–5, 764n; Truman Doctrine 7, 24; and Visegrad group 642
unity
    causes of disunity 667; and diversity 615–18; historical overview 662; and neighbouring states 663–4; *see*

also Economic and Monetary Union; political union
urban regions 402–4, 422, 425, 626, 742n

Val Duchesse meetings 387, 491, 718n
van den Broek, Hans 221, 224, 243, 311
van der Groeben, Hans 46, 56, 561
van Miert, Karel 745n
    at DG4 221, 332, 507, 511, 515, 526, 528–9, 563, 609, 754n; on evolving policy 753n; and joint ventures 510; and liberalization 588; and Social Protocol 488; and steel restructuring 574–5; as transport Commissioner 526; van Miert-Andreatta agreement 527
variable geometry 101, 122, 151, 190, 201, 428
Visegrad group
    applicants 203, 327, 482, 616, 625, 631, 641–57, 662; attitude to EU 647; conversion process 644–5, 648, 650–1; creation of 644; elections in 645; and European unity 664; *see also* Eastern Europe
Volkswagen 577, 606
Vredeling Directive 120
    Council rejection of 84; opposition to 102, 104–5, 137, 149; Social Charter and 181; UNICE and 492, 710n, 711n, 751n

waste 264, 306, 329, 334, 337, 350
welfare systems xv, 4, 5, 98, 165, 182, 607, 694, 695
Werner Committee and Report 65, 69, 87, 532, 755n
West Germany *see* Germany
Westendorp, Carlos 302, 722n
Western European Union (WEU) 28, 67, 116, 639, 663
    Council 45; enlarged status sought 185; increased competence of 642; and NATO 187, 193; as part of EU 193
White Papers 566

economic and industrial (1993) 204,
223, 239, 320, 332, 387, 454, 488,
491, 547, 563, 568–70, 597, 599,
638, 750n; Single European Act
(1985) 104, 105, 111, 124, 129,
135, 142–3, 145–6, 159, 218, 235,
481; Telecoms 587
Williamson, David 221–2
Wilson, Harold 83, 724n
worker participation
Vredeling Directive 84, 102, 104–5,
710n, 711n; Works Council Directive 488, 599
working groups 243, 246–7, 273,
726–7n
central banks 757–9n; Commission

445, 450, 460, 462, 680, 746n;
Council 266, 267, 270, 281, Fig
7.1
World Trade Organization 372, 601,
604, 609, 673, 689, 734n

Yaounde Convention 50–1, 75, 600
Yugoslavia 664
bilateral agreement with 82; break up
of 165, 184, 193; civil war 185,
186, 190, 204, 327, 616, 617,
636–7, 640, 642, 644, 647, 663,
665, 666, 697

ZVEI 469, 470

Fontana History

☐ A HISTORY OF THE SOVIET UNION Geoffrey Hosking   0-00-686287-X   £9.99

☐ A HISTORY OF THE
SCOTTISH PEOPLE 1560–1830 T. C. Smout   0-00-686027-3   £8.99

☐ BLACK IVORY: A HISTORY OF
BRITISH SLAVERY James Walvin   0-00-686292-6   £8.99

☐ THE RUSSIAN REVOLUTION 1899–1919 Richard Pipes   0-00-686233-0   £12.99

☐ WAR WITHOUT AN ENEMY:
A HISTORY OF ENGLISH CIVIL WARS Richard Ollard   0-00-686189-X   £12.99

☐ PATRIOTS AND LIBERATORS: REVOLUTION IN
THE NETHERLANDS 1780–1813 Simon Schama   £9.99

☐ THE CULTIVATION OF HATRED Peter Gay   0-00-686089-1   £9.99

☐ RISE AND FALL OF THE GREAT POWERS Paul Kennedy   0-00-686052-4   £10.99

These books are available from your local bookseller or can be ordered direct from the publishers.

To order direct just list the titles you want and fill in the form below:

Name:_____

Address:_____

_____

Postcode:_____

Send to HarperCollins Paperbacks Mail Order, Dept 8, HarperCollins *Publishers*, Westerhill Road, Bishopbriggs, Glasgow G64 2QT.
Please enclose a cheque or postal order or your authority to debit your Visa/Access account –

Credit card no:_____

Expiry date:_____

Signature:_____

to the value of the cover price plus:
UK & BFPO: Add £1.00 for the first book and 25p for each additional book ordered.
Overseas orders including Eire Please add £2.95 service charge.
Books will be sent by surface mail but quotes for airmail despatches will be given on request.

**24 HOUR TELEPHONE ORDERING SERVICE FOR ACCESS/VISA CARDHOLDERS –
TEL: GLASGOW 0141 772 2281 or LONDON 0181 307 4052**